Applied Welfare Economics and Public Policy

RICHARD E. JUST
University of California

DARRELL L. HUETH
Oregon State University

ANDREW SCHMITZ
University of California

PRENTICE-HALL, INC., Englewood Cliffs, N.J. 07632

Library of Congress Cataloging in Publication Data

Just, Richard E.
    Applied welfare economics and public policy.

    Bibliography: p.
    Includes index.
    1. Welfare economics.   2. Economic policy.
I. Hueth, Darrell L.   II. Schmitz, Andrew.
III. Title.
HB846.J87   338.9   81-13802
ISBN 0-13-043398-5   AACR2

Editorial/production supervision and interior design by *Barbara Grasso*
Cover design by *Dawn Stanley*
Manufacturing buyer: *Edward O'Dougherty*

Printed in the United States of America

10 9 8 7 6 5 4 3 2 1

ISBN 0-13-043398-5

PRENTICE-HALL INTERNATIONAL, INC., *London*
PRENTICE-HALL OF AUSTRALIA PTY. LIMITED, *Sydney*
PRENTICE-HALL OF CANADA, LTD., *Toronto*
PRENTICE-HALL OF INDIA PRIVATE LIMITED, *New Delhi*
PRENTICE-HALL OF JAPAN, INC., *Tokyo*
PRENTICE-HALL OF SOUTHEAST ASIA PTE. LTD., *Singapore*
WHITEHALL BOOKS LIMITED, *Wellington, New Zealand*

To Jane, Karen, and Carole

Contents

8

Aggregation and Economic Welfare Analysis of Market Oriented Policies   147

9

Multimarket Analysis and General Equilibrium Considerations   177

10

The Welfare Economics of Imperfect Competition   215

11

Stochastic Welfare Economics: Applications in Agricultural Policy Analysis   237

12

Nonmarket Welfare Measurement: Applications in Environmental Economics 268

13

Dynamic Considerations in Cost-Benefit Analysis: Applications in Natural Resource Economics 296

14

Conclusions   331

Appendix A

Duality of Surpluses in Factor and Product Markets: The Case of the Single Competitive Firm   337

Appendix D

Welfare Measures for Multimarket Equilibrium   **445**

Preface

This book develops economic welfare theory in the context of application to public policy questions. The authors' view is that knowledge of applied welfare theory is essential to the provision of useful and appropriate policy information. Moreover, empirical work by applied economists must be guided by the general equilibrium considerations of welfare theory as well as the empirical possibilities suggested by econometric theory and data availability. This book provides a thorough review of economic welfare theory and illustrates how this theory can be used to obtain policy information in the areas of international trade, the economics of technological change, agricultural economics, environmental economics, and the economics of extractive natural resources, just to name a few.

The general equilibrium presentation of welfare theory emphasizes the shortcomings of the Pareto criterion as a guide to policy analysis and policy decisions. The compensation criterion of Kaldor and Hicks is then considered as a more promising approach to making public policy decisions. The compensation criterion is found to fall short of providing guidance to determine the optimum optimorium for society but is found to be useful in terms of identifying potential improvements in the economic well-being of society. The need for a social welfare function to enable an economist to make statements about what ought to be done in any given situation is, however, clearly illustrated.

The emphasis of the book is on providing quantitative information on the welfare effects of alternative policy measures. This book takes as given that the willingness-to-pay measures of Professor Hicks provide the foundation for applied welfare economics although some justification is discussed. The problems which one confronts when attempting to use consumer surplus as a measure of welfare gain for the individual or household with single and multiple price changes are discussed verbally and explained graphically. Willingness-to-pay measures are developed for firms and households where households are viewed as both consumers and sellers of resources. In each case, the foremost concern is for the potential for applications. Thus, the recent results on the possibilities for using consumer surplus as an approximation for these measures in the cases of price changes, income changes, or commodity grants are presented.

The welfare measures for individual agents are then aggregated to provide market measures of welfare gain and loss which satisfy the compensation criteria. The relationship between the compensating and equivalent variation measures of Professor Hicks and the compensation criterion is explained in detail. A number of new issues in applied welfare economics are treated at the market level in this book. For example, considerable emphasis is placed on the possibilities for measuring welfare effects on consumers and producers in horizontally and vertically related markets to the market in which a policy change occurs. Also, the possibilities for disaggregation of welfare effects to analyze distributional issues arising from policy decisions are investigated in detail. Some econometric considerations which arise in multimarket welfare analysis are also emphasized, and suggestions are made with regard to the choice of market in which to do empirical analysis and the conditions under which one should choose to estimate partial (or ordinary) rather than equilibrium demand and supply curves.

Some of the later chapters cover specific areas of application and emphasize problems associated with welfare measurement under uncertainty, nonmarket welfare measurement and the modern approaches to measurement in environmental economics, dynamic issues and the welfare economics of extractive natural resources, and choice of the social rate of discount.

This book is designed to be highly flexible from the user's standpoint. The chapters are written at a level which is accessible to the upper division economics students. The bulk of the analysis in the chapters is graphical, but some simple algebra is used. Heuristic proofs are provided for major results whenever possible. For a graduate level text, instructors and its users will want to draw on the mathematical appendices provided. These appendices rigorously establish the results found in the general text of the book. The proofs follow modern approaches utilizing the concepts of duality and the envelope theorem. The only mathematical tools necessarily required even for the appendices, however, are differential and integral calculus.

The topics covered by this book form a body of reading that is essential for practitioners of applied welfare economics. Government economists and engineers who are charged with providing cost effectiveness studies and with doing benefit-cost analysis will be particularly interested in reading those portions of the book that deal with multimarket analysis, multiprice change analysis, and intertemporal or dynamic analysis both with and without uncertainty and risk. Natural resource economists will find Chapter 13, which deals with the economics of extractive resources, unique in that it treats the theory of intertemporal optimization in a manner understandable to students who have had only intermediate economic theory.

The origin of this book can be directly traced to a course taught by Professor Andrew Schmitz at the University of California at Berkeley in the spring of 1970. The other two authors of this book were students in that course. It was there that their interest in applied welfare economics was sparked. Professor Schmitz, with two other students of a previous class, Martin Currie and John Murphy, had just published in the *Economic Journal* what has subsequently become a classical survey of consumer surplus. In the process of the preparation of that manuscript, Professor Schmitz had uncovered a number of holes in the theory of consumer surplus, and his great enthusiasm stimulated considerable effort on the part of a number of students to fill these gaps. While the other authors have worked in a number of areas, Professor Schmitz's interest in applied welfare economics has continued unabated since that time. He has been particularly concerned with the income distributional issues that arise in applied welfare studies which many of his less courageous contemporaries have been unwilling to address. His work with David E. Seckler in the *American Journal of Agricultural Economics* on the adoption of the tomato harvester in California has become a classic in this area.

In addition, the authors would like to thank either individually or collectively Robert G. Chambers, Ronald G. Cummings, Steven M. Goldman, J. Arne Hallam, Harry G. Johnson, Abba P. Lerner, Ezra J. Mishan, Rulon D. Pope, and Morris Taylor for providing inspiration and encouragement to continue pursuing this subject area and for providing various insights into welfare economics and its applications. We would also like to extend special thanks to Daniel W. Bromley, Ralph C. d'Arge, W. Michael Hanemann, Wallace E. Oates, Robert D. Willig, and Pan A. Yotopoulos for reviewing and commenting on earlier versions of the manuscript (although any remaining errors are solely the authors' responsibility).

The authors would like to acknowledge financial support from the Experiment Stations at the University of California, the University of Rhode Island, and Oregon State University and to Dr. Kenneth R. Farrell and the Economics and Statistics Cooperative Service of the U.S. Department of Agriculture.

Our thanks also go to Ikuko Takeshita, Gertrude Halpern, Francis Hammond, and their associates at the University of California, Berkeley, for their impeccable job of typing and revising this manuscript—often under rush conditions. In addition, the understanding encouragement of our wives—Jane, Karen, and Carole—has been indispensable; and we thank them for the many hours of companionship they sacrificed to see this book completed.

Richard E. Just
Darrell L. Hueth
Andrew Schmitz

1

Introduction

Societies must make choices of how to use their scarce resources. The United States has enormous coal and shale resources in its western states. The exploitation of these resources could eliminate reliance on Mideast oil supplies and could indeed result in energy self-sufficiency. Production from these resources, however, has major environmental implications. Air and water quality as well as beauty of the natural environment will undoubtedly suffer with development. Suppose that you are an economist and are asked to provide expert testimony at a public meeting regarding such a development. Would you support or oppose the development? What would be the economic basis for your remarks? Is there an objective theoretical justification for government involvement, or should the decision to develop or not develop be left to free-market forces? One must bear in mind that public officials must and will make these decisions whether or not they can get objective advice.

Decisions must also be made by the federal government regarding import tariffs and quotas. Some American industries with strong support from labor unions argue for protection from "unfair" foreign competition. Yet economic theory suggests that "free trade" is optimum assuming competitive conditions within and among trading countries. On the other hand, Japan today imposes a substantial duty on some imports from the U.S. (e.g., beef); similarly, U.S. grain exports to the European Economic Community have been curtailed by heavy levies. When asked to advise the U.S. International Trade Commission regarding increased protection for U.S. industry in such an economic environment, what should the position of an economist be? Would knowledge of the structure or degree of competitiveness of the industry be helpful in taking a position? Should a position be taken at all? Perhaps one should simply point out the economic ramifications of the decision. Also in the context of trade policy, suppose that the decision has been made to embargo grain exports to a foreign country for political reasons. You are asked to assess the economic impacts. Do you need to consider effects other than those on the buyers and sellers of grain? If you find it necessary to consider impacts of lower grain prices on the beef sector, need you then also go on to consider markets such as for poultry which are related to the beef market? Where does the chain of analysis end?

Frequently, in natural resource industries, the major effects are along the chain of markets leading from the basic resource to the eventual household consumer. Decisions regarding the elimination of foreign fishing effort within the 200-mile economic zone, for example, will be felt primarily in the domestic harvesting sector (by fishermen), the seafood processing sector, and finally by household and institutional consumers of fishing products. With reductions in foreign effort, all of these groups could gain. From a more general viewpoint, however, the public might have gained more if the foreigners were allowed to continue fishing but were forced to pay taxes or fees on their catch. How can the trade-off between the gains to fishermen and the losses to the public be evaluated? Should the gains and losses to these different groups be added independently of the group to whom they accrue or should the gains to one group, the lowest-income group, for example, be considered more important? Is there merit to the argument that each individual looks out for himself or herself, so the responsibility of economists is merely to put forth the *efficient* solution—which eliminates concern about income-distributional issues?

In fishing, forestry, and minerals policy and in extractive resource industries in general, the decisions made today have important consequences for future generations. Society tends to use its highest-valued and most accessible resources first. Hence, future production costs are increased as a result of decisions to produce today. Future generations, of course, do not have either political or "dollar" votes in these affairs. Although the present generation tends to be willing to pay a premium for present consumption over future consumption, perhaps elected or appointed officials should act as the guardians for future generations, as the famous welfare economist A. C. Pigou argued long ago.[1] Thus, economic analysis for public policy evaluation must consider future generations.

The branch of economics that deals with how economists answer the foregoing questions is known as welfare economics. The objective of welfare economics is to help society make better choices. This book contains a methodology for compiling feasible economic evidence for the political process of public policy choice.

---

[1] A. C. Pigou, *The Economics of Welfare* (London: Macmillian & Company Ltd., 1952).

1.1 POSITIVE VERSUS NORMATIVE ECONOMICS

Welfare economics is concerned with what "ought" to be; that is, welfare economics is *normative economics*. Welfare economics focuses on using resources optimally so as to achieve the maximum well-being for the individuals in society. The other branch of economics—*positive economics*—is concerned with understanding and predicting economic behavior; that is, positive economics deals with what "is." What determines the price of houses, the price of ocean beach property, or the value of Iowa farmland, or what will happen to the output of a competitive firm when the price for its product increases are the types of questions that positive economics tries to answer. The theoretical parts of positive economics, insofar as they possess empirical content, provide hypotheses that can be tested and perhaps rejected. For example, the idea that a rise in price will always reduce quantity demanded can be refuted by observing market phenomena. As with positive economics, the propositions of welfare economics are also logical deductions from a set of definitions and assumptions which may or may not themselves be realistic. Unlike positive economics, however, a difficulty with welfare economics is that economic "welfare" is not an observable variable such as the number of machines, houses, market prices, or profits. The economic welfare status of an individual is formally given by his or her utility level, which is unobservable.

Utility is a term generally used synonymously with happiness or satisfaction. The utility level of an individual depends upon the goods and services the individual buys in the marketplace, but it also depends upon a number of nonmarket or nonpriced goods, such as clean air, clean water, public parks, and recreation areas. Welfare economics is concerned with the total welfare of the individual, not simply with the welfare level resulting from market goods and services.

A basic proposition of utility theory is that utility increases as the amount of goods consumed increases. One cannot, however, measure the increase in utility or additional *utils* obtained from consumption increases. This is not a problem for positive economics since all of the basic propostions about how consumers will respond to changing prices and income can be derived from a system where the consumer only ranks consumption bundles without intensities. Such a system is called an *ordinal* system. That is, an ordinal system assumes that individuals can only rank alternatives: for example, decide if two ski trips are preferred to two concerts, or vice versa.

In welfare economics, however, it is helpful to know how much two ski trips are preferred to two concerts. That is, it is helpful to know the intensities of preference or the difference in utils obtained from two ski trips or two concerts. A system where intensities of preferences can be determined is known as a *cardinal* system. In a cardinal system, it is possible to know exactly how many additional utils each affected individual would gain or lose from a proposed policy decision. Such information would surely be helpful to those concerned with determining the maximum well-being for society and would simplify the subject of welfare economics substantially.

Measurability of utility, however, is not sufficient to determine optimal social choices. To see why this is the case, suppose that two individuals come to lunch—one who prefers tea and one who prefers coffee. Assume, further, that one can serve only a single beverage. Even if the tea drinker receives 50 utils from a cup of tea and the coffee drinker receives only 30 utils from a cup of coffee, one cannot conclude that it is socially desirable to serve tea. Society may well consider the coffee drinker twice as important as the tea drinker; and, if so, coffee should be served. The point is that, even if utility were measurable, there would still be the problem of how to weight individuals. No objective way exists for solving this problem of interpersonal comparisons.

In practice, to test a welfare proposition is exceedingly difficult. In contrast to positive economics, where the normal way of testing a theory is to test its conclusions, the procedure used to test a welfare proposition is to examine its assumptions. That is, in positive economics, the proof of the pudding is in the eating. The welfare cake, on the other hand, is so difficult to taste that its ingredients must be sampled before the baking. Hence, when working with economic welfare analysis, assumptions take on increased importance.

One view of welfare economics (especially that of many applied studies) is to consider it as a branch of economics which carries positive economics one step further. As one example, studies have been done in energy economics to forecast the future prices of major petroleum products. These forecasts are based on complex models which are positive in nature. However, given the supply and demand equations on which these forecasts are based, one can easily compute effects on consumers' income and oil company profits of various government policy changes. One can show, for example, the effects of industry deregulation. However, conclusions should be checked carefully by scrutinizing the assumptions used to build the positive forecasting model. Models may forecast well even though the underlying assumptions may be unrealistic, but the economic welfare implications of two positive economic models that forecast equally well may be vastly different.

Another often misunderstood point in welfare economics is whether economists need to talk about the "desirability" of a policy change such as the "goodness" or "badness" of technological change or whether or not tariffs "should" be imposed. A frequent misunderstanding in performing economic welfare analysis relates to whether or not the analysis should be carried to the point of making recommendations to policymakers concerning whether or not a bridge or dam should be built, whether or not supersonic aircraft or the mechanical lettuce harvester should be introduced, and the like. This is *not* necessary and may not be an appropriate role for an economist to play.

A concrete example can serve to illustrate this point. Several studies have been done on the welfare effects of U.S. quotas to restrict the importation of beef.[2] Although these studies estimate the losses to consumers and the gains to cattle producers associated with removing the restrictions, they do not necessarily use their estimates of gains and losses as a basis upon which to recommend whether or not the U.S. government should remove quotas or increase them above current levels. To politicians representing their constituencies in policymaking, political factors such as international relations or related economic considerations such as trade deficit management may be more important; but only with adequate economic welfare analysis can policymakers undertake informed decisions with an understanding of the extent and magnitude of their economic consequences.

1.2   SOME CONTROVERSIES IN WELFARE ECONOMICS

Welfare economics, as a field of inquiry within the broad scope of the study of economics, has a long history. Such concepts as economic rent or producer surplus (the area above the supply curve bounded by price) and consumer surplus (the triangle-like area under the demand curve and above price), which are very much in use today, were presented in the 19th century. Ricardo introduced the concept of economic rent in 1829 when discussing the effects of England's corn laws.[3] Dupuit, a French engineer, used the notion of consumer surplus in 1844 to analyze the effects of building a bridge.[4] These concepts were developed more fully by Marshall[5] in the early 20th century and have since formed the basis for most empirical economic welfare studies.

Often, however, a distinction is made between the "old" welfare economics of Marshall and what has come to be called the "new" welfare economics. The *old welfare economics* accepts the principle that social gains are maximized by competitive markets; and, therefore, where noncompetitive interferences exist, the economist is justified in recommending policy measures that eliminate those "distortions." Also, the old welfare economics employs the technique of partial-equilibrium analysis in developing recommendations. Partial-equilibrium or piecemeal analysis considers the welfare effects of a change in one market assuming the effects in other markets are negligible. Finally, from an empirical standpoint, the old welfare economics holds that the triangle-like area

[2] See, for example, U.S. International Trade Commission, *Conditions of Competition in U.S. Markets between Domestic and Foreign Live Cattle and Cattle Meat Fit for Human Consumption,* No. 842, 1977, pp. 1–126.

[3] David Ricardo, *The Principles of Political Economy and Taxation* (London: McMillian Press, 1829).

[4] J. Dupuit, "On the Measurement of the Utility of Public Works," *Annals des Ponts et Chaussees,* Second Series, Vol. 8 (1844).

[5] Alfred Marshall, *Principles of Economics* (London: McMillian Press, 1930).

to the left of the demand curve and above price is a serviceable money measure of utility to the consumers in a market and that the triangle-like area to the left of the supply curve and below price is similarly an adequate money measure of welfare for producers in a market. Changes in these areas can then be used to measure welfare changes to society.

The principles of the old welfare economics have been attacked on several grounds by those economists associated with the *new welfare economics*. For example, beginning in 1942, economists such as Paul A. Samuelson[6] demonstrated that the basic welfare measure of the old welfare economics—consumer surplus—is not well defined. That is, consumer surplus is not generally a unique money measure of utility, and uniqueness can imply contradictions depending on the use of empirical data. This criticism of the use of consumer surplus put applied welfare economics on somewhat shaky grounds until Willig's work appeared in the mid 1970's.[7]

Another criticism of the old welfare economics is based upon an argument advanced as early as 1896 by Pareto.[8] He argued that any policy that makes any person worse off cannot be supported on objective grounds. As further elaborated by Kaldor[9] and Hicks,[10] the welfare weights attached to each individual need not be the same; and, hence, simply adding changes in consumer or producer surpluses across individuals is not a sufficient basis for evaluating change. Pareto argued that the only objective basis under which one can say society is better off is when some people are made better off and no one is made worse off. This criterion has come to be known as the *Pareto principle*.

In an attempt to extend the class of questions that can be addressed objectively by welfare economics, Kaldor and Hicks introduced the "compensation principle" in 1939 by which a change should be made if *potential* gain exists so all *could* be made better off by some redistribution of goods or income follow-

---

[6] P. A. Samuelson, "Constancy of the Marginal Utility of Income," *Studies in Mathematical Economics and Econometrics in Memory of Henry Schultz*, ed. O. Lange *et al.* (Chicago: University of Chicago Press, 1942), reprinted in *Collected Scientific Papers of Paul A. Samuelson*, ed. J. Stiglitz (Cambridge, Massachusetts: MIT Press, 1966), Vol. I, pp. 37–53; see, also, Eugene Silberberg, "Duality and the Many Consumer Surpluses," *American Economic Review*, Vol. 62, No. 5 (December, 1972), pp. 942–952.

[7] See Robert D. Willig, "Consumer's Surplus Without Apology," *American Economic Review*, Vol. 66, No. 4 (September, 1976), pp. 589–597, and Robert D. Willig, *Consumer's Surplus: A Rigorous Cookbook*, Technical Report No. 98 (Stanford University Press: Institute for Mathematical Studies in the Social Sciences, 1973).

[8] Vilfredo Pareto, *Cours d' Economie Politique*, Vol. 2 (Lausanne, 1896).

[9] Nicholas Kaldor, "Welfare Propositions of Economics and Interpersonal Comparisons of Utility," *The Economic Journal*, Vol. 49, No. 195 (September, 1939), pp. 549–552.

[10] J. R. Hicks, "The Foundations of Welfare Economics," *The Economic Journal*, Vol. 49, No. 196 (December, 1939), pp. 696–712.

ing the change. The associated measurement problem was addressed by Hicks who suggested that alternative money measures of welfare, while not directly related to utility gains and losses, can be given "willingness to pay" interpretations (e.g., how much money is each individual willing to pay to go to a new park?)[11] These measures, called *compensating and equivalent variations*, are unique measures in any situation and are hence not subject to the Samuelson criticism of consumer surplus. The notion of compensating and equivalent variations and the associated compensation criteria are key concepts and form the foundation of applied welfare economics.

But even the compensation principle did not escape criticism. Scitovsky,[12] in what has become known as the "reversal paradox" illustrated how inconsistencies can arise in using this principle in policy analysis. Later, Gorman[13] extended this analysis to illustrate the "intransitivity" problem associated with inconsistent rankings of three or more situations.

Yet another criticism of the old welfare economics has to do with its piecemeal approach. Lipsey and Lancaster[14] showed, using the Pareto principle, that there are circumstances under which distortions in one market or economic sector imply that distortions must also exist in other sectors in order to make everyone as well off as possible. Since one can hardly argue that the total economy is free of noncompetitive interferences, this result suggests that the partial approach to welfare economics may not be appropriate.

How have applied welfare economists—the practitioners—responded to these attacks? John V. Krutilla has recently asked and answered this question.[15] "Did we observe—as might be expected—hesitancy in using welfare economics in the applied area? Quite the contrary. Applied welfare economics flourished throughout this period *as though* (if not actually) innocent of the controversy." Applied welfare economists have continued to use partial equilibrium models for policy recommendations; and recommendations have been made, although there were some losers. In some cases, this analysis has even been legislatively mandated. The Flood Control Act of 1936 required that the benefits from water resource development projects must exceed the costs

---

[11] J. R. Hicks, "The Four Consumer's Surpluses," *Review of Economic Studies,* Vol. XI, No. 1 (Winter, 1943), pp. 31–41; see also, *idem, A Revision of Demand Theory* (Oxford, England: Clarendon Press, 1956).

[12] T. Scitovsky, "A Note on Welfare Propositions in Economics," *Review of Economic Studies,* Vol. 9, No. 1 (November, 1941), pp. 77–88.

[13] W. M. Gorman, "The Intransitivity of Certain Criteria Used in Welfare Economics," *Oxford Economic Papers* (New Series), Vol. 7, No. 1 (February, 1955), pp. 25–35.

[14] R. G. Lipsey and R. K. Lancaster, "The General Theory of the Second Best," *Review of Economic Studies,* Vol. 24 (1956–57), pp. 11–32.

[15] John V. Krutilla, "Reflections of an Applied Welfare Economist," presidential address at the Annual Meeting of the Association of Environmental and Resource Economists, Denver, Colo., September 1980.

"to whomever they may accrue" (section 701a). To measure these benefits and costs in project evaluation work, economists continue to use the areas behind supply and demand curves. Policymakers demand economic analyses of policy decisions, and applied welfare economists have used the only tools they have had available to provide information.

Fortunately, however, some theoretical justification for feasible empirical practices has followed. For example, the piecemeal approach has been shown to be appropriate when some markets or sectors have little economic impact on others (e.g., the effect of corn price supports on the automotive industry).[16] Where market interdependencies exist, welfare economists now have better guidance as to how far they need to look to obtain the total welfare effects of a policy change. Similar advances have been made in other areas and under other assumptions and one of the objectives of this book is to show how these many advances fit together to constitute a complete methodology for applied economic welfare analysis.

1.3 COMPENSATION IN WELFARE ECONOMICS

In its original Kaldor/Hicks form, the *compensation principle* states that policy B is preferred to policy A if, in the move from policy A to policy B, everyone can potentially be made better off. A difficulty arose with the original formulation of this principle when Tibor Scitovsky pointed out that cases exist where the gainers can compensate losers in going from policy A to policy B using the initial prices and income distribution to evaluate the change; but from the subsequent prices and income distribution, the losers can compensate gainers in going back from policy A to policy B.[17] Thus, cases can arise where both policy B is preferred to policy A and policy A is preferred to policy B. This was resolved by the adoption of the double criterion of Scitovsky, which stated that policy B is preferred to policy A only if the gainers can compensate the losers in making the change and the losers cannot bribe the gainers into not making the change. This potential compensation criterion was further broadened later by Samuelson[18] to compare all possible prices and income redistributions of the

[16] O. A. Davis and A. B. Whinston, "Welfare Economics and the Theory of the Second Best," *Review of Economic Studies,* Vol. 32 (1965), pp. 1–14, and O. A. Davis and A. B. Whinston, "Piecemeal Policy and the Theory of Second Best," *Review of Economic Studies,* Vol. 34 (1967), pp. 323–331.

[17] T. Scitovsky, "A Note on Welfare Propositions in Economics," *Review of Economic Studies,* Vol. 9, No. 1 (November, 1941), pp. 77–88.

[18] P. A. Samuelson, *Foundations of Economic Analysis* (Cambridge, Massachusetts: Harvard University Press, 1947), and P. A. Samuelson, "Social Indifference Curves," *Quarterly Journal of Economics,* Vol. LXX, No. 1 (February, 1956), pp. 1–22, reprinted in *Collected Scientific Papers of Paul A. Samuelson,* ed. J. Stiglitz (Cambridge, Massachusetts: MIT Press, 1966), Vol. II, pp. 1073–1094.

outcome associated with policy *A*. The word "potential" is critical here since policy *B* is preferred to policy *A* as long as it is *possible* for the gainers to compensate the losers—not only when the gainers *actually* compensate the losers. The principle is based on potential compensation only.

The principle of potential compensation was proposed originally with an argument that to recommend the actual payment of compensation (i.e., that the gainers in moving from policy *A* to policy *B* actually compensate the losers) would involve a value judgment. But a welfare gain is clear only when everyone is made better off or, at least, no one is made worse off. If one goes beyond making statements of potential gains and recommends that changes be made on the basis of these potential gains, then the application of the compensation principle may lead to changes that make some people worse off and others better off by a greater amount. However, if society has a high regard for the individual made worse off and a low regard for the individual made better off (perhaps because one is poor and the other is rich), then society as a whole may be worse off with the change. Thus, the application of the compensation principle when compensation is not actually paid also clearly involves a value judgment. With this in mind, appropriate economic welfare analysis must investigate the effects on both groups and leave the subjective evaluation of which distribution is better to the policymaker elected to fulfill that responsibility. Economic welfare analysis of the effects of specific policies which do not indicate to a policymaker the impacts on individual groups that are affected differently represents, in effect, an attempt to usurp the policymaker's authority to make such judgments.

An example will serve to show the importance of the distinction between potential and actual compensation. Suppose that tomatoes are hand-picked, and the industry is labor intensive. Then a mechanical harvester is introduced that displaces a substantial number of workers. Under the compensation principle, the harvester is desirable if the gains are sufficient so that the gainers (e.g., the landowners, producers, consumers, and machine manufacturers) could compensate the displaced workers if they so desired (i.e., there are potential gains for all). For the United States, this was indeed found to be the case for mechanical harvesting of tomatoes.[19] However, if compensation does not take place, there actually are losers, as well as gainers, even though there are potential gains for all. Depending on society's valuation of changes in the distribution of real income, perhaps the harvester should not have been introduced unless displaced workers actually were paid compensation. This is an issue to be decided by elected officials once economic welfare analysis is used to determine the distributional implications.

In any event, the natural approach to determining whether or not the intro-

---

[19] Andrew Schmitz and David Seckler, "Mechanized Agriculture and Social Welfare: The Case of the Tomato Harvester," *American Journal of Agricultural Economics*, Vol. 52, No. 4 (November 1970), pp. 569–77.

duction of the tomato harvester represented a potential Pareto gain according to the compensation criterion is to sum the compensating variations of gainers and losers. That is, the tomato harvester represents a potential Pareto gain if the maximum amount of money that producers and other gainers are willing to pay rather than give up the harvester exceeds the minimum amount of money that farm laborers would have to be paid to tolerate the harvester.

1.4 COMPENSATING AND EQUIVALENT VARIATIONS

Compensating and equivalent variations are welfare measures first proposed by John R. Hicks.[20] These measures relate to the classical welfare measures of the old welfare economics but do not suffer the same deficiencies. Most important, these measures can be directly employed in performing the compensation tests of the new welfare economics.

In welfare economics, different considerations arise between the theoretical formulation of a problem or issue and the actual measurement in quantitative terms of the welfare effects. When welfare economics is carried to the empirical level, one must be concerned about whether or not the relevant variables are observable. Since utility is not measurable, an alternative measure must be chosen. *An observable alternative for measuring the intensities of preferences of an individual for one situation versus another is the amount of money the individual is willing to pay or accept to move from one situation to another.* This principle has become a foundation for applied welfare economics and in particular is a foundation for the methodology developed in this book.

This position is, perhaps, somewhat subtle. As previously mentioned, a basic premise of some of the early welfare economists was that consumer surplus, the triangle-like area behind the demand curve and above the price line, is the appropriate welfare measure for the consumer. The correct stream of thought, however, is that the consumer surplus area has welfare significance only insofar as it approximates the "true" willingness-to-pay measure. Recently, a relatively simple technique for determining the goodness of this approximation has been developed.[21]

The two most important willingness-to-pay measures are compensating and equivalent variations. *Compensating variation* is the amount of money which, when taken away from an individual after an economic change, leaves the person just as well off as before. (For a welfare gain, it is the maximum amount that the person would be willing to pay for the change; for a welfare loss, it is the negative of the minimum amount that the person would require as compen-

---

[20] Hicks, "The Four Consumer's Surpluses," *op. cit.*

[21] Robert D. Willig, "Consumer's Surplus Without Apology" and Robert D. Willig, *Consumer's Surplus: A Rigorous Cookbook.*

sation for the change.) *Equivalent variation* is the amount of money paid to an individual which—if an economic change does not happen—leaves the individual just as well off as if the change had occurred. (For a welfare gain, this is the minimum compensation that the person would need to forgo the change; for a welfare loss, it is the negative of the maximum amount that the individual would be willing to pay to avoid the change.)

Compensating variation and equivalent variation can also be used to measure producer welfare effects. On the producer side, these measures are shown in Chapter 4 to coincide with more well-known welfare quantities, such as quasi-rents and, in some cases, profits. However, there are still a number of empirical problems on the supply side. It is not easy in today's complex environment to define the producer or the firm. Many firms are legal entities that do not own all of the factors of production they use. As an example, in agriculture, a great deal of farmland is leased by growers. This type of problem makes empirical welfare economics difficult but not unmanageable (one needs to split producers into groups). To illustrate this issue, consider the controversy surrounding the Soviet grain purchases in 1973, which, in turn, caused the price of U.S. farmland to increase. Clearly, renters of farmland did not obtain the same benefits as did producers who owned the land they farmed.

1.5   EFFICIENCY AND EQUITY

Almost without exception, the great works in economics have focused on some aspect of the operation of the economy in terms of such criteria as efficiency and equity. *Economic efficiency* has to do with producing and facilitating as much consumption as possible with available resources, whereas *equity* has to do with how equitably goods are distributed among individuals. Do competitive markets lead to the most preferable state of society? What are the distributional effects of imperfect competition and monopoly power? How can the effects of monopoly power be measured? These are some of the fundamental questions of efficiency and equity that can be addressed with welfare economics.

Given an initial distribution of income and resources, one can possibly improve market efficiency and hence make society better off. However, a system may be very efficient but not very equitable in how the output is distributed. Efficiency can be defined only with reference to a given income distribution. If one changes the distribution, one changes the optimal or competitive output product mix. There is no objective way to determine both the ideal output and its distribution. There are many economically efficient states, each corresponding to different income distributions. The choice of income distribution, however, is a political matter that can be solved only by value judgments through the political process.

In spite of this, welfare economics can provide a useful input in the policy making process by pointing out the efficiency and distributional implications of a policy change. For example, the Organization of Petroleum Exporting Countries (OPEC) was formed and seemed to be an effective monopolistic device for pricing oil. The associated welfare impacts have, no doubt, been considerable. Partially as a response, there have been several proposals for forming an international grain export cartel. But how might the associated welfare impacts be evaluated? Efficiency can be improved for grain exporting countries through such a cartel arrangement, but what about the distributional effects? Is there a difference between a government export cartel and a producer cartel? Which groups would oppose a cartel? To form such a cartel in grains, would prices have to be set by governments and/or marketing boards; or could pricing be done by the private grain companies, many of which are large, multinational firms? Welfare economics can and has been used to determine such effects.[22] For example, results show that a government export cartel has very different effects on the welfare of producers than does a producer export cartel.[23]

1.6 WELFARE WEIGHTINGS

Because the question of optimal income distribution cannot be resolved on objective grounds, one approach has been to try to develop "welfare weights" for various groups of individuals. In dealing with welfare analysis, some economists attach "equal" welfare weights to the various market groups in their models. For example, suppose that a competitive market becomes monopolistic. This change would cause a welfare loss to consumers and a gain to the producing sector. In this type of analysis, equal weighting implies that a dollar lost by the consumers exactly offsets a dollar gained by producers. A policymaker, however, may prefer a change that gives $10 to the poor at the expense of $11 to the rich. A graduated income tax scale with welfare assistance for the poor is evidence of such preferences and perhaps gives some basis for determining which weighting scheme matches revealed policy preferences.

Clearly, the choice of welfare weights is a value judgment unless it is done on the basis of policy preferences revealed in previous policy choices. Attempts to base such weights on previous policy choices, however, are plagued by problems of frequent changes in policymaking bodies and problems associated with noneconomic forces playing a role in many policy decisions. An alternative approach in applied economic welfare analysis is to derive results under various welfare weightings. A policymaker can then decide what action to take based on his or her choice of weights. Thus, the economic analyst need not select the weighting that he or she would, in fact, prefer; and thus, a value judgment is not necessary in the economic analysis even when compensation is

---

[22] Andrew Schmitz, Alex F. McCalla, D. O. Mitchell, and Colin C. Carter, *Grain Export Cartels* (Cambridge: Ballinger Publishing Company), forthcoming, 1981.

[23] Colin C. Carter, Nancy Gallini, and Andrew Schmitz, "Producer-Consumer Trade-Offs in Export Cartels," *American Journal of Agricultural Economics*, Vol. 62, No. 4 (November, 1980), pp. 812–818.

not considered. When applied economic welfare studies focus on the distribution of effects across major groups of individuals, rather than only on the aggregate effects of a policy, this more detailed information can rightfully be used in augmenting information available to policymakers who represent different constituencies. This book provides a framework for supplying such information.

Of course, this type of information may or may not be the deciding factor in specific policy choices. Policy formulation and the theory of policy choice is a much broader subject area; while economic welfare analysis should be viewed as an integral step in policy formation and evaluation, it is *not* the only component. A broad coverage of the theory of public choice in democracy, for example, can be found in texts such as those by Mueller[24] and Doel.[25] There are also many other topics in welfare economics which focus on issues of a more esoteric nature such as the "ideal" society or social choice mechanism. This includes such subjects as the illusive "social welfare function" (i.e., a hypothetical function which resolves conflicts of efficiency and equity)[26] and theories of justice (e.g., Rawls' theory of justice which argues that analysis should be directed to helping the most miserable person).[27] Some of these concepts are discussed briefly but the mainstream of the book does not focus on such issues because of their limited use for applied economic welfare analysis.

1.7   OVERVIEW OF THE BOOK

The topic of this book is applied welfare economics. The major emphasis is on concepts which have empirical possibilities. However, before proceeding to the more applied aspects of welfare economics, Chapters 2 and 3 discuss theoretical welfare economics in a general equilibrium context. A discussion and understanding of such concepts as Pareto optimality, optimum income distribution, the social welfare function, and the compensation tests are necessary in order to meaningfully interpret the content of the later chapters which focus on concepts of applied welfare economics.

Chapter 4 deals with producer welfare measurement and discusses concepts such as producer surplus, economic rent, and profits. The appropriate use of each is analyzed. Measurement is considered in both input and output markets.

Chapters 5 and 6 focus on consumer welfare measurement. Chapter 5 deals with the notion of consumer surplus and why it may not provide a unique

[24] Dennis C. Mueller, *Public Choice* (London: Cambridge University Press, 1979).

[25] Hans van den Doel, *Democracy and Welfare Economics* (London: Cambridge University Press, 1979).

[26] Abram Bergson, "A Reformulation of Certain Aspects of Welfare Economics," *Quarterly Journal,* Vol. 52 (February, 1938), pp. 310–334.

[27] J. Rawls, *A Theory of Justice* (New York: Oxford University Press, 1971).

measure of welfare change for consumers. Chapter 6 looks at consumer welfare measurement in a willingness-to-pay context. It discusses the various measures that have been proposed. Then the extent to which the triangle-like area under a demand curve can approximate these measures is investigated.

Chapter 7 focuses on decision making by resource owners and factor suppliers. Economic rent for a factor supplier is shown to have a welfare interpretation symmetrical with consumer surplus. Chapter 7 also demonstrates how willingness-to-pay measures can be approximated by areas above factor supply curves.

Chapters 8 and 9 focus on aggregation and multimarket general equilibrium considerations. In Chapter 8, aggregation is carried out for a single market, and policy evaluation is discussed in this context. The effects of taxes, subsidies, quotas, price supports, price controls, tariffs, and other trade barriers are analyzed and possibilities for estimating welfare effects are discussed. Chapter 9 shows how applied welfare analysis can be done when more than one market (either input or output) is affected.

Chapters 10 through 13 consider applications of welfare economics in specific areas. Chapter 10 deals with imperfect markets and shows the welfare effects of monopoly and monopsony practices. Antitrust economics is briefly discussed. Chapter 11 considers stochastic welfare economics with applications in agricultural policy analysis. Chapter 12 looks at nonmarket welfare measurement as applied to environmental economics. Such concepts as externalities, property rights, and public goods are introduced. Empirical approaches are also discussed. Chapter 13 considers cost-benefit analysis with applications in natural resource economics. Dynamic methods of economic welfare analysis and social discounting of benefits and costs over time are introduced.

Chapter 14 presents conclusions. It ends with a note of optimism and suggests that, despite the criticisms of classical welfare economics, the body of applied economic welfare methodology as now constituted can provide a useful input into the policy process.

2

Pareto Optimality
and the Pareto Criterion

The Pareto criterion was introduced in the nineteenth century by the eminent Italian economist Vilfredo Pareto.[1] Its potential for application to public policy choices, however, is still very much discussed. By this criterion, a policy change is socially desirable if by the change everyone can be made better off or at least some are made better off while no one is made worse off. If there are any who lose, the criterion is not met. In his book *The Zero-Sum Society: Distribution and the Possibilities for Economic Change,* Lester Thurow contends that many good projects do not get under way simply because project managers are unwilling to pay compensation to those who would actually be made worse off.[2] If this is correct, perhaps policy measures should be considered that meet the Pareto criterion. That is, perhaps policy measures that include the payment of compensation, so that everyone is made better off, should be considered. For example, those who support tariffs argue that their removal results in short-term loss of jobs for which workers are not adequately compensated. Trade theory shows that there are economic gains from free trade, but the distribution of these gains is what the workers object to. This objection would probably not arise if only policies that met the Pareto criterion were considered. However, as will become clear, there are also limitations to using the Pareto criterion to rank policy choices.

---

[1] Vilfredo Pareto, *Cours d'Economie Politique,* Vol. 2 (Lausanne, 1896).

[2] Lester C. Thurow, *The Zero-Sum Society: Distribution and the Possibilities for Economic Change* (New York: Basic Books, Inc., 1980).

A large part of theoretical welfare economics and its application are based on the Pareto principle and the concept of Pareto optimality. This chapter discusses both Pareto optimality and the Pareto criterion in a general equilibrium setting. The consideration of these concepts in a general equilibrium context enables greater understanding of the assumptions, limitations, and generalizations associated with applying welfare economics to real-world problems discussed in later chapters.

2.1   PARETO OPTIMALITY AND THE PARETO CRITERION DEFINED

The *Pareto criterion* is a technique for comparing or ranking alternative states of the economy. By this criterion, if it is possible to make at least one person better off in moving from state A to another state B without making anyone else worse off, state B is ranked higher by society than state A. If this is the case, a movement from state A to state B represents a *Pareto improvement,* or state B is *Pareto superior* to state A. As an example, suppose that a new technology were introduced which resulted in lower food prices and at the same time did not harm anyone by (for example) causing unemployment or reduced profits. The introduction of such a technology would be a Pareto improvement.

To say that society should make movements that are Pareto improvements is, of course, a value judgment but one that enjoys widespread acceptance. Some would disagree, however, if policies continuously made the rich much richer while the poor are unaffected.

If society finds itself in a position from which there is no feasible Pareto improvement, such a state is called a *Pareto optimum.* That is, *a Pareto-optimal state is defined as a state from which it is impossible to make one person better off without making another person worse off.* It is important to stress that, even though a Pareto-optimal state is reached, this in no way implies that society is *just* in terms of income distribution. For example, as will become evident later, a Pareto-optimum position is consistent with a state of nature in which the distribution of income is highly skewed.

If the economy is not at a Pareto optimum, there is some inefficiency in the system. When output is divisible, it is always theoretically possible to make everyone better off in moving from a *Pareto-inferior* position to a *Pareto-superior* position. Hence, Pareto-optimal states are also referred to as *Pareto-efficient* states; and the Pareto criterion is referred to as an *efficiency criterion.* Efficiency in this context is associated with getting as much as possible for society from its limited resources. Note, however, that the Pareto criterion can be used to compare two inefficient states as well. That is, one inefficient state may represent a Pareto improvement over another inefficient state.

Of course, it may be politically infeasible to move from certain inefficient states to certain Pareto-superior states. If Thurow is correct, the only feasible options may be moves to positions where at least one person is made worse off. States where one person is made better off and another is made worse off are referred to as *Pareto-noncomparable states*.

Note that, in the context of this section, these concepts have been defined independently of societies' institutional arrangements for production, marketing, and trade.

2.2   THE PURE CONSUMPTION CASE

Now consider the concepts of Pareto optimality and the Pareto criterion for the pure exchange case, that is, the optimal allocation of goods among individuals where the goods are, in fact, already produced. In this context, a set of marginal exchange conditions characterizing Pareto–efficient states can be developed. Suppose that there are two individuals, A and B, and quantities of two goods, $\bar{q}_1$ and $\bar{q}_2$, which have been produced and can be distributed between the two individuals. This situation is represented by the *Edgeworth–Bowley box* in Figure 2.1, where the width of the box measures the total amount of q_1 produced and the height of the box measures the total amount of q_2 produced.

The indifference map for individual A is displayed in the box in standard form with O_A as the origin. Three indifference curves for individual A—labeled $U_1{}^A$, $U_2{}^A$, and $U_3{}^A$—are drawn in the box. The indifference map for individual B with indifference curves $U_1{}^B$ and $U_2{}^B$ has O_B as the origin and thus appears upside down and reversed. Displaying the indifference maps of individuals A and B in this manner ensures that every point in the box represents a particular distribution of $\bar{q}_1$ and $\bar{q}_2$ or a "state of the economy" in the pure exchange

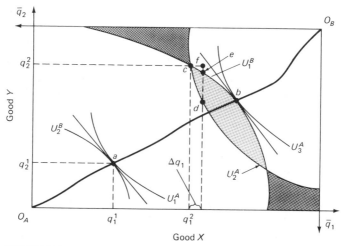

FIGURE 2.1

case. For example, at point a, individual A is endowed with q_1^1 of good q_1 and q_2^1 of good q_2, while the remainder of each, $\bar{q}_1 - q_1^1$ and $\bar{q}_2 - q_2^1$, respectively, is distributed to individual B.

The solid line in Figure 2.1 running from O_A to O_B through points a and b is known as the *contract curve* and is constructed by connecting all points of tangency between indifference curves for individuals A and B. At all points on this line, both consumers' indifference curves have the same slope or, in other words, both consumers have equal *marginal rates of substitution* for goods q_1 and q_2. The marginal rate of substitution measures the rate at which a consumer is willing to trade one good for another at the margin. The marginal rate of substitution for each consumer generally varies along the contract curve for both consumers; the slope of the indifference curves at point a, for example, is not the same as the slope at point b.

Now, consider the possibility of using the Pareto criterion to compare or rank alternative states of the economy. For example, compare point c with other points in the Edgeworth box. First, compare point c with points inside the lightly shaded area. At point c, the marginal rate of substitution of q_1 for q_2 for individual A, denoted by $\text{MRS}_{q_1q_2}^A$, is greater than the marginal rate of substitution of q_1 for q_2 for individual B, denoted by $\text{MRS}_{q_1q_2}^B$. This implies that the amount of q_2 that individual A is willing to give up to obtain an additional unit of q_1 exceeds the amount individual B is willing to accept to give up a unit of q_1. For the marginal increment Δq_1 in Figure 2.1, this excess corresponds to the distance de. That is, individual A is willing to pay df of q_2 to obtain Δq_1, whereas individual B requires only ef of q_2 to give up Δq_1. If this excess of willingness to pay over willingness to accept is not paid to individual B and individual B is paid only the minimum amount necessary, then point e is Pareto superior to point c since individual A is made better off and individual B is no worse off. If the excess is paid to individual B, the movement is to point d, which is again Pareto superior to point c since individual B is made better off and individual A is no worse off. If any nontrivial portion of the excess is paid to individual B, both are made better off. Thus, all points, including end points on the line de, are Pareto superior to point c. Similar reasoning suggests that a movement from point c to any point in the lightly shaded area can be shown to be an improvement on the basis of the Pareto criterion. Thus, all points in the lightly shaded area are Pareto superior to point c.

Now consider comparison of point c with any point in the heavily shaded areas. All points in the heavily shaded areas in Figure 2.1 are on indifference curves which are lower for both individuals A and B; hence, points in the heavily shaded regions are Pareto inferior to point c since at least one individual is worse off and neither individual is better off.

Finally, consider comparison of point c with all remaining points that are not in shaded areas in the Edgeworth box to discover a major shortcoming of the Pareto criterion: at all these points, one person is made better off and the other person is worse off relative to point c; that is, at point a, individual B is better off than at point c but individual A is worse off. Hence, these points are noncomparable using the Pareto principle. *Improvements for society using the Pareto criterion can be identified only for cases where everyone gains or at least no one loses.*

Now suppose that society starts at point c and moves to point e making a Pareto improvement. At point e, $\text{MRS}_{q_1 q_2}^A > \text{MRS}_{q_1 q_2}^B$, and hence further gains from trade are possible. Suppose that individuals A and B continue trading with individual A giving up each time the minimum amount of q_2 necessary to obtain additional units of q_1. In this manner, the trade point moves along the indifference curve U_1^B until point b is reached. At point b, the amount of q_2 that individual A is willing to give up to obtain an additional unit of q_1 is just equal to the amount of q_2 that individual B would demand to give up a unit of q_1. With any further movement, individual A would not be willing to pay the price that individual B would demand; in fact, a movement in any direction from point b must make at least one person worse off. Thus, point b is a Pareto optimum.

In this manner, one can verify that the marginal condition that holds at point b,

$$\text{MRS}_{q_1 q_2}^A = \text{MRS}_{q_1 q_2}^B \tag{2.1}$$

holds at all points on the contract curve. Thus, *in the pure exchange case, any point on the contract curve is a Pareto optimum; Pareto optimality implies that the marginal rate of substitution between any two goods is the same for all consumers.* The intuition of this condition is clear since improvements for both individuals are possible (and Pareto optimality does not hold) if one individual is willing to give up more of one good to get one unit of another good than another individual is willing to accept to give up the one unit.

2.3   PRODUCTION EFFICIENCY

Efficiency in production must also be considered when discussing Pareto optimality. Consider once again Figure 2.1—but now assume that more of good q_1, good q_2, or both can be made available by improving the efficiency with which inputs are used. This would imply that individual B's origin O_B could be moved rightward, upward, or both. In any of these cases, any two indifference curves that were previously tangent on the contract curve would now be separated by a region such as the cigar-shaped, lightly shaded region in Figure 2.1. Thus, individual A, individual B, or both could be made better off. If production possibilities are considered and more of q_1, q_2, or both can be produced, the points on the contract curve in Figure 2.1 will no longer be Pareto-optimal points generally. Stated conversely, where alternative production possibilities exist, the points on the contract curve $O_A O_B$ can be Pareto efficient only if the point $\bar{q}_1$, $\bar{q}_2$ is an efficient output point. A *Pareto-efficient output bundle* is one where more of one good cannot be produced without producing less of another.

However, an output point can only be efficient if inputs are allocated to their most efficient uses. To see this, consider the production-efficiency Edgeworth box in Figure 2.2. This box is constructed by drawing the isoquant map for output q_1 as usual with isoquants q_1^1, q_1^2, and q_1^3 but with the insoquant map for q_2 upside down and reversed with origin at O_{q_2}. The total amounts of inputs x_1 and x_2 available are given by $\bar{x}_1$ and $\bar{x}_2$. Any point in this box represents an allocation of inputs to the two production processes. For example, at point g, x_1^1 of x_1 and x_2^1 of x_2 are allocated to the production of q_1. The remainder of inputs, $\bar{x}_1 - x_1^1$ and $\bar{x}_2 - x_2^1$, are allocated to the production of q_2.

Point g does not represent an efficient allocation of inputs because at point g the *rate of technical substitution* of x_1 for x_2 in the production of q_1, denoted by $\text{RTS}_{x_1 x_2}^{q_1}$, is greater than the *rate of technical substitution* of x_1 for x_2 in the production of q_2, denoted by $\text{RTS}_{x_1 x_2}^{q_2}$. The rate of technical substitution measures the rate at which one input can be substituted for another while maintaining the same level of output. Thus, if an increment of x_1, say Δx_1, is shifted from the production of q_2 to q_1, then an increment of x_2, say Δx_2, could be shifted to the production of q_2 without decreasing the output of q_1 from q_1^1. But only an increment of $ab < \Delta x_2$ of x_2 is necessary to maintain the output of q_2 at the original level q_2^1. This results from the fact that the marginal rate at which x_1 substitutes for x_2 in q_2 is less than the rate at which it substitutes for x_2 in the production of q_1. If, in the exchange of Δx_1 for an increment of x_2, the output of q_2 is kept constant at q_2^1, the output of q_1 can be increased to q_1^2. Thus, point g is an inefficient point; the output of q_2 can be increased without decreasing the output of q_1. Clearly, if any amount of x_2 on the segment bc is allocated to q_2 as Δx_1 is allocated to q_1, the outputs of both q_1 and q_2 are increased.

By identical reasoning, point b can be established as an inefficient point. The output of q_1 can again be increased, holding q_2 constant, by reallocating x_1 to q_1

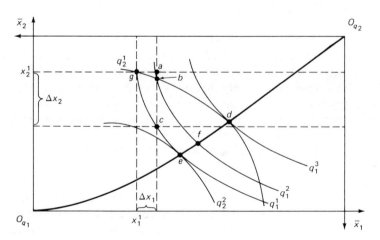

FIGURE 2.2

and x_2 to q_2. This process can be continued until a state such as point d is reached. At point d, the amount of x_2 that can be given up in exchange for an increment of x_1, keeping q_1 constant at $q_1{}^3$, is precisely equal to the amount of x_2 needed to keep q_2 constant at $q_2{}^1$ if an increment of x_1 is removed from the production of q_2. It is impossible to increase the output of q_1 without decreasing the output of q_2. Point d is thus a Pareto-efficient output point. But it is not unique. For example, point e, a point of tangency between $q_1{}^1$ and $q_2{}^2$, is also a Pareto-efficient output point, as is point f. In fact, all points on the *efficiency locus* $O_{q_1}O_{q_2}$ are Pareto-efficient output points.

Tangency of the isoquants in Figure 2.2 implies that

$$\text{RTS}_{x_1 x_2}^{q_1} = RTS_{x_1 x_2}^{q_2} \tag{2.2}$$

Thus, to the earlier exchange conditions, this second set of conditions for Pareto optimality can now be added. That is, *Pareto optimality in production implies that the rate of technical substitution between any two inputs is the same for all industries that use both inputs.* The intuition of this condition is clear since greater production of both goods is possible (and Pareto optimality does not hold) if one production process can give up more of one input in exchange for one unit of another input than another production process requires to give up that one unit (holding the quantities produced constant in each case).

The set of Pareto-optimal points (or the efficiency locus) $O_{q_1}O_{q_2}$ can also be represented in output space. In Figure 2.3, the curve connecting $q_1{}^*$ and $q_2{}^*$ corresponds to $O_{q_1}O_{q_2}$. That is, $q_2{}^*$ is the maximum output possible if all resources, $\bar{x}_1$ and $\bar{x}_2$, are used in the production of q_2. This point corresponds to

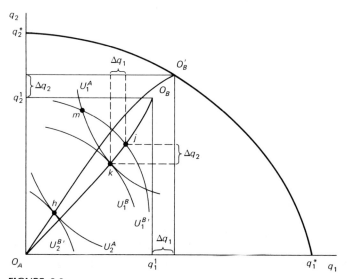

FIGURE 2.3

point O_{q_1} in Figure 2.2. Likewise, q_1^* in Figure 2.3 corresponds to point O_{q_2} in Figure 2.2. Similarly, one can trace out the entire set of production possibilities corresponding to the contract curve $O_{q_1}O_{q_2}$ in Figure 2.2. This efficiency locus in output space is called the *production possibility curve or frontier;* thus *all Pareto-efficient production points are on the production possibilities frontier.*

The Pareto inferiority of point g in Figure 2.2 is clear in Figure 2.3. The Edgeworth exchange box corresponding to output point g is drawn with individual A's origin at O_A and individual B's origin at O_B with the output associated with point g in Figure 2.2 efficiently distributed at point k. A movement to point f in Figure 2.2 corresponds to providing the increments Δq_1 and Δq_2 in Figure 2.3, which shifts individual B's origin to O_B'. Thus, individual B's initial indifference curve U_1^B shifts to position $U_1^{B'}$, and his or her initial consumption point shifts to point j. The increase in output, $\Delta q_1 + \Delta q_2$, can then be used to make individual A, individual B, or both better off; hence, point g in Figure 2.2 is not a Pareto optimum.

Although point g in Figure 2.2 is not a Pareto optimum, one cannot conclude that a movement from point g to any Pareto-efficient production point is a Pareto improvement. That is, the Pareto criterion cannot be used to compare all inefficient production points with all efficient ones. For example, a movement from O_B to O_B' in Figure 2.3 can be accompanied by a distribution of the larger output at point h which, although an efficient exchange and production point, results in individual A being made worse off and individual B being made better off than if output O_B is distributed at point m. Without a priori knowledge of the distribution of a larger bundle of goods, one cannot say whether or not a Pareto improvement results. *A Pareto improvement with a larger bundle of goods is attained only if it is distributed such that all individuals are made better off or no one is made worse off.* Thus, using the Pareto criterion, society cannot choose between states with more goods and states with fewer goods unless distributional information is also available.

2.4 THE PRODUCT-MIX CASE

From the foregoing, it should not be surprising that the Pareto criterion cannot be used to rank bundles of goods where one bundle has more of one good but less of another good without knowledge of how the goods are distributed. In what follows, this point is demonstrated, and the notion of Pareto optimality is discussed for the more general case where society has a choice over product mix.

First, however, the concept of the *Scitovsky indifference curve* (SIC) will be introduced. In Figure 2.4, society produces q_1^1 of q_1 and q_2^1 of good q_2. The SIC labeled C in Figure 2.4 corresponds to point a on the contract curve, where the level of utility is represented by U_1^A for individual A and by U_1^B for individual B. To determine the SIC, hold O_A stationary, thus holding individual A's indifference curve stationary at U_1^A. At the same time, move O_B, thus shifting

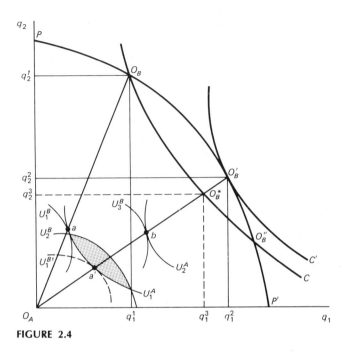

FIGURE 2.4

B's indifference map; but do this such that individual B's indifference curve U_1^B remains tangent to individual A's indifference curve U_1^A with axes for both goods parallel between individuals. Thus, C consists of the locus of all output bundles to which every member of society is indifferent if the bundle is initially distributed at point a.

Now consider comparing a particular distribution of one bundle of goods on the production possibility frontier with the distribution of another bundle also on the frontier. For example, in Figure 2.4 consider comparing the output bundle at O_B, which is distributed between individuals A and B at point a, with the output bundle at O_B' distributed at point a'. The Scitovsky curves corresponding to the distribution at points a and a' are C and C', respectively. Note that C is not tangent to the production possibility curve at O_B while C' is tangent at O_B'. Both individuals can be made better off by choosing the bundle at O_B' since C' lies above C and since only output at O_B^* (instead of O_B') distributed at point a' is needed to yield the same level of total utility as at O_B. The additional product $q_1^2 - q_1^3$, $q_2^2 - q_2^3$ can be divided in any way desired to make both individuals better off in moving from O_B^* to O_B'.

Even though C' lies entirely above C, however, both individuals need not be made actually better off in moving from O_B to O_B' in Figure 2.4. That is, the bundle represented by O_B' may be distributed at point b, where individual A is made better off and individual B is worse off relative to the bundle represented by O_B distributed at point a. The SICs can lie with one entirely above the other,

23

and one individual may still be worse off at the higher SIC. However, it is possible to redistribute the output bundle at $O_B{'}$ to make everyone better off than at point a (the distribution of the initial bundle) by choosing a distribution of the product at $O_B{'}$ in the shaded region.

Now consider comparing output bundle $O_B{'}$ distributed at point a' (which generates the SIC denoted by C' tangent to PP') with any other efficient output bundle with all possible distributions. Since there are no feasible production points above C', it is impossible to generate a SIC that lies above C'. That is, if one starts at $O_B{'}$ distributed at point a', one person cannot be made better off without making another person worse off; in other words, $O_B{'}$ distributed at point a' is a Pareto-optimal point.

The requirement of tangency of the SIC to the production possibility curve thus establishes a third set of marginal equivalences which must hold for Pareto optimality in the product-mix case. That is, the slope of the production frontier must be the same as the slope of the SIC at the optimum. But the negative of the slope of the production possibility curve is the *marginal rate of transformation* of q_1 for q_2 (which measures the rate at which one output can be traded for another with given quantities of inputs), denoted by $MRT_{q_1 q_2}$, and the negative of the slope of the SIC is the marginal rate of substitution of q_1 for q_2 for both individuals A and B. Thus, *Pareto optimality in product mix implies that the marginal rate of transformation must be equal to the marginal rate of substitution for consumers;* that is,

$$MRT_{q_1 q_2} = MRS_{q_1 q_2}^A = MRS_{q_1 q_2}^B \qquad (2.3)$$

The intuition of this condition is clear since improvements for one individual are possible without affecting any other individual if production possibilities are such that the incremental amount of one output that can be produced in place of one (marginal) unit of another output is greater than the amount that some individual is willing to accept in place of that one unit. Of course, this condition does not define a Pareto optimum uniquely. *Any* point on the production possibility frontier distributed such that the corresponding SIC is tangent to the production possibility curve satisfies the condition. And, as in the pure exchange case, the Pareto criterion does not provide a basis for choosing among these points.

2.5 PARETO OPTIMALITY AND COMPETITIVE EQUILIBRIUM

As mentioned earlier, Pareto-optimal production and consumption points can be identified independently of societies' institutional arrangements for organizing economic activity. However, a fundamental relationship exists between the notion of Pareto optimality and the competitive market system as a mechanism for determining production, consumption, and the distribution of commodities.

Before this relationship can be fully understood, however, the concept of competitive equilibrium for a market system must be defined. Suppose that consumers are utility maximizers and producers are profit maximizers. Also, suppose that consumers and producers act competitively, taking prices as given. Let the resulting quantities demanded of good q_k follow the functions $D_A(p_k)$ for individual A and $D_B(p_k)$ for individual B, where p_k is the price of good q_k, $k = 1, 2$. Also, let the quantity supplied of good q_k follow the function $S_k(p_k)$, $k = 1, 2$. Then suppose that there exists a set of positive prices $\bar{p}_1$ and $\bar{p}_2$ such that the sum of quantities demanded over consumers is equal to the amount supplied for each commodity. That is, suppose that

$$D_A(\bar{p}_1) + D_B(\bar{p}_1) = S_1(\bar{p}_1)$$

and

$$D_A(\bar{p}_2) + D_B(\bar{p}_2) = S_2(\bar{p}_2)$$

The set of prices $\bar{p}_1$ and $\bar{p}_2$ then gives a competitive equilibrium. Thus, *a competitive equilibrium is simply a set of prices such that all markets clear;* there is no excess demand or excess supply. Of course, this concept generalizes easily to the case with many consumers and many producers where supplies and demands depend possibly on prices of competing products as well.

A competitive equilibrium can be shown to exist if (1) all consumers have preferences which can be represented by indifference curves that are convex to the origin, and (2) if no increasing returns exist for any firm over a range of output that is "large" relative to the market.[3] Of course, *many competitive equilibria may exist depending upon the distribution of factor ownership or consumer income.*

The important relationship between competitive equilibria and Pareto optimality is that, *when a competitive equilibrium exists, it attains Pareto optimal-*

---

[3] The first condition is a standard assumption of economic theory and needs no further comment. The problem that arises with increasing returns is that the average cost curve for the firm is continuously decreasing and the marginal cost curve is always below the average cost curve. With falling average costs, if it pays the firm to operate at all, it pays the firm to expand its scale of operations indefinitely as long as output price is unaffected since the marginal revenue is greater than the marginal cost on each additional unit produced. If there are increasing returns over a large range of output, the percentage of the industry output produced by such a firm eventually reaches sufficient size to have some influence over price, and thus the firm will no longer be competitive. Hence, there is no profit-maximizing equilibrium for competitive firms in this case. As long as increasing returns are "small," on the other hand, a competitive industry will consist of a great number of firms with the usual U-shaped average cost curves; and all of these profit-maximizing firms will operate at either the minimum or on the increasing portion of their average cost curve. For a rigorous development of the problem of existence and uniqueness of competitive equilibrium, see James Quirk and Rubin Saposnik, *Introduction to General Equilibrium Theory and Welfare Economics* (New York: McGraw-Hill Book Company, 1968) or K. J. Arrow and F. Hahn, *Competitive Equilibrium Analysis* (San Francisco: Holden-Day, Inc., 1971).

ity.[4] This result, formerly known as the first optimality theorem, is sometimes referred to as the theorem of Adam Smith.[5] In *The Wealth of Nations,* published in 1776, Smith argued that consumers acting selfishly to maximize utility and producers concerned only with profits attain a "best possible state of affairs" for society, given its limited resources, without necessarily intending to do so. Although more than one best (Pareto-efficient) state of affairs generally exists, Smith was essentially correct.

To see this, first consider the case of consumer *A* displayed in Figure 2.5. To maximize utility, given the *budget constraint II'* associated with income *m*, consumer *A* chooses the consumption bundle $\bar{q}_1, \bar{q}_2$, which allows him or her to reach the highest possible indifference curve. Thus, the consumer chooses the point of tangency between *II'* and the indifference curve $\bar{U}^A$. At this tangency, $\mathrm{MRS}^A_{q_1 q_2} = \bar{p}_1/\bar{p}_2$ since the former is the negative of the slope of the indifference curve and the latter is the negative of the slope of the budget constraint. But under perfectly competitive conditions, all consumers face the same prices. Thus, $\mathrm{MRS}^B_{q_1 q_2} = \bar{p}_1/\bar{p}_2$ for consumer *B* and, hence,

$$\mathrm{MRS}^B_{q_1 q_2} = \mathrm{MRS}^A_{q_1 q_2} \tag{2.4}$$

which is the Pareto-optimality exchange condition derived in equation (2.1). That is, since all consumers face the same relative prices of the two goods, their marginal evaluations must be the same in equilibrium.

Now recall that a firm cannot maximize profits for any level of output unless it is producing that output at minimum cost. That is, profit maximization implies cost minimization. Assuming that $\bar{q}_1$ is the profit-maximizing level of output for the firm producing q_1 in Figure 2.6, the minimum cost of producing this output given input prices $\bar{w}_1$ and $\bar{w}_2$ is obtained by using $\bar{x}_1$ of x_1 and $\bar{x}_2$ of x_2. That is, the cost-minimizing input bundle is selected by finding the point of

---

[4] Technically, this result requires that (1) *firms are technologically independent* and (2) *consumers' preferences are independent.* The first assumption implies that the output of each firm depends only on the input-use decisions it makes, not on production or input decisions of other firms. The latter assumption implies that the utility function for each consumer contains as variables only items over which the consumer has a choice and not those quantities chosen by other consumers or producers. Assumptions (1) and (2) jointly imply that no externalities exist. For a further discussion of externalities, see Chapter 12. For a rigorous proof of this result, see Arrow and Hahn, *Competitive Equilibrium Analysis,* or Quirk and Saposnik, *Introduction to General Equilibrium.* A detailed discussion is also given in Kenneth J. Arrow, "The Organization of Economic Activity: Issues Pertinent to the Choice of Market Versus Nonmarket Allocation," in *Public Expenditures and Policy Analysis,* J. Margolis and Robert H. Haveman, eds. (Markham Publishing Company, 1970), Chapter 2, pp. 59–73; also found in, U.S. Congress, Joint Economic Committee, *The Analysis and Evaluation of Public Expenditures, the PPB System,* Compendium, 91st Cong., 1st Sess., Volume I, 1969.

[5] Adam Smith, *An Inquiry into the Nature and Courses of the Wealth of Nations,* 2 Vols., Edwin Cannan, ed. (London: Methuen and Company, Ltd., 1904).

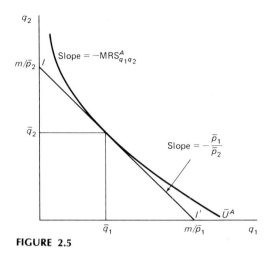

FIGURE 2.5

tangency of the *isocost curve CC'* (associated with cost level $\bar{C}$) with the isoquant associated with output $q_1 = \bar{q}_1$. Finding this point of tangency involves equating the slope of the isoquant, which is equal to the negative of the rate of technical substitution of x_1 for x_2, with the slope of the isocost curve, which is equal to the negative of the ratio of input prices. But all producing firms that use x_1 and x_2 face the same input prices; hence,

$$\text{RTS}_{x_1x_2}^{q^2} = \text{RTS}_{x_1x_2}^{q^1} \tag{2.5}$$

which yields the production efficiency condition of equation (2.2).

To establish that the product-mix condition of equation (2.3) is satisfied, first consider increasing the output of q_1 by Δq_1 and decreasing the output of q_2 by Δq_2 along the production possibility curve. Suppose this change is accomplished by transferring at the margin either one unit of x_1 or one unit of x_2 from production of q_2 to production of q_1. Then the increase in output of q_1 is equal to the marginal physical product of input x_k in production of q_1. That is,

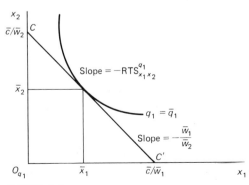

FIGURE 2.6

$\Delta q_1 = \text{MPP}_{x_k}^{q_1}$. Similarly, the decrease in output of q_2 is $\Delta q_2 = \text{MPP}_{x_k}^{q_1}$. But the amount of q_2 that must be given up to obtain an increment of q_1 is given by the marginal rate of transformation between q_1 and q_2. Thus,

$$\text{MRT}_{q_1 q_2} = \frac{\Delta q_2}{\Delta q_1} = \frac{\text{MPP}_{x_k}^{q_2}}{\text{MPP}_{x_k}^{q_1}} \tag{2.6}$$

Now recall that cost minimization by a producer requires that producers equalize the marginal physical product per dollar spent on each input. That is, the least-cost combination $\bar{x}_1, \bar{x}_2$ in Figure 2.6 is characterized by the conditions

$$\frac{\text{MPP}_{x_1}^{q_j}}{w_1} = \frac{\text{MPP}_{x_2}^{q_j}}{w_2}, \qquad j = 1, 2 \tag{2.7}$$

But the marginal physical product of an input is equal to the increase in output Δq_j divided by the increase in input Δx_k required to obtain the increase in output. Thus, $\text{MPP}_{x_k}^{q_j} = \Delta q_j / \Delta x_k$. Using this result in equation (2.7) and inverting yields

$$\bar{w}_1 \frac{\Delta x_1}{\Delta q_j} = \bar{w}_2 \frac{\Delta x_2}{\Delta q_j}, \qquad j = 1, 2 \tag{2.8}$$

where $\bar{w}_k \, \Delta x_k / \Delta q_j$ is simply the marginal cost, MC_{q_j}, of obtaining an additional unit of q_j. Thus,

$$\text{MC}_{q_j} = \frac{\bar{w}_k}{\text{MPP}_{x_k}^{q_j}} \qquad j = 1, 2 \tag{2.9}$$

Finally, recall that all profit-maximizing producers equate marginal revenue, which is simply the competitive producer's output price, with marginal cost; thus, substituting $\bar{p}_j$ for MC_{q_j} in equation (2.9) and dividing the equation with $j = 1$ by the one with $j = 2$ yields

$$\frac{\bar{p}_1}{\bar{p}_2} = \frac{\text{MPP}_{x_k}^{q_2}}{\text{MPP}_{x_k}^{q_1}} \tag{2.10}$$

But from equation (2.6), the right-hand side of equation (2.10) is simply $\text{MRT}_{q_1 q_2}$; and since consumers face these same commodity prices, the product-mix condition in equation (2.3),

$$\text{MRS}_{q_1 q_2}^A = \text{MRT}_{q_1 q_2}^B$$

must hold with competitive market equilibrium.

Thus, under the assumptions of this chapter, *competitive markets result in an equilibrium position from which it is impossible to make a change without making someone worse off; competitive markets are Pareto efficient.* This conclusion is probably the single most powerful result in the theory of market economies and is widely used by those economists who believe that markets are competitive and hence that government should not intervene in economic activity. Milton Friedman and the "Chicago School" are the best known defenders of this position.[6]

In general, a particular Pareto optimum can be achieved by competitive markets given a particular initial distribution of factor ownership. But if one changes the distribution of ownership, a new competitive equilibrium and thus a new Pareto optimum is reached. Hence, many Pareto optima may exist which are competitive equilibria associated with different factor endowments. This is why one cannot solve the problem of efficiency and distribution in two stages by first maximizing the value of the social product by correctly allocating resources and then distributing the product equitably. The relative value of products depends on income distribution, which depends, in turn, on factor ownership.

Figure 2.7 demonstrates this point by considering only two possible states. The two goods produced are q_1 and q_2, and PP' is the production possibility frontier. The Scitovsky indifference curve C pertains to the output bundle O_B distributed among the individuals at point a. Alternatively, the output bundle O_B' distributed at point b yields the Scitovsky indifference curve C'. As points O_B and O_B' show, both bundles and their distributions lead to Pareto-optimal states. Thus, points O_B and O_B' with corresponding distributions at points a and b, respectively, are called *first-best states*, but in no sense does either represent a unique optimum since the other is also optimum in the same sense.

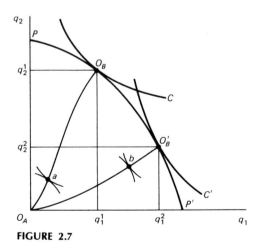

FIGURE 2.7

---

[6] See, for example, the best-seller by Milton Friedman and Rose Friedman, *Free to Choose* (New York: Harcourt, Brace, and Jovanovich, 1980).

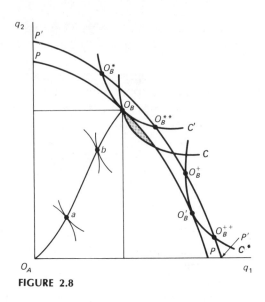

FIGURE 2.8

2.6 LIMITATIONS OF PARETO OPTIMALITY
AND THE PARETO PRINCIPLE

Although the Pareto principle gives a plausible criterion for comparing different states of the world, its limitations are great. The greatest shortcoming of the Pareto principle is that many alternatives are simply not comparable. For example, in Figure 2.8, if production possibilities are represented by PP and production is initially O_B with distribution at point b corresponding to Scitovsky indifference curve C, then the only Pareto-preferred alternatives are in the shaded, cigar-shaped area. All other production points are either infeasible, non-Pareto comparable or Pareto inferior. If production is initially at O_B with distribution at point a corresponding to Scitovsky indifference curve C', then no other feasible alternatives are Pareto superior. In fact, once *any* competitive equilibrium is reached in the framework of this chapter, no other feasible alternatives are Pareto superior. For example, production at O_B with distribution corresponding to Scitovsky indifference curve C' is not Pareto comparable to production at O_B' with distribution corresponding to social indifference curve C^*. Thus, alternative Pareto optima are not Pareto comparable. Hence, without, say, technological change the Pareto criterion prevents consideration of income distributional considerations once a competitive equilibrium is attained.

Another serious problem with the Pareto principle is that no unique choice of distribution is apparent when improvements are possible. For example, suppose that a technological change takes place in Figure 2.8, shifting the production possibilities frontier out to $P'P'$. If production was initially at O_B with distribution at point a corresponding to Scitovsky indifference curve C', the only points that are Pareto superior are those above C' and below $P'P'$. The only points that are Pareto superior and also possibly correspond to Pareto optimality with the new technology are those on the $P'P'$ frontier between $O_B{}^*$ and $O_B{}^{**}$. But the points along this interval may be associated with a wide variation in income distribution (assuming, for example, that only one distribution exists at each production point with tangency between the Scitovsky indifference curve and the new production possibilities frontier). The Pareto criterion gives no basis for choosing among these alternatives. On the other hand, however, this problem may be viewed as an advantage since possibilities can exist for altering income distribution while fulfilling the simply appealing nature of the Pareto criterion. For example, in a rapidly growing economy (one with rapidly expanding production possibilities), the possibilities for altering income distribution while still fulfilling the Pareto criterion are great even though the Pareto criterion gives no guidance on how this should be done.

Even with expanding production possibilities, however, the Pareto principle strongly favors the status quo. For example, if production is originally at O_B with distribution associated with Scitovsky indifference curve C', a new point of Pareto optimality is possible only at points between $O_B{}^*$ and $O_B{}^{**}$ on the new frontier $P'P'$ in Figure 2.8, assuming that the Pareto principle is satisfied in such a change. But if the initial production point is at $O_B{}'$ with distribution associated with Scitovsky indifference curve C^*, a new Pareto optimum is possible only at points between $O_B{}^+$ and $O_B{}^{++}$ on the frontier $P'P'$, again assuming the Pareto principle is satisfied in the change. In each case the set of feasible Pareto improvements does not represent a substantial departure from the initial point unless technological improvements are large. Again, alternatives with widely varying income distributions may be neither comparable nor attainable from a given initial state by strict adherence to the Pareto criterion.

In a policy context, however, decisions often must be made in which someone is made worse off while someone else is made better off. Furthermore, some policies are directly intended to change the distribution of income (i.e., narrow the gap between high- and low-income people). Hence, to evaluate such changes, a device other than the Pareto principle is needed.

2.7 CONCLUSIONS

This chapter has focused on the concept of Pareto optimality and the Pareto criterion. A Pareto improvement is a situation where a move results in at least one person becoming better off without anyone else becoming worse off. Pareto optimality is achieved when it is no longer possible for a policy change to make someone better off without making someone else worse off.

From a policy point of view, the Pareto criterion favors the status quo since the range of choices that represent Pareto improvements depends critically on the initial distribution of income. The Pareto criterion cannot be used to choose among widely different income distributions. Furthermore, many Pareto-optimal policy choices may exist which correspond simply to different income distributions. Perhaps not all first-best, Pareto-optimal choices are superior to some second-best choice. Although it is possible to make a Pareto improvement from a second-best state, it does not follow that any Pareto-optimal state is preferred to any second-best state. For example, if a second-best and a first-best state have markedly different income distributions, the situation that is second best may not be inferior to the first-best situation. Thus, the Pareto criterion alone appears to constitute an insufficient basis for applied economic welfare analysis of public policy alternatives.

3

The Compensation Principle
and the Welfare Function

In Chapter 2, emphasis was given to the Pareto criterion as a means for selecting among alternative policies. Results show that unfortunately many "first-best" bundles or many Pareto-optimal points usually exist for an economy, and the Pareto principle does not give a basis for selecting among them. To narrow the range of possibilities to a single first-best bundle (which essentially requires determining the ideal income distribution) requires a more complete criterion. One such criterion, which was introduced much later than the Pareto principle in the hope that it would be a more powerful device for choosing among policies, is the *compensation principle* (sometimes called the *Kaldor–Hicks compensation test*).[1] The development of the compensation principle was thus an attempt to broaden the states of the world which could be compared using an accepted welfare criterion. Simply stated, state B is preferred to state A if all individuals *could* be made better off at state B—not that all individuals *are necessarily* made better off—by some feasible redistribution following the change. Unlike the Pareto principle, the compensation criterion does not require the actual payment of compensation.

The issue of compensation payments is at the heart of many policy discus-

---

[1] The compensation principle is due to Kaldor and Hicks; see Nicholas Kaldor, "Welfare Propositions of Economics and Interpersonal Comparisons of Utility," *The Economic Journal,* Vol. 49, No. 195 (September 1939), pp. 549–52; and, J. R. Hicks, "The Foundations of Welfare Economics," *The Economic Journal,* Vol. 49, No. 196 (December 1939), pp. 696–712.

sions. Some argue that compensation should be paid in certain cases. According to Lester Thurow: "If we want a world with more rapid economic change, a good system of transitional aid to individuals that does not lock us into current actions or current institutions would be desirable."[2] However, most policies that have been introduced have not entailed compensation. Bans on DDT and other pesticides, for example, have resulted in producer losses in many cases. Producers have not, however, been compensated for their losses in revenue.

Although the compensation principle does, in fact, expand the set of comparable alternatives (at the expense of additional controversy), some states remain noncomparable. The latter part of this chapter turns to considering the necessary features of a criterion that ranks all possible states of an economy. However, empirical possibilities for the resulting more general theoretical constructs appear bleak.

3.1 THE COMPENSATION PRINCIPLE

According to the compensation principle, state B is preferred to state A if, in making the move from state A to state B, the gainers can compensate the losers such that everyone can be made better off. The principle is stated in terms of *potential* compensation rather than *actual* compensation since, according to the founders of the principle, the payment of compensation involves a value judgment. That is, to say that society should move to state *B* and compensate losers is a clearly subjective matter, just as recommendation for change on the basis of the Pareto criterion is a subjective matter. For example, if a Pareto improvement is undertaken, then, as demonstrated in Section 2.6, the possibilities that represent further Pareto improvements may be more restricted. Conceivably, the true optimum state of society may not be reachable by further applications of the criterion if the wrong initial Pareto improvement is undertaken. Similarly, to say that society should move to state *B* without compensating losers is also a subjective matter of perhaps a more serious nature. Thus, nonpayment of compensation also involves a value judgment. In terms of objective practice, one can only point out the potential superiority of some state *B* without actually making a recommendation that the move be made.

The Pure Consumption Case[3]

Consider the application of the compensation principle to comparing different distributions of a given bundle of goods, again using the basic model of two

---

[2] Lester C. Thurow, *The Zero-Sum Society: Distribution and the Possibilities for Economic Change* (New York: Basic Books, Inc., 1980), p. 208.

[3] This section is largely based on M. J. Bailey, "The Interpretation and Application of the Compensation Principle," *The Economic Journal*, Vol. 64, No. 253 (March 1954), pp. 39–52.

goods and two individuals developed in Chapter 2. In Figure 3.1, point a is preferred to point b on the basis of the Pareto principle. But how does one compare point b with a point such as c, where c is not inside the cigar-shaped area? The compensation principle offers one possibility. For example, suppose that one redistributes the bundle such that, instead of being at point b, individual A is at point d and individual B is at point e. Note that the welfare of each is thus unchanged. However, at these points there is an excess of q_2 equal to $q_2^3 - q_2^2$ and an excess of q_1 equal to $q_1^3 - q_1^2$. Now, if the move *actually* takes place to point c, individual A is clearly worse off while individual B is better off; individual A loses $q_2^2 - q_2^1$ of q_2 and $q_1^2 - q_1^1$ of q_1, but individual B gains $q_2^3 - q_2^1$ of q_2, and $q_1^3 - q_1^1$ of q_1. The amount individual B gains in physical amounts of q_1 and q_2 is greater than the loss to individual A. Hence, point c is potentially preferred to point b. *By the compensation principle, everyone is potentially better off by moving from point b to point c because the amount individual B gains is greater than the amount individual A loses.* This result holds even though compensation is not actually paid. If compensation is paid in terms of q_1 and q_2, both parties would, in effect, not agree to move to point c; instead, a move would only take place from point b to somewhere within the cigar shape. But points within the cigar shape are comparable with point b by the Pareto principle; thus, the application of the compensation criterion does not increase the ability to make statements about *actual* increases in welfare.

To view the problem in a different way, consider to what extent individual B would have to bribe individual A in order to make the move from point b to point c. The minimum amount is $q_2^2 - q_2^1$ of q_2 and $q_1^2 - q_1^1$ of q_1. Hence, in equilibrium, one would move from point b to point d only if compensation were paid; individual B would gain $q_2^3 - q_2^2$ of q_2 and $q_1^3 - q_1^2$ of q_1 in the move if the minimum bribe is paid. Thus, point c is never actually reached if compensation is paid.

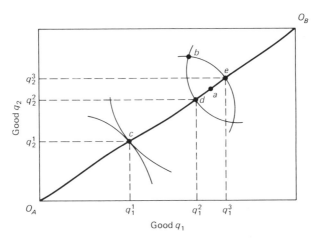

FIGURE 3.1

Distribution of Different Bundles

Consider next how the compensation principle can be used to compare different distributions of *different output bundles*. Recall from the preceding case that potential gains can be made in a move from point b to point c if, in the actual move to point c, the amount one individual loses is less than the amount the other individual gains. With this in mind, consider Figure 3.2, where the indifference curve C corresponds to production at O_B and distribution at point a. Similarly, with production at O_B*, the Scitovsky curve corresponding to distribution at point b is $C*$. At point b, one individual is worse off than at point a, and the other individual is better off. However, potential gains are possible in the move from point a to point b since the amount the loser loses is less than what the gainer gains. Potential gains are clear since production at O_B* can be distributed to keep welfare the same as at point a by moving along Scitovsky indifference curve C to point f; by so doing, hf of q_2 and fg of q_1 are left over. Thus, if the compensation principle is used as a policy criterion, the move would be made (even though at point b one of the individuals may be actually worse off than at point a).

At this point, a comparison and contrast can be drawn between the compensation principle and the Pareto principle. Using the compensation principle with initial production bundle at O_B and distribution at point a, a move to the production bundle at O_B* is supported regardless of the way it is actually distributed. Using the Pareto principle, however, the move is supported only if the actual distribution corresponds to moving along Scitovsky curve C to point f keeping the welfare of each individual constant and then dividing the excess of

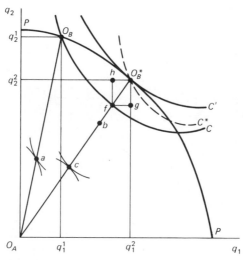

FIGURE 3.2

fg of good q_1 and *fh* of good q_2 among the two individuals in some way so that neither is worse off.

The reason that production at O_B^* is preferred to production at O_B in either case is that the starting point with distribution at point *a* is a second-best state. The corresponding Scitovsky curve C is not tangent to the production possibilities frontier *PP*. Like the Pareto criterion, the compensation principle does not support a move away from a first-best state such as production at O_B^* with distribution at point *c* corresponding to Scitovsky indifference curve C'. Thus, the compensation criterion, like the Pareto criterion, cannot be used to rank two first-best states. A movement from one to the other would not be supported regardless of which is used as a starting point. The compensation criterion, on the other hand, gives a means of comparing all pairs of second-best states and for comparing all second-best states with all first-best states.

The Reversal Paradox

An important class of problems in applying the compensation principle falls under the general heading of the reversal paradox.[4] In the case where gainers can potentially compensate losers, a conclusion that one position is better than another is not always warranted. *One must ask, also, whether the losers can bribe the gainers not to make the move.* The crux of the argument is presented in Figure 3.3. The production possibility curve is *PP*, and the two bundles to be compared are O_B and O_B^*. Each of the bundles is distributed such that the

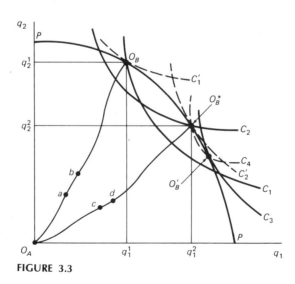

FIGURE 3.3

---

[4] This paradox was pointed out by T. Scitovsky, "A Note on Welfare Propositions in Economics," *Review of Economic Studies*, Vol. 9, No. 1 (November 1941), pp. 77–88.

corresponding Scitovsky indifference curves cross; in other words, both are second-best states since neither indifference curve is tangent to the production possibility curve. The curves C_1 and C_2 correspond to points a and c on the contract curves, respectively. Now, by the compensation principle, production at $O_B{}^*$ with distribution at point c is better than production at O_B with distribution at point a because production at $O_B{}^*$ can generally be redistributed such that all are actually better off at point d (where distribution at point d corresponds to Scitovsky curve $C_2{}'$, which lies above curve C_1 and is associated with improved welfare for both individuals). However, by this criterion, $O_B{}^*$ is only potentially better; compensation is not actually paid. Since compensation is not actually paid, a reversal problem arises. That is, the new state with production at $O_B{}^*$ and distribution at point c is a second-best state with Scitovsky curve C_2. Thus, according to Figure 3.3, there must be some distribution—say, at point b—such that production at O_B is preferred to production at $O_B{}^*$ by the Scitovsky criterion (where distribution at point b corresponds to Scitovsky curve $C_1{}'$ which is associated with improved welfare for both individuals as compared with C_2). Thus, each is preferred to the other.

This reversal occurs because in each case a given distribution of the first bundle is compared with all possible distributions of the alternative bundle. The reversal paradox suggests that all distributions of the initial bundle should also be considered. In other words, a *reversal test* (sometimes called the *Scitovsky reversal test*) is passed if one determines, first, that gainers can bribe losers to make a change and second, that losers cannot bribe gainers not to make the change. Unless the reversal test is passed in addition to the Kaldor–Hicks compensation test, one cannot really say that one state is even potentially preferred to another.

Some additional points that must be borne in mind with respect to the Scitovsky reversal paradox are as follows:

1. *The reversal paradox occurs only in comparing two second-best bundles.* It does not arise if one of the bundles is a first-best or Pareto-efficient bundle. For example, in Figure 3.3, if production at $O_B{}^*$ with distribution corresponding to indifference curve C_2 is compared to production at $O_B{}'$ with distribution corresponding to indifference curve C_3, a reversal problem does not occur.

2. *The reversal paradox does not always occur in comparing two second-best bundles* even though compensation is not actually paid. For example, in Figure 3.3, production at $O_B{}^*$ with distribution corresponding to Scitovsky indifference curve C_4 does not lead to a paradox when comparing with production at O_B and distribution corresponding to Scitovsky curve C_1. The paradox occurs only when the relevant Scitovsky curves cross in the interior of the feasible production region. This problem may not occur when income distributions do not change substantially.

Intransitive Rankings

If the compensation criteria (both the direct Kaldor–Hicks and Scitovsky reversal tests) are employed to rank all possible states, a further problem can arise even if the reversal problem is not encountered. That is, compensation tests can lead to intransitive welfare rankings when more than two states are compared.[5] This problem arises, for example, when one must choose among, say, *states where all of the alternative policies are of a second-best nature* (i.e., there is no single policy in the policy set which leads to a bundle of goods distributed with the Scitovsky community indifference curve tangent to the production possibility curve). In Figure 3.4, given the production possibility curve PP, bundle O_B^2 is preferred to O_B^1, O_B^3 is preferred to O_B^2, and bundle O_B^4 is preferred to O_B^3 using the compensation test. However, O_B^1 is also preferred to O_B^4; hence, the Kaldor–Hicks compensation test leads to welfare rankings that are intransitive. But note that some form of a distortion exists for each bundle since the Scitovsky indifference curves are not tangent to the production possibility curve in any of the four cases. All the bundles are of a second-best nature.

Suppose, on the other hand, that one policy results in a bundle of goods that is economically efficient (with the Scitovsky indifference curve tangent to the production possibility curve). For example, consider bundles O_B^1, O_B^2, O_B^3, and O_B^5. Here O_B^5 is clearly the optimum choice; there is no desire, once at O_B^5, to return to bundles O_B^1, O_B^2, or O_B^3. As a second example, suppose that the bundles to be compared are O_B^1, O_B^2, O_B^3, and O_B^6. Again, once at O_B^6, no potential gain is generated in returning to O_B^1, O_B^2, or O_B^3; hence, no ambiguity is encountered in choosing a top-ranked policy if the policy set contains exactly one first-best state. Thus, as with the reversal problem discussed earlier,

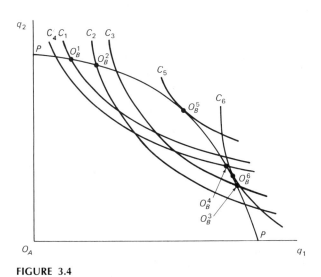

FIGURE 3.4

---

[5] The results in this section are due to W. M. Gorman, "The Intransitivity of Certain Criteria Used in Welfare Economics," *Oxford Economic Papers* (New Series), Vol. 7, No. 1 (February 1955), pp. 25–35.

intransitivity results only when all the bundles being compared are generated from second-best policies.[6]

Consider, on the other hand, one further case where the possibilities consist of O_B^1, O_B^5, and O_B^6. In this case, the Kaldor–Hicks compensation test shows that O_B^5 is preferred to O_B^1; the possibility associated with O_B^6 is not preferred to O_B^1 even though O_B^6 is a first-best bundle. Among these three states, however, the rankings are not complete since, once at either O_B^5 or O_B^6, the compensation test does not suggest a move to either of the other states. In other words, the compensation test does not lead to a ranking of policy sets containing more than one first-best state.

3.2 UTILITY POSSIBILITY CURVES AND THE POTENTIAL WELFARE CRITERION

Another approach related to the choice of alternative income distributions and the reversal problem is based on the concept of utility possibility curves.[7] To develop this approach, consider Figure 3.5, where the utilities of two

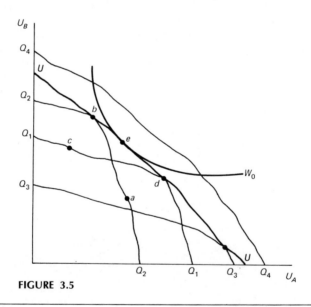

FIGURE 3.5

---

[6] Partly in response to the problems associated with using the compensation principle as a basis for welfare comparison, Kenneth Arrow developed the impossibility theorem, which proves that no reasonable rule exists for combining rankings of various states of society by individuals into a societal ranking; see Kenneth J. Arrow, *Social Choice and Individual Values* (New York: John Wiley & Sons, Inc., 1951).

[7] This concept was introduced by Paul A. Samuelson, *Foundations of Economic Analysis* (Cambridge, Mass.: Harvard University Press, 1947). Also see "Social Indifference Curves," *Quarterly Journal of Economics,* Vol. LXX, No. 1 (February 1956),

individuals, A and B, are represented; the utility of individual B is measured on the vertical axis, while that for individual A is measured along the horizontal axis. Three utility possibility curves are represented, each of which is derived by changing the distribution of a given bundle of goods along a contract curve. For example, Q_2Q_2 shows the maximum utility both individuals can receive from a fixed production at O_B* in Figure 3.3; Q_1Q_1 corresponds to a different bundle of goods, and so on.

To demonstrate the reversal paradox, consider Q_2Q_2 and Q_1Q_1. Points a and b represent particular distributions of the bundle from which Q_2Q_2 is derived. Similarly, points c and d represent particular distributions of the bundle from which Q_1Q_1 is derived. Suppose that the initial distribution is at point c. Then one can redistribute production in moving from Q_1Q_1 to Q_2Q_2 such that both individuals A and B would be better off at point b than at point c. Similarly, one could redistribute the other bundle so that both are better off at point d than at point a. The paradox arises because point d lies to the northeast of point a while point b lies to the northeast of point c. Thus, one comparison implies a preference for the production bundle associated with Q_1Q_1, whereas the other comparison favors the production bundle associated with Q_2Q_2. This paradoxical situation would not arise if compensation were actually paid.

These results, of course, correspond directly with the analysis in commodity space in Figure 3.3. Points a and c in Figure 3.5 correspond to distributions which are second-best states. In other words, these points correspond to points a and c in Figure 3.3, which are also distributions giving rise to second-best states. Note that points b and d in Figure 3.5 and points b and d in Figure 3.3 correspond to first-best states.

If one considers all possible production bundles that can be obtained from a given production possibility frontier and all possible distributions of these bundles (which in utility space correspond to considering all utility possibility frontiers such as Q_3Q_3 associated with all other possible production bundles), then the "grand utility possibilities frontier" UU can be constructed as an envelope of the utility possibility curves. All points on this envelope curve correspond to first-best optima, that is, bundles distributed such that the Scitovsky curves are tangent to the production possibility curve.

Samuelson has argued that, even if gainers can profitably bribe losers into accepting a movement and the losers cannot profitably bribe the gainers into rejecting it (i.e., both the Kaldor–Hicks and Scitovsky criteria are satisfied), a potential gain in welfare is not necessarily attained.[8] He argues that one has to consider all possible bundles and all possible distributions of these bundles before statements can be made about potential gains. The problem then be-

---

pp. 1–22, reprinted in *Collected Scientific Papers of Paul A. Samuelson*, ed. J. Stiglitz (Cambridge, Mass: MIT Press, 1966), Vol. II, pp. 1073–1094.

   [8] P. A. Samuelson, "Evaluation of Real National Income," *Oxford Economic Papers* (New Series), Vol. 2, No. 1 (January 1950), pp. 1–29.

comes one of selecting among many first-best states to which there is no solution unless a social ranking of first-best utility possibilities can be determined. He proposes an alternative *potential welfare criterion* which is demonstrated in Figure 3.5. Simply stated, *if there is some utility frontier such as Q_4Q_4 which lies entirely on or outside another utility frontier—Q_2Q_2, for example— owing perhaps to technological change, any position on this new frontier is clearly at least potentially superior to any position on the old one.* Only if the new frontier lies entirely outside the other, however, are potential increases in real income necessarily obtained. Of course, this criterion can be used to compare either grand utility possibilities before and after, say, a technological change or utility possibilities associated with given alternative production bundles.

In the absence of a rule for ranking alternative first-best utility possibilities, Samuelson argues that this is the only appropriate criterion to apply.[9] In a strict sense, this argument is correct. But in a practical sense, this approach leads to few cases in which beneficial empirical evidence can be developed for policymakers (see Section 8.3 for a discussion of the related empirical approach). On the other hand, the arguments in favor of this approach are based on an attempt to determine optimal policy without relying on policymaker preferences or judgment. Such information may not be necessary in a practical policymaking setting where political institutions exist for the express purpose of providing policymakers to make such choices.

3.3 THE SOCIAL WELFARE FUNCTION

Because the potential welfare criterion may not be satisfied often even if utility possibilities curves can be identified, economic inquiry has continued to search for a rule that can rank all states of society and thus determine which first-best state on the grand utility possibilities frontier represents *the* social optimum. In theory, the social welfare function is such a concept. The *social welfare function* is simply a function—say, $W(U_A, U_B)$—of the utility levels of all individuals such that a higher value of the function is preferred to a lower one. Such a welfare function is called a *Bergsonian welfare function* after Abram Bergson,[10] who first used it. The properties one would expect in such a social welfare function with respect to the utilities of individuals are much like those one would expect in an individual's utility function with respect to the quantities of commodities consumed. That is, one would expect that (1) an increase in the utility of any individual holding others constant increases social welfare (the Pareto principle); (2) if one individual is made worse off, then another

---

[9] *Ibid.*

[10] Abram Bergson, "A Reformulation of Certain Aspects of Welfare Economics," *Quarterly Journal of Economics*, Vol. 52 (February, 1938), pp. 310–334.

individual must be made better off to retain the same level of social welfare; and (3) if some individual has a very high level of utility and another individual has a very low level of utility, then society is willing to give up some of the former individual's utility to obtain even a somewhat smaller increase in the latter individual's utility, with the intensity of this trade-off depending on the degree of inequality.

The properties described above suggest the existence of welfare contours such as W_0 in Figure 3.5, which correspond conceptually to indifference curves for individual utility functions. By property (1), social welfare increases by moving to higher social welfare contours, either upward or to the right. By property (2), the social welfare contours have negative slope; and by property (3), the welfare contours are convex to the origin.

Social welfare is maximized by moving to the highest attainable social welfare contour which thus leads to tangency of the grand utility possibilities frontier with the resulting social welfare contour such as the point e in Figure 3.5.[11] This tangency condition is sometimes called the *fourth optimality condition*. This condition, together with conditions (2.1), (2.2), and (2.3), completely characterizes the social optimum.

Although a social welfare function is a desirable concept in theory, its practicality has been illusory. Apparently, little hope exists for determining a social welfare function on which everyone can agree. Early students of the utilitarian school (e.g., Bentham[12]) believed that changes in happiness should simply be added up. If the net gain is positive, policy implementation is recommended. In this case,

$$W(U_A, U_B) = U_A + U_B$$

---

[11] Note that the slope of the welfare contour can be represented by

$$-\frac{\partial W/\partial U_A}{\partial W/\partial U_B} \equiv -\frac{W_{U_A}}{W_{U_B}}$$

if $W(U_A, U_B)$ is continuous and first derivatives exist. The slope of the utility possibilities frontier is

$$-\frac{\partial U_B/\partial q_1}{\partial U_A/\partial q_1} = -\frac{\partial U_B/\partial q_2}{\partial U_A/\partial q_2}$$

Thus, the tangency condition can be represented mathematically by

$$\frac{W_{U_A}}{W_{U_B}} = \frac{\partial U_B/\partial q_i}{\partial U_A/\partial q_i}, \qquad i = 1, 2$$

Cross-multiplying yields

$$\frac{\partial W}{\partial U_B}\left(\frac{\partial U_B}{\partial q_i}\right) = \frac{\partial W}{\partial U_A}\left(\frac{\partial U_A}{\partial q_i}\right), \qquad i = 1, 2$$

which, simply stated, implies that the marginal social significance of consumption must be equated across individuals for each commodity.

[12] Jeremy Bentham, *Introduction to Principles of Morals and Legislation*, 1823 Edition (New York: Doubleday Book Company, 1961).

Some economists have argued, however, that one needs a social welfare function that is simply symmetric but that, the happier individual A is relative to individual B, the less socially valuable is an addition to individual A's happiness compared with an addition to individual B's. The social welfare contours of a symmetric welfare function are symmetric about a 45° line from the origin in a utility possibilities diagram such as Figure 3.5. Thus, when all individuals have identical utility functions (in which case the utility possibilities frontier is symmetric about the 45° line), a symmetric welfare function leads to identical utility levels of all individuals (assuming marginal utility is always decreasing for all goods). On the other hand, if one individual always receives far more utility from consuming the same bundles as another individual, such a welfare function would lead to more consumption for such an individual. Thus, in effect, such a welfare function could correspond to assigning different welfare or utility weights to individuals.

In contrast to this approach, the Pareto criterion and compensation principle are based on ordinal utility. For example, application of the Pareto criterion does not require weighing the utilities of different groups or individuals. On the other hand, the welfare function relies on cardinal measures in that welfare weights are, in effect, assigned to different groups or individuals to make interpersonal comparisons. Generally, the greatest weight is given to low-income groups, although that need not be the case. Of course, the choice of such welfare weights is highly controversial because their choice essentially determines income distribution.[13]

There is a voluminous literature on the theory of income distribution, the social welfare function, and justice.[14] For example, a recent theory of justice contends that policy should be evaluated by the welfare of the most miserable person. Making this person better off even though others are made worse off is socially desirable.[15] This only requires comparing the levels of utility of different people in different situations.

Another of the more celebrated treatises is that of *Arrow's impossibility theorem*.[16] This theorem addresses the question of whether a general rule exists that can rank social states based only on the way these states are ranked by individual members of society. Arrow showed that there can be no such rule

---

[13] One objective approach in this case is to estimate the policy preference functions corresponding to observed government decisions. Some studies of this type have shown that neither the Pareto nor compensation criterion has been used. See, for example, the study of Gordon C. Rausser and John W. Freebairn, "Estimation of Policy Preference Functions: An Application to U.S. Beef Import Quotas," *The Review of Economics and Statistics*, Vol. 56, No. 4 (November 1974), pp. 437–49.

[14] See, for example, A. K. Sen, *Collective Choice and Social Welfare* (Edinburgh: Oliver & Boyd Ltd., 1970).

[15] J. Rawls, *A Theory of Justice* (New York: Oxford University Press, 1971).

[16] Arrow, *Social Choice*.

under reasonable requirements (an example of an ethical rule that does not work is the principle of majority voting). Thus, to make ethical judgments theoretically, one is forced to compare the utilities of different people.

In applied welfare economics, one should keep the notion of a welfare function clearly in the background; but this does not mean that one should abandon the study of welfare economics because the function cannot be specified in terms of any practical meaning. Even those who are critical of welfare economics for this reason must agree that it is still often possible to point out who loses and who gains, as well as the magnitude of losses and gains for particular policies, and that this information is useful to policymakers.

In summary of the welfare function controversy, it suffices to quote a notable welfare economist, E. J. Mishan:

> The social welfare function, even when it is more narrowly defined as a ranking of all conceivable combinations of individual welfare, remains but a pleasing and nebulous abstraction. It cannot be translated into practical guidance for economic policy. Even if there were no fundamental obstacles to its construction, or even if one could think up reasonable conditions under which a social welfare function could exist, there would remain the virtually impossible task of arranging for society to rank unambiguously all conceivable combinations of the individual welfares and moreover—in order to utilise this massive apparatus—to discover (without much cost) the effect on the welfare of each person in society (in terms of utilities, goods, or money) of the introduction of alternative economic organisations. For only if we have such data can we rank all existing and future economic possibilities and pronounce some to be socially superior to others. Although one can always claim that "useful insights" have emerged from the attempts to construct theoretical social welfare functions, the belief that they can ever be translated into useful economic advice is chimerical.
>
> In contrast, the more pedestrian welfare criteria, although analyzed in abstract terms, can be translated into practical propositions. Modern societies do seek to rank projects or policies by some criterion of economic efficiency and to take account also of distributional consequences.[17]

3.4 POTENTIAL VERSUS ACTUAL GAINS

Because the social welfare function is a concept upon which general agreement has not been reached[18] and because the potential welfare criterion is one that renders many policy alternatives noncomparable, the compensation principle has emerged as the criterion that is empirically the most widely applicable. But this conclusion underscores the controversy about whether compensation should actually be paid in adopting policy changes that satisfy the criterion. If possible, should the gainers from a new policy actually compensate the losers

---

[17] E. J. Mishan, "Welfare Criteria: Resolution of a Paradox," *The Economic Journal,* Vol. 83, No. 331 (September 1973), pp. 747, 748.

[18] For a further discussion of the difficulties related to determination of a social welfare function, see A. B. Atkinson, "On the Measurement of Inequality," *Journal of Economic Theory,* Vol. 2, No. 3 (September, 1970), pp. 244–63, and Amartya Sen, *On Economic Inequality* (Oxford: Clarendon Press, 1973).

such that "everyone" is actually made better off? Can a policy change be recommended only on the basis of "potential" gains alone recognizing that, if the change is made, someone is actually made worse off? As an example, the United Automobile Workers (UAW) union has taken the stand that new technology which displaces workers should not be introduced unless the workers are fully compensated for their losses. This is a case where the *potential* gains criterion is not supported; but, of course, to the extent that the UAW represents displaced workers, objections from the losing group are not surprising.

However, an economist can often analyze the distributional impacts of policy choices that can be carried out without getting into the issue of compensation. For example, suppose that one did an analysis of the impact of removing quotas on the importation of steel into the United States. A proper analysis would show the separate effects on government revenues, producers, consumers, and the like (possibly by disaggregated groups if, say, several groups of consumers are affected differently); thus, the losers, the gainers, and the magnitudes of losses and gains would be identified. Such an analysis would be useful to government officials who are elected or appointed to decide, among other things, the issue of compensation. In fact, a welfare analysis that does not adequately indicate individual group effects may be misleading or useless to government officials endowed with authority to make interpersonal comparisons. Thus, as emphasized in Chapter 1, studies can be done on the impact of policy choices using welfare economics without getting into the debate as to what "ought to be."

3.5 SUMMARY

This chapter has focused on the compensation principle and the welfare function as devices to aid policymakers in using resources optimally. The compensation principle states that state B is preferred to state A if, in making the move from state A to state B, the gainers can compensate the losers such that everyone could be made better off. The principle is based on potential rather than actual compensation. As a result, some could be made actually worse off from a policy change, yet the change would be supported if the gainers could have compensated the losers so that everyone could have been better off. Because the principle is based on potential rather than actual gains, two problems arise: the reversal paradox and the intransitivity problem. However, even though the criterion is based on potential gains, these problems can arise only if no first-best bundle is considered.

The concept of a utility possibility curve was introduced, and a parallel was drawn between the utility possibility approach to welfare economics versus that based on production possibility frontiers and Scitovsky indifference curves. The notion of a potential welfare criterion was introduced. If this criterion is adhered to by policymakers, all possible bundles of goods have to be considered together with all possible distributions of these bundles. Such an approach is apparently not empirically practical (although it is considered further in Section 8.3).

Since it is impossible by the compensation principle to rank first-best bundles, the concept of a welfare function was introduced. If such a function were available and agreed upon, the optimum organization could be obtained. But since agreement on such a function cannot be reached, the compensation principle is apparently the most widely applicable, yet empirically practical, criterion. However, one of the problems with the principle is that it is based on potential rather than actual gains. Thus, in any policy context, the payment of compensation is a matter that must be decided by policymakers endowed with the authority to determine income distributional issues.

4

Producer Welfare: The Case of the Single Competitive Firm

Production is a crucial component of economic activity. Many firms produce the goods and services consumed by the general public. Some industries (for example, steel) are made up of only a few firms, whereas others are made up of many firms (for example, the U.S. wheat-producing industry). Also, some firms are multinational in scope (that is, they manufacture and sell products in more than one country).

Increasing attention has been devoted to the question of how well producing firms and marketing firms perform. That is, do they price competitively or not? Does competitive pricing lead to economic efficiency? Do producers adequately consider the costs imposed on society by pollution of the environment? Are producers affected (and, if so, by how much) by government policy? For example, what is the effect on the steel industry of the use of import quotas?

This chapter focuses on producer welfare measurement. Several different producer welfare measures are defined and compared. The chapter proceeds on a rather simple level, dealing only with a single competitive firm under the assumption of profit maximization. Clearly, firms may operate with more criteria in mind than simply profit maximization. A vast literature exists in positive economics about firms that maximize sales, growth, market shares, and the like. Although the approach developed in this chapter and throughout the rest of this book could be used in contexts where firms have such objective criteria, the major emphasis is on profit maximization since it is the more popular and perhaps more relevant approach. The profit-maximization approach requires some generalization when price or production is random. For example, a more appropriate assumption is that producers maximize the expected utility from profits. But this distinction makes no difference when prices and production are nonrandom, as in the case of this chapter. The case with risk (random prices and production) in which utility maximization may be important is introduced in Chapter 11 and considered in detail in Appendices A and C.

Welfare analysis of an individual firm, even in a competitive industry, is often required. Examples are the analysis of effects of selective labor strikes against individual firms and analysis of the effects of antitrust litigation brought against a single processor or retailer by a single producer of a product. However, in most cases, empirical welfare analysis focuses on an entire industry. This requires aggregating producer responses and effects. This issue will be delayed until Chapter 8. The concepts derived in this chapter, however, form the basis for aggregation.

4.1 THE PROFIT-MAXIMIZING FIRM

The basic framework for the analysis of this chapter is the neoclassical model as presented in Figure 4.1. Under the assumption of profit maximization, the producer equates price and marginal cost (MC) assuming price exceeds the minimum of the average variable cost (AVC) curve; hence, with a fixed output price of p_1, the producer chooses output level q_1. Suppose that output price is increased to p_2 because of a policy change, such as introducing a tariff or a price-support program. To maximize profits, the firm will increase output from q_1 to q_2. *Is the producer better off, and by how much?* Or put another way, has there been an increase in revenue that may be "taxed away" without making the firm any worse off than it was before the price change?

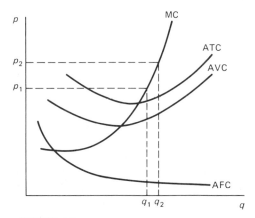

FIGURE 4.1

Alternatively, consider the case where the firm is faced with the prospect of having to discontinue production as a result of some policy decision; for example, an air quality control board closes down factories in an urban area during a temperature-inversion period, or farmers are not allowed to harvest and market their crops because it has been found that seed treatments included a carcinogenic compound. *How would one determine the welfare loss to producers forced to shut down production?* There are some measures—profits, for example—that may be appropriate for answering questions related to changes in welfare for a producing firm but are not appropriate for questions relating to the change in welfare of a firm when it cannot produce.

A clear definition of a producer is needed to address the foregoing issues. The *producer* (that is, the firm) is defined as a legal entity that supplies either intermediate or final goods and possibly uses both variable and fixed inputs in the production process. This chapter assumes that the firm is able to purchase all the variable inputs it needs at a fixed price; that is, the supply curve for variable inputs is perfectly price elastic. With respect to the fixed factors, the analysis is appropriate for cases where the producer is either an owner and/or a renter. The fixed factors that the firm does not own are rented at a market-determined "rental" price which is not negotiable during the period under consideration. The fixed factors owned by the firm are valued at their opportunity cost at the beginning of the period. The fixed costs associated with the fixed factors are sunk; that is, they cannot be avoided even if the firm goes out of business (for example, as when a farm firm rents land and pays a cash rental at the beginning of the season). Within this framework, *the rents to primary factor owners will be unaffected by any short-run policy change imposed on the producer.*

This point is illustrated in Figure 4.2. Initially, the firm is producing output q_0 at price p_0 using x^0 of a variable factor that has a perfectly elastic supply at w^0 and R_0 of a fixed factor that has been rented at (or has an opportunity cost of) r_0. Suppose, then, that a policy change is considered which increases output price to p_1. The firm expands its level of output to q_1 and increases its variable input use from x^0 to x^1 as the derived demand for x shifts from $D_x(p_0)$ to $D_x(p_1)$ in Figure 4.2(c). Hence, in the short run, the increase in price from p_0 to p_1 affects only the producing firm, not the owners of fixed factors. However, if the output price remains at p_1 and the supply of fixed factors remains perfectly elastic at w^0, rents to the fixed factor will increase under competition to perhaps r_1 in Figure 4.2(b) in the subsequent period. Thus, the welfare position of the firm may be reduced if the fixed factors are owned by individuals outside the firm.

This is important because very often firms rent factors of production. A clear illustration is in agriculture, where many farmers rent land from landowners on a cash-lease basis. As a result, an increase in the price of farm products can improve the welfare position of the farmer in the short run. However, how long

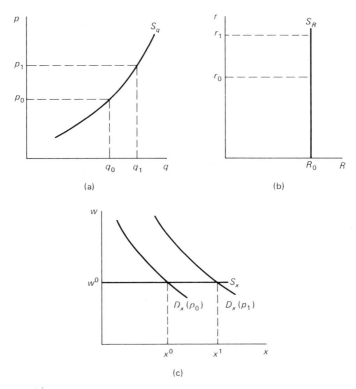

FIGURE 4.2

the firm can maintain this position depends on the extent to which the owners of the fixed factor increase the rental price. Also, the observation that the increase in price in the output market in Figure 4.2(a) shifts the demand curve for the variable input in Figure 4.2(c) suggests another question: Given that the producer's welfare has been affected as a result of some policy change, can the extent of change in welfare be measured in the input market, the output market, or both?

Before proceeding further, it is necessary to adopt clear and concise definitions of the concepts and measures of producer welfare. Such terms as producer surplus and quasi-rent are often used in this connection, but unfortunately, there remains a considerable amount of confusion in economics as to just what these terms mean. To avoid this confusion, the following section focuses on definitions of producer welfare measures. Sections 4.3 and 4.4 then evaluate the extent to which these concepts are reflective of producer welfare in terms of the general criteria for welfare measurement discussed in the preceding chapters. Sections 4.5 and 4.6 contain a number of alternative possibilities for measuring benefits accruing to a single producer. Finally, the use of producer welfare measures over multiple time periods is considered.

4.2 WELFARE MEASURES FOR THE PRODUCING FIRM

Profit

Profit is perhaps the most obvious candidate for a measure of producer welfare since, at this point, maximizing profit is the assumed objective of the firm. Profit is also the best understood. Profit is defined as gross receipts minus total costs; that is, profit (π) is given by

$$\pi = \text{TR} - \text{TC} = \text{TR} - \text{TVC} - \text{TFC}$$

where

$$\text{TR} = \text{total revenue}$$
$$\text{TC} = \text{total cost}$$
$$\text{TVC} = \text{total variable cost}$$
$$\text{TFC} = \text{total fixed cost}$$

To what extent does profit measure producer welfare? To determine this, the general criteria of compensating and equivalent variation discussed in Chapters 1 and 3 are used. First, the case is considered where the firm produces a positive level of output before and after a policy change.

The competitive firm in Figure 4.3 with supply (short-run marginal cost) curve S is faced with price p_1 and must consider the higher price p_2.[1] Profit-maximizing quantities at p_1 and p_2 are q_1 and q_2, respectively. *The compensating variation associated with the price increase is the sum of money that, when taken away from the producing firm, leaves it just as well off as if the price did*

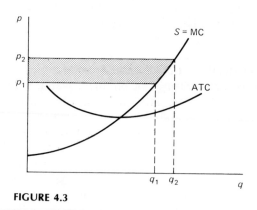

FIGURE 4.3

---

[1]Again, it is assumed for convenience that the average cost curve (at its minimum) intersects marginal cost at a small output.

not change, given that it is free to adjust production (to profit-maximizing quantities) in either case. Since profit at p_2 (and q_2) is higher than at p_1 (and q_1) by the shaded area, this area is exactly the compensating variation. *The equivalent variation associated with the price increase is the sum of money which, when given to the firm, leaves it just as well off without the price change as if the change occurred, again assuming freedom of adjustment.* Since profit at p_1 is lower than at p_2 by the amount of the shaded area, this area must also represent the equivalent variation. Thus, the change in profit associated with such a price change provides an exact measure of both the compensating and equivalent variations.

Although profit can serve as an appropriate measure of the welfare effects of a price change, however, it is not always appropriate in other cases. For example, consider the case where a policy change prevents a firm from producing during a period. The compensating variation of such a change is the sum of money which, when taken away from the firm, leaves the firm just as well off as if it were allowed to remain in production. This sum is generally negative. The equivalent variation is the sum of money which, when given to the firm, leaves the firm just as well off in production as if it were forced to shut down. This sum is also generally negative.

A firm with marginal cost MC, average variable cost AVC, average total cost ATC, and product price p_1 is depicted in Figure 4.4. Only by giving the firm a transfer payment in the amount of area $a + b$ is it just as well off without producing as if production continued as usual. The firm is willing to pay more than its current profits a to remain in production because its fixed costs in the amount of area b cannot be avoided even if production is shut down. But it would be better off shutting down and absorbing fixed costs if a payment any greater than area $a + b$ were required. With any transfer payment (in lieu of production) smaller than area $a + b$, the firm would be worse off (after covering unavoidable fixed costs) than in its previous profit position. The total benefit to the producer from remaining in business is thus given by profit plus fixed cost

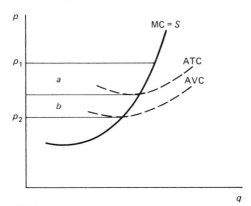

FIGURE 4.4

(area $a + b$) rather than simply profit (area a). Thus, an alternative to profit is required to measure producer welfare in this case.

Producer Surplus and Quasi-rent

As an alternative to profit, Alfred Marshall defined a producer's net benefit as the excess of gross receipts which a producer receives for any commodities produced over their prime cost—that is, over the extra cost that the firm incurs in order to produce those things which it could have escaped if it had not produced them.[2] This concept has been called quasi-rent for the firm because it is a rent on fixed factors employed by the firm but, unlike factor rent, may not persist over a long period of time. Specifically, *quasi-rent (R) is defined as the excess of gross receipts (TR) over total variable costs (TVC)*, $R = \text{TR} - \text{TVC}$. Marshall went on to suggest the area below the price line and above the supply curve—commonly called producer surplus—as a *measure* of this benefit. Thus, *producer surplus is defined as the area above the supply curve and below the price line of the corresponding firm or industry.*[3]

Although Marshall did not emphasize the distinction between quasi-rent as an economic concept and producer surplus as a geometric area, more general cases (such as those in Chapter 9) suggest the need for such a distinction. For purposes of this chapter, which corresponds to Marshall's framework, however, producer surplus and quasi-rent are equivalent.[4]

Given the assumptions of this chapter, the welfare significance of quasi-rent or producer surplus can be usefully investigated by a comparison with profits. To determine the relationship among profit (π), quasi-rent (R), and producer surplus (P), note from above that

$$P = R = \text{TR} - \text{TVC}$$

That is, the area above a competitive firm's short-run supply curve and below the price line provides a measure of the "excess of gross receipts over prime costs" since the firm's short-run supply curve coincides with its marginal cost curve. Hence, based on the analysis of Figure 4.4, one finds that

---

[2]See Alfred Marshall, *Principles of Economics* (London, 1930); also for a discussion of producer welfare measurement, see John M. Currie, John A. Murphy, and Andrew Schmitz, "The Concept of Economic Surplus and Its Use in Economic Analysis," *The Economic Journal*, Vol. 81 (December 1971), pp. 741–99.

[3]George J. Stigler, *The Theory of Price* (New York: The Macmillan Company, 1952), p. 163.

[4]The equivalence of quasi-rent and producer surplus has led Mishan to argue that the term "producer surplus" is unnecessary jargon. Nevertheless, although producer surplus could be discarded in the context of this chapter, it is still useful to retain for measurement purposes in later chapters. See E. J. Mishan, "What Is Producer's Surplus?" *American Economic Review*, Vol. 58, No. 5, Part 1 (December 1968), p. 1279.

$$R = P = \pi + \text{TFC}$$

or that both quasi-rent and producer surplus are given by profit plus total fixed cost.

Now, evaluating quasi-rent or producer surplus with the same criteria as for profit above (that is, by comparison with compensating and equivalent variation), one finds that the change in either is an exact measure of the compensating or equivalent variation of a price change (since the change in each is equal to the change in profit). Where the firm is forced to cease production, however, quasi-rent or producer surplus is also appropriate (where the profit measure is not) since they exceed profit by fixed cost; this is exactly the amount by which profit underestimates the true welfare cost of a forced shutdown.

The total benefit to the producer from remaining in business, given by profit plus fixed cost, is thus equal to quasi-rent, which in the present case of fixed factor prices is equivalent to producer surplus. Since profit underestimates the benefits accruing to a firm from doing business, producer surplus and quasi-rent are more useful focal points for economic welfare analysis.

4.3 A DIAGRAMMATIC COMPARISON OF PROFIT, QUASI-RENT, AND PRODUCER SURPLUS[5]

In various empirical and theoretical economic welfare problems, it can be advantageous to recognize the variety of ways that producer welfare gains can be computed. The most common approach in empirical and graphical theoretic work is simply to determine (according to the definition of producer surplus) the area above the short-run supply curve and below price. For a firm with marginal cost curve MC and average variable cost curve AVC in Figure 4.5, the short-run supply curve is given by $S'S'$ in Figure 4.5(a) (since, at any price below p_1 the firm can no longer recover any of its fixed costs and thus ceases to operate). Hence, producer surplus or, equivalently, quasi-rent can be calculated as the shaded area in Figure 4.5(a).

Another possibility demonstrated in Figure 4.5(b) is suggested by the definition of quasi-rent. At price p_0, the profit-maximizing total receipts are given by the area below p_0 and left of quantity q_0, or

$$\text{TR} = \text{area } a + b + c + d = p_0 \cdot q_0$$

---

[5]For a diagrammatic discussion similar to that in this section, see Charles E. Ferguson, *Microeconomic Theory* (Homewood, Ill.: Richard D. Irwin, Inc., 1969), p. 376. Also, note that the "area" operator is used in this section and throughout this book without parentheses to denote the sum of areas of all terms following it. If any quantities are to be added to the area, they appear in front of the operator.

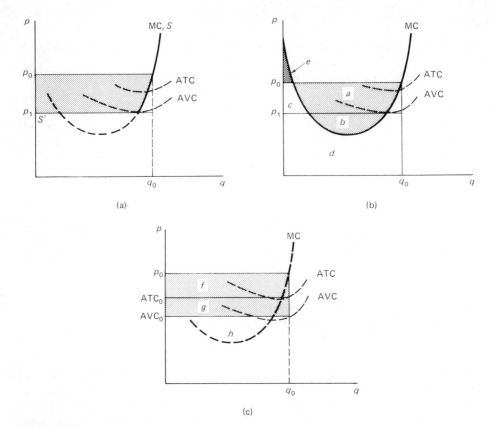

FIGURE 4.5

Also, one measure of total variable costs is the total area below the marginal cost curve (and left of quantity q_0):

$$\text{TVC} = \text{area } c + d + e$$

Thus, quasi-rent can be calculated as the difference,

$$R = \text{TR} - \text{TVC} = \text{area } a + b - e$$

which is the lightly shaded area minus the heavily shaded area. This is the more common theoretical approach suggested by the calculus and is the one used in the appendices of this book.

A third possibility also based on the definition of quasi-rent is suggested in Figure 4.5(c). Again, total receipts can be measured by the area below price p and left of quantity q_0 or by

$$\text{TR} = \text{area } f + g + h = p_0 \cdot q_0$$

Noting that, by definition,

$$\text{TVC} = \text{AVC} \cdot q$$

it is possible to calculate total variable costs as the profit-maximizing output (q_0) multiplied by the average variable cost at that output (AVC_0) which is the area h,

$$\text{TVC} = \text{area } h = \text{AVC} \cdot q_0$$

Hence, quasi-rent or, equivalently, producer surplus can also be calculated as

$$R = \text{area } f + g = (p_0 - \text{AVC}_0) \cdot q_0$$

With this approach it is a simple matter to determine what part of quasi-rent overlaps fixed cost as opposed to profit. By definition, total cost (TC) is given by the product of average total cost (ATC) and quantity,

$$\text{TC} = \text{ATC} \cdot q$$

Hence, total fixed cost (TFC) is given by

$$\text{TFC} = \text{TC} - \text{TVC} = (\text{ATC} - \text{AVC}) \cdot q$$

At output q_0 where average total cost is ATC_0, total fixed cost is thus given by area g with profit given by the remainder of the shaded area (so long as p_0 is greater than ATC_0).[6]

4.4   PRODUCER WELFARE MEASUREMENT IN THE INPUT MARKET AND RELATED ISSUES

Measuring producer welfare effects in the output market is a useful approach in applied economic welfare analysis provided that data are available to estimate supply curves for final products. Cases arise, however, where this is not possible. Data may be sufficient only to estimate the producer's derived de-

---

[6]This latter case suggests another algebraic approach to calculating producer welfare. That is, suppose that the firm uses quantities $x_1, x_2, \ldots, x_n$ of n respective inputs with fixed variable input prices of $w_1, w_2, \ldots, w_n$. Then, by definition,

$$\text{TVC} = w_1 x_1 + w_2 x_2 + \cdots + w_n x_n$$

Hence, quasi-rent or producer surplus is given by

$$R = \text{TR} - \text{TVC} = p_0 q_0 - w_1 x_1 - w_2 x_2 - \cdots - w_n x_n$$

mand in an intermediate product market. For example, it may be possible to estimate the derived demand curve for iron ore at the firm or industry level even though the marginal cost curve for steel production for an individual firm or industry cannot be estimated. In such a case, is it possible to obtain welfare estimates by looking only at input markets? To answer this question, it is essential to understand the welfare significance of changes in areas under derived demand curves and how these relate to the quasi-rent or the producer surplus in the output-market. This section explores these relationships; and, fortunately, for the practitioner, a transition can be made from the input to the output market.

First, the possibilities for measuring the producer welfare effect of an input and/or an output price change in either the input or output markets (at the investigator's choice) are considered for the single-variable-factor case. These arguments are generalized to the case of evaluating a multiple price change (input and/or output) in any arbitrarily chosen market in the many-variable-factor case. In each case, an alternative sequential method of evaluation is also suggested.

The Single-Variable-Input Case

The following sections present welfare measures for cases when prices change in the input market only, when prices change in the output market only, and when both prices change together. In this simple framework, in addition to fixed factors, the firm uses only a single variable input.

Input price changes in the input market. The consideration of welfare effects of changes in factor market conditions can be made as before through application of the general willingness-to-pay welfare criteria of Chapters 1 and 3. Consider a single competitive firm (with fixed product price) using a single variable input x. The input demand schedule D for such a firm is determined as in Figure 4.6(a) by the value of marginal product (defined as output price multiplied by the marginal physical productivity of the input). The compensating variation of a fall in input price from w^0 to w^1 is the sum of money the producer would be willing to pay to obtain the privilege of buying at the lower price (that is, which would leave the firm just as well off at the lower price). The equivalent variation is the sum of money the producer would accept to forgo the privilege of buying at the lower price (that is, which would leave the firm just as well off at the original price). But note that, at input price w^0 and corresponding profit-maximizing input use x^0, total variable cost is given by the area $b + d$ (or

---

This suggests a rather simple empirical approach of simply using income-expense accounts in producer welfare measurement. In Chapter 9, which carries analysis to sector and general economy levels, this type of approach is generalized to suggest the use of national income accounts in measuring the distribution of producer welfare originating within a market or industry.

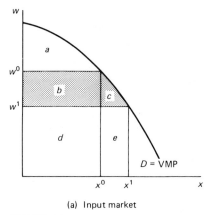

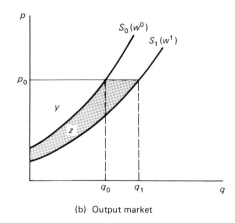

(a) Input market (b) Output market

FIGURE 4.6

w^0x^0) and total receipts are area $a + b + d$.[7] Similarly, at price w^1 and input use x^1, total variable cost is area $d + e$ and total receipts are area $a + b + c + d + e$. Thus, the shaded area $b + c$ measures the change in either quasi-rent or profit. In keeping with the definition of producer surplus provided above, the triangle-like area below a demand curve and above a price line will be called consumer surplus. For this case, the compensating and equivalent variations are identical and are measured by the change in either quasi-rent, profit, or the change in consumer surplus in the input market. Using the same approach as in Section 4.2, it can also be shown that the compensating and equivalent variation of altogether preventing the producer from obtaining the needed inputs is measured by quasi-rent or consumer surplus in the input market (rather than profit).

Input price changes measured in the output market.   Interestingly, the net welfare effect on the producer of an input price change can also be measured accurately in the output market. That is, it was shown in Section 4.3 that producer welfare (or rent) is accurately measured by the producer surplus area above the short-run marginal cost curve and below price in the output market. Thus, suppose that the shift in marginal cost brought about by the change in factor prices is represented in Figure 4.6(b) by movement from S_0 to S_1 with a corresponding output change from q_0 to q_1.[8] The resulting change in producer surplus or quasi-rent is then given by the shaded area z since producer surplus

---

[7] A mathematical proof of the latter claim is contained, as a special case, in Appendix A. For those unfamiliar with the calculus, an intuitive understanding of this point may be gained by viewing the area $a + b + d$ as a discrete summation of output price multiplied by marginal product over all levels of input usage from zero to x^0.

[8] Of course, depending on the magnitude and direction of the input price movement, the output market effect could be in either direction, but a rightward shift is assumed for illustrative purposes.

is given by area y at S_0 and by area $y + z$ at S_1. This area z must also measure the change in the factor-market consumer surplus since both areas are unambiguously equivalent to quasi-rent.

Output price changes measured in the input market.   The preceding result suggests the additional possibility of measuring the effect of an output price change in the input market. This possibility indeed exists. That is, since the output market producer surplus, the input market consumer surplus, and quasi-rent are all equal in the single-variable-input case, the increase in quasi-rent resulting from an increase in output market price can be measured by the change in input market consumer surplus as well as by the change in output market producer surplus. Geometrically, this would imply in Figure 4.7 that the increase in producer surplus resulting from an increase in output price from p_0 to p_1 is equal to the increase in consumer surplus in the input market, where D_0 is the demand curve given output price p_0 and D_1 is the demand given output price p_1. Thus, where the (unchanging) input price is w^0, area a in Figure 4.7(a) is equal to area b in Figure 4.7(b).

Simultaneous changes in input and output prices.   Finally, consider a simultaneous change in both input and output price, say, from w^0 to w^1 and from p_0 to p_1, respectively, in Figure 4.8. Producer surplus is given by area c at prices p_0 and w^0 and by area $a + b + c + d$ at prices p_1 and w^1; the change in producer surplus is area $a + b + d$. The input market consumer surplus, on the other hand, is given by area v at prices p_0 and w^0 and by area $v + x + y + z$ at prices p_1 and w^1; the change is area $x + y + z$. Since both producer and consumer surpluses measure quasi-rent in the single-input case, the change in quasi-rent from the multiple price change can be completely measured either in the output market (by area $a + b + d$) or in the input market (by area $x + y + z$).

Alternatively, the multiple price change can be evaluated by imposing the

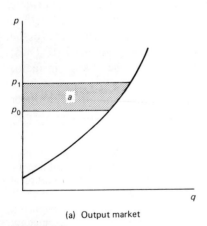

(a) Output market

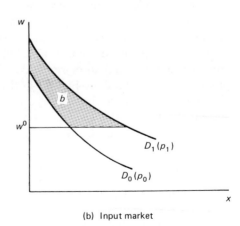

(b) Input market

FIGURE 4.7

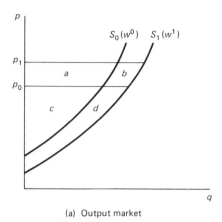

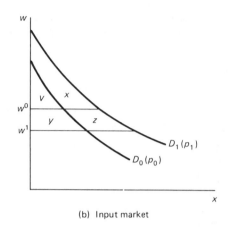

(a) Output market   (b) Input market

FIGURE 4.8

individual changes sequentially, say, first from p_0 to p_1 and then from w^0 to w^1. Moving from p_0 to p_1 and holding w fixed at w^0 results in a change in rents equal to area a. Then holding p fixed at p_1 and moving from w^0 to w^1 results in an additional change in rents equal to area $y + z$. The overall change in quasi-rent is thus area $a + y + z$. Alternatively, the input price could be changed first with p fixed at p_0 obtaining area y. Then changing p at $w = w^1$ obtains area $a + b$ for a total change of area $a + b + y$.

The change in quasi-rent associated with the dual price change from p_0 to p_1 and from w^0 to w^1 thus has at least four alternative representations in Figure 4.7:[9]

$$\Delta R = \text{area } a + b + d = \text{area } x + y + z = \text{area } a + y + z = \text{area } a + b + y$$

It can be further noted that the four approaches outlined above are generally applicable regardless of the direction of price movements. For example, if both prices increase from, say, p_0, w^1 to p_1, w^0, then total evaluation in the output market implies a welfare change of area $a - d$. Evaluated completely in the input market, the change is area $x - y$. Using the sequential approach, the change is area $a + b - y - z$ or, equivalently, area $a - y$ depending on whether output price or input price is changed first.

The Case of Multiple Inputs

Attention is now turned to the multiple-variable-factor case. When the analysis is extended with multiple inputs, a definition of the concept of consumer surplus in input markets is somewhat more difficult because the demand

---

[9]Additionally, noting that area d = area y, area a = area x, and area b = area z, the change in rents associated with the change from p_0, w^0 to p_1, w^1 can be represented in several other ways. As will become clear, however, the alternatives are of doubtful interest from either a theoretical or an empirical perspective.

curves for inputs differ from the value-of-marginal-product curves. That is, the value-of-marginal-product curves correspond to demand for an input when uses of other inputs are held constant. Derived demand curves, on the other hand, take account of optimal adjustment in output and other input uses as the associated input price varies.[10] In generalizing the results of the preceding section, however, it turns out that the derived demand curve is the appropriate concept to use in measuring quasi-rent since it reflects the producer's marginal evaluation of the input as its price and quantity vary. Hence, *the area under the derived demand curve and above price measures quasi-rent for the producer in the case where production requires positive use of the input* (this result is established rigorously in Appendix A). *If production is possible without use of the input,* that part of quasi-rent which can be earned without use of the input would, of course, not be reflected by the area under its derived demand. Furthermore, that amount of quasi-rent may change with changes in other prices. Hence, because quasi-rent is possible without use of the input, *a multiple price change cannot be completely evaluated in the single-input market if production is possible without use of the input.* Nevertheless, the *change* in quasi-rent with respect to the *change* in a good's price can be accurately measured by the change in the consumer surplus area under its derived demand curve since other prices, and hence quasi-rent possible without use of the input, do not change in this case (Appendix A). This suggests the possibility of extending the sequential approach of evaluating welfare changes over markets suggested above to the case of many factor markets.

Thus, again, two general approaches to evaluating producer welfare changes associated with multiple price changes are possible: (1) complete evaluation in a single market for a necessary input or output and (2) sequential evaluation over the markets where prices are changed. Suppose that a producer produces output q using two inputs x_1 and x_2. The first approach is illustrated in Figure 4.9 for a multiple price change from (p_0, w_1^0, w_2^0) to (p_1, w_1^1, w_2^1). Product supply is S_0 at initial prices and S_1 at final prices. Derived demands are given by D_1^0 and D_2^0 at initial prices and by D_1^1 and D_2^1 at final prices. Since quasi-rent is equal to producer surplus in this case, the change in producer welfare or quasi-rent is given by the change in producer surplus. Producer surplus is given by area $a + b$ at initial prices and by area $b + c$ at final prices; the change, area $c - a$, thus completely measures the welfare effect of the multiple price change on the producer.

If some use of input x_1 is necessary for any positive level of production, then the change in consumer surplus in the x_1 market is also equal to the change in producer welfare or quasi-rent. The x_1-market consumer surplus is given by area $r + s + t$ at initial prices and by area $r + u$ at final prices; the change, area $u - s - t$, thus also completely measures the welfare change (i.e., area $u - s -$

---

[10]For a detailed discussion of this relationship, see Ferguson, *Microeconomic Theory,* pp. 144–53.

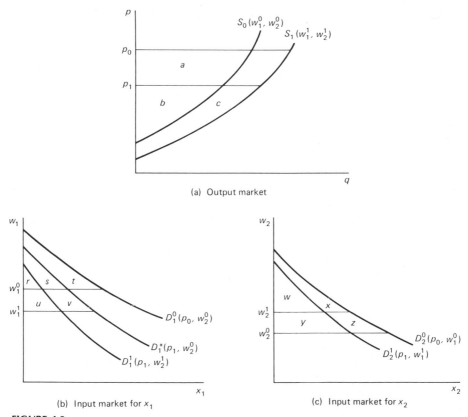

(a) Output market

(b) Input market for x_1

(c) Input market for x_2

FIGURE 4.9

t = area $c - a$). Finally, if some use of input x_2 is necessary for any positive level of production, the change in consumer surplus in the x_2 market from area $w + x + y + z$ to area w is also equal to the change in quasi-rent; that is, $-$area $x + y + z$ = area $c - a$ = area $u - s - t$.

Consider now the alternative approach of sequential evaluation over the markets where prices change. For exemplary purposes, consider changing first p, then w_1, and finally, w_2. The order of imposing these changes does not affect the final result when demand and supply functions satisfy profit-maximization conditions from economic theory (Appendix A). If output price is changed from p_0 to p_1 while input prices are held constant at w_1^0, w_2^0, then producer surplus changes from area $a + b$ to area b for a loss of area a. Next, holding output price and x_2 price constant at p_1 and w_2^0, respectively, and changing x_1 price from w_1^0 to w_1^1, the consumer surplus in the x_1 market changes from area $r + s$ to area $r + s + u + v$ for a gain of area $u + v$. Note that consumer surplus in this case is evaluated using D_1^*, the derived demand curve corresponding to prices p_1 and w_2^0. Finally, holding output price and x_1 price constant at p_1 and w_1^1, respectively, and changing x_2 price from w_2^0 to w_2^1, the x_2-market consumer

63

surplus changes from area $w + y$ to area w for a loss of area y. Summing the sequential changes over the three markets obtains area $u + v - a - y$, which measures the overall gain (loss if negative) in quasi-rent or producer welfare associated with the multiple price change from (p_0, w_1^0, w_2^0) to (p_1, w_1^1, w_2^1).[11]

Although the convenience of completely evaluating a multiple price change in a single market may appear to be far more desirable than the sequential methodology because of simplicity, this is not necessarily the case. The sequential approach, in fact, has distinct advantages from an empirical point of view. As explained in Sections 8.7 and 8.8, the sequential approach reduces the importance of obtaining good estimates of supply and demand outside the range of observed or contemplated changes (such as near the axes). Such estimates, however, are necessary if one follows the approach of making a complete evaluation in a single market when more than one price changes. On the other hand, evaluation of changes in a single market requires less information (data) relating to other markets and may be the only feasible approach when data are limited. Hence, each of the two general approaches of this section may be interesting from an empirical point of view.

4.5 LENGTH-OF-RUN ANALYSIS AND TEMPORAL AGGREGATION

For producer welfare measurement over longer periods of time where some fixed factors become variable, the appropriate definition of the marginal cost curve *vis-à-vis* factor fixity requires further discussion. For example, over longer periods of time, some fixed costs become adjustable and play the role of moving the firm from one marginal cost curve to another.

Consider a firm with short-run marginal cost curve S_1 operating at initial price p_0 in Figure 4.10. Suppose that price increases from p_0 to p_1 over two production periods. In the short run (during the first period), production increases from q_0 to q_1 along the short-run marginal cost curve. Thus, the increase in producer surplus or quasi-rent in the first period is given by area a. By the second period, however, the producing firm will have had time to adjust some of its fixed factors in response to the price increase. These investments result in a rightward shift in the short-run supply curve to S_1' and a corresponding increase in production to q_2 for the second period.

The change in short-run producer surplus or quasi-rent for the second period can be found as follows. First, if the initial price had continued (thus inducing no adjustment), producer surplus would have been given by area d. With the

---

[11]In terms of Figure 4.9, one can show rigorously on the basis of results in Appendix A that

$$\text{area } a - c = \text{area } s + t - u = \text{area } x + y + z = \text{area } a + y - u - v$$

so that no contradiction is implied by the results above.

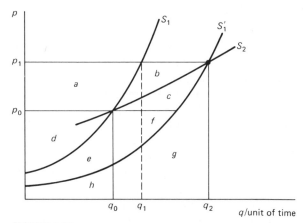

FIGURE 4.10

change, however, the producer surplus area above short-run marginal cost S_1' and below price p_1 is given by area $a + b + c + d + e + f$. The change in short-run producer surplus or rents in the second period resulting from increased price is thus given by the difference, area $a + b + c + e + f$. Consider, however, that the movement from the initial position (p_0, q_0) to the final position (p_1, q_2) traces out an intermediate run marginal cost or supply curve S_2 corresponding to two-period production adjustment possibilities.[12] In this case, as is ordinarily true with marginal cost curves, the total adjustment costs (considered variable over two production periods) incurred to increase production from q_0 to q_2 are given by the change in area under the corresponding marginal cost curve S_2, that is, the area $c + f + g$. This implies, by the development in Section 4.3, that the correct measure of the change in producer welfare in the second time period (as viewed from the beginning of the first time period) is given by the intermediate-run producer surplus area $a + b$, that is, the increase in total receipts, area $a + b + c + f + g$, less the total adjustment costs, area $c + f + g$ (which are total variable costs in the two-period time horizon). Thus, *the correct measure of the total producer welfare impact over the two time periods is not the sum of all the short-run producer surpluses over affected production periods but, rather, the sum of producer surpluses of*

---

[12]Although it is usually assumed in neoclassical economics that investments can be readily reversed with the same time lags as those required to bring them into productive capacity, the more general case (with varying degrees of irreversibility) would simply result in a kink in the two-period (or longer) marginal cost curve at the prevailing output level. The analysis in Figure 4.10 would not be substantively affected except that, once two-period adjustment to price p_1 is made, two-period adjustment back to q_0 would not be possible without incurring greater costs than originally [the two-period marginal cost curve to the left of q_2 would rotate upward about (p_1, q_2) owing to irreversibility].

variable lengths of run (as viewed from the initial point in time) over the affected production runs.[13]

For example, in Figure 4.10, simply adding the change in producer surplus in the first time period (area a) to the simple change in short-run producer surplus for the second time period (area $a + b + c + e + f$) does not yield a correct measure of the change in producer welfare resulting from a price increase from p_0 to p_1 over the two periods. The correct change in producer welfare is the sum of the change in surplus corresponding to S_1 in the first period (that is, area a) and the change in surplus corresponding to S_2 in the second period (that is, area $a + b$). In general, the change in producer welfare is determined by calculating the change in producer surplus corresponding to the one-period supply curve for the first period, the two-period supply curve for the second period, the three-period supply curve for the third period, and so on.[14]

It may seem at first as though the area (or, perhaps, twice the area) above the two-period marginal cost curve and below price should appropriately measure two-period producer welfare. To understand clearly that this is *not* the case, one must note, first, that the lower axis in Figure 4.10 measures quantities for a single time period regardless of the supply curve depicted and, second, the supply curve S_2 is not attainable even when investments are begun immediately in the first period because the supply curve S_1 represents the minimum possible marginal cost attainable during the first time period. The appropriate marginal cost or supply curve which applies over the aggregate two-period time interval, on the other hand, corresponds to the horizontal summation of the supply curves S_1 and S_2 (depicted as S_{1+2}) in Figure 4.11 (note that the lower axis

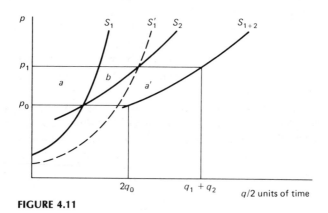

FIGURE 4.11

---

[13]These statements are made without regard to time preferences of producers at this point. The appropriate social discounting procedures for these considerations will be discussed in Chapter 13.

[14]For a more rigorous and complete derivation of this procedure and for a stochastic generalization, see Appendix C.

measures quantity over two time periods). Since the area a' is geometrically equivalent to area a, the change in the producer surplus (area $a + b + a'$) with appropriate temporal aggregation provides an accurate measurement of the producer welfare impact of the two-period price increase from p_0 to p_1. This result (and its straightforward extension) is of interest in generalizing later theoretical results over all time horizons. However, the equivalent approach with greater temporal disaggregation exemplified in Figure 4.10 is often of important practical applicability when time preferences must be considered.[15]

Yet another alternative approach to calculating a correct measure of producer welfare effects over several time periods identifies the investment costs associated with shifts in short-run marginal cost schedules. In particular, consider the investment cost associated with movement from S_1 to S_1' in Figure 4.10. As indicated above, the total adjustment cost from the initial situation at (p_0, q_0) to the final situation at (p_1, q_2) is given by the change in area under the corresponding two-period marginal cost curve S_2 (i.e., area $c + f + g$). The total adjustment cost includes both the change in short-run variable cost and investment. But short-run total variable cost is initially area $e + h$ and finally area $g + h$, so the increase in total variable cost is area $g + h$ − area $e + h$, or area $g - e$. The change in investment associated with the price change must thus be the increase in total adjustment cost minus the increase in total variable cost, or area $c + f + g$ − area $g - e$ = area $c + f + e$. Alternatively, the change in investment can be viewed as the difference in the sum of short-run producer surpluses with and without the two-period price change (area $2a + b + c + e + f$) minus the net welfare gain summed over the two periods (area $2a + b$). This implies, conversely, that the net welfare gain over the two periods is given by the sum of the changes in short-run surpluses minus the change in investment. Indeed, under certainty and with time preferences aside, Appendix C shows that, for any general time horizon, the net producer welfare change can be accurately measured by the sum of changes in short-run producer surpluses minus the sum of changes in investment over the entire time horizon.[16] In addition, details are given in Appendix C for calculation of investment effects of changes in price over time using standard dynamic supply equations. Similar

---

[15]For a further discussion, see Chapter 13 and Appendix C.

[16]For exemplary applications of this rule, the reader is referred to the following: C. Riordan, "General Multistage Marginal Cost Dynamic Programming Model for the Optimizations of Investment-Pricing Decisions," *Water Resources Research,* Vol. 7, No. 2 (April 1971), pp. 245–53; C. Riordan, "Multistage Marginal Cost Model of Investment-Pricing Decisions: Applications to Urban Water Supply Treatment Facilities," *Water Resources Research,* Vol. 7, No. 3 (June 1971), pp. 463–78; Jack Hirshleifer, James C. De Haven, and Jerome W. Milliman, *Water Supply: Economics, Technology, and Policy* (Chicago: University of Chicago Press, 1960); and I. E. Strand and D. L. Hueth, "A Management Model for a Multispecies Fishery," in *Economic Impacts of Extended Fisheries Jurisdiction,* ed. Lee G. Anderson (Ann Arbor, Mich.: Ann Arbor Science Publishers, Inc., 1977).

results are also developed in Appendix C for temporal aggregation of consumer surplus measures.

4.6 SUMMARY

This chapter has dealt with the welfare analysis of a single competitive, profit-maximizing firm which may or may not own the primary factors of production. A basic distinction has been made between the suppliers of primary inputs and the producing firm itself. The focus has been specifically on welfare measures for the producing firm. An exact measure of producer welfare is provided by producer surplus, quasi-rent, or consumer surplus in any basic input market—a basic input being any input such that production without the use of some of the input is impossible. The firm's welfare can be measured in either the output or input market. The latter possibility is of particular interest when sufficient data for examining welfare impacts are available only at a primary product level. It is often easier to estimate derived demand curves for intermediate products than supply schedules for final products.

The possibility of aggregating producer welfare measures over time was also investigated. Results indicate that short-run producer surpluses, quasi-rents, or input-market consumer surpluses cannot simply be aggregated over time but, rather, that investment costs must be subtracted from the sum of short-run surpluses or quasi-rents.

The results of this chapter are based on the crucial assumption that the variable factors of production used by the firm are in perfectly price-elastic supply. Since most industries contain more than one firm, however, welfare analysis at the industry level requires aggregation; input supplies may not be perfectly elastic at the industry level. For example, the worldwide rapid rise in grain prices in 1972–1975, due largely to large Soviet purchases, is an obvious case where it is important to recognize that input supplies can be positively sloped. During this period of phenomenal world grain price increases, to assume that the basic inputs used by producers, such as land, fertilizer, petroleum products, and machinery, were in perfectly elastic supply would be unrealistic in calculating the consequent welfare effects on farm producers. During this period, prices of most of these inputs more than doubled. Thus, for analyzing this case, the perfectly elastic supply assumption is unrealistic, and if used would apparently lead to a substantial overestimate of the welfare gains to farm producers from a price rise. Chapters 8 and 9 focus on relaxing the perfect elasticity assumptions of this chapter.

Finally, the notion of consumer surplus was introduced with reference to producer derived-demand curves. Hence, it was associated with producer welfare measurement. Chapter 5 focuses on welfare measurement for final consumers, where the notion of consumer surplus plays the vital but more controversial role discussed in Chapter 1.

5

Consumer Surplus
and Consumer Welfare

The definition of a measure of economic welfare for the consumer has been one of the most controversial subjects in economics. Unlike the producer's case, where observable measures of well-being such as profit can be clearly determined, no equally appealing *observable* measure exists for a utility-maximizing consumer. That is, the criterion of the consumer—utility—is not observable. In most practical situations the applied welfare economist can, at best, observe income and consumption decisions at various prices and then, on the basis of these economic transactions, try to compute some money-based measure of welfare effects.

A source of confusion in deriving measures of consumer welfare lies in not distinguishing between "cardinal" and "ordinal" analysis. In Chapters 2 and 3, the analysis was largely ordinal in that only consumer indifference curves were used. No attempt was made to measure the intensity of change in satisfaction or utility the consumer derived when moving from one indifference curve to another; rather, only qualitative concerns were important (for example, which indifference curve was preferred to the other). In applied welfare economics, measures of consumer welfare are generally not *cardinal* in the strict usage of the term. They are money measures of welfare change where money reflects "willingness to pay" on the part of consumers, which in turn, is related to the "utility function" of the consumer. Thus, most measures do not seek to measure utility directly; rather, they estimate a revealed willingness to pay in terms of money.

"Consumer surplus" is the vehicle most often used in empirical work to measure consumer welfare. Unfortunately, it is at the center of the controversy surrounding consumer welfare measurement.[1] For example, one critique of consumer surplus states: "Probably no single concept in the annals of economic theory has aroused so many emphatic expressions of opinion as has consumer's surplus; indeed even today the biting winds of scholarly sarcasm howl around this venerable storm centre."[2] Indeed, the issues that arise when considering consumer surplus as a welfare measure are varied and complex, and their proper resolution requires advanced mathematical techniques. Appendix B provides a rigorous analysis of these issues. This chapter attempts to simplify these issues without avoiding the substantive concerns. It provides heuristic developments of each issue based upon results found in Appendix B and then resolves them in a manner that leads to a practical approach for applied welfare economics.

5.1 THE NOTION OF CONSUMER SURPLUS

Consider the problem of measuring the effect of a price change in terms of something that is observable (for example, dollars spent on the good). In Figure 5.1, the consumer is initially in equilibrium consuming q_0 at price p_0 on the demand curve D. With a reduction in price to p_1, the consumer expands consumption to quantity q_1. How much better off is the consumer? Since the consumer now must spend only $p_1 q_0$ to consume the same quantity that had required an expenditure of $p_0 q_0$, one might argue that the consumer's gain is $(p_0 - p_1)q_0$, or area b. That is, if the consumer continued to consume q_0, there would be additional income in the amount of area b available to spend on other

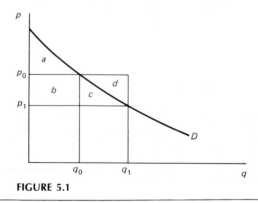

FIGURE 5.1

---

[1] A historical perspective on consumer's surplus is given in J. M. Currie, J. A. Murphy, and A. Schmitz, "The Concept of Economic Surplus and Its Use in Economic Analysis," *The Economic Journal*, Vol. 81 (December 1971), pp. 741–99. See also, Ezra J. Mishan, "The Plain Truth about Consumer Surplus," *Nationalokonomie Journal of Economics*, Vol. 37, No. 1–2 (Spring 1977), pp. 1–24.

[2] R. W. Pfouts, "A Critique of Some Recent Contributions to the Theory of Consumer's Surplus," *Southern Economic Journal*, Vol. 19 (1953), p. 315.

goods and services. This is one money measure of consumer welfare change due to a price change. As shown later, however, other money measures with perhaps better properties also exist.

Consider the alternative case of a price rise from p_1 to p_0, where the consumer is initially consuming quantity q_1. How much worse off is the consumer? In this case the consumer would require an increase in income of $(p_0 - p_1)q_1$ or area $b + c + d$, to continue buying quantity q_1.[3] This raises a paradox since the consumer apparently loses more with the price rise than is gained with the price fall; intuition would suggest, on the contrary, that the two changes should exactly offset one another.

To consider one way this paradox can be resolved, suppose that the price reduction is made in a series of small steps, as in Figure 5.2, from p_0 to p_2, then from p_2 to p_3, and so on until finally reaching price p_1. The corresponding income equivalents in this context would be areas v, w, x, y, and z, respectively. Summing these effects over the entire price change, one would thus obtain the shaded area in Figure 5.2 as a measure of the consumer's gain. Obviously, as one divides the price change more finely, the shaded area begins

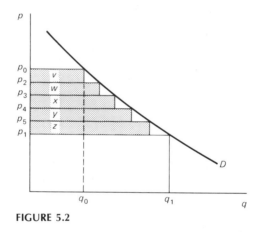

FIGURE 5.2

---

[3]Hicks refers to the changes in area associated with expenditures as the inner cost difference if the associated quantity represents initial consumption; he defines this change in area as the outer cost difference if the quantity represents subsequent consumption. Thus, area b is the inner cost difference of the price fall and the outer cost difference associated with the price rise, and area $b + c + d$ corresponds to the converse cases; see J. R. Hicks, *A Revision of Demand Theory* (Oxford: Clarendon Press, 1956). Because the inner cost difference corresponds closely with the Lespeyers index number formula, where price index weights are based on initial quantities, the inner cost difference is sometimes called a Lespeyers variation. Similarly, the outer cost difference corresponds to the Pasche index number formula, where price index weights are final or current quantities; hence, the outer cost difference is sometimes called a Pasche variation. As these cases suggest, a close relationship exists between consumer surplus theory and index number theory generally, as discussed in Appendix B.

to approach and become essentially synonymous with the area $b + c$ in Figure 5.1. Similarly, if one were to repeat this process in the case of a price rise, the corresponding income-equivalent measure of loss for the consumer would also approach the area $b + c$ in Figure 5.1 as the number of price increments (adding up to $p_0 - p_1$) becomes large. The area $b + c$ results from a summing of the cost differences in consumption bundles as price is continuously and incrementally varied from p_0 to p_1, or vice versa. Area $b + c$ is referred to as a change in consumer surplus, and area $a + b + c$ is the total consumer surplus for price p_1 and area a is the consumer surplus for price p_0. That is, *consumer surplus is defined as the area under the demand curve and above the price line.*

In 1844, Jules Dupuit,[4] who actually coined the phrase consumer surplus, postulated that the price associated with any quantity on a consumer's demand curve is the maximum price the consumer is willing to pay for the last unit consumed; hence, the demand curve is a marginal willingness-to-pay curve. Thus, in Figure 5.3, the consumer is viewed as willing to pay p_1 for the first unit, p_2 for the second, p_3 for the third, and so on. If the consumer actually pays only p_0 for the entire quantity q_0, then the consumer gains a "surplus" of $p_1 - p_0$ on the first unit purchased since willingness to pay exceeds what is actually paid by that amount. The consumer gains similar but declining increments of surplus on each of the units purchased up to q_0. In this context, the total area below the demand curve and left of the quantity consumed q_0 (the lightly shaded area plus the heavily shaded area) is called *gross benefits*, while the area below the

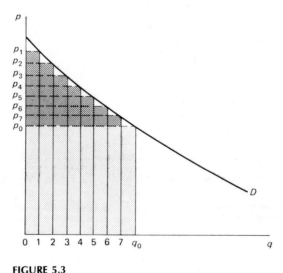

FIGURE 5.3

---

[4]Jules Dupuit,"On the Measurement of the Utility of Public Works," *Annales des Ponts et Chaussees,* Second series, Vol. 8 (1844). Translation reprinted in D. Munby, *Transport,* 1968.

demand curve and above price p_0 (the heavily shaded area) obtained by subtracting costs from gross benefits is the net surplus accruing to the consumer from buying q_0 at p_0. Clearly, if the commodity q is perfectly divisible, the Dupuit surplus from buying q_0 at p_0 will simply be given by the triangle-like area above the price line p_0 and to the left of or behind the demand curve.

Referring back to Figure 5.1, the benefits to the consumer of a price reduction from p_0 to p_1, following Dupuit, would be given by area $b + c$, since this is the increase in the triangle-like area resulting from the price fall. Thus, on the surface, there are at least two reasons why the change in consumer surplus is appealing as a measure of consumer benefits: (1) it represents the sum of cost differences as price is continuously reduced from p_0 to p_1 and (2) it gives the change in what the consumer is willing to pay over that which is actually paid with the price change if the demand curve is a marginal willingness-to-pay curve.

Before proceeding into the theoretical complexities of consumer surplus, however, an *important* point should be noted. That is, neither the cost difference approach (Figure 5.1) nor the excess of willingness to pay over actual payments approach (Figure 5.3) claims to provide a measure of utility gains to the consumer. These approaches, except in certain cases, have only an ordinal significance since they do not measure utility directly.[5] They are money measures of welfare change where the money saved or what the consumer is willing to spend reflects only relative changes in utility of the consumer.

5.2 PATH DEPENDENCE OF CONSUMER SURPLUS

On the basis of the arguments in Section 5.1, consumer surplus appears to be a possibly useful construct in consumer welfare measurement. It turns out, however, that the change in consumer surplus is not so well defined for the case where several prices change simultaneously or where income changes together with price. In point of fact, the change in consumer surplus in the case of a multiple price change or a simultaneous price-income change depends on the order in which these price changes are considered or, more generally, on the path of adjustment. The associated problem is called the *path-dependency problem*.

Consider, for example, the price–income change from price p_0 and income m_0 to price p_1 and income m_1 in Figure 5.4. As suggested in Figure 5.4(a), one might evaluate the price adjustment first and then the income adjustment as along path L_1; or income could be changed first and then price as along path L_2. But consider the associated welfare measurements suggested by Section 5.1. If the price change is considered first, the change in consumer surplus associated

---

[5]For example, two individuals with different utility functions may behave the same way and thus have identical demand curves and consumer surpluses.

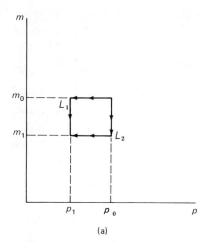 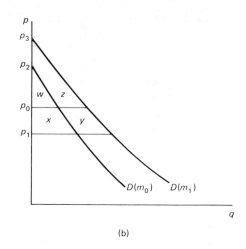

(a)   (b)

FIGURE 5.4

with the price change from p_0 to p_1 is area x where $D(m_0)$ represents demand for q at initial income. To that money-equivalent measure of the price change is added the change in income $m_1 - m_0$, thus obtaining the total measure of change, $m_1 - m_0 +$ area x. Now suppose that income is changed first, obtaining the income effect $m_1 - m_0$. The demand curve for q is shifted to $D(m_1)$; hence, the income-equivalent measure of the price change in completing the path of adjustment L_2 is area $x + y$. Thus, along path L_2 the total change is $m_1 - m_0 +$ area $x + y$, which clearly differs from that obtained along path L_1.[6] The difference in these two alternatives suggests that differences can also exist among other paths of adjustment between the points (p_0, m_0) and (p_1, m_1) in Figure 5.4(a). That such differences can indeed exist is borne out by the results in Appendix B.

---

[6]The reader may also be concerned with whether or not the area z in Figure 5.4(b) has welfare significance since consumer surplus is defined in Section 5.1 as the total area above price and behind the demand curve. Indeed, the total change in this triangle-like area in this case is area $x + y + z$. Note, however, that the motivation for consumer surplus in Section 5.1 was developed in the case where income and prices of other goods—and thus the relevant demand curve—were held fixed. Thus, any application of the same intuition in this section would suggest breaking a price–income or price–price change into steps where the effects of individual price changes could be evaluated along a demand curve that remains stationary with respect to the individual price change.

To further investigate the meaning of area $x + y + z$, consider the case where income is first held at m_0 while increasing price from p_0 to p_2, thus creating a surplus loss of area w. Then consider holding income at m_1 while lowering price from p_3 to p_1, thus creating a surplus gain of area $w + x + y + z$ for a net gain of area $x + y + z$. Obviously, a problem exists since the intervening welfare effect of changing from price p_2 and income m_0 to price p_3 and income m_1 is ignored. In terms of Figure 5.4(a), this approach does not correspond to a complete path between (p_0, m_0) and (p_1, m_1).

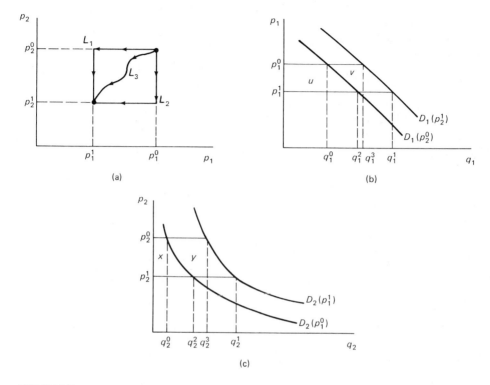

FIGURE 5.5

A similar kind of path dependency exists for the case where several prices change even though income may be held constant. Consider the case in Figure 5.5, where the prices of q_1 and q_2 change from p_1^0 and p_2^0 to p_1^1 and p_2^1, respectively. Two possible paths of adjustment to use in consumer surplus calculations are depicted in Figure 5.5(a) by L_1 and L_2. Along path L_1, the price of q_1 is first changed from p_1^0 to p_1^1, generating a gain of area u under the initial demand curve $D_1(p_2^0)$ in Figure 5.5(b). In the process, the demand curve for q_2 shifts from $D_2(p_1^0)$ to $D_2(p_1^1)$; thus, an additional gain of area $x + y$ results in Figure 5.5(c) in subsequently moving the price of q_2 from p_2^0 to p_2^1. Alternatively, if path L_2 is followed, a gain of area x is first generated in the q_2 market; then a gain of area $u + v$ is obtained in the q_1 market. The resulting measures of welfare change associated with paths L_1 and L_2—areas $u + x + y$ and $u + v + x$, respectively—need not be equal and in general will not be equal except in some special cases discussed in the following sections. Furthermore, these examples merely demonstrate the measures of welfare change resulting from two of many possible paths of price adjustment between prices (p_1^0, p_2^0) and (p_1^1, p_2^1). Many other price paths such as L_3 also exist and lead, in principle, to an endless number of measures of welfare change.

75

Thus, there is an ambiguity in determining the consumer surplus change associated with a multiple price and/or income change affecting consumers. (Recall that such was not generally the case with producers in Chapter 4.) The reason that the producer's case is by comparison unambiguous is that, under profit maximization, the owner or shareholder of the firm (producer) does not have preferences over any aspects of the firm's operation outside of its net money income (or profits). Price changes simply lead to an unambiguous expansion or contraction of the producer's or shareholder's budget constraint with no tilting of the budget surface in the space over which the producer has preferences. That is, an increase in profits to the producer is identical in effect with an increase in income to the consumer, so there is no divergence between the compensating and equivalent measures. In the consumer case, however, changes in prices lead to both income effects and substitution effects between commodities over which the interested party holds preferences.

5.3 UNIQUENESS OF CONSUMER SURPLUS

In view of the problems of path dependence, under what conditions does a *unique* money measure of welfare change exist? Of course, the problem of nonuniqueness arises only in the context of *money measurement* of welfare change (in contrast to the change in utility which is unique); *but money measurement of welfare change is the only reasonable approach for most applied economic welfare problems since consumer utility is not directly observable.* It should also be emphasized that *even though a money measure is unique, it does not necessarily follow that it measures utility change.*

Consider first the case of a simultaneous price–income change, as depicted in Figure 5.4, and the conditions under which the surplus change is unique. Examining the two particular paths L_1 and L_2, it is clear that the same result is obtained for any arbitrary price change if and only if the demand curves $D(m_0)$ and $D(m_1)$ coincide. Indeed, if the demand curve is uninfluenced by income changes, then the consumer surplus change in Figure 5.4(b) is the same regardless of which path may be followed between (p_0, m_0) and (p_1, m_1) in Figure 5.4(a). Thus, when both price and income change, *the consumer surplus measure is unique if and only if the income effect is zero*—meaning that the change in quantity consumed, Δq, associated with a change in income, Δm (i.e., $\Delta q/\Delta m$), is zero (note that this does not imply a zero welfare effect). Trivially, this condition is associated with zero income elasticity since income elasticity is defined by $(\Delta q/\Delta m) \cdot (m/q)$.[7] As shown in Appendix B, this result can be generalized to the case where many prices, as well as income, change, in

---

[7]More precisely, income elasticity of demand at a particular set of prices and income is defined as the percentage change in quantity demanded associated with a small unit percentage change in income and is given mathematically by $(\partial q/\partial m) \cdot (m/q)$, which is approximated in discrete terms by $(\Delta q/\Delta m) \cdot (m/q)$.

which case *uniqueness holds if and only if the income effects (or elasticities) of all goods for which prices possibly change along the path of adjustment are zero.* This condition cannot possibly hold if all prices and income change, since the change in income would not be offset by adjusting expenditures; thus, the consumer's budget constraint would be violated.

It is also instructive to investigate the implications of uniqueness of the surplus measure in terms of the consumer's indifference map. The case where indifference curves lead to the same demand curve regardless of income level is demonstrated in Figure 5.6. The indifference curves in Figure 5.6(a) are I_1 and I_2. As income is changed from m_0 to m_1 at price p_1, the quantity consumed remains at q_1 since the associated tangencies of the budget lines with indifference curves lie directly above one another at a quantity of q_1. Thus, the demand curves for both levels of income include the point (p_1, q_1). Similarly, the budget line/indifference curve tangencies all occur at quantity q_0 when price is p_0. In other words, the same demand curve D results in Figure 5.6(b) regardless of income level. Furthermore, since the budget lines for different income levels

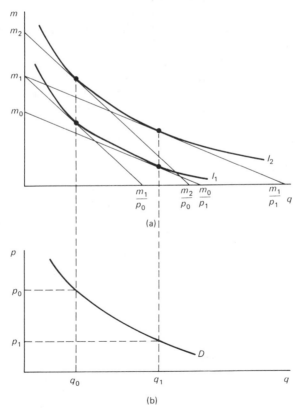

(a)

(b)

FIGURE 5.6

but the same price must be parallel, it is clear that coincidence of the demand curve at different income levels is obtained if and only if the consumer's indifference curves are vertically parallel. In the latter case the income-expansion path is a vertical straight line for any set of prices.

Turn now to the price–price change case depicted in Figure 5.5. In this case the two paths L_1 and L_2 lead to the same consumer surplus change if area $u + v + x =$ area $u + x + y$ (that is, if area $v =$ area y). Under what conditions would these areas be equal? To answer this question, consider arbitrary price changes, $\Delta p_1 = p_1^0 - p_1^1$ and $\Delta p_2 = p_2^0 - p_2^1$. If these price changes become small, v and y are approximately parallelograms, in which case the corresponding areas are given by the product of the price changes and the respective quantity changes, $\Delta q_1 = q_1^3 - q_1^0 \doteq q_1^1 - q_1^2$ and $\Delta q_2 = q_2^3 - q_2^0 \doteq q_2^1 - q_2^2$. Thus, the conditions of equality of areas v and y become $\Delta p_1 \cdot \Delta q_1 = \Delta p_2 \cdot \Delta q_2$, or

$$\frac{\Delta q_1}{\Delta p_2} = \frac{\Delta q_2}{\Delta p_1}$$

In intuitive terms, this condition implies that demand must be such that the change in consumption of the first good associated with a small unit change in the price of the second good must be the same as the change in consumption of the second good associated with a small unit change in the price of the first. If area $v =$ area y for all arbitrary sets of price changes, this condition must hold all along both sets of demand curves. As shown in a more rigorous mathematical framework in Appendix B, this condition must hold for all pairs of goods for which prices possibly change in order to have uniqueness of consumer surplus in the general case where many prices change.

Consider, however, the economic implications of these conditions. As in the preceding case, an interesting implication can be developed by relating the conditions to a change in income. To do this, one can use the concept of *zero-degree homogeneity of demand in prices and income*. This implies that a consumer's consumption bundle choice is not altered as all prices and income are adjusted proportionally (for example, consider redenominating the unit of currency).

In this context, suppose that all prices are adjusted proportionally so that $p_1^1 = \alpha p_1^0$ and $p_2^1 = \alpha p_2^0$, in which case

$$\frac{\Delta p_2}{\Delta p_1} = \frac{(\alpha - 1) p_2^0}{(\alpha - 1) p_1^0} = \frac{p_2^0}{p_1^0}$$

Using the path-independence conditions above, which correspond to equality of areas v and y, one thus finds that

$$\frac{\Delta q_1}{\Delta q_2} = \frac{\Delta p_2}{\Delta p_1} = \frac{p_2^0}{p_1^0}$$

Hence, the ratio of adjustments of q_1 and q_2 corresponding to any proportional changes in prices is a constant (that is, the ratio determined by initial prices) no matter how much prices are adjusted.

Using homogeneity of demand, as indicated above, indicates that this proportional change in prices is equivalent to an inversely proportional change in income. For example, doubling income has the same effect on the consumer (excluding wealth considerations) as cutting all prices by half. Hence, the foregoing arguments also imply that the ratio of consumption adjustments in response to an income adjustment is a constant determined completely by prices regardless of income level. Interpreting these results in the context of the consumer's indifference map thus implies straight-line income-expansion paths emanating from the origin, for example, $E(p_1{}^0, p_2{}^0)$ and $E(p_1{}^1, p_2{}^1)$ in Figure 5.7. As income is adjusted upward from zero with prices $p_1{}^0$ and $p_2{}^0$, the changes in quantities are always proportional; thus, the ratio between quantities is a constant $(p_2{}^0/p_1{}^0)$. An indifference map with these properties is generally called *homothetic*.[8] Geometrically, from Figure 5.7, homotheticity clearly implies that any percentage change in income (holding prices fixed) leads to an equal percentage change in all quantities consumed; hence, all income elasticities of demand must be 1.

These results are indeed borne out by the mathematical derivation in Appendix B. That is, *when all prices facing the consumer change, the consumer*

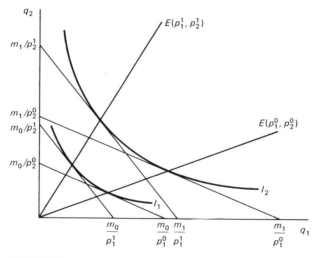

FIGURE 5.7

[8]Mathematically, a homothetic function is any function $U(x)$ such that $U(x) = f[g(x)]$, where $g(x)$ is any function such that $g(tx) = tg(x)$ for some scalar t, and $f(\cdot)$ is any monotonic function.

surplus change is uniquely defined if and only if the consumer's indifference map is homothetic, which occurs if and only if all income elasticities of demand are unity. However, Appendix B further shows that if only some subset of prices change, then homotheticity is merely necessary with respect to the subset of goods for which prices change.[9] *A necessary and sufficient condition for uniqueness of consumer surplus change is that all income elasticities for the subset of goods with changing prices must be equal* (but not necessarily unity).

Having determined the conditions under which the consumer surplus change is uniquely defined, one may consider the possibility of fulfilling these conditions in reality. For example, in the price–income change case, is one likely to find consumers in the real world who do not change their consumption of some goods as income changes? For a good such as salt, there may be many such consumers, but for most commodities there is overwhelming empirical evidence suggesting income effects. Similarly, in the price–price change case, one may consider the likelihood of finding consumers who adjust consumption of all or, indeed, even several goods proportionally in response to income changes. For example, if a consumer receives a 10 percent increase in income, is he or she likely to increase consumption of both bread and movies by exactly 10 percent (or even the same percentage)? Again, empirical evidence suggests different responses for many goods. Increases in income tend to be spent more on luxury goods and less on necessities at higher income levels. Thus, generally, the conditions for uniqueness of consumer surplus change may be so restrictive as to be unrealistic for many cases. Nevertheless, the applicability of the necessary conditions for applied work can be investigated empirically by estimating the associated income elasticities.

5.4 CONSTANCY OF THE MARGINAL UTILITY OF INCOME

Section 5.2 has shown that the consumer surplus measurement of the effect of a price–income or price–price change may depend on the path of adjustment followed in making the calculations. Section 5.3 has developed necessary and sufficient conditions under which the path-dependency problem vanishes and has further investigated the implications of these conditions for the preference structure of the consumer. A further important issue relates to whether or not the consumer surplus change provides a meaningful *money measure of utility change*. That is, under what conditions does a unique correspondence exist between the change in consumer surplus and the change in the consumer's actual utility?

The source of the present problem is depicted in Figure 5.8. With the utility

---

[9]Homotheticity with respect to a subset of goods implies that the budget-expansion paths in the associated subspace are straight lines through the origin where the relevant budget consists of income spent on only the subset of goods.

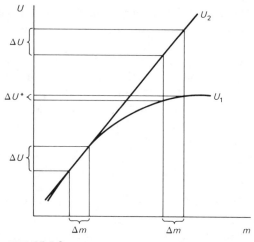

FIGURE 5.8

function U_1, the same income change Δm may lead to a much different change in utility, ΔU or ΔU^*, depending on the initial income. With utility function U_2, however, the associated change in utility is the same regardless of the initial income. The utility function U_2 thus implies a constant marginal utility of income, at least with respect to income changes. As suggested by Section 5.1, the consumer surplus change is simply a money-equivalent measure of the effect of changing prices as well as possibly income. Hence, an unambiguous conversion of the surplus change ΔS into utility change ΔU can be made only when the slope of the utility function is constant, that is, when the marginal utility of income is constant with respect to all prices that change as well as with respect to income if it changes (note that Figure 5.8 depicts constancy of the marginal utility of income only with respect to income changes, not with respect to price changes).

Consider, for example, the price–price change case, as depicted in Figure 5.9, where prices change from p_1^0, p_2^0 to p_1^1, p_2^1. To abstract from the problem of path dependence, consider only the path shown in Figure 5.9 and suppose

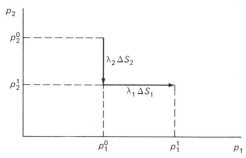

FIGURE 5.9

that the surplus change associated with changing p_1 is ΔS_1 and the subsequent surplus change associated with changing p_2 is ΔS_2, where $\Delta S_2 = -\Delta S_1$. To examine the case where the marginal utility of income is not constant, suppose for simplicity that λ_1 is the marginal utility of income along the first segment of the path and that λ_2 is the marginal utility of income along the second segment of the path. Since ΔS_1 is the income-equivalent change along the first segment and λ_1, the change in utility per unit change in income, is constant along that segment, the surplus or income-equivalent change can be converted into utility change by multiplying by λ_1. Thus, $\Delta U_1 = \lambda_1 \Delta S_1$, where ΔU_1 is the utility change along the first segment of the path in Figure 5.9. Similarly, $\Delta U_2 = \lambda_2 \Delta S_2$, where ΔU_2 represents the utility change along the second segment of the path. The total utility change is thus $\Delta U = \Delta U_1 + \Delta U_2$.

To see the problem that can arise (even when path-independence conditions hold), note that the total surplus change is $\Delta S = \Delta S_1 + \Delta S_2 = 0$, whereas $\Delta U \neq 0$ if $\lambda_1 \neq \lambda_2$. In other words, *even with path independence, ΔS may not behave in a way qualitatively similar to ΔU. Thus, uniqueness of ΔS is not sufficient to guarantee any meaningful interpretation of ΔS as a money measure of utility change.* To be a meaningful money measure of utility change, ΔS must be at least qualitatively related to ΔU; that is, ΔS and ΔU must be of the same arithmetic sign regardless of the particular price change. As shown in Appendix B, this relationship holds only when the factor λ, which converts income (equivalent) change into utility change, is constant over the entire set of price changes under consideration, that is, when the marginal utility of income is constant.

Appendix B also shows that *constancy of the marginal utility of income guarantees path independence of ΔS* (but not vice versa). Hence, the condition of constancy of λ is at least as restrictive as the implications of path independence outlined in Section 5.3 (in fact, more so). As indicated there, the economic implications of these conditions on the consumer indifference map are so restrictive as to prevent use of the "money measure of utility change" approach in an a priori sense for essentially all practical purposes. That is, one would have little basis for estimating money measures of utility change without first carrying out considerable empirical analysis to determine, for example, whether or not all income elasticities of demand are consistent with the implications of path independence. Even then, constancy of the marginal utility of income may not hold.

It is important to stress that *constancy of the marginal utility of income guarantees path independence of ΔS, but not vice versa.* This has been a major source of confusion underlying the theory of welfare measurement; often the phrases "zero-income effect" and "constancy of the marginal utility of income" have been treated as meaning the same thing. They simply do not. Once they are viewed separately, it becomes clear that, *even though one can obtain a unique measure of consumer surplus, that surplus need not measure utility* *change*. *Consumer surplus* only measures utility change when the marginal utility of income is constant.

5.5 CONCLUSIONS

The famous economist Alfred Marshall[10] instigated the search (and the many controversies that followed) for money measures of gain that could be uniquely related to utility changes for the consumer. That is, Marshall was concerned with the conditions under which the change in consumer surplus could measure a *true surplus* of utility. This chapter has shown that the assumptions which guarantee that consumer surplus is a measure of such a *true surplus*—namely, that the marginal utility of income is constant with respect to the prices and/or income which change—are highly restrictive with respect to the preference structures of individuals. To obtain uniqueness of consumer surplus, income elasticities must be the same for all goods for which prices change and these elasticities must be zero if income changes. Such preference structures are contradicted by the bulk of empirical evidence.

Because of the conditions outlined in this chapter, consumer welfare measurement may appear bleak at this point. However, further possibilities exist for determining whether or not given changes are in a consumer's best interest. Having determined that the original definitions and their later refinements have some serious problems from the standpoint of empirical application, Chapter 6 returns to the general concepts of willingness to pay set forth in Chapters 1 and 3. These concepts, although also not having a direct correspondence with utility change, at least lead to unambiguous interpretation in empirical work.

---

[10]Alfred Marshall, *Principles of Economics* (London: Macmillan Co, 1930).

6

Willingness to Pay
and Consumer Welfare

Chapter 5 has shown that conditions under which consumers will exhibit preference structures that ensure uniqueness of the change in consumer surplus as a money measure of utility gain or loss are very stringent. Thus, in this chapter attention is turned to consideration of a number of alternative but less demanding money measures of consumer welfare which are partially justified on the grounds originally proposed by Dupuit.[1] In other words, attention is turned to measures of consumer welfare change that have simple but plausible willingness-to-pay interpretations.

The welfare measures discussed and adopted in this context were originally developed by John R. Hicks.[2] Hicks suggested four measures of consumer gain or loss, but only two of these—compensating and equivalent variation—allow the consumer freedom of choice in responding to a changing economic environment.[3] Since the vast majority of policy decisions allow consumer adjustment, attention is focused on these two measures.

---

[1]J. Dupuit, "On the Measurement of the Utility of Public Works," *Annales des Ponts et Chaussees*, Second Series, Vol. 8 (1844). Translation reprinted in D. Munby, *Transport*, 1968.

[2]J. R. Hicks, "The Four Consumer's Surpluses," *Review of Economic Studies*, Vol. 11 (Winter 1943), pp. 31–41.

[3]The other two measures proposed by Hicks, compensating surplus and equivalent surplus, constrain the consumer to buy the same consumption bundle as he or she did in the subsequent and initial situations, respectively. There are in principle an infinite

Compensating and equivalent variations have been generally defined in Chapter 1. This chapter focuses on price and/or income changes for the consumer; hence, the Chapter 1 definitions imply that *compensating variation (C) is the amount of income which must be taken away from a consumer (possibly negative) after a price and/or income change to restore the consumer's original welfare level.* Similarly, *equivalent variation (E) is the amount of income that must be given to a consumer (again possibly negative) in lieu of price and income changes to leave the consumer as well off as with the change.*

Thus, compensating and equivalent variations are defined as income adjustments which maintain the consumer at particular levels of welfare. Compensating variation focuses on the initial level of welfare, that which the consumer held prior to price and/or income changes; and equivalent variation focuses on the subsequent level of welfare, that which the consumer would obtain with the price and/or income changes.

6.1 WILLINGNESS-TO-PAY MEASURES

To demonstrate how compensating and equivalent variation may be directly related to the consumer's ordinal preferences, consider a consumer with preferences over the good q with price p and the good y (which can be regarded as

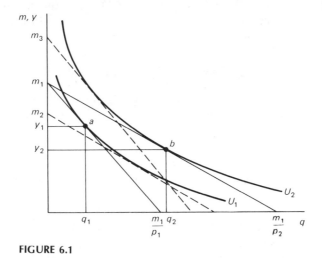

FIGURE 6.1

number of measures which can be generated by alternative kinds of constraints on consumer response to price and/or income change, but only compensating and equivalent variations are consistent with competitive behavior in most situations. Hence, in applied settings, measures other than compensating and equivalent variation are seldom applicable. There are, however, nonprice change cases where compensating or equivalent surplus is the conceptually appropriate measure. An explanation of these concepts is given in Section 7.9.

a composite of all other commodities) with a price of 1.[4] Faced with the budget constraint, $p_1 q + y = m_1$, where m_1 is initial income, the consumer chooses the optimum consumption point a with q_1 of q and y_1 of y in Figure 6.1. With a lower price p_2, the consumer increases the consumption of q to q_2 and decreases the consumption of y to y_2, hence moving to consumption point b.

Now recall that a change in income m results in a new budget line parallel to the old one. Hence, to find the measure of the compensating variation going from point a to point b, the budget line through point b is shifted downward (income is reduced) until it is just tangent to the original welfare level U_1. Thus, the compensating variation (C_{12}) associated with the price fall is given by $m_1 - m_2 > 0$. That is, the consumer's income must be reduced by the amount $m_1 - m_2$ after the price is reduced to p_2 for the consumer's welfare to remain unchanged.

The equivalent variation associated with the price fall (E_{12}) is found in Figure 6.1 by increasing the consumer's income, given the old price p_1, until the consumer has sufficient income to attain the utility level attained with the price fall. Thus, the budget line through point a is shifted upward until it is just tangent to U_2; the measure of equivalent variation is thus given by the vertical distance, $m_3 - m_1 > 0$.

With a price rise, the amount of income that must be *taken away* to restore the consumer's original welfare level is negative. That is, the consumer in this case must be given income to maintain the same level of welfare as before the price increase. Hence, in Figure 6.1, the compensating variation associated with an increase in price from p_2 to p_1 is given by $m_1 - m_3 < 0$.

Similarly, the amount of income that must be *given to* the consumer in lieu of the price increase is negative, or income must be taken away to make the consumer as poorly off as with the price increase. Thus, the equivalent variation in Figure 6.1 associated with an increase in price from p_2 to p_1 is $m_2 - m_1 < 0$.

Clearly, the compensating variation associated with a price fall is equal in magnitude but of opposite sign to the equivalent variation for the reverse movement in prices. That is, in Figure 6.1, $C_{12} = m_1 - m_2 = -(m_2 - m_1) = -E_{21}$.

Using the graphical approach described above, one can easily verify that the compensating variation for a price fall is bounded by the initial income, whereas equivalent variations may be infinite when indifference curves are asymptotic to the vertical axis. For price increases, the opposite result holds. That is, equivalent variation is bounded and compensating variation is unbounded. Moreover, both compensating variation and equivalent variation are ordinally related to utility. That is, equivalent variation varies ordinally with utility as the subsequent welfare position (point b in Figure 6.1) is continuously

---

[4] In this framework good y serves as the numéraire, so its price serves as the accounting price.

varied, and compensating variation varies ordinally as the initial welfare position (point a in Figure 6.1) is continuously varied.

As suggested earlier, compensating and equivalent variation can be given more strict willingness-to-pay interpretations. For example, compensating variation for a price fall can be interpreted as the maximum amount of income the consumer would be *willing to pay* rather than relinquish the price reduction. For a price increase, compensating variation is the minimum amount the consumer must be paid or is willing to accept to tolerate the higher price. Thus, compensating variation questions measure gains or losses associated with *taking* the proposed action, in this case changing price.

Equivalent variation, on the other hand, measures gains and losses to the consumer associated with *not taking* the proposed action. That is, equivalent variation for a price fall can be interpreted as the minimum amount of income the consumer is *willing to accept* to forgo the lower price; for a price rise, it is the maximum amount the consumer is *willing to pay* to avoid the higher price. Thus, equivalent variation is the maximum bribe the consumer is willing to pay to avoid an adverse change in economic conditions or the minimum bribe necessary to gain relinquishment of a claim on an improvement in economic conditions.[5]

To see how these concepts are related to observed quantities and prices, it is necessary to introduce the concept of the Hicksian or compensated demand curve and show how both it and the Marshallian (or ordinary) demand curve can be related to the consumer's ordinal preference map. The *Hicksian compensated demand curve* is a relationship giving quantities demanded at various prices when utility is held constant by varying income (alone). By contrast, the *Marshallian demand curve* is a relationship giving quantities demanded at various prices when income is held constant by varying utility (alone).

Consider again the consumer with budget constraint $p_1q + y = m_1$ and preferences as given by the indifference curves in Figure 6.2(a). The consumer's optimum, initial consumption point is again point a, which implies the purchase of q_1 of commodity q. This establishes point c as one point on the ordinary demand curve D and the compensated demand curve H_1 in Figure 6.2(b). With a reduction in price to p_2 and no change in income, the consumer's budget constraint is shifted to $(m_1, m_1/p_2)$, and the consumer optimally responds by choosing point b. This implies a second point f in Figure 6.2(b) on the consumer's ordinary demand curve as the consumer increases purchases with the lower price to q_2. By continuously varying price upward and down-

---

[5]These interpretations underscore the attractiveness of compensating and equivalent variation for the compensation tests discussed in Chapter 3. A full discussion of how these questions naturally relate to the Kaldor–Hicks and Scitovsky compensation criteria, however, is deferred to Chapter 8, where the case of many consumers is considered since the compensation criteria make sense only in a setting with more than one individual.

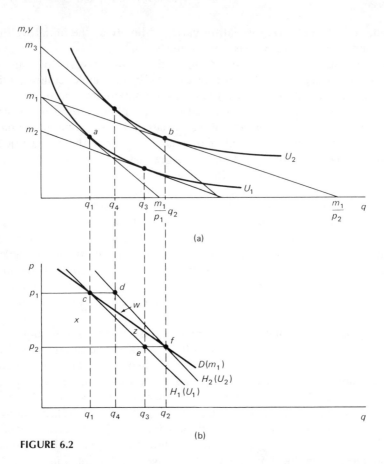

FIGURE 6.2

ward from p_1 in Figure 6.2(a), one can in the same manner trace out a continu-ous locus of price–quantity combinations and hence generate the ordinary demand curve D along which income is held constant at m_1.

The Hicksian compensated demand curve going through point c in Figure 6.2(b) is generated by starting at point a in Figure 6.2(a) and determining the amounts of q purchased as price is varied but income is adjusted to maintain the consumer at utility level U_1. Thus, as price is reduced to p_2 and the compensat-ing variation of $m_1 - m_2$ is taken away from the consumer to restore the original welfare level, the consumption of q increases to q_3, which implies in Figure 6.2(b) a second point e on the compensated demand curve H_1. The increase in consumption from q_1 to q_3, as a result of the price fall, is entirely due to the desire to substitute q for other goods as the relative price of q falls. As long as the commodity q is a normal good (one with a positive income effect or one with an income expansion path having a positive slope), the point q_3 will lie to the left of q_2. Similar reasoning suggests that all points on the Hicksian demand curve H_1 for prices less than p_1 will lie to the left of the ordinary demand curve D.

Since the compensated demand curve considers the effects of a combined price and income change that leaves the consumer indifferent to the initial position, there will be a compensated demand curve corresponding to each level of utility or each possible initial position. For example, H_2 in Figure 6.2(b) corresponding to indifference curve U_2 in Figure 6.2(a) can be developed in a similar manner. If the consumer's initial position is point b in Figure 6.2(a) [point f in Figure 6.2(b)], a new compensated demand curve H_2 is generated, corresponding to indifference level U_2, in Figure 6.2(a) passing through point f and, for price decreases, will again lie to the left of the ordinary demand curve D.

For price increases, consider starting at point f and increasing price from p_2 to p_1. In Figure 6.2(a), the consumer must be given $m_3 - m_1$ in income (compensating variation of $m_1 - m_3$ must be taken away) to maintain the same level of welfare at the higher price. When this increase in income is combined with the higher price, the consumer optimally chooses amount q_4 of commodity q. As long as the commodity is a normal good, q_4 will lie to the right of q_1, the point on the ordinary demand curve to which the consumer would move at the higher price if income compensation were not provided. Thus, starting at any price–quantity combination on the ordinary demand curve, there exists a Hicksian compensated demand curve passing through that point which, for normal goods, will lie to the left of the Marshallian demand curve for lower prices and to the right at higher prices.

With this framework in mind, it is possible to develop compensating and equivalent variation measures in the price–quantity space of Figure 6.2(b). One can show that the compensating variation associated with a price fall from p_1 to p_2 is exactly equal to area x in Figure 6.2(b) and hence is equal to the vertical distance $m_1 - m_2$ in Figure 6.2(a). Similarly, the compensating variation associated with a price rise from p_2 to p_1 can be shown to be the negative of area $w + x + z$ in Figure 6.2(b), which is thus equal to $-(m_1 - m_3) = m_3 - m_1 = E_{12}$ in Figure 6.2(a). That is, the area $w + x + z$ in Figure 6.2(b) measures the equivalent variation associated with the price fall from p_1 to p_2. Thus, for a normal good, the change in consumer surplus resulting from a price fall from p_1 to p_2 is bounded from below by compensating variation and from above by equivalent variation ($C \leq \Delta S \leq E$) and differs from these two amounts by area z and area w, respectively, in Figure 6.2(b).

To begin the development of the foregoing results—that is, to show that the vertical distance measure of compensating variation in Figure 6.2(a) is equal to the change in area under the Hicksian compensated demand curve in Figure 6.2(b)—consider the consumer initially in equilibrium at point a in Figure 6.3(a). The compensating variation associated with a price fall from p_1 to p_2 is $m_1 - m_2$. To show that $m_1 - m_2$ = area $x + w$ in Figure 6.3(b), consider the budget line $(m_3, m_3/p_2)$ passing through point a. This budget line can be determined by taking sufficient income away from the consumer at the lower price to just allow purchase of the old bundle (y_1, q_1) at the new prices. That is, $m_1 = p_1q_1 + y_1$ and $m_3 = p_2q_1 + y_1$. This implies by subtracting that $m_1 - m_3 =$

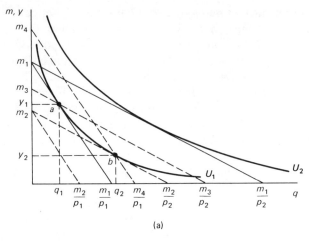

(a)

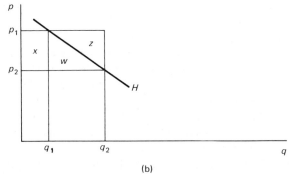

(b)

FIGURE 6.3

$(p_1 - p_2) q_1$, which is the inner cost difference of the original bundle of goods and is measured by area x in Figure 6.3(b). As long as the indifference curves in Figure 6.3(a) are convex to the origin, the inner cost differences will be less than compensating variation, or $m_2 < m_3$. That is, this cost difference is a lower bound on compensating variation in Figure 6.3(b) since at least this amount of income can be taken away after the price fall and yet leave the consumer at least as well off as before.

Now consider the possibility of establishing an upper bound on compensating variation in Figure 6.3(b). If the consumer is initially in equilibrium at point b in Figure 6.3(a) with income m_2 and price p_2, the absolute value of the compensating variation associated with a price rise from p_2 to p_1 is $m_1 - m_2$. But this is also the compensating variation determined above for the reverse price movement with initial income m_1. That is, the compensating variation for an increase in price from p_2 to p_1 with income m_2 is equal to the compensating variation for a decrease in price from p_1 to p_2 with income m_1. Thus, to place an upper bound on compensating variation beginning at point a for the price fall, consider first an upper bound on compensating variation for a price increase starting at point b. This upper bound is established by asking how much additional income must be paid to the consumer when price is increased to p_1 to enable the consumer to buy the old commodity bundle (y_2, q_2). The associated budget line with price p_1 must pass through the point b; hence, income of $m_4 - m_2$ in Figure 6.3(a) must be paid to the consumer to make the bundle (y_2, q_2) feasible. However, $m_4 - m_2 = (p_1 - p_2)q_2$; thus, the outer cost difference measured by area $w + x + z$ in Figure 6.3(b) is an upper bound on compensating variation.

With compensating variation now bounded in Figure 6.3(b) by area x below and by area $w + x + z$ above, the establishment of $w + x$ as the measure of compensating variation proceeds by breaking up the price change from p_1 to p_2 into a sequence of smaller and smaller price changes. For example, consider proceeding from p_1 to p_2 via the sequence $p_1, p_3, p_4, \ldots, p_2$ in Figure 6.4. The lower bound on compensating variation for the first step is area v; the second, area w; and, finally, the fifth, area z. Clearly, the sum of these lower bounds (area $v + w + x + y + z$) can be made closer to the change in area under the compensated demand curve [area x in Figure 6.3(b)] by dividing the price change into more and smaller increments. A similar approach can be used to show that an upper bound formed by outer cost differences for the series of small price changes also becomes equal to the area behind the compensated demand curve between the two price lines.

To obtain area $w + x + z$ in Figure 6.2 as a measure of equivalent variation, observe that area $w + x + z$ is the compensating variation for an increase in price from p_2 to p_1 and that the negative of compensating variation for a price increase is equal to equivalent variation for the corresponding price decrease.

Finally, to complete the argument, it must be shown that the compensating variation from the single price change from p_1 to p_2 is equal to the sum of the

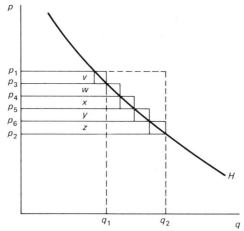

FIGURE 6.4

compensating variations from the sequential price changes $p_1, p_3, \ldots, p_2$. To see this, consider Figure 6.5, where the consumer is initially in equilibrium at point a with price p_1 and income m_1. The compensating variation of the single price change from p_1 to p_2 is given by $m_1 - m_2$. The compensating variation of the sequential price change from p_1 to p_2 is $m_1 - m_3$ for the change from p_1 to p_3 plus $m_3 - m_2$ for the price fall from p_3 to p_2, the sum of which is $m_1 - m_2$. That is, the total amount of income that must be taken away from the consumer with a given price reduction to restore the consumer to the original welfare level is the same regardless of whether or not it is taken in pieces as prices are incrementally reduced or if it is taken in one amount with a single price change.

6.2 THE NIBBLE PARADOX

It is important to note that the compensating variation which is calculated for the price adjustment from p_3 to p_2 above is done after the consumer's income has been reduced by the compensating variation for the previous price adjustment from p_1 to p_3. This points out an important principle in making any stepwise computation of compensating or equivalent variation. To calculate an overall compensating (equivalent) variation in a stepwise manner (for example, impose a change of one price, then another, and so on), one must assume that the compensating (equivalent) variation for any previous price or income change is already extracted from (paid to) the consumer before making further calculations.

The problem that arises when this principle is not adhered to is known as the *nibble paradox*. To demonstrate the nibble paradox, note that the compensating variation of the single price change from p_1 to p_4 in Figure 6.6 is given by area $a_0 + b_0 + c_0$. It appears that, if the overall price change is attained by a

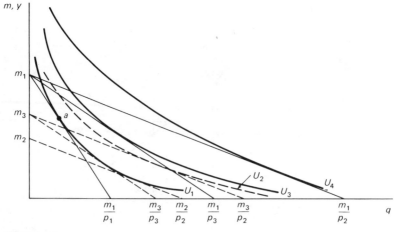

FIGURE 6.5

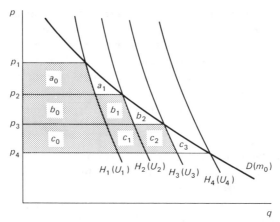

FIGURE 6.6

series of smaller changes—first, from p_1 to p_2, then from p_2 to p_3, and finally from p_3 to p_4—the compensating variation is area a_0 for the first change, area $b_0 + b_1$ for the second change, and area $c_0 + c_1 + c_2$ for the third change, the sum of which exceeds the compensating variation for the single price change. But if, for each interval, the compensating variation is extracted from the consumer before proceeding to consider the next price change (extraction of area a_0, for example, before reducing the price from p_2 to p_3), the consumer is always constrained to utility level U_1, and hence the sum of the incremental compensating variations is properly calculated as area $a_0 + b_0 + c_0$.

6.3 COINCIDENCE OF COMPENSATING AND EQUIVALENT VARIATIONS

The focus thus far has been on two alternative willingness-to-pay measures: compensating variation and equivalent variation. This raises a dilemma about which to use in any given situation. There is, however, one circumstance in which these measures coincide and a choice need not be made. This is the case of zero-income effects or vertically parallel indifference curves for the goods for which prices change (illustrated in Figure 5.6). Given a price fall, the compensated demand curve, the equivalent demand curve (the compensated demand curve for the reverse movement in price), and the ordinary Marshallian demand curve all coincide; hence, given any single price change, $C = \Delta S = E$. Similarly, if more than one price changes and the goods for which prices change have zero-income effects, the compensated and ordinary curves will coincide in every case, so again both compensating and equivalent variation will be given by the change in consumer surplus.

Section 5.3 argues, however, that conditions for a zero-income effect, which imply that the consumer surplus measure is unique, are not likely to occur in the real world. Thus, the conditions that eliminate the dilemma of choice among willingness-to-pay measures are just as stringent as those which are required to establish consumer surplus as a unique money measure of welfare gains. Indeed, there are cases where the only reasonable course of action for the applied welfare economist is to present estimates of *both* compensating and equivalent variation; in such cases, a project that is justified using one measure may not be justified using the other. In such a case, both measurements can be provided to policymakers and the associated value judgment of which to use can be left in their hands.

A further complication which then arises is how does one estimate compensated and equivalent variation since the estimation of Hicksian compensated demand curves is a difficult issue in many situations. Fortunately, however, as long as the proportion of income spent upon the good is small, the income effect is likely to be quite small.[6] Hence, in many cases compensating variation, equivalent variation, and changes in consumer surplus are all likely to be of similar magnitude; that is, areas w and z in Figure 6.2 are likely to be quite small. Recently, substantial progress has been made in providing a precise quantitative meaning for the word "small." Techniques have been developed whereby the applied welfare economist can obtain estimates of either compensating or equivalent variation with knowledge of only Marshallian consumer surplus changes and income elasticity estimates. Note that the *Marshallian consumer surplus* is the consumer surplus associated with the ordinary or Marshallian demand curve. By contrast, the consumer surplus triangle associated with a Hicksian compensated demand curve is sometimes called a *Hicksian consumer surplus*.

6.4 ALTERNATIVE GRAPHICAL ANALYSIS OF WILLINGNESS TO PAY

To lay the foundation for much of the mathematical derivation in Appendix B and to provide understanding of the development of the remainder of this chapter, this section uses the indirect utility function and the expenditure function.[7] The *indirect utility function* specifies the highest attainable utility level for a consumer as a function of prices p and income m. For example, in Figure 6.7(a), where prices are p_1^0 and p_2^0, income is m_0, and U_1 denotes an indifference curve with utility level U_1, no higher utility level is attainable. Thus, in Figure 6.7(b), the indirect utility function is such that an isoutility curve V_1 corresponding to utility level U_1 passes through (p^0, m_0), where, for

---

[6]J. R. Hicks, *A Revision of Demand Theory* (Oxford, England: Clarendon Press, 1956), p. 65.

[7]The graphical approach in this section was developed by E. E. Zajac, "An Elementary Road Map of Integrability and Consumer's Surplus" (Murray Hill, N.J.: Bell Telephone Laboratories, Inc., 1976).

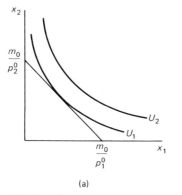

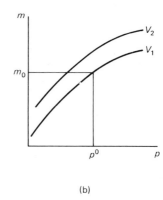

(a)   (b)

FIGURE 6.7

convenience, both prices are combined along the lower axis. Thus, the curves V_1 and V_2 represent contours of the indirect utility function in price–income space.

The *expenditure function,* on the other hand, is defined as the amount of money income that allows a consumer to attain (at most) a specified utility level at a specified set of prices. The expenditure function is very closely related to the indirect utility function. The contours of the indirect utility function represented by V_1 and V_2 in Figure 6.7(b) give the money incomes required to attain the respective utility levels as functions of prices. Thus, the expenditure function in price–income space is given by the corresponding indirect utility contour. For example, to attain utility level $V_1 = U_1$ at prices p^0 would require income m_0.

Now, in the context of Figure 6.7(b), return to the concepts of consumer surplus and willingness to pay. The compensating variation of a price change from p^0 to p^1 is demonstrated in Figure 6.8. The consumer is originally at prices p^0, income m_0, and utility level V_1. With a price fall to p^1, the income level m_0 now allows the consumer to move to a higher utility level V_2. Clearly, the

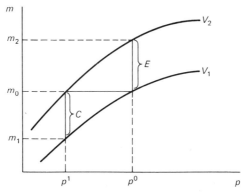

FIGURE 6.8

consumer could give up $m_0 - m_1$ in income at the new prices and remain at the initial utility level V_1. Thus, the distance C between the expenditure functions (or indirect utility contours) at new prices measures the compensating variation. Similarly, considering the equivalent variation, an increase in income from m_0 to m_2 would be required to reach the higher utility level V_2 if prices remained at initial levels p^0. Hence, the increase in income measured by the distance E between the contours V_1 and V_2 at old prices p_0 is the equivalent variation of the price change.[8]

Finally, consider interpretation of the ordinary Marshallian consumer surplus in the context of the indirect utility function. As shown in Section 5.1, the ordinary consumer surplus measure corresponds approximately to evaluation of the sum of income-equivalent effects of a series of small price changes when such income equivalents are not extracted. Consider the price change from p_0 to p_1 in Figure 6.9. If this price change is divided into a series of small steps of length Δp, the corresponding income effects can be found as follows. First, consider the price change from p_0 to $p_0 - \Delta p$. As indicated by the indirect utility contours, this price fall results in the same utility as an increase in income of Δm_1 in the absence of the price change. Given the change to $p_0 - \Delta p$, a further price fall to $p_0 - 2\,\Delta p$ has the same effect on utility as an increase in income of Δm_2. Continuing in this manner generates a series of income-equivalent effects which sum to $\Delta m_1 + \Delta m_2 + \Delta m_3 + \Delta m_4$. The exact Marshallian consumer surplus is obtained by allowing the size of the price increments which add up to the overall change from p_0 to p_1 to become smaller and smaller.

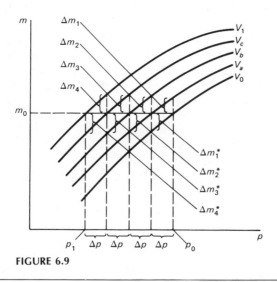

FIGURE 6.9

---

[8]Of course, if the price change were reversed from p^1 to p^0, distance E would measure the compensating variation and distance C would measure equivalent variation.

Since this measure is, in effect, obtained by summing a series of equivalent variations of small price falls, Figure 6.9 formally demonstrates the nibble paradox (the consumer surplus is obtained by considering the sum of equivalent variations of small price changes where each successive calculation assumes that the initial income level m_0 is unaltered). A similar interpretation of consumer surplus is the sum of compensating variations associated with small price decreases as evaluated by the sum of income effects, $\Delta m_1^* + \Delta m_2^* + \Delta m_3^* + \Delta m_4^*$, which measure willingness to pay for the successive price decreases assuming payments are not extracted. Clearly, as the size of price increments becomes smaller, the two sums approach the same result (the Marshallian consumer surplus change) if the indirect utility contours are not kinked at m_0.

Finally, suppose in the context of Figure 6.9 that the marginal utility of income is constant. This implies that the slope of the indirect utility contours is constant. Thus, $\Delta m_1 = \Delta m_2 = \Delta m_3 = \Delta m_4 = \Delta m_1^* = \Delta m_2^* = \Delta m_3^* = \Delta m_4^*$. In this case, $C = E = \Delta m_1 + \Delta m_2 + \cdots = \Delta m_1^* + \Delta m_2^* + \cdots$ regardless of how finely Δp divides the price interval between p_0 and p_1. Thus, in Figures 6.8 and 6.9, the change in consumer surplus would be exactly equal to both the compensating and equivalent variations if the contours of the indirect utility function are parallel in the interval of price changes and income effects considered. These results thus confirm and add intuition to those obtained in Sections 6.1 through 6.3.

6.5   CONSUMER SURPLUS AS AN APPROXIMATION OF WILLINGNESS TO PAY: THE SINGLE-PRICE-CHANGE CASE[9]

As shown in Chapter 5, the ordinary consumer surplus measure (1) is an intuitively appealing measure of the consumer welfare effect of a price and/or income change, (2) is generally an ambiguous (that is, nonunique) measure, (3) requires very restrictive path-independence conditions on the utility function for uniqueness, and (4) requires even more restrictive conditions of constancy of the marginal utility of income to guarantee even an ordinal (qualitative) relationship with the actual utility change. For these reasons, major problems may be encountered with the use of consumer surplus, and hence the classical intuitive arguments are not sufficient to justify its use. Alternatively, the concepts of compensating and equivalent variation associated with the willingness-to-pay approach have been advanced in the context of consumer

[9]This and the following sections of this chapter are based on Robert D. Willig, "Consumer's Surplus without Apology," *American Economic Review*, Vol. 66, No. 4 (September 1976), pp. 589–97; and Willig, *Consumer's Surplus: A Rigorous Cookbook*, Technical Report No. 98, Institute for Mathematical Studies in the Social Sciences (Stanford, Calif.: Stanford University Press, 1973).

welfare measurement as being at least unique and ordinally (or qualitatively) related to actual utility changes. Nevertheless, the compensating and equivalent variations can be difficult to determine empirically since actual utility levels cannot be observed. A researcher cannot generally determine what change in income leaves a consumer just as well off after or in the absence of a price change and, even when interviewed, a consumer is tempted to exaggerate one way or the other to serve his personal interest. Thus, to develop an empirically tractable approach to measurement, this section considers indirectly estimating the compensating and equivalent variations. Even though the ordinary consumer surplus cannot be justified directly, an approximate relationship exists with the willingness-to-pay concepts under a broad range of conditions. Hence, the use of consumer surplus may be justified indirectly or a modification of it may serve to estimate the welfare effects.

To develop these results, consider Figure 6.10, where price is initially p_0 and falls to p_1 causing quantity consumed to increase from q_0 to q_1 (the ordinary demand curve D is conditioned on a given income level). The Hicksian or compensated demand curves corresponding to initial and subsequent utility levels are represented by $H(U_0)$ and $H(U_1)$, respectively. Thus, the ordinary consumer surplus change, ΔS, is area $a + b$, and the compensating and equivalent variations, C and E, are areas a and $a + b + c$, respectively. Two important observations motivate the following results. First, if areas b and c are negligible, the consumer surplus change may be used directly as an approximation of both the compensating and equivalent variations. Second, if areas b and c can be estimated from observable phenomena by some means, the consumer surplus change can be appropriately modified to produce approximations of the compensating and equivalent variations.

An estimate of areas b and c can be developed by noting that each is approximately a triangle at least for small price changes and that the height of each, Δp, is determined by the extent of the price change. Also, the base of

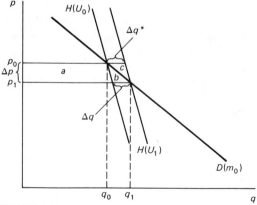

FIGURE 6.10

each triangle, Δq or Δq^*, is essentially an income effect, that is, the effect of changing income by a certain amount while holding price fixed. Furthermore, the size of the income effect is related to the income elasticity of demand, which is an estimable parameter. In simple terms, the income elasticity is given by

$$\eta = \frac{\Delta q}{\Delta m} \frac{m}{q}$$

where Δm is the real income change precipitated by the price change which leads to the quantity change, Δq, when price is held constant. Thus, to determine Δq in Figure 6.10, note that the above equation implies that

$$\Delta q = \eta \cdot q \cdot \frac{\Delta m}{m} \tag{6.1}$$

and that the income change that leads to reduction in consumption by Δq is approximately ΔS (for small Δp), that is,[10]

$$\Delta m \doteq \Delta S$$

Substituting into equation (6.1) thus yields

$$\Delta q \doteq \eta \cdot q \cdot \frac{\Delta S}{m} \tag{6.2}$$

When the functions in Figure 6.10 are nearly linear (for example, when Δp is small), area b can thus be approximated using equation (6.2):

$$\text{area } b \doteq \tfrac{1}{2} \Delta q \cdot |\Delta p| \doteq \tfrac{1}{2} \eta \cdot \Delta S \cdot q \cdot \frac{|\Delta p|}{m}$$

Finally, note that $\Delta S \doteq q |\Delta p|$ for small Δp; hence, the compensating variation ($C = $ area a) can be approximated by subtracting the foregoing approximation of area b from area $a + b$ ($= \Delta S$),

$$\hat{C} = \Delta S - \frac{\eta}{2m} (\Delta S)^2 = \Delta S - \hat{\epsilon}|\Delta S| \tag{6.3}$$

---

[10]Of course, one could also consider use of $C = $ area a as the measure of the income change. Indeed, this is exactly the change in income that reduces consumption by Δq. However, C is not directly observable, whereas ΔS is. As verified by Appendix B, the errors introduced by this approximation are not serious for the class of cases described below.

where

$$\hat{\epsilon} = \frac{\eta|s|}{2}, \qquad s = \frac{\Delta S}{m} \tag{6.4}$$

A similar approximation of the equivalent variation (E = area $a + b + c$) is obtained using

$$\Delta q^* \doteq -\eta \cdot q \; \frac{\Delta S}{m}$$

and

$$\text{area } c \doteq -\tfrac{1}{2} \Delta q^*|\Delta p| \doteq \tfrac{1}{2} \eta \cdot \Delta S \cdot q \cdot \frac{|\Delta p|}{m}$$

that is, the equivalent variation can be approximated by

$$\hat{E} = \Delta S + \frac{\eta}{2m} (\Delta S)^2 = \Delta S + \hat{\epsilon}|\Delta S| \tag{6.5}$$

The approximations in (6.3) and (6.5) have an important use both in determining the extent of error involved in using consumer surplus change to approximate compensating and equivalent variations and in suggesting appropriate modifications of the consumer surplus change to serve as more precise estimates of the compensating and equivalent variations. First, note from (6.3) and (6.5) that $\hat{\epsilon}$ is approximately the fraction of error in each case. Thus, using (6.4), *if the product of income elasticity and the ratio of surplus change to total income divided by 2 is less than 0.05 in absolute value, no more than about a 5 percent error* ($|\hat{\epsilon}| = |\eta s/2| \leq 0.05$) *is made by using consumer surplus as a measure of either compensating or equivalent variation* (without modification).[11] As argued by Robert D. Willig in his seminal paper, this is a condition that is likely to hold in many cases.[12] That is, for many goods, the change in consumer surplus or the income-equivalent change of any price change within reason is a very small fraction of total income; hence, for any reasonable income elasticity the condition will hold. For other goods, the income elasticity is small, so that the change in consumer surplus would have to be a very large fraction of total income to create a large error (which suggests a commodity for which actual expenditures may be large—at least at some intermediate prices).

For common everyday items such as clothing and stereo sets, the percentage of income that would be spent at any relevant price is probably small enough

---

[11]A precise examination of these errors in Appendix B confirms these results.
[12]Willig, "Consumer's Surplus."

that the condition $|\eta s/2| < 0.05$ will not be violated even if the income elasticity is 2 or 3. For items such as housing, however, the income equivalent of a large price change may represent a substantial proportion of income (e.g., half); furthermore, the income elasticity may well be 1 or greater in some cases. Hence, this would be an instance in which more than a 5 percent error may be made by using consumer surplus as a direct estimate of the compensating or equivalent variation.

If $|\eta s/2|$ is greater than 0.05 in absolute value or if a more precise estimate of the willingness-to-pay concepts is desired, C or E can be estimated following (6.3) or (6.5). This can be accomplished by estimating the average income elasticity η over the price-change interval and obtaining data on total income so that $\hat{e}$ can be calculated using ΔS. Neglecting errors in statistical application, Appendix B shows that these *modified formulas for estimating the compensating and equivalent variations lead to less than about 2 percent error when* $|\eta s/2| \leq 0.08$ *and income elasticity changes by less than 50 percent over the interval of a price change.* The latter condition is much less restrictive than that developed above for direct use of ΔS as an estimate of C or E.

To exemplify application of these results, suppose that a consumer's demand for beef is given by the relationship

$$q = 11 - 5p + \tfrac{8}{75} m \qquad\qquad (6.6)$$

where

q = quantity of beef consumed in hundred pounds per year
p = price of beef in dollars per pound
m = income in thousand dollars per year

Assume that initial price is $p^0 = 1$ and consumer income is $m_0 = \tfrac{75}{2}$. Now consider the consumer welfare effect of adding a luxury tax which thus increases consumer price to $p^1 = 2$. Substituting m_0 into equation (6.6) leads to the equation $q = 15 - 5p$, shown graphically in Figure 6.11. As is obvious from the graph, the change in consumer surplus is thus $\Delta S = -\tfrac{15}{2}$, which suggests a real income loss of $750 per year (note that areas in Figure 6.11 are measured in hundred dollars per year). But how accurate is ΔS as a measure of the compensating or equivalent variation? If one is sure that $|\eta s/2| \leq 0.05$ and any absolute error up to about 5 percent is tolerable, then ΔS can be used directly as an estimate of C or E. If not, this question can be answered by appealing to the approximation given above.

To do this, note that the change in quantity, Δq, caused by a change in income, Δm, must always satisfy $\Delta q / \Delta m = \tfrac{8}{75}$ according to equation (6.6). Hence, the income elasticity is

$$\eta = \frac{m}{q}\,\frac{\Delta q}{\Delta m} = \frac{\tfrac{75}{2}}{q}\,\frac{8}{75} = \frac{4}{q}$$

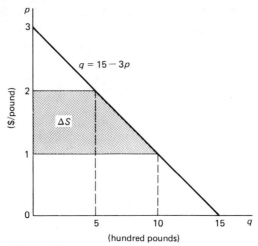

FIGURE 6.11

Over the price interval from p^0 to p^1, the quantity q is between 5 and 10, as indicated by Figure 6.11; hence, the income elasticity varies between $\eta_1 = \frac{4}{10}$ and $\eta_2 = \frac{4}{5}$. Further noting that $s = \Delta S/m = (-\frac{15}{2})/(\frac{75}{2}) = -\frac{1}{5}$, one thus finds that $\hat{\epsilon}$ is between $\eta_1|s|/2 = 0.04$ and $\eta_2|s|/2 = 0.08$. Following equation (6.3), this implies that ΔS overestimates the compensating variation by about 4 to 8 percent (note that both C and ΔS are negative, so the compensating variation is larger in absolute value). Similarly, equation (6.5) implies that ΔS underestimates the equivalent variation by about 4 to 8 percent.

If a 4 to 8 percent error is unacceptable,[13] equations (6.3) and (6.5) suggest a further improvement. That is, if ΔS overestimates the compensating variation by 4 to 8 percent, then increasing ΔS by 6 percent (or in this case reducing it by 6 percent in absolute terms) will neither overestimate nor underestimate the compensating variation by more than about 2 percent. A reasonable approach thus amounts to choosing η equal to the average of the minimum and maximum income elasticities $[\bar{\eta} = (\eta_1 + \eta_2)/2]$ for the purpose of making the calculations in equations (6.3) through (6.5). Thus, $\bar{\epsilon} = \bar{\eta}|s|/2$ is the midpoint of the interval generated by $\hat{\epsilon}$ over the course of the price change—in this case the midpoint of the interval (0.04, 0.08). Thus, substituting $\bar{\epsilon}$ for $\hat{\epsilon}$ in equation (6.3) obtains

$$\bar{C} = \Delta S - \bar{\epsilon}|\Delta S| = \Delta S - 0.06|\Delta S| = 1.06(-\tfrac{15}{2}) \tag{6.7}$$

---

[13]For the purposes of the discussion in this chapter, it is assumed that the parameters of equation (6.6) are known exactly. However, an equation of the type in (6.6) would ordinarily be estimated statistically; and the possible errors resulting from inaccurate estimation may make bounding the error by, say, 4 or 8 percent impossible.

Similar reasoning suggests estimating the equivalent variation using equation (6.5) in the same way:[14]

$$\bar{E} = \Delta S + \bar{\epsilon}|\Delta S| = \Delta S + 0.06|\Delta S| = 0.94(-\tfrac{15}{2}) \tag{6.8}$$

6.6 CONSUMER SURPLUS AS AN APPROXIMATION OF WILLINGNESS TO PAY: THE MULTIPLE-PRICE-CHANGE CASE

Section 6.5 has discussed approximating willingness to pay with consumer surplus change only in the case of a single price change. However, these results may be simply extended to the case of a multiple price change. That is, even though the consumer surplus change may be path dependent, the compensating

---

[14]To exemplify the size of errors introduced by the approximation in this section, one may use Appendix Table B.1 as explained in Appendix B (note the symmetry about $s = 0$, which allows bounds for $s = -0.2$ to be deduced from those for $s = 0.2$) to find that

$$0.08326 \geq \frac{\Delta S - C}{|\Delta S|} \geq 0.03948$$

and

$$0.07686 \geq \frac{E - \Delta S}{|\Delta S|} \geq 0.04055$$

Thus,

$$\Delta S - 0.08326|\Delta S| \leq C \leq \Delta S - 0.03948|\Delta S|$$

and

$$\Delta S + 0.07686|\Delta S| \geq E \geq \Delta S + 0.04055|\Delta S|$$

Clearly, in this case $\hat{\epsilon}$ is a good approximation of the actual percentage error (compare 0.04 to 0.03948 and 0.04055 in the case of the small income elasticity, and compare 0.08 to 0.07686 and 0.08326 in the case of the larger income elasticity). Also, using these results from Appendix Table B.1, error bounds on the modified estimates of C and E in equations (6.3), (6.5), (6.7), or (6.8) can be developed. For example, in the context of (6.7) and (6.8), the preceding results in this footnote imply that

$$0.08326 - 0.06 = 0.02326 \geq \frac{\bar{C} - C}{|\Delta S|} \geq -0.02052 = 0.03948 - 0.06$$

and

$$0.07686 - 0.06 = 0.01686 \geq \frac{E - \bar{E}}{|\Delta S|} \geq -0.01945 = 0.04055 - 0.06$$

Thus, only about a 2 percent error is made by using modifications of consumer surplus change for a case where the income elasticity changes by 100 percent and $|\eta s/2| \leq 0.08$ over the course of the price change.

and equivalent variations are unique. For example, compensating variation in its willingness-to-pay version measures the maximum amount of income the consumer is willing to pay for a change in prices, and the order in which prices are reduced cannot affect this amount. A time-path problem simply does not exist. Hence, if the path of price changes is segmented into small steps, large errors in calculating compensating and equivalent variation can be avoided by following the procedures in Section 6.5.

In Figure 6.12, suppose that prices are p_1^0 and p_2^0 for commodities q_1 and q_2 and that prices change to p_1^1 and p_2^1, respectively. To calculate compensating or equivalent variation, the Hicksian compensated demand curves must be used rather than the ordinary demand curves. Thus, in calculating compensating and equivalent variation in Figure 6.12, one may arbitrarily choose the path in Figure 6.12(a), changing p_1 first and then p_2. As in preceding cases, compensated demand curves are distinguished from ordinary demand curves by condi-

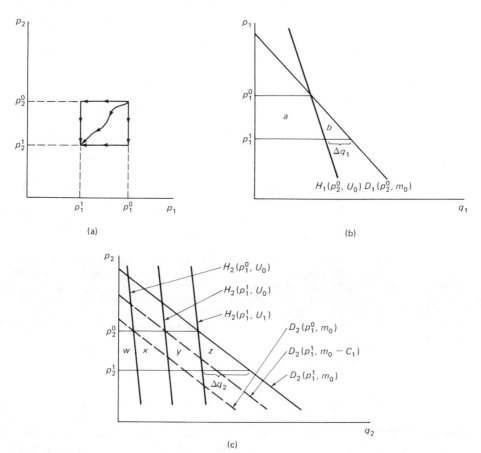

FIGURE 6.12

tioning on utility levels rather than income levels. Initially, income is m_0 and utility is U_0. Changing prices along the first segment of the path in Figure 6.12(a), holding the price of q_2 fixed at p_2^0, the associated change in consumer surplus, ΔS_1, is area $a + b$ in Figure 6.12(b); and the compensating variation associated with this part of the path, C_1, is area a. Analogous to the single-price-change case, area b can be estimated by

$$\text{area } b \doteq \tfrac{1}{2} \Delta q_1 \cdot |\Delta p_1| \doteq \tfrac{1}{2} \eta^1 \cdot \Delta S_1 \cdot q_1 \cdot \frac{|\Delta p_1|}{m_0}$$

where $\Delta p_1 = p_1^1 - p_1^0$, $\Delta S_1 = $ area $a + b$, η^1 is the income elasticity of demand for q_1 [i.e., $\eta^1 = (\Delta q_1/\Delta m)/(m/q_1)$, where Δm is the income change which leads to the change in quantity demanded, Δq_1, holding prices fixed], and Δq_1 is as shown in Figure 6.12(b). Thus, following the derivation leading to equation (6.3), C_1 can be approximated by

$$\hat{C}_1 = \Delta S_1 - \frac{\eta^1}{2m_0} (\Delta S_1)^2 \tag{6.9}$$

Now consider the additional compensating variation C_2 generated by the second part of the path where p_2 is changed, holding p_1 fixed at p_1^1. Of course, the associated change in surplus, ΔS_2, is given by the area $w + x + y + z$, which is the area behind the ordinary demand curve in the q_2 market after p_1 is changed to its terminal level. Based on this surplus change, one may thus be led to estimate C_2 by

$$\tilde{C}_2 = \Delta S_2 - \frac{\eta^2}{2m_0} (\Delta S_2)^2 \tag{6.10}$$

where η^2 is the income elasticity of demand for q_2. Note, however, that $\tilde{C}_2$ is an approximation of area $w + x + y$ where area z is approximated by

$$\text{area } z \doteq \tfrac{1}{2} \Delta q_2 \cdot |\Delta p_2| \doteq \tfrac{1}{2} \eta^2 \cdot \Delta S_2 \cdot \frac{|\Delta p_2|}{m_0}$$

where $\Delta p_2 = p_2^1 - p_2^0$. But area $w + x + y$ measures the willingness to pay for the price change from p_2^0 to p_2^1 starting from the initial prices (p_1^1, p_2^0) rather than from (p_1^0, p_2^0). Thus, the utility level is held constant at U_1, which is the utility level corresponding to prices p_1^1 and p_2^0 and income m_0.

The compensating variation of moving from prices $(p_1{}^0, p_2{}^0)$ to $(p_1{}^1, p_2{}^1)$, on the other hand, must hold the utility level at U_0 along the entire path. Thus, the compensating variation of the entire price change is obtained by adding to C_1 the change in area behind $H_2(p_1{}^1, U_0)$, the compensated demand curve conditioned on the initial utility level (and the terminal level of p_1), that is, area $w + x$. The error obtained by using $C_1 + \tilde{C}_2$ as an approximation of the compensating variation of the overall price change is thus approximately area y.

The problem that arises here is thus similar to that of the nibble paradox. As resolved in Section 6.2, when a price change is broken into intervals, the sum of compensating variations over the intervals does not generally measure the overall compensating variation unless income is first reduced by the compensating variations associated with previous price-change intervals in calculating the compensating variation of subsequent price-change intervals. Thus, in this case income must be reduced by C_1 before calculating or estimating C_2 if $C_1 + C_2$ is to measure the overall compensating variation.

Since that adjustment in income just equates the utility at $(p_1{}^0, p_2{}^0)$ with the utility at $(p_1{}^1, p_2{}^0)$, the ordinary demand curve for q_2 at price $p_1{}^1$ and income $m_0 - C_1$ must just coincide with the compensated demand curve for q_2 at price $p_1{}^1$ and utility U_0 when $p_2 = p_2{}^0$ [Figure 6.12(c)]. Hence, for small price changes, area y is approximately a parallelogram with approximate area $|\Delta p_2| \cdot \widetilde{\Delta q}_2$ where $\widetilde{\Delta q}_2$ is the horizontal difference in ordinary demand curves conditioned on the same prices and different incomes, $m_0 - C_1$ and m_0. Knowledge of the income elasticity permits approximation of $\widetilde{\Delta q}_2$. That is, using equation (6.1) in the context of the q_2 market, where $\Delta m = C_1$, obtains

$$\widetilde{\Delta q}_2 = \eta^2 \cdot q_2 \cdot \frac{C_1}{m_0}$$

Thus, using equation (6.8) and the fact that $\Delta S_2 \doteq q_2 |\Delta p_2|$ for small Δp_2,

$$\text{area } y \doteq |\Delta p_2| \cdot \widetilde{\Delta q}_2 \doteq |\Delta p_2| \cdot \eta^2 \cdot q_2 \cdot \frac{C_1}{m_0} \doteq \frac{\eta^2}{m_0} \Delta S_2 \, \Delta S_1 \qquad \textbf{(6.11)}$$

Note that, in making the approximation in the last step, a term with $(m_0)^2$ in the denominator is discarded. Since m_0 is generally large relative to surplus changes, this approximation is not serious.[15] Recalling that $\tilde{C}_2$ overestimates

---

[15] Actually, the discarded term is

$$\frac{\eta^1 \eta^2}{2 m_0{}^2} \Delta S_2 (\Delta S_1)^2 = |\pm 2 \hat{\epsilon}^1 \hat{\epsilon}^2| \, \Delta S_1$$

where $\hat{\epsilon}^1 = \eta^i |s_i|/2$ and $s_i = \Delta S_i/m_0$. Under conditions similar to those suggested above in the one price-change case, $|\hat{\epsilon}_i| \leq 0.05$, so that the discarded term represents less than 0.5 percent of ΔS_1 (i.e., $|2\hat{\epsilon}^1\hat{\epsilon}^2| < 0.005$).

the correct component of compensating variation C_2 corresponding to the second part of the price path by area y, an appropriate estimate of C_2 is thus obtained by subtracting equation (6.11) from equation (6.10):

$$\hat{C}_2 = \Delta S_2 - \frac{\eta^2}{2m_0} (\Delta S_2)^2 - \frac{\eta^2}{m_0} (\Delta S_2) \cdot (\Delta S_1) \qquad (6.12)$$

Aggregating equations (6.9) and (6.12) thus estimates the sum of compensating variations or the overall compensating variation associated with the price change from $(p_1{}^0, p_2{}^0)$ to $(p_1{}^1, p_2{}^1)$:

$$\hat{C}_1 + \hat{C}_2 = \Delta S_1 + \Delta S_2 - \frac{\eta^1}{2m_0} (\Delta S_1)^2 - \frac{\eta^2}{m_0} (\Delta S_1)(\Delta S_2) - \frac{\eta^2}{2m_0} (\Delta S_2)^2 \qquad (6.13)$$

If the income elasticities are the same in each market ($\hat{\eta} = \eta^1 = \eta^2$) or are estimated by $\hat{\eta} = (\eta^1 + \eta^2)/2$, then the overall compensating variation is estimated by

$$\hat{C} = \Delta S_1 + \Delta S_2 - \frac{\hat{\eta}}{2m_0} (\Delta S_1)^2 - \frac{\hat{\eta}}{m_0} (\Delta S_1)(\Delta S_2) - \frac{\hat{\eta}}{2m_0} (\Delta S_2)^2$$

$$= \sum_{i=1}^{2} \Delta S_i - \frac{\hat{\eta}}{2m_0} \left(\sum_{i=1}^{2} \Delta S_i \right)^2 \qquad (6.14)$$

$$= \sum_{i=1}^{2} \Delta S_1 - \hat{\epsilon} \left| \sum_{i=1}^{2} \Delta S_i \right|$$

where

$$\hat{\epsilon} = \frac{\hat{\eta}|s|}{2}, \qquad s = \sum_{i=1}^{2} \frac{\Delta S_i}{m_0}$$

Similarly, if one defines

$$\eta_1 = \min (\eta^1, \eta^2)$$
$$\eta_2 = \max (\eta^1, \eta^2)$$

where the minimization and maximization are performed with respect to the (arbitrary) price path as well as commodities, then approximate bounds on the true compensating variation are given by

$$\bar{C}_1 = \sum_{i=1}^{2} \Delta S_1 - \epsilon_1 \left| \sum_{i=1}^{2} \Delta S_1 \right| \qquad (6.15)$$

and

$$\bar{C}_2 = \sum_{i=1}^{2} \Delta S_1 - \epsilon_2 \left| \sum_{i=1}^{2} \Delta S_i \right| \tag{6.16}$$

where

$$\epsilon_i = \frac{\eta_i |s|}{2}, \quad i = 1, 2$$

As shown in Appendix B, these approximations generalize for the case of price changes in many markets; and the associated errors of approximation are not much more serious than in the single-price-change case. A similar approximation of the equivalent variation is also possible and, as confirmed by Appendix B, leads to the estimate

$$\hat{E} = \sum_{i=1}^{n} \Delta S_i + \hat{\epsilon} \left| \sum_{i=1}^{n} \Delta S_i \right| \tag{6.17}$$

with approximate bounds

$$\bar{E}_1 = \sum_{i=1}^{n} \Delta S_i + \epsilon_2 \left| \sum_{i=1}^{n} \Delta S_i \right| \tag{6.18}$$

and

$$\bar{E}_2 = \sum_{i=1}^{n} \Delta S_i + \epsilon_1 \left| \sum_{i=1}^{n} \Delta S_i \right| \tag{6.19}$$

Again, the errors of approximation are small for most practical cases. *If income elasticities are constant and the same in all markets for which prices change, then no more than about 1 percent error is incurred by using $\hat{C}$ or $\hat{E}$ as estimates of the associated willingness-to-pay measures as long as $|\hat{\epsilon}| = |\hat{\eta}s/2|$ ≤ 0.1. If income elasticity is not constant, then no more than about 2 percent error is made by using $\hat{C}$ or $\hat{E}$ if $|\hat{\epsilon}| = |\hat{\eta}s/2| \leq 0.08$ and income elasticity varies less than 50 percent among commodities and over the path of the price change.* As discussed earlier, these conditions are satisfied in a wide variety of (but not all) practical cases.[16]

From equations (6.14) through (6.19), it is also evident that ϵ_1 and ϵ_2 reflect the extent of error incurred by using the raw consumer surplus change, $\sum_{i=1}^{n} \Delta S_i$,

---

[16]Appendix B also discusses an algorithm that can estimate the compensating or equivalent variations even more precisely using information about the difference in income elasticities over intervals composing the overall price change [e.g., as in equation (6.13)].

as a direct estimate of C or E. That is, since approximate bounds are given by $\bar{C}_2 \le C \le \bar{C}_1$ and $\bar{E}_2 \le E \le \bar{E}_1$, subtraction of $\sum_{i=1}^{n} \Delta S_i$ and division by $\left| \sum_{i=1}^{n} \Delta S_i \right|$ obtains approximate bounds

$$\epsilon_2 \ge \cdot \frac{\sum_{i=1}^{n} \Delta S_i - C}{\left| \sum_{i=1}^{n} \Delta S_i \right|} \ge \cdot \epsilon_1 \qquad (6.20)$$

and

$$\epsilon_2 \ge \cdot \frac{E - \sum_{i=1}^{n} \Delta S_i}{\left| \sum_{i=1}^{n} \Delta S_i \right|} \ge \cdot \epsilon_1 \qquad (6.21)$$

on the respective percentage errors.

To exemplify application of the results above, consider demand relationships

$$q_i = 12 - 5p_i + 2p_j + \tfrac{3}{200} m$$
$$q_j = 5 - 5p_j + 3p_i + \tfrac{2}{200} m$$

for, say, beef and pork, the quantities of which are represented respectively by q_i and q_j. Suppose that respective prices change from $p_i^0 = p_j^0 = 1$ to $p_i^1 = p_j^1 = 2$ while income remains at $m_0 = 400$. First, consider the change in consumer surplus along the path where p_i is first adjusted from p_i^0 to p_i^1, then p_j is adjusted from p_j^0 to p_j^1. Holding p_j at p_j^0, the demand curve for q_i is thus

$$q_i = 20 - 5p_i$$

which, as is apparent from Figure 6.13(a), generates a change in surplus of

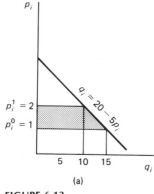
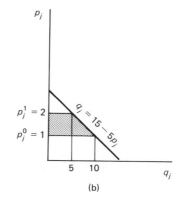

(a)

(b)

FIGURE 6.13

$$\Delta S_i = -\tfrac{25}{2}$$

as p_1 moves from $p_i{}^0$ to $p_i{}^1$. Now holding p_i at $p_i{}^1$, the demand curve for q_j is

$$q_j = 15 - 5p_j$$

which, as suggested by Figure 6.13(b), generates a surplus change of

$$\Delta S_j = -\tfrac{15}{2}$$

as p_j moves from $p_j{}^0$ to $p_j{}^1$. Thus, the consumer surplus change is

$$\Delta S_i + \Delta S_j = -20$$

But how accurate is this figure as an estimate of the compensating or equivalent variation, and how might it be modified to obtain greater accuracy? To use equations (6.14) through (6.19) to answer these questions, one must first compute income elasticities over the path of price adjustment. Using the demand equation for q_i, one finds that

$$\frac{\Delta q_i}{\Delta m} = \tfrac{3}{200}$$

for any change in income holding prices fixed; hence, the income elasticity is

$$\eta_i = \frac{\Delta q_i}{\Delta m} \; \frac{m}{q_i} = \frac{6}{q_i}$$

Similarly,

$$\frac{\Delta q_j}{\Delta m} = \tfrac{2}{200}$$

and

$$\eta_j = \frac{4}{q_j}$$

Noting from Figure 6.13 that $10 \le q_i \le 15$ and $5 \le q_j \le 10$ along the selected price path implies that $0.4 = \tfrac{6}{15} \le \eta_i \le \tfrac{6}{10} = 0.6$ and $0.4 = \tfrac{4}{10} \le \eta_j \le \tfrac{4}{5} = 0.8$ along the respective segments of the price path. Thus, the minimum and maximum income elasticities along the price path are $\eta_1 = 0.4$ and $\eta_2 = 0.8$, respectively, and

$$\hat{\eta} = \frac{(0.4 + 0.8)}{2} = 0.6$$

$$s = \frac{\Delta S_i + \Delta S_j}{m_0} = -\frac{20}{400} = -0.05$$

$$\hat{\epsilon} = \frac{0.6\,|-0.05|}{2} = 0.015$$

$$\epsilon_1 = \frac{0.4\,|-0.05|}{2} = 0.01$$

$$\epsilon_2 = \frac{0.8\,|-0.05|}{2} = 0.02$$

Substituting these calculations into equations (6.14) through (6.19) implies the following:

1. From equation (6.14), $\Delta S_i + \Delta S_j$ overestimates the compensating variation by about 1.5 percent ($\hat{\epsilon} \times 100$).

2. From equation (6.17), $\Delta S_i + \Delta S_j$ underestimates the equivalent variation by about 1.5 percent.

3. Thus, using equations (6.14) and (6.17), better estimates of the compensating and equivalent variations are

$$\hat{C} = -20 - 0.015\,|-20| = -20.3$$

and

$$\hat{E} = -20 + 0.015\,|-20| = -19.7$$

respectively.

4. From equations (6.15) and (6.16), the compensating variation is approximately bounded by

$$-20.4 \leq C \leq -20.2$$

and from equations (6.18) and (6.19), the equivalent variation is approximately bounded by[17]

$$-19.8 \leq E \leq -19.6$$

---

[17]For cases such as this where income elasticities vary along the price path, one may use the accurate bounds from Appendix B to determine, for example, that

$$0.02019 \geq \frac{\Delta S_i + \Delta S_j - C}{|\Delta S_i + \Delta S_j|} \geq 0.00996$$

(Footnote continued on pg. 112)

6.7 CONSUMER SURPLUS AS AN APPROXIMATION OF WILLINGNESS TO PAY: THE PRICE–INCOME CHANGE CASE

One final note is necessary in using the methods of the preceding two sections in estimating willingness to pay when income also changes. Consider, for example, changing price(s) and income according to the paths demonstrated in Figure 6.14(a), that is, either changing prices and then income (L_1) or first income and then prices (L_2). A key point to note here is that the methods for evaluating the effect of a price change in Sections 6.5 and 6.6 assume that the initial set of prices corresponds to the initial utility level. If one uses path L_1, the initial utility level on the segment where price(s) change is, indeed, the initial utility level for the overall change, so the methods of Sections 6.5 and 6.6 apply. Thus, to the compensating variation corresponding to the price change must be added the subsequent willingness to pay for the income change continuing to hold utility at the overall initial level. The latter effect is trivially equal to the change in income. On the other hand, if one first changes income, thus generating compensating variation equal to the change in income, the level

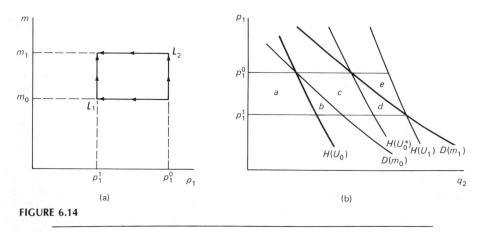

FIGURE 6.14

Substituting $\Delta S_i + \Delta S_j = -20$ thus implies that

$$-20.4038 \leq C \leq -20.1992$$

Comparing with the approximated bounds above suggests, and rightfully so, that the width in error bounds caused by income elasticity variation is great enough to make further adjustments according to the accurate methods of Appendix B inconsequential—at least when income elasticities vary to any substantial degree. For practical purposes, the bounds in (6.20) and (6.21) are so close to accurate that common usage of the more complicated (accurate) methods of Appendix B is not worth the additional computational burden.

of utility at which the price-change segment of the path begins is different from the initial utility level, and modifications in the methods to correct for this difference would be required.

The methods of Sections 6.5 and 6.6 can thus be employed directly in evaluating compensating variation for the price–income-change case only if the income change is considered after the price change(s) (by merely adding the income change to the compensating variation generated by the price change). In the case of equivalent variation, just the reverse is true because computations correspond to the terminal utility level. That is, the price change(s) must be considered after the income change, so that the terminal utility of the price-change segment of the path is the same as the terminal utility level of the overall price–income change.

Application of these arguments is considered graphically in Figure 6.14(b) for the case where income and a single price change from (m_0, p_1^0) to (m_1, p_1^1), respectively. Initially, the ordinary and compensated demand curves are $D(m_0)$ and $H(U_0)$, respectively, and subsequently change to $D(m_1)$ and $H(U_0^*)$, respectively. Thus, U_0 is the initial utility level, and U_0^* is the utility level after the income change but before the price change. Consider, first, the case of estimating compensating variation. Of course, since $H(U_0)$ is the appropriate compensated demand curve (it is conditioned on the initial utility level), the compensating variation is

$$C = m_1 - m_0 + \text{area } a$$

Area a is estimated by correcting the change in consumer surplus, area $a + b$, associated with $D(m_0)$ by an estimate of area b. If one uses the change in surplus, area $a + b + c + d$, associated with $D(m_1)$, on the other hand, the correction approximates area d and gives a resulting estimate of area $a + b + c$. Hence, the associated estimate of compensating variation would approximate (area $a + b + c) + m_1 - m_0$ and be in error by approximately area $b + c$. Thus, *to estimate compensating variation using the methods of Sections 6.5 and 6.6, one must evaluate the effects of the price change at the initial income level and then add to that effect the change in income.*

Turning to estimation of equivalent variation, let U_1 represent the terminal level of utility following the price–income change. Both the price and income segments of the path of adjustment are properly evaluated at the terminal utility level. This is accomplished by evaluating the price change conditioned on the terminal income level. Thus, the change in area behind the terminal compensated demand curve, area $a + b + c + d + e$, is obtained by adding an estimate of area e to the surplus change, area $a + b + c + d$, associated with the ordinary demand curve conditioned on the terminal income. Thus, *to estimate equivalent variation, one must evaluate the effects of the price change at the terminal income level and then add that effect to the change in income.*

6.8 CONCLUSIONS

The development of measures of gain based upon what a consumer is willing to pay for an improved situation began in 1844 with the French engineer Dupuit.[18] Following Alfred Marshall's[19] shift in emphasis to money measures of utility change, Professor Hicks[20] reestablished willingness-to-pay measures as the foundation for applied welfare work. The two chief measures he proposed— compensating and equivalent variation—are directly related to the consumer's preference map, and each yields a unique measure of gain for any price path from the initial to the terminal situation. Moreover, since each can be given willingness-to-pay interpretations, each can be used to perform the Kaldor-Hicks and Scitovsky compensation tests when more than one consumer is involved. That is, asking if the gainer can compensate the loser and still prefer a change is equivalent to asking if the compensating variation of the gainer (or willingness to pay to keep the change) is greater than the compensating variation of the loser (or willingness to accept payment to make the change). Of course, the same questions can be asked for the reverse movement and, as Scitovsky[21] pointed out, can lead to the paradoxical situation where the test suggests a change be made—but once made, the same test suggests the reverse movement be made. This situation arises because compensating variation is unequal to equivalent variation for each of the consumers involved. Only in the case where compensating and equivalent variation coincide are they both equal to consumer surplus, so no reversal occurs.

The definition of consumer surplus for the purpose of these comparisons is that of simply an area—the calculated dollar area behind the demand curve and above the price line. This area obtains welfare significance in the context of this chapter only insofar as it can be related to the Hicksian willingness-to-pay measures of consumer welfare change. Hicks[22] has argued that, if the income effect is "small," consumer surplus will provide a "good" approximation of either compensating or equivalent variation. But Willig[23] has provided precise quantitative guidance as to how "small" the income effect must be to obtain a "good" approximation. The Willig formulas in Sections 6.5 and 6.6 can indeed be used to calculate error bounds on consumer surplus as an approximation of either welfare quantity. These empirical embellishments of Hicks' conceptual results thus provide a sound foundation for consumer welfare measurement.

---

[18]Dupuit, "On the Measurement of the Utility of Public Works."

[19]Alfred Marshall, *Principles of Economics* (London, 1930).

[20]J. R. Hicks, *A Revision of Demand Theory.*

[21]T. Scitovsky, "A Note on Welfare Propositions in Economics," *Review of Economic Studies,* Vol. 9, No. 1 (November, 1941), pp. 77–88.

[22]J. R. Hicks, *A Revision of Demand Theory.*

[23]R. D. Willig, "Consumer's Surplus Without Apology."

These results are made possible by an important dual relationship which exists between demands and preferences. That is, just as demands can be derived from preferences through utility maximization, one can, in principle, determine preferences in an ordinal context from consumer demand equations. This relationship is discussed rigorously in Appendix B, and Section B.13 in particular outlines an alternative approach to estimation of demands based on the theory of this duality.

7

Factor Supply Decisions
and Resource Owners

In the preceding two chapters, consumer welfare was analyzed in terms of the effect on consumers from changing the prices of products that consumers purchase and/or from introducing a new commodity. However, in order to purchase goods, consumers must earn income (excluding for the moment government welfare payments to consumers) from such sources as work, interest on savings, rental income from landholdings, and the like.

The owners of factors of production such as labor and land derive "economic rent" from the services provided by these factors for which there is a positive market demand (see Section 4.1). Economic rent has a symmetrical welfare interpretation with consumer surplus in that they are "both measures of the change in the individual's welfare when the set of prices facing him are altered or the constraints upon him are altered."[1] Hence, the approach of Chapter 6 can be generalized in a straightforward fashion, although the Willig results require a somewhat different interpretation.

7.1 INITIAL CONSIDERATIONS IN RESOURCE
OWNER WELFARE MEASUREMENT

To use the same framework developed earlier, consider the labor supply curve in Figure 7.1, for example. Initially, the wage earner is willing to work longer

---

[1]E. J. Mishan, "Rent as a Measure of Welfare Change," *American Economic Review,* Vol. 49, No. 3 (June 1959), p. 394.

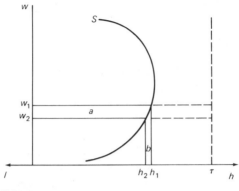

FIGURE 7.1

hours (h) if the wage rate (w) is increased (although perhaps at higher incomes the same wage increment may lead to reduced willingness to work; see Section 7.4 for a further explanation). As pointed out by Gary Becker,[2] the consumer's labor supply curve represents the mirror image of his or her demand for leisure. That is, with units of time of length τ (e.g., 24-hour days), a decision to work h_1 hours automatically entails a decision to allocate $\tau - h_1$ hours to nonwork or leisure. Thus, one may further consider Figure 7.1 in the context of the demand for leisure. In point of fact, with prevailing wage rate—say, w_1—at which h_1 hours of labor are supplied, w_1 not only represents the marginal income from an additional hour of labor but also the marginal cost of obtaining an additional hour of leisure.

With this interpretation of the labor supply curve, consider a reduction in the wage rate to w_2 at which working hours are reduced to h_2. Following the earlier approach (Figure 5.3) the change in gross benefits from consuming leisure in Figure 7.1 is the change in area below the demand curve—area b. From this must be subtracted the costs of obtaining the additional leisure. In this case the cost is the reduction in income resulting from the wage change and the induced change in hours worked, that is, $w_1 h_1 - w_2 h_2$ or area $a + b$. Subtracting this cost from the change in gross benefits obtains area a as a net loss for the consumer/labor supplier as a result of the wage reduction. Note, however, that area a is simply the change in area above the labor supply curve and below the wage rate.

The area behind a resource supply curve is fully analogous to use of the consumer surplus area behind a consumer demand curve. To maintain symmetry of terminology with Chapter 4, however, the triangle-like area above a supply curve and below price will be called the *producer surplus* associated with the supply curve. This area is also sometimes called *economic rent* in the

---

[2]Gary S. Becker, "A Theory of the Allocation of Time," *The Economic Journal,* Vol. 75 (September 1965), pp. 493–517.

context of this chapter because it is a net benefit earned as a return on the resource.

However, not all resources supplied by individuals enter into their preferences (apart from the implicit purchasing power of the income they earn) as does labor. For example, suppose that in Figure 7.2 an individual owns a quantity of land q_1. As a consumer, the individual may receive no explicit benefit from using the land for himself. Thus, he would be willing to rent the land to someone else who could make beneficial use of the land at the prevailing rental price p_1. If the rental price is too low, the landowner may seek to sell the land, but this would be a longer-run decision. Hence, the vertical line at q_1 may be regarded as a short-run supply curve analogous to S in Figure 7.1. For example, with an increase in rental price to p_2, the increase in producer surplus or economic rent in the short run is area a and is equivalent to the change in nominal rental income (the change in $p \cdot q$) on the land.

7.2 ENDOGENOUS VERSUS EXOGENOUS INCOME

The case associated with Figure 7.2 suggests yet a further distinction which becomes important from the standpoint of empirical practice, especially in applying the Willig results, to approximate willingness to pay via the consumer or producer surplus triangles. Consider, for example, the case where the vertical supply curve in Figure 7.2 is determined in the short run strictly by the amount of resource controlled by the individual (for example, amount of owned land) rather than by prices of other commodities. For example, suppose that land purchases and sales require more time to implement than other consumption/resource supply decisions, and hence short-run price variations cannot induce a shift in the supply curve of rental land. In this case the short-run income from land rental is essentially imposed on the individual rather than determined by the individual according to his preferences.

In economics, the term *exogenous* is used to refer to forces or variables that are determined from the outside, whereas *endogenous* variables are determined, jointly or simultaneously, from within (for example, within the consumer's decision problem) in the context of existing exogenous forces. Thus,

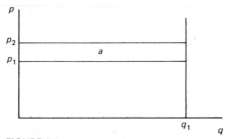

FIGURE 7.2

for purposes of making the foregoing distinction, *exogenous income* will be defined as that component of income which the consumer has no ability to increase and that he will not voluntarily decrease in the short run. *Endogenous income,* on the other hand, will be defined as that component of income which may generally be altered by the consumer as a response to changes in prices or other exogenous forces.[3]

These concepts become important in delineating the determinants of a resource supply curve. Conceptually, *a resource supply curve for the consumer is determined by exogenous income and the prices of consumption commodities and other resources for which quantities may generally be adjusted by the consumer.* For example, a labor supply curve may be determined by consumption prices, the interest rate, and exogenous income composed of rents, dividends on shareholdings (profits), and transfer payments from government or possibly private sources. That is, if the quantity of savings supplied by the consumer at a given interest rate depends on the wage rate, total interest income could not be included in exogenous income as a determinant of labor supply since interest income would itself be determined or influenced by movement along the labor supply curve. The amount of land offered for rental, on the other hand, may not generally respond to changes in the wage rate at least in the short run; hence, the income from land rental rather than simply the rental rate may serve as a determinant of labor supply.[4]

Consumption demand may also be treated in the same way in the context of this chapter. That is, if the consumer's decision problem is one of maximizing utility through choice of the quantities of consumption goods and resources supplied, the exogenous forces affecting the consumer are the prices of all consumption goods and resources which are subject to variation in the short run plus the exogenous income resulting from transfers, profits, and resource sales which are not subject to short-run alteration. Thus, the determinants of each consumer demand or supply curve consist of exogenous income and the prices of all other consumption goods and resources subject to short-run variation.

7.3 PATH DEPENDENCY AND RELATED ISSUES

Having defined an intuitive measure of welfare change for a resource owner— producer surplus—and having discussed the alternative roles of resource prices

---

[3]In some earlier literature, endogenous and exogenous income have been called earned and unearned income. See, for example, Michael Abbott and Orley Ashenfelter, "Labour Supply, Commodity Demand, and the Allocation of Time," *Review of Economic Studies,* Vol. 43, No. 135 (October 1976), pp. 389–411.

[4]In a longer-run application, where the quantity of land offered for rental may respond to price changes, however, the rental rate rather than total rental income is the appropriate determinant or exogenous variable in the consumer's decision problem.

as determinants of supply and demand, consider now the applicability of such desirable properties as uniqueness and path dependency when several prices and possibly income change. Because of the similarities between producer surplus arising from resource supply and consumer surplus arising from final consumption demand, the problems discussed in Sections 5.2 through 5.4 generalize to include the case where resource supply decisions are coupled with consumption decisions. Consider, for example, Figure 7.3, where wages rise from w_0 to w_1 while exogenous income rises from m_0^* to m_1^*. Of course, both changes entail a change in income; the former generally causes a change in endogenous income while the latter is a change in exogenous income. Again, this distinction is important since the labor supply curve is generally determined by the level of exogenous income; for example, a change in exogenous income causes a shift in the supply curve—say, from S_0 to S_1—whereas a change in wage rate causes movement along the labor supply curve and thus a change in endogenous income. As in Section 5.2, however, the surplus effect is ambiguous. Consider, for example, the two possible paths of adjustment, L_1 and L_2, depicted in Figure 7.3(a). Along path L_1, wages rise, leading to a gain of area $a + b$ along the initial supply curve S_0 with the subsequent adjustment in exogenous income $m_1^* - m_0^*$. Along path L_2, income is first adjusted by the same amount, but the subsequent producer surplus change along the supply curve is a gain of only area a. The two paths, therefore, suggest the same welfare impact only if area b is zero, in which case (for arbitrary price changes) the two supply curves must coincide. Such a condition is characterized by a zero exogenous income effect; that is, a change in exogenous income does not induce a change in the associated quantity of resource supplied when all other prices are held constant. Analogous to the Section 5.3 fixed-income case, a zero exogenous income effect also implies zero exogenous income elasticity for the associated commodity. In simple terms the exogenous income elasticity is the percentage change in consumption or resource quantity supplied associated with a small percentage change in exogenous income.

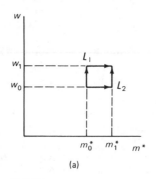

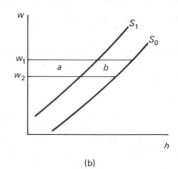

(a)   (b)

FIGURE 7.3

Since these same arguments can also be developed in the consumption case, just as in the resource supply case (simply substitute the term "exogenous income" for "income" in the Section 5.2 and 5.3 arguments), results may be summarized as follows.[5] For arbitrary changes of prices and exogenous income, the change in surplus is unique if and only if exogenous income effects are zero; or, equivalently, exogenous income elasticities are zero for all commodities (supplied or demanded) for which prices change.

In the case where more than one commodity price changes without a simultaneous change in exogenous income, the associated conditions for uniqueness of the surplus change are somewhat different. Consider Figure 7.4, where the wage rate changes from w_0 to w_1 and the price of a consumption commodity changes from p_0 to p_1. Initially, consumption demand is D_0 and labor supply is S_0. Following the wage–price change, demand for the consumer good is D_1 and labor supply is S_1. The change in surplus may be evaluated along any one of an infinite number of paths between initial and final wages and prices. Two possible paths, L_1 and L_2, are shown in Figure 7.4(a). Along path L_1, one obtains first a gain in consumer surplus of area $x + y$ and then labor supply shifts due to the consumer price change obtaining a loss in producer surplus or economic rent of area a. Along path L_2, one obtains first a loss in producer surplus of area $a + b$ and, after consumption demand has shifted to D_1, a gain in consumer surplus of area x. The two surplus measures are the same if and only if area b is equal to area y. Following the approach of Section 5.3 and using Δ to represent changes, these areas are equal with small wage–price changes if and only if

$$\frac{\Delta q}{\Delta w} = \frac{\Delta h}{\Delta p}$$

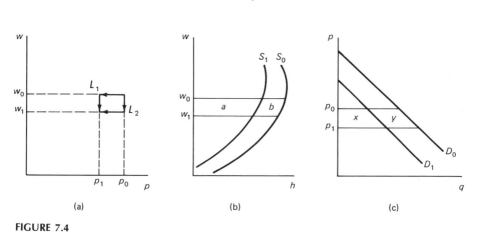

(a)　　　　　　　　(b)　　　　　　　　(c)

FIGURE 7.4

---

[5]For a rigorous derivation, see Section B.7.

By comparison with Section 5.3, this is the same condition required for uniqueness between consumption goods with a multiple consumer price change. Thus, the same results also apply which require homothetic preferences or unitary income elasticities for uniqueness of the surplus change. The case above, however, demonstrates that *these conditions extend over resources sold by the consumer as well as over the commodities consumed.* Furthermore, the condition of unitary income elasticities is somewhat altered since only the exogenous part of income serves as the determinant of consumption demand and resource supply analogous to the income in Chapter 5. The resource prices serve as the determinants associated with endogenous income. Hence, the appropriate conclusions in the present context (verified rigorously in Appendix B) are as follows. *The surplus change associated with a multiple change of both final consumption prices and resource supply prices for a single competitive consumer (holding exogenous income fixed) is unique if and only if preferences are homothetic or, equivalently, exogenous income elasticities are identical with respect to all commodities for which prices change.*

Having generalized the conclusions of Section 5.3 to the case where income is not fixed but, rather, is influenced by the consumer's decisions to sell resources, it suffices to say that the prospects of uniqueness in surplus measurement of welfare change are no brighter than the fixed-income case implies. Indeed, the same restrictiveness is implied for preferences relating to consumption, while further restrictions of a similar nature are implied with respect to resource supply.

7.4 WILLINGNESS TO PAY REVISITED

Because of problems associated with interpretation and nonuniqueness of surplus measures, a further application of willingness-to-pay analysis is useful for the resource supply case. For this purpose, the definitions of compensating and equivalent variation specific to cases of price and income changes given in Chapter 6 may be used. The term "prices," however, is interpreted more broadly to include prices of resources sold by the consumer (e.g., labor) as well as prices of commodities consumed.

To develop the willingness-to-pay approach with respect to resource supply, the concept of a compensated supply curve is needed. *Compensated supply* is defined by the relationship between the quantity of a resource supplied and its price for a given level of utility (holding other prices fixed). That is, by contrast with ordinary supply, it is conditioned on the level of utility rather than on the level of exogenous income. Consider the indifference map in Figure 7.5(a) between leisure (l) and income (m), where the leisure axis runs leftward. Thus, the corresponding work (h) axis runs rightward, although with a different origin. The individual can allocate total time (τ) to either leisure or work, thus implying a "budget" line between the point τ on the leisure axis and the point

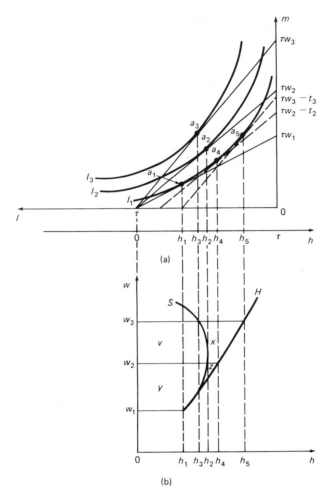

FIGURE 7.5

$\tau \cdot w$ on the income axis where w is again the wage rate.[6] Thus, three different budget lines are obtained for wage rates w_1, w_2, and w_3 with respective optimal consumer decision points a_1, a_2, and a_3. Transferring these results to Figure 7.5(b) demonstrates the relationship of the ordinary labor supply curve S with leisure–income preferences. The ordinary supply curve, of course, is the relationship between the quantity of resource supplied by the consumer and its price for a given level of exogenous income (holding other prices fixed). Hence, the example in Figure 7.5 clearly demonstrates that the ordinary labor supply curve may be backward bending at higher wages.

---

[6] If income is also earned from other sources, that income can be included in a nonzero origin on the income axis. The amounts $\tau \cdot w$ would then be additional income.

To develop a corresponding compensated supply curve, suppose that the wage rate is initially w_1 and falls successively to w_2 and w_3. The compensating variation of the change from w_1 to w_2 is the amount of income that must be taken away from the consumer to restore the original utility level I_1. Since wage w_2 leads to the higher utility level I_2, the original utility level can be obtained by imposing a lump-sum tax on the consumer without changing the wage rate. In this case the budget line contracts to one with maximum income $\tau w_2 - t_2$ and tangency with indifference curve I_1 at a_4. Hence, the compensating variation of the wage change from w_1 to w_2 is precisely t_2. Furthermore, since the utility level at a_4 with wage w_2 is the same as the utility level at a_1 with wage w_1, a pair of points on a single compensated supply curve H is obtained. A third point is obtained by changing the wage rate from w_1 to w_3 and then imposing a lump-sum tax t_3 to bring the consumer back to indifference curve I_1 with a tangency at a_5 and labor quantity h_5. By analogy, a (Hicksian) compensated labor supply curve may be constructed for any level of utility corresponding to any point on the ordinary supply curve.

One can also show in a manner analogous to results in Section 6.1 (by using inner and outer cost differences, breaking the price change into a series of small changes, and taking away the compensating or equivalent variation with each successive small change) that the income differences t_2 and t_3 are related to the change in area above the *compensated* supply curve and below price. In other words, the compensating variation of a wage change from w_1 to w_2 is given either by t_2 in Figure 7.5(a) or by area $y + z$ in Figure 7.5(b). Similarly, the compensating variation of a wage rate increase from w_1 to w_3 is measured either by the distance t_3 in Figure 7.5(a) or, equivalently, by area $v + x + y + z$ in Figure 7.5(b). In each case the distance or area also measures the negative of the equivalent variation of the corresponding wage-rate reduction. Thus, the area behind a compensated resource supply curve plays an analogous role to the area behind a compensated consumption demand curve for the individual consumer.

From Figure 7.5, when indifference curves are positively sloped in the space of income and resource quantity, the corresponding compensated supply curve is positively sloped throughout even though the ordinary supply curve may have negatively sloped portions. Under the same conditions, geometric considerations also imply that the compensated supply curve intersects the ordinary supply curve from the left unless the two curves coincide. Indeed, however, analogous to the Section 5.3 consumption case, zero exogenous income effects or, equivalently, zero exogenous income elasticities imply coincidence of the ordinary and compensated supply curves. That is, when the indifference curves in Figure 7.5(a) are vertically parallel, points a_2 and a_4 correspond to the same level of labor ($h_2 = h_4$), while a_3 and a_5 correspond to another single level of labor ($h_3 = h_5$). Given the foregoing results associated with positively sloped indifference curves, it is a simple matter to show that $C \geq \Delta S \geq E$ for increases or decreases in resource prices, where C is compensating variation, E the equivalent variation, and ΔS the change in producer surplus (all three are negative in the case of price decreases).

7.5   SURPLUS CHANGE AS AN APPROXIMATION OF WILLINGNESS TO PAY

Given the similarities of the results described above and those obtained in Chapter 6 for the fixed-income case, an obvious approach at this point is to attempt approximation of the empirically difficult willingness-to-pay measures using the simple surplus concept. Since common sense suggests doubt that exogenous income effects (or elasticities) are zero in most cases, the desirable equality $C = \Delta S = E$ probably does not hold in general. Nevertheless, the approximate relationships in Sections 6.5 and 6.6 can be readily extended.

To develop these results, consider Figure 7.6, where the wage rate is initially w_0 and rises to w_1 causing the labor quantity to increase from h_0 to h_1, following the ordinary labor supply curve $S(m_0^*)$, along which the level of exogenous income (m_0^*) and all other prices are held fixed. The compensated labor supply curves corresponding to initial and final wage rates are represented, respectively, by $H(U_0)$ and $H(U_1)$. Thus, ΔS = area $a + b$, C = area $a + b + c$, and E = area a.

Following the approach of Section 6.5, note that areas b and c associated with the accuracy of ΔS, as a measurement of C or E, are related to the exogenous income elasticity. That is, consider small wage changes where area $b + c$ is approximately a parallelogram with $\Delta h \doteq \Delta h^*$. Using the exogenous income elasticity definition

$$\eta^* = \frac{\Delta h}{\Delta m^*} \frac{m^*}{h}$$

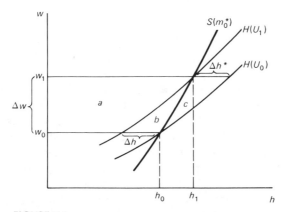

FIGURE 7.6

the horizontal base of the parallelogram is obtained as an income effect of changing exogenous income,

$$\Delta h = \eta^* \cdot h \cdot \frac{\Delta m^*}{m^*} \tag{7.1}$$

Based on the intuitive arguments of Section 7.1, the approximate size of the change in income that induces this change is

$$\Delta m^* \doteq \Delta S \tag{7.2}$$

Thus, substituting equation (7.2) into (7.1) and calculating areas b and c obtains

$$\text{area } b \doteq \text{area } c \doteq \tfrac{1}{2} \Delta h \cdot |\Delta w| \doteq \tfrac{1}{2} \eta^* \cdot \Delta S \cdot h \cdot \frac{|\Delta w|}{m^*}$$

Finally, note that $h \cdot |\Delta w|$ in the equation above is approximately equal to ΔS for small Δw (it is a simple cost-difference approximation of ΔS). Hence, $C = $ area $a + b + c$ is approximated by adding the foregoing approximation of area c to area $a + b \ (= \Delta S)$,

$$\hat{C} = \Delta S - \hat{\epsilon} |\Delta S| \tag{7.3}$$

and $E = $ area a is approximated by subtracting the foregoing approximation of area b from area $a + b$,

$$\hat{E} = \Delta S + \hat{\epsilon} |\Delta S| \tag{7.4}$$

where

$$\hat{\epsilon} = \frac{\eta^* |s^*|}{2}, \ s^* = \frac{\Delta S}{m^*}$$

From these results, the conclusions of Section 6.6 generalize immediately to the case of resource supply, as well as consumer demand, where income has both exogenous and endogenous components (the generalization relating to consumer demand follows the derivation of Section 6.6, where the income term m is interpreted as only that component of income which is exogenous). That is, as suggested by equations (7.3) and (7.4), the term $\hat{\epsilon} \times 100$ is approximately the percentage error of the surplus change as a measure of compensating or equivalent variation. Hence if $|\hat{\epsilon}| = |\eta^* s^* / 2| < 0.05$, the surplus change is in error by no more than about 5 percent. Furthermore, if accurate estimates of η^* and m^* are available, much more precise estimation of C and E is possible on the basis of surplus changes following equations (7.3) and (7.4). Rigorous results in Appendix B, which verify all of the intuitive derivations discussed above, imply that one can avoid more than about 2 percent error by using the estimates in equations (7.3) and (7.4) if $|\eta^*s^*/2| \leq 0.08$ and η^* changes by less than 50 percent over the course of the price change.

One must continue to bear in mind in the present context of evaluating changes in resource prices, however, that the income elasticity η^* and relative surplus change, $s^* = \Delta S/m^*$, are computed with respect to exogenous rather than total income—even for consumption goods. To facilitate understanding of the implications of using exogenous income rather than total income in the cases of consumer demand for—say, q—note that

$$\hat{\epsilon} = \frac{\eta^*|s^*|}{2} = \frac{1}{2}\frac{\Delta q}{\Delta m^*}\frac{m^*}{q}\frac{|\Delta S|}{m^*} = \frac{1}{2}\frac{\Delta q}{\Delta m^*}\frac{|\Delta S|}{q} \tag{7.5}$$

If in this case the change in quantity demanded associated with a small change in exogenous income (i.e., $\Delta q/\Delta m^*$) is the same as the change in quantity demanded associated with a small but equal change in total income (i.e., $\Delta q/\Delta m$) then substitution in equation (7.5) yields

$$\hat{\epsilon} = \frac{1}{2}\frac{\Delta q}{\Delta m}\frac{|\Delta S|}{q} = \frac{1}{2}\frac{\Delta q}{\Delta m}\frac{m}{q}\frac{|\Delta S|}{m} = \frac{\eta|s|}{2} \tag{7.6}$$

Comparing equations (7.5) and (7.6) reveals that the percentage error and associated correction factor for consumer surplus, as a measure of compensating or equivalent variation, are exactly the same as in the results of Chapter 6 for the case of consumer price changes as long as consumers do not distinguish between incomes from different sources in their marginal propensities to consume. Thus, the results of Chapter 6 relating to total income continue to hold for determining error bounds and correction factors on measurements of *consumer surplus changes*. However, an important difference also exists with respect to evaluating *income changes*. That is, the welfare effects of changes in endogenous income directly due to consumer price changes are automatically reflected in the associated consumer surplus changes (because of the consumer's ability to adjust endogenous variables to equate marginal utilities), whereas changes in exogenous income or changes in endogenous income due to changes in resource prices are not.

To see this more clearly, consider Figure 7.7(a), where q is the quantity of a consumption good and h is the quantity of labor. Initially, the wage rate is w_0, and the price of the consumption good is p_0. Also, suppose these are the only two commodities considered by the consumer and that the exogenous income is zero. With a decline in the price of the consumption good to p_1, the budget line rotates about the origin from a slope of p_0/w_0 to a slope of p_1/w_0. Utility maximization with indifference curves U_0 and U_1 thus implies an increase in consumption from q_0 to q_1 and a decrease in labor from h_0 to h_1. Transferring these results to Figure 7.7(b) thus yields the ordinary demand curve D; or

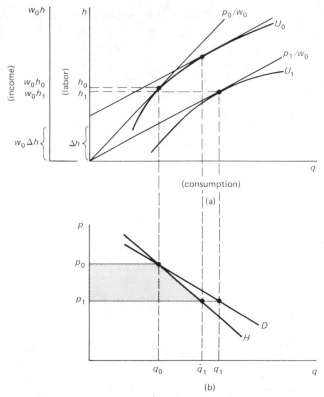

FIGURE 7.7

taking away Δh, or $w_0 \, \Delta h$ in terms of income (note that the wage rate is constant), to remain on the same indifference curve implies a smaller adjustment to $\bar{q}_1$ and thus determines the Hicksian compensated demand curve H.

Again, recall the approach of using inner or outer cost differences, breaking the price change into small intervals, and taking away the compensating variation with each successive small price change to remain on the same compensated demand curve to show that the shaded area behind H measures the overall compensating variation Δh (or $w_0 \, \Delta h$ in money terms) of the price change. Note, however, that income has also changed as a result of the price change from $w_0 h_0$ to $w_0 h_1$ because of the endogenous possibilities of adjustment. Clearly, this change in income should not be subtracted from the welfare gain represented by the shaded area in arriving at a final measure of the effect. This, then, is in contrast to the case of Chapter 6, where any change in exogenous income must be considered as an additional welfare effect over and above the compensating or equivalent variations induced by accompanying price changes.

7.6 THE GENERAL CASE OF RESOURCE SUPPLY/CONSUMER DEMAND PRICE CHANGE

Having discovered the simple extension of the Chapter 6 results to resource supply price changes and the revision in approach that is necessary when resource quantities are influenced by consumption prices, it is a simple matter to extend the results to consider multiple price changes, as in Section 6.6, or to consider multiple price changes connected with income changes, as in Section 6.7. For exemplary purposes, this section considers only the case of a multiple price change analogous to Figure 7.4, involving one resource price and one consumption good price. Other cases may be developed as exercises, or the reader may refer to Appendix B, which treats the general case of many resources and many consumption goods.

Suppose that, initially, the wage rate is w_0 and the price of a consumption good is p_0 with a respective change to w_1 and p_1, as in Figure 7.8. To calculate, say, the compensating variation measure of welfare change, consider first adjusting wages from w_0 to w_1 and then prices from p_0 to p_1. The choice of path is again arbitrary in evaluating willingness to pay, as in the pure consumer case. Initially, exogenous income is m_0^* (and endogenous income is $w_0 h_0$) and utility is U_0. Ordinary supplies and demands (S and D) are represented by conditioning on exogenous income, while compensated supplies and demands (HS and HD) are represented by conditioning on utilities.

To generate the compensating variation along the path holding price at p_0 and changing wages from w_0 to w_1, the results of the preceding section can be used directly. Thus,

$$\text{area } b \doteq \tfrac{1}{2} \Delta h \cdot |\Delta w| \doteq \tfrac{1}{2} \eta_h^* \cdot \Delta S_h \cdot h \cdot \frac{|\Delta w|}{m_0^*}$$

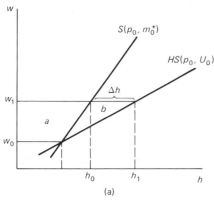

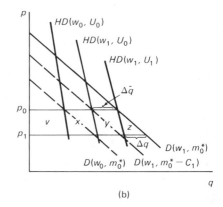

(a)

(b)

FIGURE 7.8

where $\Delta w = w_1 - w_0$, $\Delta S_h =$ area a, and $\eta_h{}^*$ is the exogenous income elasticity of labor supply. Thus, following equation (7.3), the compensating variation associated with the first part of the path is approximated by

$$\hat{C}_1 = \Delta S_h + \frac{\eta_h{}^*}{2m_0{}^*} (\Delta S_h)^2$$

Now consider the additional compensating variation C_2 generated by the fall in price from p_0 to p_1, holding the wage rate at w_1. Again, recalling the fundamental implication of the nibble paradox, this calculation must be made holding utility fixed not at the level afforded by the new wage rate and old price but at the level corresponding to the initial wage rate and initial price. Thus, the compensating variation along the second part of the path is the change in area behind the compensated demand curve, $HD(w_1, U_0)$, in Figure 7.8(b) (that is, area $v + x$). This contrasts with the associated change of area $v + x + y + z$ in simple consumer surplus. To determine the extent of error and approximate the correct area, the approach of Section 6.6 may be applied almost directly. That is, area z can be approximated by

$$\text{area } z \doteq \tfrac{1}{2} \Delta q \cdot |\Delta p| \doteq \tfrac{1}{2} \eta_q{}^* \cdot \Delta S_q \cdot q \cdot \frac{|\Delta p|}{m_0{}^*} \doteq \frac{\eta_q{}^*}{2m_0{}^*} (\Delta S_q)^2$$

and area y can be approximated by

$$\text{area } y \doteq |\Delta p| \cdot \Delta \tilde{q} \doteq |\Delta p_2| \cdot \eta_q{}^* \cdot q \cdot \frac{C_1}{m_0{}^*} \doteq \frac{\eta_q{}^*}{m_0{}^*} \Delta S_q \cdot \Delta S_h$$

where $\Delta \tilde{q}$ is as indicated in Figure 7.8(b), $\eta_q{}^*$ is the exogenous income elasticity of consumption demand, and $\Delta S_q =$ area $v + x + y + z$ is the consumer surplus change along the second segment of the wage–price adjustment path. Thus, approximating area $v + x$ by subtracting the approximated areas y and z from the surplus change (area $v + x + y + z$) yields

$$\hat{C}_2 = \Delta S_q - \frac{\eta_q{}^*}{2m_0{}^*} (\Delta S_q)^2 - \frac{\eta_q{}^*}{m_0} \Delta S_q \cdot \Delta S_h$$

Adding $\hat{C}_1$ and $\hat{C}_2$ then yields an estimate of the overall compensating variation,

$$\hat{C} = \hat{C}_1 + \hat{C}_2 = \Delta S_h + \Delta S_q + \frac{\eta_h{}^*}{2m_0{}^*} (\Delta S_h)^2 - \frac{\eta_q{}^*}{m_0{}^*} \Delta S_q \cdot \Delta S_h - \frac{\eta_q{}^*}{2m_0{}^*} (\Delta S_q)^2$$

Hence, if the elasticities are additive inverses of one another ($\eta_q{}^* = -\eta_h{}^* = \hat{\eta}^*$) or are estimated by $\hat{\eta}_h{}^* = -\hat{\eta}^*$, $\hat{\eta}_q{}^* = \hat{\eta}^*$, $\hat{\eta}^* = (\eta_q{}^* - \eta_h{}^*)/2$, the overall compensating variation is estimated by

$$\hat{C} = \sum_{i=h,q} \Delta S_i - \hat{\epsilon} \left| \sum_{i=h,q} \Delta S_i \right|$$

following the same derivation as in equation (6.14), where

$$\hat{\epsilon} = \frac{\hat{\eta}^*|s^*|}{2}, \qquad s^* = \sum_{i=h,q} \frac{\Delta S_i}{m_0^*}$$

Or, perhaps more usefully, if one defines

$$\eta_1^* = \min\ (-\eta_h^*, \eta_q^*)$$
$$\eta_2^* = \max\ (-\eta_h^*, \eta_q^*)$$

where the minimization and maximization are over the arbitrary price path used in calculating s, as well as over commodities, then approximate bounds on compensating variation are given by

$$\bar{C}_1 = \sum_{i=h,q} \Delta S_i - \epsilon_1 \left| \sum_{i=h,q} \Delta S_i \right|$$

and

$$\bar{C}_2 = \sum_{i=h,q} \Delta S_i - \epsilon_2 \left| \sum_{i=h,q} \Delta S_i \right|$$

where

$$\epsilon_i = \frac{\eta_i^*|s^*|}{2}, \qquad i = 1, 2$$

Thus, the ϵ_i ($\times$ 100) reflect approximate percentage bounds on the error of the surplus change ($\Sigma_i \Delta S_i$) as a measure of compensating or equivalent variation. The maximum exogenous income elasticity (over the course of a particular price change) times the magnitude of surplus change relative to initial exogenous income ($\times$ 100) is about twice the maximum percentage error (in absolute terms) that can possibly be incurred.

As shown in Appendix B, the foregoing results generalize to include the case of many consumption goods and many resources; also, similar results hold in the case of equivalent variation.[7] To summarize the results, suppose that the consumer faces prices $p_1^0, \ldots, p_n^0$ for consumer goods $q_1, \ldots, q_n$ and resource prices $w_1^0, \ldots, w_k^0$ for resources $x_1, \ldots, x_k$. Suppose that prices change to p_1^1, $\ldots, p_n^1$ and $w_1^1, \ldots, w_k^1$, respectively, and that the surplus change is determined by calculating first the change ΔS_1 associated with q_1 holding other prices at $p_2^0, \ldots, p_n^0, w_1^0, \ldots, w_k^0$; then calculating ΔS_2 holding other prices

---

[7]Note, however, that in Appendix B sales of resources are represented by negative quantities so that minus signs are not attached to the exogenous income elasticities of resource sales as they are here.

at $p_1{}^1, p_3{}^0, \ldots, p_n{}^0, w_1{}^0, \ldots, w_k{}^0; \ldots$; then calculating ΔS_n holding other prices at $p_1{}^1, \ldots, p_{n-1}^1, w_1{}^0, \ldots, w_k{}^0$; then calculating ΔS_{n+1} holding other prices at $p_1{}^1, \ldots, p_n{}^1, w_2{}^0, \ldots, w_k{}^0; \ldots$; and finally calculating ΔS_{n+k} holding other prices at $p_1{}^1, \ldots, p_n{}^1, w_1{}^1, \ldots, w_{k-1}^1$. Suppose that ρ^i is the exogenous income elasticity of demand for q_i and ν^i is the exogenous income elasticity of the supply of x_i. Then approximate bounds on the compensating variation are given by

$$\bar{C}_1 = \sum_{i=1}^{n+k} \Delta S_i - \epsilon_1 \left| \sum_{i=1}^{n+k} \Delta S_i \right| \tag{7.7}$$

and

$$\bar{C}_2 = \sum_{i=1}^{n+k} \Delta S_i - \epsilon_2 \left| \sum_{i=1}^{n+k} \Delta S_i \right| \tag{7.8}$$

where

$$\epsilon_i = \frac{\eta_i{}^* |s^*|}{2}, \qquad i = 1, 2; \qquad s^* = \sum_{i=1}^{n+k} \frac{\Delta S_i}{m_0{}^*}$$

$$\eta_1{}^* = \min \left(\rho^1, \ldots, \rho^n, -\nu^1, \ldots, -\nu^k \right)$$

and

$$\eta_2{}^* = \max \left(\rho^1, \ldots, \rho^n, -\nu^1, \ldots, -\nu^k \right)$$

Approximate bounds on the equivalent variation are given by

$$\bar{E}_1 = \sum_{i=1}^{n+k} \Delta S_i + \epsilon_2 \left| \sum_{i=1}^{n+k} \Delta S_i \right| \tag{7.9}$$

and

$$\bar{E}_2 = \sum_{i=1}^{n+k} \Delta S_i + \epsilon_1 \left| \sum_{i=1}^{n+k} \Delta S_i \right| \tag{7.10}$$

Thus, the maximum error in either case of using the simple surplus change, $\sum_{i=1}^{n+k} \Delta S_i$, as a measure of willingness to pay, is no more than about 5 percent as long as $|\eta_i{}^* s^*/2| < 0.05$, $i = 1, 2$. Recalling the discussion of Section 7.5, which examined the implications of using exogenous rather than total income elasticities, these conditions are just as likely fulfilled when only consumer prices change as in the pure consumer case of Chapter 6. Turning to the resource side, this condition also seems reasonable except where large changes in the wage rate or possibly the interest rate are involved. That is, most resources such as land rental would seem to have very small (short-run) exogenous income elasticities since the amount offered for rental is largely, if not totally, determined by ownership in the short run. With labor or savings, the response to changes in exogenous income would probably be more dramatic, but again it seems that elasticities would probably be less than unity in absolute terms. Thus, if the change in surplus is less than 10 percent of initial exogenous income, then no more than about 5 percent error is incurred in using the surplus change as a measure of willingness to pay. Thus, while this condition may be unlikely in some cases, there are a large number of applied economic welfare problems that fall within its bounds.

If the conditions above are not met or more accurate estimates are desired, the bounds in equations (7.7) through (7.10) can be used to create more specific estimates,

$$\hat{C} = \frac{(\bar{C}_1 + \bar{C}_2)}{2}$$

$$\hat{E} = \frac{(\bar{E}_1 + \bar{E}_2)}{2}$$

of the compensating and equivalent variations, respectively. According to the results discussed in Appendix B, these estimates will be in error by no more than about 2 percent if $|\hat{\eta}^* s^*/2| \leq 0.08$ and η_1 and η_1 differ by no more than 50 percent, where $\hat{\eta}^* = (\eta_1^* + \eta_2^*)/2$. Finally, even tighter bounds and better estimates of C and E can be established by applying the algorithm discussed in Appendix B if the foregoing bounds or conditions are not acceptable.

7.7   EVALUATION OF MULTIPLE PRICE CHANGES WITH CHANGES IN EXOGENOUS INCOME

Thus far in this chapter, exogenous income has been considered truly fixed. Nevertheless, since exogenous income includes such factors as profits or dividends, which may change even in the short run, an extension of the results follows immediately in a fashion analogous to that described in Section 6.7. If both prices and exogenous income change, the compensating variation can be measured by following the methods of the preceding section holding exogenous income at the initial level, and then adding the change in exogenous income to the resulting compensating variation of the price change. If the change in exogenous income is considered first, the compensating variation of the price change must be determined holding utility at the level prior to the income change; thus, further modifications of the approach in the preceding section would be required. Similarly, the equivalent variation of a multiple price–income change can be measured by considering the change in income first and then following the methods of the preceding section to determine the additional equivalent variation associated with price movements, holding income at its terminal level. Thus, both the price and income changes can be associated with the terminal level of utility.

7.8 AN EXAMPLE

An example can serve to demonstrate the methodology of Sections 7.6 and 7.7. Consider a consumer with demand for manufactured goods represented by[8]

$$q = 11 - 5p + 2w + \tfrac{3}{50} m^* \qquad (7.11)$$

and supply of labor,

$$h = -20 + 5w + 3p - \tfrac{2}{50} m^* \qquad (7.12)$$

where

q = quantity of manufactured goods purchased
p = price of manufactured goods
h = quantity of labor supplied
w = wage rate
m^* = exogenous income

Suppose that the consumer initially faces prices and wages $p_0 = 3$ and $w_0 = 5$ with exogenous income $m_0^* = 100$. Now suppose the government establishes tight controls on production (safety and pollution standards) which cause the industry to contract and, as a result, lower wages to $w_1 = 4$. Also, because of reduced wages, the demand for manufactured goods falls thus lowering price to $p_1 = 2$. In addition, suppose that the consumer's exogenous income falls to $m_1^* = 97$ because of reduced dividends on stockholdings in the manufactured goods industry.

In the context of Section 7.6, consider first the wage change, then the price change, and, finally, the income change. At initial price and income, the consumer's labor supply curve is

$$h = -15 + 5w$$

Thus, the surplus change associated with the wage reduction from $w_0 = 5$ to $w_1 = 4$ shown in Figure 7.9(a) generates a surplus loss, $\Delta S_h = -\tfrac{15}{2}$. Also, for purposes of applying the Willig results, note that the exogenous income elasticity of labor supply is

---

[8]The possibility of estimating relationships of the type in equations (7.11) and (7.12) from observed behavior will be discussed in Section 8.8. However, for a discussion of several empirical studies which estimate relationships of this type, see John T. Addison and W. Stanley Siebert, *The Market For Labor: An Analytical Treatment* (Santa Monica, Calif.: Goodyear Publishing Company, Inc., 1979).

$$\eta_h = \frac{\Delta h}{\Delta m^*} \frac{m^*}{h} = -\tfrac{2}{50} \frac{100}{h} = -\frac{4}{h}$$

where $\Delta h / \Delta m^* = -2/50$ is the slope or change in labor associated with a small unit change in exogenous income. Thus, the smallest exogenous income elasticity associated with the wage change is $\nu_1{}^h = -4/10 = -0.4$ and the largest is $\nu_2{}^h = -\tfrac{4}{5} = -0.8$.

Next, consider the price change holding the wage rate at its new level, $w_1 = 4$, and exogenous income at its initial level, $m_0{}^* = 100$. Thus, the demand curve is

$$q = 25 - 5p$$

and the associated surplus indicated geometrically in Figure 7.9(b) is $\Delta S_q = \tfrac{25}{2}$. Again, for purposes of applying the Willig results, the exogenous income elasticity of demand is

$$\eta_q = \frac{\Delta q}{\Delta m^*} \frac{m^*}{q} = \tfrac{3}{50} \frac{100}{q} = \frac{6}{q}$$

where $\Delta q / \Delta m^*$ is the change in q induced by a 1-unit change in exogenous income. The elasticity bounds associated with the price change are thus $\rho_1{}^q = \tfrac{6}{15} = 0.4$ and $\rho_2{}^q = \tfrac{6}{10} = 0.6$.

Using the simple surplus approach gives a welfare change of $\Delta S_h + \Delta S_q = -\tfrac{15}{2} + \tfrac{25}{2} = 5$, to which must be added (subsequently) the change in income, $m_1{}^* - m_0{}^* = 97 - 100 = -3$, for a net welfare change of $\Delta S_h + \Delta S_q + m_1{}^* - m_0{}^* = 2$. Suppose, however, that the compensating variation is of interest to a policymaker who plans to pay compensation only if the policy is adopted. Then equations (7.7) and (7.8) can be used to develop a more precise estimate based on the estimated surplus change. The Willig approach of equations (7.7) and

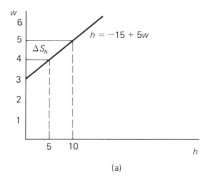

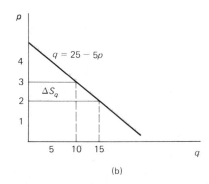

(a)

(b)

FIGURE 7.9

(7.8) would be applied only in improving the estimates $\Delta S_h + \Delta S_q$ associated with the wage–price change since the income change is an accurate measure of its money impact on willingness to pay. One finds that

$$\eta_1^* = \min\ (\rho^q,\ -v^h) = 0.4$$

$$\eta_2^* = \max\ (\rho^q,\ -v^h) = 0.8$$

$$s^* = \frac{\Delta S_q + \Delta S_h}{m_0^*} = \tfrac{5}{100} = 0.05$$

$$\epsilon_1^* = \frac{\eta_1^*|s^*|}{2} = \frac{0.4 \cdot 0.05}{2} = 0.01$$

$$\epsilon_2^* = \frac{\eta_2^*|s^*|}{2} = \frac{0.8 \cdot 0.05}{2} = 0.02$$

$$\bar{C}_1 = 5 - 0.01\ |5| = 4.95$$

$$\bar{C}_2 = 5 - 0.02\ |5| = 4.90$$

Thus, adding the change in income ($m_1^* - m_0^* = -3$) obtains bounds on the overall compensating variation of the wage–price–income change of 1.95 and 1.90. Thus, whereas the surplus change is possibly in error by 0.1, the estimate obtained by using the average of the latter bounds (1.925) is in error by no more than 0.025. Thus, the possible percentage error is reduced from 5 percent to 1.25 percent. It may also be noted that these percentage errors of the combined wage–price–income change are greater than for the associated wage–price change because the income change is in an opposite direction and thus leads to comparison of the same absolute errors with a smaller surplus change.

7.9 IMPOSED QUANTITY CHANGES

Thus far in Chapters 4 through 7, attention has focused on evaluating welfare impacts of price changes. Proposed policies, however, often constrain amounts of production or consumption. For example, if the U.S. Food and Drug Administration decides that some substance under its control is harmful, it may ban the substance. Hence, consumption of zero quantity is imposed. In the producer case, evaluation of such constraints poses no special problem since, in effect, compensated and ordinary supply and demand curves coincide. In the consumer and resource owner case, however, imposing quantity changes requires special consideration because the error in consumer or producer surplus as a measure of willingness to pay may be much different.

For example, consider Figure 7.10, where initially the price is p_0 and the free-market quantity is q_0. Now suppose that a smaller quantity q_1 is imposed. From the standpoint of actual consumption, this would be equivalent to raising price to p_1, so that consumption would fall to q_1 along the ordinary demand curve D. Suppose that this price rise in fact accompanies the reduced quantity restriction. The compensated demand curves associated with the final and initial states are thus H_1 and H_2, respectively. The change in consumer surplus is a reduction of area $b + c + d$. The equivalent variation is $-$area $b + c$, so the associated error in consumer surplus change is $-$area d. Assuming that the price p_1 where D crosses q_1 can be determined, the approximation of this error can follow the earlier Willig calculations. On the other hand, the compensating variation of changing price from p_0 to p_1, $-$area $b + c + d + e$, does not measure the willingness to pay for the quantity restriction in the event of change. The consumer is not free to adjust q following the price change, and so is worse off than otherwise. *The necessary compensation for an imposed quantity change is given by the change in area under the compensated demand curve less the change in what is actually paid* (i.e., $-$area $a + b + c + d + e$ in this case); the consumer loses gross benefits of area $a + c + d + e + f$ but reduces expenditure by area $f - b$ for a net loss of area $a + b + c + d + e$. Thus, the error in consumer surplus change as a measure of compensating variation is not simply area e, as in the price change case, but area $a + e$. This implies that special considerations are required for compensating variation when a quantity is imposed; a similar result holds for resource supply as well as consumption demand. Similarly, special considerations are required in both resource supply and consumption demand for the equivalent welfare measure when a quantity imposition is removed; if both initial and terminal quantities are restricted, both variations require special consideration.

These considerations may be particularly bothersome because the area a in

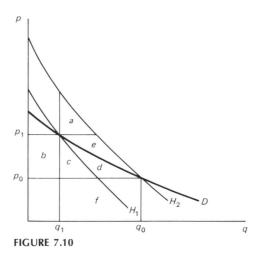

FIGURE 7.10

Figure 7.10 can be infinite in some cases. For example, consider Figure 7.11, where the price of q is initially p_0 with exogenous income m_0^*. The ordinary demand for q induced by a utility function with indifference curves U_0 and U_1 is D. Now, imposition of quantity q_1 leads to the same actual consumption of q as raising the price from p_0 to p_1. The compensated demand curve associated with the subsequent situation is thus H_1 and the equivalent variation E_v is given

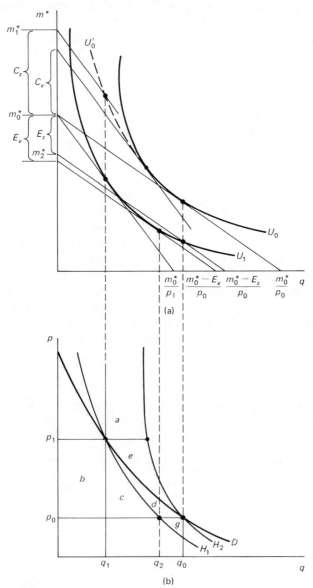

FIGURE 7.11

by $-$area $b + c$. What compensation is required to keep the consumer at his initial utility level U_0 if quantity q_1 is imposed? If the indifference curve U_0 does not cross a vertical line at q_1 in Figure 7.11(a), no amount of compensation can retain the initial utility level. This implies that the compensated demand curve H_2 associated with the initial consumption point does not cross a vertical line at q_1 in Figure 7.11(b), so that area a is infinite. While this result is quite disturbing, one may also argue that there are relatively few goods in the economy for which consumers could not be induced to reduce consumption for sufficiently large sums of money. Nevertheless, this possibility must be borne in mind in evaluating welfare effects of quantity restrictions.

To see what compensation is required if the same utility level is attainable at the new restricted quantity q_1, consider indifference curve U_0' in Figure 7.11(a). This utility level is attainable at quantity q_1 with the new price if income is m_1^*; thus, the necessary compensation is $m_1^* - m_0^*$. The corresponding welfare measure, *the amount of income that must be taken away from a consumer (possibly negative) after a change to restore him to his original welfare level where quantity cannot be adjusted (from the postchange case) is called the compensating surplus* (C_s in Figure 7.11). It differs from the compensating variation, C_v, because the compensating variation allows adjustment of consumption following compensation. The difference in C_v and C_s is given by area a. *If the subsequent quantity is restricted so that adjustment is not possible following compensation, compensating surplus should be used in place of compensating variation for welfare analysis.*

In the equivalent variation case, if the initial quantity is a restricted quantity, necessary compensation in the event of forgoing a change may also be different. Suppose, for example, in Figure 7.11 that q_0 is a restricted quantity so that, if the consumer is compensated not to make the change to q_1, he is not free to adjust consumption to q_2. He is thus worse off, so less income need be taken away. He can only attain his subsequent utility level U_1 when the change is not made if his income is m_2^* rather than $m_0^* - E_v$. The necessary welfare measure in this case, *the equivalent surplus* (E_s), *is defined by the amount of income that must be given to a consumer (again possibly negative) in lieu of a change to leave him as well off as he would be with the change given that quantity cannot be adjusted from the initial situation.* The equivalent surplus of the change depicted in Figure 7.11(b) is $-$area $b + c - g$. That is, since the consumer is forced to move down along his compensated demand curve H_1 but yet pay price p_0, the additional loss not captured by the equivalent variation, E_v, is given by area g. *If the initial quantity is restricted so that adjustment is not possible in the event of compensation, equivalent surplus should be used in place of equivalent variation in welfare analysis.*

The terms "compensating" and "equivalent" surplus were introduced by John R. Hicks[9] as simply additional alternatives for welfare measurement.

---

[9]J. R. Hicks, "The Four Consumer's Surpluses," *Review of Economic Studies*, Vol. 11 (Winter 1943), pp. 31–41.

They have not found common use in evaluating price changes because consumer/resource suppliers are generally free to adjust in a market economy. However, these measures are, in fact, much more appropriate in a few instances, such as when government restricts quantities. Another case where these considerations can be important is when goods are "lumpy" (thus far, commodities have been assumed perfectly divisible so that consumption of any fractional unit of a commodity is possible). For example, a given family may, under reasonable circumstances, consume only one or two automobiles, not 1.5 automobiles. Since consumption quantities are essentially limited in this case, the surplus rather than the variation measurements may be more appropriate.

Having determined appropriate welfare measures for the case where quantities are restricted, a natural question is how accurate are consumer/producer surplus changes as measures of compensating and equivalent surplus? Consider initial restricted quantity q_0 and subsequent restricted quantity q_1 with prevailing price p_0 in each case, as shown in Figure 7.12. Let D^* represent a marginal valuation curve for consumption (a similar concept can be developed for resource supply). The curve D^* would coincide with the free-market ordinary demand curve if the price corresponded to quantity along D^*. Otherwise, D^* differs from the true ordinary demand curve by an income effect associated with paying a different amount for the good than otherwise specified by the demand curve. This distinction is important since with market quotas as developed in Chapter 8, competition among individuals rations a given quota so that all individuals react along their ordinary demand curve. In some free or low-cost public good problems as presented in Chapter 12, however, no market mechanism operates, so that marginal valuations follow a different schedule than would be specified by the ordinary demand pertaining to a free market.

In this context, the error of $\Delta S = -$ area $c + d + f + g$ as a measure of

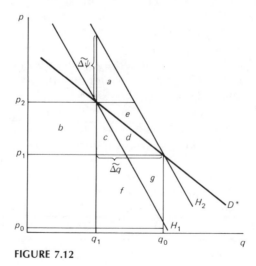

FIGURE 7.12

compensating surplus is $-$area $a + e$ and the error as a measure of equivalent surplus is $-$area $d + g$. For small changes, area $d + e$ and area $a + d + e + g$ are approximately parallelograms, so area $a + e \doteq$ area $d + g$. In fact, as drawn in Figure 7.12,

$$\text{area } a + e = \text{area } d + g = \tfrac{1}{2}\widetilde{\Delta\psi}|\widetilde{\Delta q}| \tag{7.13}$$

where $\widetilde{\Delta q} = q_1 - q_0$. To approximate this area, define income flexibility ϕ^* as

$$\phi^* = \frac{\widetilde{\Delta\psi}}{\Delta m^*}\,\frac{m^*}{\bar{\psi}} \tag{7.14}$$

where $\bar{\psi}$ is the vertical distance between price p_0 and the marginal valuation curve D^* and $\widetilde{\Delta\psi}$ is the change in the distance associated with a change in exogenous income that causes movement from the initial welfare level to the terminal level. Solving equation (7.14) for $\widetilde{\Delta\psi}$, substituting equation (7.2)—which is again applicable in the same sense as earlier where $\Delta S = -$area $c + d + f + g$—and using equation (7.13) yields

$$\text{area } a + e = \text{area } d + g \doteq \tfrac{1}{2}\,\phi^* \cdot \bar{\psi} \cdot \Delta S \cdot \frac{|\widetilde{\Delta q}|}{m^*} \tag{7.15}$$

Next, note that $\bar{\psi} \cdot |\widetilde{\Delta q}| \doteq \Delta S$, where $\Delta S = -$area $c + d + f + g$. Hence, (7.15) becomes

$$\text{area } a + e = \text{area } d + g \doteq \bar{\epsilon}|\Delta S|$$

where $\bar{\epsilon} = \phi^*|s^*|/2$, $s^* = \Delta S/m^*$. Or, finally,

$$C_s = \Delta S - \text{area } a + e \doteq \Delta S - \bar{\epsilon}|\Delta S| \tag{7.16}$$

$$E_s = \Delta S + \text{area } d + g \doteq \Delta S + \bar{\epsilon}|\Delta S| \tag{7.17}$$

In other words, $\bar{\epsilon} \times 100$ approximates the percentage error of consumer surplus change as a measure of compensating and equivalent surplus.

The approximate results obtained here are also borne out by the rigorous development in Sections B.6 through B.10. Furthermore, although the results in Figure 7.12 pertain to consumption, analogous results are obtained for the resource supply case, and the formulas in equations (7.16) and (7.17) summarize the relevant results. Thus, if $|\phi^*s^*/2| \leq 0.05$, the errors in either the consumer demand or resource supply case will be no greater than about 5 percent. As explained by Randall and Stoll,[10] who are responsible for extending

---

[10]Alan Randall and John R. Stoll, ''Consumer's Surplus in Commodity Space,'' *American Economic Review*, Vol. 70, No. 3 (June 1980), pp. 449–57.

Willig's results to this case, this condition is likely to be reasonable when small quantity changes or small budget items are involved, but large budget items with strong income effects (for example, housing) may not satisfy the condition. Nevertheless, applicability of the approximation can be investigated on the basis of estimated income and price elasticities of demand or supply upon noting that

$$\phi^* = \xi \cdot \eta^*$$

where ξ is the price elasticity of the associated demand or supply [defined in simple terms as $\xi = (\Delta q / \Delta p) \cdot (p/q)$] and η^* is the income elasticity of the demand or supply. Hence, estimates of any consumer demand or resource supply, which must generally include price elasticity and income elasticity at least implicitly, provide sufficient information to determine the accuracy of consumer/producer surplus as a measure of willingness to pay or accept when quantities are constrained. Furthermore, if the approximation is not sufficiently accurate, equations (7.16) and (7.17) can be used to develop more accurate specific estimates of the compensating and equivalent surpluses.[11]

7.10   THE MEANING OF AREAS BETWEEN RESOURCE SUPPLY CURVES OR CONSUMER DEMAND CURVES: CONSUMER WELFARE MEASUREMENT OF MULTIPLE PRICE CHANGES IN A SINGLE MARKET

Sections 7.6 through 7.8 present the sequential approach to calculating consumer welfare effects of multiple price and/or income changes. As will be discussed in Section 8.9, this approach is desirable when enough information is available to determine how all demand and resource supply curves shift as multiple price changes are imposed sequentially. Often, however, computational infeasibility prevents explicit consideration of supply and demand shifts in more than one or a few markets in any given economic welfare study. If this is true, yet prices change in many markets, measurement of welfare effects of other price changes in the market(s) of focus is desirable and necessary. Recall that such an approach was indeed possible in the producer case of Chapter 4. In point of fact, as shown in Section 4.4, the welfare effects of a multiple price change on a producer could be calculated by observing the change in a single

---

[11]Again, these results are developed in rigorous detail in Appendix B, and results show that the same order of approximation is attained as in the case where quantity adjustments are possible. Also, the table in Appendix B can again be used to determine accurate error bounds and, hence, examine error bounds on the modified estimates in equations (7.16) and (7.17).

producer surplus triangle in an output market or the change in a single consumer surplus triangle in an input market (assuming necessity of the output or input). This simplification is also possible for consumer/resource suppliers in some cases, at least as an approximation.

To see this, the producer's short-run problem can generally be stated as

$$\text{maximize } \pi = \sum_{i=1}^{m} p_i q_i - \sum_{j=1}^{n} w_j x_j$$

subject to

$$f(q_1, \ldots, q_m, x_1, \ldots, x_n) = 0$$

where π is quasi-rent, p_i the price of output i, q_i the quantity of output i produced, w_j the price of variable input j, x_j the quantity of variable input j purchased, and f represents the implicit production function.[12] One form of the consumer/resource supplier's problem, on the other hand, can be written as

$$\text{minimize } m^* = \sum_{j=1}^{n} w_j x_j \quad \sum_{i=1}^{m} p_i q_i$$

subject to

$$U(q_1, \ldots, q_m, x_1, \ldots, x_n) = U_0$$

that is, minimize exogenous income required to meet a given utility level U_0, where m^* is exogenous income, w_j is the price of consumption good j, x_j is the quantity consumed of good j, p_i is the price of resource i, q_i is the quantity of resource i supplied by the consumer, and U represents the consumer's utility function. Upon defining

$$f(q_1, \ldots, q_m, x_1, \ldots, x_n) = U(q_1, \ldots, q_m, x_1, \ldots, x_n) - U_0$$

for the consumer case, it is clear that the two problems are mathematically equivalent.[13] Hence, any mathematical result pertaining to one problem also pertains to the other.

Mathematical equivalence of these two problems thus implies that areas

---

[12]For the reader unfamiliar with implicit production functions, an ordinary single output production function that gives $q = f^*(x_1, \ldots, x_n)$ can be converted to implicit form by simply writing $f(q, x_1, \ldots, x_n) \equiv f^*(x_1, \ldots, x_n) - q = 0$.

[13]Actually, one must also consider assumptions regarding slopes, curvature, and smoothness of f in each case, but the standard neoclassical assumptions are also the same and imply that f is strictly increasing (in the relevant range), quasi-concave, and (in most work) twice differentiable in $(-q_1, \ldots, -q_m, x_1, \ldots, x_n)$.

behind firm supply and demand curves are related to the firm's quasi-rent exactly as areas behind a consumer's compensated supply and demand curves are related to (the negative of) expenditures necessary to attain a given utility level. That is, since the utility level is held constant in the consumer problem above, the solution of the problem gives quantities supplied or demanded at a given utility level (i.e., compensated supplies and demands). Thus, the change in area behind the compensated supply or demand of any essential commodity is reflective of the change in welfare associated with any other price change.

Consider Figure 7.13, where initial labor supply and food consumption demand for a particular consumer are S_0 and D_0, respectively. As a result of price changes from w_0 to w_1 and p_0 to p_1, however, the supply and demand shift to S_1 and D_1, respectively. The issue is whether areas d and x are of importance in measuring changes in economic welfare. For example, if, say, wages fall from w_0 to w_1 while food price remains at p_0, does area x reflect the welfare effect (i.e., is area x = area a)? The foregoing results answer this question in the affirmative if the demand curves in Figure 7.13(b) are compensated curves associated with the same utility level and the good is an essential good in the sense that it will always be consumed in positive amounts as long as any other goods are consumed in positive amounts or labor or other resources are sold in positive amounts. Similarly, area d is an exact measure of the welfare effect of a price change from p_0 to p_1 with wages fixed at w_1 if S_0 and S_1 are compensated supplies associated with the same utility level and labor is essential for the consumption process; area d is the compensating (equivalent) variation if supplies are based on initial (final) utility.[14]

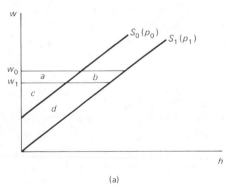

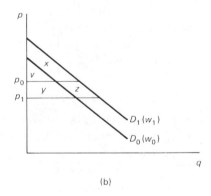

(a)   (b)

FIGURE 7.13

---

[14]Of course, labor is not essential to consumption if exogenous income is sufficiently high or economic assistance for the poor is available to a sufficient degree. Nevertheless, if the range of considerations for all other prices and exogenous income are such that quantities in the market of interest are never zero, the commodities are sufficiently essential so that the results of this section may hold approximately.

Under these necessity assumptions, the overall welfare effect of changing both wages and prices can be measured in a single (essential) market. In Figure 7.13(a), the producer surplus is area $a + c$ at wage w_0 and price p_0 and area $c + d$ at wage w_1 and price p_1 for a net change of area $d - a$. In Figure 7.13(b), the consumer surplus is area v at wage w_0 and price p_0 and area $v + x + y + z$ at wage w_1 and price p_1 for a net change of area $x + y + z$. If labor is essential to the consumer's well-being, then area $d - a$ is an exact measure of compensating or equivalent variation, depending on whether supply of labor is conditioned on the initial or subsequent utility level; and/or if food is essential, area $x + y + z$ is an exact measure of compensating or equivalent variation, depending on whether food demand is conditioned on the initial or subsequent utility level.

If the change in surpluses associated with shifts in compensated curves can have useful meaning in the consumer/resource supplier case, what about the surplus associated with ordinary curves? Mishan[15] has argued that the change in surplus associated with shifts in ordinary consumer demand curves has no welfare significance. Strictly speaking, he is correct for the general case. However, given the Willig results and the possibility of equivalence of ordinary and compensated curves, an accurate or approximate welfare measure may result. For example, *with a zero-income effect (zero income elasticity), the ordinary and compensated curves coincide so that the change in surplus associated with shifting consumer demand or resource supply curves for necessary goods is an exact measure of both compensating and equivalent variation associated with other price changes generating those shifts.* If not, each ordinary surplus may be viewed as an approximation of the surplus associated with a compensated curve. However, the approximation may not be as accurate as in direct price-change cases because the ordinary curve must be used as an approximation of the compensated curve over a much wider range of prices (quantities). Nevertheless, the accuracy of the approximation can be investigated using the results discussed in Section 7.9. For example, in Figure 7.13(b), the accuracy of area v can be determined by comparing with a case where zero quantity is imposed in the initial price-wage situation. Then the accuracy of area $v + x + y + z$ can be determined by comparing with a case where zero quantity restrictions are removed in the subsequent price–wage situation. This approach will generally overstate error bounds since both cases are likely to be in error in the same direction and hence partially cancel one another. But a complete treatment of this case is beyond the scope of this chapter.

7.11 SUMMARY AND CONCLUSIONS

This chapter has extended the results and concepts of Chapters 5 and 6 to the case where the consumer also makes decisions regarding quantities of re-

---

[15]E. J. Mishan, *Cost–Benefit Analysis: An Introduction* (New York: Praeger Publishers, Inc., 1971).

sources to sell. This leads to an important distinction between exogenous income that is essentially uncontrolled by short-run consumer decisions and endogenous income that is determined on the basis of the consumer's individual decisions. In this context results indicate that areas above supply curves of resources play roles analogous to areas below demand curves for consumption.

Nonuniqueness of money measures of utility change presents problems in the resource supply case just as in the pure consumer demand case. The willingness-to-pay approach associated with compensating and equivalent variation, however, again has reasonable properties when multiple prices— including resource prices—change. Furthermore, the results introduced in Chapter 6 readily extend to the case of resource supply, so that simple producer surplus measurements associated with resource supply provide approximate measures of welfare effects.

Finally, the concepts of compensating and equivalent surplus have been introduced to deal with the case where quantity changes are imposed. Again, results indicate that simple consumer and producer surplus changes provide reasonable approximations in much the same sense as do the earlier Willig results. These results are applied further in determining the welfare connotations of areas between shifting supply (demand) curves which are caused by changing prices in other markets. The welfare measurement possibilities associated with the latter result are significant because in many cases lack of sufficient data forces a welfare analyst to evaluate the welfare effects of many price changes within a single market. This result will also be of particular use in dealing with instability and welfare analysis in the context of random shifts in supply and demand (see Chapter 11).

Having now derived the possibilities for welfare measurement for the producer, the consumer, and the resource supplier, Chapter 8 turns to market analysis, where the responses of many such decision makers and the associated welfare effects are aggregated and then investigated on the basis of market information.

8

Aggregation and Economic Welfare Analysis of Market Oriented Policies

Chapters 4 through 7 have focused on welfare measurement for individual decision makers: consumers, producers, and resource owners. In many practical cases, however, public policies affect a large number of people, and a determination of the effects on each individual decision unit is impractical both computationally and from the standpoint of data availability. Furthermore, because of the number of people affected by most policies, a specific welfare analysis for each decision maker is too cumbersome and incomprehensible from the point of view of presenting a policymaker with conveniently useful information. Thus, to perform useful welfare analysis of alternative policies, some aggregation is usually necessary.

Chapters 4 through 7 are used as a basis for the aggregation discussed in this chapter. The willingness-to-pay approach is considered first since it is apparently the most practically applicable approach in terms of analysis of individual welfare. Individual supply and demand functions are aggregated and willingness-to-pay interpretations of changes in areas behind supply and demand curves apply to aggregate market groups just as for individuals. The willingness-to-pay approach is attractive since market supply and demand curves can be empirically estimated. The advantages of this approach are emphasized by contrast with empirical use of money measures of utility change in the context of Samuelson's utility possibilities approach. Based on the market approach to applied welfare economics, this chapter also shows how to analyze various simple government policies, such as taxes, quotas, and price controls.

8.1   AGGREGATION OF WILLINGNESS TO PAY: THE PRODUCER CASE

Consider the possibilities for aggregation of willingness-to-pay measures of welfare change. As shown in Chapter 4, willingness to pay (either compensating or equivalent variation) for a price change by a producer is simply the change in area behind the firm's supply curve or derived demand curve, as the case may be. Consider first the aggregation of several such effects over several producers. Suppose in Figure 8.1 that the representative supply curves for firms 1 and 2 are S_1 and S_2, respectively, and that summing these supply curves horizontally over all firms in an industry obtains the supply curve S. Under competition, where all firms perceive no individual influence on price, S represents the market supply curve and specifies how much will be produced by the industry at various prices.

Now suppose that the price increases from p_0 to p_1. According to Chapter 4, the associated welfare effects are a gain of area a for firm 1 and area b for firm 2; that is, areas a and b are the compensating or equivalent variations of the price increase for firms 1 and 2, respectively. However, geometry verifies that area c, the change in area behind the market supply curve, is the sum of the changes in areas behind individual supply curves since all firms face the same prices and the market curve is obtained by horizontal summation. Thus, the change in producer surplus associated with a market supply curve has a willingness-to-pay interpretation for the market group analogous to the individual firm case of Chapter 4. Thus, area c measures the sum of compensating or equivalent variations over all firms included in the market supply.

A similar exact aggregation property holds with respect to derived demand by all firms in an industry. Where derived demands by firms 1 and 2 are

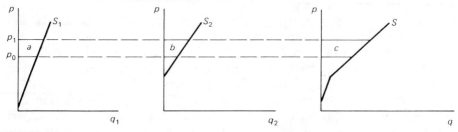

FIGURE 8.1

represented by D_1 and D_2, respectively, in Figure 8.2, the market demand curve D under competition is obtained by summing firm demands horizontally over all firms in the industry. Thus, if price falls from w^0 to w^1, the change in market consumer surplus, area z, is the sum of changes in individual firm consumer surpluses (i.e., the sum of areas x and y), since all firms face the same prices under competition. Since areas x and y are exact measures of compensating and equivalent variation for the individual firms, area z is an exact measure of the sum of compensating or equivalent variations for the industry.

Thus, based on these results, the Kaldor–Hicks and Scitovsky compensation criteria (discussed in Chapter 3) can be applied among a group of producers for, say, a policy-controlled price change. *If the change in market producer (or consumer) surplus associated with a market supply (or derived demand) curve is positive, then both the Kaldor–Hicks and Scitovsky criteria are satisfied among the producing group; otherwise, neither is satisfied.* Furthermore, if a particular policy affects several different producer market groups differently, the market surplus changes for each group can be added together to obtain the sum of compensating or equivalent variations over all affected producers. *If the sum of producer surplus changes over several markets is positive, both criteria are satisfied among all producers considered jointly; otherwise, neither is satisfied.* That is, if the criteria are met, some producers can compensate other producers so that all producers are better off with the change; otherwise, some producers can compensate other producers so that all are better off without the change.

There are important cases, however, when different producer groups should be considered separately. Consider Figure 8.3, where long-run average total cost is ATC. Suppose that the industry is highly heterogeneous with respect to costs of production. As an example, one firm's marginal and average total costs are represented by MC′ and ATC′ and the other firm's costs are represented by MC^0 and ATC^0, respectively. Suppose, in the absence of a price support system, that prices are p_0. Clearly, the small firm would go out of business. However, a price support system that raises price to p_1 in order to keep this firm in business helps the large firm proportionately more (the large firm gains

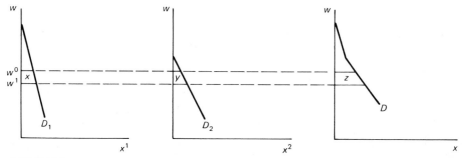

FIGURE 8.2

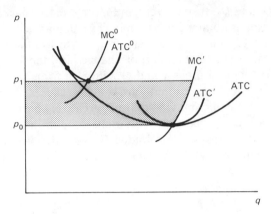

FIGURE 8.3

excess profits equal to the shaded area). An example of such a support system is that in dairying. Because of the large variation in the size of dairy herds (ranging, say, from 50 cows up to several thousand cows) and, hence, differences in efficiency, the dairy price support system helps the large producer relatively more than the small one. Only welfare analysis at a disaggregated level can point out this distributional detail. In some cases, disaggregated analysis can lead to useful information even though, when changing price along a market supply curve, all producers are affected in the same direction. In the foregoing case, disaggregated analysis shows that consumers pay the cost of subsidizing a few relatively large firms who could function very well without price supports.

Another case where disaggregation is crucial is shown in Figure 8.4. Suppose that S_D is the supply curve for a product produced on land that is not irrigated. Now suppose that a new hybrid variety is introduced together with irrigation which brings new land into production. Because of lack of access to water,

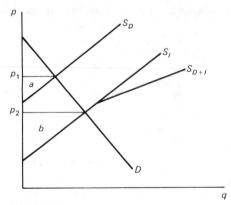

FIGURE 8.4

150

dryland farmers cannot irrigate. Let the supply curve from irrigated land be represented by S_I. The total supply is thus $S_D + S_I$. With demand D, the price thus declines from p_1 to p_2, but this price is not sufficient to cover costs of production on dryland. The producers who gain access to the government financed irrigation project gain a quasi-rent of area b. However, those who do not lose a quasi-rent of area a. Compensation is possible, but if it is not paid, an economic welfare analysis should point out to policymakers that there are both losers and gainers and what the magnitudes of those losses and gains are.

8.2   AGGREGATION OF WILLINGNESS TO PAY: THE CONSUMER/RESOURCE SUPPLIER CASE

Turning to the case of consumers and resource suppliers, the aggregation problem is a bit more complicated because surplus changes are not, in general, accurate measures of compensating or equivalent variation. Clearly, however, the derivation of Figures 8.1 and 8.2 shows that, under competition, the consumer (producer) surplus associated with a market demand (supply) curve is the same as the sum of individual consumer (producer) surpluses over all market participants; this result holds regardless of whether or not the market participants are producers, consumers, or resource suppliers. Hence, one must consider only aggregation of the errors associated with surplus changes as measurements of compensating and equivalent variation (or as measurements of compensating and equivalent surpluses where quantity changes are imposed). But if assumptions for accuracy of surplus change hold for all individuals buying (selling) in a particular market, the same accuracy will hold for the market surplus change since, with competition, all individual surplus changes will be in the same direction.

For example, following Chapter 7, suppose that $|\eta_j^* s_j^*/2| < 0.05$ for all individuals, where η_j^* is the exogenous income elasticity of demand for individual j and $s_j^* = \Delta S_j/m_{0j}^*$, where ΔS_j is consumer surplus change and m_{0j}^* is initial exogenous income, both for individual j. Also, suppose that market price decreases as in Figure 8.2. Then $\Delta S_j > 0$ for all individuals and, based on results from Chapter 7, approximate bounds on compensating (equivalent) variation are given by $0.95 \Delta S_j$ and $1.05 \Delta S_j$; that is, the consumer surplus change is no more than about 5 percent in error. Adding the lower bounds over all individuals thus obtains a lower bound on the sum of compensating (equivalent) variations, $0.95 \Delta S$, where ΔS is the market consumer surplus change and, similarly, adding upper bounds over all individuals obtains an upper bound, $1.05 \Delta S$. Thus, the market change in consumer surplus is no more than 5 percent in error if corresponding conditions are met that limit errors to 5 percent for all individuals.

Thus, for empirical purposes where errors in estimation are comparatively large, the simple changes in market surplus (changes in areas behind supply and demand curves) provide useful economic welfare quantities for cases where $\eta_j{}^*s_j{}^*$ is not large for any individual. Again, as in the producer case, however, one must bear in mind that aggregation of all consumers into a simple market curve for welfare calculations corresponds to application of equal welfare weights. If unequal weights are considered, consumer demand or resource supply must be considered separately for each group that is to receive a different weight. Again, disaggregation into *groups* of similar consumers may be necessary to point out any serious distributional effects.

8.3   AGGREGATION OF MONEY MEASURES OF UTILITY CHANGE

Before proceeding to show how the foregoing results can be used to analyze policy changes, a short digression on money measures of utility change serves to emphasize the practicality of the willingness-to-pay approach. Remember that, as discussed in Chapter 5, early welfare economists sought a unique money measure of utility change. An obvious approach is then to add money measures of utility change across individuals. However, to use only the sum of individual utilities as the criterion for policy decisions implicitly assumes that a Bergsonian social welfare function is known and, in fact, equally weights utility changes for all individuals. As explained in Section 3.3, use of such a welfare function entails a value judgment any time such an objective is not explicitly mandated by the policymaker.

In addition, maximization of the simple sum of money measures of utility change does not generally lead to the same policy choices as maximization of the simple sum of utilities. For example, suppose that one seeks to maximize the sum of utilities for two individuals with proportional utility functions, U_A and U_B, where $U_A = 2U_B$. That is, suppose that the utility of consumer A is twice that of consumer B whenever the two consume identical consumption bundles. In this case, the consumers will possess identical demand curves in identical situations (indifference maps will coincide even though indifference curves represent different utility levels for different individuals), and the corresponding money measures of utility change for any price–income change will be identical even though the utility change for one will be twice that of the other. Hence, a social welfare function that implies maximization of the sum of utilities would weight the money measure of utility change for consumer A twice as much as that for consumer B. Obviously, to maximize the simple sum (or almost any weighted sum) of consumer utilities using money measures of utility change thus requires some rather specific and generally unobtainable information about the relationship of individuals' utility functions (e.g., their marginal utilities of income). Empirical aggregation of money measures of utility change in applied analysis of economic welfare is thus seemingly impossible without value judgments.

Alternatively, consider money measures of utility change in empirical economic welfare analysis along the lines suggested by Samuelson's utility possibility curve approach and his potential welfare criterion (see section 3.2). Suppose that a unique money measure of utility change with respect to a particular price change exists and can be measured for each of two individuals and that no other individuals are affected by the price change. Since the money measures of utility change are ordinally related to the respective individuals' utility levels, the approach of Section 3.2, as demonstrated in Figure 3.5, can be employed simply by making the appropriate monotonic transformation of axes. Thus, rather than using U_A and U_B on the axes, one can use the corresponding money measures ΔS_A and ΔS_B (which are ordinally related to U_A and U_B, respectively, as demonstrated in Figure 5.8). Since both ΔS_A and ΔS_B are functions of the price change, a money-measure utility possibility curve such as Q_1Q_1 in Figure 8.5 can be generated by considering all possible levels of feasible policy controls.

Now suppose that the two consumers trade in more than one commodity and the prices of several such goods possibly change (or alternatively, consider a change in production organization as in Figure 3.5). In this case, a host of money-measure utility possibility curves such as Q_1Q_1, Q_2Q_2, Q_3Q_3, and Q_4Q_4 can be developed by changing one price, holding others fixed at diffcrent levels or by changing several simultaneously in specific ways. One can apply the same rules of choice developed by Samuelson for utility possibilities curves; that is, an envelope curve or grand possibility frontier UU can be determined along which any optimal policy must lie. Similarly, if the money-measure utility possibility curve associated with one policy lies entirely outside the money-measure utility possibility curve associated with another policy, as Q_1Q_1 lies outside Q_2Q_2, then the first policy is clearly preferable to the second. Similar comparisons may be possible using grand utility frontiers for policies that affect several prices.

Thus, using money measures of utility change, a locus of efficient points

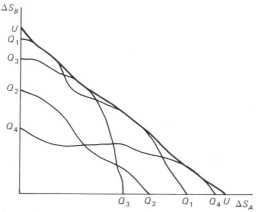

FIGURE 8.5

(*UU* in Figure 8.5) can be developed; furthermore, because of the ordinal relationship of utility and money measures, these efficient points correspond to exactly the same actions that lead to efficient points in the utility possibilities space of Figure 3.5. The problem of choosing a single point on the efficiency locus then requires a social welfare function unless one utility possibilities curve dominates all others. If a social welfare function in terms of money measures of utility is not available, the policymaker must construct one. Without such a value judgment, ideally all a welfare economist can do is present the policymaker with the efficient locus of points *UU* in Figure 8.5. The policymaker must then choose a point on that locus.

In terms of empirical application of the foregoing approach, if many individuals are affected by a policy change, the diagram in Figure 8.5 takes on many dimensions, as does the empirical measurement. The problem thus becomes intractable empirically once the number of individuals gets large. In addition, because this approach introduces many dimensions, it may be impossible to comprehend from a policymaker's standpoint even if the analysis could be carried out empirically. Furthermore, as pointed out in Chapter 5, the conditions that lead to unique money measures of utility change are likely not to be met. For these reasons, the willingness-to-pay approach appears far more useful on empirical grounds.

8.4 AGGREGATION OF WILLINGNESS TO PAY ACROSS PRODUCERS AND CONSUMERS

Turning once again to willingness-to-pay measures, this section demonstrates economic welfare analysis of simple government policies. Consider the market in Figure 8.6, with supply curve S_0, demand curve D, and equilibrium at price p_0 and quantity q_0. Consumer surplus is area a and producer surplus is area

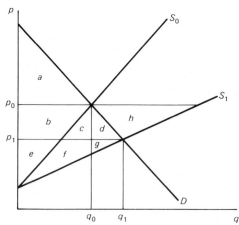

FIGURE 8.6

$b + e$. Now consider a policy which leads to development of a new technology such as hybrid corn. The supply curve shifts to S_1 because of accompanying cost-reducing or output-increasing possibilities. As a result, equilibrium price falls to p_1 as output is increased to q_1. But what are the welfare effects of the new technology? Consumer surplus increases from area a to area $a + b + c + d$ for a gain of area $b + c + d$. If D represents the derived demand of a producing industry that maximizes profits, then area $b + c + d$ represents the combined willingness to pay (either compensating and equivalent variation) of that industry for the reduction in their input price. If D represents an ordinary consumer demand, then area $b + c + d$ approximates the combined willingness to pay of all consumers under the Willig conditions discussed in Chapter 7. If D is a compensated consumer demand, then area $b + c + d$ is an exact measure of the compensating or equivalent variation, depending on the conditional utility level.

If S_0 and S_1 represent industry supply curves, the change in area behind the supply curve represents the combined willingness to pay of the innovative industry for the new technology. Producer surplus is area $b + e$ before innovation and is area $e + f + g$ after innovation, so the gain for the innovating industry (or loss if negative) is area $f + g - b$. Note that *this welfare effect can be quite different from the usual cost-savings calculations, which would be attached by simple engineering studies of a new technology.* For example, if one were simply to consider the cost savings that could be obtained by producers under the new technology by continuing to produce the same output at the same price, the effect would be a gain of area $c + f$ (in cost savings). But with reduced marginal costs, all firms will expand output so the associated net welfare effects are, in fact, greater while the producer's welfare effect may be much less or even negative. If an engineering study further considers the increase in profit-maximizing production but fails to consider product price adjustment, the producer gains would be incorrectly estimated by area $c + d + f + g + h$. But as output is increased, product prices must fall unless demand is perfectly elastic. Hence, the correct welfare effects can be assessed only by determining the shift in both equilibrium price and quantity.

As pointed out in Chapter 9, other possible price adjustments must also be considered if present. For example, expansion of output q may entail an increase in demand for inputs used in producing q and thus the input prices may increase as a result of the technology. Or perhaps the new technology is capital intensive and displaces labor. Then wage rates for a particular type of labor may fall, and wage earners may be left unemployed. Thus, welfare effects may also be experienced by other groups not directly involved in the market in Figure 8.6. Typical engineering cost studies are sometimes deficient in considering these economic consequences and hence this is an area in which proper economic welfare analysis can make a contribution. These latter considerations relating to other markets, however, will be introduced in Chapter 9.

To facilitate simple discussion of direct economic consequences in this chapter, prices in all other markets are assumed unaffected by changes in the market of interest. Such an assumption may be reasonable if the producing industry accounts for only a small component of each of its input markets (and thus has little price impact) and if the demand has very small cross-price elasticities or represents derived demand by an industry that is relatively unimportant in each of the other markets in which it is directly involved.

With this in mind, consider the net welfare consequences of the technological change in Figure 8.6. Adding the consumer and producer surplus gain obtains area $c + d + f + g$, which is simply the change in area above supply and below demand. What welfare connotations can be attached to this area? Subject to applicability of the Willig approximation criteria, this area represents the combined willingness to pay of all producers and consumers in the marketplace. Unlike the case with area behind a market demand curve or behind a market supply curve, however, not all individuals are necessarily affected in the same direction in this case. All producers may lose while all consumers gain. In Figure 8.6, producers gain if area $f + g >$ area b; otherwise, producers lose. Thus, the combined willingness to pay represents a net willingness to pay after losers have just been compensated for losses. As Figure 8.6 shows, technological change generates a positive economic surplus which can be distributed in any manner whatever to attain a Pareto optimum.

Pareto optimality, however, necessarily involves compensation for any losers. If some individuals lose, as producers would if area $b >$ area $f + g$, then a decision to change (introduce the technology) without compensation involves a value judgment. That is, *some system of welfare weights must be used as a criterion to make a change unless all individuals gain or unless compensation is paid when only net gains are possible.* For example, if the producer gain is -10 and the consumer gain is 20, then—without compensation—the change is not justified unless the producer weight is no more than twice the consumer weight. Only when all welfare weights are equal can simple aggregate producer and consumer willingness to pay be used as a criterion for change unless compensation is paid. Thus, an adequate welfare analysis of the effects of a change should generally determine the effects on each of the market groups (e.g., producers and consumers) separately unless compensation is planned. Note also, however, that compensation should not always be paid. Some policies are designed with the specific objective of aiding some group even when an expense is involved for another group because of a specific problem confronting the first group. When a policymaker has such an objective, a constraint that compensation always be paid can severely limit the policymaker's ability to help the former group. Section 8.5 presents several such examples.

8.5 WELFARE ANALYSIS OF SIMPLE MARKET DISTORTIONS

Given the framework developed thus far, the welfare effects of a number of government-imposed market distortions can be considered. Some common distortions imposed by government include price ceilings/floors, support prices, taxes, subsidies, and quotas. This section considers each of these possibilities and shows that such government intervention leads to a Pareto-inferior state where some economic agents lose. The assumptions underlying these conclusions, however, are crucial, as shown in succeeding chapters.

Price Ceilings

Consider first the effects of price ceilings. In Figure 8.7, D represents demand and S represents supply. At market equilibrium, price is p_0 and quantity is q_0. Now, suppose that a price ceiling of p_1 is imposed. At price p_1, producers are willing to supply only q_1 rather than q_0, and hence they lose area $d + e$ in producer surplus. At price p_1, however, consumers would like to buy a larger quantity q_4, but since only q_1 is produced, consumption is thus restricted. Assuming efficiency in rationing (those excluded from the market are not willing to pay more than those who are not), the effect on consumer surplus is equivalent to raising price to p_2 and then giving the consumer a payment of $(p_2 - p_1) \cdot q_1$. Thus, consumer surplus changes by area $d - b$. The net effect on producers plus consumers obtained by adding these two effects is thus a loss of area $b + e$. If S and D are compensated supply and demand curves wherever they represent consumer/resource suppliers, these areas represent exact measures of compensating or equivalent variations for each level of aggregation, depending on conditioned utility levels (otherwise, they are approximations in the Willig sense). Thus, a compensation scheme must exist such that everyone is better off without the price ceiling. For example, producers who lose area $d + e$ could instead pay only area d to consumers, and thus consumers could gain area d without giving up area b. Clearly, the adoption of a price ceiling, if either group is benefited, represents an attempt to help one group at the expense of

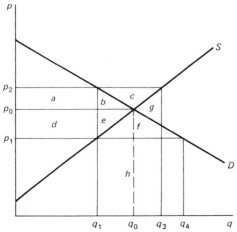

FIGURE 8.7

another and thus requires implicitly an unequal welfare weighting on the part of the policymaker.

The price controls that were enacted in the U.S. economy in the early 1970s were of this nature. The Administration was increasingly concerned about the adverse effect of inflation on consumers, and price controls or ceilings were imposed to give some short-run relief to consumers at the expense of producers. Figure 8.7 shows that such controls do indeed aid consumers (if area $d >$ area b) but only at the expense of producers. Figure 8.7 also shows, however, that—with the price ceiling—a shortage of $q_4 - q_1$ develops so that either each individual is not able to consume as much as desired at the new price or else some consumers are not able to gain access to the lower price at all. In the case of natural gas, where prices were regulated over a longer period of time, the latter effects are more apparent. When gas supplies were not sufficient, new customers were simply not allowed in some cases. This points to a possible need to disaggregate consumer welfare effects into groups that continue to have market access and those who do not (including or possibly considering another group for those who begin to desire market access at the lower price). The welfare effects on each of these groups may be different, and thus a policymaker may wish to assign different weights to each. By this disaggregation, welfare analysis may reveal that the price ceiling actually has a severe adverse effect on at least part of the group it is intended to serve.

Price Floors

The welfare effects of a price floor can be considered similarly. If price p_2 is imposed in Figure 8.7, consumers will only purchase q_1. Once this is realized by producers, they will adjust output accordingly, since no other sales opportunities exist. Thus, consumers lose area $a + b$ while producers gain area $a - e$. The net loss due to the price ceiling is area $b + e$. Thus, without doubt, a compensation scheme exists so that everyone is better off without a price floor than with the price floor, regardless of welfare weights. For example, through a lump-sum transfer of area a from consumers to producers with equilibrium maintained at price p_0 and quantity q_0, producers would be better off by area e and consumers would be better off by area b than under the price floor. Furthermore, no one would thus be denied entrance into the market. Nevertheless, one should bear in mind that some set of welfare weights may exist such that a price floor is preferred to free market equilibrium.

A prime example of a price floor that has existed in the U.S. economy is the minimum wage law. Under the assumptions in this chapter, where S represents compensated labor supply and D represents labor demand by industry, Figure 8.7 implies that the minimum wage reduces the quantity of labor demanded (increases unemployment). Industry is adversely affected while labor, in general, benefits. Some workers, however, are denied access to the market under the minimum wage (those represented by $q_3 - q_1$).[1] An adequate welfare analysis should point out the latter effects specifically, since the losses per individual by the unemployed may be substantial as compared with the gains per individual of those who remain in the market.

Price Supports

Sometimes price floors or controlled prices have been imposed by government in such a way that no one is denied market access. This is accomplished by government entrance in the market to make up the difference in supply and demand. For example, suppose that p_2 in Figure 8.7 represents a price support. Government can enforce price p_2 by purchasing $q_3 - q_1$, which just makes up the difference in supply and demand at that price. The associated welfare effects are a loss of area $a + b$ for consumers and a gain of area $a + b + c$ by producers. Thus, producers and consumers jointly gain area c over the market equilibrium case. Note, however, that this gain is financed by a government expenditure of $p_2 \cdot (q_3 - q_1)$ or area $b + c + e + f + g + h$. This expenditure must be financed by taxpayers and hence leads to a net loss of area $b + e + f + g + h$ when all three groups are considered jointly. This quantity purchased by the government, however, may not be entirely worthless and may be resold on an international market or saved for periods of shortage. If this is the case, the ultimate welfare effects may be different, as shown in Chapter 11.

The most common examples of price supports have been in the agricultural economy (e.g., support prices for milk and grains). Price supports have been established to protect farmers from inadequate incomes due to the unstable nature of farm prices. But, from Figure 8.7, when possibilities for dumping in international markets or carrying government stocks over into periods of shortage do not exist, much better schemes of aiding producers are possible. For example, a lump-sum transfer of area a from consumers to producers and of area $b + c$ from taxpayers to producers entails as much gain for producers, with less loss for consumers and substantially less expense for taxpayers.

Taxes

The case of an *ad valorem* tax is represented in Figure 8.8. An ad valorem tax is a tax paid per unit of quantity, such as a sales tax. If p is the price of a good charged by the producer and t is the ad valorem tax that the consumer must pay on each unit of the good purchased, the effective price to the consumer is $p + t$. Thus, with p on the vertical axis, the effect of the tax is to lower the effective demand curve by a distance of t. Where equiiibrium without

---

[1]Of course, $q_0 - q_1$ may also represent a gap in the amount of work per individual from desired levels by individuals remaining in the market, but because of the institution of a fixed-length workweek, the difference tends to represent displacement of workers.

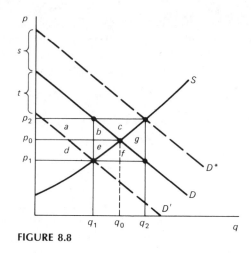

FIGURE 8.8

the tax is at price p_0 and quantity q_0, the tax t lowers effective demand to D', thus reaching a new equilibrium at price p_1 and quantity q_1; the vertical distance between D and D' at that point, given by $p_2 - p_1$, is equal to t, so p_2 represents the effective consumer price. The welfare effects of the tax are thus a loss of area $d + e$ for producers and a loss of area $a + b$ for consumers. Both producers and consumers lose as the tax drives a wedge between supply and demand. The government component, however, gains $(p_2 - p_1) \cdot q_1$, or area $a + d$, in tax revenues. Thus, the tax leads to a net welfare loss, sometimes called a *deadweight loss,* of area $b + e$.

The tax has a distorting effect because it induces producers to adjust to a different marginal price than effectively experienced by consumers. A better possibility in theory and under the simple assumptions of this chapter is to impose lump-sum taxes in the amounts of areas a and d on consumers and producers, respectively, while leaving marginal prices unaffected. In this way, market equilibrium at price p_0 and quantity q_0 can still be maintained so that area $b + e$ need not be lost. In reality, however, lump-sum taxes that truly do not affect marginal conditions are difficult to determine. Perhaps the closest approximations to a lump-sum tax that are imposed in popular practice are property and income taxes. But an income tax, for example, is by no means free of effects on marginal conditions.

Subsidies

The case of a subsidy is very similar to the ad valorem tax. Sometimes, if government wants to encourage production of some commodity or to aid failing producers in an industry, a subsidy of, say, s per unit of output is paid from the public treasury. In Figure 8.8, this effectively increases the demand curve by a vertical distance of s, so that equilibrium shifts from price p_0 and quantity q_0 to price p_1 and quantity q_2. With the subsidy, the effective producer price is thus

p_2. Producers gain area $a + b + c$ while consumers gain area $d + e + f$. Government, however, pays $(p_2 - p_1) \cdot q_2$ in subsidy payments, which represents a loss of area $a + b + c + d + e + f + g$ to taxpayers. The subsidy thus leads to a net welfare loss of area g. Without other considerations (such as national security associated with a well-developed production sector), a better approach in aiding producers is to make a lump-sum transfer of area $a + b + c$ from taxpayers to producers. Consumers can also be made as well off without the subsidy as with it by transferring a lump-sum area $d + e + f$ from taxpayers to consumers. Thus, area g can be saved for taxpayers while producers and consumers are just as well off as with the subsidy. On the other hand, if such factors as national security are important (where security is gained by developing a well functioning production sector), an adequate economic welfare analysis can inform the policymaker of exactly what the costs of that security are and how much cost must be incurred for incremental amounts of security.

Quotas

Finally, consider the case of quotas imposed by government or other institutional arrangements. If a quota of q_1 is imposed in the market in Figure 8.8 such that no quantity greater than q_1 can be marketed by producers, consumers will bid up the price to p_2 in order to ration what is produced. Producers, however, only incur costs based on the short-run supply curve S and hence, in addition to the producer surplus normally realized at price p_1, they gain $(p_2 - p_1) \cdot q_1$. Thus, consumers lose area $a + b$ while producers gain area $a - e$. The quota thus leads to a net or deadweight welfare loss of area $b + e$.

In this welfare analysis, producer sales are assumed limited by the quota. Alternatively, consumer purchases could be limited by the quota. In this case, the producers would respond along their supply curve and bid the price down to p_1 in a competitive effort to capture some of the available market. Thus, producers would lose area $d + e$ while consumers would gain area $d - b$. The net effect, however, would still be a loss of area $b + e$.

These two examples suggest that quotas may be imposed in several ways. The way they are imposed may give more advantage to either producers or consumers so that the area $a + d$ may be allocated in various ways between the two groups. Nevertheless, a deadweight loss of restricting the market of area $b + e$ is clear. Thus, some compensation scheme exists so that both groups are better off without the quota. However, one must also consider the fact that a policymaker may still prefer to restrict a market if the restriction has desirable effects elsewhere in the economy, such as in the case of chemicals that are harmful to the environment. Such considerations are made in Chapter 12.

It should also be noted that the quota case is one in which quantities rather than prices are directly controlled. Hence, the compensating or equivalent surplus considerations of Section 7.9 come into play. When the supply (demand) curve represents ordinary consumer behavior, the true welfare measure for imposing a quota is the compensating surplus rather than the compensating variation (although the equivalent variation may be applied to the question in lieu of change), and the true welfare measure for removing a quota is the equivalent surplus if the question is necessary compensation in lieu of change (although compensating variation may be used if the question is compensation in the event of change). Thus, the conditions for accuracy of the consumer/ producer surplus change in assessing willingness to pay for quotas may follow the discussion of Section 7.9 rather than Sections 7.5 through 7.7, depending on the policy question.

An Example

An example can serve to illustrate the above analyses of simple distortions. Suppose that consumer demand for wheat (and wheat equivalent in wheat products) is represented by

$$q = 18 - 2p + 2m$$

and producer supply of wheat is given by

$$q = 2 + 4p - 2w$$

where

q = quantity of wheat in hundred million bushels per year
p = price of wheat in dollars per bushel
m = consumer disposable income in thousand dollars per capita per year
w = price of fertilizer in hundred dollars per ton

Suppose that the best projections for consumer income and fertilizer price for next year are $m = 3$ and $w = 1$, respectively. In this case, the projected demand is represented by $q = 24 - 2p$ and projected supply is represented by $q = 4p$, as shown in Figure 8.9, with equilibrium at price $p = 4$ and quantity $q = 16$ (obtained by solving the two equations simultaneously).

Now consider the expected welfare effects of imposing a quota on wheat marketings as was done in the United States during the 1950s and early 1960s. If, say, producers are forbidden to market more than 1.2 billion bushels ($q = 12$), then consumer price will be bid up according to the demand curve to $p = 6$ (obtained by solving the demand equation for p with $q = 12$). As in the case of Figure 8.8, the producer gain is area $a - e$, and the consumer loss is area $a + b$. To calculate these effects, note that area a is $(6 - 4) \times 12 = 24$, and area e is a triangle with base 1 and height 4 (or vice versa) so the area is $1 \times 4 \times \frac{1}{2} = 2$. Similarly, area b is a triangle with base 4 and height 2 so the area is $4 \times 2 \times \frac{1}{2} = 4$. Thus, area $a - e = 22$, and area $a + b = 28$. Noting that quantity is measured in hundred million bushels and price is measured in dollars per bushel, the areas

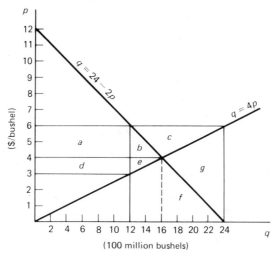

FIGURE 8.9

are measured in hundred million dollars. Thus, the implications of the quota in this example are a gain of $2.2 billion for wheat producers and a loss of $2.8 billion for wheat consumers. The deadweight loss is $600 million.

An alternative policy control that has been used to support wheat producers' incomes is a price support. Suppose that, instead of a quota, a price support of $6.00 per bushel is established. The quantity produced at that price is $q = 4p = 24$, while the quantity demanded is $q = 24 - 2p = 12$ (Figure 8.9). Thus, with a $6.00 per bushel price support, the model implies excess production of 1,200 million bushels that would have to be purchased by government to make the support effective (assuming no production controls). As in the analysis in Figure 8.7, producers gain area $a + b + c$, consumers lose area $a + b$, and government spends area $b + c + e + f + g$ on excess production. In terms of the present example, areas a, b, and e are the same as above, while area c is a triangle of base 12 and height 2; thus, area $c = 12 \times 2 \times \frac{1}{2} = 12$. Area $b + c + e + f + g$ is a rectangle of dimensions 6 and 12 so the area is 72. Thus, again recalling that the areas in Figure 8.9 are measured in hundred million dollars, producers gain $4.0 billion (area $a + b + c = 40$) and consumers lose $2.8 billion (area $a + b = 28$), while government spends $7.2 billion in accumulating 1.2 billion bushels of wheat in reserves.

Of course, the effects of other types of policies or combinations of policies can also be considered in the context of this example, but the above cases serve to demonstrate how quantitative measurements or estimates of supply and demand relationships can be used to produce meaningful quantitative information about the economic welfare consequences. One should also bear in mind in this analysis, however, the possibility that actual willingness to pay may diverge from the ordinary consumer and producer surpluses calculated in this manner as demonstrated in the examples in Sections 6.5, 6.6, and 7.8.

8.6 INTERNATIONAL TRADE

A topic of considerable interest in international trade has been whether or not countries are better off with trade and, if so, what kind of trade relations are best. That free trade is the "first best" policy for two countries considered jointly is demonstrated in Figure 8.10. In Figure 8.10, demand and supply in the importing country are given by D' and S', respectively. Demand and supply in the exporting country are represented by D and S and appear backward in the left side of Figure 8.10. Without international trade, equilibrium price is p_i and p_e in the two respective countries. But since price is higher in one country than the other, there is an incentive for the first to buy from the second. The amount that the exporting country will sell at each price can be determined by horizontally subtracting D from S, thus obtaining the excess supply curve ES. Similarly, the amount that the importing country will import at each price can be determined by horizontally subtracting S' from D', thus obtaining the excess demand curve ED. Equilibrium in international trade is obtained where the importer's excess demand is equal to the exporter's excess supply (i.e., at international price p_t).

The welfare effects of opening trade can be examined by evaluating the effect of a price change to p_t in each country. In the exporting country, producers gain area $a + b$, and consumers lose area b; the net effect in the exporting country is a gain of area a, which is equal to area $h + j$ since ES represents the horizontal difference in S and D. In the importing country, producers lose area $c + d$ while consumers gain area $c + d + e + f + g$. The net effect in the importing country is thus a gain of area $e + f + g$, which is equal to area $c + e$ since ED represents the horizontal difference in S' and D'. Thus, both countries gain from opening trade even though only one country buys

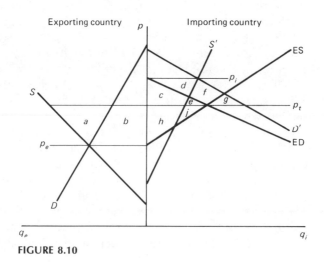

FIGURE 8.10

164

from the other. The overall gain is area $c + e + h + j$, that is, the area behind excess demand and excess supply.

One may note, however, that the distributional effects are quite different in the two countries. In the exporting country, producers gain and consumers lose, whereas in the importing country, producers lose and consumers gain. However, since both countries gain, any necessary compensation need only be made within countries.

The results in this section are one proof of the gains from free international trade over no trade. For example, these results suggest that both the United States and the People's Republic of China gained when trade relations were opened in the 1970s. Furthermore, since the net welfare effects on each country (in the context of compensation) are reflected entirely by the excess supply and excess demand curves in Figure 8.10, all of the analysis in Figures 8.7 and 8.8 can be repeated in an international context to show that both countries considered jointly lose from any deviation from the free-trade solution. Thus, some form of international compensation must exist such that both countries are better off without intervention. Cases exist, however, where one country or the other can gain by imposing certain trade controls. These cases are discussed in Sections 10.1, 10.2, and 10.6.

8.7 LAISSEZ-FAIRE AND GOVERNMENT INTERVENTION

The cases above demonstrate that Adam Smith's "invisible hand," associated with market competition (see Section 2.5), results in an optimal allocation of resources. That is, given the assumptions to this point, there is no way that the government can increase welfare in a Pareto-superior fashion by changing output price or quantity in either direction from the competitive equilibrium. Government intervention, however, does not always lead to net losses and hence Pareto suboptimality—even when compensation is not considered. Some counterexamples arise in the cases of instability (see Chapter 11), externalities and public goods (see Chapters 12 and 13), and government intervention in international trade on behalf of a single country or group of countries (see Chapter 10).

8.8 EMPIRICAL CONSIDERATIONS IN MARKET-LEVEL WELFARE ANALYSIS

Thus far, the analysis has centered on theoretical issues in welfare economics, notwithstanding that issues have been developed to lay foundations for empirical applications. This section begins to consider empirical issues surrounding the econometric applications.[2] For example, in some cases, several alternative

---

[2] For the reader unfamiliar with econometrics, this is the term pertaining to the application of statistics in the estimation of economic relationships.

measurements of the same welfare effect are possible. It stands to reason that more precise estimation may be possible in one case than another on econometric grounds. Thus, when data are sufficient to permit a choice among estimates of alternative welfare measures, it is important to know which estimators entail greater precision.

To estimate the welfare triangles defined by consumer or producer surplus, one must first estimate the associated demand or supply curves.[3] The science of estimating such relationships is called *econometrics* and occupies a large part of the economics literature. This book is not intended, nor could it presume, to provide a thorough discussion of all the related issues. Nevertheless, a somewhat heuristic discussion of some of the basic issues provides a sufficient foundation to discuss the related problems which frequently arise in estimating economic welfare quantities. A more detailed and general derivation of the underlying econometric results can be found in any standard econometrics text, such as those by Intriligator, Theil, and Goldberger.[4] A simple but complete coverage of the properties of linear regression presented in this section is given by Draper and Smith.[5]

The usual approach in econometrics is to assume a particular functional form that is, hopefully, sufficiently general to describe adequately the mechanism generating a particular set of data. For example, a supply curve may be linear and thus suggest the relationship

$$q = \alpha_0 + \alpha_1 p \tag{8.1}$$

where q is quantity supplied and p is price; α_0 and α_1 would thus be unknown parameters that one would seek to estimate on the basis of observed price and quantity data. The price–quantity data may be generated by observing a particular market over several periods of time (e.g., for several years) or by observing several firms, individuals, or groups during a given period of time.[6]

---

[3]As shown in Section 4.3, producer surplus calculation may be accomplished through quasi-rent calculations for individual firms; thus, estimation of supply may not be necessary. For example, if accurate data are available on costs and returns, quasi-rent may be calculated without error on that basis. To evaluate alternative policies, however, one must be able to estimate producers' response under the alternative policies, and this requires information about either the supply curve or the cost curves of producers. Since information on price and quantity is more often available than information on costs, this chapter focuses on estimation of supply. Similar principles apply to use of estimated cost functions in welfare economics since welfare calculations with producer supply curves are equivalent to welfare calculations with producer marginal cost curves under competition and profit maximization.

[4]Michael D. Intriligator, *Econometric Models, Techniques, and Applications* (Englewood Cliffs, N.J.: Prentice-Hall, Inc., 1978; Henri Theil, *Principles of Econometrics* (New York: John Wiley & Sons, Inc., 1971); Arthur S. Goldberger, *Econometric Theory* (New York: John Wiley & Sons, Inc., 1964).

[5]N. R. Draper and H. Smith, *Applied Regression Analysis* (New York: John Wiley & Sons, Inc., 1966), Chap. 1.

[6]In each of these cases, the supply relationship may be affected by different sets of

The former set of data is called a *time series*, whereas the latter is called a *cross section*.

Since, with "real-world" data, not all of the observations thus generated are likely to fall on a straight line (or any other functional form specified prior to estimation), the usual econometric practice is to consider the relationship in equation (8.1) as stochastic (which means random) by adding a random disturbance term, say ϵ,

$$q = \alpha_0 + \alpha_1 p + \epsilon$$

where $E(\epsilon) = 0$; that is, one expects ϵ to be zero on average, and in this context one usually denotes var $(\epsilon) = E(\epsilon^2) = \sigma^2$.[7] The parameters α_0 and α_1 are often then estimated by choosing the $\hat{\alpha}_0$ and $\hat{\alpha}_1$ that minimize the sum of squared deviations of the observed quantities from the estimated linear relationship, $\hat{\alpha}_0 + \hat{\alpha}_1 p$. Geometrically, consider Figure 8.11, where one has four observations (p_i, q_i), $i = 1, \ldots, 4$.[8] The sum of squared deviations is $a^2 + b^2 + c^2 + d^2$.

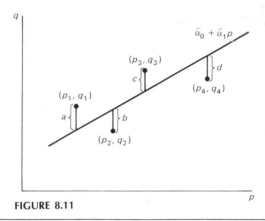

FIGURE 8.11

determinants, in which case variation in determinants should be considered in estimation as discussed below.

[7]Mathematically, the expectation of a function $g(\cdot)$ of a random variable y is the associated point of central tendency and is defined by

$$E[g(y)] \equiv \int_{-\infty}^{\infty} g(y)f(y)dy$$

where $f(y)$ is the probability density function of y (which describes the relative frequency of various values of y). The variance of a random variable measures the dispersion of the associated distribution and is defined by $\text{var}[g(y)] = E\{g(y) - E[g(y)]\}^2$.

[8]Note that, in contrast to diagrams in previous chapters, Figures 8.11 and 8.12 have the price and quantity axes reversed. This is done since quantity appears as the dependent or left-hand-side variable in the regression equation in (8.1); discussion in this context is more consistent with the econometrics literature and the notion that individual producers and consumers make quantity decisions in response to price changes following profit or utility maximization. That is, quantities are usually used as

The estimates $\hat{\alpha}_0$ and $\hat{\alpha}_1$ which minimize this sum are called *least-squares* or *ordinary least-squares* (OLS) estimates.[9]

Using these estimates, one can then estimate the supply curve for various levels of p by

$$\hat{q} = \hat{\alpha}_0 + \hat{\alpha}_1 p$$

and the corresponding estimated change in producer surplus for a particular price change from p_1 to p_2 would be[10]

$$\Delta P = \hat{\alpha}_0(p_2 - p_1) + \frac{\hat{\alpha}_1(p_2^2 - p_1^2)}{2}$$

In statistics a key parameter that measures the accuracy of an estimate or prediction is its variance (defined by the expected value of the square of its deviation from its mean or expected average).

The variance of an estimated supply curve and its implications for the

---

dependent or left-hand-side variables in estimating supply; the same is often true in estimating demand. The case with price as the left-hand-side variable, however, can be treated in a similar manner with analogous results for the purposes of this chapter.

[9]Where one generally has, say, n observations, the sum of squared deviations can be represented algebraically as

$$\text{SS} = \sum_{i=1}^{n} (q_i - \hat{\alpha}_0 - \hat{\alpha}_1 p_i)^2$$

Using calculus, the conditions that $\hat{\alpha}_0$ and $\hat{\alpha}_1$ must satisfy to minimize this sum are

$$\sum_{i=1}^{n} (q_i - \hat{\alpha}_0 - \hat{\alpha}_1 p_i) = 0$$

$$\sum_{i=1}^{n} (q_i - \hat{\alpha}_0 - \hat{\alpha}_1 p_i)p_i = 0$$

which can be solved to find

$$\hat{\alpha}_1 = \frac{\sum_{i=1}^{n} q_i p_i - \bar{q}\sum_{i=1}^{n} p_i}{\sum_{i=1}^{n} p_i^2 - \bar{p}\sum_{i=1}^{n} p_i} = \frac{\sum_{i=1}^{n} (q_i - \bar{q})p_i}{\sum_{i=1}^{n} (p_i - \bar{p})^2}$$

$$\hat{\alpha}_0 = \bar{q} - \hat{\alpha}_1 \bar{p}$$

where

$$\bar{q} = \frac{1}{n}\sum_{i=1}^{n} q_i \quad \text{and} \quad \bar{p} = \frac{1}{n}\sum_{i=1}^{n} p_i$$

[10]Using calculus, this is simply verified since

$$\Delta P = \int_{p_1}^{p_2} (\hat{\alpha}_0 + \hat{\alpha}_1 p)dp = \hat{\alpha}_0(p_2 - p_1) + \hat{\alpha}_1 \frac{(p_2^2 - p_1^2)}{2}$$

variance of estimated producer surplus are depicted in Figure 8.12. Where observed data are represented by the scatter of points around means $\bar{p}$ and $\bar{q}$, the estimated supply curve is $\hat{\alpha}_0 + \hat{\alpha}_1 p$. A general result in econometrics is that the variance of $\hat{\alpha} + \hat{\alpha}_1 p$ increases as p moves away from $\bar{p}$. Hence, the region in which one may have reasonable confidence of containing the supply curve may be represented by the area between B_L and B_U, where B_L and B_U diverge as p is farther from $\bar{p}$. Similarly, this implies that *there is an increasing loss in precision in estimating a surplus change as the corresponding price limits diverge from the mean of observed data* (i.e., as p_1 or p_2 diverges from $\bar{p}$). In Figure 8.12, the estimated surplus change is area $b + c$, but at B_U it is area $a + b + c$, and at B_L it is only area c. Obviously, these areas diverge as the price interval (p_1, p_2) moves away from $\bar{p}$.[11]

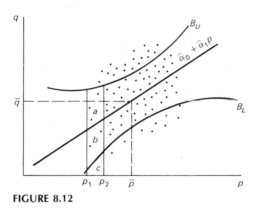

FIGURE 8.12

---

[11]These results can be derived more formally as follows. Using the identity $\mathrm{var}(y) = \sum_{i=1}^{n} k_i^2 \, \mathrm{var}(z_i)$, where $y = \sum_{i=1}^{n} k_i z_i$ and z_i and z_j are uncorrelated for all $i \neq j$, one can determine the variance of the estimated supply by noting from footnote 9 that

$$\hat{\alpha}_1 = \sum_{i=1}^{n} k_i q_i, \qquad \hat{\alpha}_0 = \sum_{i=1}^{n} k_i' q_i$$

where

$$k_i = \frac{(n-1)p_i}{n \sum_{j=1}^{n} (p_j - \bar{p})^2}, \qquad k_i' = \frac{1}{n} - \bar{p} k_i; \qquad i = 1, \ldots, n$$

Hence, in the context of the identity, one finds a predicted quantity of

$$\hat{q} = \hat{\alpha}_0 + \hat{\alpha}_1 p = \sum_{i=1}^{n} k_i^* q_i$$

where

$$k_i^* = k_i' + k_i p_i = \frac{1}{n} + k_i(p_i - \bar{p})$$

(Footnote continued on pg. 170)

One may also note that similar conclusions hold in estimation of demand and consumer surplus. That is, simply considering equation (8.1) as a demand curve with $\alpha_1 < 0$, one would estimate the demand curve in a similar way, with the corresponding variance increasing as prices and quantities move farther from $\bar{p}$ and $\bar{q}$. Consumer surplus change for a given price change from p_1 to p_2 would be estimated by

$$\widehat{\Delta S} = -\hat{\alpha}_0(p_2 - p_1) - \frac{\hat{\alpha}_1(p_2{}^2 - p_1{}^2)}{2}$$

with variance again increasing as prices move away from $\bar{p}$. That is, in estimating demand and consumer surplus, the accuracy in estimation decreases or variance increases as the difference of prices from the mean of observed prices increases (that is, from the mean of prices used in estimating demand) just as in the supply case.[12]

Although the foregoing results illustrate the general statistical properties of estimated supply and demand curves which have important implications for applied welfare economics, several additional complications should also be

---

and, similarly, using footnote 10,

$$\Delta\hat{P} = \sum_{i=1}^{n} k_i{}^{**} q_i$$

where

$$k_i{}^{**} \equiv k_i'(p_2 - p_1) + k_i \frac{(p_2{}^2 - p_1{}^2)}{2}$$

Thus, assuming that the disturbance in the supply relationship (ϵ) is uncorrelated from observation to observation and that p is uncorrelated with ϵ,

$$\text{var}(\hat{q}) = \sum_{i=1}^{n} (k_i{}^*) \, \text{var}(q_i)$$

$$= \sum_{i=1}^{n} \left[\frac{1}{n^2} + \frac{1}{n}k_i(p - \bar{p}) + k_i{}^2(p - \bar{p}) \right]\sigma^2$$

$$= \frac{\sigma^2}{n} + (p - \bar{p})\frac{\sigma^2}{n}\sum_{i=1}^{n} k_i + \sigma^2(p - \bar{p})^2 \sum_{i=1}^{n} k_i{}^2$$

and, similarly,

$$\text{var}(\Delta P) = \frac{\sigma^2}{n}(p_2 - p_1)^2 + \frac{\sigma^2}{n}\left[(p_2 - p_1)\frac{p_2{}^2 - p_1{}^2}{2 - \bar{p}(p_2 - p_1)^2}\right]\sum_{i=1}^{n} k_i$$

$$= \frac{\sigma^2}{n}(\Delta p)^2 + \frac{\sigma^2}{n}\left[\frac{p_1 + p_2}{2} - \bar{p}\right](\Delta p)^2 \sum_{i=1}^{n} k_i + \sigma^2\left[\frac{p_1 + p_2}{2} - \bar{p}\right]^2(\Delta p)^2 \sum_{i=1}^{n} k_i{}^2$$

In each of these cases, it is clear that the precision of estimation falls (variance increases) as the supply curve or welfare change is estimated for prices farther from the mean of observed data. Similar results also hold when p is correlated with ϵ as in a simultaneous equations problem.

[12]These results follow from the mathematical framework in footnotes related to the supply case.

borne in mind. First, other determinants of supply or demand generally vary from time period to time period or from individual to individual or group to group. These determinants lead to corresponding movements in supply and demand which must generally be taken into account in estimation to avoid biased results. This can be done, however, by simply including the appropriate determinants as additional variables in regression. For example, one could specify a supply or demand equation as

$$q = \alpha_0 + \alpha_1 p + \alpha_2 z_1 + \alpha_3 z_2 + \cdots + \alpha_{n+1} z_n \qquad (8.2)$$

where $z_1, \ldots, z_n$ are the determinants of the supply or demand, respectively.[13] In this context the intercept of the supply or demand curve on the quantity axis in the price–quantity diagram in Figure 8.12 is $\alpha_0 + \alpha_2 z_1 + \cdots + \alpha_{n+1} z_n$.

Following previous chapters, $z_1, \ldots, z_n$ would include prices of other consumer goods and income. In the context of Chapter 7, $z_1, \ldots, z_n$ would include the prices of (other) consumer goods, wage rates and prices of other resources supplied by consumers, and exogenous income from other sources. In the context of Chapter 4, $z_1, \ldots, z_n$ would include the prices of other variable inputs and outputs of the firm or industry as well as quantities of fixed inputs (as indicated by Section 4.5).[14] Equations of this type can be estimated by the same general OLS approach discussed above, although the computational formulas for the coefficients (e.g., α_0, α_1, etc.) are different.[15]

---

[13] A further discussion of the choice of determinants in this context is given in Section 9.5.

[14] Actually, depending on length of run, the consumer demand and resource supply equations may also be conditioned on quantities of durable consumer goods that have been purchased in the past and are thus fixed at present. That is, durable consumer goods play a somewhat analogous role to fixed inputs in producer supply. A producer seeks to maximize profit by selecting quantities of variable inputs $x_1, \ldots, x_{n_1}$ subject to given variable input prices, output prices, and quantities $\bar{x}_{n_1+1}, \ldots, \bar{x}_n$ of the fixed inputs determined by previous decisions. Thus, the resulting input demands and output supplies are functions of the variable input prices, output prices, and quantities of fixed inputs. Similarly, if the consumer's decisions depend on quantities of durable goods purchased in previous decisions, then the consumer's utility-maximizing demands for nondurables are functions of *prices of nondurables* and *quantities of durables* as well as income and prices of resources sold by the consumer. For example, if a consumer has purchased an energy-efficient refrigerator, his or her electricity consumption decision will tend to be different from that of a consumer with an energy-inefficient refrigerator, even though facing the same prices with the same preferences. The decision to replace an old durable, on the other hand, would depend on its obsolescence, cost of use relative to other durables, and quality of services produced. Another specification for using both prices and quantities as determinants of demand is given by Phlips in the context of dynamic demand where tastes and preferences depend on previous consumption; see L. Phlips, *Applied Consumption Analysis* (Amsterdam: North-Holland Publishing Company, 1974).

[15] For example, see Draper and Smith, *Applied Regression Analysis;* Goldberger, *Econometric Theory;* or Theil, *Principles of Econometrics.*

A second generality that must be considered in many applications is that supply and demand curves may not follow linearity. A common alternative specification, for example, follows log linearity, which implies that[16]

$$q = A p^{\alpha_1} z_1^{\alpha_2} z_2^{\alpha_3} \cdots z_n^{\alpha_{n+1}}$$

Such an example for the case of both supply and demand is given specifically in Appendix A in equations (A.14) through (A.18). As is apparent from the results there, the surplus change associated with a price change from p_1 to p_2 where determinants are held at fixed levels $\bar{z}_1, \ldots, \bar{z}_n$ is

$$\frac{A}{\alpha_1 + 1} (p_2^{\alpha_1+1} - p_1^{\alpha_1+1}) \bar{z}_1^{\alpha_2} \bar{z}_2^{\alpha_3} \cdots \bar{z}_n^{\alpha_{n+1}}$$

which represents an increase in the supply case or a decrease in the demand case (both possibly negative).

Statistical estimation in this case can be carried out in much the same way as the linear case if data are represented in logarithmic form. That is, ordinary linear least squares can be used to choose $\hat{A}, \hat{\alpha}_1, \hat{\alpha}_2, \ldots, \hat{\alpha}_{n+1}$ to minimize the sum of squares of $\log q - (\log \hat{A} + \hat{\alpha}_1 \log p + \hat{\alpha}_2 \log z_1 + \cdots + \hat{\alpha}_{n+1} \log z_n)$ over all observations. Such an approach does not lead to convenient estimates of variances for the estimator of surplus change as suggested by equation (8.2).

---

[16]The linear and log-linear functions are often used in econometrics because of their convenience. From a technical standpoint, however, one must also be concerned about whether or not specified functional forms for supply and demand make sense in terms of economic theory. For example, it can be shown that there is no utility function which, when maximized subject to a consumer budget constraint, yields demand equations that are linear in all prices and income for all goods. When a system of demand equations actually corresponds to maximizing some underlying utility function subject to a budget constraint, there are a number of conditions that must be satisfied for all possible prices and income: the budget constraint, homogeneity, Slutsky negativity and symmetry, and several aggregation conditions. These conditions and a few functional forms which are satisfactory by these criteria are discussed in Intriligator, *Econometric Models,* Chap. 7. For a more advanced treatment, see Phlips, *Applied Consumption Analysis* (Amsterdam: North-Holland/American Elsevier, 1974); Charles Blackorby, Daniel Primont, and R. Robert Russell, *Duality, Separability, and Functional Structure: Theory and Economic Applications* (New York: Elsevier/North-Holland, Inc., 1978). A similar set of issues is also of concern with respect to a producer supply function which, under competition, is equivalent to the producer's marginal cost curve (for prices above minimum average variable costs). The theory of duality implies that cost functions are, in fact, determined by the underlying production functions. Hence, concern arises about whether or not a supply (or marginal cost) curve specification corresponds to a reasonable underlying production function. A brief discussion of these issues is also given in Intriligator, *Econometric Models,* Chap. 8. At a more advanced level, see M. Fuss and D. McFadden, *Production Economics: A Dual Approach to Theory and Applications,* Vols. 1 and 2 (Amsterdam: North-Holland Publishing Company, 1978); and Blackorby, Primont, and Russell, *Duality.*

But following the derivation in the linear case, one finds that the variance of $\widehat{\log q} \equiv \log \hat{A} + \hat{\alpha}_1 \log p + \hat{\alpha}_2 \log z_1 + \cdots + \hat{\alpha}_{n+1} \log z_n$ increases as $p - \bar{p}$ increases, where $\bar{p}$ represents the mean of observed price data. Thus, the same general property of obtaining poorer estimates of supply and demand and associated surplus changes when using prices outside the range of observed prices is again suggested.

A third generality that must be considered in many cases is simultaneity of supply and demand. The problem of simultaneity must be considered unless production lags are longer than the intervals at which data are observed. That is, if the quantity supplied is determined by previous price—say, at the time of production decisions—and the price for the next period is determined subsequently when the production is actually realized, then supplies and demands are determined recursively rather than simultaneously.

If demands and supplies are determined simultaneously, the expectations for the ordinary estimators of the structural parameters α_0 and α_1 and also any corresponding surplus estimates ΔP or ΔS are biased (that is, after repeating the estimation procedure many times with different sets of data, one would *not* expect to obtain, even on average, the parameter values and welfare quantities sought). This phenomenon is referred to as *simultaneous-equations bias*. Moreover, the magnitude of bias does not necessarily get small as the number of observations gets large, and thus the resulting estimates are said to be statistically *inconsistent*. A number of alternative estimators exist which at least attain the latter criterion of consistency (that is, the magnitude of bias becomes inconsequential and also the likely variation of estimators around the associated parameters gets small as the number of observations gets large). The more popular of these estimation methods are two-stage least squares, three-stage least squares, indirect least squares, limited-information maximum likelihood, and full-information maximum likelihood.[17]

While these estimators and other more sophisticated techniques attain desirable statistical properties, however, the resulting estimators for supply or demand or associated surplus changes have the same general properties suggested by Figure 8.12. That is, the resulting estimators become less precise as the points of evaluation are farther from the observed data used in estimation. The following section investigates the implications of these general properties of surplus estimation for applied welfare economics.

8.9 THE CHOICE OF MARKET
FOR ESTIMATION

In Section 4.4, the results suggest that several alternatives exist for measurement of a producer welfare change associated with some (multiple) price

---

[17]For a thorough coverage of these and other simultaneous equations estimation methods, see Intriligator, *Econometric Models,* Chap. 11; Theil, *Principles of Econometrics,* Chaps. 9 and 10; or Goldberger, *Econometric Theory,* Chap. 7.

change. These possibilities include (1) measuring the change in producer surplus associated with an essential output, (2) measuring the change in consumer surplus associated with an essential input, and (3) measuring the sum of producer and consumer surplus changes obtained by sequentially imposing price changes in the respective markets. The results of the preceding section have important implications regarding which of these approaches should be used, depending on data availability. Consider, for example, evaluation of the effect of changing one particular price (which may be only a part of an overall price change). In Figure 8.13, the price change from w_1^0 to w_1^1 for input x_1 causes the derived demand by an industry for another input to increase from D_2^0 to D_2^1 and industry supply increases from S_0 to S_1. According to the results of Section 4.4, the compensating (or equivalent) variation of this price change is given equivalently by either area a, b, or c if both inputs are essential in the production process.

The results of Section 8.8, on the other hand, suggest that supply and demand estimates are relatively accurate only near observed prices and quantities. Thus, the precision or confidence in estimates of supply and demand prior to the change in Figure 8.13 may be limited, as represented by the broken lines on either side. Similarly, the subsequent supply and demand estimates

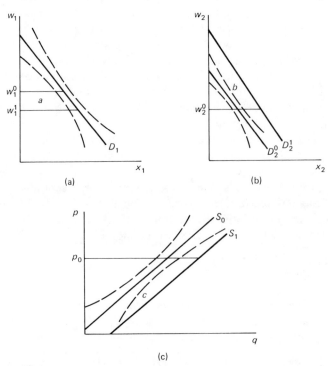

FIGURE 8.13

would also be associated with less precision outside the range of normal prices and quantities. As a result, the precision in estimation of areas b and c is probably very poor compared with the precision in estimation of area a, since area a calculations rely on information about the demand curve only in the range of normal price variation. Exceptions to this rule would occur only if very imprecise estimates of the demand D_1 were obtained or if data used in estimation of D_2 or S tend to cover a broad interval of the quantity axis from zero up to the equilibrium points depicted in Figure 8.13.

These observations imply that, when data permit, the welfare effects associated with a multiple price change can be calculated more accurately by estimating supply and demand in each market for which prices change and then using the *sequential* approach, where the welfare change associated with each price change is evaluated in its respective market as illustrated in Sections 4.4 and 7.10 in Figures 4.8, 4.9, and 7.13. As implied by the aggregation in this chapter, this approach extends to calculation of welfare effects for groups of individuals or firms (for example, industries) as well. Hence, the overall or group welfare effects would be obtained by aggregating the resulting trapezoidal welfare effects between pairs of price lines from individual markets.

On the other hand, alternative policies may involve changing so many prices that estimation of all the associated supplies and demands may be impractical or even impossible because of lack of data for some markets. In these cases, economic welfare analysis is possible only by using the observable data in related markets. For example, if quantity data are not available for x_1 and x_2 in Figure 8.13, the use of area c estimated from data on p, q, w_1, and w_2 (the latter two variables serve as determinants of the ordinary supply curve) may be the only observable or estimable welfare quantity. To evaluate two alternative policies, a welfare quantity of this kind would be estimated for each market group affected by the (possibly multiple) price change induced by the change in policies.[18]

8.10 CONCLUSIONS

This chapter has demonstrated that producer and consumer welfare effects can be examined using market supply and demand relationships in much the same sense as suggested by Chapters 4, 6, and 7. In this context it becomes possible to analyze the welfare effects of a number of policies that affect an individual market. These effects may be analyzed using either ordinary supply and demand curves or compensated supply and demand curves. When compensated curves are used, the changes in producer and consumer surplus are exact reflections of compensating or equivalent variation of imposed or induced

---

[18]It must be noted on the basis of results in Chapters 4, 6, and 7, however, that this type of surplus change has welfare meaning only in the case of commodities that are essential in the associated production or consumption processes.

changes. When ordinary curves are used, the changes in producer and con-sumer surplus must be viewed as approximations (in the Willig sense) of the true compensating or equivalent variation whenever the supply or demand curve pertains to a consumer or resource supplier group.

As indicated in this chapter, two considerations are crucial in the aggregation of welfare effects. One has to do with whether or not compensation is paid when changes lead to adverse impacts on some of the individuals involved. The second has to do with appropriate interpersonal comparisons (welfare weights) for policies that may be desirable but yet not meet the Pareto criterion. The results of this chapter indicate that, depending on a policymaker's welfare weights, policies may be appropriate which involve gains for one group at the expense of another—even when compensation is not paid. Thus, appropriate welfare analysis should investigate the welfare impact on at least each group that is affected differently by a particular policy. On the other hand, policies may exist where compensation is considered that can make further improve-ments over those associated with a particular set of welfare weights without compensation. One example is when a policymaker wishes to aid a failing industry by means of a subsidy or price support but yet can offer the same aid without as much welfare loss for other groups through a different policy, such as a lump-sum transfer that does not affect market behavior in a distorting fashion.

This chapter also explores empirical possibilities for applying the theoretical concepts developed. The associated econometric theory is not developed in rigorous fashion but is drawn upon in a semiformal sense to illuminate pos-sibilities and potential problems in estimation of welfare quantities. Generally, the results suggest that more accurate estimation of the welfare effects asso-ciated with multiple price changes is possible by means of sequential calcula-tions. This approach, however, necessarily involves estimation of supply and demand in all markets for which prices change. For many practical problems, such extensive estimation is not feasible. But, fortunately, estimation of the welfare effects of many price changes is often possible in a single market if not.

In all the welfare analysis presented in this chapter, one must bear in mind that prices in other markets have been assumed fixed or unaffected by interven-tion in the market of consideration. Such an assumption is certainly unrealistic in many interesting welfare analyses. For example, when an agricultural price support is introduced, it tends to increase the price of agricultural inputs because of increased demand for inputs. These related price changes cause a further adjustment in the market of consideration as well as some additional welfare effects on the producers of inputs. Chapter 9 turns to consideration of these further adjustments and the related welfare impacts in other markets.

9

Multimarket Analysis and General Equilibrium Considerations

The analysis of Chapter 8 is conducted under the premise that price changes occur only in the market of interest. In many policy evaluation and cost–benefit studies, however, such an assumption is unrealistic. For example, suppose that the government establishes a quota on, say, Middle Eastern oil imports. Although this policy would clearly affect domestic crude oil prices and hence oil refinery profits, some of the increased cost would probably be passed along the marketing channel to gasoline distributors and retailers and, finally, to gasoline consumers. Similarly, increased petroleum prices can lead to higher fertilizer prices, which, through competition, tend to be passed along to processors, retailers, and consumers of agricultural products. In such cases, economic agents involved in markets other than the restricted market can obviously experience important economic welfare consequences. These consequences should be considered in any decision regarding adoption of the policy.

This chapter, accordingly, extends the framework of Chapter 8 to consider the welfare effects of price changes in markets related to the one in which some change is introduced. The analysis begins with the relationship of input markets to output markets. Alternative possibilities for discerning the welfare effects of output market price changes on input suppliers and of input market price changes on consumers are discussed. Such cases, where a clearly defined marketing channel exists—for example, the petroleum production–refining–

distributing–retailing channel—are called *vertical market structures*. Consideration is then given to welfare measurement of the effects of a price change on producers or consumers of competing commodities. The situations where one industry sells different products to different industries—for example, refineries sell different petroleum derivatives to gasoline distributors and fertilizer manufacturers—or where one industry buys different inputs from several different industries are called *horizontal market structures*.

These vertical and horizontal considerations suggest a methodology for measuring the general equilibrium effects of governmental intervention, which occur, to various degrees, throughout the entire economy. Consideration and modification of this methodology is then examined for the case where these other markets are already distorted by existing taxes, subsidies, quotas, and so on. Finally, econometric considerations in the multimarket context are discussed.

9.1   WELFARE EFFECTS IN VERTICALLY RELATED MARKETS

Producer Surplus Associated with Equilibrium Supply

To evaluate the welfare consequences of price changes in vertically related markets, consider a competitive final-goods industry that uses a single factor of production where the input-producing industry is also competitive but faces perfectly elastic supplies (fixed prices) for all its factors of production. The final-goods industry, depicted in Figure 9.1(b), is initially confronted with input price p_{n-1}^0 and output price p_n^0 and thus produces output q_n^0 along its short-run

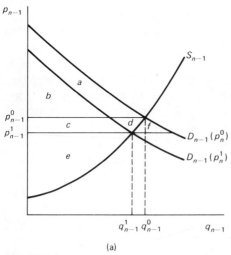

(a)

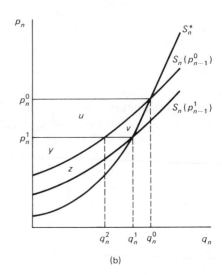

(b)

FIGURE 9.1

supply curve $S_n(p_{n-1}^0)$. Now, suppose that the output price is decreased to p_n^1 because of governmental action. Initially, the final-goods industry will attempt to adjust output along its short-run supply curve to q_n^2 because individual producers do not perceive the effects of their actions on prices. Since the industry is the sole user of its input (q_{n-1}), however, the input price will not remain at p_{n-1}^0; a decrease in output price causes a decrease in derived demand for the input from $D_{n-1}(p_n^0)$ to $D_{n-1}(p_n^1)$. Given input supply S_{n-1}, input price thus decreases from p_{n-1}^0 to p_{n-1}^1. In turn, the lower input price leads to decreased costs for the final-goods industry; hence, its supply shifts rightward from $S_n(p_{n-1}^0)$ to, say, $S_n(p_{n-1}^1)$. Thus, the new equilibrium output at price p_n^1 is q_n^1.

Now consider the welfare implications of the output price change. First, from Section 8.1 the quasi-rent for an industry is given by the area above its short-run supply curve (at the associated input price) and below its product price. Hence, it is clear that quasi-rent in the final-goods industry changes from area $y + u$ to area $y + z$. Thus, the welfare loss (compensating or equivalent variation) for final-goods producers is area $u - z$; and this loss is obviously less than area u, the loss that would occur if input price remained at p_{n-1}^0. Also, from Section 8.1, quasi-rent for the final goods industry can be measured by consumer surplus associated with derived demand. In Figure 9.1(a), quasi-rent for the final goods industry thus changes from area $a + b$ to area $b + c$ for a loss of area $a - c$ (thus, area $y + z$ = area $b + c$, area $u + y$ = area $a + b$, and area $u - z$ = area $a - c$). As suggested by the examples in the introduction to this chapter, however, additional welfare effects from the initial price change will be experienced in related markets where prices also change—in this case by the producers of the input. From Figure 9.1(a), quasi-rent for the input-producing industry decreases from area $c + d + e$ to area e; hence, their welfare effect is a loss of area $c + d$.

Determination of the net social gains from the output price change requires summing the welfare effects over the two individual industries. Collecting these effects over both industries, as reflected in the input market, yields a net social loss of area $a + d$ $[= (a - c) + (c + d)]$.

Observation of the net social welfare effects in the output market is somewhat more difficult because both industries are not explicitly represented. To explore the possibilities for measurement in the output market, consider first the implications of aggregating the two industries into a single vertically integrated industry. This hypothetical industry faces perfectly elastic supplies (those in reality pertaining to the input producing industry) as well as the same output prices considered earlier (those facing the output industry). Profit maximization for this hypothetical (competitive) industry leads to the same output decisions as when the former final-goods industry is in equilibrium—for example, at (p_n^0, q_n^0) with input price p_{n-1}^0 or (p_n^1, q_n^1) with input price p_{n-1}^1—since individual decisions associated with the separate industries are based on competitive profit maximization.[1] Thus, the hypothetical integrated industry would possess an output supply $S_n{}^*$ in Figure 9.1(b) necessarily passing through both $(p_n{}^0, q_n{}^0)$ and $(p_n{}^1, q_n{}^1)$. Based on results in Section 8.1, the welfare effect on the integrated industry of the price change from $p_n{}^0$ to $p_n{}^1$ is a loss equal to area $u + v$, the change in producer surplus associated with $S_n{}^*$.

To relate this loss to the sum of losses over the two original individual industries, merely note that the integrated industry makes the same decision with respect to output q_n and input(s) q_{n-2} used in producing q_{n-1} as the individual industries. Hence, quasi-rent for the hypothetical industry, $R_n{}^*$, is the sum of quasi-rents over the two individual industries, R_{n-1} and R_n:

$$R_n{}^* = p_n q_n - p_{n-2} q_{n-2} = (p_n q_n - p_{n-1} q_{n-1})$$
$$+ (p_{n-1} q_{n-1} - p_{n-2} q_{n-2}) = R_n + R_{n-1}$$

Thus, the change in quasi-rent represented by area $u + v$ in Figure 9.1(b) must be the same as the sum of changes in quasi-rents over the two industries, which is given by area $a + d$ in Figure 9.1(a).

By way of comparison with the case where prices in related markets do not change, it is apparent that incorrectly assuming perfectly elastic input supply at initial price p_{n-1}^0 leads to an underestimate of the welfare effect by area v in the output market or area d in the input market.

A further interesting observation at this point is that the welfare effect for industry $n - 1$ (which produces q_{n-1}) can also be observed in the output market for q_n. From above, one has

$$\text{area } a - c = \text{area } u - z$$
$$\text{area } a + d = \text{area } u + v$$

---

[1]To see that this is indeed the case, consider a final-goods industry with production function $q_n(q_{n-1})$ and an input-producing industry with production function $q_{n-1}(q_{n-2})$, where the price of its factor of production, q_{n-2}, is p_{n-2}. Profit maximization within individual industries implies that input price is equated to the marginal value of product, that is,

$$p_{n-1} = p_n \frac{\partial q_n(q_{n-1})}{\partial q_{n-1}}, \qquad p_{n-2} = p_{n-1} \frac{\partial q_{n-1}(q_{n-2})}{\partial q_{n-2}}$$

Substituting the first relationship into the second yields

$$p_{n-2} = p_n \frac{\partial q_n(q_{n-1})}{\partial q_{n-1}} \frac{\partial q_{n-1}(q_{n-2})}{\partial q_{n-2}}$$

Now consider the hypothetical combined industry with output price p_n, input price p_{n-2}, and production function $q_n[q_{n-1}(q_{n-2})] \equiv q_n(q_{n-2})$. The associated parallel condition for profit maximization is thus (by the chain rule)

$$p_{n-2} = p_n \frac{\partial q_n(q_{n-2})}{\partial q_{n-2}} = p_n \frac{\partial q_n(q_{n-1})}{\partial q_{n-1}} \frac{\partial q_{n-1}(q_{n-2})}{\partial q_{n-2}}$$

which is identical to the implications of separate industry profit maximization.

Hence, subtracting the first equation from the second yields

$$\text{area } c + d = \text{area } v + z$$

which is the industry $n - 1$ welfare loss.

To gain practical insight into appropriate application of the principles of welfare economics, further interpretation of the meaning of the curve S_n^* in Figure 9.1(b) is useful. That is, it may be difficult to perceive how an industry resulting from a hypothetical merger might react to various parametric price changes. However, S_n^* may also be interpreted as the competitive supply curve for the final-goods industry, which takes account of equilibrium adjustments in the input market (conditioned, of course, on prices of factors used in producing the input). If input price is intimately related to output price, as it would be under competition, then such a supply curve may be readily discernible; after all, only the locus of points along S_n^* would be observed in response to any series of output price changes (holding p_{n-2} fixed). For this reason, a supply curve, such as S_n^*, may be called an *equilibrium supply curve*. That is, the supply curve S_n^* is different from an "ordinary" short-run industry supply curve, such as $S_n(p_{n-1}^0)$, which indicates how the industry will respond to alternative output prices given that all input (and other output) prices are held fixed as with perfectly elastic input supply (output demand). *It is, rather, a supply curve that allows for equilibrium adjustment of input use and input price as output price changes.* The important property of such a curve is that the change in producer surplus defined with respect to an equilibrium supply curve measures the net change in quasi-rent for all affected producing industries for which adjustments are considered in the supply curve. That is, where ΔP_j^* represents the change in producer surplus associated with the equilibrium supply curve in market j and ΔR_j represents the change in quasi-rent in industry j (i.e., the industry producing q_j), one has $\Delta P_n^* = \Delta R_n + \Delta R_{n-1}$ and $\Delta P_n^* = \Delta P_{n-1}^* + \Delta R_n$ upon noting that $\Delta R_{n-1} = \Delta P_{n-1}^*$.

Consider now the case where the factor q_{n-2} used by the input industry is also not available in perfectly elastic supply. Assume that the only use of the factor q_{n-2} is in the production of the input q_{n-1} and hence that the market for q_{n-2} bears the same relationship to the q_{n-1} market as the q_{n-1} market has previously borne to the q_n market. Even more generally, consider a sequence of competitive markets for $q_0, q_1, \ldots, q_n$, where q_{j-1} is the only input used in producing q_j and is not available in perfectly elastic supply in each stage of the marketing channel, $j = 1, \ldots, n$; hence, any change in price p_n causes a change through competition in the respective prices $p_1, \ldots, p_{n-1}$ at all intermediate stages of the marketing channel. Finally, suppose that the basic input of the sector q_0 is available in perfectly elastic supply.

On the basis of the two-good case above, one is inclined to speculate that the change in producer surplus P_n^* defined with respect to the equilibrium supply curve in the market for q_n would measure the net change in quasi-rent over the entire producing sector (consisting of the industries selling $q_1, \ldots, q_n$). Indeed, Appendix D rigorously establishes for the vertically related market case that the total welfare effects over industries 1 through n of a price change in the market for q_n can be measured entirely by the change in producer surplus associated with the equilibrium supply curve in the market for q_n; that is,

$$\Delta P_n^* = \sum_{j=1}^{n} \Delta R_j \qquad (9.1)$$

from which one finds (subtracting a similar equation for ΔP_{n-1}^*) that

$$\Delta P_n^* = \Delta P_{n-1}^* + \Delta R_n \qquad (9.2)$$

Again, the intuition of the basic results in equation (9.1) can be developed much as in the two-industry case in Figure 9.1. That is, consider a hypothetical competitive industry formed by merging individual firms vertically throughout the marketing channel so that each firm purchases input q_0 and produces output q_n. In this case the supply curve S_n^* of a hypothetical integrated industry would coincide with the actual set of equilibrium price-production points (the equilibrium supply curve) in market n [just as in Figure 9.1(b)], since profit maximization in the hypothetical industry is equivalent to profit maximization (in equilibrium) among all individual industries.

Intermediate-Market Consumer Surplus Associated with Equilibrium Demand

As suggested earlier, the welfare effects of an input price change on an industry facing a perfectly elastic output demand (fixed output price) are reflected by the change in the consumer surplus measure associated with industry demand for the input. In the case where output price responds to a change in output supply induced by an input price change, however, equilibrium considerations can be made in a manner similar to the producer surplus case above.

Suppose that, initially, the industry producing q_{n+1} in a vertical market sector faces input price p_n^0 and output demand $D_{n+1}(p_{n+2})$; thus, the output market equilibrium depicted in Figure 9.2(b) is at price p_{n+1}^0 and quantity q_{n+1}^0. If input price is raised to p_n^2 through, say, government price control, output supply shifts leftward from $S_{n+1}(p_n^0)$ to $S_{n+1}(p_n^2)$. This shift, after succeeding rounds of adjustment, induces an increase in output price from p_{n+1}^0 to p_{n+1}^1; hence, the ordinary industry demand for the input increases from $D_n(p_{n+1}^0)$ to $D_n(p_{n+1}^1)$. The input market equilibrium thus shifts from (p_n^0, q_n^0) to (p_n^2, q_n^1) assuming that output price p_{n+2} for industry $n + 2$ which purchases q_{n+1} as an input is fixed (i.e., demand for q_{n+2} is perfectly elastic). The relationship D_n^* connecting these equilibrium points as price p_n is altered is, in fact, the equilibrium demand for q_n, since it takes account of equilibrium adjustments in other affected markets.

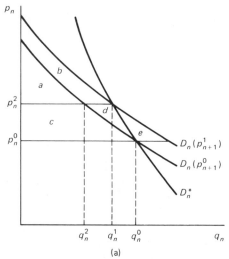
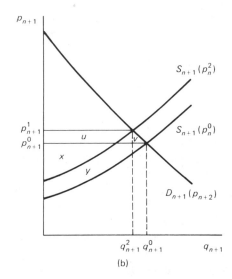

FIGURE 9.2

Again, the welfare effects can be evaluated in either the input or the output market. First, in the output market, the change in quasi-rent is clearly a decrease of area $u + v$ for industry $n + 2$ and a loss of area $y - u$ for industry $n + 1$; the latter area results since quasi-rent for industry $n + 1$ changes from area $x + y$ to area $u + x$. The net social welfare loss from the input price change, obtained by aggregating effects over industries, is thus area $v + y$ ($= u + v + y - u$).

Turning to evaluation in the input market, quasi-rent for industry $n + 1$ is area $a + b$ at prices p_n^2 and p_{n+1}^1 and area $a + c$ at prices p_n^0 and p_{n+1}^0; hence, the industry n welfare loss is area $c - b$. To determine the net social welfare effect in the input market, it is again instructive to consider a hypothetical vertical integration of industries $n + 1$ and $n + 2$. Such an industry, operating under competition and facing fixed price p_{n+2} in the market for its output, would have demand D_n^* for its input q_n. Thus, the results of Section 8.1 would imply a decrease in its quasi-rent of area $c + d$ as the input price increases from p_n^0 to p_n^2. Again, as in the previous supply case, profit maximization for the hypothetical industry leads to the same decisions as profit maximization by the individual industries; thus, the integrated industry profit would be the same as the sum of individual industry profits in equilibrium. Hence, the sum of changes in quasi-rent for the two industries can be measured in the input market by area $c + d$ ($=$ area $v + y$). That is, where ΔC_j^* represents the change in consumer surplus associated with a general equilibrium demand curve in market j, one finds that $\Delta C_n^* = \Delta R_{n+1} + \Delta R_{n+2}$ and $\Delta C_n^* = \Delta C_{n+1}^* + \Delta R_{n+1}$ upon noting that $\Delta R_{n+1} = \Delta C_n^*$.

From these results, it is also interesting to note that the welfare effect on industry $n + 2$ can be identified in the q_n market. As noted above,

$$\text{area } y - u = \text{area } c - b$$
$$\text{area } v + y = \text{area } c + d$$

Subtracting the first equation from the second yields

$$\text{area } u + v = \text{area } b + d$$

which gives the welfare loss for industry $n + 2$ in terms of input market measurements.

Consider now the more general case of consumer surplus in a vertical market sequence. That is, suppose that competitive industries $n + 1$, $n + 2$, . . . , N are characterized by a relationship where q_{j-1} is the only input used in producing q_j which is not available in perfectly elastic supply, $j = n + 1, \ldots ,$ N. Also, suppose that industry N faces a perfectly elastic demand for q_N. Again, the equilibrium demand $D_n{}^*$ in market n can be traced out by determining the equilibrium quantities q_n associated with various prices p_n assuming equilibrium or competitive profit-maximizing adjustments in all industries, $n +$ 1, ..., N (as their prices change). As in previous cases, this equilibrium curve reflects the behavior of a hypothetical competitive industry composed of all industries $n + 1, \ldots , N$ affected by a change in p_n; hence, the change in consumer surplus associated with $D_n{}^*$ in market n reflects the net welfare effect for the entire group of industries. Thus, for the general vertical market case,

$$\Delta C_n{}^* = \sum_{j=n+1}^{N} \Delta R_j \tag{9.3}$$

and, subtracting the similar equation for ΔC_{n+1}^*

$$\cdot \Delta C_n{}^* = \Delta C_{n+1}^* + \Delta R_{n+1} \tag{9.4}$$

Indeed, these results are developed rigorously in Appendix D.

Vertical-Sector Welfare Analysis

On the basis of the foregoing results, the overall social welfare effect of intervention in market n which alters either or both the supply and demand prices can be obtained by aggregating the producer and consumer surplus measures in market n,

$$\Delta P_n{}^* + \Delta C_n{}^* = \sum_{j=1}^{N} \Delta R_j \tag{9.5}$$

assuming that industry 1 faces a perfectly elastic input supply and that industry N faces a perfectly elastic output demand. For example, consider the vertical sector depicted in Figure 9.3, where equilibrium supply and demand are represented by $S_j{}^*$ and $D_j{}^*$ respectively; ordinary supply and demand are rep-

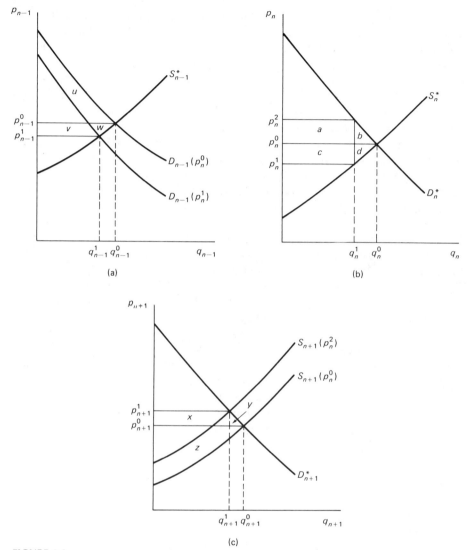

FIGURE 9.3

resented by S_j and D_j, respectively; and equilibrium price and quantity are represented by $p_j{}^0$ and $q_j{}^0, j = n - 1, n, n + 1$, respectively.[2] Now suppose that an ad valorem tax of $p_n{}^2 - p_n{}^1$ or a quota of $q_n{}^1$ is imposed on producers in

---

[2] Here markets $n - 1$, n, and $n + 1$ are regarded as part of an extended vertical sector, so it is useful to define equilibrium curves in markets $n - 1$ and $n + 1$. If industry $n - 1$ faces perfectly elastic input supply and industry $n + 1$ faces perfectly elastic output demand, then $S_{n-1}{}^*$ and $D_{n+1}{}^*$ would, in fact, coincide with ordinary curves as in Figures 9.1 and 9.2.

market n. The new equilibrium price and quantity would thus be p_n^2 and q_n^1 in market n, p_{n-1}^1 and q_{n-1}^1 in market $n-1$, and p_{n+1}^1 and q_{n+1}^1 in market $n+1$. Using the analysis of Section 8.5, as modified for the sector equilibrium case by equation (9.5), the net social welfare loss is thus area $b+d$ in Figure 9.3. Using equation (9.3), the joint welfare loss for industries $n+1, \ldots, N$ is area $a+b$; and using equation (9.1) the joint welfare effect for industries $1, \ldots, n$ is a loss of area $c+d$ in the tax case or a gain of area $a-d$ in the quota case. In the tax case the government also collects a tax revenue gain of area $a+c$.

The specific welfare effects for various industries involved in Figure 9.3 can be determined using ordinary supplies and demands. The welfare loss for industry $n+1$ is area $z-x$ in Figure 9.3(c), which can also be determined in market n using ordinary demands $D_n(p_{n+1}^0)$ and $D_n(p_{n+1}^1)$ according to the methodology suggested by Figure 9.2, and the effect on industries $n+2, n+3$, $\ldots, N$ is a loss of area $x+y$. The accounting for industry n, however, is somewhat different from that suggested in Figure 9.1. That is, industry n may be actually realizing output price p_n^2 after controls are imposed. Nevertheless, the resulting ordinary industry demand for q_{n-1} is not $D_{n-1}(p_n^2)$ but, rather, $D_{n-1}(p_n^1)$, since industry n is forced to act as though it were receiving price p_n^1 for its output. Hence, the welfare effect for industry n is, in fact, a gain of area $v-u$ in Figure 9.3(a) plus any additional rewards received in market n by actually receiving a price different than p_n^1. In the tax case all additional rewards above price p_n^1 are taxed away, so area $v-u$ is negative and represents a welfare loss for industry n. In the quota case the industry actually receives p_n^2 for its output and thus receives an additional reward of $(p_n^2 - p_n^1) \cdot q_n^1 = $ area $a+c$ above that which it would have received if price p_n^1 were applicable; hence, industry n has a welfare gain of area $a+c+v-u$. Finally, note that the joint effect on industries $1, 2, \ldots, n-1$ is a loss given by area $v+w$ in Figure 9.3(a).

Extension to Resource Supply and Final Consumer Demand

Extension of the vertical market structure to include resource supply and final consumer demand is of considerable interest in many cases. For example, imposition of a quota on petroleum imports may have serious implications for petroleum industry workers as well as for consumers. Such an extension is possible *in a purely vertical framework* in the special case where the resource supply price and final product price do not affect other consumer resource and consumption prices (including each other's price except as suggested explicitly in the vertical sector framework). In this case consumers and producers in the economy outside the vertical sector are indeed unaffected by intervention in the sector; furthermore, all welfare effects on consumers (resource suppliers) involved in the sector are reflected in the markets associated with the sector even though the quantities of goods taken in other sectors can change.

The intuition of this extension can be developed by reinterpreting Figures 9.1

and 9.2. If S_{n-1} is a resource supply curve in Figure 9.1 (consider $n = 1$), then S_n^* is the equilibrium supply curve in market n, which takes account of equilibrium adjustments of resource prices as output price p_n is altered. Hence, the change in producer surplus associated with S_n^* is the sum of changes in producer surplus associated with S_{n-1} and quasi-rent for industry n. Where ΔP_0 represents the change in surplus associated with resource supply, the relationship in (9.1) can thus be extended using equation (9.2) for the relationships of intermediate markets, together with $\Delta P_1^* = \Delta P_0 + \Delta R_1$, to obtain

$$\Delta P_n^* = \Delta P_0 + \sum_{j=1}^{n} \Delta R_j \qquad (9.6)$$

Similarly, for the final consumer, Figure 9.2 can be reinterpreted where D_{n+1} represents final consumer demand (consider $n = N - 1$), in which case the change in consumer surplus associated with D_n^* includes both the change in rent for industry $n + 1$ plus the change in consumer surplus associated with D_{n+1}. Denoting the latter change in surplus by ΔC_N, one has $\Delta C_N = \Delta C_{N-1}^* + \Delta R_N$. Thus, the relationship in (9.3) can be extended using equation (9.4) (which continues to apply for intermediate markets), obtaining

$$\Delta C_n^* = \Delta C_N + \sum_{j=n+1}^{N} \Delta R_j \qquad (9.7)$$

Finally, combining equations (9.6) and (9.7) yields the welfare effect of introducing a distortion in any market n in the sector,

$$\Delta C_n^* + \Delta P_n^* = \Delta P_0 + \Delta C_N + \sum_{j=1}^{N} \Delta R_j$$

Hence, where market 0 is a resource market and market N is a final-goods market (so that the related chain of markets, $n = 0, \ldots, N$, comprises a vertical economic sector), it is found that the sum of changes in equilibrium producer and consumer surpluses from distorting some market in the sector actually measures the change in total sector welfare to the extent that resource supply surplus and final consumer demand surplus (each computed along ordinary rather than compensated curves) measure welfare effects for the associated groups (to the extent that Willig conditions apply). Furthermore, since other sectors are unaffected by this change by assumption, the change in welfare for the economy as a whole is also obtained.

Thus, it turns out that the restrictive perfect-elasticity assumptions that have been made in earlier chapters for *all* related markets are unnecessary. Surplus welfare measures (defined with respect to equilibrium curves) have validity regardless, at least in a purely vertical economic framework. More important, the equilibrium surplus measures provide an overall rather than a partial picture of welfare change. Hence, the failure of perfect-elasticity assumptions in a vertical market structure has no serious consequences as long as one is interested in aggregate welfare rather than the welfare of a particular set of producers or consumers. Furthermore, the change in welfare for a particular set of producers or consumers can still be examined using surplus measures associated with ordinary supply and demand curves to obtain distributional information.

9.2 WELFARE EFFECTS IN HORIZONTALLY RELATED MARKETS

Input Market Relationship for Industries

Consider next horizontal market relationships and the possibilities for measuring the overall social welfare effect of market intervention. Consider first a horizontal relationship of markets due to use of multiple inputs by a single industry. Suppose that inputs q_1 and q_2 are the only inputs used by some industry A facing perfectly elastic demand for its output where q_2 is produced by an industry B facing perfectly elastic supplies of its inputs. The supply of q_2 is represented by S_2 in Figure 9.4(b), and the respective industry A demands for inputs are initially $D_1(p_2{}^0)$ and $D_2(p_1{}^0)$ in equilibrium when faced with a (controlled) price $p_1{}^0$ for q_1. Now let the price for q_1 increase from $p_1{}^0$ to $p_1{}^1$ because of some intervention in the market for q_1. Initially, the competitive industry A attempts to reduce q_1 input use from $q_1{}^0$ to $q_1{}^2$ but, because of complementarity or substitution of inputs, the higher price for q_1 causes alteration in the industry A demand for q_2 (an increase if q_1 and q_2 are substitutes or a decrease if q_1 and q_2 are complements). This shift in demand for q_2 from $D_2(p_1{}^0)$ to $D_2(p_1{}^1)$ thus causes a change in q_2 price from $p_2{}^0$ to $p_2{}^1$, which, in turn, leads to a shift in

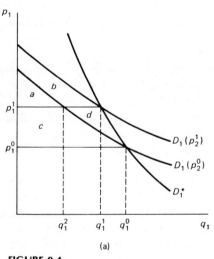

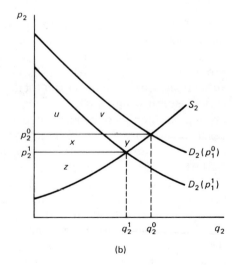

(a)   (b)

FIGURE 9.4

industry A demand for q_1 from $D_1(p_2^0)$ to $D_1(p_2^1)$. The new equilibrium finally occurs at price p_1^1 and quantity q_1^1. Thus, the demand relationship D_1^* for q_1, which takes account of equilibrium adjustments in other markets, is obtained.

To see the welfare significance of D_1^*, again consider a hypothetical merger—in this case of industries A and B—into a single competitive industry. Competitive profit maximization by the joint industry would imply behavior identical to that of the individual industries with the same resulting aggregate quasi-rent. So, quasi-rent for the hypothetical firm decreases by area $c + d$ as q_1 price increases from p_1^0 to p_1^1. Thus, the net social welfare effect over all affected industries is a loss of area $c + d$.

Again, the welfare effects for individual industries can be determined under various assumptions by aggregating and using results shown in Section 8.1. That is, if q_1 is an essential input for industry A (meaning that industry A cannot produce without using q_1, then its quasi-rent changes from area $a + c$ to area $a + b$ for a net welfare loss of area $c - b$. Similarly, if input q_2 is essential for industry A production, alternative but equivalent market 2 measurements indicate a change in quasi-rent from area $u + v$ to area $u + x$ for a net welfare loss of area $v - x$. Industry B quasi-rent decreases from area $x + y + z$ to area z for a net welfare loss of area $x + y$. If both q_1 and q_2 are essential inputs for industry A, industry B welfare effects can also be measured in market 1. That is, since the overall net welfare loss for both industries taken together is area $v + y$ [= area $(v - x) + (x + y)$], which must be the same as area $c + d$, the welfare loss for industry B in the q_1 market is area $b + d$ (that is, the overall loss of area $c + d$ minus the Industry A loss of area $c - b$ implies an industry B loss of area $b + d$).

These results can be extended to the case of many horizontally related input markets in a straightforward manner by adding any number of markets, such as market 2 in Figure 9.4, where the associated producers face perfectly elastic supplies of their inputs. In this case the general equilibrium demand D_1^*, which accounts for equilibrium adjustments in all other markets, thus leads to a consumer surplus which reflects joint welfare effects over all the associated industries. Hence, the type of analysis in Figure 9.4(a) is again applicable except that area $b + d$ reflects the joint welfare effects of all competing input industries if all the inputs are essential for industry A production.

Output-Market Relationships for Industries

Similar analysis is also possible in the case where one industry sells products in several output markets. For example, suppose that a competitive industry X faces a perfectly elastic input supply and sells products q_1 and q_2. Initially, product prices are p_1^0 and p_2^0 in Figure 9.5, respectively; thus, industry sales are q_1^0 and q_2^0 as determined by the respective industry supplies $S_1(p_2^0)$ and $S_2(p_1^0)$. Also, assume that industry Y, which purchases q_2 as an input, faces perfectly elastic demand for its output; thus, the consumer surplus associated

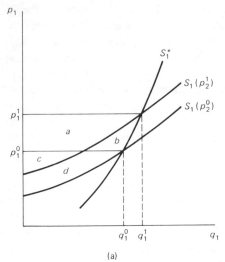

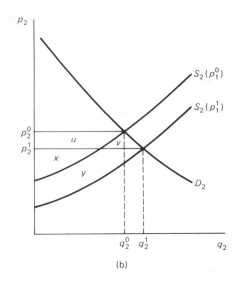

(a)   (b)

FIGURE 9.5

with its demand curve, D_2, reflects the welfare effects of changes in p_2 on industry Y. Now, suppose that the price of q_1 is increased from p_1^0 to p_1^1 through some intervention. As a result, output supply of q_2 is altered (increased in the case of complements or reduced in the case of substitutes). Where this movement is represented by a shift in q_2 supply from $S_2(p_1^0)$ to $S_2(p_1^1)$, as in the case of complements, one finds a welfare gain for industry Y of area $u + v$. If q_2 is an essential output for industry X, then Figure 9.5(b) implies a welfare gain for industry X of area $y - u$ for a net social gain, taking both industries together, of area $v + y$.

Turning to the market for q_1, the p_2 increase causes a shift in supply of q_1 from, say, $S_1(p_2^0)$ to $S_1(p_2^1)$ thus leading to a new equilibrium at price p_1^1 and quantity q_1^1. Again, it is useful to define the general equilibrium supply curve S_1^*, which specifies equilibrium output associated with various prices in market 2, taking account of all equilibrium adjustments in affected markets. The change in producer surplus associated with this supply curve (which can again be interpreted as the supply of a hypothetical competitive industry formed by merging industries X and Y) again measures net social welfare effects (assuming industries other than X and Y are unaffected). Thus, the price increase from p_1^0 to p_1^1 leads to a net social welfare gain of area $a + b$. If q_1 is an essential output for industry X, its specific welfare effect is reflected in market 1 by a change from area $c + d$ to area $a + c$ for a net gain of area $a - d$. In the case where both q_1 and q_2 are essential outputs of industry X, the industry Y welfare effect is also indicated in market 1 by a loss of area $b + d$; that is, area $a + b =$ area $v + y$, and area $a - d =$ area $y - u$, implying that area $b + d =$ area $u + v$.

Again, as in the input case, the results can be extended to many horizontally related output markets by adding any number of markets, such as market 2, in

190

Figure 9.5, where the associated consuming industry faces perfectly elastic demands for their outputs.

Horizontal Relationships for Consumers/Resource Suppliers

Consider next the possibilities for determining the welfare effects on consumers and resource suppliers of price changes in horizontally interrelated markets. For example, reconsider Figure 9.4, where the two markets pertain to a pair of consumer goods and the demands represent final demands by a consumer group. In the firm or industry case, the demands $D_1(p_2^0)$ and $D_1(p_2^1)$ reflect the marginal value of an additional unit of q_1 holding other prices fixed; and the demand D_1^* reflects the marginal value of q_1 when adjustments of other prices are taken into account. By analogy, a logical extension of the industry results suggests that consumer demand curves reflect marginal values of additional consumption—in the one case holding prices fixed and, in the other, allowing prices to vary. Indeed, the demand curves in each case represent the maximum amount that would be paid for the marginal consumption unit. Thus, as in the industry case, it seems that the area under a demand curve, even when other prices are allowed to adjust, represents the sum of marginal values over all marginal units of consumption from zero up to the level in question. If this were true, the total area under an equilibrium demand curve D_1^* would be a money measure of the total value of consumption of q_1.

The only problem with this simple extension of the industry results to the final consumer case is that the standard of measurement is not well defined for the consumer case. That is, the change in area under the equilibrium demand curve D_1^* is a clear measure of the change in value of consumption (of all goods) only if the utility levels of the individual consumers are held constant; only in this case can money values of one commodity be translated unambiguously into money values of another commodity. Otherwise, if utility is not held constant, the translation of marginal money values from one market into another (as is needed if all money value effects are to be represented neatly under one curve) is confounded by changing marginal utilities. Of course, consumer adjustments are also influenced by these changing marginal utilities if utility is not constant. As suggested by Section 5.2, uniqueness is thus lost because the appropriate order of imposing price changes is not clear.

Nevertheless, where D_1^* is a compensated equilibrium demand curve (defined as the price–quantity demand relationship where all consumers are held at constant utility levels and all other prices adjust to equilibrium levels as the price in question changes), the change in area under D_1^* is equivalent to the sum of changes in areas behind individual market compensated demand curves obtained by sequentially imposing all the price changes suggested by the new equilibrium.[3]

---

[3]In the case of compensated curves, it is easy to see that these results follow in the same way as the industry case since the compensated consumer problem is formally

Turning to the resource owner side, the situation in Figure 9.5 can also be reconsidered in the context of one group of consumer/resource owners selling resources in more than one market. Again, the supply curves represent marginal costs in terms of value given up by the resource owners as successive units of a commodity are supplied. In the compensated case where uniqueness is clear, the change in area above the compensated equilibrium supply curve represents the appropriate measure of welfare effects for resource suppliers.

The results of this section, although presented on a somewhat superficial level, follow directly from the rigorous development in Appendix D.

9.3   GENERAL EQUILIBRIUM
WELFARE MEASUREMENT

An implication of the results of the previous two sections is that net social welfare effects over the economy as a whole of intervention in any single market can be measured completely in that market using equilibrium supply and demand curves of sufficient generality. That is, Section 9.1 implies that all welfare effects extending into vertically related markets can be captured in the single market; Section 9.2 implies that all welfare effects extending into horizontally related markets can be captured in the single market. It seems a small step to extend the methodology to include effects in the rest of the economy. Although the graphical analysis becomes too cumbersome in this case for practical exposition, this generalization of the results can be developed rigorously, as in Appendix D, using more sophisticated mathematical techniques.

Thus, a summarization of the results in their full generality is useful at this point. Consider an economy with N goods including all consumer goods and all basic resources used in production where any industry producing good j uses as inputs in their production process any subset of the N goods, $j = 1, \ldots, N$. Assume all industries, resource suppliers, and consumers operate competitively and are initially in general competitive equilibrium characterized by prices p_j^0 and quantities q_j^0, $j = 1, \ldots, N$.[4] Now suppose that some intervention, such as an ad valorem tax in the amount of $p_n^2 - p_n^1$ or a quota of q_n^1, is imposed. Where J represents the set of all other markets, $J = \{1, \ldots, n - 1, n + 1, \ldots, N\}$, ordinary supply and demand (conditioned on all other prices in the economy) are initially $S_n(p_j^0, j \in J)$ and $D_n(p_j^0, j \in J)$, respectively. After intervention, ordinary supply and demand shift to $S_n(p_j^1, j \in J)$ and $D_n(p_j^1, j \in J)$, respectively, as all other prices are induced through competition to change from p_j^0 to p_j^1, $j \in J$.

The consumer surplus for industries or consumers directly consuming q_n in

---

equivalent to the producer problem (see Section 7.10); hence, the same relationship of areas under equilibrium curves with areas under market curves must be obtained in the compensated consumer/resource owner case, as in the industry case.

[4]The assumption of competition is relaxed somewhat in Appendix D.

Figure 9.6 changes from area $b + c + f$ to area $a + b$ for a net loss of area $c + f$ $- a$. The latter area necessarily carries welfare significance only if all of q_n is purchased by industry rather than final consumers and then only if q_n is an essential input in all industries that use it; even approximate significance holds in the consumer case only under conditions discussed in Section 7.10. The producer surplus for resource suppliers or industries directly selling q_n in market n changes from area $u + v + y$ to area $y + z$ (or $y + z + c + d + u + w$ in the quota case) for a net loss of area $u + v - z$ (or a gain of area $c + d - v$ in the quota case). The net effect in this case again necessarily carries welfare significance only if all of q_n is supplied by profit-maximizing industry and then only if q_n is an essential output of all industries that sell it; approximate significance holds for resource suppliers only under conditions indicated by Section 7.10, for the multiple-price-change case.[5]

Nevertheless, regardless of whether or not the group-specific measurements above carry welfare significance, the compensated general equilibrium supply

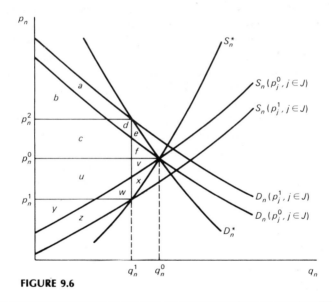

FIGURE 9.6

[5] It is also interesting to consider welfare measurement in market n for a broader set of industries. For example, suppose that the set J is reduced in size by excluding indices of markets which have, say, a vertical market relationship with market n. Then the supply and demand curves in Figure 9.6 conditioned on prices outside the vertical sector become, in a sense, sector equilibrium curves. To the extent that such industries are related by essential inputs or outputs, as the case may be, the areas discussed above carry welfare significance for the whole set of vertically related industries for which indices are excluded from the set J. Calculating these areas for all such feasible variations in the set J thus makes possible calculation of industry-specific welfare effects for all such related industries.

and demand curves can be used to measure the net social welfare effects of intervention in market n. That is, suppose that S_n^* and D_n^* in Figure 9.6 are, respectively, the compensated general equilibrium supply and demand curves which specify the respective marginal cost and price that result in market n for various levels of the tax or quota assuming (1) competitive adjustments in all other markets and (2) no distortions in other markets. In this case the net social welfare effect of introducing an ad valorem tax of $p_n^2 - p_n^1$ or a quota of q_n^1 in market n is given by area $e + f + v + x$. This represents a loss for all producers and consumer/resource suppliers taken together in the quota case. In the tax case the area $c + d + u + w$ represents a tax gain for government, so the loss for all private parties taken together is area $c + d + e + f + u + v + w + x$.

These areas apply exactly if consumers/resource suppliers respond along *compensated* demand/resource supply curves in the markets for which prices change.[6] If instead the consumers/resource suppliers make noncompensated adjustments, then the foregoing general equilibrium welfare effects are approximate to the extent that noncompensated equilibrium approximates compensated equilibrium and to the extent that noncompensated equilibrium supply and demand approximates compensated equilibrium supply and demand. The Willig results of Chapters 6 and 7 suggest that the latter approximation is sufficiently close to be useful. The former approximation should also be close for small changes but more investigation is needed for the case of large changes. Appendix D suggests an empirical approach that can be used when these approximations are not acceptable.

One further and easily misunderstood issue relating to definition and use of single-market general equilibrium curves for welfare measurement requires discussion. That is, the usual (noncompensated) general equilibrium supply and demand curves used above are defined with respect to the variation in the *particular kind of distortion* that is being considered rather than with respect to variation in individual supply or demand prices. This is necessary because any redistribution of area $c + d + u + w$ in Figure 9.6, say, from government to resource suppliers can cause those resource suppliers to alter their consumption decisions thus (perhaps indirectly) affecting the demand for the same good.[7] Thus, a noncompensated general equilibrium demand curve cannot be

---

[6]In some earlier work on general equilibrium economic welfare analysis, Boadway argued that a paradox existed in that general equilibrium could no longer be maintained in the event that compensation is paid. This paradox, however, is resolved in Appendix D by using compensated general equilibrium supply and demand concepts as opposed to the noncompensated general equilibrium concepts used by Boadway. See Robin W. Boadway, "The Welfare Foundations of Cost-Benefit Analysis," *The Economic Journal*, Vol. 84, No. 336 (December 1974), pp. 926–39.

[7]If (some of) the buyers are final consumers or some of the sellers are resource suppliers in market n, the lump-sum transfer would be equivalent to a change in their exogenous income, which would affect their marginal behavior and thus lead to different general equilibrium curves.

determined uniquely irrespective of the way (effective) supply price varies in relation to demand price. The appropriate noncompensated general equilibrium curves, therefore, can be determined only in the context of a specific type of distortion.

To demonstrate an alternative distortion which can lead to different general equilibrium curves, consider Figure 9.7. Initial equilibrium is the same as in Figure 9.6, but now a price support of p_n^2 is enacted by the government such that all excess supply at that price is purchased by the government. After adjustment to equilibrium in all markets, the resulting quantity demanded in market n is q_n^2 and the quantity supplied is q_n^1; the government buys $q_n^1 - q_n^2$ at price p_n^2 at a loss of area $b + c + d + e + f$ (assuming that government acquisitions are disposed costlessly without affecting private concerns or recouping some of the loss). The net welfare effect for all private concerns taken jointly is a gain of area c; thus, the net social welfare loss resulting from the distortion is area $b + d + e + f$.

Obviously, comparing Figure 9.7 with Figure 9.6, production takes place at a higher level under the price support than under the tax or quota case. The higher production is associated with greater use of resources at higher prices, thus creating higher incomes for consumers. Some of these increased incomes can thus percolate through the economy in the form of increased consumption, causing higher demand for q_n at prices above the free-market equilibrium. This suggests that the portion of the noncompensated general equilibrium demand curve above p_n^0 in Figure 9.7 may lie to the right of the noncompensated general equilibrium demand curve in Figure 9.6.

This problem, however, is not as severe as it might seem on the surface. In point of fact, if welfare effects are calculated on the basis of compensated general equilibrium supply and demand surves, then no such dependence on the form of distortion beyond dependence on the supply and demand prices

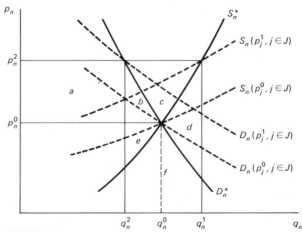

FIGURE 9.7

occurs. For example, when one considers all possible redistributions of area c + d + u + w in Figure 9.6, compensated supplies and demands remain invariant; any such lump-sum payments to (from) individuals are taken away (given back) to return them to initial utility levels (see Appendix D). Thus, even though forms of distortions may differ for given changes in supply and demand prices, the noncompensated general equilibrium welfare measures approximate the same compensated general equilibrium welfare measures (which are the accurate measures) to the extent that ordinary supplies and demands approximate compensated supplies and demands.

In the context of the preceding discussion, however, the change in consumer surplus associated with a general equilibrium demand curve cannot necessarily be interpreted as an effect on consumer welfare and on the welfare of industries involved in transforming q_n into final consumption goods. Neither can the change in producer surplus associated with the general equilibrium supply curve be interpreted as a welfare effect on resource suppliers and those industries using various resources to produce q_n. Through competitive adjustments, *some* of the consumer surplus change may represent effects on producers and conversely. Nevertheless, such conclusions may be reasonable as approximations in a variety of practical situations.

9.4 WELFARE MEASUREMENT WITH EXISTING DISTORTIONS IN OTHER MARKETS

A general criticism of welfare economics has been that distortions existing elsewhere in the economy are usually not taken into account. And, indeed, consideration thus far has been given only to the case of introducing a single distortion in an economy otherwise completely free of distortions. In reality, however, taxes exist on many commodities (for example, a sales tax on final goods), quotas exist on some commodities (for example, some agricultural commodities), and price controls or ceilings are occasionally used to control inflation or encourage development. Thus, for practical application of welfare analysis of any proposed additional distortion or removal of any existing distortion, the framework of Section 9.3 must be generalized to consider existing distortions.

Consider the situation in Figure 9.8, where a vertical relationship exists between industries n, $n + 1$, and $n + 2$. Industry n faces perfectly elastic supplies of its inputs, thus leading to supply $S_n(p_{n-1})$ in market n, and industry n + 2 faces perfectly elastic demand for its product, thus leading to demand $D_{n+1}(p_{n+2})$ in market $n + 1$. Initially, an ad valorem tax of $p_{n+1}^0 - p_{n+1}^1$ exists in market $n + 1$ which is associated with equilibrium ordinary demand $D_n(p_{n+1}^1)$, price p_n^0, and quantity q_n^0 in market n. The equilibrium ordinary supply is $S_{n+1}(p_n^0)$ in market $n + 1$, the quantity transacted is q_{n+1}^0, and the price is p_{n+1}^0 or p_{n+1}^1, depending on whether or not the tax is included or excluded.

Now suppose that a tax of $p_n^2 - p_n^1$ is introduced in market n. This reduces

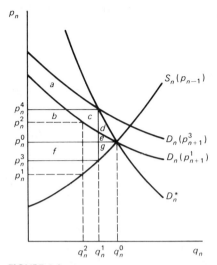
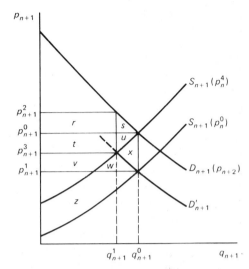

FIGURE 9.8

the supply of q_{n+1}, which, in turn, raises the effective supply price (excluding tax) in market $n + 1$ so that demand in market n tends to increase. As a result, a new equilibrium is achieved after sufficient adjustment at quantity q_n^1 and price p_n^4 (including tax), where $p_n^4 - p_n^3 = p_n^2 - p_n^1$. The set of equilibrium points associated with various levels of the tax in market n—for example, (p_n^0, q_n^0) and (p_n^4, q_n^1)—thus traces out an equilibrium demand curve D_n^* for q_n, *given the existing distortion.*

Now consider the welfare effects of imposing the second distortion. Given the vertical framework and elasticity assumptions above, industry $n + 2$ experiences a welfare loss of area $r + s$, industry n loses area $f + g$, and industry $n + 1$ loses area $b + e - a$ as measured in market n or area $z - v$ as measured in market $n + 1$. In addition, the government loses area $u + v + w + x - r$ in taxes in market $n + 1$ while gaining area $b + c + f$ in market n.

In this case the net social welfare effect cannot be observed in a single market except through use of the concept of equilibrium curves, and even then some changes in government tax revenues can be omitted. To see this, one need merely note that all behavior and welfare effects for industries $n + 1$ and $n + 2$, included in the equilibrium demand curve D_n^* in this case, are exactly the same as if demand were D_{n+1}' and no distortion existed in market $n + 1$ [where D_{n+1}' differs vertically from $D_{n+1}(p_{n+2})$ by the amount of the tax in market $n + 1$]. Hence, the welfare effect of area $r + s$ for industry $n + 2$ can be equivalently measured by area $v + w$. Based on the analysis in Figure 9.2, the welfare effect for both industries $n + 1$ and $n + 2$ is thus reflected by the consumer surplus associated with D_n^*. These observations imply that the net social welfare effect of adding the additional distortion in market n exclusive of the reduction in tax revenue in market $n + 1$ is reflected in market n by a loss of area $d + e + g$. Net

197

private welfare loss is area $b + c + d + e + f + g$, which is partially offset by the tax revenue gain of area $b + c + f$.

Such a problem with failure to account for all social welfare effects, even those of the government, does not occur, however, when the existing distortion is a quota. Because of such differences in methodology, depending on the form of distortion, examination of at least one other case is useful before discussing general conclusions. For an alternative problem, consider the case in Figure 9.9, where industries 1 and 2 have a horizontal relationship with both selling their output to industry 3 and facing perfectly elastic supplies of their inputs. Initially, a quota of q_2^0 exists in market 2 with equilibrium at prices p_1^0 and p_2^0 and market 1 quantity q_1^0. Consider the introduction of an ad valorem tax in the amount of $p_1^2 - p_1^1$ in market 1. The tendency toward higher q_1 prices leads to reduced demand for the (complementary) input q_2, as in the case of Figure 9.4, and hence leads to the lower price p_2^1. The lower q_2 price thus leads to an increase in the ordinary demand for q_1 to $D_1(p_2^1)$ with a new equilibrium at price p_1^4 including tax or price p_1^3 excluding tax. Such variations in the q_1 tax map out an equilibrium demand curve D_1^* which is conditioned on the level of the q_2 quota.

Determination of the overall welfare effects of introducing the new distortion in this case, given that the distortion in market 2 already exists, follows easily from the analysis in Figure 9.4. That is, imagining a hypothetical supply for industry 2 of S_2' (which coincides with S_2 at quantities below q_2^0), all of the welfare effects for industries 2 and 3 would be reflected by the change in consumer surplus associated with D_1^*. But the welfare effects on industry 1 are reflected by the producer surplus associated with S_1, which in this case is also

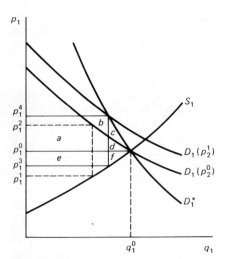
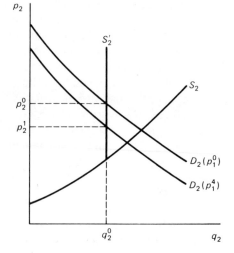

FIGURE 9.9

an equilibrium supply. Thus, the net social welfare effect of introducing the tax in market 1, given the existence of the quota in market 2, is a loss of area $c + d + f$. The net private welfare loss is area $a + b + c + d + e + f$, which is offset to some extent by the gain in government tax revenues of area $a + b + e$.

Obviously, many other useful simple cases of introducing one distortion when another exists could be examined. For example, one could consider introducing a tax, subsidy, quota, price support, or some other price or production control where any one of those kinds of distortions exists in another market even in a simple two-market framework. This could be done in horizontally related input markets, horizontally related output markets, vertically related markets where the first distortion exists in the input market, or vertically related markets where the first distortion exists in the output market. Even these simple cases are too numerous to consider here, but using the framework developed thus far, the reader can investigate any further simple cases of interest.

At this point, the general conclusions suggested by the cases above, which are developed rigorously with full generality in Appendix D, may be simply summarized. The general conclusion is that the analysis of Chapter 8 extends directly to take account of all *private* social welfare effects (not necessarily government effects) in the entire economy of intervention in a single market if (1) the supply and demand curves used for analysis in the market of interest are conditioned on all other distortions which exist in the economy, (2) all consumers and resource suppliers adjust along compensated demand and supply curves, (3) no existing distortions are in the form of price ceilings or floors, and (4) competitive behavior prevails throughout the economy. To the extent that consumers and resource owners do not react along compensated curves, the actual private welfare effects are approximated to the extent that compensated equilibrium prices and adjustments approximate noncompensated equilibrium prices and adjustments.

A few additional comments about social welfare analysis relating to governmental effects are also in order. For example, as in the cases of Figures 9.6 and 9.7, any change in government revenues or losses due to taxes, subsidies, or acquisition of commodities under price-support programs that result directly from the new distortion under consideration are reflected directly in the market of interest. However, if some *existing* distortions are of the type that lead to government revenues or losses, the net social welfare effects of any new distortion can be determined only by measuring the effects on these government revenues and losses in their respective markets and adding them to the net social welfare effects that are reflected in the newly distorted market (the net private welfare effects plus any government revenues or losses associated directly with the new distortion). Appendix D gives additional details for cases where some markets are distorted by use of market power or by price ceilings or floors.

9.5 GENERAL EQUILIBRIUM CONSIDERATIONS IN ESTIMATION, MULTICOLLINEARITY, SPECIFICATION, AND INTERPRETATION

To discuss the empirical approach suggested by this chapter, an understanding of the econometric problem of multicollinearity and its relationship to specification is helpful. The problem of multicollinearity is a condition in econometrics where the variables on the right-hand side of the estimated equation in (8.2) are so closely related that statistical procedures cannot attribute changes in observed data to one variable versus another variable with very much accuracy. This condition occurs when one variable happens to be approximately a linear function of another (e.g., $p = 2 + 5z_2$) or if one variable happens to be approximately a linear function of several other variables (e.g., $z_1 = 4 + 3z_2 + 2z_3 - 4z_4$) during the sample period.

Intuitively, the problem of multicollinearity can be exemplified by a situation where all observed data for, say, p and z_1 take on either values 1 and 2 or 4 and 6, respectively (thus, $z_1 = 2 + 2p$ in every observation). Suppose, also, that q is 8 in the first case and 4 in the second case. Then from observed data, it is impossible to determine whether or not the data were generated by the equation $q = 12 - 4p + 0 \cdot z_1$ or by the equation $q = 8 - 8p + 2z_i$. In the first case the curve is $q = 12 - 4p$ as represented in Figure 9.10; for the latter equation, the curve would be $q = 8 - 8p + 2 \cdot 4 = 16 - 8p$ or $q = 8 - 8p + 2 \cdot 6 = 20 - 8p$, depending on whether or not $p = 1$, $z = 4$ or $p = 2$, $z = 6$, respectively (again, see Figure 9.10). Thus, on the basis of observed data, the coefficients could be

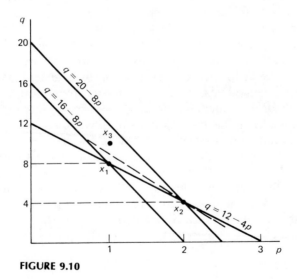

FIGURE 9.10

either $\alpha_0 = 12$, $\alpha_1 = -4$, $\alpha_2 = 0$ or $\alpha_0 = 8$, $\alpha_1 = -8$, $\alpha_2 = 2$; and no distinction is possible without additional data. Similarly, many other alternatives also exist.[8]

On the other hand, suppose that more observations are obtained where $p = 1$, $z_1 = 5$, and the q distribution is centered on 10. Then the case with $\alpha_0 = 8$, $\alpha_1 = -8$, and $\alpha_2 = 2$ is the only set of coefficients consistent with the data; obviously, $10 \neq 12 - 4 \cdot 1 + 0 \cdot 5$, so the other alternative must now be rejected. But this distinction is possible only by obtaining more data so that p and z_1 are no longer collinear (now $z_1 = 2 + 2p$ no longer holds for all observations).

This problem of multicollinearity or near multicollinearity is a problem that plagues many empirical studies of demand and supply. That is, appropriate practice from a theoretical point of view is to include in a demand or supply specification all the variables that serve as determinants of the demand or supply equation. Such a set of determinants generally includes a number of prices of competing consumer goods and income or of competing input prices. Because inflation tends to be reflected in all prices, these sets of variables tend to be characterized by a high degree of multicollinearity (all prices tend to rise together with time).

One possibility for avoiding these problems is to use *real* prices rather than *nominal* prices. Nominal prices reflect the actual price paid or received in terms of current dollars. Real prices, on the other hand, reflect the price level relative to some base period so that the effects of inflation tend to be removed. Real prices can be constructed by dividing observed or nominal prices by a suitable price index which reflects the level of inflation. For example, consumer prices are generally deflated or converted to real terms by dividing by the consumer price index. Prices of intermediate or manufactured goods are deflated by dividing them by the wholesale price index, and so on.

Although use of real prices rather than nominal prices tends to reduce multicollinearity, bothersome and sometimes unacceptable problems may still persist. This tends to occur, for example, on the producer side, where "booms" or "busts" occur for particular industries relative to the rest of the economy. Hence, all the prices associated with a particular industry (which thus serve as determinants in the same supply or demand equation) often increase or decrease together even relative to some overall price level. Because of the competitive nature of free economies, close relationships also tend to exist among the more closely competing consumer goods as well.

Because most data on determinants of supply and demand are characterized by multicollinearity, a dilemma must be faced. On the one hand, there are advantages to specifying demand and supply equations with fewer variables serving as determinants in order to reduce multicollinearity and thus increase accuracy (or reduce variance) in estimation of the most important parameters (like the parameter of the price in question). On the other hand, omitting

---

[8]For example, let $\alpha_0 = 12\theta - 8(1 - \theta)$, $\alpha_1 = -4\theta + 8(1 - \theta)$, and $\alpha_2 = 0 \cdot \theta - 2(1 - \theta)$ for any real value of θ.

important determinants tends to bias estimates of the coefficients, so that one can no longer expect to get correct results even on average (even as the sample size gets large). That is, suppose that the data are represented in Figure 9.10 by points x_1, x_2, and x_3. Then if the determinant z_1 is ignored, the OLS regression results would correspond to the broken line in Figure 9.10 rather than the true equation, $q = 8 - 8p + 2z$. Where the number of observations around x_1 is the same as around x_3, the broken line would lie halfway between the two and thus have a coefficient of $\alpha_1 = -5$ for p rather than -8. An estimate of the corresponding consumer surplus—say, at x_1—would thus be in error by the wedge-shaped area to the right of x_1 and between the broken line and the line corresponding to $q = 20 - 8p$.

In response to this dilemma, a common practice that has arisen in econometrics is to shorten the list of variables representing the determinants to the point that reasonable accuracy can be attained for the remaining coefficients. Suppose, for example, that one estimates a supply equation,

$$q = \alpha_0 + \alpha_1 p + \alpha_2 \gamma \qquad (9.8)$$

in the market for q, where p represents the price in that market and γ represents the price of the input (or index of prices of all inputs) used in producing q. For prices $p = p^*$, $\gamma = \gamma^*$ and the corresponding quantity $q^* = \alpha_0 + \alpha_1 p^* + \alpha_2 \gamma^*$, the simple or ordinary surplus measure S^* which holds the input price γ fixed at γ^* is given by area a, the area above the ordinary demand curve represented by $q = \alpha_0 + \alpha_1 p + \alpha_2 \gamma^*$ and below price p^* in Figure 9.11. Since p_0, the price at which supply just falls to zero, is given by $p_0 = -(\alpha_0 + \alpha_2 \gamma^*)/\alpha_1$ [simply set the right-hand side of equation (9.8) equal to zero and solve for p], the surplus triangle may be calculated from geometry as[9]

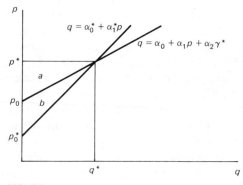

FIGURE 9.11

---

[9]Note that $\alpha_0 + \alpha_2 \gamma^*$ is assumed to be negative to simplify the example.

$$S^* = \text{area } a = \frac{1}{2}(p^* - p_0)q^*$$

$$= \frac{1}{2}\left(\frac{1}{\alpha_1}q^*\right)q^* = \frac{(q^*)^2}{2\alpha_1}$$

(9.9)

As implied by the results in Section 8.1, the area S^* measures quasi-rent only to producers selling in that market.

The equilibrium surplus, which reflects welfare effects for a broader group of producers (and consumers), is calculated on the basis of an equilibrium supply curve which is not conditioned on the input price γ. Instead, the equilibrium supply curve takes account of variation in γ induced by equilibrium adjustments in response to changes in p. For example, if cattle prices fall, cattle feeders generally respond by reducing supply through lowering the number of cattle on feed. This response, in turn, reduces demand for feed grain and causes a fall in feed price. Thus, suppose that the market in question is one of several that form a vertically related sector of the economy in the same sense as discussed in Section 9.1. Also, suppose for simplicity that the equilibrium relationship between p and γ is represented by

$$\gamma = c_0 + c_1 p \tag{9.10}$$

Then, substituting equation (9.10) into (9.8) yields

$$q = (\alpha_0 + \alpha_2 c_0) + (\alpha_1 + \alpha_2 c_1)p$$
$$= \alpha_0^* + \alpha_1^* p \tag{9.11}$$

as the equilibrium supply curve, which takes account of varying input prices where $\alpha_0^* = \alpha_0 + \alpha_2 c_0$ and $\alpha_1^* = \alpha_1 + \alpha_2 c_1$. The equilibrium surplus which reflects quasi-rent for all industries on the supply side of the market in the sector is given by area $a + b$ in Figure 9.11. Solving for p_0^* (setting $q = 0$) implies that $p_0^* = -\alpha_0^*/\alpha_1^*$. Thus, geometric calculation of the triangular area $a + b$ implies that the equilibrium producer surplus is

$$S = \text{area } a + b = \frac{1}{2}(p^* - p_0^*)q^*$$

$$= \frac{1}{2}\left(\frac{1}{\alpha_1^*}q^*\right)q^*$$

$$= \frac{(q^*)^2}{2\alpha_1^*}$$

$$= \frac{(q^*)^2}{2(\alpha_1 + \alpha_2 c_1)}$$

(9.12)

Since reasonable conditions imply that both α_1 and α_1^* are positive (both ordinary and equilibrium supply are upward sloping), that $\alpha_2 < 0$ (an increase in the price of inputs causes a reduction in supply), and that $c_1 > 0$ (an increased price of the output leads to increased input prices through increased derived demand), a casual examination of equations (9.9) and (9.12) reveals that $S^* < S$, so that the quasi-rent of all producers on the supply side of the sector is greater than quasi-rent for producers involved directly in the supply side of the individual market.

Returning now to the econometric problems of multicollinearity, recall that the general approach of the preceding chapter in estimating a supply curve is to include as determinants all of the input prices (at least of variable factors). In the context of the discussion above, this practice would correspond to estimation of equation (9.8). For this equation, however, the mere existence of competition tends to cause multicollinearity through equilibrium adjustments that lead to the relationship in equation (9.10). In equation (9.10), the input and output prices indeed have a perfectly linear relationship, as in the first case discussed in this section; hence, direct estimation of equation (9.8) is not possible as long as observations on p and γ have such a linear relationship.

Although the usual relationship between input and output prices in supply estimation is not one of perfect collinearity as in equation (9.10), problems are often sufficiently manifest to prevent much accuracy in estimation of the associated coefficients. In practice, the severity of this condition has often led investigators to drop input prices from the supply equation specification altogether, thus estimating instead an equation of the form

$$q = \tilde{\alpha}_0 + \tilde{\alpha}_1 p \tag{9.13}$$

But clearly, the interpretation of parameters and associated surpluses for equation (9.13) is different from that in equation (9.8). Indeed, equation (9.13) is equivalent to equation (9.11). Hence, an estimate of $\tilde{\alpha}_1$ in equation (9.13) must be interpreted as an estimate of α_1^* in equation (9.11) so that the producer surplus associated with the supply in equation (9.13) is the equilibrium surplus in equation (9.12).

If, on the other hand, the relationship between p and γ is not so close as to cause problems of multicollinearity in estimating the ordinary supply equation (9.8) [say, because of a random disturbance in (9.10)], then the equilibrium supply in equation (9.11) can also be estimated in indirect fashion by computing

$$\alpha_0^* = \hat{\alpha}_0 + \hat{\alpha}_2 \hat{c}_1$$
$$\alpha_1^* = \hat{\alpha}_1 + \hat{\alpha}_2 \hat{c}_2$$

where $\hat{\alpha}_0$, $\hat{\alpha}_1$, and $\hat{\alpha}_2$ are the estimated parameters of the ordinary supply curve in equation (9.8).

From a practical standpoint, it seems that the latter approach is the more reasonable to follow when both alternatives exist and, in fact, some generalizations can be easily considered. That is, the relationship of p and γ may not be so close as to create acute multicollinearity problems in estimation of the ordinary supply in equation (9.8) because some force elsewhere in the sector or economy (such as government intervention or prices outside the sector) may have altered equation (9.10) during the sample period. Suppose that this force is represented by z and that its effect in equation (9.10) can be represented linearly,

$$\gamma = c_0{}^* + c_1{}^*p + c_2{}^*z \qquad (9.14)$$

If this is the case, the appropriate equilibrium supply curve is found by substituting equation (9.14) into equation (9.8), thus obtaining

$$q = \alpha_0 + \alpha_1 p + \alpha_2(c_0{}^* + c_1{}^*p + c_2{}^*z) \qquad (9.15)$$
$$= \bar{\alpha}_0 + \bar{\alpha}_1 p + \bar{\alpha}_2 z$$

where $\bar{\alpha}_0 = \alpha_0 + \alpha_2 c_0{}^*$, $\bar{\alpha}_1 = \alpha_1 + \alpha_2 c_1{}^*$, and $\bar{\alpha}_2 = \alpha_2 c_2{}^*$.

With this type of phenomenon in mind, it seems that direct estimation of ordinary supply may be preferable to direct estimation of equilibrium supply since problems of bias due to mis-specification (e.g., leaving out important variables) are not likely to be so great. With the equilibrium supply equation in (9.15), on the other hand, the set of determinants corresponding to z is sometimes difficult to determine or narrow down to manageable proportions.[10] In point of fact, when one considers the context of the sector equilibrium approach given in Section 9.1, it indeed conditions results on fixed prices and incomes in the rest of the economy. These prices from the rest of the economy

---

[10]Another point of interest that will be clear to a practicing econometrician has to do with the possible pitfalls of, by chance, considering as a determinant some variable z in equations (9.14) and (9.15) that does not rightfully serve as a determinant. When additional variables are considered in linear regression, they can only reduce rather than increase the sum of squares of errors. Furthermore, when one investigates a large number of variables as possibilities, chances are that some will be found that cause a significant reduction (have a t ratio greater than 2 in absolute value). With this in mind, one must consider adding variables in (9.14) which tend to take away from the explanation of γ by p, thus reducing the estimate of c_1. Substituting in the ordinary supply curve will thus lead to a smaller coefficient for p in the equilibrium estimate of supply, which thus implies more inelastic equilibrium supply. If, instead, the equilibrium relationship is turned around to estimate

$$p = \bar{c}_0 + \bar{c}_1\gamma + \bar{c}_2 z$$

then a smaller estimate of $\bar{c}_1$ after substitution in equation (9.8) is reflected by a more elastic estimate of equilibrium supply. Thus, one check on whether or not the right set of determinants is employed is to estimate the induced equilibrium curve both ways. One may note that direct estimation of the equilibrium curve in (9.15) will tend to yield more inelasticity if incorrectly included z terms detract from the explanation of q by p. The alternative conclusion would be reached if the supply equation were estimated with p rather than q as the left-hand-side or dependent variable.

thus serve as determinants for the equilibrium supply and demand curves. Although the number of such prices that must be considered is overwhelming in most cases, the approach of constructing suitable indices may serve as a reasonable means of reducing the number of variables that must be considered econometrically (the theory of separability of demand and resource supply is directly applicable with respect to the prices of all goods that are not traded directly with the sector if, in fact, appropriate separable groupings exist).[11]

In addition to the considerations raised in this section on the supply side, symmetrical arguments can be made with respect to the area under estimated demand curves for intermediate goods in a sector. That is, reinterpreting γ as the price of a product that uses q in its production process and S as a consumer surplus, all the derivation in equations (9.8) through (9.15) continues to hold.

The General Vertical Market Approach

The essence of the approach can be generalized to consider problems of econometric estimation and identification in the case where the equilibrium price relationships in a sector are changing because of varying prices and government policies (or determinants) imposed on the sector by the rest of the economy. That is, one can estimate an equilibrium supply curve in market j in the vertical sector case [encompassing endogenous adjustments of $(p_0, \ldots, p_{j-1}, p_{j+1}, \ldots, p_N)$] by regressing the quantity supplied, q_j^s, on the effective market j price for producers (e.g., output price less any ad valorem tax, as in Figure 9.3) and all determinants γ_j^- affecting resource suppliers and industries $1, \ldots, j,$[12]

$$q_j^s = q_j^s(p_j^s, \gamma_j^-) \tag{9.16}$$

Similarly, the market j equilibrium demand can be estimated in the form

$$q_j^d = q_j^d(p_j^d, \gamma_j^+) \tag{9.17}$$

where q_j^d is quantity demanded, p_j^d is the effective market price for purchasers, and γ_j^+ a vector of all determinants associated with the rest of the economy affecting industries $j + 1, \ldots, N$ and final consumer demand. If the small vertical-sector assumption applies, sector equilibrium functions are, indeed, general equilibrium curves and can be used to estimate the overall welfare effects of a distortion.

---

[11]For a detailed discussion of separability, see Charles Blackorby, Daniel Primont, and R. Robert Russell, *Duality, Separability, and Functional Structure: Theory and Economic Applications* (New York: North-Holland Publishing Company, 1978).

[12]For purposes of the remainder of this chapter, the inclusion of variables in a functional form $q(\cdot, \cdot)$ is meant to imply which variables should be considered in the regression equation without necessarily specifying the functional form (in terms of linearity, log linearity, etc.).

On the other hand, if one estimates (ordinary) supply and demand in the same intermediate market by considering prices in vertically related markets, that is, using a supply function of the form

$$q_j^s = \tilde{q}_j^s(p_j^s, p_{j-1}, \gamma_j) \tag{9.18}$$

and a demand function of the form

$$q_j^d = \tilde{q}_j^d(p_j^d, p_{j+1}, \gamma_{j+1}) \tag{9.19}$$

respectively, where γ_j and γ_{j+1} include only those determinants from the rest of the economy that affect industries j and $j + 1$ directly, one can obtain (assuming identifiability) partial equilibrium welfare measures, that is, measures of welfare for only the producers and consumers in the market in question. If in addition, one estimates the equilibrium price relationships,

$$p_{j-1} = p_{j-1}^s(p_j^s, \gamma_j^-) \tag{9.20}$$

$$p_{j+1} = p_{j+1}^d(p_j^d, \gamma_j^+) \tag{9.21}$$

then estimates of the equations (9.20) and (9.21) can be substituted into equations (9.18) and (9.19) to obtain estimates of the equilibrium functions in equations (9.16) and (9.17). Then equilibrium producer and consumer surplus can be calculated from the associated graphs of q_j against p_j for given values of determinants γ associated with the rest of the economy.

The General Equilibrium Approach

Turning to the general equilibrium results of Section 9.3 (which also encompass the case of Section 9.2), similar conclusions with respect to econometric practice may again be drawn. That is, one can estimate an equilibrium supply equation of the form

$$q^s = q^s(p^s, \gamma_s) \tag{9.22}$$

and an equilibrium demand equation of the form

$$q^d = q^d(p^d, \gamma_d) \tag{9.23}$$

in any particular market where q^s and q^d are quantities supplied and demanded, p^s and p^d are effective supply and demand prices, and γ_s and γ_d are determinants of the economy that affect equilibrium supply and demand, respectively. In this context all prices in the economy are viewed as being determined by the determinants of the economy. Specifically, the determinants of the economy would thus include such factors as government policy instruments (taxes, quotas, and so on), which introduce distortions in the economy, as well as all exogenous forces on the economy (weather, social and political factors, and so on) including any short-run production factor fixity or consumer durable asset fixity, and if the relevant economy does not pertain to the world as a whole, world prices of traded goods and exogenous income earned from external sources. In the latter case, conditioning of supply and demand estimates on external prices of traded goods will result in measuring equilibrium welfare for only the constituents of the economy in question, just as the sector equilibrium approach of Section 9.1 measures welfare for only the constituents of the sector in question.

From a practical standpoint, however, each of the determinants of the equilibrium supply in equation (9.22) may also affect the equilibrium demand in equation (9.23); thus, γ_s and γ_d may be synonymous. That is, once all the effects of any exogenous force have filtered through the economy, the equilibrium adjustments brought about by competition may lead to a change in both the equilibrium supply and equilibrium demand in the market of interest because of the circular relationship among producers, consumers, and resource suppliers in the general economy (see Section 9.3 for a similar discussion related to introducing different types of distortions).[13] An econometric problem that arises in this context is that if equations (9.22) and (9.23) compose a pair of simultaneous equations (Section 8.8), then structural identification problems can prevent estimation with reasonable properties.

For example, consider a simultaneous equations system where the same determinant affects both equations,

$$q = \alpha_0 + \alpha_1 p + \alpha_2 y \qquad \qquad (9.24)$$

$$q = \beta_0 + \beta_1 p + \beta_2 y \qquad \qquad (9.25)$$

Solving the system for p and q implies that

---

[13]One case in which this would not be true is where the economy can be segmented into two groups of decision makers such that all the interaction between the two groups, direct or indirect, takes place in a single market. Thus, determinants that affect the net equilibrium supply of one group of individuals do not necessarily affect the net equilibrium demand of the other group. In particular, a change in the supply price in the single connecting market, holding the demand price fixed, does not cause adjustments within the segment of the economy associated with demand and or of the resulting equilibrium demand. Similarly, a change in demand price in the connecting market, holding the supply price fixed, does not cause a shift in the equilibrium supply. Using the framework of Section D.2, one can show, in this case, that the change in producer surplus associated with compensated equilibrium supply measures the net welfare effect (in terms of willingness to pay) for the segment of the economy associated with that supply; and a similar statement holds for the other segment of the economy with respect to the change in consumer surplus associated with compensated equilibrium demand. The vertical market structure is such a special case. See Section D.2 for more detailed analysis of this case.

$$p = a_0 + a_1 y$$
$$q = b_0 + b_1 y$$

where

$$a_0 = \frac{\beta_0 - \alpha_0}{\alpha_1 - \beta_1}, \quad a_1 = \frac{\beta_2 - \alpha_2}{\alpha_1 - \beta_1} \tag{9.26}$$

$$b_0 = \frac{\alpha_0 \beta_1 - \alpha_1 \beta_0}{\beta_1 - \alpha_1}, \quad b_1 = \frac{\alpha_2 \beta_1 - \alpha_1 \beta_2}{\beta_1 - \alpha_1} \tag{9.27}$$

But given estimates of a_0, a_1, b_0, and b_1, there is no way to solve the corresponding four equations in (9.26) and (9.27) uniquely for the six parameters α_0, α_1, α_2, β_0, β_1, and β_2 of the structural demand and supply equations in (9.24) and (9.25). In this case, methods which can generally attain at least consistent estimators of structural equation parameters, fail.[14]

An alternative approach is to estimate conventional ordinary supply and demand equations,

$$q^s = \bar{q}^s(p^s, p_d{}^s, \gamma_s{}^*) \tag{9.28}$$
$$q^d = \bar{q}^d(p^d, p_d{}^d, \gamma_d{}^*) \tag{9.29}$$

where q^s, p^s, q^d, and p^d are as defined earlier; $p_d{}^s$ and $p_d{}^d$ represent all prices and exogenous income in the economy that serve as determinants of ordinary supply and demand, respectively; and $\gamma_s{}^*$ and $\gamma_d{}^*$ represent all determinants of the economy that affect this particular ordinary supply and demand directly With estimates of these equations, the ordinary surpluses may be calculated and used to determine welfare effects on the participants of the market from changes in policy instruments (taxes, quotas, etc.) represented in $\gamma_s{}^*$ or $\gamma_d{}^*$

Such calculations, however, require knowledge of the equilibrium adjustments of $p_d{}^s$ and $p_d{}^d$. These prices and incomes may, in fact, be observed both before and after a policy change so that the ordinary surpluses can be appropriately calculated on the basis of the location of the ordinary supply and demand curves before and after the change as determined by the determinants. Even in most *ex post* policy analyses, however, it is necessary to estimate the effects of a particular policy change on equilibrium prices because the effects of many other coincidental changes must be removed in order to isolate the effects of interest.

---

[14] For further details on structural identification in simultaneous equations estimation, see Henri Theil, *Principles of Econometrics* (New York: John Wiley & Sons, Inc., 1971); Arthur S. Goldberger, *Econometric Theory* (New York: John Wiley & Sons, Inc., 1964), Chap. 7; or Michael D. Intriligator, *Econometric Models, Techniques, and Applications* (Englewood Cliffs, N.J.: Prentice-Hall, Inc., 1978), Chap. 10.

One possible approach to estimating equilibrium price adjustments is to estimate equations that specify how prices in the economy adjust to changes in the determinants of the economy,

$$p_d^s = p_d^s(p^s, \gamma_s) \qquad (9.30)$$

$$p_d^d = p_d^d(p^d, \gamma_d) \qquad (9.31)$$

These equations, however, must be considered as simultaneous equations and hence may suffer from the same structural identification problems associated with equations (9.22) and (9.23).[15] Alternatively, if the functional forms in (9.30) and (9.31) are such that the equations can be rewritten as

$$\frac{p_d^s}{p^s} = \tilde{p}_d^s(\gamma_s) \qquad (9.32)$$

$$\frac{p_d^d}{p^d} = \tilde{p}_d^d(\gamma_d) \qquad (9.33)$$

then no such problems exist. The latter set of equations can, in principle, be estimated without structural identification problems (although stochastic identification problems associated with multicollinearity may occur).[16] Thus, substitution of estimates of equations (9.32) and (9.33) into estimates of equations

---

[15]Technically, one must also note that the prices in p^s and p^d are determined simultaneously with p_d^s and p_d^d. If this is the case, equations must also be specified for p^s and p^d and used in estimation of (9.30) and (9.31) to avoid simultaneous equations bias (Section 8.8). Similar statements also apply to estimation of the price relationships in (9.14), (9.20), and (9.21). Also, the price variables p_d^s and p_d^d on the right-hand side of equations (9.28) and (9.29) are generally determined simultaneously with q^s, q^d, p^s, and p^d; and this simultaneity must also be considered in estimation. A similar statement applies to p_{j-1} and p_{j+1} in equations (9.18) and (9.19). In all these cases, however, a 2SLS or instrumental variables approach of first regressing the jointly dependent variables on all exogenous forces (e.g., on γ) and then replacing the right-hand side jointly dependent variables by estimates suggested by these regressions can lead to an acceptable estimation procedure. Consideration of additional equations is not necessary for estimation of equations (9.11), (9.13), (9.15) through (9.17), (9.22), and (9.23), since jointly dependent variables from other markets do not appear, so that simultaneity with other equations need not be considered (although some additional precision or efficiency in estimation may be possible by so doing). In econometric terms, these equations behave like (partially) reduced forms; for a discussion of related econometric issues, see Theil, *Principles of Econometrics*, Chap. 9.

[16]The principle of separability may again suggest the use of index numbers to reflect groups of determinants of the economy so that multicollinearity problems may be circumvented. For example, a basket exchange rate may adequately reflect trade prices for an economy, so that perhaps all individual trade prices may not need to be included. Again, see Blackorby, *et. al.*, *Duality, Separability, and Functional Structure*.

(9.28) and (9.29) obtains estimates of the equilibrium supply and demand equations in (9.22) and (9.23):

$$q^s = \tilde{q}^s[p^s, p^s \cdot p_d{}^s(\gamma_s), \gamma_s{}^*] = q^s(p^s, \gamma_s)$$
$$q^d = \tilde{q}^d[p^d, p^d \cdot p_d{}^d(\gamma_d), \gamma_d{}^*] = q^d(p^d, \gamma_d)$$

In this framework the equilibrium welfare effects of altering any policy variable in the market (reflected in $\gamma_s{}^*$ and/or $\gamma_d{}^*$) can be determined following the results in Section 9.3.

Practical Aspects of Equilibrium Welfare Analysis

The preceding material in this section provided a methodology for estimating equilibrium welfare effects, which is applicable in theory. In reality, however, one cannot expect to identify all of the determinants of an economy. Furthermore, even if all determinants of an economy could be identified and corresponding data could be collected, little hope exists for estimating equations such as (9.22) and (9.23) involving all such determinants because problems of multicollinearity become more acute as variables are added (assuming a fixed number of observations on each variable). In reality, an applied welfare economist must abstract somewhat from the true case in an effort to represent the *important* phenomena in a *tractable* model.

Early economists met this challenge by examining individual markets assuming that prices in all other markets remained fixed as alterations were made in the market in question. But this assumption is unacceptable for those markets that are closely related to the market in question. For example, if the price of beef is increased sharply by a tightening of import quotas, assumptions that cattle, pork, and feed grain prices remain unchanged seem inappropriate.

A more acceptable yet tractable approach based on the results in this chapter is to choose a subset of markets from the entire economy that is affected in important ways by contemplated policy changes in the market in question. This subset of markets should be made as large as possible while maintaining tractability. And generally, the more important the relationship between a distant market and the market in question, the more tractable a model involving that distant market should be. That is, more important relationships are apt to generate data that make those relationships discernible.

Once such a subset of markets is determined, a reasonable approach in the context of practical possibilities is to treat that subset of markets as an economy in and of itself. Determinants of that economy would consist of prices in markets outside the designated subset of markets (which can possibly be summarized by index prices) plus government policy instruments and natural, social, and political phenomena which affect the subset of markets directly. In this context, the estimated welfare quantities would capture effects for all individuals involved directly in the subset of markets and, by assumption (or econometric implication) all other welfare effects are unimportant.

Consider, for example, the problem of relaxing beef import quotas. The direct effects of such a change in policy are experienced by beef consumers and by restaurants and fast food chains who buy imported beef (for more completeness, wholesalers and retailers could also be considered along with consumers). However, with an increased supply of foreign beef, domestic suppliers of meat may find reduced demand for their products and these effects must also be considered. Suppose that one either postulates or determines through econometric means that the other important effects are experienced by meat packers who find reduced demand for both their beef and pork products, by feedlot operators, hog producers, and cow-calf producers who find a related reduced demand for their live animals by meat packers, and finally, by feed grain producers who find the reduced demand transmitted to the feed grain market by reduced activity in feeding hogs and cattle.

This intermarket structure is represented in Figure 9.12 where each circle represents a group of decision makers and each line segment between two circles represents a market. The circle at the top end of each line segment is the demander and the circle at the bottom end of each line segment is the supplier in the associated market. By estimating a supply and demand equation for each market, which is sensitive to the other prices faced by the relevant group of

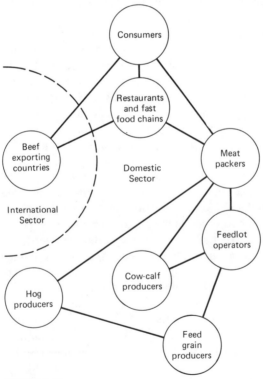

FIGURE 9.12

decision makers, one obtains a system of equations that allows computation of the effects of various levels of quotas on prices, quantities traded, and ordinary consumer and producer surpluses in each market. Thus, one can determine the overall welfare effect, as well as the distribution of welfare effects, among the groups of decision makers represented in Figure 9.12 to the extent that ordinary surpluses approximate willingness to pay. Alternatively, one can estimate equilibrium demand for beef imports (by consumers, restaurants, and fast food chains combined) by using as determinants those factors that are exogenous to the entire set of domestic markets represented in Figure 9.12 (such as the wage rate of labor in the meat packing industry, the price of fertilizer for feed grain producers, and so on). By the results for the segmented market case in Section D.2, the change in equilibrium consumer surplus associated with this general equilibrium demand captures the net welfare effect of a quota change on all domestic concerns assuming prices in other markets not represented in Figure 9.12 are truly unaffected.[17]

This discussion of the beef-import quota problem is far from complete. For example, the livestock feeding sector is a highly dynamic one with long lags in adjustment because of the time required to carry animals to maturity. These characteristics of the problem likely make the dynamic considerations discussed further in Chapter 13 and Appendix C crucial. The present example, however, provides a flavor for the type of equilibrium analyses that are practically possible in the context of results in this chapter and serves to illustrate that applied economic welfare analyses need not be subject to criticisms of ignoring important effects in other markets when those effects are econometrically discernible. For a further discussion of empirical considerations in estimating equilibrium welfare effects, see Appendix D and particularly Section D.4.

9.6   CONCLUSIONS

Based on the results of this chapter, rather comprehensive applied welfare analysis is possible. Depending on empirical conditions, all of the private social welfare effects of a proposed new or altered government policy can be measured completely, at least in an approximate sense, in the single market, which is thereby distorted or in which a distortion is altered. If the policy introduces or alters several distortions, approximate measurement of all private effects is possible by considering the changes sequentially in the respective markets they affect directly (path independency holds in terms of the exact results relating to

---

[17]Incidentally, this net effect, plus the change in producer surplus associated with supply from beef exporting countries, should be the same as the sum of changes in ordinary surpluses over all the markets in Figure 9.12. This equivalence, however, will be obtained in practice only when appropriate specifications are used; see Section D.4 for a further discussion.

compensated consumer adjustments). The determination of all governmental effects is more troublesome and requires measurement in all markets in which government revenues or losses are being realized for exact results. Since changes in all prices may be induced by a single distortion, determination of the welfare effects for individual firms, industries, consumers, or consumer groups generally requires measuring all of their ordinary (compensated, to be exact, in the consumer case) supply and demand curves and then calculating the sum of changes in their surpluses by imposing price changes sequentially or, in the firm or industry case, by measuring the overall change in surplus associated with their demand or supply for an essential output or input, respectively (see Appendix B for some alternative but related possibilities).

Drawing upon both the theoretical and the econometric results outlined in this chapter, fairly accurate estimates of welfare effects can in some cases be developed by estimating supply and demand only in those markets where distortions change. In this way, welfare effects consist of areas between price lines rather than between shifting supply curves or shifting demand curves and, thus, the property of more accurate estimation suggested by Section 8.9 is apparently applicable. The discussion indicates that problems of multicollinearity will generally be less acute when this approach is taken although problems of specification may be more severe.

This chapter has dealt with the possibilities of estimating and using equilibrium supply and demand curves. Depending on how the determinants of supplies and demands are defined, the generality of welfare effects estimated from supply and demand curves appears to depend directly on the generality with which determinants of supply and demand are specified for econometric estimation. These considerations suggest that the consumer and producer triangles may be used to evaluate the welfare effects of changes on a very extensive basis rather than on a very partial basis, as has been presumed in much of the classical welfare economics literature. With this discussion in mind, the results go a long way toward making the general equilibrium theoretical considerations of Chapters 2 and 3 possible at an empirical level of analysis.

10

The Welfare Economics
of Imperfect Competition

The theory of perfect competition and perfectly competitive markets underlies a great deal of economic thinking. To this point, this book has been based on the assumption of perfectly competitive markets. In many markets, however, the assumptions of competition break down. Market participants often do not have perfect information. More important, goods are often not homogeneous, and the number of buyers or sellers is not large. Sometimes entry into an industry is blocked for one reason or another. If these variations from competitive assumptions are not serious, a market may still behave essentially *as if* it were perfectly competitive. If so, the foregoing competitive theory may be a sufficient basis for welfare analysis. If such variations from competitive assumptions are serious, however, some alternative theoretical considerations are necessary. Such theories fall generally under the heading of imperfect competition. The economic welfare implications of some alternative cases of imperfect competition are examined in this chapter.

Throughout this and succeeding chapters, little distinction is made between the cases where supplies and demands are ordinary, compensated, equilibrium, or compensated equilibrium relationships. The reason is that such distinctions needlessly complicate the discussion whereas the theoretical concepts can apply to many levels of generality. Except in a few cases as noted where the differences are important the reader should simply bear in mind that the conclusions hold with respect to as broad a group as for which adjustments are considered in the definition of the supply or demand and that conclusions are only approximate in cases of noncompensated curves involving consumer or

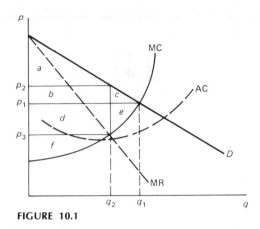

FIGURE 10.1

resource supplier responses. The related empirical considerations thus follow the discussion in Sections 8.8, 8.9, and 9.5.

10.1 THE SIMPLE MONOPOLY MODEL

The simplest and most distinctive case of imperfect competition is that of monopoly. *Pure monopoly* is a market situation in which there is a single seller of a product for which no good substitutes exist. Thus, pure monopoly is a polar case just as perfect competition is a polar case of the opposite nature.

A simple monopoly model is given in Figure 10.1. The demand for the monopolist's product is D. Average cost for the monopolist is AC, and marginal cost is MC. If the monopolist acts as a competitor, the industry output is q_1 and price p_1 prevails. However, under monopoly pricing, output is less and the price is higher. The monopolist maximizes profits by equating the marginal cost MC with the marginal revenue from sales represented by MR—not the demand curve D.[1] The monopolist then charges price p_2 and produces output q_2. (*Note that sales decline when price is increased.*)

In terms of the welfare effects of moving from the competitive solution to one of monopoly, there is a gain in short-run profits or producer quasi-rent from area $d + e + f$ to area $d + b + f$. However, there is a loss in consumer welfare from area $a + b + c$ to area a. Furthermore, there is a net loss from monopoly of area $c + e$. This area is often called the "deadweight loss" from monopoly. As in Section 8.5, the general conclusion is again that gainers gain less than the amount that losers lose when a distortion from the competitive solution is introduced. In the case above, if antitrust authorities could not or would not be

---

[1]For a simple presentation of the monopoly solution, see Richard H. Leftwich, *The Price System and Resource Allocation*, 7th ed. (Hinsdale, Ill.: The Dryden Press, 1979), Chap. 11.

willing to break up the monopolist, consumers would be better off to band together and bribe the monopolist to behave as a competitor.

In the model above, demand is viewed as the demand for a product in a region or country; and the industry is in private hands. However, the model in Figure 10.1 can also be viewed as a simple model of an export cartel. In this case, D is the demand by importing countries and MC is the supply curve for exporting countries. If some of the good is produced in the importing country, D can be viewed as an excess demand curve; similarly, if some of the good is consumed in the exporting countries, exporters' supply can be viewed as an excess supply. Under free trade, the importing countries import q_1 of the good and pay price p_1.

Under a cartel arrangement, the exporters can ban together to restrict exports and raise price. This can be done as a matter of government policies in exporting countries by setting an "optimal export tax" equal to $p_2 - p_3$ per unit of export. In this case, competitive suppliers in the exporting countries and competitive consumers in the importing nations would be induced to reduce trade to q_2, where marginal consumer willingness to pay is just equal to the marginal cost of exporting plus the marginal tax. Thus, market participants in exporting countries suffer a loss in welfare from area $d + e + f$ to area f; market participants in the importing countries suffer a welfare loss from area $a + b + c$ to area a. However, tax proceeds in exporting countries increase by area $b + d$, so the net effect on exporting countries is a gain from area $d + e + f$ to area $b + d + f$. Again, the net effect is a welfare loss of area $c + e$, which suggests that everyone could be made better off if importing countries could bribe exporters not to impose export taxes.

The model in Figure 10.1 is also useful in demonstrating the effects of cartel arrangements such as the Organization of Petroleum Exporting Countries (OPEC) where the exporting countries band together in determining an export price, say, p_2. The model thus demonstrates that, if importers cannot successfully block an export cartel in a major product such as oil, both exporters and importers would be better off if importers bribed exporters not to form a cartel. (Of course, matters of political feasibility also require consideration.)

10.2   THE SIMPLE MONOPSONY MODEL

While the case with only one seller of a good is called monopoly, a corresponding case with only one buyer of a good can also be considered. *Pure monopsony* is the term used to describe a market situation with one buyer of a product for which no good substitutes exist.

Consider the model in Figure 10.2, where S represents the supply curve facing a monopsonistic firm and MRP is the marginal revenue of product that the monopsonist gains from sale in its output market. The marginal outlay curve associated with the supply curve is given by MO and gives the marginal change in expenditure for good q which the monopsonist must make for

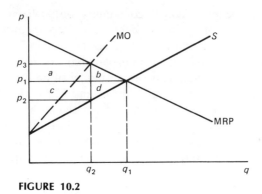

FIGURE 10.2

successive units of q (much like a marginal revenue curve in Section 10.1 gives the marginal change in total revenue for the monopolist of selling successive units of output). The monopsonist maximizes its profits by equating marginal outlay and marginal revenue of product, thus purchasing quantity q_2 at price p_2. Of course, if the buyer alternatively acts competitively, then quantity q_1 is traded at price p_1. The welfare effects of monopsony are thus a loss of area $c + d$ for producers and a gain of area $c - b$ for the monopsonist for a net loss of area $b + d$. Again, the triangular area $b + d$ is referred to as a deadweight loss and suggests that producers could afford to bribe the monopsonist to act competitively and still be better off.

As in the simple monopoly case, the monopsony case can be viewed as a model of an importing cartel. In this case the net or excess competitive supply among all exporting countries is given by S, and the net or excess competitive demand among all importing countries in the cartel is given by MRP. By lowering bid prices from competitive levels (p_1) to p_2 and reducing the quantity demanded to q_2, a gain for importing countries of area $c - b$ is possible. This result could be achieved in practice by means of imposing trade tariffs in the importing countries. The optimal import tariff is given by $p_3 - p_2$ per unit according to Figure 10.2.

10.3 THE CASES OF OLIGOPOLY AND OLIGOPSONY

The monopoly and monopsony cases of the preceding sections are extreme cases where only one buyer or seller for a product exists. A more common case is where there are several buyers or sellers of a product that may or may not be homogeneous among firms. A group of firms comprising the total supply in a given market is called an *oligopoly* if at least one of the selling firms is large enough to influence the overall market price for sales and thus affect other firms single handedly. A group of firms comprising the total demand in a given market is called an *oligopsony* if at least one of the buying firms is large enough to influence the overall market price for purchases.

Many theories of oligopoly (oligopsony) have been developed.[2] A discussion of all such theories and the economic welfare analysis of each is too lengthy to undertake at this point. Alternatively, consider one of the most common and tractable theories—that of dominant firm or dominant share price leadership. Oligopolistic dominant share price leadership is described by Figure 10.3, where D represents market demand for the product. The dominant share may be composed of one or several firms that collusively band together to raise price and restrict output to maximize their joint profits. The associated marginal cost of the dominant share is MC_d and is derived as the horizontal summation of marginal cost curves over firms that are part of the dominant share. In addition, there are additional firms (few or many) outside of the dominant share that do not have a direct influence on market price either because they are individually too small or because they fear retaliation by the dominant share if they attempt to affect market price directly. Hence, these firms (called price followers) act competitively, simply maximizing profits by taking the price set by the dominant share as given. The aggregate supply from all price-following firms is represented by S_f.

In this context the behavior of the dominant share is determined as follows. First, horizontally subtract the supply S_f for the price-following firms from the market demand curve D to determine the effective demand D_d facing the dominant share. Then determine the marginal revenue MR_d associated with D_d.

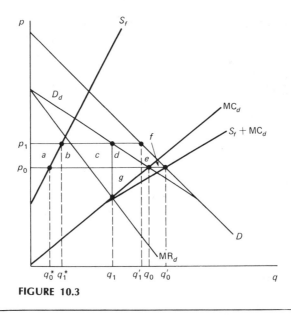

FIGURE 10.3

[2]Kalman J. Cohen and Richard M. Cyert, *Theory of the Firm: Resource Allocation in a Market Economy* (Englewood Cliffs, N. J.: Prentice-Hall, Inc., 1965).

The profit-maximizing price and quantity for the dominant share are p_1 and q_1, respectively, as determined by the intersection of MC_d and MR_d. This compares with a competitive price and quantity of p_0 and q_0, respectively, by the dominant share. The output of the price-following firms is $q_0^* = q_0' - q_0$ when the dominant share acts competitively and is $q_1^* = q_1' - q_1$ when the dominant share exercises market power. The welfare effects of oligopolistic pricing are thus a gain of area $a + b + c - g$ for the dominant share, a gain of area $a =$ area $e + f$ for the price-following firms, a loss of area $a + b + c + d + e + f$ for consumers, and thus an overall net loss of area $d + g$. The case of dominant share price leadership oligopoly is thus very similar to monopoly once the excess demand curve D_d facing the dominant share is determined.

The case of oligopsony is treated similarly by simply turning the curves in Figure 10.3 upside down and reversing the supply and demand notation as well as the marginal cost and marginal revenue notation. In this way, one finds an excess supply curve facing a dominant share, and the remaining analysis becomes very similar to the case of monopsony.

Because these cases of oligopoly and oligopsony are similar to monopoly and monopsony, respectively, the remainder of this chapter focuses on monopoly and monopsony. Extension to these cases of oligopoly and oligopsony follows in a straightforward fashion.

10.4   DEMAND AND COST CONDITIONS

In studying specific industries, a crucial assumption used in the foregoing models is that both the demand and the cost conditions are the same under competition as under monopoly. The importance of this assumption is demonstrated in Figure 10.4. In Figure 10.4(a), costs under monopoly are assumed to be lower than under competition, perhaps because of lower costs of coordination or information acquisition. The marginal cost schedule under competition is MC, while MC' is the marginal cost schedule under monopoly.[3] Thus, in comparing monopoly to competition, the gain of area c must be considered in addition to the usual efficiency loss. Thus, if area c is greater than area b, monopoly is preferred to competition on efficiency grounds.

Suppose, on the other hand, that costs under monopoly are higher than under competition because of an increased tendency for waste with greater profits. For example, it has been argued that costs may be higher under monopoly because a monopolist fails to minimize costs in the absence of the "competitive stick." Thus, in Figure 10.4(a), suppose MC is the monopolist's cost curve, and MC' is the competitive cost curve.. The net loss from monopoly power is then area $a + b + c + d$.[4]

---

[3]This case was developed by Oliver E. Williamson, "Economics as an Antitrust Defense: The Welfare Tradeoffs," *American Economic Review*, Vol. 58, No. 1 (March 1968), pp. 18–36.

[4]This case was suggested by William S. Comanor and Harvey Leibenstein, "Alloca-

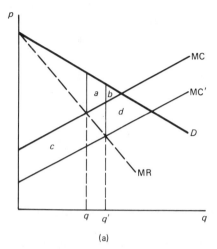

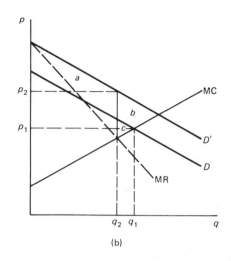

FIGURE 10.4

The case where demand differs with market structure is depicted in Figure 10.4(b). Suppose, for example, that the monopolist is much more aggressive than a competitive industry in selling the product and creates demand through advertising. Thus, suppose that demand for the monopolist is represented by D', whereas demand is D under competition. The competitive output is q_1, which sells for a price of p_1. Under monopoly, output is q_2 and price is p_2. The welfare effects of monopoly are thus a net gain for society of area $a - c$. Of course, similar considerations could be made in the case of monopsony, oligopoly, or oligopsony as well.

10.5 ECONOMIES OF SCALE

One case where monopolies tend to develop is when average costs decline substantially at larger levels of output, or in other words where economies of scale exist. Economies of scale arise from several sources, including technical (e.g., economies of scale in assembly-line automobile plants) and pecuniary (e.g., buying inputs in bulk rather than on a small-scale basis) sources. The extent to which economies of scale exist is industry specific. As an example, there may be large economies of scale in beef-packing plants but few economies of scale in the production of strawberries.

The importance of this issue is discussed with reference to Figure 10.5. Consider, first, the industry or firm long-run average cost curve AC. Clearly, from an efficiency standpoint, society is better off with output q_0 produced by a firm having costs AC* and MC* (under the assumption for the moment of

tive Efficiency, X-Efficiency and the Measurement of Welfare Losses," *Economica*, Vol. 36, No. 143 (August 1969), pp. 304–9.

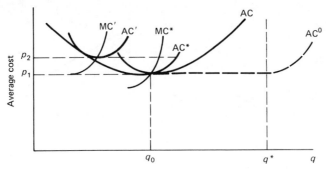

FIGURE 10.5

competition—price then being p_1) than with the same output produced by several firms having costs MC′ and AC′.

Suppose, alternatively, that a single firm produces output $q*$. If the planning curve is AC, society could do better from an efficiency standpoint by "splitting up" the firm into smaller producing units in order to produce the output under maximum efficiency. However, if the cost curve were AC^0, output $q*$ may be produced just as efficiently with one firm as with several. From a "market power" position, society may prefer to break up the industry into smaller units to avoid monopoly losses even though it has nothing to gain on cost-efficiency grounds.

The slope of the long-run cost curve is vital in any discussion of antitrust policy or monopoly power control. With fewer economies of scale, less social justification can be made for large firms. Another important point relates to the distinction between price surveillance policies versus breaking up large businesses. In Figure 10.5, suppose that the firm with costs MC* and AC* charges price p_2 because of its monopoly power and earns excess profits. Ideally, society should try to force the monopoly to charge price p_1 and have the industry produce output q_0 rather than keep price at p_2 and break the industry into small units with costs MC′ and AC′. Regulating monopolies in this case may involve keeping the economies of scale intact by not breaking up the industry; rather, a competitive price may be imposed as supposedly is the case in a regulated utility industry. Whether or not it is possible to prevent large companies from engaging in monopolistic practices in individual cases is another matter. In some cases, perhaps the only solution is to break up large firms into smaller units.

10.6 MARKET INTERMEDIARIES

In the equilibrium models presented in Chapters 2 and 3 the "actors" in the economic system are producers and consumers. Market intermediaries are not considered. However, goods seldom move directly from producers to consumers. Marketing firms (either private or public) buy the goods from producers and eventually sell them, usually in a modified form, to consumers. For example, a Kansas wheat farmer rarely sells wheat directly to consumers in the Soviet Union; the actual trade is carried out by multinational private grain companies.

In elementary monopoly theory, one views the monopolist also as the producer of the good. However, monopoly power can exist in an industry because of power in marketing a good even though the industry producing the good is competitive. As an example, in producing wheat in North America, no single producer can influence aggregate market price. However, this does not necessarily imply that the pricing of wheat is competitive since, to reach this conclusion, one must examine the structure, conduct, and performance of the associated marketing board in Canada and the large private grain traders in the United States.

In this section, markets are viewed as consisting of producers, consumers, government, and marketing intermediaries.[5] How pricing can depend on the type of market intermediary is demonstrated. The following discussion is not intended to imply that all marketing boards necessarily behave as monopolists or that private firms behave as "pure middlemen." Rather, several extremes are presented which can serve as a basis for interpretation of observed market behavior. This behavior may occur in some industries and not in others and hence is an empirical question.

Producer Marketing Boards and Associations

Many commodities, especially those of an agricultural nature, are distributed through marketing boards or associations. A marketing board is an association charged with the responsibility of marketing a product on behalf of a given market group—in this case, producers. In countries such as Canada, Great Britain, and Israel, marketing boards are widespread.[6] A producer marketing board has many different objectives, depending on its type and the country in which it is located. Among its objectives are price stability, equity to producers, enhancement of producer returns, and the provision of tax revenue to governments. Only two objectives are considered here: maximizing producer returns and providing revenue to governments.

To demonstrate this case, the demand for the product is represented by D, and the supply is represented by S in Figure 10.6(a). Suppose that the industry producing the good is perfectly competitive, and assume zero marketing costs

---

[5]This characterization of market participants was suggested by Richard E. Just, Andrew Schmitz, and David Zilberman, "Price Controls and Optimal Export Policies under Alternative Market Structures," *American Economic Review,* Vol. 69, No. 4 (September 1979), pp. 706–14.

[6]Sidney Hoos, ed., *Agricultural Marketing Boards: An International Perspective* (Cambridge, Mass.: Ballinger Publishing Company, 1979).

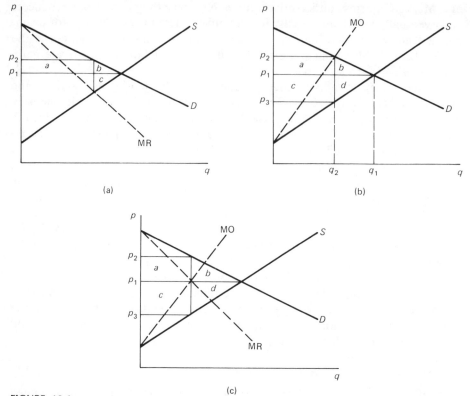

FIGURE 10.6

for the board. If the board's objective is to maximize producer returns, it behaves as a monopolist and charges price p_2 to consumers instead of p_1. If the board is to be successful in this effort, it must restrict output by such devices as production quotas on producers. In doing so, the board—operating in the best interest of producers—extracts economic surplus from consumers and returns it to producers. As in the monopoly case discussed above, this leads to inefficiency since a loss of area $a + b$ must be imposed on consumers in order for producers to benefit by area $a - c$.

Suppose, instead, that the board is created by government and seeks to gain tax revenues from the producing sector in order to benefit consumers. This case is shown in Figure 10.6(b). The government, acting in the best interest of consumers (assuming that tax revenues are redistributed to consumers) will extract surplus from producers to give to consumers. The board will thus behave as a monopsonist—not as a monopolist. The board will equate its marginal outlay curve (MO) to the demand curve. It will charge consumers price p_2 and pay producers price p_3. Clearly, producers are worse off than under competition, and consumers are better off provided that the loss in consumer surplus is more than offset by the additional government revenue, which is $(p_2 - p_1)q_2$. Specifically, producers lose area $c + d$, and consumers (including benefits of redistributed taxes) gain area $c - b$. The overall effect of such a marketing board, however, is a loss of area $b + d$.

In each of these cases, there is a welfare loss from the operation of a marketing board since output is restricted below the competitive level. Who gains and who loses from the operation of the board depends on the board's objective, which depends partly on the power given to it by government.

Consumerism

Recent years have experienced an increase in "consumerism." Many argue that consumer groups and consumer marketing boards are organized to provide "countervailing" power to big business. This may well be the case. However, conceptually, consumerism can lead to welfare losses just as producer and government monopolies can. Consider again Figure 10.6(b). Under competition, consumers would pay price p_1 for quantity q_1. However, if they can exert monopsony power in the market by forming a cooperative or similar organization, they can be made better off than under competition. By behaving as a monopsonist, they extract surplus from producers for themselves. The cooperative, by charging its members p_2, gives rise to a loss in consumer welfare of area $a + b$; but this is more than offset by the area $a + c$, which is the difference between the amount consumers pay and the amount producers receive. Of course, the cooperative profits of area $a + c$ must be redistributed in such a way as not to affect marginal behavior in order to attain quantity q_2. If dividends are paid on the basis of purchases, consumers will buy more in order to receive a larger share of the high dividends until aggregate quantity increases to q_1 and no dividends are paid. Thus, the mere presence of a large consumer cooperative does not necessarily imply imperfect competition. This example points out that how the economic surplus is distributed depends on who *exercises* power in the marketplace, regardless of who *has* power in the marketplace.

The Pure Middleman

The pure middleman case was one of the first monopoly models developed and encompasses elements of both monopoly and monopsony power.[7] In Figure 10.6(c), the competitive price is p_1, S represents supply by an industry made up of many small producing firms, and D represents demand by many small consumers. For simplicity, zero marketing costs are assumed. Suppose that a private marketing firm that buys the product from producers and sells to consumers desires to maximize profits. At the extreme, the firm will act as *both*

---

[7]This case is due to Abba P. Lerner, "The Concept of Monopoly and the Measurement of Monopoly Power," *Review of Economic Studies*, Vol. 1, Nos. 1–3 (1933–34), pp. 157–75.

a monopolist and monopsonist. It will extract surplus from *both* producers and consumers by setting consumer price at p_2 and producer price at p_3 (which corresponds to the intersection of MO and MR). The monopolist–monopsonist thus makes excess profits of area $a + c$. Producers lose area $c + d$, and consumers lose area $a + b$. The deadweight welfare loss to society is area $b + d$. Note that the loss with both monopoly and monopsony power exercised is greater than if only one of these were exercised. In this context, two distortions give rise to a greater welfare loss than one distortion.

An Example

An example can serve to illustrate the dramatic differences in economic welfare consequences of the three cases discussed in this section. Suppose that the excess demand for crude oil by the United States is represented implicitly by

$$p = 60 - q + 5m$$

and the marginal cost of producing crude oil in the Organization of Petroleum Exporting Countries (OPEC) is given implicitly by

$$p = 16 + 2q - 0.02w$$

where

p = price of crude oil in dollars per barrel
q = quantity of crude oil in 100 million barrels
m = total disposable personal income in the United States in trillion dollars
w = index of costs of oil production in OPEC countries.

For simplicity, suppose that demand by other countries and consumption in OPEC countries can be ignored. Also, suppose that $m = 2$ and $w = 300$ so with current levels of determinants, competitive demand and supply are given implicitly by

$$p = 70 - q$$
$$p = 10 + 2q$$

respectively, as depicted in Figure 10.7. With competitive trading, market equilibrium is found by solving the demand and supply equations simultaneously for p and q, which obtains $p = 50$ and $q = 20$ (see Figure 10.7).

Suppose, however, that the OPEC countries unite and sell monopolistically to the United States. Their marginal revenue[8] from sales to the United States is given by

$$MR = 70 - 2q$$

---

[8]Marginal revenue can be found by multiplying q by the price indicated by the demand curve,

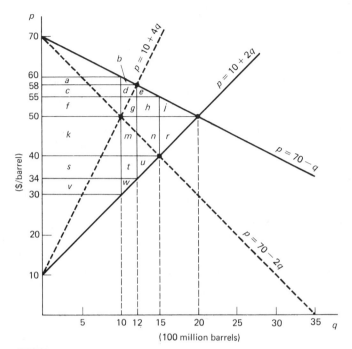

FIGURE 10.7

Equating this marginal revenue to their marginal cost given by $10 + 2q$ implies that $q = 15$, and at $q = 15$, the United States is willing to pay price $p = 55$ (obtained by substituting $q = 15$ into the U.S. demand curve). At the same time, the marginal cost of production falls from 50 to 40 (obtained by substituting the respective quantities into the marginal cost relationship $10 + 2q$). Following Figure 10.7, the welfare effects of OPEC cartelization are as follows. The United States loses area $f + g + h + j = 87.5$ or \$8.75 billion (note that areas in Figure 10.7 are measured in 100 million dollars). The OPEC countries gain area $f + g + h - r = 50$ or \$5 billion.

Suppose alternatively that, instead of OPEC countries forming a cartel, the United States were to set an optimal import tariff or set up a marketing board to exercise monopsony power in crude oil purchases. Optimality for the United States occurs where the marginal outlay[9] intersects the demand curve where marginal outlay is

$$pq = 70q - q^2$$

and then differentiating with respect to q,

$$\text{MR} = \frac{\partial pq}{\partial q} = 70 - 2q$$

[9]Marginal outlay can be found by multiplying q by the price indicated by the supply curve,

227

$$MO = 10 + 4q$$

These two relationships intersect where $p = 58$ and $q = 12$ (see Figure 10.7). The OPEC countries would be willing to supply this quantity at a price $p = 34$ (obtained by substituting $q = 12$ into the OPEC supply relationship). Thus, a U.S. marketing board should offer \$34 per barrel for crude oil, or an import tariff of \$24 per barrel ($58 - 34$) should be imposed. Compared to a purely competitive market, the welfare effects are as follows. The United States gains area $k + m + s + t - e - h - j = 160$ or \$16 billion, while OPEC loses area $k + m + n + r + s + t + u = 256$ *or* \$25.6 billion. The reason these welfare effects are considerably larger than the welfare effects of cartelization is that the supply curve is more inelastic than the demand curve (in an absolute sense).

Finally, suppose that instead of OPEC forming a cartel or the United States adopting an optimal import tariff (or marketing board) policy, the international trade is carried out by a large private company who buys monopsonistically from OPEC and sells monopolistically to the United States. The company profits are maximized by equating marginal outlay and marginal revenue which implies

$$10 + 4q = 70 - 2q$$

or $q = 10$. The OPEC countries will supply $q = 10$ at $p = 30$ while the United States will buy $q = 10$ at $p = 60$ (Figure 10.7). At these prices, the private company earns a profit of \$30 per barrel on one billion barrels for a total of \$30 billion. Compared to a competitive market, the United States (excluding the private trading company) loses area $a + b + c + d + e + f + g + h + j = 150$ or \$15 billion while OPEC countries lose area $k + m + n + r + s + t + u + v + w = 300$ or \$30 billion. Thus, the welfare implications of the three cases differ widely.

10.7 LABOR UNIONS

Another area in which the theory of imperfect competition finds application is in labor negotiations. The extent to which labor is organized in the form of unions varies from country to country. For example, the percentage of the work force in Great Britain belonging to unions is much greater than that in the United States. Yet even in the United States the numbers are significant (in 1975 over 20 million U.S. workers belonged to unions); also, there have been

---

$$pq = 10q + 2q^2$$

and then differentiating with respect to q,

$$MO = \frac{\partial pq}{\partial q} = 10 + 4q$$

recent attempts to form new unions. For example, farm workers in the United States historically have not been unionized. But a serious effort has been made over the last decade to organize laborers in this sector to bargain for higher wages and better living conditions.

A Simple Model

Consider Figure 10.8(a), where w is the wage rate, S is the supply curve of labor, and q is the quantity of labor supplied. The derived demand curve for labor is represented by D. Under competitive equilibrium, w_1 is the wage rate and q_1 denotes the number of workers employed. In the simplest case, if a union were established to raise the real wage rate for the workers in this

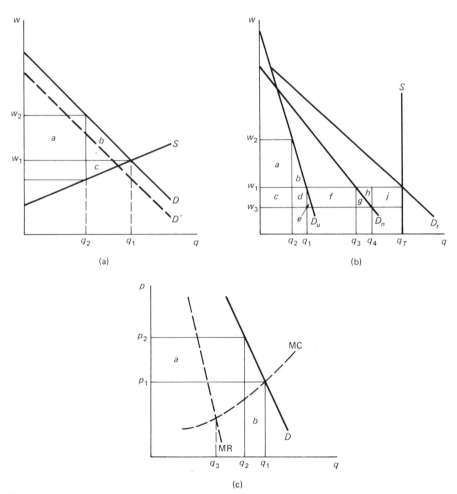

FIGURE 10.8

particular industry, employment would drop. If wage rate w_2 were negotiated, only q_2 would be employed in the industry, and $q_1 - q_2$ workers would have to seek employment elsewhere.[10] For the workers now represented by the union, the total wage bill increases by area a. This is desirable for the workers who remain in the industry but not for those who must seek work elsewhere; the workers who must seek employment elsewhere suffer a loss of area c.

The foregoing model can also be used to study the impact of restricted entry by unions for workers entering a profession. Suppose that a union restricts the entry of people into the medical profession, dentistry, plumbing, and the like. Restricted entry has a positive or beneficial effect for persons already in the profession and those who gain entry but not for those excluded. Also, if unions restrict entry, there is a loss to society. Area $b + c$ reflects the extent of loss where area $a + b$ consists of the loss to consumers using the service provided by the industry and area c is the loss to the workers who, because of union restrictions, cannot enter the industry.

Another possible impact of the threat or reality of unionization is to bring about technological change which displaces workers; hence, the derived demand under unionization may be D' instead of D. If this is the case, the gains from unionization may be less than anticipated, even for those who gain entry into the unionized labor force.

Two Markets

To extend the model described above, consider Figure 10.8(b).[11] Suppose that the supply of labor is perfectly inelastic at S and that D_u, D_n, and D_t represent the demand for labor in the unionized sector, the nonunionized sector, and the two combined. Under competition the wage rate is w_1. If union wages increase to w_2, employment in the unionized sector declines from q_1 to q_2. As a result, employment in the nonunionized sector increases from q_3 to q_4, where $q_4 - q_3 = q_1 - q_2$, so that wages drop to w_3. As a result, the total wage bill drops by area $d + e + f + g + h + j - a$, which is a welfare loss for labor as a whole in the case of perfectly inelastic labor supply even though those who remain in the unionized labor force gain area a. Producers who hire labor also lose area $a + b$ in the unionized industry but gain area $c + d + e + f + g$ in nonunionized industries. The net welfare effect is thus a loss of area $b + h$ (note that area $c = $ area j by construction). Again, it is not surprising that the overall effect of partial unionization is an economic loss since it represents a distortion from the competitive equilibrium.

---

[10]The assumption here is that the amount of work per worker remains fixed while varying the total amount of labor.

[11]This case was developed by Albert Rees, "The Effects of Unions on Resource Allocation," in *Readings in Labor Market Analysis*, ed. John F. Burton, Jr., et al. (New York: Holt, Rinehart and Winston, 1971).

Consider, finally, the simple model in Figure 10.8(c), which depicts the producers' output market rather than their labor input market. This model shows that, if a union can control industrial production, it will prefer demand for the product to be inelastic.[12] That is, if the labor union can cause a small reduction in output from, say, q_1 to q_2, that reduction will have a greater impact on price when producers' output demand is more inelastic. If the union controls production to the extent that it could close down the industry with a strike, employers will be willing to bargain with the union concerning who should get the increase in sales revenue of area $a - b$.

However, it is one thing for a union to control output to the extent of having economic power over the industry. It is quite another matter if the union cannot control output sufficiently so that the employer will bargain with the union (agriculture appears to be a case in point partly because the supply of farm workers in many labor-intensive crops is wage elastic). Note in Figure 10.8(c) that if the union can only reduce output from q_1 to q_3 due to a strike, producers become better off since the strike actually places them in a monopoly position. For the union to be effective, it has to reduce output beyond q_3. Hence, whereas an inelastic demand is desirable once the union can completely control output, it may be undesirable otherwise, since it requires the union to restrict output substantially before employers are willing to bargain with workers.[13] The analysis in Figure 10.8(c) points out the importance of considering extended market effects as suggested in Chapter 9.

10.8 ANTITRUST ECONOMICS

Another important area of application of the welfare economics of imperfect competition is in legal proceedings related to control of market power. There have been literally thousands of lawsuits brought against entire industries or certain firms within industries for price fixing. These suits have been initiated both by the private sector and by federal monopoly regulatory agencies such as the Federal Trade Commission. The number of suits appears to be growing at an exponential rate which makes the integration of law and economics an important area of inquiry. There are, in fact, some interesting contrasts, as shown earlier, between estimating the aggregate welfare effects from monopoly pricing and determining damages in individual lawsuits. For example, the amount of damages awarded in antitrust cases is often determined by seemingly

---

[12]This case is due to F. R. Warren-Boulton, "Vertical Control by Labor Unions," *American Economic Review*, Vol. 67 (June 1977), pp. 309–22.

[13]This result is pointed out by Colin Carter, Darrell Hueth, John Mamer, and Andrew Schmitz, "Labor Unions and Grower Returns: The Case of Lettuce," University of California, Department of Agricultural and Resource Economics, Working Paper No. 83, Berkeley, Calif., 1980.

arbitrary means. Figure 10.9 illustrates the problem in two different cases, which differ by whether or not the marketing firm exercises monopoly as well as monopsony power. Suppose that a group of competitive producers with supply S sues a marketing firm for buying at a "fixed price" p_3 instead of a competitive price p_1. One could compute the competitive solution and the monopsony solution and hence the excess profits given by area $a + c$. From an economic standpoint, however, it is not clear that the producers should receive all the excess profits, since they lose only area $c + d$ as a result of price fixing; part of the loss from monopsony pricing is borne by consumers (i.e., the loss in consumer surplus is area $a + b$). However, the monopsonist's unfair gains are not sufficient to compensate both consumers and producers according to their losses if a court so ordered; therefore, how the settlement should be made is unclear. Court rulings usually do not compensate consumers at all if producers win their lawsuits against a middleman. Furthermore, the comparison of Figure 10.9(a) and (b) shows that the extent of damages for producers depends on whether or not monopoly was exercised in the middleman's sales to consumers. Yet the weight of evidence in most court cases suggests that producers only sue for price fixing in their dealings with a middleman; any lawsuit for price fixing in the middleman's sales to consumers must normally be brought independently by consumers (or government regulatory agencies). Thus, even though the producers' damages may be area $c + d$ in Figure 10.9(b), they may recover only the smaller area $c + d$ in Figure 10.9(a).

To consider further peculiarities, suppose that three industries exist in a chain where the middle industry acts as a monopsonist as in Figure 10.9(a). Although price fixing in this case occurs on the input side, consumers lose area $a + b$. Thus, consumer losses are substantial even though the price fixing is not exercised directly against them; the monopsonist is, in effect, selling competitively to consumers. However, legal precedent does not suggest the possibility of, say, consumers filing suit against middlemen or processors for their price fixing against producers. Similar statements hold for the reverse case, where a

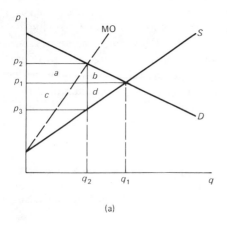

(a)

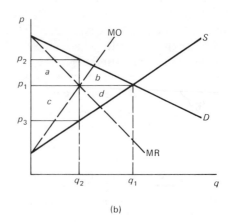

(b)

FIGURE 10.9

middleman buys competitively and sells as a monopolist; producers lose substantially even though the price fixing is exercised against consumers, yet legal precedent does not suggest the possibility of producers filing suit against processors and retailers for their price fixing in retail sales.

Similar problems are demonstrated by the famous "pass-through" ruling.[14] Stated simply, if three market groups A, B, and C are related in a chain—for example, beef producers, meat packers, and retail grocery chains—then individuals in A cannot sue C for price fixing; neither can individuals in C sue A. Such rulings are peculiar in the context of economic theory because effects of price fixing tend to be passed through market chains in varying degrees. Such a ruling often implies, for example, that consumers cannot sue producers for price fixing because processing firms handle the product before it is finally sold.

To consider this case in greater detail, suppose initially that an entire economic sector is competitive (i.e., only "normal profits" are being made by each industry in the sector). Now introduce monopoly pricing by industry A. If industries B and C remain competitive, a pass-through effect occurs since prices for industry C will increase because of a rise in "production costs" for industry B due to monopoly pricing by industry A. This effect is demonstrated in Figure 10.10, where in Figure 10.10(a), S is the supply of the input and D is the derived demand for the input and, in Figure 10.10(b), S' is the supply of the final product and D' represents final consumer demand. Under competition, the input quantity demanded is q_0 and its price is p_0. The competitive output market

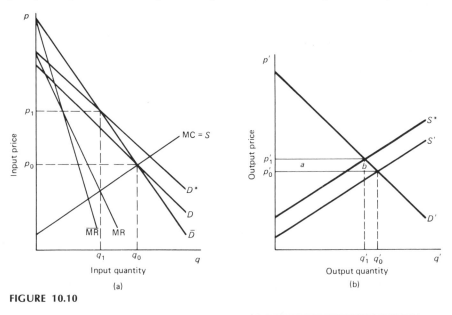

FIGURE 10.10

[14]See, for example, Elmer Schaefer, "Passing-On Theory in Antitrust Treble Damage Actions: An Economic and Legal Analysis," *William and Mary Law Review,* Vol. 16, No. 4 (Summer 1975), pp. 883–936.

equilibrium price and quantity are p_0' and q_0', respectively. Now suppose that monopoly power is created in the input market. Following the framework of Chapter 9, an increase in price in the input market causes supply to decline in the output market. This results in higher price in the output market, which, in turn, causes derived demand in the input market to increase somewhat so that eventually derived demand becomes D^* and output supply becomes S^*. As a result, price in the output market increases to p_1', and consumers suffer a loss of area $a + b$ as a result of monopolization of a market in which they do not deal directly.

Note that the price and quantity in the input market in this case thus change according to an equilibrium demand curve $\bar{D}$, which takes account of adjustments in other markets. This consideration suggests that a monopolist could maximize profits naively considering the demand curve D^* and its associated marginal revenue curve MR; or alternatively, the monopolist could maximize profits with respect to the equilibrium demand curve $\bar{D}$ and its associated marginal revenue $\overline{MR}$. Of course, the latter would be appropriate for true profit maximization and would generally entail larger welfare effects. Arguments quite similar to this could also be developed where, say, a consumer cooperative exercises monopsony in the output market. In such a case it maximizes consumer welfare by equating marginal consumer benefits to an equilibrium marginal outlay curve which takes account of input market adjustments. As a result, input suppliers would suffer welfare effects even though they are not involved in the same market as the monopsonist.

These cases suggest that a wide gap yet exists between legal practice and economic theory. But these problems may exist for some time because empirical methods have often not been sufficiently accurate to determine whether or not price-fixing practices have been followed. Traditionally, such investigations have attempted to rely on estimation of cost functions for which data are often unobservable or difficult to assimilate.[15] Without agreement on the extent of

---

[15] For a recent study that develops an approach of statistical testing for price-fixing practices based on observable market data alone, see Richard E. Just and Wen S. Chern, "Tomatoes, Technology, and Oligopsony," *Bell Journal of Economics,* Vol. 11, No. 2 (Autumn 1980), pp. 584–602. Alternatively, courts have attempted to verify whether *formal* collusive agreements have existed among firms (comprising a dominant share) in an industry. But as Adam Smith remarked, "People of the same trade seldom meet together, even for merriment and diversion, but the conversation ends in a conspiracy against the public, or in some contrivance to raise prices." In other words, social gatherings provide a vehicle by which informal gentlemen's agreements can be reached. But the consequences of such agreements can be as serious as with formal collusive agreements, and the illegality is just as great, even though proof in a court of law may be more difficult; see Adam Smith, *An Inquiry into the Nature and Causes of the Wealth of Nations,* 2 Vols. Edwin Cannan, ed. (London: Methuen and Company, Ltd., 1904). For a further discussion of the problems of making objective court rulings, see Richard Posner, "Oligopoly and the Antitrust Laws: A Suggested Approach," *Stanford Law Review,* Vol. 21 (June 1969), pp. 1562–1606.

price-fixing practices, little potential exists for agreement on the extent of damages.

10.9 SOME EMPIRICAL ESTIMATES OF THE SOCIAL COST OF MONOPOLY

Until recently, many of the estimates of monopoly effects in the United States presented a picture of very small monopoly costs both in terms of restricted output due to monopoly power of firms and in terms of restricted entry into the labor force due to unions. In 1954, Harberger estimated the efficiency welfare losses from monopoly for the United States to be 0.1 percent of gross national product.[16] These estimates established the idea that efficiency welfare losses from monopoly are insignificant.

More recent estimates suggest, however, that the social cost from monopoly power is quite high in some industries. In Table 10.1, estimates of social costs of market power are presented for the top 20 U.S. firms. The losses from market power associated with General Motors alone approach $2 billion. Thus, even though one may find that the aggregate effects of monopoly power are relatively small, the monopoly effects of any one firm or industry could be large in terms of the consumers and/or producers that such a firm or industry affects.

TABLE 10.1   Monopoly Welfare Losses by Firm
United States, Annual Average, 1963–66

Company	Social Loss (million dollars)	Company	Social Loss (million dollars)
1. General Motors	1,780.3	11. American Cyanamid Co.	240.8
2. American Telephone & Telegraph	1,025.0	12. Genesco, Inc.	292.6
3. Unilever	490.5	13. Exxon Corp.	197.8
4. Procter & Gamble	427.0	14. Colgate-Palmolive Co.	160.3
5. E. I. du Pont de Nemours	375.3	15. Chrysler Corp.	155.5
6. Ford Motor Co.	331.7	16. General Electric Co.	148.8
7. IBM	319.8	17. Pan American Airways	147.2
8. R. J. Reynolds Industries	278.8	18. Pacific Telephone & Telegraph	138.1
9. Sears, Roebuck and Co.	272.5	19. Gillette Co.	129.2
10. Eastman Kodak	258.5	20. Minnesota Mining & Manufacturing	129.1

Source: Keith Cowling and Dennis C. Mueller, "The Social Costs of Monopoly Power," The Economic Journal, Vol. 88, No. 352 (December 1978), p. 740.

[16] Arnold C. Harberger, "Monopoly and Resource Allocation," *American Economic Review, Proceedings*, Vol. 44 (May 1954), pp. 77–87. Harberger's estimates were also supported by David Schwartzman, "The Burden of Monopoly," *Journal of Political Economy*, Vol. 68, No. 6 (December 1960), pp. 627–30; F. M. Scherer, *Industrial Market Structure and Market Performance* (Chicago: Rand McNally & Company, 1970); and D. A. Worcester, Jr., "Innovations in the Calculations of Welfare Loss to Monopoly," *Western Economic Journal*, Vol. 7 (September 1969), pp. 234–43.

10.10 CONCLUSIONS

This chapter has focused on economic welfare analysis when markets are imperfectly competitive. The major cases considered were monopoly, monopsony, and dominant share price leadership oligopoly or oligopsony. Although firm behavior under other forms of imperfect competition is more cumbersome to model analytically, the economic welfare considerations can be made in similar fashion.

The economic welfare analysis in this chapter shows that, in some cases, monopoly may be preferable. This occurs if returns to scale from a large firm lead to production cost savings that outweigh the social costs of monopoly pricing. Even in this case, however, some further form of price regulation may attain both production and social efficiency. For example, government regulation of utility companies (government-sanctioned monopolies) is supposedly a case in point.

One of the plausible applications of imperfect competition relates to the role of market intermediaries. In many sectors of the economy, large marketing firms buy from many producers and sell to many consumers. The analysis shows that the distributional as well as efficiency implications of such firms depend critically on the objectives and clientele of the marketing firm. Producer cooperatives and marketing boards benefit producers at the expense of consumers. And pure middlemen adversely affect both consumers and producers and cause greater market contraction than other marketing arrangements.

Another important area of application of market power considerations is in the analysis of labor unions. Here the results show that labor union market power not only benefits labor union members at the expense of employers but also that nonunionized labor may suffer substantially as well. Thus, the distributional consequences can be large even when efficiency effects are small.

Finally, another application of the welfare economics of imperfect competition is in the legal area of antitrust. Economic welfare analysis has much to say about the effects of market power on various market groups. And some of the implications of such analysis are contrary to some current legal precedents. Much of the inconsistency may have resulted from inaccurate estimation which tends to diminish the effect of formal economic considerations in a courtroom. But in many cases an important issue has been a failure to convey sufficient understanding of complex multimarket effects.

11

Stochastic Welfare Economics: Applications in Agricultural Policy Analysis

Thus far in this book, producers and consumers have been assumed to know all the prices that can possibly affect their decisions. Furthermore, prices have been assumed nonrandom or *nonstochastic*. In reality, however, prices move about with a good deal of instability. Instability is generally thought to lead to adverse effects on both producers and consumers for two reasons. First, when prices change substantially, costs of adjustment must generally be incurred to undertake new profit or utility maximization decisions. Second, when prices are changing substantially, decision makers may not anticipate all price changes and hence may make a worse decision than would otherwise be made. The first situation might be characterized as one of instability with certainty because unstable price movements are anticipated with certainty so that adjustments can be made. The second situation is one of instability with uncertainty because price movements are not known in advance.

Of course, reality usually presents some mixture of these two extremes. For example, a manufacturing firm might expect the price of the product that it is currently producing to rise before sale, but it may not know by how much. Since the choice of government policies can affect both price stability and uncertainty, an examination of the associated welfare effects is important.

Similarly, random variation in production can lead to adverse welfare effects, although policy instruments may not be as readily available for reducing these welfare effects.

This chapter first examines the effects of instability in prices on both producers and consumers in the traditional economic welfare framework of certainty (price changes are anticipated in time to make adjustments). A variety of applications in this framework are discussed. Then the welfare measures of earlier chapters are generalized for the case of uncertainty where decisions must be made before prices are known. In this framework some of the classical economic welfare analyses of price instability are reconsidered, and applicability of the alternative approaches for realistic problems is considered.

11.1 CONSUMER WELFARE UNDER STOCHASTIC BUT CERTAIN PRICE

The welfare effects of price instability were first studied by Frederick V. Waugh in 1944.[1] Contrary to popular opinion, he concluded that consumers should prefer price instability. His results are developed in Figure 11.1, where D represents demand and consumers face prices p_1 and p_2, each of which occurs half the time (i.e., with probability 0.5). These price variations may be caused, for example, by random fluctuations in supply between S_1 and S_2. When price is p_1, consumers buy q_1 so that consumer surplus is area $a + b + c$. When price is p_2, consumers buy q_2 so that consumer surplus is area a. If, on the other hand, prices are stabilized by means of, say, some government policy

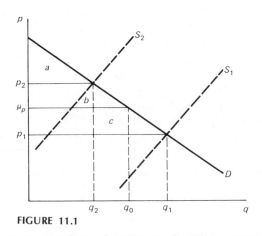

FIGURE 11.1

---

[1]Frederick V. Waugh, "Does the Consumer Benefit from Price Instability?" *Quarterly Journal of Economics,* Vol. 58, No. 4 (August 1944), pp. 602–14.

at the average price level, $\mu_p = (p_1 + p_2)/2$, then consumption takes place at q_0 with a consumer surplus of area $a + b$.

To investigate the welfare effects of price stabilization, note that half the time consumers gain area b as the price is lowered from p_2 to μ_p, but the other half of the time consumers lose area c as the price is raised from p_1 to μ_p. Since $p_2 - \mu_p = \mu_p - p_1$, the loss obviously outweighs the gain; the average loss is $\frac{1}{2}$ (area b − area c). This result implies that consumers prefer price instability if they can take advantage of it by buying more at low prices and less at high prices.

Although this result holds in terms of consumer surplus, it is worthwhile in this case reexamining the results by means of the compensating or equivalent variation concepts. These arguments concerning consumer surplus associated with an ordinary consumer demand curve are directly applicable if income elasticity is zero (Section 6.3). This holds for both the single-consumer case and for a group of consumers as in the market demand case (Section 8.2). Alternatively, the demand curve in Figure 11.1 may be viewed as a Hicksian compensated demand curve associated with utility attained at the stabilized price μ_p. Then the surplus analysis above applies to measuring the equivalent variation of moving from destabilized prices or to measuring the compensating variation of moving from stabilization to destabilization—regardless of income elasticity.

On the other hand, to measure the compensating variation of stabilization or the equivalent variation of destabilization would require use of the compensated demand curves associated with p_1 and p_2, the latter of which would lie entirely left of the former for positive income elasticities (with steeper slope than ordinary demand). The latter would be used to compare p_2 with μ_p, thus generating an area smaller than area b in Figure 11.1 (where D, again, represents ordinary demand); the former compensated curve would be used to compare p_1 with μ_p, thus generating an area larger than area c. Thus, the loss from stabilization would be even greater in terms of compensating variation than in terms of consumer surplus. Similarly, the gain from destabilization would be even greater in terms of equivalent variation than in terms of consumer surplus. In lieu of these kinds of arguments, however, one can simply claim, on the basis of the Willig results (Sections 6.5, 6.6, 7.5, and 7.6), that areas b and c in Figure 11.1 are in error by no more than 5 percent under reasonable conditions (which can be investigated empirically) and interpret the results given above on that basis.

Finally, the consumer surplus results above apply directly to the case of quasi-rent for a producer where the demand curve represents derived demand for an input. Similarly, the results apply to a sector equilibrium demand curve in the sense discussed in Section 9.1, although, again, one must be concerned with compensation of final consumers if final consumption prices are affected by the price variation in the market in question.

11.2 PRODUCER WELFARE UNDER STOCHASTIC BUT CERTAIN PRICE

The effect of stochastic output price on producers was first examined in 1961 by Oi.[2] Assuming a fixed supply curve, he concluded that producers also prefer price instability when they can adjust instantaneously to price changes. To understand his results, consider Figure 11.2, where supply is represented by S and producers are confronted with two prices—p_1 and p_2—each of which occurs with probability 0.5. These price variations may be caused, for example, by random variation in demand between D_1 and D_2. When price is p_1, producers sell q_1 so that quasi-rent is given by area a. When price is p_2, producers sell q_2 so that quasi-rent is given by area $a + b + c$. If, on the other hand, prices are stabilized by some means such as government policy at the average price level $\mu_p = (p_1 + p_2)/2$, then production is q_0 and producer surplus is area $a + b$. Where price would otherwise be p_1, producers thus gain area b; but where price would otherwise be p_2, producers lose area c with stabilization. Since $p_2 - \mu_p = \mu_p - p_1$, the latter loss is larger than the former gain; and since each occurs half the time, producers lose on average from price stabilization (unless supply is completely inelastic). In terms of compensating or equivalent variation, producers would require an average compensation of $\frac{1}{2}$ (area c − area b) to be equally well off under stabilization.

Again, the interpretation of these results can be generalized. For example, these results apply directly to the case of measuring the compensating or equivalent variation associated with stabilization for one or many competitive producers, to one or many consumers with a zero exogenous income elasticity in resource supply, and to a sector equilibrium supply curve of the type described in Section 9.1. The results can also be used to investigate the

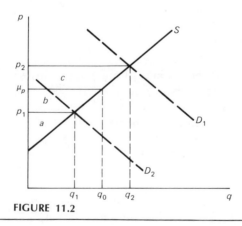

FIGURE 11.2

---

[2]W. Y. Oi, "The Desirability of Price Instability under Perfect Competition," *Econometrica*, Vol. 27, No. 1 (January 1961), pp. 58–64.

equivalent variation of stabilization or compensating variation of destabilization for a group of resource suppliers with nonzero exogenous income elasticity. The alternative measures in this case also lead to somewhat different results as in the case of Section 11.2 and can only be approximated using the Willig results (e.g., Section 7.5) or, again, can be investigated by noting the relationship of compensated curves to ordinary curves.

11.3 PULLING BY THE BOOTSTRAPS

These two counterintuitive results favoring economic instability led economists to consider the issue of stabilization more closely. Samuelson argued that, in fact, an economy cannot "pull itself up by the bootstraps" by simply generating instability.[3] Both Samuelson and Massell[4] showed that these two results (Sections 11.1 and 11.2) cannot be simultaneously applicable and that, when effects on both sides of the market are considered, there is a net gain from stabilization. Considering the Massell approach, suppose as in Figure 11.3 that consumer demand is represented by D and that stochastic supply is represented by S_1 and S_2, each of which occurs with probability 0.5. Thus, equilibrium prices are p_1 and p_2, respectively, again with probability 0.5 each. Now, suppose that prices are stabilized at μ_p, say, by means of a buffer stock authority which buys excess supply, $q_1' - q_0$, when S_1 occurs and sells excess demand, $q_0 - q_2'$, when S_2 occurs. In the event of S_1, consumers thus lose area $c + d$ in consumer surplus while producers gain area $c + d + e$ in producer

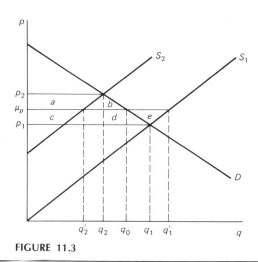

FIGURE 11.3

---

[3]Paul A. Samuelson, "The Consumer Does Benefit from Feasible Price Stability," *Quarterly Journal of Economics,* Vol. 86, No. 3 (August 1972), pp. 476–93.

[4]B. F. Massell, "Price Stabilization and Welfare," *Quarterly Journal of Economics,* Vol. 83, No. 2 (May 1969), pp. 285–97.

surplus for a net gain of area e. In the event of S_2, producers lose area a in producer surplus, but consumers gain area $a + b$ in consumer surplus for a net gain of area b. The average overall effect of price stabilization is thus a gain of $\frac{1}{2}$ (area b + area e). This result implies that the gain from destabilization for consumers in Section 11.1 comes at the expense of producers who are plagued by instability. Furthermore, the expense for producers more than offsets the consumer gains.

Similar considerations apply to the results in Section 11.2, as demonstrated in Figure 11.4. With instability represented by demand and price varying between D_1 and p_1 and D_2 and p_2, respectively, price stabilization at μ_p via a buffer stock leads to a gain of area e if D_1 occurs or of area c if D_2 occurs. On average, the producer loss of $\frac{1}{2}$ (area $a + b - d - e$) is more than offset by a consumer gain of $\frac{1}{2}$ (area $a + b + c - d$).

These results may, again, be interpreted in a variety of contexts. For example, the interpretation of welfare effects for buyers in Figure 11.3 follows the discussion in Section 11.1, and the interpretation for sellers in Figure 11.4 follows the discussion in Section 11.2. The interpretation must be somewhat more careful on the other sides of the markets. For example, suppose that randomness in a derived demand curve is due to random output prices. Then, as shown in Section 4.4, the area behind the shifting derived demand curve does not necessarily reflect accurately the change in quasi-rent for a producer unless the input is essential to the production process. If, however, the good is essential to the production process (either as an input or output) or to the well-being of a consumer or resource supplier (see Section 7.10), the area behind the associated supply or demand curve has welfare significance even when other prices (or income) are changing. Under these conditions, the area is an exact measure of quasi-rent for producers. For consumers/resource suppliers, the area is an exact measure of compensating or equivalent variation if the random supply or demand curve is a compensated curve or the area is an approximation in the sense of Section 7.10 if the random supply or demand is ordinary. Furthermore, based on the aggregation results of Sections 8.1 and

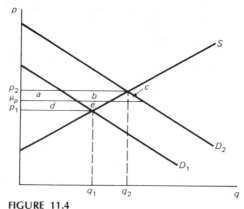

FIGURE 11.4

8.2, these statements apply for groups of producers and consumers; or using the results of Chapter 9, these statements apply for equilibrium supply and demand in an individual market (with equilibrium variation defined with respect to buffer stock intervention), where instability is caused by forces that are exogenous to the sector or economy (e.g., external prices or perhaps weather).

This section suggests that welfare gains for both producers and consumers are possible by stabilizing prices of storable commodities. That is, if one group gains by more than the other loses, a simple compensation scheme must exist such that gainers can compensate losers by enough so that both are better off under stabilization. If this compensation is actually paid, then stabilization is preferred even in a Pareto sense.[5]

The foregoing framework can be easily extended to consider the issue of price stabilization in international trade. In this context, the supply curve in Figures 11.3 and 11.4 can be considered as an excess supply by exporting countries, and the demand curve can be considered as an excess demand by importing countries. Thus, it follows from Figure 11.3 that exporters gain and importers lose from price stabilization when supply is unstable. Alternatively, from Figure 11.4, exporters lose and importers gain from stabilization when demand is unstable. In both cases, the net international effect of price stabilization is positive. In either case, however, some additional implications for distribution of gains and losses within countries can be considered. For example, consider Figure 11.5, which represents supply and demand within an importing country. Prices p_1, p_2, and μ_p correspond to those in Figure 11.3 interpreted in the context of free international trade versus stabilized international trade. In this context, producers in the importing country gain area c from stabilization when excess supply by the exporting countries is high and

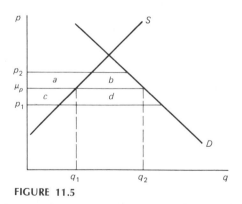

FIGURE 11.5

[5]As shown in a more general algebraic framework by Massell (ibid.), these conclusions may be generalized to include any joint stochastic distribution of fluctuations in supply and demand as long as supply and demand are linear and fluctuations manifest themselves in parallel shifts of the supply and demand curves.

lose area a when excess supply by the exporting countries is low. Consumers in the importing country, on the other hand, lose area $c + d$ when exporters' excess supply is high and gain area $a + b$ when exporters' excess supply is low. Thus, producers in the importing country suffer a net loss on average of $\frac{1}{2}$ area $a - c$, and consumers in the importing country lose on average $\frac{1}{2}$ area $c + d - a - b$. For example, if demand in an importing country is highly inelastic, consumers lose relatively little while producers may suffer substantial losses if supply is highly elastic. Effects under alternative elasticities and effects for producing and consuming groups in different countries can be worked out for alternative cases similarly.[6]

11.4 ADDITIONAL CONSIDERATIONS REGARDING THE WELFARE EFFECTS OF PRICE STABILIZATION

Subsequent analysis has shown that the foregoing conclusions regarding who gains and who loses from price stabilization and how instability can come about are highly sensitive to market structure and to shape, movement, and other aspects of specification regarding demand and supply. Some of the more important considerations have to do with (1) nonlinearity, (2) the form of disturbance, (3) private response to public intervention, (4) the role of market intermediaries, (5) instability with certainty versus uncertainty, (6) ex ante versus ex post benefits, and (7) risk aversion and risk response. The first four issues are discussed in this section and the latter three are investigated in the following two sections.

Nonlinearity

The simple framework of Sections 11.1 through 11.3 is based on the assumption of linearity in supply and demand. To see the implications of nonlinearity, consider Figure 11.6, where the demand curve D is nonlinear and supply fluctuates randomly between S_1 and S_2 with each having probability 0.5. Now suppose that price is stabilized via a buffer stock authority which purchases some production when supply is high and sells from buffer stocks when supply is low. For such a buffer stock to operate for a long period of time, the increase in stocks when supply is high must be the same as the decrease in stocks when supply is low. Otherwise the buffer stock would either tend to accumulate until some of the stock would require disposal by other means or stocks would tend to run out so that the stable price could not be enforced. With this requirement, excess supply, $q_1 - q_0$, at S_1 is equal to excess demand, $q_0 - q_2$, at S_2 so that the buffer stock authority's receipts in a short supply period are the same as its

---

[6]For further details, see Darrell L. Hueth and Andrew Schmitz, "International Trade in Intermediate and Final Goods: Some Welfare Implications of Destabilized Prices," *Quarterly Journal of Economics*, Vol. 86, No. 3 (August 1972), pp. 351–65.

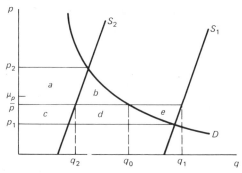

FIGURE 11.6

expenses in a long supply period; thus, its net welfare effect is zero on average (excluding storage and transaction costs). It may also be noted that this requirement is satisfied by the analysis in Figures 11.3 and 11.4 under linearity, where shifts in supply or demand curves are parallel.

With this in mind, the stable price $\bar{p}$ in Figure 11.6 must be chosen so that the horizontal distance between S_1 and D is the same as between S_2 and D. Hence, if demand is upward bending (convex) as in Figure 11.6, the stabilized price is lower than the average destabilized price is; if demand is downward bending (concave), stabilized price is above the average destabilized price. The welfare gains and losses for producers and consumers—in terms of areas a, b, c, d, and e in Figure 11.6—are exactly the same as in Figure 11.3 except that areas a and b are now relatively large and areas c, d, and e are relatively small. As a result, an average net gain of $\frac{1}{2}$ (area b + area e) is still possible, but now the average consumer effect of $\frac{1}{2}$ (area $a + b - c - d$) may be positive rather than negative (with sufficient nonlinearity) because the stabilized price is lower than the average destabilized price. Also, the average producer effect of $\frac{1}{2}$ (area $c + d + e - a$) can possibly become negative, thus obtaining exactly the opposite qualitative impacts on producers and consumers as suggested by Figure 11.3.

A similar generalization of the analysis in Figure 11.4 for the case of upward-bending (convex) supply also shows that sufficient nonlinearity in supply can reverse the qualitative effects of price stabilization when instability is due to fluctuations in demand. Thus, these results show that the functional forms used for supply and demand in analyzing policies that affect price instability may determine to a large extent the suggested welfare effects. Furthermore, a simple change between the popular functional forms of linearity and log linearity with elasticities of usual magnitudes may be sufficient to induce changes in *qualitative* implications of price stabilization.[7] On the basis of these results one

---

[7]This result was shown by Richard E. Just, Ernst Lutz, Andrew Schmitz, and Stephen Turnovsky, "The Distribution of Welfare Gains from International Price Stabilization under Distortions," *American Journal of Agricultural Economics,* Vol. 59, No. 4 (November 1977), pp. 652–61. The role of nonlinearity has also been examined in

must conclude that any investigation of the effects of a policy that affects price stability should be undertaken only after econometric estimation of the degree of curvature.[8]

The Form of Disturbances

Another issue that has proven to be of importance in analyzing policies that affect price stability is the form of the disturbance in fluctuating supply or demand. In Figures 11.3 through 11.6, the random fluctuations take place in a parallel or additive fashion. The form of the disturbances is additive in the sense that, if supply or demand is written with quantity q as a function of price p, say $f(p)$, then the actual demand or supply curves correspond to $q = f(p) + \epsilon$, where ϵ is a random disturbance, $E(\epsilon) = 0$. One alternative form of disturbance, defended, for example, by Turnovsky, is the multiplicative specification $q = f(p) \epsilon$, $E(\epsilon) = 1$.[9]

To demonstrate the comparative implications of these two specifications, suppose that demand is stable at D as in Figure 11.7 but that supply is unstable with multiplicative variation represented by fluctuations between S_1 and S_2, where each occurs with probability 0.5. By comparison additive variation in supply is represented in Figure 11.3. For buffer stocks to be self-liquidating, prices must be stabilized at $\bar{p}$, where $q_1 - q_0 = q_0 - q_2$, rather than at the average destabilized price, $\mu_p = (p_1 + p_2)/2$. Again, the welfare effects in Figure 11.7 are the same as in Figure 11.3 in terms of areas a, b, c, d, and e; but again, as with nonlinearity, areas c, d, and e are smaller relative to areas a and b. As supplies S_1 and S_2 diverge (as the slope of S_1 falls), these results are accentuated until area $c + d + e = 0$. Hence, with sufficiently strong multiplicative disturbances, net overall gains $\frac{1}{2}$ (area $b + e$) are still possible; but again, even the qualitative implications for individuals or groups may switch. Producers may lose (if area $c + d + e - a < 0$) and consumers may gain (if area $a + b - c - d > 0$).

Results similar to those in Figure 11.7 can also be developed for the case of

---

a more elegant and advanced framework using the indirect utility function approach by S. J. Turnovsky, H. Shalit, and A. Schmitz, "Consumer's Surplus, Price Instability and Consumer Welfare," *Econometrica* Vol. 48, No. 1 (January 1980), pp. 135–52. Their results show that reversal is obtained depending on the curvature of the utility function, which they measure by the Arrow–Pratt risk-aversion parameter (even though their framework is not one of risk, as the next section makes clear). Since the curvature in demand curves is related to curvature in underlying utility functions, the results of their approach are equivalent with those of the simplistic framework of this chapter. The indirect utility approach in the case of risk is considered in Appendix C.

[8]Richard E. Just and J. Arne Hallam, "Functional Flexibility in Analysis of Commodity Price Stabilization Policy," *Proceedings, Journal of the American Statistical Association*, Business and Economic Statistics Section, 1978, pp. 177–86.

[9]Stephen J. Turnovsky, "The Distribution of Welfare Gains from Price Stabilization: The Case of Multiplicative Disturbances," *International Economic Review*, Vol. 17, No. 1 (1976), pp. 133–48.

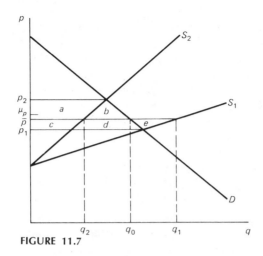

FIGURE 11.7

multiplicative disturbances in demand, in which case the qualitative implications can possibly be just the opposite of those in Figure 11.4, where demand disturbances are additive.[10] Again, welfare effects of price stabilizing policy cannot be adequately evaluated empirically without sufficient econometric estimation of the form of disturbances.[11]

Response of Private Storage to Public Intervention

Another issue that must be considered with any potential government policy is that economic stability may be affected not only directly but also indirectly because of private decision makers' reactions to the direct effects of the policy. For example, when a large government buffer stock is established to stabilize prices, the demand for private inventories will probably change because of greater certainty concerning future supplies. For example, if—in addition to working stocks—some private stocks are held for speculation (that future price will be higher than present price plus storage costs), the purpose of holding speculative stocks would be removed by a government policy of price stabilization at some announced price. But this leads to a greater reliance of private concerns on public stocks. In fact, this consideration raises the question as to

---

[10]The literature also implies that these conclusions carry over into models of general stochastic distributions. This is evident by comparing the results of Massell and of Hueth and Schmitz under additivity and linearity with those that pertain to the case of nonlinearity of Turnovsky and Just, Lutz, Schmitz, and Turnovsky (where multiplicity is assumed); see Massell, "Price Stabilization"; Hueth and Schmitz, "International Trade"; Turnovsky "Distribution of Welfare Gains"; and Richard E. Just, Ernst Lutz, Andrew Schmitz, and Stephen Turnovsky, "The Distribution of Welfare Gains from Price Stabilization: An International Perspective," *Journal of International Economics*, Vol. 8, No. 4 (November 1978), pp. 511–63.

[11]Just and Hallam, "Functional Flexibility."

whether or not private stocks may be held in optimal amounts in absence of government held stocks. so that no public stocks are needed.

Consider, for example, the diagrammatic analysis of Figure 11.3. If storage costs are negligible and producers gain from price stabilization, the same gains can be assured if producers undertake stock operations on their own. They need simply carry stocks of $q_1 - q_0$ from high-supply years over to periods of low supply. Alternatively, other private decision makers would be induced to enter the private storage industry if they were assured of receiving a sales price higher than their purchase price, as in Figure 11.3.

With nonzero storage costs, on the other hand, private storage would not be induced to such a great extent. For example, consider Figure 11.8, where storage costs are $p_2' - p_1'$ per unit.[12] Then, if price with supply S_1 is less than p_1' and price with supply S_2 is greater than p_2', profits could be made by private firms by purchasing at the low price and storing and selling at the high price. Private storage would increase until price at S_1 is p_1' and price at S_2 is p_2'—in other words, to the point where the stock purchased with S_1 is $q_1'' - q_1'$ and is equal to the amount sold from stocks, $q_2' - q_2''$, with short supply S_2. In this case the welfare areas a, b, c, d, and e measure benefits for the same groups as in Figure 11.3, except that, with storage costs considered, all welfare effects are smaller because the sales from stocks are at a price high enough to cover purchase and storage costs.

Now suppose in this framework that a public storage program is undertaken

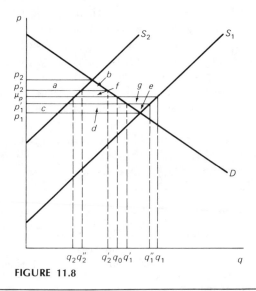

FIGURE 11.8

[12]The framework of Figure 11.8 was first introduced by Massell to demonstrate that welfare gains from price stabilization can be possible even when storage costs are positive; see Massell, ''Price Stabilization.''

to further stabilize prices. If the government attempts to increase total stock purchases to $q_1 - q_0$ when S_1 occurs by purchasing public stocks of $(q_1 - q_0) - (q_1'' - q_1')$ and selling an equal amount in periods of low supply, private storers of the commodity can no longer cover their storage costs and will reduce private inventories until prices again vary between p_1' and p_2' or until private storage ceases. It should be further noted, however, that any public storage beyond $q_1'' - q_1'$ would lead to reduced overall benefits considering consumers, producers, *and government* jointly (where consumer and producer surpluses have strict willingness-to-pay interpretations) since the increase in storage cost would be greater than the increase in net consumer plus producer surplus.

The framework used in this section to demonstrate the reaction of private concerns to price-stabilizing effects of public policy is admittedly quite simple and serves only illustrative purposes. A number of other issues must also be considered, such as differences in private and public storage costs, time preference discounting (Chapter 13), the length of time in storage, credit availability, risk preferences (Section 11.6), and so on. Using only some of these considerations, it can be shown that the free market level of private stocks may not be optimal.

The Role of Market Intermediaries

The analysis of the instability issue is also somewhat different in the case with market intermediaries. To show the importance of market intermediaries, the following discussion demonstrates how, in an imperfect market setting, certain market intermediaries can "manufacture" price instability to their own advantage while other types of intermediaries will attempt to stabilize producer prices.[13] Consider a market as in Figure 11.9(a), where AR is the average revenue or demand curve and MR is the corresponding marginal revenue schedule. For simplicity, again consider supplies S_1 and S_2 to occur with probability 0.5 each, as in the earlier cases of this chapter. Thus, for the two periods taken together, AR coincides with the horizontal summation of the marginal revenue schedules, Σ MR, which indicates marginal revenue over the two periods considered jointly. A pure middleman (one who, as defined in Chapter 10, has both monopoly and monopsony power) will maximize profits over the two periods by equating the horizontal summation of marginal cost, denoted by Σ MC, and the horizontal summation of marginal revenue, denoted by Σ MR. The middleman then sets prices and quantities in each period to attain this marginal level in both buying and selling. Thus, he sells quantity q_0 at price p_0 in both periods. But he buys quantity q_1 at price p_1 in short-supply periods and quantity q_2 at price p_2 in long-supply periods [Figure 11.9(a)].

---

[13]This problem was pointed out by Jurg Bieri and Andrew Schmitz, "Market Intermediaries and Price Instability: Some Welfare Implications," *American Journal of Agricultural Economics,* Vol. 56, No. 2 (May 1974), pp. 280–85.

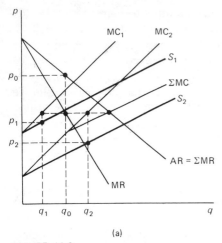

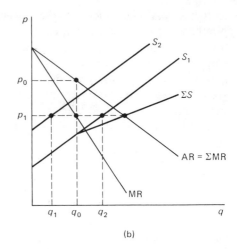

FIGURE 11.9

Thus, quantity $q_2 - q_0$ is stored in long supply periods to facilitate sale of quantity $q_0 - q_1$ in short-supply periods, $q_2 - q_0 = q_0 - q_1$. Therefore, through the use of stocks, the pure middleman will stabilize prices on the demand side but destabilize prices on the supply side. Interestingly, a pure middleman finds it to his advantage not to stabilize producer prices even though he does store part of the good produced. The associated welfare effects can be calculated by comparison with the competitive solution in both stabilized and destabilized cases; but these effects are not pointed out here explicitly because they are tedious to represent diagrammatically.

Consider alternatively the producer marketing board case in Figure 11.9(b), where the board maximizes producer returns as in Section 10.6. The producer marketing board would equate the sum of the marginal revenue schedules, Σ MR (which is the AR schedule), with the horizontal summation of the producer supply schedules over the two periods (denoted as ΣS). Again, the board would stabilize prices to the consumer at p_0 selling quantity q_0. However, unlike the previous case, the board maximizes producer profits by stabilizing producer prices at p_1. The board then stores $q_2 - q_0$ in long supply periods to fill the excess demand $q_0 - q_1$ in short supply periods, $q_2 - q_0 = q_0 - q_1$. Thus, the marketing board undertakes price stabilization in the absence of a government stabilization policy, which is very different from the pure middleman case. Again, the welfare implications can be easily determined, although they are somewhat tedious to discuss in the context of Figure 11.9. An interesting question in the marketing board case is to compare the gains from stability with a marketing board to the associated efficiency loss. It turns out that the latter loss always outweighs the former gain.[14]

[14]Models have also been developed to compare instability in a free-trade case with that where tariffs exist. The results concerning who gains and who loses from instability

11.5 INSTABILITY WITH UNCERTAINTY

Thus far in this chapter, producers and consumers have been assumed to adjust instantaneously along their supply or demand curve or, equivalently, to have *certainty* with respect to prices even though prices are *unstable*. For example, in Figure 11.4 producers can respond by producing the high quantity q_2 by correctly anticipating high demand. This approach has been criticized, for example, by Tisdell[15] and, more recently, by Anderson and Riley.[16] Random prices are rarely known in advance with certainty and, at best, a producer may have only some idea of the distribution of prices for its output at the time production decisions are made. Consider, for example, Figure 11.10, where prices p_1 and p_2 each have probability 0.5, but the producer must determine the quantity q before price is known. In contrast to Figure 11.2, this situation is one of *instability with uncertainty*.

If the producer anticipates price p_1 and produces q_1, then quasi-rent will be area j if p_1 prevails but will be area $a + e + j$ if p_2 occurs [costs are unchanged, but total revenue increases by $q_1 \cdot (p_2 - p_1)$]; the average quasi-rent at q_1 is area $e + j$. Similarly, if production q_2 is chosen, then quasi-rent is area $a + b + c + e + f + j$ when price is p_2 but is area $j - d - g - h$ when price is p_1 [the latter is obtained by simply subtracting $q_2 \cdot (p_2 - p_1) =$ area $a + b + c + d + e + f + g + h$ from the former]; the average quasi-rent at q_2 is area $e + f + j - d$. Finally, in a similar manner, average quasi-rent at q_0—the quantity determined by equat-

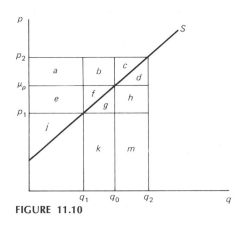

FIGURE 11.10

are quite different. See Jurg Bieri and Andrew Schmitz, "Export Instability, Monopoly Power and Welfare," *Journal of International Economics,* Vol. 3, No. 4 (November 1973), pp. 389–96.

[15]C. Tisdell, "Uncertainty, Instability, and Expected Profit," *Econometrica,* Vol. 31, No. 1–2 (January–April, 1963), pp. 243–47.

[16]James Anderson and John G. Riley, "International Trade with Fluctuating Prices," *International Economic Review,* Vol. 17, No. 1 (February 1976), pp. 76–97.

ing expected price μ_p to marginal cost—is area $e + f + j$. Clearly, the optimal production decision (with expected profit maximization) is q_0 since average or expected quasi-rent is greatest.

The interesting aspect of the result in Figure 11.10, however, is that the expected quasi-rent under instability is exactly the same as if prices are stabilized at their mean, in which case the certain price μ_p calls forth production q_0 which leads to a certain quasi-rent of area $e + f + j$. Hence, producers are not affected by stabilization as they were in Figure 11.2 if instability is accompanied by uncertainty.[17]

Also under uncertainty, expected welfare quantities are generally not the ones actually realized. Whereas producers in Figure 11.10 expect quasi-rent of area $e + f + j$, the actual price realized by producers is either p_1 or p_2, and thus the actual quasi-rent differs from the expected quasi-rent. For purposes of this distinction, ex ante producer surplus is defined as the area above the supply curve and below expected price while ex post producer surplus is further adjusted to account for the difference in actual and expected returns. In Figure 11.10, area $e + f + j$ is thus the ex ante producer surplus and is associated with expected returns $\mu_p \cdot q_0$. Suppose, however, that price p_1 is realized. Costs incurred by the producer continue to be represented by the same area under the supply curve and left of q_0 assuming that input decisions are made and costs are incurred prior to realization of price. Actual returns, on the other hand, are $p_1 \cdot q_0$ so that the actual quasi-rent is less than the expected quasi-rent by an amount $(\mu_p - p_1) \cdot q_0 =$ area $e + f + g$. Making this adjustment in ex ante producer surplus thus obtains the ex post producer surplus of area $j - g$ associated with price p_1. Similarly, the ex post producer surplus associated with price p_2 is area $a + b + e + f + j$.

Thus far, only random prices have been considered. However, another phenomenon that can lead to further differences in ex ante and ex post surpluses is random production. In agriculture, for example, producers make decisions regarding planted acreage and other inputs such as fertilizer, but neither actual production nor actual price are generally known until some time later when the crop is harvested. In Figure 11.10, producers may plan to produce q_0, but because of random yields, actual production is either q_1 or q_2. Thus, whereas ex ante surplus is area $e + f + j$, the ex post surplus would be area $j - g - k$ if p_1 and q_1 occur, area $j - g + m$ if p_1 and q_2 occur, and so on. In each case, this ex post surplus simply corresponds to subtracting production cost (the area below the supply or marginal cost curve and left of planned production) from the actual returns realized.

The latter phenomenon of random production has led to yet an additional problem, where random prices are induced by random production through a

---

[17]The consumer effects of stabilization for the case with producer uncertainty (Figure 11.10) may be investigated along the lines in Section 11.3 but in this case from the consumer standpoint, the market behaves as if supply is perfectly inelastic at q_0.

demand relationship. Consider, for example, Figure 11.11, where planned production is q_0 but actual production is either q_1 or q_2, each occurring with probability 0.5. With linear demand D, the resulting actual prices are thus p_1 or p_2, respectively. The ex ante producer surplus obtained by planning production q_0—so as to equate expected price, $\mu_p = (p_1 + p_2)/2$, and marginal cost—is area $c + d + g$. If production is q_1, however, then actual returns are $p_1 \cdot q_1$ rather than $\mu_p \cdot q_0$ [where $q_0 = (q_1 + q_2)/2$], so that ex post producer surplus is area $a + c + g - e - h$. On the other hand, if production is q_2, then actual returns are $p_2 \cdot q_2$ instead of the planned $\mu_p \cdot q_0$, so that ex post producer surplus is area $g - e + j$.

The peculiar problem in this case is that the expected ex post producer surplus, $\frac{1}{2}$ [area $(a + c + g - e - h)$ + area $(g - e + j)$] = area $a + g - e$, is less than the ex ante producer surplus area $c + d + g$ (note that area a = area c and area j = area h). This result is obtained because a negative correlation of price and quantity is induced by the downward-sloping demand curve so that expected returns (price times quantity) is less than expected price times expected quantity.

This raises a question regarding which welfare quantity policymakers should consider. If each individual producing firm perceives only a distribution of price and not the effect its production may have on price (which is the usual competitive assumption) and makes decisions accordingly, then the producer expected ex ante surplus does not reflect how well off the firm is likely to be in an ex post sense. When individual producers do not perceive the correlation of their production with price because of their smallness relative to the market, then the aggregate of all producers or the industry also behaves as though there is no correlation of production and price. A policymaker who realizes this relationship in the aggregate can thus be faced with the question of whether to formulate policy according to what producers say they want (ex ante surplus) or according to what is actually in producers' best interest (expected ex post surplus).

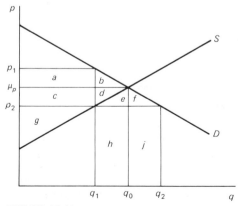

FIGURE 11.11

This question was raised in an agricultural context by Hazell and Scandizzo.[18] They found that if producers make decisions on the basis of expected returns per acre rather than on the basis of expected prices and expected yields, the correlation of prices and yields is adequately considered even though the individual producers do not perceive their individual impact on prices. For example, if a producer attempts to produce q_0 in Figure 11.11 for several periods and realizes returns $p_1 \cdot q_1$ half of the time and returns $p_2 \cdot q_2$ the other half, then he or she would come to expect returns $\frac{1}{2}(p_1 \cdot q_1 + p_2 \cdot q_2)$ on average even though the average price times average quantity, $\mu_p \cdot q_0$, is larger by area $d + e$ in Figure 11.11. Hazell and Scandizzo concluded that, if producers act on the basis of expected prices and expected production (ignoring correlation of the two) rather than on the basis of expected returns, free-market competition does not lead to Pareto optimality. On the contrary, area $d + e$ must be imposed as an ad valorem tax [for any given q_0, (area $d + e)/q_0$ would be the per unit tax] and then redistributed as a lump-sum payment to induce producers to form the correct ex ante expectations of ex post welfare. This type of tax is called an *optimal distortion* by Hazell and Scandizzo since it is required to reach Pareto optimality.

Although the issue of instability with certainty versus uncertainty has been discussed in this section only from the standpoint of the producer, similar generalizations are also applicable for the consumer or resource owner, where decisions must be made before prices are known. The usual consumer choice problem, however, involves deciding how much to buy or sell given prevailing market prices. Only rarely must a consumer decide upon a quantity before a price is quoted. Nevertheless, in the dynamics of the real world, a consumer must often begin to allocate a budget among consumption items before all the prices are known. For example, a consumer may decide how much to allocate to buying an automobile, gasoline, and food before knowing all gasoline and food prices over the life of the car. In this case, however, the consumer is still free to adjust food and gasoline consumption decisions after purchasing the automobile although the budget constraint may be altered. The consumer problem with durable choice and instability thus becomes much like the producer problem with instability. In fact, the compensated consumer problem is mathematically equivalent, just as in the case of certainty discussed in Section 7.10 (see Appendix C).

11.6 STOCHASTIC WELFARE ECONOMICS WITH RISK PREFERENCES

Thus far in this chapter, any preferences for stable or unstable prices have been discussed solely in terms of gains in expected surplus. For individuals who

---

[18]P. B. R. Hazell and P. L. Scandizzo, "Market Intervention Policies When Production Is Risky," *American Journal of Agricultural Economics,* Vol. 57, No. 4 (November 1975), pp. 641–49.

neither like nor dislike random outcomes per se (that is, for risk-neutral individuals), these results are appropriate. A risk-neutral individual is one who is indifferent to randomness in the economic surplus as long as expected surplus is unaltered. Some individuals, however, may have either a great affinity or a great aversion for risk. For example, a producer may prefer earning a quasi-rent of $20,000 year after year to earning a quasi-rent of $10,000 or $40,000 each with probability 0.5. This preference may be due to economic reasons, such as more efficient planning possibilities, as well as to purely psychological factors such as emotional trauma. To reflect these kinds of preferences, the surplus concepts used thus far must be further modified.

Consider, for example, a risk-averse producer operating in a competitive market with random product price p and expectation $\mu_p = E(p)$. Thus, consistent with the assumption of competition, the firm's output has no effect on the product price distribution. Suppose that the firm makes short-run decisions by maximizing a mean-variance expected utility function,[19]

$$E[U(\pi)] = E(\pi) - \alpha q^2 \sigma^2$$

$$- \mu_p q - \sum_{i=1}^{n} \omega_i X_i - \alpha q^2 \sigma^2 \qquad (11.1)$$

where U is utility, π is quasi-rent (profit plus fixed cost), the X_i are input quantities, the ω_i are respective input prices, α is a risk aversion parameter, and σ^2 is the variance of price, $\sigma^2 = E(p - \mu_p)^2$; thus $q^2\sigma^2$ is the variance of quasi-rent. To simplify the discussion below, suppose that minimum variable costs for each level of output are given by $C(q)$, so that

$$E[U(\pi)] = \mu_p q - C(q) - \alpha q^2 \sigma^2 \qquad (11.2)$$

is simply a function of q. A condition for maximization of (11.2) with respect to q (the first-order condition of calculus) is

$$\mu_p - C'(q) - 2\alpha q \sigma^2 = 0 \qquad (11.3)$$

where $C'(q)$ represents marginal cost. Recall that the condition for maximization of profit or quasi-rent from the theory of the firm under certainty is $\mu_p = C'(q)$. Thus, in the mean-variance expected utility formulation, the term $2\alpha q\sigma^2$ represents a discounting of the expected price because of the uncertainty associated with it. Specifically, where $\alpha q^2 \sigma^2$ is called a risk premium associated with output price uncertainty, the term $2\alpha q\sigma^2$ is a marginal risk premium.

---

[19]As shown by James Tobin, expected utility follows a mean-variance specification if either the utility function is quadratic or price is distributed normally. Kenneth Arrow has argued that a quadratic utility function is not plausible because it implies increasing

The compensating or equivalent variation associated with various parametric changes for this problem can be determined by comparing the risk-averse firm's decision problem with a risk-neutral decision problem. That is, in the case of risk neutrality, the maximand in (11.2) becomes

$$E[U^*(\pi)] = E(\pi)$$
$$= \mu_p q - C(q)$$
(11.4)

for which the maximization condition in (11.3) becomes

$$\mu_p - C'(q) = 0$$
(11.5)

Identical decisions are thus implied if the expected price μ_p^* facing the risk-neutral firm in (11.4) is related to the expected price μ_p' facing the risk-averse firm in (11.1) by the equation

$$\mu_p^* = \mu_p' - 2\alpha q' \sigma^2$$
(11.6)

where q' is the optimal output of the risk-averse firm with expected price μ_p'; this is evident upon substituting μ_p' into equation (11.3) and μ_p^* into equation (11.5) and noting that $C'(q)$ must be the same in the two cases (assuming that marginal cost is strictly upward sloping). The relationship in (11.6) allows construction and comparison of supply curves with different levels of risk as in Figure 11.12. In point of fact, equation (11.6) implies that the risk-averse supply curve $S_\alpha(\sigma^2)$ (conditioned on the risk-aversion coefficient α) lies above the risk-neutral supply curve $S_0(\sigma^2)$ at a distance $2\alpha q \sigma^2$.

Now consider the case where the firm is risk averse but faces no risk. Clearly, without risk, the maximand in (11.1) also reduces to

$$E[U(\pi)] = E(\pi)$$
$$= \mu_p q - C(q)$$
(11.7)

since $\sigma^2 = 0$. Hence, resulting decisions must be the same as for the maximand in (11.4), so the corresponding supply curve $S_\alpha(0)$ in Figure 11.12 coincides with the risk-neutral supply curve $S_0(\sigma^2)$ and the maxima of the objective functions in the two cases are the same. But the results of Chapter 4 apply to the supply curve $S_\alpha(0)$ and show that area $e + f + g$ measures quasi-rent for the producer associated with expected price μ_p^*. Hence, area $e + f + g$ also

absolute risk aversion. Normality of price, however, may be a plausible assumption; see James Tobin, "Comment on Borch and Feldstein," *Review of Economic Studies*, Vol. 36 (1), No. 105 (January 1969) pp. 13, 14. For a more general discussion of the Von Neumann-Morgenstern utility framework underlying this analysis, see Walter Nicholson, *Microeconomic Theory: Basic Principles and Extensions*, 2nd ed. (Hinsdale, Ill.: The Dryden Press, 1978), Chapter 6.

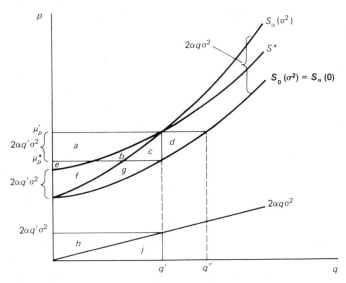

FIGURE 11.12

provides an appropriate measure of producer welfare associated with a random price with mean $\mu_p{}^*$ under risk neutrality.[20] And from Chapter 4 any change in this quasi-rent measure under price certainty (associated with a change in some parameter affecting the firm) is an exact measure of both the compensating and equivalent variations. Thus, also under uncertainty and risk neutrality, this dual interpretation of area $e + f + g$ implies that the change in the area above the supply curve (taken as a function of mean price) and below mean price is a measure of both compensating and equivalent variation of any change affecting the firm. This is clear since the objective criteria in equations (11.4) and (11.7) are identical.

Finally, suppose that risk is introduced in the certainty problem with risk aversion; that is, suppose that product price has mean $\mu_p{}'$ and variance σ^2. Since mean price $\mu_p{}'$ leads to output q' under uncertainty, expected utility is given by

$$V' = \mu_p{}'q' - C(q') - \alpha(q')^2\sigma^2 \qquad (11.8)$$

But note that price $\mu_p{}^*$ under certainty also leads to expected-utility-maximizing quantity q' so that the corresponding expected utility is

$$V^* = \mu_p{}^*q' - C(q') \qquad (11.9)$$

and substituting for $\mu_p{}^*$ in equation (11.9) using equation (11.6) obtains

---

[20]This result is, in fact, a version of the result associated with Figure 11.10.

$$V^* = \mu_p{}'q' - C(q') - 2\alpha(q')^2\sigma^2 \qquad (11.10)$$
$$= V' - \alpha(q')^2\sigma^2$$

where the latter equality follows by using equation (11.8). Also as noted above, the expected utility at price $\mu_p{}^*$ under certainty is $V^* = $ area $e + f + g$. Hence, comparing (11.8) and (11.10) reveals that expected utility at mean price $\mu_p{}'$ with uncertainty is $V' = $ (area $e + f + g$) $+ \alpha(q')^2\sigma^2$.

To consider welfare measurement in the context of Figure 11.12, note that $2\alpha(q')^2\sigma^2 = $ area $h + j = $ area $b + c + f + g$ where S^* is a curve constructed vertically parallel to $S_0(\sigma^2)$ at a distance of $2\alpha q'\sigma^2$. Thus, $\alpha(q')^2\sigma^2 = $ area $h = $ area $b + f$ again by construction and, hence, $V' = $ area $e + f + g + b + f$. Finally, note that area $a + e = $ area $e + f + g$ by construction so that $V' = $ area $a + b + e + f$. From this result, one learns that the expected utility under risk aversion is represented by the area below expected price and above the supply curve taken as a function of expected price and conditioned on the variance of price.

Thus, to examine the welfare effects of changing risk, consider a given mean price $\mu_p{}'$ but changing the variance of price from 0 to σ^2. With variance zero, production is q'' and the expected utility in Figure 11.12 is area $a + b + c + d + e + f + g$; whereas with variance σ^2, expected utility is area $a + b + e + f$. The welfare effect of risk on the producer is thus a loss of area $c + d + g$. With mean-variance utility, a certain payment of area $c + d + g$ makes the producer just as well off under risk as with no risk. Hence, the area $c + d + g$ is an exact measure of both the compensating and equivalent variation of the risk.

These results thus imply that the change in producer surplus associated with a supply curve taken as a function of expected price and conditioned on respective observed levels of risk in price before and after a change gives an exact measure of both compensating and equivalent variation associated with any parametric change in the input prices or in the distribution of output price (mean or variance).[21] For example, in a mean-variance framework, suppose that the mean price is changed from $\mu_p{}^0$ to $\mu_p{}^1$, the variance of price is changed from $\sigma_0{}^2$ to $\sigma_1{}^2$, input prices are changed from $\omega_i{}^0$ to $\omega_i{}^1$, $i = 1, \ldots, n$, and the induced change in production is from q_0 to q_1. Suppose that the supply curve as a function of mean price μ_p with determinants consisting of the variance of price and all input prices is represented by $S(\sigma^2, \omega_1, \ldots, \omega_n)$, as in Figure 11.13. Then both the compensating and equivalent variation of the change is given by area $b - a$.

---

[21]Although these results have been derived in a simple mean-variance framework for intuitive purposes, they can be readily extended. The only alteration in results is that the appropriate supply curve to use for welfare calculations depends on the entire distribution of price exclusive of location (i.e., on all moments about the mean) rather than simply on the variance. Also note that some important alterations are necessary when production is stochastic. See Appendix A for further details.

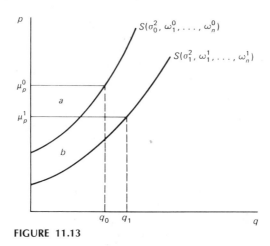

FIGURE 11.13

The case of risk response in demand may be considered similarly. For example, because of the need for advance planning, an industry may be determining quantities before prices are known. Thus, the response in derived demand to greater stability would follow the same type of framework as developed in this section for supply. That is, the effects of changes in output price risk are reflected (completely) by the area under input derived demand (for necessary inputs with nonstochastic prices). Similar statements hold for compensated consumers' demand and supply as well since their problem is equivalent to the producers' problem in the compensated case. A reasonable application in the consumer case is in making durable choices (automobiles or appliances) when faced with risk regarding what prices of related goods, such as fuels, will be over the life of the durables (see Appendix C). Other considerations would include the risk associated with technological change and the range of new products which may come on the market during the life of alternative durables.

The results of this section can also be partially extended to handle the case of random production at least with respect to measurement of welfare effects in input markets. For example, agriculture is a common example where both production and price are stochastic and such considerations are necessary. The results do not generalize for measurement of welfare effects in output markets where production is random at the time of decision making. Alternatively, however, this methodology extends generally to the case of measuring welfare effects in any market where quantities are determined with certainty by the decision maker at the time of decision making and for which the good is essential in the related production process.[22]

---

[22]For a mean-variance expected utility function, these results can be shown in much the same way as above. The general results, however, are developed in Appendices A and C.

11.7 AN EXAMPLE

An example can serve to illustrate application of some of the concepts of this chapter. Suppose the government is considering setting up a buffer stock of wheat for the purpose of stabilizing wheat farmers' incomes. Suppose that farmers are risk averse and behave according to an objective criterion of the form in equation (11.1) and that, upon estimating a supply equation for wheat farmers and after accounting for current levels of all determinants of supply other than price risk, one obtains

$$q = \mu_p - 1.5q\sigma^2$$

where

$$q = \text{quantity of wheat in billion bushels}$$
$$\mu_p = \text{expected price of wheat in dollars per bushel}$$
$$\sigma^2 = \text{variance of wheat price}$$

(suppose for simplicity that wheat production is nonstochastic). Suppose that the estimated demand equation, after accounting for current levels of all determinants of demand, is

$$q = 4.5 - 0.5p + 0.5\epsilon$$

where

$$p = \text{actual price of wheat in dollars per bushel}$$
$$\epsilon = \text{a random term associated with consumer preferences which is not known at the time farmers decide how much to produce.}$$

Suppose for simplicity that $\epsilon = 1$ or $\epsilon = -1$, each with probability 0.5.
  Solving each of these equations for implicit form (solving for p or μ_p) obtains

$$\mu_p = q + 1.5q \, \sigma^2$$

for supply and

$$p = 9 - 2q + \epsilon$$

for demand. The supply curve is depicted in Figure 11.14 for $\sigma^2 = 0$ and $\sigma^2 = 1$, while the demand curve is shown with $\epsilon = 1$ and $\epsilon = -1$ and also where ϵ is at its expected value, $E(\epsilon) = 0$. The latter relationship shows how expected price is determined with given quantities of production; that is, simply taking expectations in the demand equation implies

$$\mu_p = 9 - 2q + E(\epsilon) = 9 - 2q$$

260

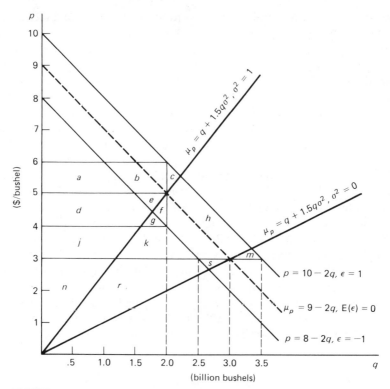

FIGURE 11.14

Note that the supply equation is of the form in equation (11.3) where $C'(q) = q$ and $\alpha = 0.75$. Since equation (11.3) gives the farmers' condition for optimization, the stochastic market equilibrium is obtained by equating the supply curve with the expected price implied by the demand curve; that is,

$$q + 1.5q\,\sigma^2 = 9 - 2q$$

which implies

$$q = \frac{9}{3 + 1.5\sigma^2}$$

Also, note that the variance of price if the market is freely competitive is

$$\sigma^2 = E[(p - \mu_p)^2] = E\{[(9 - 2q + \epsilon) - (9 - 2q)]^2\} = E(\epsilon^2) = 1$$

Thus, in a free market, the equilibrium quantity is $q = 9/(3 + 1.5 \cdot 1) = 2$, in which case price is $p = 9 - 2 \cdot 2 + 1 = 6$ or $p = 9 - 2 \cdot 2 - 1 = 4$, each with probability 0.5 (see Figure 11.14).

Now suppose that a buffer stock is introduced which completely stabilizes price, thus implying $\sigma^2 = 0$. In this case, the equilibrium supply is represented implicitly by $\mu_p = q$. If the government fixes a stable price at $p = 3$, then the quantity produced is $q = 3$. Also, following the demand curve, the quantity consumed is $q = 4.5 - 0.5 \cdot 3 + 0.5 = 3.5$ if $\epsilon = 1$, and $q = 4.5 - 0.5 \cdot 3 - 0.5 = 2.5$ if $\epsilon = -1$. Hence, on average, the buffer stock neither grows nor declines; the expected quantity demanded is equal to the quantity supplied. Note alternatively that the buffer stock is expected to grow if stabilized price is set above $p = 3$, and a decline in the buffer stock is expected if stabilized price is set below $p = 3$.

The welfare effects of this buffer stock policy are thus as follows. Consumers gain area $a + b + c + d + e + f + g + h + j + k + m = 8.25$ or \$8.25 billion in periods where $\epsilon = 1$ (note that areas in Figure 11.14 are measured in billion dollars) and gain area $j + k = 2.25$ or \$2.25 billion in periods where $\epsilon = -1$. Their expected gain is thus \$5.25 billion. The expected utility of wheat farmers (measured in money terms), on the other hand, changes from area $d + e + j + n = 5$ or \$5 billion to area $n + r + s = 4.5$ or \$4.5 billion for a loss of \$0.5 billion. In this case, there is a net gain for producers and consumers considered jointly of \$4.75 billion, but the buffer stock policy actually makes farmers—an intended beneficiary group—worse off. The relative worsening of the farmers' position is due to a substantial risk response and the accompanying price-depressing impact.

11.8   APPLICATIONS IN AGRICULTURAL POLICY

As suggested by the example of Section 11.7, perhaps the most important area of application of the framework of this chapter is agricultural price stabilization. A great deal of this type of analysis was precipitated by the extreme price fluctuations of agricultural commodities in the early 1970s. The Food and Agriculture Act of 1977, for example, was one policy response intended to deal with these wide price fluctuations in the United States. The grain stock policy instituted with this Act represented an important departure from previous agricultural policy. Before 1977, U.S. grain policy relied mainly on price supports, sometimes augmented by marketing quotas for the purpose of protecting farm incomes from down-side risk. When huge grain stocks began to accumulate, however, officials quickly realized that any rule for accumulating stocks (for example, a price support program) must be accompanied by an orderly rule for liquidating those stocks. When stock liquidation was undertaken as soon as prices exceeded price supports, as in the late 1950s and early 1960s, the huge grain stocks caused the price support to act somewhat like a price ceiling as well as a price floor.

In this context, the spread between the price support and the release price (or trigger price where stock liquidation is encouraged) in the Food and Agriculture Act of 1977 provided a margin that makes government storage seem more justified on efficiency grounds according to the analysis of this chapter. By comparison, when only a price support is instituted, as with earlier policies, the analysis of Section 8.5 indicates an economic efficiency loss.[23] That is, in light of the extreme price instability of the early 1970s and the observed price-depressing effect of stock liquidation a decade or so earlier, the Food and Agriculture Act of 1977 represented an effort to bound price variations both above and below, as in Figure 11.8. Under the current reserve policy, increased storage from bumper crops is encouraged to prevent excessively low prices; then, in years of shortage, stock liquidation is encouraged to mitigate excessively large price increases which would otherwise destabilize the industry.

As shown by the various theoretical cases of this chapter, however, an evaluation of the distributional impact of a grain stock policy that shrinks the price distribution by means of a self-liquidating buffer stock rule is necessarily sensitive to such considerations as curvature of supply and demand, the form of disturbances, risk response, and so on.[24] The results show that almost nothing can be determined on the basis of economic theory alone about which groups gain and which lose from price stabilization with such a buffer stock policy. If demand and supply are linear, producers may gain and consumers lose, whereas if demand and supply are nonlinear (with the same price elasticities and price levels), consumers may gain while producers lose. The same difference may apply if disturbances in supply and demand are multiplicative rather than additive. In other words, theory alone cannot determine whether produc-

---

[23]One should also note, however, that equity rather than efficiency was apparently the goal of earlier agricultural policies. But, of course, the occurrence of efficiency loss implies that some more efficient redistribution plan may have existed (apart from political acceptability considerations).

[24]A number of studies have been performed to estimate the economic welfare effects of grain price stabilization, including: Willard W. Cochrane and Yigal Danin, *Reserve Stock Grain Models: The World and United States, 1975–1985*, Minnesota Agricultural Experiment Station Technical Bulletin No. 305, 1976; J. A. Sharples, R. L. Walker, and R. W. Slaughter, Jr., "Buffer Stock Management for Wheat Price Stabilization," Commodity Economics Division Economic Research Service, U.S. Department of Agriculture, Washington, D.C., 1976; C. Robert Taylor and Hovav Talpaz, "Approximately Optimal Carryover Levels for Wheat in the United States," *American Journal of Agricultural Economics*, Vol. 61, No. 1 (February 1979), pp. 32–40; and, A. C. Zwart and K. D. Mielke, "The Influence of Domestic Pricing Policies and Buffer Stocks on Price Stability in the World Wheat Industry," *American Journal of Agricultural Economics*, Vol. 61, No. 3 (August 1979), pp. 434–47. These studies, however, use essentially the Massell framework in Figures 11.3 and 11.4, although some of these studies consider specific nonflexible nonlinear supply and demand. Another study that examines the distributional issues of grain price stabilization empirically in the context of international trade using the framework of Figure 11.5 is Panos A. Konandreas and Andrew Schmitz, "Welfare Implications of Grain Price Stabilization: Some Empirical Evidence for the United States," *American Journal of Agricultural Economics*, Vol. 60, No. 1 (February 1978), pp. 74–84.

ers benefit from a buffer stock policy that stabilizes prices. Nor can theory alone determine whether consumers benefit from a buffer stock policy.

The theoretical results, however, indicate some important generalities that must be considered in an empirical analysis of buffer stock policy. Consider, for example, the implications of the results relating to nonlinearity in Section 11.4 for empirical and simulation studies of stabilization. The theory implies that any empirical study that does not adequately investigate nonlinearity may determine the estimated impacts (even qualitatively) through arbitrary specifications and assumptions. The same is true with respect to disturbance form. Unfortunately, these considerations have generally not been made in empirical stabilization studies nor are they easy to make. Nonlinearity and disturbance form are problems that have often plagued econometricians. The usual empirical or simulation approach which has been continued in stabilization studies has been simply to specify a linear form with additive disturbances or log-linear form with multiplicative disturbances. Hence, simplistic as the theoretical cases of this chapter may be, they lead to serious reservations about the use of such empirical work on distributional aspects of applied economic welfare analysis.

These conclusions for functional form are supported, for example, by the empirical work of Reutlinger, who, in using crude, piecewise-linear demand curves, concluded that "the storage impact on gains and losses by consumers and producers is particularly sensitive to the assumed shape of the demand function."[25] Similarly, with respect to the form of disturbances, Turnovsky concludes that "unless the policy maker has reliable information on this question, any stabilization policy may have undesirable effects on the group it is intended to assist."[26] In a rare empirical stabilization study considering risk response, Hazell and Scandizzo, conclude that "the potential welfare gains to be had from optimal intervention policies are surprisingly large, in fact far greater than might be anticipated" in the case where risk response is considered.[27]

There has been some limited effort to consider the necessary generalities outlined in this chapter in empirical work, but the evidence is not yet sufficiently substantial to be conclusive. One study has found that estimation can be accurate enough to make the qualitative distributional effects reasonably

---

[25]Shlomo Reutlinger, "A Simulation Model for Evaluating Worldwide Buffer Stocks of Wheat," *American Journal of Agricultural Economics,* Vol. 58, No. 1 (February 1976), pp. 1–12.

[26]Turnovsky, "Distribution of Welfare Gains."

[27]P. B. R. Hazell and P. L. Scandizzo, "Optimal Price Intervention Policies When Production Is Risky," in *Risk, Uncertainty and Agricultural Development,* ed. James A. Roumasset, Jean-Marc Boussard, and Inderjit Singh (Philippines: Southeast Asian Regional Center for Graduate Study and Research in Agriculture/ New York: Agricultural Development Council, 1979), p. 378.

clear.[28] But as more functional generality is added in specification, the esti-mated econometric accuracy declines.

Another issue that arises in stabilization policy considerations relates to optimal policy design. In the framework of this chapter, zero storage costs were assumed for the most part. Thus, in the absence of risk response or private storage response to government intervention, complete price stabilization is the most efficient policy. When storage costs are substantial, however, the problem of optimal policy design is more difficult. Consider, for example, Figure 11.15, where storage cost per unit is $p_1 - p_2$, and supply alternates between S_1 and S_2. With complete price stabilization, consumers and producers gain $\frac{1}{2}$ area $a + c + f + h$ on average. However, storage costs are $\frac{1}{2}$ area $b + c + d + e + f + g$ on average, so costs of stabilization outweigh the gains if area $b + d + e + g >$ area $a + h$. Thus, quite obviously, when storage costs are high, complete price stabilization is not preferable to no price stabilization. On the other hand, application of the analysis in Figure 11.8 clearly implies a gain of $\frac{1}{2}$ area $a + h$ on average from partial price stabilization. Thus, when storage costs are con-sidered, there is generally an optimal degree of price stabilization which can be greater than no stabilization and less than complete stabilization.

Furthermore, altering the parameters of Figure 11.15 suggests that the opti-mal degree of price stabilization depends on storage costs and the extent of free-market fluctuations. Consider, for example, Figure 11.16, where D repre-sents demand and supply is either S_1, S_2, S_3, or S_4. Using the framework of Figure 11.8, where storage costs are present, suppose that the optimal price band in Figure 11.16 is given by p_2 and p_3 if supply alternates between S_2 and S_3 and marginal per unit storage cost is $p_2 - p_3$.[29] Alternatively, suppose that the optimal price band is given by p_1 and p_4 if supply alternates between S_1 and S_4 and marginal per unit storage cost is $p_1 - p_4$. In the former case, the amount

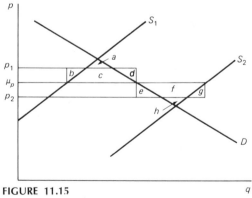

FIGURE 11.15

[28]See Just and Hallam, "Functional Flexibility."

[29]Note that the optimal price band is not necessarily the one that equates the band width to marginal storage cost per unit. This assumption is used here merely for demonstrative purposes and to relate more clearly to the analysis in Figure 11.8.

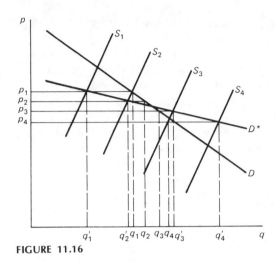

FIGURE 11.16

stored or carried over from high-supply periods to low-supply periods is $q_3' - q_3$, whereas in the latter case, the amount carried over is $q_4' - q_4$.

Suppose now that the marginal cost of storage is increasing in the quantity stored because of capacity constraints, cost of conversion of facilities, and so on. Then the higher marginal storage costs of $p_1 - p_4$ would reasonably correspond to the case of greater storage (i.e., where $q_4' - q_4$ is larger than $q_3' - q_3$). This argument suggests the existence of a function such as D^*, which prescribes the optimal regulated price and storage transaction as a function of the supply fluctuation. That is, the optimal price is given by the intersection of D^* and supply, while the optimal storage transaction is given by the horizontal difference in D^* and D at that price.[30]

When storage costs are introduced, it becomes apparent that the quantity variability of stock transactions caused by complete price stabilization significantly reduces benefits because a much larger buffer stock is required. Although more price stabilization may benefit producers and consumers jointly, the costs incurred by the buffer authority in additional price stabilization increase sharply. The buffer authority is better off with quantity stabilization of buffer stock transactions. Thus, a trade-off between price stabilization and quantity stabilization must be considered; the question of economic stabilization that should properly be addressed involves finding an optimal trade-off between the two.

---

[30]The superiority of such a stabilization rule relative to price bands and other popular recommendations has been shown empirically by Cochrane and Danin, *Reserve Stock Grain Models,* for the case of wheat. A practical means of implementing such a policy is discussed by Richard E. Just, "Theoretical and Empirical Considerations in Agricultural Buffer Stock Policy under the Food and Agriculture Act of 1977," prepared for the U.S. General Accounting Office, Washington, D.C., 1981.

Another issue that must be considered empirically is how price regulation should be altered depending on current stock levels. In reality, supply does not vary systematically as in Figures 11.15 and 11.16. Thus, buffer stocks may unexpectedly begin to accumulate or be depleted. The consideration of these problems involves dynamic issues such as those discussed in another context in Chapter 13. Such problems can only be addressed with advanced tools such as dynamic stochastic programming and stochastic control theory, although the welfare theoretic considerations follow those outlined in this chapter, together with possible dynamic modifications as suggested by Chapter 13.[31]

11.9 CONCLUSIONS

This chapter has focused on economic welfare analysis in markets affected by random phenomena. Although the discussion has focused on the welfare implications of price stabilization, the principles are applicable in evaluating any policy or project that affects the underlying stochastic phenomena or individual response to such phenomena. Thus, for example, the issues raised in this chapter should be considered in the analysis of any policy that affects uncertainty with respect to the future. And policy uncertainty itself may create substantial welfare effects. That is, when policymakers begin to consider several alternative policies with widely different provisions, private decision makers may become uncertain about future policies and thus hold back on replacement or expansionary investments until future policy becomes clear. As a result, supply is reduced. The effects of such policy uncertainty can, thus, be examined in the framework of Section 11.6.

The framework of this chapter also points out that the welfare effects of policies that affect market stability can be substantial even when decision makers are not inherently averse to risk depending on their ability to respond quickly to developing market situations. Thus, in addition to the importance of properly determining the degree of nonlinearity and form of random variation in supply and demand already pointed out in this chapter, the determination of time lags in response by individual decision makers is also crucial from both efficiency and distributional points of view. The benefits of stability are very different for individuals who can respond relatively little than for those who can adjust to take advantage of price swings. Thus, the results discussed in this chapter underscore the need for sound empirical work as a basis for applied economic welfare analysis.[32]

---

[31]For an application of dynamic programming in this context, see, for example, Oscar R. Burt, Won W. Koo, and Norman J. Dudley, "Optimal Stochastic Control of U.S. Wheat Stock and Exports," *American Journal of Agricultural Economics,* Vol. 62, No. 2 (May 1980), pp. 172–87.

[32]For a further survey of economic welfare implications of stability, see S. J. Turnovsky, "The Distribution of Welfare Gains from Price Stabilization: A Survey of Some Theoretical Issues," in *Stabilizing World Commodity Markets,* ed. F. G. Adams and S. A. Klein (Lexington, Mass.: Heath—Lexington Books, 1978), pp. 119–48.

12

Nonmarket Welfare Measurement: Applications in Environmental Economics

Thus far, this book has dealt with market welfare measurement—that is, the measurement of welfare effects that are directly reflected through market phenomena. This chapter turns to nonmarket welfare measurement where individual preferences are not necessarily completely reflected in observable decisions in the marketplace. In a modern economy with large corporations, a growing government sector, and increasing pollution problems, the measurement of nonmarket welfare effects is of increasing importance. For example, when an industry pollutes either air or water through its production process, it does not generally take account of those adverse effects in deciding how much to produce, given the market prices of its products. Similarly, when a government decides to build a bridge, it may be able to determine the demand for crossing the bridge; but it may not measure in any way the utility or disutility derived by individuals from looking at the bridge. Problems of the former type are termed externalities, whereas problems of the latter type have to do with public goods. This chapter deals first in some detail with externalities and then discusses the problem of public goods, which is, in fact, a special type of externality problem. The latter part of the chapter then turns to possibilities for measuring the associated welfare effects.

12.1   EXTERNALITIES

An *externality* is defined as the case where an action of one economic agent affects the utility or production possibilities of another in a way that is not reflected in the marketplace. External effects are often classified into the effects of consumers on consumers, producers on producers, producers on consumers, and consumers on producers. Smoking is a common example of a consumer–consumer externality. When a smoker enters a restaurant and chooses to light a cigarette, it may create an unpleasant odor for a nonsmoker also patronizing the restaurant. Since the smoker pays for cigarettes, those actions are partially reflected in the marketplace, but the smoker does not pay the nonsmoker for the right to smoke nor does a market exist for the nonsmoker to pay the smoker to cease smoking in the restaurant! Another example of a consumer–consumer externality is the common phenomenon of "keeping up with the Joneses." When the family next door buys a new Cadillac or Mercedes, one may become more unhappy with his Volkswagen than previously. Again, the behavior of the family purchasing the new car is partially reflected in the marketplace by the automobile purchase, but no market exists to reflect the effect of that purchase on the neighbors. Thus, market behavior cannot possibly reflect any utility or disutility derived by one individual associated with another's consumption.

Perhaps the most widely publicized external effects are those of producers on consumers. These include the effects of industrial pollution which are generally opposed by environmental groups. For example, when a steel plant pollutes air or water, it may detract from the aesthetic qualities of the environment and may even lead to disease or other adverse effects on consumers which are not reflected in the marketplace. Similarly, if a lumber company removes all the trees from a mountainside, it may lead to flooding as well as a decrease in the aesthetic value of the mountain. The value of the lumber for building purposes will be reflected in the market for lumber, but if the lumber company does not pay for the damage due to flooding and does not compensate consumers for the loss of aesthetic pleasures in viewing the mountain, it will generally be inclined to remove too many trees from the mountainside.

With respect to external effects on producers, the effects of consumers on producers have received much less attention; perhaps the most common external effect of consumers on producers involves theft and vandalism. The external effects of producers on producers, on the other hand, have received substantial attention and have involved a large number of legal disputes in the courts. A common agricultural producer externality involves the case where a farmer applies pesticides to his crop to control damaging insects but, as a result of adverse winds, kills a neighboring beekeeper's bees. The benefits of the farmer's increased production are reflected in the marketplace, but unless the beekeeper sues for damages, the farmer does not pay for the beekeeper's losses and hence will tend to overuse pesticides. Another common producer–producer externality is involved in the case where an industry pollutes a river through its production process and, as a result, the fish in the river are killed or contaminated so that fishermen suffer adverse effects.

Each of these examples involves a case where one individual is adversely affected by another's actions. External effects are not necessarily negative, however. Some consumers may be positively affected by an increase in the consumption of others; for example, a rich person may enjoy seeing the consumption of a poor person increase. Giving to charities designed to help the poor is one evidence that this type of positive consumption–consumption externality can exist. In the producer–producer case, one farmer may find his pesticide application much more effective if neighboring farmers also apply the same types of pesticides, so that new pest populations do not immediately move into his fields from neighboring fields as soon as the effects of the pesticides have worn off.

Social Optimality

When externalities exist, a competitive economy will generally no longer attain a Pareto equilibrium as in the case of Chapter 2. To consider a concrete example, suppose that a producer–producer externality exists between two firms. Let the production function of the first firm be given by $q_1 = x_1^{1/2}$ and the production function of the second firm be given by $q_2 = x_2^{1/2} - x_0$ where x_0 is considered as a constant by the second firm. Suppose that both firms are profit maximizers with the prices of q_1, q_2, x_1, and x_2 given, respectively, by p_1, p_2, w_1, and w_2. Assume, further, that the second firm purchases only x_2 as an input and that $x_0 = x_1^{1/2}$ is imposed upon it as an externality by the first firm's input decision.

The first firm will maximize its profits $p_1 q_1 - w_1 x_1$, by equating its output price p_1 with its marginal costs, $2w_1 q_1$, thus choosing an output quantity, $q_1 = p_1/(2w_1)$.[1] The second firm maximizes its profits, $p_2 q_2 - w_2 x_2$, by equating its price p_2 with its marginal costs $2w_2(q_2 + x_1^{1/2})$, given the amount of x_1 used by the first firm, thus obtaining the quantity, $q_2 = (p_2 - 2w_2 x_1^{1/2})/(2w_2)$. In other words, what constitutes optimal behavior for the second firm depends on what the first firm does.

These solutions represent a competitive equilibrium in the presence of the externality. Obviously, the first firm imposes a cost on the second firm in its choice of x_1 that is not reflected in the marketplace and is not considered in its

---

[1]The firm's marginal cost is determined here by expressing total variable cost, $w_1 x_1$, as a function of q_1 through substitution of the production function and then computing the derivative of total variable cost with respect to q_1.

profit maximization. The external effect as a function of x_1 is given by $p_2 x_1^{1/2}$ and represents the damages imposed on the second firm by decisions of the first firm. This function is called the *damage function*. The damage function gives the total external costs as a function of the amount of the pollutant (x_1 is the pollutant in this case). Social or Pareto optimality is not attained by the competitive equilibrium because this cost or damage by the first firm is not considered in its actions. In point of fact, the costs considered by the first firm in its profit maximization are only its *private costs*, where private costs are defined as those costs actually incurred by an individual as a result of his actions. The social costs that should actually be considered are the sum of the firm's private costs and its external costs. Social optimality for the decisions of firm 1 is attained by equating its output price with its marginal social costs rather than the marginal private costs, $2w_1 q_1$, used above. The social costs, $w_1 x_1 + p_2 x_1^{1/2}$, are obtained as the sum of private costs, $w_1 x_1$, and external costs. Similarly, the marginal social costs, $2w_1 q_1 + p_2$, are determined by the sum of marginal private costs, $2w_1 q_1$, and marginal external cost, p_2.[2] The social optimum production for firm 1 obtained by equating its product price with its marginal social costs is thus $q_1 = (p_1 - p_2)/(2w_1)$.

To see more clearly that this indeed represents a social optimum, consider the approach of *internalization*.[3] Internalization is an approach commonly used to determine social optimality in the presence of externalities by considering all of the involved economic agents jointly, as, for example, in a hypothetical merger of firms. In the preceding case, where the prices of both inputs and outputs are truly fixed for both firms, the externality can be internalized by maximizing the joint profits of the two firms as if the two firms were merged. Joint profits are given by $p_1 q_1 + p_2 q_2 - w_1 x_1 - w_2 x_2$. Substituting for q_1 and q_2 using the respective production functions yields $p_1 x_1^{1/2} + p_2 x_2^{1/2} - p_2 x_1^{1/2} - w_1 x_1 - w_2 x_2$, and the associated first-order conditions of calculus for maximization require $(p_1 - p_2)/(2x_1^{1/2}) - w_1 = 0$ and $p_2/(2x_2^{1/2}) - w_2 = 0$. Solving the first condition and substituting the first production function indeed verifies that $q_1 = (p_1 - p_2)/(2w_1)$ under social optimality.

Substituting the resulting decisions in the case of competitive equilibrium in the presence of externalities leads to profits of $p_1^2/(4w_1)$ for the first firm and $p_2^2(4w_2) - p_2 p_1/(2w_1)$ for the second firm. Using the results for the internalized solution, however, implies joint profits for the two firms of $(p_1 - p_2)^2/(4w_1) + p_2^2/(4w_2)$. The latter profits are obviously larger by $p_2^2/(4w_1)$, indicating that the competitive equilibrium in the presence of externalities is Pareto subopti-

---

[2] The marginal cost associated with q_1 production is determined here by expressing the total external cost as a function of q_1 rather than x_1 through substitution of the production function for q_1 and then computing the derivative with respect to q_1.

[3] For a detailed discussion of externalities and the approach of internalization, see F. M. Bator, "The Anatomy of Market Failure," *Quarterly Journal of Economics*, Vol. 72, No. 3 (August 1958), pp. 351–79.

mal; *that is, by moving to the internalized solution, the second firm gains more than the first firm loses and can thus compensate the first firm for its losses and still be better off.*

To understand these concepts diagrammatically and to demonstrate the general externality problem, consider Figure 12.1, where the marginal private cost of production of q is represented by MPC, which is, of course, the competitive supply curve in the presence of externalities, marginal external cost is represented by MEC, and marginal social cost is represented by MSC. Note that, in general, the marginal external cost represents the change in the sum of external costs on all agents affected externally associated with a change in q. This definition is unambiguous in the case where all external effects are on profit-maximizing firms. In the case where some external effects are on consumers, external costs may be represented by willingness to pay for increments or decrements of q; in doing so, one must bear in mind the results of Section 7.9 which discuss consumer surplus changes as approximations of willingness to pay when quantity changes are imposed. Thus, the marginal external cost curve is a marginal willingness-to-pay curve which represents either the sum of changes in compensating variations or the sum of changes in equivalent variations *over all agents* affected externally depending on whether the associated utility levels are held at initial or final states.

If the price of q is initially p_0, then competitive production in the presence of the externality will be q_0 in Figure 12.1. External costs are represented by area $k + h$. Social optimality, however, is obtained by equating price and marginal social cost at q_1. Since cutting production will, in general, lead to an increase in price along the demand curve, however, the equation of price and marginal social costs will result in equilibrium production at q_2.

Where for simplicity the ordinary and compensated demand curves coincide, the welfare effects of moving from competitive equilibrium at q_0 to social

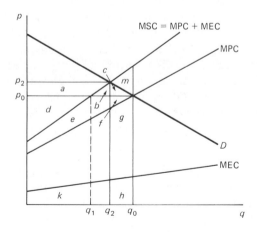

FIGURE 12.1

optimality at q_2 can be analyzed as follows. Production costs decrease by area $g + h$. Total revenue for producers decreases by area $f + g + h - a - b$ (which is an increase if demand is inelastic). Producers can thus be actually better off by area $a + b - f$ as a result of moving to social optimality. Consumers, on the other hand, lose area $a + b + c$ as a result of the increase in price and reduction in production. Finally, external agents gain area h as a reduction in external costs. The net social gain is thus area $h - c - f =$ area m since, by construction, area h = area $c + f + m$.

An interesting implication of Figure 12.1 is that social optimality does not necessarily imply that externalities should be restricted to zero. In other words, if a firm is polluting the atmosphere and external effects are represented by MEC, then the optimal reduction in production from q_0 to q_2 will generally entail only a reduction in the rate of pollution rather than a complete curtailment. That is, as the rate of pollution is reduced, marginal external costs are also reduced while marginal market benefits, as represented by the vertical difference in the demand curve and the marginal private cost curve, are increasing and may soon outweigh the marginal external costs. This phenomenon is ignored by some environmental groups that argue for extreme policies of environmental preservation.

The externality represented in Figure 12.1 is a negative externality; however, some positive externalities may possibly be derived from the production of q or its side effects. For example, in Figure 12.2 the vertical distance between MSC and MPC represents marginal external costs or the sum of changes in compensating variation (or equivalent variation as the case may be) with respect to a change in q over all those individuals affected negatively by an increase in q. The vertical distance between marginal social benefits, MSB, and marginal private benefits, MPB, represents marginal external benefits or the sum of changes in compensating variation (equivalent variation) with respect to

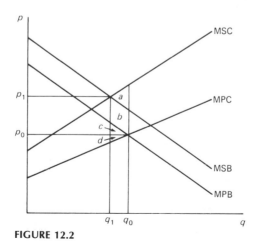

FIGURE 12.2

a change in q over all those individuals affected positively by an increase in q. The private equilibrium for a competitive economy in the presence of externalities is attained at the intersection of MPC, which represents competitive supply, with MPB, which represents competitive demand (i.e., at price p_0 and quantity q_0). The social optimum, on the other hand, is obtained by equating marginal social cost and marginal social benefits (i.e., at price p_1 and quantity q_1). In this case, producers and consumers jointly lose area $c + d$, those who suffer external costs gain area $a + b + c + d$, and those who derive external benefits lose area b. The net impact is thus a gain of area a. Although the case in Figure 12.2 suggests that optimum social production is smaller than optimum private production, the same methodology can be used to show that optimum social production can be larger than optimum private production in the case where marginal external benefits exceed marginal external costs at the private optimum production.

Another consideration in determining the social optimum relates to possibilities for pollution control and the installation of pollution abatement equipment.[4] For example, it could be that a factory can build taller smoke-stacks to gain more condensation within stacks and thus lead to less resulting air pollution. Suppose that marginal external cost differs in the cases of pollution control and no control, as exemplified in Figure 12.3. Also, suppose that operation of pollution control equipment increases the marginal private cost, again as indicated in Figure 12.3. In this case the marginal social cost, obtained by adding external costs and marginal private costs in the two situations, may fall with the consideration of pollution control. If so, the social optimum will

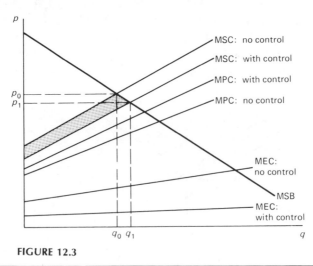

FIGURE 12.3

---

[4]For an excellent exposition on corrective policies in the presence of pollution abatement equipment and a discussion of the property rights issue, see J. H. Dales, *Pollution, Property, and Prices* (Toronto, Canada: University of Toronto Press, 1968).

result in a decrease in price from p_0 to p_1 and an increase in quantity from q_0 to q_1 as pollution abatement equipment is implemented. The resulting increase in social welfare is indicated by the shaded area in Figure 12.3. However, since marginal private costs may be higher with pollution abatement equipment, some incentives may be required to induce firms to adopt such equipment.

Policies for Obtaining Social Optimality in the Presence of Externalities

Policies for dealing with externalities of the type discussed above generally include Pigouvian taxes or subsidies, standards (pollution quotas), and assignment of property rights. For the purpose of illustrating these three approaches, assume that only three groups are affected: producers, consumers, and those suffering adverse externalities. This case seems to be the most commonly encountered situation in policymaking. Other cases can be handled with the same principles by simply considering external benefits associated with production or external benefits or costs associated with consumption.

A *Pigouvian tax* is a tax that imposes the external cost of pollution on the generator of that pollution.[5] For example, where marginal external cost is represented by the vertical difference in MSC and MPC in Figure 12.4, a Pigouvian tax is determined by that vertical difference at the associated production level. For example, at production level q_1 the Pigouvian tax imposed on an ad valorem or per unit basis is $p_1 - p_2$. When the marginal tax is equal to the marginal external cost associated with the resulting output, the firm is made to bear the full marginal cost of its production, and thus its marginal private cost in the presence of the tax is equal to the marginal social cost. Hence, in a

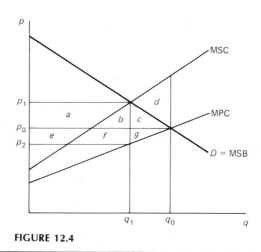

FIGURE 12.4

---

[5]A. C. Pigou, *The Economics of Welfare,* 4th ed. (London: Macmillan & Company Ltd., 1932).

competitive economy, the imposition of a tax rate of $p_1 - p_2$ automatically induces a reduction in production from q_0 to q_1 as equilibrium consumer price adjusts from p_0 to p_1. Along the lines of the methodology in Chapter 8, the associated welfare effects are as follows. Producers lose area $e + f + g$ in producer surplus, consumers lose area $a + b + c$ in consumer surplus, government gains area $a + b + e + f$ in tax revenues, and external agents gain area $c + d + g$ as a reduction in external costs; the net effect is thus a gain of area d. Hence, with both competition and externalities, some lump sum redistribution is possible so that all parties gain by imposing the optimal Pigouvian tax.

In the foregoing example, the relationship of pollution to production is assumed fixed, as when pollution abatement equipment is not available. If pollution can be reduced without a similar reduction in output (through use of pollution abatement equipment), the Pigouvian tax must generally be imposed directly on pollution rather than on output. Otherwise, production is discouraged, and the appropriate incentive for use or installation of pollution abatement equipment is not conveyed to the polluter. Aside from these considerations, however, the analysis described above is valid.

The use of *standards* to control externalities can also be represented in Figure 12.4. That is, since q_1 represents the socially optimal production point, the government may simply limit production to q_1. With the imposition of such a restriction, production is thus reduced from q_0 to q_1, which induces a price increase from p_0 to p_1. The welfare effects associated with such a standard are as follows. Producers gain area $a + b - g$, consumers lose area $a + b + c$, and external agents gain area $c + d + g$. The potential net gain under competition, which is area d, is thus the same with standards as with Pigouvian taxes. However, in the case with standards, producers are better off than under taxes, whereas other parties are equally well off under both sets of controls. Since consumers and external agents are equally well off under the two controls, whereas producers are better off, legislative lobbying interests are inclined to favor standards as opposed to taxes. This fact has been used to explain the predominance of standards or quotas in governmental policies which have been used to deal with externalities.

Again, with quotas as with Pigouvian taxes, these considerations must be modified slightly when pollution abatement equipment is available for altering the relationship between output and pollution. In fact, to properly encourage the adoption of pollution control equipment without overly discouraging output, the standard must be imposed directly on pollution rather than on the overall production activity. Analysis of the welfare effects in this case is similar to that described above except that the pollution standard acts as a determinant of supply and simply rotates the private supply curve upward and counterclockwise but not necessarily to a point of perfect inelasticity as with a quota on production.[6]

---

[6]The literature on environmental economics deals with several types of pollution

Finally, consider the method of assigning *property rights* when externalities are present. Laws are developed either to give the polluter the right to pollute or the pollutee the right to no pollution. The permissive pollution law whereby the polluter has the right to pollute is called L law. The prohibitive pollution law that gives a pollutee the right to no pollution is then called $\bar{L}$ law.

The assignment of property rights is intended to encourage the development of a market for the externality. If a polluter clearly owns the right to pollute, the pollutee may be willing to pay the polluter to either reduce or cease pollution. If the pollutee owns the right to no pollution, a potential polluter may buy the right to pollute from the pollutee. R.H. Coase was first to show in his famous *Coase Theorem* that *Pareto optimality* is attained when such markets are developed.[7] The assignment of property rights, however, can have a profound effect on income distribution; under one law, one agent can sell the right to pollute while, under the other law, the other agent can sell that right.

The results of assigning property rights can be demonstrated in the framework of Figure 12.4. To do this clearly, however, consider Figure 12.5, where

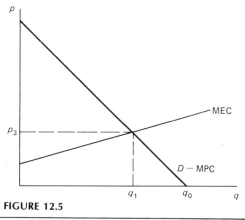

FIGURE 12.5

problems. The controls considered explicitly here, however, are those which relate to effluents or omissions generated by individual firms, i.e., those which deal with point source pollution problems. *Point source pollution* problems are those in which the amount of pollution produced by individual firms is identified for purposes of imposing controls. In *nonpoint source pollution* problems, where amounts of pollution generated by individual firms cannot be determined (for practical purposes), similar principles apply but controls can only relate indirectly to pollution. In such cases, controls usually take the form of taxes or quotas on production or standards on technologies used. In the latter case, the effect of imposing a technology standard is to shift cost curves and supply curves much as discussed above where a standard is imposed on pollution. An example of standards dealing with point source pollution would be an effluent standard where effluent generation is monitored by a control agency. An example in the case of nonpoint source pollution would be ambient air quality standards which are attained by means of emission standards imposed on the technology incorporated in automobiles.

[7]R. H. Coase, "The Problem of Social Cost," *Journal of Law and Economics*, Vol. 3 (October 1960), pp. 1–44.

the marginal external costs, MEC, represent the vertical difference in MSC and MPC in Figure 12.4 and $D - MPC$ represents the vertical difference in demand and marginal private costs in Figure 12.4. In this context, MEC represents a marginal damage function, whereas $D - MPC$ represents a marginal (opportunity) *cost of control*.[8] Now suppose that the pollutee has the right to no pollution, as under $\bar{L}$ law. Then MEC will represent the supply of pollution rights since it is simply the marginal cost to the pollutee of allowing pollution. The $D - MPC$ curve, on the other hand, represents the demand by the producer for the right to pollute. Thus, if a market for the pollution right develops, the resulting price will be p_3 at a quantity of q_1. Comparing with Figure 12.4, social optimality is thus obtained when the price of pollution rights, p_3, is equal to $p_1 - p_2$, which is also the optimal Pigouvian tax.

Now suppose that the right to pollute is assigned to the polluter as under L law. In this case, the lower axis of Figure 12.5 may simply be reversed so that MEC represents the demand by the pollutee for pollution reduction. Similarly, the $D - MPC$ curve will represent the supply of pollution reduction. Equilibrium will again result at price p_3 and quantity q_1, obtaining the social optimality point of Figure 12.4.

Contrasting the results under L law and $\bar{L}$ law, however, reveals a substantial difference in income distribution. Under $\bar{L}$ law, the pollutee sells the polluter the right to pollute, associated with the quantity q_1 at a price p_3, thus involving a transfer of $p_3 q_1$ from the polluter to the pollutee. Under L law, on the other hand, the polluter receives a price of p_3 per unit for reducing production from q_0 to q_1, which thus involves a transfer of $p_3(q_0 - q_1)$ from the pollutee to the polluter. In effect, the polluter's income is higher by $p_3 q_0$ under $\bar{L}$ law than under L law, while the pollutee's income is higher by the same amount in the opposite situation.

Important Considerations in Comparing Policies

In comparing policies that are implemented to control externalities, as in the framework described above, several crucial assumptions must be borne in mind—the failure of which may reverse some of the implications. For example, if the assumption of competition is replaced by one of monopoly, the effects of a tax may be quite different from those in Figure 12.4. Consider, for example, Figure 12.6, where the monopolist's marginal private cost is given by MPC and

---

[8]The *control cost function* is defined as the cost incurred by a polluter (due to reduced output and other opportunity costs in addition to direct pollution abatement costs) to reduce pollution from the level that would occur with a free market in the absence of control policies. In Figure 12.5, both the control cost function and the damage function are represented as functions of output to relate to Figure 12.4, since production and pollution are assumed to have a fixed relationship. In general, however, control cost and damage are expressed as functions of the amount of pollution, so that possibilities for use of pollution abatement equipment are taken into account.

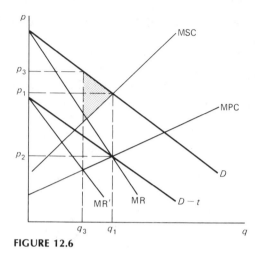

FIGURE 12.6

the marginal social cost that accounts for externalities is MSC. The demand curve facing the monopolist is represented by D with the associated marginal revenue curve MR. As demonstrated in Figure 12.6, the production point selected by the monopolist where marginal revenue is equal to marginal private cost at q_1 can possibly coincide with the point where marginal social cost is equal to marginal social benefits represented by the demand curve, even though no corrective taxes, standards, or other controls are used (similarly, Figure 12.6 could be redrawn so that the monopoly solution involves either more or less production than under social optimality). On the other hand, if the Pigouvian tax, $p_1 - p_2$, is imposed, then the free-market solution which reaches social optimality would be distorted. With the tax, the demand curve perceived by the monopolist would shift to $D - t$ (assuming an ad valorem tax of $t = p_1 - p_2$), and the associated marginal revenue curve would be MR'. Thus, the production point selected by the monopolist would fall from q_1 to q_3, and raise consumer prices from p_1 to p_3. An accounting of welfare effects on individual groups in this case will demonstrate a net social loss equal to the shaded area in Figure 12.6.

The case in Figure 12.6 exemplifies the problem of *second best*.[9] The general premise of the theory of second best is that when two or more distortions exist—for example, a monopoly and an externality—then the imposition of a corrective control for one of the distortions may drive the economy further from the point of social optimality than if the distortions are allowed to (par-

---

[9]The problem of second best was introduced by R. G. Lipsey and K. Lancaster, "The General Theory of Second Best," *Review of Economic Studies*, Vol. 24 (1956–57), pp. 11–32, and was discussed for the particular problem presented here by J. Buchanan, "External Diseconomies, Corrective Taxes, and Market Structure," *American Economic Review*, Vol. 59, No. 1 (March 1969), pp. 174–77.

tially) offset each other. In Figure 12.6, the imposition of a Pigouvian tax to correct the externality, or changing the structure of the production industry from monopoly to competition, drives the economy away from social optimality; only if both measures are undertaken is Pareto optimality attained. In the latter case, production and consumption would be unchanged with respect to the commodity in question, although income distribution may be altered.

A simple analogy of the tax case with the property rights case also reveals that an assignment of property rights to correct the externality may lead to a similar problem of second best if production does not take place under competition. On the other hand, if a standard or quota is imposed, production can be maintained at q_1 if the quota corresponds to the socially optimum production point.

Another point to keep in mind in Figures 12.4 and 12.5 is the case where changes in income cause supply or demand curves to shift—that is, where ordinary and compensated curves do not coincide. In this case the point of social optimality depends upon the income distributional effects of the control adopted.

Consider, for example, Figure 12.7, where the various MEC curves and $D - $ MPC curves correspond to different income distributions. Under the case of a tax, for example, both polluters' and pollutees' incomes are not affected, and thus they react along their initial ordinary curves, $D - MPC_0$ and MEC_0. The corresponding equilibrium is at point t with quantity $q_1{}^t$ and price $p_3{}^t$. With a quota, on the other hand, external agents' income is unaffected directly, whereas the producers or sellers of q receive an additional amount, corresponding to $q_1(p_1 - p_2)$ in Figure 12.4, over the amount they would ordinarily receive when reacting along their private supply curve. To examine the case in Figure 12.7, consider the marginal external cost curve MEC_0 and the pollution demand curve $D - MPC_2$, which corresponds to an increase in sellers' income of $p_3{}^Q q_1{}^Q$

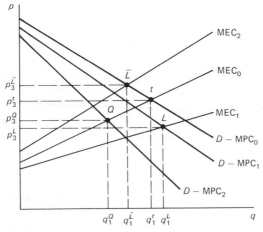

FIGURE 12.7

above the tax solution. The resulting social optimum obtained with this alternative income distribution is thus at point Q with quantity q_1^Q and price p_3^Q.

The assignment of property rights, of course, corresponds to other distributions of income. Under L law, external agents make a payment of $p_3^L(q_0 - q_1^L)$ to sellers of q. With the effective reduction in income, the marginal external cost curve of external agents shifts to MEC_1, and the increase in income for sellers causes a shift of the demand for pollution to $D - MPC_1$. The associated equilibrium is at point L in Figure 12.7. Finally, under $\bar{L}$ law, the income of external agents is increased by $p_3^{\bar{L}}q_1^{\bar{L}}$, thus shifting the marginal external cost curve to MEC_2, while the income of sellers is the same as it would ordinarily be at the resulting equilibrium. That is, turning to Figure 12.4, sellers sell at price p_1 but pay $q_1(p_1 - p_2)$ to external agents, thus leaving their income the same as if price p_2 were received at quantity q_1 along their ordinary private supply curve. Thus, equilibrium under $\bar{L}$ law is at point $\bar{L}$ in Figure 12.7. The analysis in Figure 12.7 thus demonstrates along much the same lines as the pure exchange economy in Chapter 2 that the point of Pareto optimality depends critically upon income distribution and that the choice of policy controls for dealing with externalities can involve a choice among income distributions. And of course, to evaluate the welfare differences between these controls accurately, one must additionally consider divergence of compensated curves from ordinary curves (not shown) in Figure 12.7.

Finally, the following points are important in the choice of policy instruments for controlling externalities. First, property rights may be a reasonable approach only when a few parties are involved as polluters and pollutees. Otherwise, the costs involved in developing and operating a market for the externalities (commonly called *transactions costs*) may quickly outweigh the associated social gains and become prohibitive.

Even when few parties are involved, however, transactions costs may become prohibitive or impose substantial costs on other parts of the economy because competitive forces do not operate in such cases. For example, a number of legal suits have involved pollutees suing polluters, thus leading to substantial court costs. And court costs are just as much a cost to society as an equal amount of production costs.

The assignment of property rights for the purpose of controlling externalities also assumes that the source of pollution can be identified. However, many pollution problems are of a *non-point-source* nature, meaning that the particular firm or individual generating the pollution is not identifiable. For example, when groundwater (water associated with the underground water table) becomes polluted with salts, identification of the relative contribution of various sources to that salt pollution problem may be impossible.

Also, in the assignment of property rights where few parties are involved, the individuals on one side or the other of the market in Figure 12.7 may be able to exercise market power and thus influence the price of pollution rights above or below the point of social optimality. For this reason and those cited above, the assignment of property rights has found very limited application in the solution of externality problems except where pollution rights and associated damages have been decided in the courts.

Another consideration that can alter the conclusions of this section relates to the presence of stochastic phenomena. If pollution is stochastic and depends, for example, on wind direction or amount of rainfall, then standards may be imposed only with respect to production plans or the operation of pollution abatement equipment. Taxes, on the other hand, may be imposed either on actual pollution or on the act of production without use of abatement equipment. The various risk effects of these policies are quite different. For example, a standard on production technology imposes all of the risk of pollution on the pollutee as with the case of taxes on ex ante production decisions. In the case of a tax on actual stochastic pollution, however, some of the risk is transferred to the polluter. The relative social benefits of one system versus the other depend upon the extent of risk aversion by polluters versus pollutees. It has also been shown that a subsidy on nonpollution versus a tax on pollution in a case where the event of pollution is stochastic can have different outcomes as well. The relative social benefits of these two controls depend upon whether the likelihood of pollution is high or low, since the degree of risk involved can be much different with the alternative controls in these extremes. In point of fact, it turns out that an increase in the tax on pollution can even lead to an increase in the likelihood of pollution in this case because of the effects of risk aversion when the probability of pollution is high.[10]

Even when pollution is nonstochastic, however, there may be definite advantages of one control over the other. For example, Baumol and Oates have shown that the optimal imposition of standards or quotas may require a substantial amount of information on individual cost curves, which, if not obtained, can suggest a preference for use of taxes in controlling externalities.[11] For example, consider the two firms exemplified in Figure 12.8, where the marginal private cost of the first firm is given by MPC_1 and the marginal private cost of the second firm is given by MPC_2. Suppose that demand facing the two firms is perfectly elastic at p_0 but that a Pigouvian tax of t is imposed, thus reducing effective output price to p_1. Each firm will thus reduce its production along its marginal private cost curve to q_i', $i = 1, 2$. Now suppose instead that a quota is imposed on production in order to reduce pollution. Also, suppose for simplicity that pollution occurs in constant proportion to output and that the

[10]On these points, see Richard E. Just and David Zilberman, "Asymmetry of Taxes and Subsidies in Regulating Stochastic Mishap," *Quarterly Journal of Economics*, Vol. 93, No. 1 (February 1979), pp. 139–48; and Eithan Hochman, David Zilberman, and Richard E. Just, "Internalization in a Stochastic Pollution Model," *Water Resources Research*, Vol. 13, No. 6 (December 1977), pp. 877–81.

[11]W. Baumol and W. Oates, "The Use of Standards and Prices for Protection of the Environment," *Swedish Journal of Economics*, Vol. 73, No. 1 (March 1971), pp. 42–54.

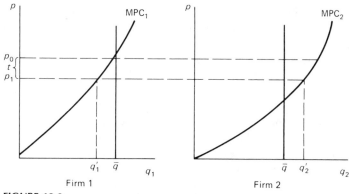

FIGURE 12.8

rate of pollution is the same for both firms. In this case, if t is the appropriate tax, the quota that will achieve the same social optimality will be q_1' for firm 1 and q_2' for firm 2.

However, unless the policymaker has knowledge of the marginal private cost curves of the individual firms, these quota levels can generally not be computed. An alternative that is employed in practice is to select an overall quota level and then allocate it among firms. If this is done and the quota level is allocated equally among firms, for example, the quota level $\bar{q}$ may be imposed upon each firm individually so as to obtain the same overall output as if the tax t were imposed. If this is done, however, the quota may be economically inefficient because, for example, firm 1 will be producing at much higher marginal costs than firm 2, and hence overall costs could be reduced by increasing firm 2's production and reducing firm 1's production by an equal amount from the quota level. If pollution is proportional to production by firm, equating marginal costs across firms would result in the same level of pollution and thus lead to Pareto superiority.[12]

The imposition of either taxes or standards, however, requires information about the damage function associated with externally affected agents. Unless a market for property rights is established, information regarding damages can generally not be ascertained from market data; in fact, it may be quite difficult even to determine all externally affected individuals. Approaches for dealing with this estimation problem are discussed later in this chapter, but first a related externality problem—public goods—will be discussed in some detail.

12.2 PUBLIC GOODS

The goods considered thus far in this book have been both private and excludable. A *private good* is a good that, once consumed by one consumer, cannot be

---

[12] For a detailed discussion on this point, see Martin L. Weitzman, "Prices vs. Quantities," Vol. 41, No. 128 (October 1974), pp. 477–91.

consumed by another. An *excludable good* is a good for which there exists some mechanism whereby consumption can be rationed or controlled so that someone cannot consume the good without paying a price. A *public good,* on the other hand, is a good for which consumption by one individual does not prevent consumption by another individual.[13] Also, in its purest sense, a public good is nonexcludable in the sense that a positive price cannot be enforced. Examples of public goods include such things as national defense, a view of a mountain, clean air, and the welfare of future generations. Each individual may derive some benefit from the good without preventing another from enjoying the same benefit. Also, it is impossible to force an individual to pay for the good according to the benefit derived. One can simply claim that no benefits are derived and leave it up to other individuals to make sure that the good is provided. Such an individual is often called a *free rider*. Public goods are associated with externalities since such an individual's preference for the good may not be registered in the marketplace. That is, each individual may be willing to pay a given amount for the good if assured that everyone else will pay a fair share, but in a large economy where an individual does not perceive his own individual actions as affecting the overall amount of the good, a natural inducement exists to enjoy the good without paying for it. On the other hand, since each individual probably derives a different marginal benefit from the change in the quantity of a public good, equality of payments among all individuals may also not be the best approach.

To understand these concepts, consider Figure 12.9, where the lower axis in each case represents the amount of a public good and the vertical axis represents marginal valuations. The D_1 curve in Figure 12.9(a) represents the marginal benefits derived by individual 1 in consuming the public good. Similarly, D_2 represents the marginal benefits derived by individual 2. Supposing that the economy is made up of two individuals, the marginal social benefits associated with the public good are derived by adding the individual marginal benefit curves vertically as in Figure 12.9(c). Thus, if a quantity $\bar{q}$ of the public good is produced, the marginal benefit derived by individual 1 is p_1 as indicated in Figure 12.9(a), the marginal benefit of individual 2 is p_2 as indicated in Figure 12.9(b), and the marginal social benefit is $p_1 + p_2$ as indicated in Figure 12.9(c). Social optimality is obtained by equating the marginal cost of producing the good with the marginal social benefits derived by its consumption; thus, $\bar{q}$ represents the point of social optimality.

The case of public goods is another instance in which a free competitive economy fails to reach social optimality. For example, suppose that a private firm attempts to produce the public good according to the marginal cost curve, MC, in Figure 12.9. First, if the private firm does not know the individual

---

[13]For a seminal paper on public goods, see P. A. Samuelson, "The Pure Theory of Public Expenditure," *The Review of Economics and Statistics*, Vol. 36, No. 4 (November 1954), pp. 387–89.

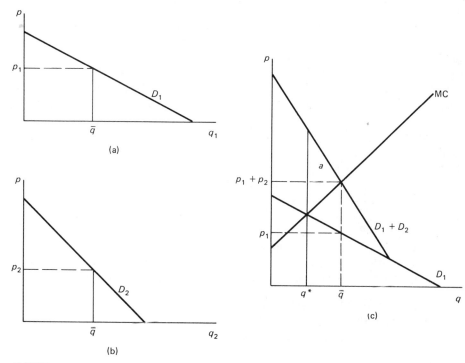

FIGURE 12.9

marginal benefit curves, it will not be able to determine the appropriate prices to charge each individual. Second, because the good is nonexcludable, it would not be able to, say, induce individual 2 to pay for the good at all, given that some is produced for individual 1. Thus, individual 2 is inclined to be a "free rider" who merely benefits from the expenditure of others.

Thus, even if the private producer is successful in reaching an equilibrium price and quantity with individual 1, if individual 2 decides to be a free rider, the equilibrium would result at quantity q^* in Figure 12.9(c). Social welfare could thus be increased by area a by increasing production to $\bar{q}$.

Because of these problems associated with public goods, optimality cannot be attained by the private market; some form of governmental intervention is necessary. The common form of intervention for public goods—such as bridges, highways, police forces, dams, and recreation areas—is for the government to play the direct role of the producer, thus deciding upon $\bar{q}$. In determining the point of social optimality, however, the government is faced with the problem of determining marginal social benefits in order to equate them with marginal costs of production. The problems thus encountered are similar to the case of externality measurement associated with Section 12.1. That is, willingness to pay by various individuals must be determined even though equilibrium market prices may not be observable or may not adequately indicate willingness to pay. The government cannot simply set a price on use of the good and observe how much is taken by individual consumers, because of the free-rider problem.

Another difficulty that must be considered in any cost–benefit analysis of public goods production is the fact that many so-called public goods are not public goods in their purest sense—namely, for such goods as streets and highways, the use of the public good by one individual may detract from the benefits derived by another individual (although both may still use the public good) due to congestion costs as the number of users increases. Thus, appropriate evaluations of individual marginal benefits must adequately consider the dependence on the number of users and the quantity of use. Also, with respect to some public goods, a nominal user's fee is imposed in the form of a toll on bridges and turnpikes or an entry fee for campgrounds and recreation areas in national parks. These fees lead to a difference in the real income of the consumers. Thus, the marginal social benefits derived from a public good may depend on whether nominal use fees are imposed (because of the differences in income available to the consumer for expenditure on other commodities).

12.3   MEASUREMENT OF EXTERNAL PROFITS AND COSTS: APPLICATIONS IN ENVIRONMENTAL ECONOMICS

How does one develop a methodology for estimating marginal benefits and costs that are not reflected in the marketplace? A number of methodologies with various advantages and disadvantages exist for this purpose. As one would expect, these methodologies are more complicated and controversial in the case of evaluating consumer benefits and costs than in evaluating producer benefits and costs. The remainder of this chapter will discuss some of the more popular of these approaches.

Estimation of Damage and Control Cost Functions

Estimation of damage and control cost functions follows a rather straightforward approach for the case of producer–producer externalities, as suggested by the mathematical example at the beginning of Section 12.1. For example, the demand for the product given by D in Figure 12.4 can be simply estimated along the lines suggested in Section 8.8. Similarly, for a competitive industry, the supply curve corresponds to the marginal private cost curve MPC in Figure 12.4 and can thus also be estimated following the methodology in Section 8.8. The vertical difference for a given set of determinants of supply and demand can then be computed, as in Figure 12.5, to represent the marginal (opportunity) cost of control. This approach, of course, assumes that the level of damages has a direct relationship with the amount of production that cannot be altered, for example, by employing pollution abatement equipment.

If pollution abatement equipment exists for reducing the extent of the externality, a more extensive study of the production function of the firm or industry must be carried out. In this case the level of production, as well as the level of pollution, can be estimated as functions of the productive inputs and the amount of pollution abatement equipment employed. Then under the assumption of producer profit maximization subject to the given demand curve by consumers, a demand for pollution rights or a supply of pollution can be derived by imposing various prices on pollution in profit maximization. The resulting schedule will thus correspond to $D - \text{MPC}$ in Figure 12.5 when possibilities for pollution abatement are taken into account. The most common approaches for carrying out this kind of work are either to estimate the production function econometrically (much as in the methodology considered in Section 8.8) or to consider optimization directly through means of linear or nonlinear programming.

Turning to the damage function or the MEC curve in Figure 12.5, when all external agents are producers and all such agents can be identified, the estimation of damages can follow a similar methodology. That is, the production function of an external agent (or group) can be estimated with production specified as depending on the firm's (or group's) productive inputs and the pollution imposed upon it externally following the simple single equation estimation methodology discussed in Section 8.8. Thus, damages can be easily calculated for varying levels of pollution using prevailing prices for inputs and output. If these inputs and output do not face perfectly elastic supplies or demand, respectively, then the associated adjustments in prices resulting from changes in pollution levels must also be considered in calculating marginal damages. Again, another approach in this case is to consider the external agent's production problem by means of linear or nonlinear programming where changes in pollution are imposed on the firm through varying pollution constraints.[14] In either case, estimation of marginal damages (that is, marginal external costs) is a rather straightforward matter, given the existence of sufficient data to estimate the associated production functions and, possibly, the input supply and output demand functions.

When external costs are also imposed on consumers, the problem of estimating marginal external costs is much more complicated and must rely on other techniques. Some of these are related to specific types of externalities or public goods such as discussed in the remainder of this chapter.

Bidding Game Techniques

In the case of consumers, there is no simply measureable (observable) concept such as profits which can be used to assess the effects of changing the

---

[14]A discussion of programming methods is beyond the scope of this book. The reader may, however, find a popular example of the linear programming approach in Chap. 10 of O. C. Herfindahl and A. V. Kneese, *Economic Theory of Natural Resources* (Columbus, Ohio: Charles E. Merrill Publishing Company, 1974).

magnitude of an externality. The ultimate criterion is utility, but utility is unobservable. Thus, as in the earlier market cases, the problem is to induce consumers to reveal willingness to pay for changes. When markets exist, the indirect means exist for assessing this willingness to pay. With externalities, however, no markets exist which force individuals to reveal their preferences. One alternative is to interview the individuals involved and ask them how much they are willing to pay for specific changes. Such methods fall under the headings of *surveys* and *bidding games.*

For example, if an industry pollutes air or water in a certain locality, an externality is imposed on individuals living in the area. One may be able to determine through fairly objective means the cost of pollution control for the industry. But to determine whether the benefits of cleaner air or water merit industry incurrence of these costs, one must determine how much better off the individuals would be. Such an evaluation requires determining the direct effects of pollution on the well-being of individuals (i.e., the aesthetic value of surroundings) and the indirect effects resulting from employment cutbacks, and so on, which may result from pollution controls. The employment cutbacks and their effects on economic welfare can also be assessed on fairly objective grounds using market and production data, but the aesthetic benefits are generally not reflected by market data. In this case, surveys can be used to ask individuals how much they would be willing to pay for various qualities of air or water.[15] If the responses to such questions are accurate, honest, and representative (in the case of a partial sample), then the implied aggregate marginal willingness to pay by all individuals can be compared to the marginal cost of pollution control to determine socially optimal pollution levels. Similar issues arise in evaluating the benefits from developing public recreation facilities, public highways, and so on.

---

[15] Alternatively, the interviewer could ask whether a proposed value is too high or too low and then adjust the proposed value accordingly; see, for example, David S. Brookshire, Berry C. Ives, and William D. Schultze, "The Valuation of Aesthetic Preferences," *Journal of Environmental Economics and Management,* Vol. 3, No. 4 (December 1976), pp. 325–46; and Alan Randall, Berry C. Ives, and Clyde Eastman, "Bidding Games for Evaluation of Aesthetic Environmental Improvement," *Journal of Environmental Economics and Management,* Vol. 1, No. 2 (August 1974), pp. 132–49. Note that such bidding games can be subject to *starting point bias.* An alternative approach is to give an individual a fixed hypothetical budget or set of coupons and then ask him or her to allocate the budget or coupons among a set of possible projects; see Dilip Pendse and J. B. Wyckoff, "Scope for Valuation of Environmental Goods, *Land Economics,* Vol. 50, No. 1 (February 1974), pp. 89–92; Robert P. Strauss and G. David Hughes, "A New Approach to the Demand for Public Goods," *Journal of Public Economics,* Vol. 6, No. 3 (October 1976), pp. 191–204. The problem associated with choosing an appropriate vehicle for payment or standard of comparison in hypothetical surveys is generally called the problem of *instrument bias.*

These approaches encounter several important problems.[16] First, the results of a survey may not be representative of the affected population. One reason why a survey may not reflect all the important effects is that it may not be possible to identify all affected individuals. Some individuals may yet visit a polluted area or recreation facility from other states or countries which cannot be anticipated, and their willingness to pay for various alternatives should be properly considered. In addition, if the process must rely on a sample rather than a complete interview of all individuals who may be affected, the sample again may not be representative and may lead to inappropriate conclusions. The criteria for sample selection must be carefully scrutinized in each case. Perhaps those that satisfy the criteria for sample selection have good reasons for responding differently than other individuals. For example, in some surveys the individuals decide for themselves whether to be included or not. In this case, only those with a vested interest may care to participate, and thus the sample would show much greater concern than the population in general. The problem of self-selection is a serious drawback for voting schemes in general because voting participation generally varies with such characteristics as ethnicity, income, and education.

A second problem with the survey and bidding game approach is that responses may be biased because of the participants' beliefs, whether well founded or not, concerning how the information will be used. Suppose, for example, that a survey is intended to determine the optimal scale of a public goods project. If the individual believes that he will not incur additional costs regardless of scale, then he may be induced to claim much larger benefits than he actually derives; thus, he could enjoy a greater amount of public goods (from which he could not be excluded) without bearing additional costs. On the other hand, suppose that he believes he will have to pay exactly what he says he is willing to pay if a project is adopted. Then he may see his contribution to aggregate willingness to pay as insignificant because of population size. If he believes his contribution is so small relative to the aggregate willingness to pay (derived by such survey techniques) that it could not make the deciding difference, he would be tempted to say he is willing to pay nothing.

When an individual responds untruthfully to such a survey because of such an attempt to influence the policy outcome, his behavior is called *strategic behavior*. Several attempts have been made to deal with strategic behavior in survey or bidding game approaches. One approach is to attempt to estimate the extent of bias in respondents' claims, but such an approach is not yet fully operational.[17] An alternative approach is to convince respondents that the

---

[16]A critique of the various problems associated with the bidding game techniques can be found in W. D. Schultze, R. C. d'Arge, and D. S. Brookshire, "Valuing Environmental Commodities: A Recent Experiment," *Land Economics* (May 1981), forthcoming.

[17]Mordecai Kurz, "An Experimental Approach to the Determination of the Demand for Public Goods," *Journal of Public Economics,* Vol. 3 (1974), pp. 329–48.

survey results will not affect supply of the public good or control of an externality.[18] However, an individual may suspect that results of such a survey may have indirect effects on policy decisions beyond the immediate purpose of the questionnaire. Thus, some incentives, however small, may exist for false answers while no countervailing economic incentives for honest answers are apparent. Another approach is to confuse the respondent to the point that he is uncertain how his response will affect his liability; but it is not clear that such an approach does not simply add uncertainty to the value of the survey results.[19]

More complicated analytical attempts to use the respondents' subjective beliefs about the policy outcome have also been made.[20] Alternatively, one study has shown, for one particular policy question related to a proposed power plant siting in the Grand Canyon National Recreational Area that willingness-to-pay responses differ little among survey approaches.[21] But much remains to be learned about strategic bias in survey and bidding game approaches generally. Furthermore, when individuals have not experienced the situations posed by a survey, questions of *information bias* must be raised. That is, an individual is likely to spend less effort and, in fact, not have sufficient information to respond to hypothetical alternatives; such responses are more likely to be incorrect as an indication of real world behavior as well as an indication of actual underlying preferences. Also, one must consider problems of *hypothetical bias* than can arise if an individual does not understand the alternatives posed in a survey or if he does not believe they are possible. In such cases, responses may not reveal information about underlying preferences at all because the respondent may simply not take the survey seriously. Questions of accuracy of responses are crucial, but little or no evidence can be compiled to examine accuracy comprehensively. At best, one can conclude that surveys and bidding games may be the only feasible approach to measurement of some consumer-related externalities.

Travel Cost Methods

An alternative approach based on observable data, which is applicable for most problems related to public provision of recreation facilities, is the *travel cost method*. Many public recreation areas, such as state and national parks, are provided at a zero price or a nominal entry fee. With entry fees, these areas become excludable goods, and the empirical approach of estimating demand in Section 8.8 seemingly becomes applicable. However, entry fees change only

---

[18] For example, see Brookshire, Ives, and Schultze, "Valuation," and Randall, Ives, and Eastman, "Bidding Games."

[19] Some rather specific language for this type of approach is suggested by Peter Bohm, "An Approach to the Problem of Estimating Demand for Public Goods," *Swedish Journal of Economics,* Vol. 73, No. 1 (March 1971), pp. 94–105.

[20] Kurz, "Experimental Approach."

[21] Brookshire, Ives, and Schultze, "Valuation."

rarely; often, enough variation is not observed to enable estimation of the slope of individual or group demand curves. Furthermore and more important, the entry fees, even when nonzero, are usually insignificant compared to other user costs, such as transportation expenses. Thus, estimation of a demand equation for a recreation area based on entry fees alone would ignore the most important factors affecting use.

Since user costs associated with transportation in many cases are large enough to make recreation areas essentially excludable goods regardless of entry fees, the travel cost method employs user costs as a "price" for the good in applying the otherwise usual approach of Section 8.8 in estimating demand.[22] Where entry fees exist, they are included as part of user costs. In practice, transportation costs are determined on the basis of travel distances to and from the recreation area. Then the number of site visits is regressed on or explained by user costs of transportation plus entry as well as other determinants of demand, such as income, education, site congestion, and the like.

To use these results for welfare analysis, one assumes that a change in the entry fee of, say, $1.00 causes the same change in site visits as a $1.00 change in transportation expenses. Thus, the estimated relationship can be easily used to determine the marginal benefits of, say, an increase in site availability. The consumer surplus triangle would be the area below the demand curve for site visits and above the user cost (user cost serves as an effective price). Errors in changes in this surplus, as a measure of true willingness to pay, must be considered along the lines presented in Sections 6.5, 6.6, 7.5, and 7.6 if the quantity of site visits is a choice left in the hands of consumers. Alternatively, errors in this measure would be examined following Section 7.9 if the quantity of site visits is determined by government policy.

The travel cost approach also suffers from several problems. First, as it was developed and has often been applied, the results apply to only the specific site to which data pertain. Other sites may offer different activities, facilities, or aesthetic quality. If the determinants of demand used in estimation properly control for these factors and if data for several sites are available, this problem does not necessarily prevent application of the method.

Another problem with the travel cost approach, as it was originally developed, is that it assumed that only one recreation area was available in each region. When several recreation facilities are available in each area, cross-

---

[22]The travel cost method was developed originally by Knetsch and Clawson; see Jack L. Knetsch, "Economics of Including Recreation as a Purpose of Eastern Water Projects," *Journal of Farm Economics*, Vol. 46, No. 5 (December 1964), pp. 1148–57; and Marion Clawson and Jack L. Knetsch, *Economics of Outdoor Recreation* (Baltimore: Johns Hopkins University Press, 1966). For a clear numerical example, See Karl Goran and Ronald Wyzga, *Economic Measurement of Environmental Damage* (Paris: Organisation for Economic Cooperation and Development, 1976).

elasticities are difficult to consider.[23] This problem is approached by essentially considering demand for each site as a function of all relevant user costs (which entails determination of distances from each of several sites for each individual). In addition, with multiple sites, one must control for quality of each site so that the list of determinants used in each demand curve may involve attributes associated with activities, facilities, and aesthetic factors at a number of sites.[24] This large number of factors can, of course, complicate estimation as well as data acquisition.

Another difficulty with the travel cost approach is the unobservable value of time involved for site visits.[25] The greater the travel distance, the less attractive a site becomes, not only because of direct monetary expense but also because of time spent driving, and so on. The travel cost method normally considers only direct monetary costs of travel. But if each $1.00 in travel expense also involves the loss of, say, 10 minutes of leisure time, then a $1.00 increase in transportation costs may reduce site visits more than a $1.00 increase in entry fee. Appropriate valuation of user costs necessarily involves determination of the value of leisure time forgone; otherwise, user costs do not adequately reflect true marginal benefits. Widely accepted methods for this purpose have not yet been developed. Some have proposed the use of shadow prices of leisure time suggested by studies of commuting modes and locational preferences. But others argue that the shadow prices of leisure for recreation, travel, and commuting are not the same because of different routes and perhaps modes of travel. Others have suggested using the wage rate as the marginal value of leisure, but for many workers the institution of an eight-hour workday prevents marginal adjustments between work and leisure. Many studies have used figures more on the order of one-fourth to one-half of the wage rate.[26]

Suffice it to say that, although the travel cost method is based on more objective evidence than direct surveys, the important question of leisure-time evaluation is still in need of resolution.

---

[23]The first paper to deal with the multiple site problem integrability conditions in the recreational literature was by O. R. Burt and D. Brewer, "Estimates of Net Social Benefits for Outdoor Recreation," *Econometrica,* Vol. 39, No. 5 (September 1971), pp. 813–27.

[24]For a paper which develops an appropriate methodology for this case, see W. Michael Hanemann, "Water Quality and the Demand for Recreation," Agricultural and Resource Economics Working Paper No. 164, University of California, Berkeley, March 1981.

[25]One of the first pieces of research to consider the opportunity cost of time used in traveling to recreational sites was by K. McConnell, "Some Problems in Estimating the Demand for Outdoor Recreation," *American Journal of Agricultural Economics,* Vol. 57, No. 2 (May 1975), pp. 330–34.

[26]Frank J. Cesario, "Value of Time in Recreation Benefit Studies," *Land Economics,* Vol. 55, No. 1 (February 1976), pp. 32–41.

A further and more objective method for evaluating some types of externalities relies on determination of the indirect effects on market data. For example, air pollution or water pollution problems can have indirect effects on the values of surrounding property. This realization suggests using market data to explain property values in terms of appropriate indices of air quality or water quality as well as the usual variables, such as lot size, structural characteristics, age, room size, and commuting distances.[27] In this case, the variation in air or water quality over individuals, groups, or periods of time works much like a change in controlled quantity of a related good. Thus, following Section 7.10, if access to property (either rented or owned) is an essential good—which seems reasonable because everyone needs a place to live—then the welfare effects of changes in air quality, water quality, and noise, as well as other threats to health and life, can be captured in markets for real estate.[28] This is done by means of estimating supply and demand in housing markets, rented and owned, where determinants or exogenous forces explaining changes in supply and demand include variables measuring air and water quality or perhaps local life expectancy or probability of mortality.

Thus, suppose that supply and demand for housing are estimated to be S_0 and D_0, respectively, in Figure 12.10 prior to some environmental degradation such as increased danger to life. Subsequently, supply and demand are estimated to be S_1 and D_1, respectively. Environmental degradation would suggest reduced demand for housing because of the reluctance of consumers to suffer from its effects either physically or aesthetically. The supply of housing may increase, decrease, or remain unaffected, depending on the nature of the environmental degradation. Suppose, for purposes of exposition, that supply decreases. With a sufficiently small decrease in supply, rental rates would fall,

---

[27] For studies related to air quality, see A. Mitchell Polinsky and Daniel L. Rubinfeld, "Property Values and the Benefits of Environmental Improvements: Theory and Measurement," in *Public Economics and the Quality of Life,* ed. Lowdon Wingo and Alan Evans (Baltimore: Johns Hopkins University Press, 1977); and A. Mitchell Polinsky and Steven Shavell, "Amenities and Property Values in a Model of an Urban Area," *Journal of Public Economics,* Vol. 5, Nos. 1–2 (January–February 1976), pp. 119–29.

For studies related to water quality, see Elizabeth L. David, "Lake Shore Property Values: A Guide to Public Investment in Recreation," *Water Resources Research,* Vol. 4, No. 4 (August 1968), pp. 697–707; and Gardner M. Brown and Henry O. Pollakowski, "Economic Valuation of Shoreline," *Review of Economics and Statistics,* Vol. 59 (August 1977), pp. 272–78.

[28] This result is demonstrated in detail in the framework of Appendix B related to quantity and quality restrictions. For a related discussion of welfare measurement with hedonic pricing, see W. Michael Hanemann, "Quality Changes, Consumer's Surplus, and Hedonic Price Indices," Department of Agricultural and Resource Economics Working Paper No. 116, University of California, Berkeley, 1980.

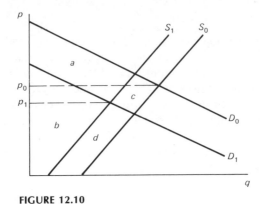

FIGURE 12.10

say, from p_0 to p_1 in Figure 12.10. Following Section 7.10, the resulting welfare effects would be a loss from area $a + b + c + d$ to area b or a net loss of area $a + c + d$.

The major difficulty with the application of this approach is that market data are difficult to obtain. A relatively small portion of housing changes hands each year; the goods exchanged are far from homogeneous, and as a result, the data in both the sales and the rental markets are sparse. Furthermore, difficulties in the estimation of both supply and demand of housing are encountered when supply cannot be considered as strictly predetermined because the same exogenous forces may affect both sides of the market; problems of econometric identification prevent estimation of supply and demand individually in a simultaneous context.[29] An alternative approach for this case has been to estimate "reduced-form" equations which explain real estate sales or rental prices or valuations as a function of all the factors affecting either supply or demand.[30] Then the notion of equilibrium by household is employed to interpret the effect of environmental quality on housing prices as an effect on marginal willingness to pay by each household.[31]

12.4 CONCLUSIONS

This chapter has focused on the theory of externalities and public goods and possible approaches to measuring welfare effects in these cases. The problem in

---

[29]For a further discussion of econometric identification, see Henri Theil, *Principles of Econometrics* (New York: John Wiley & Sons, Inc., 1971), Chap. 9.

[30]The reduced-form equations are derived by solving the supply and demand equations simultaneously for price and quantity.

[31]This approach, however, is only an approximation and corresponds to assuming fixed inelastic supply and vertically parallel shifts in demand in the context of Figure 12.10. Under such assumptions, simultaneous equations estimation methods need not be used; and thus the identification problem above is not encountered.

this type of analysis is that individual preferences are not completely reflected in ordinary market data. Nevertheless, interesting approaches have been used to analyze empirically the effects of externalities. Such information is surely needed as the externality problem becomes more severe due to such factors as growing populations and increasing resource scarcity. While these results have been developed in the context of single markets, the principles of Chapter 9 can be applied in a straightforward manner for multimarket generalizations.

Empirical work on externality effects increased phenomenally during the 1970s because of growing problems of pollution and environmental degradation. For example, during the 1940s there was no reason to study the effects of supersonic flights since such a technology did not exist. And there was little interest in controlling smog, which was not yet a serious problem. On the other hand, with the energy crisis, new and alternative sources of energy which resulted in undesirable side effects became economical in the private market. As such technologies have emerged, analysis of environmental policy and its associated economic welfare effects has and probably will become increasingly important.

13

Dynamic Considerations in Cost-Benefit Analysis: Applications in Natural Resource Economics

Thus far, welfare effects have been discussed only in a static sense. That is, all of the economic impacts occur during the same time period that the policy change is instituted. With many—if not most—policies, however, welfare effects (perhaps including both market and nonmarket effects) are realized beyond the immediate time period. For example, suppose that the government is considering building a dam with an accompanying reservoir which may generate hydroelectric power and either create or destroy recreational opportunites.[1] At the same time, those who now live where the reservoir is to be located bear the costs of relocation. With this type of project, the relocation must be borne during the early stages of the project, while the costs of building the dam will

---

[1]The famous case of the proposed Hells Canyon Dam on the Snake River, for example, has been the subject of several studies of this type of problem. In this case, economic analysis played an important role in a decision not to build the dam because of the estimated value of recreational and aesthetic opportunities that would be foregone. For further discussion, see John V. Krutilla and Anthony C. Fisher, *The Economics of Natural Environments* (Baltimore: Johns Hopkins University Press, 1978), Chap. 6.

be incurred over the first several years of the project. However, the benefits in terms of hydroelectric power and recreational opportunities will be realized only after the construction period has ended and would extend for an indefinite period of time thereafter. Thus, a question that must be answered is: How should the benefits be weighed against the costs?

Generally, a benefit is not as valuable if it is realized later rather than earlier. For example, an individual would rather obtain $1,000 today instead of 10 years from now, one reason being that the $1,000 could be gainfully invested during the 10-year period. Similarly, the same expense is more costly if incurred today rather than 10 years from now because, again, the associated amount of money can be employed usefully during that time.

When a proposed policy or project generates a time series of benefits or costs over more than a single time period, the welfare effects in each individual time period can be calculated according to procedures discussed in previous chapters. However, to decide whether or not the policy is socially preferable or to evaluate the extent of overall net social benefits, it is necessary to aggregate welfare effects over time or to develop some procedure for weighing benefits in one period versus another. The associated problem is referred to as social discounting.

This chapter first examines the problem of social discounting and the choice of a social discount rate. Then an approach for dynamic economic welfare analysis is set forth. The associated principles produce a framework for cost–benefit analysis of proposed public projects and policies that produce time streams of welfare effects. The remainder of the chapter then turns to the application of these principles in dealing with renewable and nonrenewable natural resources and technological change. Throughout this chapter, it is assumed that benefits and costs can be measured appropriately in each time period involved in the analysis, so the central question is how to aggregate the benefits and costs over time.

13.1   THE SOCIAL DISCOUNT RATE

When a private, profit-maximizing firm faces a new business venture which produces a time stream of revenues and costs, one approach for deciding whether to undertake the venture is to compute the net present value (sometimes called a discounted value) of the time stream of revenues and costs. Suppose that the time stream of revenues or benefits is denoted by $B_0, B_1, B_2, \ldots$, and the time stream of costs is denoted by $C_0, C_1, C_2, \ldots$, where the subscript represents the time period in which the revenue or cost is incurred. In this case the present or discounted value of the stream of revenues and costs for the firm is given by

$$\text{PV} = B_0 - C_0 + \frac{B_1 - C_1}{1 + r} + \frac{B_2 - C_2}{(1 + r)^2} + \frac{B_3 - C_3}{(1 + r)^3} + \ldots \qquad \textbf{(13.1)}$$

where r is the interest rate that must be incurred by the firm in carrying debts from earlier periods over to later periods, where net revenues are positive; or if the firm is using its own funds to commence the project, then r represents the opportunity cost of its funds if they are invested elsewhere.

Suppose, for example, that a firm faces a project for which it incurs an immediate cost of $10,000 which leads to a return of $25,000 in 10 years. Then $C_0 = \$10,000$ and $B_{10} = \$25,000$, while all other B_t and C_t are zero, $t = 0, 1, \ldots$. If the firm finances the project by borrowing $10,000 immediately with the intent of paying the accumulated interest and debt in 10 years at an interest rate of r, the payment required in year 10 would be $C_0(1 + r)^{10}$. The net value of the project at year 10 thus would be $B_{10} - C_0(1 + r)^{10}$. The present value, PV, represents this amount transformed into current dollars by dividing by $(1 + r)^{10}$. In other words, the present value represents the amount of money that must be borrowed today at interest rate r to supply the same time stream of net returns as would be obtained through the business venture, given the existence of a perfect capital market that can be used to carry costs or benefits at interest rate r.[2]

The mechanism in equation (13.1) similarly provides a simple approach to determining the discounted or present value of net social benefits associated with a government policy or project. That is, where B_t represents positive social benefits or the summation of willingness to pay over all those individuals affected positively in period t and C_t represents social costs or the summation of willingness to pay over all those individuals affected adversely in period t, the present value given by (13.1) represents the amount of money required at time zero to finance the same stream of net benefits or willingness to pay, given a perfect capital market with interest or discount rate r. Of course, if benefits exceed costs in every time period, a policy or project is temporally Pareto efficient; and the present value is positive for any discount rate r. Generally, however, the determination of an appropriate social discount rate is crucial in determining whether the present value is positive or negative.

Consider, for example, Figure 13.1, which gives estimates of costs and benefits over time of increased CO_2 buildup in the atmosphere as a result of coal-fired electricity generation. As the diagram shows, benefits may be positive but small for a long period of time and then turn negative and become large. Obviously, in this case, a small discount rate suggests that coal use should be controlled, whereas a large discount rate suggests that coal use should not be controlled. This example serves to illustrate that the choice of discount rate may have overriding importance in any cost–benefit analysis of government policy. For this reason, a major part of this chapter is devoted to this crucial issue.

---

[2] A *perfect capital market* is one that carries no transactions costs or limits such as might be associated with collateral. One may either borrow or invest at a prevailing interest rate in any amount.

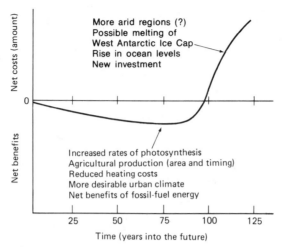

FIGURE 13.1

Ralph d'Arge, William Schutze, and David Brookshire, *Benefit–Cost Evaluation of Long Term Future Effects: The Case of CO₂*, University of Wyoming Resource and Environmental Economics Laboratory Research Paper No. 13, April 1980.

The Rationale for Social Discounting

Several arguments have been advanced to justify the discounting of future benefits and costs. First, resources that are not used for immediate consumption can be employed in investment projects yielding a return in later periods which exceeds the value of the resources. Second, consumers are generally willing to pay more for immediate consumption than for deferred consumption. And third, society may regard consumption by future generations as somewhat more or less important than that of the present generation. In the latter context, the problem of social discounting may become somewhat like the public goods problem. That is, the welfare of a future generation may be something for which all individuals in the current generation hold concerns regardless of their individual contributions to that welfare. Thus, as in the public goods case in Section 12.2, social efficiency may require government intervention on behalf of future generations.

The Market Rate of Interest as a Social Discount Rate

In a perfect market economy, the market rate of interest should correctly reflect the value of using resources in investment projects that do not exceed the life of existing firms. Similarly, the prevailing market rate of interest should reflect consumers' preferences toward financing current consumption through consumer debt as opposed to deferred consumption. The market rate of interest, however, may not reflect the value of using resources in investment projects which exceed the life of the present generation or in investment projects related to goods for which perfect markets do not exist (for example,

299

public goods). In particular, the market rate of interest will not reflect society's regard for consumption by future generations. In addition, one must note that there is no single agreed-upon market rate of interest which can be used for these purposes. Consumers receive one rate of interest for savings accounts in banks and savings and loan associations and pay other rates for home mortgages or automobile financing. Businesses pay yet another rate in financing business ventures. Furthermore, market interest rates may be altered as a result of undertaking some kinds of very large projects. Finally, it should be noted that interest rates are an important tool for macroeconomic policy; it seems unreasonable to have projects justified or not on the basis of the cyclical activity to which macroeconomic policy responds. For these reasons, the social rate of discount that is appropriate for public policies may differ from the prevailing market rate of interest.[3]

Theoretical Determination of the Discount Rate: The Time Preference Approach

One conceptual approach to the problem of determining the correct rate of social discount between two time periods is depicted in Figure 13.2, following essentially the same type of framework as in Chapters 2 and 3. The curve PP' represents a production possibilities curve depicting the trade-off between production in time period t versus production in time period t'. Production in the current period t can be given up for production in a future period t' but only at a decreasing rate. The curves I_1 and I_2 represent social indifference curves between consumption in time period t and time period t'. Social optimality is

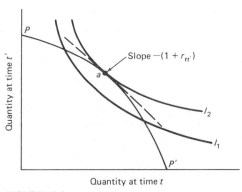

FIGURE 13.2

---

[3]One may argue that each parent's regard for the future well-being of his or her children may lead to proper regard for future generations. Although this may lead to some regard for future generations, there is no reason why it should lead to the proper regard. For example, this line of reasoning would suggest less regard for the future generation if only one-tenth of all families had 10 children each (and other families had no children) than if every family had one child.

obtained where an indifference curve is exactly tangent to the production possibilities curve at point a. Optimality thus implies the equality of the marginal rate of substitution in consumption between time periods t and t', $MRS_{tt'}$, and the marginal rate of transformation in production between time periods t and t', $MRT_{tt'}$. Of course, when markets are competitive and involve many consumers and many producers, the marginal rate of substitution and the marginal rate of transformation would be the same over all individual consumers and producers. This optimal rate of substitution or transformation corresponds to the optimal social discount rate; that is, the appropriate rate of social discount, $r_{tt'}$, is defined by[4]

$$MRS_{tt'} = MRT_{tt'} = 1 + r_{tt'} \qquad (13.2)$$

The analysis in Figure 13.2 points out that the optimal social discount rate cannot be determined without reference to a specific economy. In point of fact, a number of underlying economic factors may influence the optimal discount rate. For example, if the size of the labor force is growing rather than declining, then the production possibilities curve would be skewed toward the later time period and thus likely lead to a lower discount rate, *ceteris paribus*. Similarly, the social indifference curves may depend on wealth, so that a more wealthy society will be more willing to defer some of its consumption for the benefit of a future generation or for increased consumption at a later period. These points further suggest that the social rate of discount may depend upon which two time periods are being compared. For example, a poor developing country may weight current consumption very highly but later, after the economy develops to a certain extent, be more prone to consider future generations. A government that weights both generations equally would tend to counteract the skewed production possibilities curve by weighting current consumption more heavily (that is, choosing a social discount rate somewhat greater than 0). Finally, on the other hand, if because of depletion of resources, an economy faces decreased production possibilities in the future, a government that equally weights consumption by different generations will tend to counteract any reverse skewness in the production possibility curve through weighting more heavily the consumption of future generations as in resource conservation policy.

These points are illustrated in Figure 13.3, where I_0 represents a social indifference curve with respect to generations. The production possibilities curve for a no-growth society would be symmetric with respect to generations, as in the case of P_1P_1', thus leading to social optimality at point a. Now

---

[4]For a derivation of this equation and an excellent graphical treatment of many of the issues of this chapter at the intermediate level, see Jack Hirshleifer, *Price Theory and Applications* (Englewood Cliffs, N.J.: Prentice-Hall Publishing Company, 1976), Chapter 16.

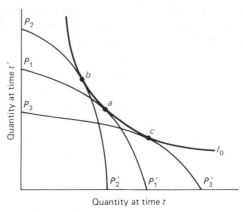

FIGURE 13.3

suppose, on the other hand, that production possibilities follow P_2P_2'; because of technological developments, much greater production may be possible at time t'. Then the point of social optimality is at point b with greater future and less present consumption even though the implied discount rate (associated with the slope at point b) is higher and more in favor of present consumption. Finally, suppose that production possibilities follow P_3P_3', as in the case where increasing resource scarcity implies that more can be produced now than later. Then social optimality is at point c. Thus, present consumption is greater and future consumption is less; nevertheless, the implied social discount rate is lower and thus is more favorable to future consumption than at cither points a or b.

Practical Determination of the Discount Rate

In a perfect economy (involving perfect markets for capital and investments with no externalities of any type including intergenerational externalities), the correct discount rate, $r_{tt'}$, represented in Figure 13.2 would result from competition. In the absence of a perfect market economy, however, the optimal social discount rate may not be reflected by observed market phenomena. For example, some individuals or firms may have projects with a much higher rate of return than the market rate of interest but are unable to qualify for credit for other reasons. Furthermore, future generations are not involved in current markets and hence cannot represent their interests. The problem of determining the appropriate social discount rate is thus similar to the externality problems discussed in Chapter 12; that is, markets fail to exist for determining the appropriate interest rate. Thus, the effects of current policies and projects on future generations are external effects, and hence the government must take those effects into account in making policy decisions. Furthermore, the problems of measurement for this purpose are much more severe since future

302

generations cannot be surveyed to determine their preferences. A policymaker is thus left in the precarious situation of having to determine for them what should be in their best interests based on his or her own values.

With these considerations in mind, the choice of a social discount rate becomes a very sensitive subject. Indeed, the choice of a social discount rate is similar to one of deciding upon income distribution; in this case, one is comparing income of different generations as opposed to different groups of the same generation. Thus, as in the earlier cases of income distribution comparison in this book, perhaps the most defensible approach from the standpoint of economic welfare analysis is to determine the distributional effects possibly performing calculations for a number of discount rates and then to leave the selection of the discount rate with its accompanying implications to the choice of policymakers who are elected or appointed for the purpose of making value judgments for society.

Other possibilities, however, are provided by either observing a policymaker's revealed discount rate implied by previously instituted policies or by comparing with opportunity costs of using the same funds in other projects. In the former case, there are probably other projects and policies, some of which have been adopted and some of which have been rejected by the same policymaker(s). *If policymakers are consistent* in their choices, there will be a (small) range of discount rates in which all rejected policies and projects have negative present values and all accepted ones have positive present values. If a proposed policy or project has a positive present value over all discount rates in this small range, it too should be accepted; if it has a negative present value for all such discount rates, it should be rejected.

With the opportunity cost approach, on the other hand, one examines other possible uses of the same funds required for the proposed policy or project, including leaving the funds in the private sector. The question of intergenerational welfare considerations is avoided using this approach by ascribing to the discount rate the more limited role of allocating capital funds to their highest-valued use. Other social instruments are assumed to be used for assuring fairness of income distribution among generations.[5] Proponents of the opportunity cost approach agree that the rate of return on a public investment should be at least as great as the rate of return that can be earned on the funds thereby displaced from the private sector. If only private investment rather than household consumption is displaced, then the highest rate of return on private investment is used as a social discount rate in the evaluation of a new proposal. The (internal) rate of return for each alternative possibility is found by determining that rate r which makes present value equal to zero in equation (13.1).

Each of these approaches also has its shortcomings. Both approaches require a large amount of information—in effect, a cost–benefit or welfare analy-

---

[5]Robert H. Haveman, "The Opportunity Cost of Displaced Private Spending and the Social Discount Rate," *Water Resources Research,* Vol. 5, No. 5 (October 1969).

sis of many projects or policies besides the one proposed. In some cases, these analyses may have been done previously but probably not in all cases. Also, some previous analyses may contain errors. In addition, the revealed preference approach will often turn up inconsistencies in previous policy decisions, so that no range of discount rates is clearly applicable for further policy decisions. Both approaches ignore the possibility that intragenerational income distributional considerations or noneconomic factors, such as national defense or political security, may influence some policy decisions. A policymaker may wish to keep economic considerations for one project independent of political considerations in another.

Finally, the opportunity cost approach can lead to some peculiar conclusions if applied indiscriminately. For example, suppose that project 1 involves an initial cost of $100 and returns $300 in one year and $400 in two years, whereas project 2 has both costs and benefits of $300 initially, as well as after one year, but then has costs of $300 and benefits of $301 two years from commencement. Clearly, project 1 appears quite lucrative and indeed has an internal rate of return of 400 percent, while project 2 appears unattractive by comparison. But project 2 has an infinite internal rate of return and would thus be favored by a ranking of rates of return. If project 2 is an investment undertaken in the private sector and one from which funds are drawn for project 1, then project 1 would not be undertaken in the public sector if the opportunity cost approach were used. Indeed, it would be impossible to find a potential public project with a higher rate of return than project 2. But unexploited opportunities, such as project 2, may conceivably exist in the private sector, and infinity is clearly a nonsensical rate to apply in discounting. The selection of any reasonable minimum rate of return leads to the favor of project 1. Thus, apparently no good substitutes for the present discounted social value criterion appear to exist in spite of the problem of determination of an appropriate social discount rate.[6]

If a policymaker uses a social discount rate which differs from private rates, however, it can have serious implications in terms of private sector effects. For example, if the social discount rate is lower than the private rate, public projects will be undertaken which return less on average than some private projects which will be displaced by the need for public funds (possibly financed by higher taxes).[7] Similarly, when private rates differ from the social rate, private decisions are being made without the appropriate consideration of impacts on future generations implied by the social discount rate. The most

---

[6]Other approaches, such as ranking proposed projects by payback period or by excess benefit–cost ratios (the ratio of discounted net benefits to discounted costs), have also been proposed but lead to similar inconsistencies; see E. J. Mishan, *Cost–Benefit Analysis,* 2d ed. (New York: Praeger Publishers, Inc., 1976), Chaps. 25–37.

[7]On this point, see Jack Hirshleifer, "Investment Decision under Uncertainty: Applications of the State Preference Approach," *Quarterly Journal of Economics,* Vol. 80, No. 2 (May 1966), pp. 270–75.

straightforward approach for a government to use in making sure all decisions carry proper regard for future contingencies may be to regulate the private market rate of interest (i.e., making it equal to the social rate of discount). This approach, however, would work only if unlimited credit were made available at the regulated market rate; otherwise, limited borrowing capacity would lead to limited investment and a higher private rate of return on investment than suggested by the market rate of interest.

Empirical Use of Discount Rates

As some of the earlier examples suggest, empirical results of dynamic economic welfare analysis can differ substantially depending on the choice of social discount rate, even in the range of those that seem reasonable. For example, many government projects involve substantial costs over the first several years of a project with substantial benefits accruing only 10, 20, 30, and even 100 years into the future. Suppose that a project involves investing $1 million immediately to gain a benefit of $50 million at the end of 50 years. With a social discount rate of 8 percent, the project will almost break even; the present value is $6,606. With a social discount rate of 12 percent, however, the present value is in the red—$826,990. Finally, with a social discount rate of 5 percent, the present value is $3,360,186. Obviously, the choice of discount rate is highly critical in deciding whether the project should be undertaken. By performing this kind of sensitivity analysis, the extent to which project outcomes are sensitive to the discount rate may be ascertained. In some cases a project may remain profitable over a wide range of discount rates, while another may be highly sensitive to the discount rate.

Social discount rates which have been employed in the literature have ranged from 0 to 16 percent. This wide range is suggestive of the great amount of controversy that has surrounded social discounting. An important distinction exists in the literature on the social discount rate, however, in that some authors concern themselves with a *real* social discount rate, whereas others work in terms of a *nominal* discount rate. The difference is, of course, associated with the rate of inflation. Where r represents the real rate of social discount, γ represents the nominal rate of social discount, and f represents the rate of inflation, these rates are related according to the following equation:

$$1 + r = \frac{1 + \gamma}{1 + f} \qquad (13.3)$$

In this context, the formula for computation of present or discounted value of a project [equation (13.1)] applies when the stream of benefits and costs is evaluated in real terms (i.e., after the effects of inflation have been removed). If benefits and costs are evaluated in nominal terms (that is, current dollars), then γ should be substituted for r in equation (13.1).

The real rates of social discount used in the literature fall in the range 0 to 4 percent; nominal rates of social discount in the literature generally fall in the range 8 to 16 percent, with the higher rates having appeared in the more recent literature since inflation and market interest rates have risen substantially. To point out the importance of this distinction, suppose, for example, that one chooses a nominal rate of social discount of 10 percent and a real rate of discount of 2 percent, thus expecting a rate of inflation of just under 8 percent. In nominal terms, this would imply that society would prefer $1.00 today in favor of $13,780 one hundred years hence. At first thought, this conclusion seems rather absurd. However, when one takes into account the effects of inflation and reduces this consideration to real terms (i.e., constant dollars), one finds that society is only trading $1.00 today for $7.24 one hundred years hence. With these considerations in mind, a real discount rate in the neighborhood of 0 to 2 percent may, in fact, appear appropriate. For example, in a no-growth economy where a government weights real consumption by a future generation with the same regard it holds for consumption by the current generation, the real rate of social discount should be zero. If, because of technological advancement, however, an economy is able to produce increasingly more goods, government would weight current consumption more heavily by choosing a real social discount rate somewhat greater than zero. Finally, on the other hand, if an economy faces decreased production possibilities in the future because of depletion of nonrenewable resources, a government would favor more heavily the consumption of future generations as in resource conservation policy by using a negative real social discount rate.

13.2 MEASURING CHANGES IN ECONOMIC WELFARE OVER TIME: COST–BENEFIT ANALYSIS

Once the choice of a (set of) social discount rate(s) is determined, the methods of previous chapters become immediately applicable in measuring welfare effects of alternative policies or changes. For example, when fixed factors remain fixed over time, the welfare effect (i.e., the discounted social welfare effect or discounted willingness to pay) of a change beginning at time t_0 is given by

$$\Delta W_{t_0} = \sum_{t=t_0}^{\infty} \delta^{t-t_0} \sum_{i=1}^{N} C^{it} \tag{13.4}$$

or

$$\Delta W_{t_0} = \sum_{t=t_0}^{\infty} \delta^{t-t_0} \sum_{i=1}^{N} E^{it} \tag{13.5}$$

(depending on which concept of willingness to pay is used), where $\delta = 1/(1 + r)$, r is the social discount rate, C^{it} is the compensating variation of the change for individual i in period t (change in area behind the relevant short-run compensated supply or demand conditioned on the initial utility level), E^{it} is the equivalent variation of the change for individual i in period t (change in area behind the relevant short-run compensated supply or demand conditioned on the terminal utility level), and N is the total number of individuals affected by the change. Following the methodology in Chapters 8 or 9, these willingness-to-pay measures for groups of individuals can be determined within individual time periods by using aggregate market demand and supply curves, possibly of an equilibrium nature. Use of market or equilibrium demand and supply curves may be necessary because proposed policies or projects may be of sufficient size to alter prices in related markets. If not, simple calculations of changes in costs and benefits based on fixed prices may be sufficient.

Accounting for Changes in Investment

Although the foregoing approach is appropriate when fixed factors are fixed over time, most problems of economic welfare analysis involve factors that are fixed in the short run but become variable in the longer run. As a result, short-run supply and demand curves shift from period to period and, in particular, investment costs are incurred in the process. In this case the formulas in (13.4) and (13.5) must be further modified. Suppose, for example, that fixed factors can be altered by producers through undertaking new investment as suggested in Section 4.5. In this case a change in policy at time t_0 can cause a series of investments (or disinvestments). Where I_t^i represents investment made by producer i at time t and N_p is the total number of producers, the discounted present value of welfare effects on producers is

$$\Delta W_p = \sum_{t=t_0}^{\infty} \delta^{t-t_0} \sum_{i=1}^{N_p} (\Delta S_t^i - \Delta I_t^i) \tag{13.6}$$

That is, ΔS_t^i represents the change in producer surplus associated with the ordinary, short-run supply curve in period t for producer i (both the supply curve and the price may differ between cases of change or no change), and ΔI_t is the change in investment undertaken or financed in period t.[8] Thus, ΔW_p is the present value of changes in receipts and expenditures. If consumers make no adjustments in fixed assets as a result of the change, their welfare effect is given by

$$\Delta W_c = \sum_{t=t_0}^{\infty} \delta^{t-t_0} \sum_{i=N_p+1}^{N} \Delta S_t^i$$

where $N - N_p$ is the number of consumers and ΔS_t^i represents the change in

---

[8]For details on calculating ΔI_t^i from standard dynamic supply equations, see Appendix C. Also, as shown in Appendix C, note that these results pertain only to the nonstochastic case.

Hicksian consumer surplus for consumer i in period t. The net overall welfare effect on private concerns is thus $\Delta W_p + \Delta W_c$.[9]

13.3 A FOOTNOTE ON DYNAMIC ASPECTS OF THE CONSUMER PROBLEM

In some problems of economic welfare analysis, consumer changes in the holdings of fixed assets are also induced. Although the dynamics of consumer adjustments in fixed assets were not considered explicitly in earlier chapters, the associated economic welfare considerations can be made in much the same framework as producer adjustments in fixed production factors using household production function theory. That is, consumers can be viewed as purchasing fixed assets or durables, such as refrigerators, televisions, automobiles, and houses, in order to combine them with other nondurable inputs, such as electricity, gasoline, and leisure to produce commodities such as entertainment, food, transportation, and shelter from which the consumer actually derives utility.[10] For example, suppose that each household commodity y_i is produced within the household by combining nondurables $q_1, \ldots, q_m$ with durables $q_{m+1}, \ldots, q_n$,

$$y_i = f_i(q_1, \ldots, q_n)$$

Then where the consumer utility function depends on household commodities,

$$U = \bar{U}(y_1, \ldots, y_c)$$

the utility function can be rewritten through substitution as

$$U = U(q_1, \ldots, q_n)$$

where it is understood that $q_{m+1}, \ldots, q_n$ are durables which are fixed in the short run just as some inputs are fixed for producers.

---

[9]For examples of this approach, see P. R. Crosson, R. G. Cummings, and K. D. Frederick, *Selected Water Management Issues in Latin America* (Baltimore: Johns Hopkins University Press, 1978), Otto Eckstein, *Water-Resource Development: The Economics of Project Evaluation* (Cambridge, Mass.: Harvard University Press, 1961), Anthony C. Fisher, "On Measures of Natural Resource Scarcity" in V. Kerry Smith (ed.) *Scarcity and Growth Reconsidered* (Baltimore: The Johns Hopkins University Press, 1979), Charles W. Howe and K. William Easter, *Interbasin Transfers of Water: Economic Issues and Impacts* (Baltimore: The Johns Hopkins University Press, 1971), and John V. Krutilla and Otto Eckstein, *Multiple Purpose River Development* (Baltimore: The Johns Hopkins University Press, 1958).

[10]Household production function theory was introduced by K. J. Lancaster, "A New Approach to Consumer Theory," *Journal of Political Economy*, Vol. 74, No. 2 (April 1966), pp. 132–57. See also R. T. Michael and G. S. Becker, "On the New Theory of Consumer Behavior," *Swedish Journal of Economics*, Vol. 75 (1973).

Now consider the dual of the utility maximization problem,

$$\min p_1 q_1 + \cdots + p_n q_n$$

subject to

$$U^*(q_1, \ldots, q_n) = 0$$

where $p_1, \ldots, p_n$ are respective prices for $q_1, \ldots, q_n$ and $U^*(q_1, \ldots, q_n) = U(q_1, \ldots, q_n) - \bar{U}$ with $\bar{U}$ representing a constrained level of utility. This problem is obviously mathematically equivalent to a producer problem (by simply reversing signs of prices),

$$\max p_1 q_1 + \cdots + p_n q_n$$

subject to

$$f(q_1, \ldots, q_n) = 0$$

where f represents an implicit production function, $q_i > 0$ represents purchases for consumers and output sales for producers, and $q_i < 0$ represents resource sales for consumers and input purchases for producers.[11] Since both problems can also contain the same kinds of fixities (consumer durables or producer fixed inputs), the areas under the associated supply and demand curves of various lengths of run must also have the same interpretation. Of course, in the consumer case, the associated supply and demand curves are compensated rather than ordinary curves, since utility is constrained to a fixed level.

Hence, by analogy with the producer case, the discounted present value of welfare effects on consumers is given by

$$\Delta W_c = \sum_{t=t_0}^{\infty} \delta^{t-t_0} \sum_{i=N_p+1}^{N} (\Delta S_t^i - \Delta D_t^i) \tag{13.7}$$

where ΔS_t^i is the change in consumer surplus for consumer i associated with Hicksian compensated short-run supplies or demands in period t and ΔD_t^i represents the change in expenditures (investment) by consumer i on durables in period t. Where direct data are not available on D_t^i, durable expenditures can be estimated from the dynamics in estimated consumer demand and supply curves just as in the case of calculating investment from producer supply and derived demand curves in Section 4.5 and Appendix C. The net overall welfare

---

[11]Technically, mathematical equivalence also requires some further conditions on concavity of f and U^* which hold under usual assumptions; see Section 7.10 for a similar case of comparing the consumer and producer problems where factor fixity is not assumed.

effect on private concerns is thus given by the sum of ΔW_p and ΔW_c in equations (13.6) and (13.7), respectively. Practical approximate applications of (13.7) in terms of ordinary Marshallian consumer surplus can be made through application of the Willig approximation arguments. Thus, the temporal distribution of welfare effects of any policy on both producers and consumers can be investigated empirically and aggregated with various discount rates to examine potential compensation schemes.

13.4 DYNAMIC WELFARE ANALYSIS OF RISKY PROJECTS AND POLICIES

In selecting an appropriate social discount rate, another consideration has to do with uncertainty regarding future time periods. For example, many policies and potential policies relate to extraction of petroleum and minerals. Although the importance of these resources in today's economy can be determined fairly accurately, there is a great deal of uncertainty about the reserves which may exist for future generations to use. Exploration may yet reveal large quantities of reserves which are as yet undiscovered. Furthermore, technological changes may occur so that these resources are less important for future generations. When these kinds of uncertainties exist, society may be much less willing to trade off current consumption for future consumption. That is, as suggested by Section 11.6, private individuals may have a tendency to discount outcomes associated with greater risk within a single time period. Similar arguments and observations suggest that decisions associated with greater risk over time would also be discounted or valued less than if no risk existed. For example, a risk-averse individual would be more willing to pay $100 today for a certain return of $200 in 10 years than for a 50–50 chance of returns of $50 or $350 each. This raises the question as to whether and how much policies or projects associated with risky outcomes should be discounted in making policy decisions.

Several schools of thought exist on this issue. One school argues that, since government is very large and undertakes many projects, it can spread or absorb risks easily and hence should act as a risk-neutral decision maker and ignore risks.[12] It has been argued, however, that pooling risk requires negative correlation among projects (that is, when one turns out bad, another tends to turn out good) and restricting consideration to such sets of projects may reduce the overall value of the investment set of projects. Actually, however, negative correlation of returns is not necessary; pooling risk is possible as long as the returns on any project are independent of other components of national income.[13] Also, even though the government may be risk neutral, certain risks

---

[12]P. A. Samuelson and W. Vickrey, "Discussion," *American Economic Review, Proceedings,* Vol. 59 (1964), pp. 88–96.

[13]Hirshleifer, "Investment Decision."

may be imposed on individuals (for example, the risk of higher taxes), and these may adversely affect private individuals just as in the cases of Chapter 12. The government should not ignore these risks (since they carry private welfare effects) unless they are neutralized—meaning the government actually intervenes to eliminate changes in private risk.

Such steps, however, may carry significant transactions costs and significant moral hazards. For example, the cost of verifying the extent to which each individual must be compensated each period for imposing risks on him may be prohibitive. Also, individuals may be induced to "cheat" by altering their behavior in response to the government spreading of risk. For example, if the government offers a crop insurance program to ensure profits associated with a specific yield and thus spread risks associated with, say, a ban on pesticides, some farmers may use less of some (possibly unobservable) productive inputs since yields are guaranteed. Claims for damages could therefore be higher than anticipated. This phenomenon is referred to as *moral hazard*. These same factors prevent the existence of perfect insurance markets which could otherwise spread risks throughout an economy and thus reduce inefficiencies due to risk.

Another school of thought on public risk discounting argues that risk should be discounted but not at market rates. Rather, a national policy should be established on appropriate rates of discount for both expected effects and risk.[14] Some have argued that the regulated public rate of discount should be determined by the desired rate of growth for an economy.[15] These approaches are based on the assumption of market imperfections such as when externalities exist for future generations. However, one must again bear in mind that a differential in public and private rates of discount can have serious implications for the allocation of funds between the public and private sectors. If the public discount rate is lower than the private rate, funds will be used in the public sector that would otherwise be used in the private sector at a higher expected rate of return. On the other hand, if the public discount rate is above the private rate, private individuals with access to credit at the private rate will redistribute to future time periods some of the public costs transferred to the private sector. These arguments suggest that, with sufficiently competitive capital markets, the government should regulate the private rate of return to that level deemed socially efficient so that both public and private sector investments would appropriately consider future contingencies.

Finally, a third school of thought argues that public-sector risks should be discounted at private rates because private individuals generally bear the

[14] O. Eckstein, "A Survey of the Theory of Public Expenditure" and "Reply," *Public Finances: Needs, Sources, and Utilization* (Princeton, N.J.: National Bureau of Economic Research, 1961), pp. 493–504.

[15] S. Marglin, "The Social Rate of Discount and the Optimal Rate of Investment," *Quarterly Journal of Economics,* Vol. 77 (1963), pp. 95–111.

risks—if not directly, then indirectly through taxes.[16] Rarely does or can the government attempt to bear all the risks of projects that are adopted. If this is the case, any use of a public discount rate that differs from a private rate could at best reach a "second-best" alternative. It seems that this third school of thought has been increasingly adopted by notable economists, although some of its favor may be due to the tractable approach it offers.

To understand these issues analytically, return again to the willingness-to-pay criteria.[17] To consider the implications of risk, suppose that each individual i is risk averse and has, for simple but practical purposes, a mean-variance expected utility function given by

$$E[U_i(S_t^i + T_t^i)] = E(S_t^i) + E(T_t^i) - \alpha V(S_t^i + T_t^i)$$

where E is the expectation operator, V is the variance operator, U_i is a utility function, S_t^i represents net benefits from market involvement as measured by Hicksian surplus at time t, T_t^i represents net benefits gained through transfers from government to individual i at time t, including commodities as well as money (possibly negative), and α is a risk-aversion coefficient. Discounting expected utility over time and aggregating over individuals obtains a welfare objective for society of[18]

$$W = \sum_{i=1}^{N} \sum_{t=0}^{T} \delta^t E[U_i(S_t^i + T_t^i)] = \sum_{t=0}^{T} \delta^t \left[E(S_t) + E(T_t) - \alpha \sum_{i=1}^{N} V(S_t^i + T_t^i) \right]$$

$$= \sum_{t=0}^{T} \delta^t \left[E(S_t) + E(T_t) - \alpha \sum_{i=1}^{N} V(S_t^i) \right.$$

$$\left. - \alpha \sum_{i=1}^{N} V(T_t^i) - 2\alpha \sum_{i=1}^{N} \mathrm{cov}(S_t^i, T_t^i) \right]$$

where $S_t = \Sigma_{i=1}^{N} S_t^i$, $T_t = \Sigma_{i=1}^{N} T_t^i$, $\delta = 1/(1 + r)$, r is the social discount rate, cov is the covariance operator, N is the total number of individuals, and T is the

---

[16]Hirshleifer, "Investment Decision."

[17]The results in the remainder of this section are based on K. J. Arrow and R. C. Lind, "Uncertainty and the Evaluation of Public Investment Decisions," *American Economic Review*, Vol. 60, No. 3 (June 1970), pp. 364–78, although the framework used here is much more simple and heuristic.

[18]This function can serve as a welfare objective for society since changes in W measure net willingness to pay by society as a whole. Aggregation over individuals is possible in a willingness-to-pay context, as in the producer case of Section 11.6, since a certain payment to any individual i is equivalent to an equal change in $E(S_t^i)$ or $E(T_t^i)$.

planning horizon. Suppose, further, that benefits from government projects are divided equally among all individuals so that $T_t^i = T_t/N$. Then

$$\sum_{i=1}^{N} V(T_t^i) = \sum_{i=1}^{N} \frac{V(T_t)}{N^2} = \frac{V(T_t)}{N}$$

$$\sum_{i=1}^{N} \text{cov}(S_t^i, T_t^i) = \sum_{i=1}^{N} \frac{\text{cov}(S_t^i, T_t)}{N} = \frac{\text{cov}(S_t, T_t)}{N}$$

Then the welfare objective of society can be written as

$$W = \sum_{t=0}^{T} \delta^t \left[E(S_t) + E(T_t) - \alpha \sum_{i=1}^{N} V(S_t^i) - \frac{\alpha}{N} V(T_t) - \frac{2\alpha}{N} \text{cov}(S_t, T_t) \right] \quad \textbf{(13.8)}$$

Now consider the spreading of government risks. If the total benefits from government are held constant as the number of individuals over which they are spread increases, the latter two terms in brackets in equation (13.8) disappear. This result implies that government can behave in a risk-neutral manner if its actions do not affect private market risk, reflected in $V(S_t^i)$, and if the benefits of each incremental project are spread over many individuals. On the other hand, if a government project affects private risk, the effects on private risk should be used to discount expected net benefits through the risk-aversion coefficient of the private sector, α. This also implies that the appropriate risk-discounting factor may vary from project to project if different groups of individuals with different degrees of risk aversion are affected by different projects.

One must bear in mind, however, that this result is not applicable when the government project produces a commodity with the characteristics of a public good described in Section 12.2. That is, when every individual derives the full benefit of the project irrespective of how many other individuals are also involved, the total benefits from a project are necessarily proportional to the number of individuals who gain benefits. In this case, one cannot hold total benefits constant while spreading the benefits over more individuals. Instead, the total benefits may be represented by $T_t = NT_t^0$, where T_t^0 represents the size of a project. Thus, W in (13.8) becomes

$$W = \sum_{t=0}^{T} \delta^t \left[E(S_t) + NE(T_t^0) - \alpha \sum_{i=1}^{N} V(S_t^i) - \alpha N V(T_t^0) - 2\alpha \, \text{cov}(S_t, T_t^0) \right]$$

This result implies that risk on public good projects should be discounted at a much higher rate than risk in the private sector, that is, N times higher where N is the number of individuals who benefit from the public good. This is clear since the coefficient of $V(T_t^0)$ is αN rather than simply α.

Even in this case, however, the risk considerations can become unimportant if one considers a small (additional) project which has benefits that are independent of other components of national income. For example, suppose that the expression in (13.8) corresponds to the current projected state of the economy. Now consider an additional project which generates benefits of ΔT_t^0 at time t, where Δ is the scale of the project. This consideration may be made where the new project has either the nature of a public good or not, but suppose for expositional purposes that it involves a public good so that ΔT_t^0 represents benefits for each individual. Then, with the addition of the project, W becomes

$$W^* = \sum_{t=0}^{T} \delta^t \left[E(S_t) + E(T_t) + \Delta NE(T_t^0) - \alpha \sum_{i=1}^{N} V(S_t^i) - \frac{\alpha}{N} V(T_t) - \Delta^2 \alpha NV(T_t^0) \right.$$

$$\left. - \frac{2\alpha}{N} \operatorname{cov}(S_t, T_t) - 2\Delta\alpha \operatorname{cov}(S_t, T_t^0) - 2\Delta\alpha \operatorname{cov}(T_t, T_t^0) \right]$$

Net willingness to pay for the new project is thus

$$W^* - W = \sum_{t=0}^{T} \delta^t [\Delta NE(T_t^0) - \Delta^2 \alpha NV(T_t^0) - 2\Delta\alpha \operatorname{cov}(S_t, T_t^0) - 2\Delta\alpha \operatorname{cov}(T_t, T_t^0)]$$

One can examine the benefits of adding a small project by determining the change in $W^* - W$ associated with a change in Δ and then evaluating that change where $\Delta = 0$,

$$\frac{\partial(W^* - W)}{\partial \Delta} \bigg|_{\Delta=0} = \sum_{t=0}^{T} \delta^t [NE(T_t^0) - 2\alpha \operatorname{cov}(S_t, T_t^0) - 2\alpha \operatorname{cov}(T_t, T_t^0)]$$

This benefit becomes simply $\sum_{t=0}^{T} \delta^t NE(T_t^0)$ if the benefits of the new project, T_t^0, are independent of other components of national income represented by S_t and T_t.[19] Hence, if a project is of sufficiently small scale and independent of other economic phenomena, no risk discounting is necessary even on public good projects.

In summary, there are two conditions where government can act as a risk-neutral decision maker: (1) if the benefits (and costs) of a project are spread over a large number of individuals, the project does not affect private risk from market activities, and the project does not involve public goods in the sense of Section 12.2, or (2) if the project is small and has benefits that are independent of economic benefits derived from other sources. Otherwise, government must discount risk using private risk-discounting factors associated with the individuals who actually bear the risks. For further considerations along this line, see Section C.4.

---

[19]In this case it is necessary only that covariance terms vanish, but it has been shown in a more general framework that independence is necessary; see Arrow and Lind, "Uncertainty and the Evaluation of Public Investment Decisions," *American Economic Review*, 60, No. 3 (June 1970), 364–78.

13.5 CASES IN NATURAL RESOURCE ECONOMICS[20]

One of the most crucial areas for the application of social discounting and cost–benefit analysis is in natural resource economics. *Natural resource economics* is concerned with the conservation of natural resources. Whereas some environmental groups would define conservation of natural resources as the nonuse of resources, *resource conservation* is defined in economics as the optimum or efficient intertemporal use of natural resources.[21]

Natural resources are often divided into two categories: renewable and nonrenewable. A *renewable resource* is one for which the stock can either increase or decrease. Increases are obtained through natural reproductive or recharging mechanisms which can possibly be altered through resource management practices. Examples of such resources are forests and fisheries. A *nonrenewable resource* is one for which the stock can only decrease. Any depletion of such a resource necessarily reduces the availability of the resource for a future period. Examples are fossil fuels and iron ore. In some cases of nonrenewable resources, the service flows can be renewed by recycling even though the resource itself cannot be renewed. For example, once iron ore is manufactured into an automobile, it cannot again be used as iron ore; but the steel in an automobile can be recovered after the life of the automobile to a large extent for, say, manufacturing other steel items. Such resources are sometimes called destructible, nonrenewable resources with renewable service flows. A third classification is that of *capital resources,* sometimes called nonrenewable resources with renewable service flows. These are resources that are available in quantities not affected by the rate at which they are exploited. Examples of such resources are solar and wind energy and land.

Social discounting is crucial in policy formulation and evaluation in each of these cases. With a nonrenewable resource, the policy questions involve intertemporal decisions about how much of the available resource should be used by the current generation and how much should be saved for use by future generations. With a renewable resource, the policy questions involve determination of resource management practices which improve the flow of goods or services from a resource over time as well as determination of optimal rates of use which appropriately balance consumption intertemporally. The use of the social discounting principle can be illustrated by its applications in policy formulation for the major natural resources in each of these categories. Some of

---

[20]This section draws on the graphical analysis developed by John McInnerney, "The Simple Analytics of Natural Resource Economics," *British Journal of Agricultural Economics,* Vol. 27, No. 1 (1976), pp. 31–52.

[21]S. V. Ciriacy-Wantrup, *Resource Conservation: Economics and Policies* (Berkeley: University of California Press, 1952), Chapter 4.

the crucial intertemporal issues with capital resources have to do with irreversibility of resource use decisions.

Nonrenewable Resources

In the case where a resource is available in fixed supply and is destructible—meaning that once it is used it cannot be used again—the problem of temporal allocation is rather simple once the appropriate social discount rate is determined. Consider, for example, a two-period allocation problem, as in Figure 13.4, where MSB_0 in the upper right quadrant represents marginal social benefits of using the resource in the current period, MSB_1^* in the lower left quadrant measures the marginal social benefits of using the resource in a future period, MXC_0 in the upper right quadrant represents the marginal costs of extraction for the raw material at time t_0, MXC_1^* in the lower left quadrant measures the marginal cost of extraction for the raw material at time t_1, and $\bar{q}$ represents the fixed amount of the resource available. The line $\bar{q}\bar{q}$ in the lower right quadrant simply indicates that the amount of resource can be traded between time periods in any way so that total use does not exceed $\bar{q}$. That is, if quantity q_0 is used at time t_0, then following the graph $\bar{q}\bar{q}$ from the right axis to the lower axis implies that q_1 remains for future consumption.

Now consider discounting future benefits and costs in such a way that present welfare effects may be weighed against future effects. This can be done by using the line with slope $1/(1 + r)$ in the upper left quadrant, where r is the appropriate social discount rate between the two time periods (note that t_1 is not

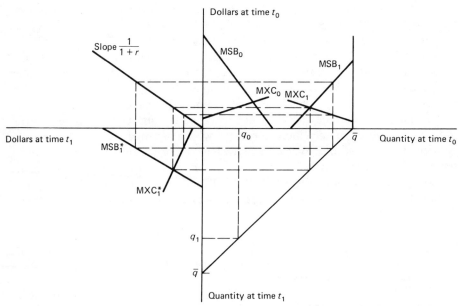

FIGURE 13.4

necessarily equal to $t_0 + 1$). That is, by using the lines drawn in the upper left and lower right quadrants, the $MSB_1{}^*$ and $MXC_1{}^*$ curves in the lower left quadrant can be transformed into the MSB_1 and MXC_1 curves in the upper right quadrant. The MSB_1 curve thus gives the *discounted* marginal social benefit of using the resource in time period t_1. The MXC_1 curve gives the *discounted* marginal extraction cost at time t_1. Both of these curves are drawn backward from quantity $\bar{q}$, representing the fact that future consumption is constrained by the amount left over from current consumption.

In this context, two cases of nonrenewable resource allocation may be depicted as in Figure 13.5. Each case corresponds to the upper right quadrant

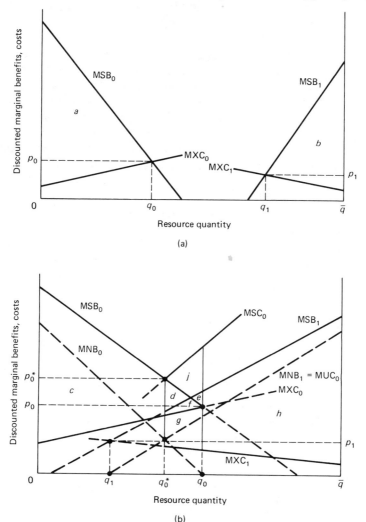

FIGURE 13.5

of Figure 13.4 after discounting. Figure 13.5(a) represents the case where a nonrenewable resource is available in unlimited quantities. The available stock exceeds the maximum that would be consumed over the planning horizon. Such resources are sometimes called *nondepletable* or *nonexhaustible* resources because free-market use levels do not lead to depletion. Competition at time t_0 results in price p_o with quantity q_0 consumed at that price, and competition at time t_1 results in price p_1 with consumption of $\bar{q} - q_1$ (assuming no intratemporal externalities). Hence, there is no need to modify the market resource price to attain proper resource use regardless of discount rate. An example of such a resource is seawater for desalination. Discounted producer plus consumer welfare in this case is represented by area a at time t_0 and area b at time t_1, so the discounted present value of net benefits from the intertemporal resource market is given by area $a + b$.

Figure 13.5(b) represents the alternative case where a destructible nonrenewable resource is available in limiting supply over the planning horizon (i.e., where the resource is *depletable* or *exhaustible*). In this case, competition at time t_0 would result in price p_0 and consumption of q_0. On the other hand, competition at a future time t_1 would result in price p_1 and consumption of $\bar{q} - q_1$ if resource supply were unlimiting. But if current consumption is q_0, then only $\bar{q} - q_0$ would be available for consumption at time t_1. An externality thus exists since the interests of the future generation are not represented in the market at time t_0. Following the principles in Section 12.1, the problem of intertemporal welfare maximization can be solved in at least two ways. First, using the principle of internalization, welfare is maximized intertemporally where the discounted excess of marginal social benefits over marginal extraction costs is just equal over all time periods (i.e., $MSB_0 - MXC_0 = MSB_1 - MXC_1$). By subtracting vertically in Figure 13.5(b) one obtains discounted marginal net benefits $MNB_0 = MSB_0 - MXC_0$ at time t_0 and $MNB_1 = MSB_1 - MXC_1$ at time t_1. The two are equal at q_0^*, which is the consumption that would result at time t_0 if the resource price were regulated upward to p_0^* from the competitive level p_0 (possibly by means of a tax) or if a quota of q_0^* on resource use were established at time t_0 (assuming that regulations also ensure efficiency in extraction and allocation).

Alternatively, this solution can be found by determining first marginal external cost. The external cost in this case is the opportunity cost associated with loss in future benefits due to current consumption. These forgone future benefits are commonly called *user costs* in natural resource economics.[22] These marginal user costs are then added together with the marginal extraction cost to determine the marginal social cost at time t_0.[23] That is, as consumption at time

---

[22]A. D. Scott, "Notes on User Cost," *Economic Journal*, Vol. 63, No. 250 (1953), pp. 68–84. Also see, A. D. Scott, *Natural Resources: The Economics of Conservation* (Canada: University of Toronto Press, 1955).

[23]These results can be obtained mathematically by letting $SB_{t_0}(q_{t_0})$ and $SB_{t_1}(q_{t_1})$

t_0 exceeds q_1, the marginal net benefit forgone by future generations, MNB_1, becomes a marginal external cost or a *marginal user cost* at time t_0, denoted by MUC_0 in Figure 13.5(b). Adding this cost to the marginal extraction cost MXC_0 obtains marginal social cost MSC_0 at time t_0. Equating marginal social cost MSC_0 with marginal social benefits MSB_0 thus leads to the optimal consumption q_0* of the resource at time t_0. Again, this consumption could be achieved under competition by imposing a quota of q_0* or by imposing a price floor or regulated price of p_0* at time t_0 assuming efficiency in extraction and allocation.[24]

To consider the welfare effects in this case, note that producer plus consumer net benefits at time t_0 are given by area $c + d + f$ if competition at price p_0 and quantity q_0 prevails. If price p_0* and quantity q_0* are achieved as a result of regulations, then net benefits at time t_0 are given by area c. Net producer plus consumer benefits at time t_1 are given by area $e + f + g + h$ if price p_0* and quantity q_0* are achieved by regulation at time t_0. However, if competition

---

represent the gross benefit functions at t_0 and t_1, respectively; $XC_{t_0}(q_{t_0})$ and $XC_{t_1}(q_{t_1})$ represent the costs of extraction at t_0 and t_1 and let $\bar{q}$ be the total amount of the resource available. The amount of the resource available at t_1 is then given by

$$q_{t_1} = \bar{q} - q_{t_0}$$

Socially optimal resource use over the two time periods assuming an interior optimum is then obtained by maximizing

$$SB_{t_0}(q_{t_0}) - XC_{t_0}(q_{t_0}) + \frac{1}{1+r} [SB_{t_1}(q_{t_1}) - XC_{t_1}(q_{t_1})]$$

subject to resource availability. The Lagrangian expression for this problem is given by

$$\pounds = SB_{t_0}(q_{t_0}) - XC_{t_0}(q_{t_0}) + \frac{1}{1+r} [SB_{t_1}(q_{t_1}) - XC_{t_1}(q_{t_1})]$$

$$- \lambda (q_{t_1} - \bar{q} + q_{t_0})$$

where λ is the Lagrangian multiplier. Optimizing with respect to q_{t_0} and q_{t_1} yields first-order conditions

$$MSB_{t_0} - MXC_{t_0} - \lambda = 0$$

$$\frac{1}{1+r} (MSB_{t_1} - MXC_{t_1}) - \lambda = 0$$

where $MSB_t = \partial SB_t / \partial q_t$ and $MXC_t = \partial XC_t / \partial q_t$. The latter condition implies that λ is the marginal user cost (MUC_{t_0}) at time t_0. That is λ is the present value of forgone marginal net benefits resulting from an incremental increase in q_{t_0}. Thus, the optimum decision rule at time t_o is given by

$$MSB_{t_0} = MXC_{t_0} + \frac{1}{1+r} (MSB_{t_1} - MXC_{t_1}) - MXC_{t_0} + MUC_{t_0}$$

[24]One might note alternatively, however, that the optimal consumption q_0* could possible result under monopoly without government intervention and that the imposition of a tax in such a case may drive the economy further from Pareto optimality (see the discussion related to Figure 12.6 for a similar case).

prevails at time t_0, then only $\bar{q} - q_0$ of the resource remains at time t_1 and, hence, net benefits at t_1 are only area h. The effects of regulation are thus a loss of area $d + f$ at time t_0 and a gain of area $e + f + g$ at time t_1 which is equal to area $d + e + f + j$ or a net gain of area $e + g - d =$ area $e + j$. Since these welfare effects are in discounted terms, a Pareto improvement is thus possible through regulation by redistributing the net gain so that all individual groups are no worse off.

Finally, consider the case where a nonrenewable resource may be recycled. Such resources include iron, copper, lead, gold, and aluminum. In this case, present consumption need not deprive future generations. However, recycling is not a costless process. The potential for recycling depends on the proportion of the extant resource services that can be recaptured; the length of time for which resource services are fixed, or the rate at which they can be recycled; and the costs of the recycling process.

For the purposes of diagrammatic discussion, assume that resources used at time t_0 can be recycled for use at time t_1. This case is depicted in Figure 13.6 using the approach of internalization, rather than calculating damages for the future generation, and then determining a related marginal social cost curve. Figure 13.6(a) gives the marginal net benefit curve MNB_0 at time t_0, which is derived in Figure 13.5(b) by subtracting marginal extraction cost MXC_0 from marginal social benefits MSB_0. The discounted marginal net benefits from consumption MNB_1 at time t_1 in Figure 13.6(b) are similarly derived, as in Figures 13.4 and 13.5(b), by discounting and then subtracting marginal extraction cost MXC_1 from marginal social benefits MSB_1. Aggregating these two marginal net benefits horizontally thus obtains the discounted intertemporal marginal net benefit curve MNB_{0+1} depicted in Figure 13.6(c). Of course, this same principle would apply in aggregating marginal net benefits across many time periods.

Now suppose that the total amount of the resource is given by $\bar{q}$ in Figure 13.6(c). Translating the intersection of MNB_{0+1} and the vertical line at $\bar{q}$ back to Figure 13.6(a) and (b) thus obtains the appropriate discounted differential between price and marginal extraction cost for time periods t_0 and t_1 which equate discounted marginal net benefits over time when no recycling is used. This is the same solution for social optimality as obtained in Figure 13.5(b),

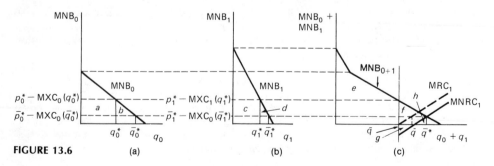

FIGURE 13.6   (a)   (b)   (c)

since $MNB_0 = MNB_1$ where the total quantity of resource is exhausted between the two periods.

Consider, finally, the opportunity of recycling which can increase total intertemporal consumption beyond $\bar{q}$. Let MRC_1 represent the *discounted* marginal cost per unit of resource recovered. With respect to recycled material, the marginal net benefits for a unit of resource recovered would be marginal social benefits less the marginal recovery cost, $\overline{MNB_1} = MSB_1 - MRC_1$, whereas the marginal net benefits in Figure 13.6(c) correspond to marginal social benefits less the marginal extraction costs (e.g., $MNB_1 = MSB_1 - MXC_1$ at time t_1). Thus, $\overline{MNB_1} = MNB_1 + MXC_1 - MRC_1 = MNB_1 - MNRC_1$, where $MNRC_1 = MRC_1 - MXC_1$. The marginal net resource cost of recycling, $MNRC_1$, depicted in Figure 13.6(c) is the marginal recycling cost less the marginal extraction cost that would have been incurred in the absence of recycling (if the available quantity of resource were great enough). The point of social optimality is thus at $\bar{q}^*$, where marginal net benefit is equal to marginal net resource cost, $MNB_{0+1} = MNRC_1$, which corresponds to recycling enough of the resource used at time t_0 to support consumption of $\bar{q}^* - \bar{q}$ at time t_1. Translating back into individual time periods in Figure 13.6(a) and (b), this implies optimal discounted marginal net benefits of $\bar{p}_0{}^* - MXC_0(\bar{q}_0{}^*)$ and $\bar{p}_1{}^* - MXC_1(\bar{q}_1{}^*)$, respectively, or respective discounted prices $\bar{p}_0{}^*$ and $\bar{p}_1{}^*$. Of course, price $\bar{p}_0{}^*$ and quantity $\bar{q}_0{}^*$ would not occur unless appropriate regulations were imposed as above in Figure 13.5(b).

Without recycling, net discounted consumer plus producer welfare is represented by area a at time t_0, by area c at time t_1, and by area e for both time periods considered jointly. With recycling, the present value of net benefits over both time periods increases by area $f + g$. The gain at time t_0 is represented by area b in Figure 13.6(a) assuming that recycling costs are incurred only at time t_1. The net gain at time t_1 is area $d + g - h$. This is clear since area $f + h$ is equal to area $b + d$ by construction; hence, area f is equal to area $b + d - h$. Substituting for area f in the overall gain of area $f + g$ and subtracting the gain at time t_0, area b, thus obtains the gains at time t_1 of area $d + g - h$. Intuitively, area g represents a cost savings associated with recycling where marginal recycling costs are lower than marginal extraction costs; area h represents the higher cost that must be incurred for consumption at time t_1 where marginal recycling costs exceed marginal extraction costs. Since the marginal net benefit curve MNB_1 in Figure 13.6(b) relates only to extraction, both of these adjustments to area d are required in calculating welfare effects of recycling at time t_1.

Of course, the solution in Figure 13.6 is valid only if the intersection of MNB_{0+1} and $MNRC_1$ is above the horizontal axis. Otherwise, recycling would be undertaken to the point of supporting consumption $\tilde{q} - \bar{q}$ at time t_1 (since recycling to this point is cheaper than extraction); then consumption in both time periods would be expanded until marginal social benefits were equated to marginal extraction costs. In this case, resource availability would exceed free-market consumption so that the competitive market would attain social optimality. One may also note that the analysis in Figure 13.6 can be easily generalized to the case where recycling takes place in both (or many) time periods by simply replacing MRC_1 with the horizontal summation over time of all relevant discounted marginal recycling cost curves.

Renewable Resources

With renewable resources, the resource, as well as the service that can be derived from it, is depleted with use, but new stocks are created by a process of regeneration. Resources of this type include fisheries, forests, and grasslands. In each of these cases, once an amount of the resource is used, it cannot be again added to the stock of resources—a house cannot again become a tree, and so on. However, unless the resource is depleted completely, it can regenerate itself, usually at a rate that depends upon the amount of the resource left.

To consider this case, define g as the rate by which 1 unit of the resource will grow from time t_0 to time t_1 if unutilized at time t_0. Thus, if $\bar{q}$ is the total stock of the resource at the beginning of time period t_0 and q_0 of this stock is utilized for current consumption in time t_0, the stock of the resource available at time t_1 is $(\bar{q} - q_0)(1 + g)$. This situation is depicted graphically in Figure 13.7, which corresponds in structure to Figure 13.4. The right axis measures quantity at time t_0, where $\bar{q}$ is the total available stock. If none of the stock is utilized at time t_0, it will grow through regeneration to a stock of $\bar{q}(1 + g)$ by time t_1 as depicted on the lower axis. Any combination of these two extremes is also possible, as indicated by the upward-sloping line in the lower right quadrant. As in Figure 13.4, the marginal social benefits and marginal extraction costs are depicted in current dollars in the upper right quadrant for time t_0 (MSB_0 and MXC_0, respectively) and in the lower left quadrant for time t_1 (MSB_1^* and MXC_1^*, respectively).

If competition prevails, then price p_0 and utilization q_0 occurs at time t_0. Equilibrium at time t_1 would lead to price p_1^* and quantity q_1^*. However, to utilize a quantity of q_1^* at time t_1, a resource stock of at least $\bar{q} - q_1$ must remain unutilized at time t_0. This would not be the case if q_0 is utilized at time t_0. Thus, utilization at t_0 imposes an externality at time t_1. These results thus suggest that, without regulations, a fishery may be overfished, rangelands may be overgrazed, or forests may be overcut at the expense of future generations. Thus, with renewable resources there are user costs associated with decisions to produce now rather than later.

To properly consider user costs in determining intertemporal marginal social cost at time t_0, one must use the appropriate social discount rate, as in Figure 13.4, but one also must consider that one unutilized unit of the resource at time t_0 supports consumption of $1 + g$ units of the resource at time t_1. This is considered by using a line of slope $(1 + g)/(1 + r)$ in the upper left quadrant. Thus, the marginal social benefit curve MSB_1 in the upper right quadrant is

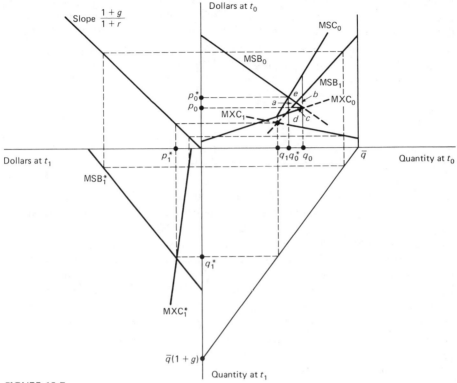

Slope $\dfrac{1+g}{1+r}$

Dollars at t_0

MSC_0

MSB_0

MSB_1

p_0^*

p_0

MXC_1

a

e

b

MXC_0

d c

Dollars at t_1

p_1^*

$q_1 q_0^*$ q_0

$\bar{q}$

Quantity at t_0

MSB_1^*

q_1^*

MXC_1^*

$\bar{q}(1+g)$

Quantity at t_1

FIGURE 13.7

derived by deflating the marginal social benefit MSB_1^* in the lower left quadrant by a social discount rate of r but then inflating by a rate of g because nonuse of 1 quantity unit at time t_0 supports consumption of $1 + g$ units at time t_1. The marginal extraction cost MXC_1 is derived similarly and then the marginal social cost at time t_0 is obtained as $MSC_o = MXC_0 + MSB_1 - MXC_1$, as in Figure 13.5(b).[25] Thus, social optimality at t_0 implies that marginal social benefits at t_0 must be equal to the sum of marginal extraction cost (at t_0) and marginal user cost. Note that marginal user cost, in the case of renewable resources, involves two distinct components: (1) the marginal scarcity value (which is the only cost component associated with exhaustible resources), and (2) the cost imposed on future generations of reduced resource regeneration.

Social optimality in Figure 13.7 is obtained where $MSB_0 = MSC_0$ or at quantity q_0^*. This quantity of resource utilization at time t_0 can be obtained by

---

[25]The renewable resource decision rules can be obtained mathematically as follows. Using the same notation as in footnote 23 for the nonrenewable resource case, the only change in the optimization problem is that the resource constraint becomes

$$q_{t_1} = \bar{q} - q_{t_0} + g(\bar{q} - q_{t_0}) = (1 + g)(\bar{q} - q_{t_0})$$

(Footnote continued on pg. 324)

323

means of a tax given by the vertical difference in MSB_1 and MXC_1 at q_0^* or by establishing a regulated price p_0^* or regulated quantity q_0^* along with some regulations to obtain efficiency in extraction and allocation. The welfare effects are a loss of area $a + c$ for market participants at time t_0 and a gain of area $b + c + d$ for market participants at time t_1 assuming any tax revenues at time t_0 are redistributed in lump-sum payments to time t_0. The net gain from regulation is thus area $b + d - a =$ area $b + e$.

Capital Resources

A final category of resources that are neither renewable nor destructible is typified by land. Regardless of how a given area of land is utilized in one time period, the same quantity of land remains to be utilized in the succeeding time period. However, the way in which land is utilized in one period may limit the set of choices regarding use in a succeeding period. For example, soil misman-agement leads to fertility depletion and erosion. Nonmaintenance of housing, overpopulation of amenity areas, and water pollution also affect choice sets for future generations. In these cases, regeneration may be possible in time so that a framework much like the case of renewable resources above is appropriate. The more serious intertemporal decisions for land relate to uses that are irreversible (or practically so). For example, when land is transferred from agricultural to urban use, fields are covered by houses and streets so that reversal is impractical. The same is true when a dam is built to create a reservoir.

This problem is examined graphically in Figure 13.8, where $\bar{q}$ represents the total quantity of land. The marginal social benefits of using land for housing are

---

Forming the Lagrangian with the same objective function as previously yields first-order conditions

$$MSB_{t_0} - MXC_{t_0} - \lambda(1 + g) = 0$$

$$\frac{1}{1 + r}(MSB_{t_1} - MXC_{t_1}) - \lambda = 0$$

In this case, λ is the present value of an increment of the resource at t_1, which can come from two sources; nonuse in t_0 or regeneration of the stock from t_0 to t_1. Substituting the latter condition into the former, the optimal use of the renewable resource at t_0 is given by

$$MSB_{t_0} = MXC_{t_0} + \frac{1}{1 + r}(MSB_{t_1} - MXC_{t_1})$$

$$+ \frac{g}{1 + r}(MSB_{t_1} - MXC_{t_1})$$

$$= MXC_{t_0} + \frac{1 + g}{1 + r}(MSB_{t_1} - MXC_{t_1})$$

$$= MXC_{t_0} + MUC_{t_0}$$

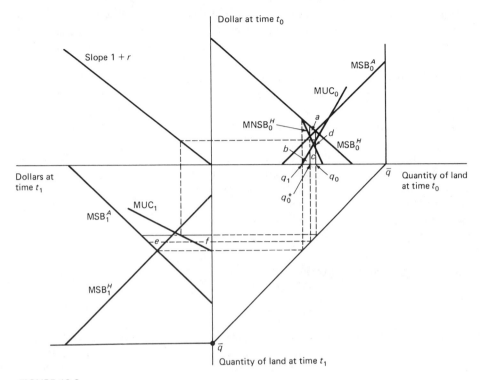

FIGURE 13.8

given by MSB_0^H at time t_0 and by MSB_1^H at time t_1. The marginal social benefits of using land for agricultural purposes are given by MSB_0^A at time t_0 and by MSB_1^A at time t_1. If the free market prevails, equilibrium at time t_0 would occur with quantity q_0 of land in housing. But suppose that population growth is declining and construction costs are rising so that marginal social benefits from housing decline from time t_0 to time t_1. Also, suppose that increasing world demand for food causes the marginal social benefits from agricultural use to increase as reflected in Figure 13.8. Then the desired use of land shifts so that only q_1 is used in housing (determined by the intersection of MSB_1^A and MSB_1^H in the lower left quadrant). However, if housing is irreversible, housing remains at q_0 in time t_1. The welfare effect of the reduced choice for the future generation is a loss of area e measured in currency at time t_1. This, of course, represents a user cost.

To determine a social optimum, first construct a marginal user cost MUC_1 by subtracting MSB_1^H from MSB_1^A in the lower left quadrant. Then area f is equal to area e, so that the area under MUC_1 measures the user cost. Next, transform this user cost curve through social discounting (in the upper left quadrant), obtaining the discounted marginal user cost curve MUC_0 in the upper right

325

quadrant. This curve represents an external cost associated with housing because of its irreversibility. Deducting the marginal user cost from the marginal social benefit MSB_0^H obtains the marginal net social benefit curve $MNSB_0^H$ associated with housing. Equating this with the marginal social benefits from agricultural use thus determines the intertemporal social optimum at q_0^*. This optimum would be achieved by limiting the free-market growth in housing at time t_0. The welfare effects of such a limitation would be a loss of area a for the current generation and a discounted gain of area $c + d$ for the succeeding generation.

The crucial assumptions in this analysis, of course, are the irreversibility of housing and a declining relative benefit from housing. If benefits from housing continue to grow more than for agriculture or if housing were (costlessly) reversible, the free market would attain social optimality in each time period individually as well as intertemporally.

13.6 A PRACTICAL FRAMEWORK FOR DYNAMIC ECONOMIC WELFARE ANALYSIS

Although the foregoing cases characterize some of the broad issues that can arise in intertemporal economic welfare analysis, one must bear in mind that not all problems can be categorized neatly into one of these frameworks. Some problems contain several of these aspects, as well as others such as discussed in Chapter 12. In general, however, the approach is to identify the economic, physical, and biological processes that are affected by policy controls and economic decision making. If private decisions are involved, the reaction of those decisions to policy controls must be considered. Then the indirect and intertemporal effects of various policies on consumer and producer welfare can be investigated.

For example, one can specify and possibly estimate a vector-valued state process

$$X_t = f(X_{t-1}, Y_t, Z_t) \tag{13.9}$$

where the coordinates of X_t represent such things as known reserves of a natural resource and capital accumulation in an industry at time t and possibly also at time $t - 1, t - 2$, etc.; the function f may entail search and discovery processes, technological development, natural or biological regeneration, and so on; Y_t represents government policy controls such as taxes, subsidies, quotas, and direct involvement at time t; and Z_t represents decisions made in the private sector at time t. Upon considering the influence of government controls on the private sector, one can write Z_t as a function of the other variables in the problem so that Z_t can possibly be eliminated.

The objective criteria for policymaking purposes can then be written as

$$\max_{Y_0, Y_1, \ldots, Y_T} \sum_{t=0}^{T} \left(\frac{1}{1 + r} \right)^t \sum_{i=1}^{N} [S_t^i(X_t, Y_t, Z_t) + E_t^i(X_t, Y_t, Z_t) + T_t^i(X_t, Y_t, Z_t)] \quad \textbf{(13.10)}$$

where r is the social discount rate, S_t^i represents market effects on individual or firm i at time t in terms of (Hicksian) consumer surplus or producer surplus, E_t^i represents external effects also in terms of willingness to pay by individual or firm i at time t, T_t^i represents transfers to individual i at time t from government (possibly negative as in the case of a tax), and T is the policy planning horizon.

Maximization of (13.10) subject to (13.9) and an initial state X_0 is a complicated mathematical problem but can be solved, in practice, using dynamic programming, linear or nonlinear programming, or discrete optimal control. Sometimes this type of problem is stated in terms of continuous rather than discrete time, in which case the techniques of continuous control theory are applicable.[26]

The framework in (13.9) and (13.10) provides a powerful and general means of examining a wide range of problems. Because of its apparent simplicity, however, some emphasis on the importance of considering all relevant components is needed. The problem associated with use of public funds for research and development can serve to illustrate this need. Particularly in the area of agriculture, a large amount of public funds has been used to finance research on seed variety improvement and machinery development. The original rationale for these expenditures was that this research requires such massive expenditures that private industry was not in a position to undertake it. Furthermore, the research product, particularly in the area of seed varieties, has the charac-

---

[26]For a further general discussion, see Charles W. Howe, *Natural Resource Economics: Issues, Analysis, and Policy* (New York: John Wiley & Sons, Inc., 1979). For some specific applications, see Oscar R. Burt, "Optimal Resource Use over Time with an Application to Groundwater," *Management Science*, Vol. 11 (1964), pp. 80–93; O. R. Burt and R. G. Cummings, "Production and Investment in Natural Resource Industries," *American Economic Review*, Vol. 60, No. 4 (1973), pp. 576–90; Colin W. Clark, *Mathematical Bioeconomics: The Optimum Management of Renewable Resources* (New York: John Wiley and Sons, 1976); R. G. Cummings, "Some Extensions of the Economic Theory of Exhaustible Resources," *Western Economic Journal*, Vol. 7 (September 1969), pp. 201–10; Partha Dasgupta and Geoffrey Heal, "The Optimal Depletion of Exhaustible Resources," *The Review of Economic Studies: Symposium on the Economics of Exhaustible Resources*, 1974, pp. 3–28; H. Hotelling, "Economics of Exhaustible Resources," *Journal of Political Economy*, Vol. 39 (April 1931) pp. 137–75; Dwight R. Lee, "Price Controls, Binding Constraints, and Intertemporal Economic Decision Making," *Journal of Political Economy*, Vol. 86, No. 2 (April 1978), pp. 293–302; Vernon L. Smith, "On Models of Commercial Fishing," *Journal of Political Economy*, Vol. 77, No. 2 (March–April 1969), pp. 181–98; and R. M. Solow, "Intergenerational Equity and Exhaustible Resources," *Review of Economic Studies: Symposium on the Economics of Exhaustible Resources*, 1974.

teristics of a public good since many producers eventually benefit by obtaining seed from neighbors if not directly from a seed company. Thus, externalities associated with the public goods case of Section 12.2 must be considered.

As more of the research product has led to market impacts, however, several objections have been raised. First, in some cases, private industry has obtained the patent rights to some public research developments, and some have thus argued that public research has only padded the pocketbooks of private industry. Others have argued that the presence of public research has reduced incentives for private research that would otherwise have been undertaken because the likelihood of capturing rents for new technology development is reduced. Still others have argued that the effects of displacement of labor by technological advances have been undesirable and more than outweigh any benefits.

Numerous studies have been undertaken to estimate and compare the costs and benefits of research and development and the associated technological changes. Many of these studies have focused on particular aspects of the problem. For example, Mansfield et al.[27] have focused on the private return to private investment. In so doing, they consider only the terms in (13.10) that relate to private industry (for example, agricultural seed and machinery companies), while disregarding the role of government and public expenditures. Ruttan[28] and others have alternatively examined the returns on public investment. These works generally focus only on the terms in (13.10) that relate to producers and consumers; the role of private industry and private industry's response to public expenditures has not been examined. But in both of these cases, returns to research and development have been found to be quite high, even when social costs have been taken into account.[29]

The framework in (13.9) and (13.10) serves to emphasize why, in spite of these high estimated returns, controversy still exists regarding the desirability of public expenditure for research and development. A complete cost–benefit analysis of public research expenditure must consider effects on all concerns (including those associated with other markets) from both public and private investment and the interactions between the two in terms of the effects of

---

[27]E. Mansfield, J. Rapoport, A. Romeo, E. Villani, S. Wagner, and F. Husic, *The Production and Application of New Industrial Technology* (New York: W.W. Norton & Company, Inc., 1977).

[28]For a list of studies done, see R. E. Evenson, P. E. Waggoner, and V. W. Ruttan, "Economic Benefit from Research: An Example from Agriculture," *Science,* Vol. 205 (September 14, 1979), 1101–7.

[29]See, for example, the paper by A. Schmitz and D. Seckler, "Mechanized Agriculture and Social Welfare: The Case of the Tomato Harvester," *American Journal of Agricultural Economics,* Vol. 52, No. 4 (November 1970), pp. 569–78. Here, even if workers displaced by the introduction of the harvester had been compensated, the payoff from investment in technology would still have been very high.

public investment on private investment decisions and the benefits captured from sales of products developed in the public sector.

13.7   CONCLUSIONS

This chapter expands the framework of economic welfare analysis to the case where costs and benefits accrue over a long period of time. In conclusion, some of the arguments can be briefly reviewed for clarity. Consider first the case where a perfect capital market exists through which a private decision maker operating in a certain environment can distribute his personal willingness to pay over time in any way he sees fit. Then when willingness to pay for a particular change (along with all its associated time stream of effects) is determined at time t_0, it will include welfare effects over all time. In this case, each individual discounts his own effects at his private discount rate (which would be the perfect capital-market rate of interest). Hence, use of the willingness-to-pay criterion necessarily implies that the (implicit) social discount rate is equal to the private rate of return (assuming all individuals face the same private rate of return as with a perfect capital market).

On the other hand, suppose that markets are not perfect. If capital markets do not permit individuals to freely redistribute their welfare effects over time, then the private rate of return may not be appropriate. In the former case, willingness to pay in individual time periods would require specific determination so that necessary compensation schemes could be considered. In the event of compensation over time, as well as within time, where funds are carried forward or backward in time by government, the appropriate discount rate is the one representing opportunity cost for government rather than the private sector (for example, the rate paid on government treasury bills). Hence, the δ in equations (13.6) and (13.7) should be associated with the public discount rate rather than respective private rates. If, however, compensation is only considered at time t_0, then the time stream of welfare effects for each individual should be discounted with his respective private discount rate which may differ substantially both among individuals and over time depending on whether deficits or surpluses are being carried.

If, on the other hand, market failure entails externalities due to unrepresented contingencies of future generations, the extent of such externalities must be estimated (as well as possible) and then a social discount rate must be used as a means of comparing relative income distributions between present and future generations. Unless a change is Pareto superior without compensation, no intratemporal compensation scheme could attain Pareto optimality; the government would be forced either to carry compensation over time or to make interpersonal comparisons between generations. In this case, the choice of a social discount rate becomes crucial in comparing welfare effects at different points in time. The theoretical analysis shows that the choice of discount rate depends on whether society foresees increasing production possibilities due to technological development or declining production possibilities due to natural resource depletion.

Since the crux of most natural resource problems has to do with comparing social welfare effects over a very long period relating to, perhaps, several generations, the choice of a discount rate is the most important issue in determining intergenerational distribution of resource use. The methodology expounded in this chapter, however, has important applications to many other problems as well. Indeed, social discounting is an important consideration in evaluation of any policy from which effects are realized over a long period of time. The technological development case discussed briefly in Section 13.6 is one such example.

14

Conclusions

This book has presented the subject of applied welfare economics including the theory underlying the methodology of application. Some of the basic concepts in applied welfare economics have been of a controversial nature for many years. Some economists have accepted the surplus framework as a basis for applied work, whereas others have not. However, those who are critical of the approach in this book either have not developed workable empirical alternatives or they have recommended equivalent approaches (for example, index number theory). The following quotes from famous economists are presented to highlight the controversial history of the subject matter. Abba P. Lerner argues:[1]

> Consumer's surplus nevertheless seems to me to be of very great use not only as a heuristic device for showing students of economics the benefits from an increase in the freedom of trade, but also for indicating where one should look for indications and estimates of the social benefits or damages from many an important governmental or other policy decision.

In regard to the general usefulness of consumer's surplus, Hicks writes:[2]

> The idea of consumer's surplus enables us to study in detail the effects of deviations from the optimum in a particular market. It is not merely a convenient way of showing when there will be a deviation (consumers' surplus is not necessary for that purpose, since the basic optimum conditions . . . show us at once when there will be a deviation); it also offers us a way of measuring the size of the deviation. This, if we are right in our general viewpoint, is a most important service.

[1]Abba P. Lerner, "Statics and Dynamics in Socialistic Economics," *Economic Journal*, Vol. 47 (June 1937), p. 80.

[2]J. R. Hicks, "The Rehabilitation of Consumer's Surplus," *Review of Economic Studies*, Vol. 8 (February 1940–41), p. 112.

Samuelson, however, states:[3]

> My ideal Principles would not include consumer's surplus in the chapter on welfare economics except possibly in a footnote, although in my perfect Primer the concept might have a limited place, provided its antidote and the alternatives were included close at hand.

In fact, Samuelson makes the most fundamental attack on the concept of consumer's surplus. In arguing that the concept is superfluous, he writes:[4]

> Even if consumer's surplus did give a cardinal measure of the change in utility from a given change, it is hard to see what use this could serve. Only in the contemplation of alternative movements which begin or end in the same point could this cardinal measure have any significance and then only because it is an indicator of ordinal preference.

In fairness to Samuelson, however, one should note that his attacks on consumer surplus were made prior to the development of the Willig results discussed in Chapters 6 and 7 and prior to much of the other sophistication which has led welfare economics to an equivalence with index number theory which he supports.[5]

Policies are continuously being introduced and modified, and it is part of the role of the economist to provide quantitative results concerning their impact. As Bhagwati has recently stressed:[6]

> Policies are maintained or changed largely for noneconomic reasons; and the (economic) 'cost' involved is a magnitude that is commonly demanded and bandied about in discussions of public policy. Whether we like it or not, this is what the policy makers do want; and the trade theorist, in consonance with the best traditions in the profession, has begun to meet this need in an attempt to bring economic analysis closer to fulfilling the objective that provides its ultimate raison d'etre. The result has been a definite and significant trend, in the welfare analysis of pure theory, towards measurement of welfare change.

During the heaviest period of criticism of surplus concepts and before the many subsequent generalizations, the primary force that caused continued surplus analysis in applied literature was this need for quantitative empirical analysis of alternative policies.

---

[3]Paul A. Samuelson, *Foundations of Economic Analysis* (Cambridge, Mass.: Harvard University Press, 1963), p. 197.

[4]*Ibid.*, p. 210.

[5]P. A. Samuelson and S. Swamy, "Invariant Economic Index Numbers and Canonical Duality: Survey and Synthesis," *American Economic Review,* Vol. 64, No. 4 (September 1974), pp. 566–93.

[6]Jagdish Bhagwati, "The Pure Theory of International Trade: A Survey," in American Economic Association and Royal Economic Society, *Surveys of Economic Theory,* Vol. 2 (New York: AEA/RES, 1965), p. 213.

14.1 EMPHASIS ON APPLICATION

This book has focused on applied economic welfare analysis on the basis of estimable market supply and demand equations. Generalizations of these methods in response to many of the classical criticisms of surplus analysis have been developed. Often in the literature, the discussion of welfare economics focuses on the validity of the concept of economic surplus as a measure of welfare change without worrying about the additional problem of empirically estimating economic surplus. Even if, for example, consumer's surplus is a valid measure of compensating or equivalent variation, how does one empirically estimate the appropriate demand curve from which the surplus is to be calculated? Even if, conceptually, the framework provided in this book is valid for applied work, errors can still be created from econometric estimation of these relationships. Thus, both the theory and the problems of empirical estimation must be considered together in assessing the usefulness of the methodology. For example, although this book points out some estimation problems and alternatives, in some cases there is no way of knowing whether or not the errors created by econometric specification and estimation with some approaches are greater than or less than the errors created by using the ordinary concept of economic surplus with other approaches. Nevertheless, this book has tried to modify standard welfare analysis in the direction of making it amenable to econometric estimation at various levels of generality.

Theoretical Applications

The concept of economic surplus with appropriate generalizations is a very powerful one. This book has shown, for example, how the concept was used very early in economics to demonstrate the welfare loss associated with monopoly and other distortions, the gains from technological change, the notion of the optimum tariff on trade, the gains from trade, and so on. These problems were subsequently reformulated and studied along general equilibrium lines, but the basic qualitative conclusions still held. The conclusions based on the early simple surplus literature were correct. The extension of surplus concepts discussed in this book reveals why this is the case. In fact, any surplus analysis based on a simple supply and demand diagram has several levels of interpretation in theory. First, if the supply and demand are interpreted as ordinary curves, the triangles represent consumer and producer surplus which offer a basis for approximating willingness to pay for participants in the market. Second, if the supply and demand are interpreted as compensated curves, the triangles are Hicksian surpluses, the changes in which reflect willingness to pay exactly for participants in the market. Thus, with a simple interpretation of the same diagrams used early in the economics literature, the analysis becomes exact rather than approximate. Finally, if supply and demand are interpreted as compensated general equilibrium curves the triangles reflect welfare effects for the economy as a whole—not just for the participants in the individual market. Thus, the economic surplus concepts can be as general, for theoretical purposes, as many of the more sophisticated general equilibrium approaches which have been advanced; yet the economic surplus approach is simple, intuitive, and forms a useful basis for empirical work.

Empirical Applications

Although this book attempts to extend partial equilibrium analysis and models toward a more general equilibrium approach, most empirical work cannot be made completely general. For example, if the government is considering allowing more steel or cars to enter the country, the decision is usually not made even partially on the basis of the effects that steel or auto imports might have on the real wages of shoe workers. Nevertheless, the large equilibrium effects in related markets can conceivably be measured empirically because it is precisely their size which makes their effects identifiable empirically in the context of methodology advanced in Chapter 9. In fact, the frontiers of methodological development in welfare economics now seem sufficient to offer guidance for how to consider all the effects that econometric or programming models are capable of identifying.

14.2 WELFARE MAXIMIZATION AND COST–BENEFIT ANALYSIS

Cost–benefit analysis has become quite popular in public circles. A seemingly endless number of proposed government projects come before policymaking bodies; rational public decision making requires some understanding of the associated costs and benefits. This has led to a great demand for cost–benefit analyses of specific projects with specific specifications. Unfortunately, however, this type of approach can lead to social suboptimality. That is, the welfare effects of some general action may depend heavily on the scale of project or on some specific design parameters. Cost–benefit analyses, as they are often undertaken upon specific requests, however, generally attempt to investigate the net social benefits of a particular project with a particular scale, design, and so on. By performing a very specific cost–benefit analysis, the potential for social welfare maximization may be forgone. For example, in some cases the adoption of a project of a particular scale may preclude any later augmentation or reduction necessary to reach a state of social efficiency or optimal scale.

For example, by one process or another, a proposed dam of a particular size and location may come before a legislative body. In many cases, preliminary costs and benefits (from perhaps electricity generation) may be based on prevailing market prices; but market prices may change as a result of project adoption. Proposed size and location may even be appropriate as a result of engineering studies—given that existing prices are not altered as a result. In many cases, however, some economic externalities may exist which, in addition to induced price changes, may invalidate initial engineering design studies. For example, recreational opportunities are benefits associated with a dam for which standard accounting prices do not exist. Congestion costs also may be experienced as externalities by surrounding residents and are generally not included in standard engineering cost studies. These considerations suggest that social welfare analysis should play an important role in determining the design or scale of a project. Otherwise, some adverse effects or possibly greater needs may be realized only after a given dam is completed. But, of course, a dam is generally too costly to relocate or modify once completed.

These considerations thus emphasize the importance of applying cost–benefit analysis more generally in the context of social welfare maximization, that is, determining the best project design to adopt rather than whether or not to adopt a given project. The concept of welfare maximization is also important in deciding which set of a large group of potential projects should be adopted. Government funds are generally limited because of political factors, and so on; hence, not all projects with positive present discounted social value can be undertaken. Of course, the set of projects to adopt should be chosen to maximize discounted net social benefits, given the funding constraint; one project may not be appropriate unless some other one is also adopted. Again, however, one should bear in mind the possibilities for improving social welfare by altering individual project designs. Also, existing prices are likely to be altered to a greater extent when many projects are undertaken than when a single project is implemented; and any cost–benefit or welfare analysis should consider the related interactions among projects where substantial cross effects may exist. Again, the methodology of applied welfare economics is sufficiently general to lend guidance on these issues at least when a sufficient empirical base of information is available.

14.3   INCOME DISTRIBUTION

In the early chapters on general equilibrium welfare economics, the notion of a social welfare function was introduced. This was necessary both to discuss the ideal income distribution (and hence the ideal production mix in society) and to illustrate the conceptual problems of applied economic welfare analysis. The search for an "ideal society" continues in some of the recent works by Rawls[7] and Nozick.[8] These studies, although belonging to the field of moral philosophy, are being studied closely by economists. Rawls offers a theory that judges the "goodness" of the distribution of social goods according to the level of welfare provided to the least advantaged members of society. According to

---

[7] J. Rawls, *A Theory of Justice* (New York: Oxford University Press, 1971).

[8] R. Nozick, *Anarchy, State and Utopia* (New York: Basic Books, Inc., 1974).

Rawls, society must be organized to (1) guarantee a maximal system of equal, basic liberties and (2) distribute all social goods (other than liberty) equally unless an unequal distribution of social goods benefits the least advantaged, provided that the positions and offices that foster this inequality are open to all. However, it does not follow, as Nozick points out, that equality in the distribution of income and wealth is prima facie desirable. For Nozick, the attempt by the state to pattern the distribution of income and wealth to accord with some concept of justice is a violation of basic rights. Thus, "utilitarians may require that the minority sacrifice itself for the sake of the majority, while a Rawlsian may demand a sacrifice by the best-off for the sake of the worst-off."[9]

The intent of this book is much less ambitious than seeking the welfare function to define the ideal society. It provides, instead, a framework for analyzing the impacts of policy changes. The underlying view is that, at best, economists can point out the economic impact of policy changes including distributional effects to the extent they can be empirically identified; the political process must use this along with other information and preferences of policymakers to formulate new policy decisions. Politicians can be expected to continue to divide on income-distributional issues since even economists or philosophers cannot reach agreement concerning an ideal distribution.

14.4 SUMMARY

The methodology developed in this book is not sufficient to provide a framework to solve the world's problems. If they can be solved, the solutions require more than economics, let alone welfare economics. To argue that applied welfare economics has all the answers to solving real-world problems is a mistake, just as it is a mistake to argue that political science or moral philosophy has all the answers. Hopefully, however, this book provides a broad basis for delving into the topic of welfare economics and understanding how its constructs can be used to promote more informed public policy formulation.

---

[9]Janusz A. Ordover, "Understanding Economic Justice: Some Recent Developments in Pure and Applied Welfare Economics," in *Economic Perspectives*, Vol. 1, ed. Maurice B. Ballabon (New York: Harwood Academic Publishers, 1979), p. 56. This article is an excellent treatment of the subject of economic justice from the viewpoint of both economics and moral philosophy.

Appendix A

Duality of Surpluses in Factor and Product Markets: The Case of the Single Competitive Firm

Rigorous analysis of the question of whether or not producer welfare changes can be measured alternatively in factor or output markets by choice of the investigator began with the papers by Richard Schmalensee,[1] Daniel Wisecarver,[2] and J. E. Anderson.[3] Although many economists had speculated or assumed that producer welfare could be measured in factor markets as well as the product market (for example, Andrew Schmitz and David Seckler,[4]

---

[1]Richard Schmalensee, "Consumer's Surplus and Producer's Goods," *American Economic Review,* Vol. 61, No. 4 (September 1971), pp. 682–87; and Schmalensee, "Another Look at the Social Valuation of Input Price Changes," *American Economic Review,* Vol. 66, No. 1 (March 1976), pp. 239–43.

[2]Daniel Wisecarver, "The Social Costs of Input-Market Distortions," *American Economic Review,* Vol. 64, No. 3 (June 1974), pp. 359–72.

[3]J. E. Anderson, "The Social Cost of Input Distortions: A Comment and a Generalization," *American Economic Review,* Vol. 66, No. 1 (March 1976), pp. 235–38.

[4]Andrew Schmitz and David Seckler, "Mechanized Agriculture and Social Welfare:

Darrell L. Hueth and Andrew Schmitz,[5] and Rachel Dardis and Janet Dennison[6]), the early works of Schmalensee[7] and Wisecarver[8] were interesting in that they apparently proved that this was not the case. More recently, however, Schmalensee[9] and Anderson[10] have identified errors in the earlier analyses; and Schmalensee has, indeed, shown that changes in producer welfare resulting from a single input price change can be accurately evaluated in either the (single) relevant input market or the output market.[11] In this appendix, the special case of Schmalensee's assumptions where product price is fixed or unaffected (as with a single competitive firm) is considered. However, a number of results and details not pointed out by Schmalensee are also established; in particular, the results are extended to the case of risk. The case where product price or input prices adjust is considered in Appendix D.

A.1 SEQUENTIAL EVALUATION OF A MULTIPLE PRICE CHANGE

Consider a multiproduct, profit-maximizing firm facing fixed product prices $p = (p_1, \ldots, p_m)$ and fixed variable input prices $w \equiv (w_1, \ldots, w_n)$. Suppose that the production functions are given by $q_i = q_i(x)$, $i = 1, \ldots, m$, where $x \equiv (x_1, \ldots, x_n)$, $q_i(0) = 0$, fixed production factors are assumed to exist but are not explicitly included as arguments in q_i, and each q_i is assumed to be concave and twice differentiable with positive marginal productivities ($q_{ij}' \equiv \partial q_i/\partial x_j > 0$) with respect to some subset of inputs, while marginal productivities are identically zero ($q_{ij}' \equiv 0$) for all other inputs (but $q_{ij}' > 0$ for some i).[12] Thus, each input may have positive marginal productivities for one or several products; any ability to influence product mix for a given set of physical inputs is represented by dummy inputs with zero prices. Profits are given by

The Case of the Tomato Harvester," *American Journal of Agricultural Economics,* Vol. 52, No. 4 (November 1970), pp. 569–77.

[5]Darrell L. Hueth and Andrew Schmitz, "International Trade in Intermediate and Final Goods: Some Welfare Implications of Destabilized Prices," *Quarterly Journal of Economics,* Vol. 86, No. 3 (August 1972), pp. 351–65.

[6]Rachel Dardis and Janet Dennisson, "The Welfare Costs of Alternative Methods of Protecting Raw Wool in the United States," *American Journal of Agricultural Economics,* Vol. 51, No. 2 (May 1969), pp. 303–19.

[7]Schmalensee, "Consumer's Surplus."

[8]Wisecarver, "Social Costs."

[9]Schmalensee, "Another Look."

[10]Anderson, "Social Cost."

[11]Anderson also showed equivalence of input and output market surplus changes but under assumptions different from those which apply in this appendix; see Chapter 7 for a further discussion.

[12]For a discussion of concavity, see James M. Henderson and Richard E. Quandt, *Microeconomic Theory: A Mathematical Approach,* 2d ed. (New York: McGraw-Hill Book Company, 1971), p. 402.

$$\pi = \sum_{i=1}^{m} p_i q_i(x) - \sum_{j=1}^{n} w_j x_j - \text{TFC}$$

hence, first-order, profit-maximization conditions are

$$\frac{\partial \pi}{\partial x_j} = \sum_{i=1}^{m} p_i \frac{\partial q_i}{\partial x_j} - w_j = 0, \qquad j = 1, \ldots, n \qquad \textbf{(A.1)}$$

and second-order conditions are satisfied under the assumptions above. In principle, these first-order conditions can be solved for derived input demand functions,[13]

$$x_j = \tilde{x}_j(p,w), \qquad j = 1, \ldots, n \qquad \textbf{(A.2)}$$

which specify optimal input levels for given prices. Through substitution of (A.2), functions specifying optimal output and optimal quasi-rent in terms of prices can also be defined,

$$q_i = \tilde{q}_i(p, w) \equiv q_i[\tilde{x}(p, w)] \equiv q_i[\tilde{x}_1(p, w), \ldots, \tilde{x}_n(p, w)] \qquad \textbf{(A.3)}$$

$$R = R(p, w) \equiv \sum_{i=1}^{m} p_i \tilde{q}_i(p, w) - \sum_{j=1}^{n} w_j \tilde{x}_j(p, w) \qquad \textbf{(A.4)}$$

Using (A.3) and (A.4), one finds that[14]

$$\frac{\partial R}{\partial p_i} = \tilde{q}_i(p, w) + \sum_{j=1}^{n} \left(\sum_{k=1}^{m} p_k \frac{\partial q_k}{\partial x_j} - w_j \right) \frac{\partial \tilde{x}_j}{\partial p_i} = \tilde{q}_i(p, w) \qquad \textbf{(A.5)}$$

and

$$\frac{\partial R}{\partial w_j} = -\tilde{x}_j(p, w) + \sum_{k=1}^{n} \left(\sum_{i=1}^{m} p_i \frac{\partial q_i}{\partial x_k} - w_k \right) \frac{\partial \tilde{x}_k}{\partial w_j} = -\tilde{x}_j(p, w) \qquad \textbf{(A.6)}$$

since the terms in brackets in each case are zero by the conditions in (A.1).

It is now possible to examine the impact of a multiple set of price changes on quasi-rent, $R = \pi + \text{TFC}$. The change in quasi-rent ΔR from initial prices (p^0,

---

[13] For a clear and detailed discussion of these results, the reader is referred to ibid., p. 127.

[14] The results in (A.5) and (A.6) are obtained directly by the envelope theorem. For further discussion, see Hal R. Varian, *Microeconomic Analysis* (New York: W. W. Norton & Company, Inc., 1978), or Eugene Silberberg, *The Structure of Economics: A Mathematical Analysis* (New York: McGraw-Hill Book Company, 1978).

w^0) to final prices (p^1, w^1) may be expressed using the results in (A.5) and (A.6) as

$$\Delta R \equiv R(p^1, w^1) - R(p^0, w^0)$$

$$= \int_L dR = \int_L \left(\sum_{i=1}^{m} \frac{\partial R}{\partial p_i} dp_i + \sum_{j=1}^{n} \frac{\partial R}{\partial w_j} dw_j \right) = \int_L \left(\sum_{i=1}^{m} \bar{q}_i \, dp - \sum_{j=1}^{n} \bar{x}_j \, dw_j \right) \quad (A.7)$$

where L is any path of integration from initial prices to final prices.

To evaluate welfare changes using (A.7), note that, since the integrand of (A.7) is the exact differential of R by derivation, there is no need to convert to a money measure as in the consumer case (it is already in money terms); the integral may be evaluated by choosing any particular path. For example, consider the path described by the following variations:

$$\hat{p}_i(p_i) \equiv (p_1^1, \ldots, p_{i-1}^1, p_i, p_{i+1}^0, \ldots, p_m^0, w^0), \quad i = 1, \ldots, m$$
$$\hat{w}_j(w_j) \equiv (p^1, w_1^1, \ldots, w_{j-1}^1, w_j, w_{j+1}^0, \ldots, w_n^0), \quad j = 1, \ldots, n$$
(A.8)

In this case, one finds that

$$\Delta R = \sum_{i=1}^{m} \int_{p_i^0}^{p_i^1} \bar{q}_i[\hat{p}_i(p_i)] dp_i - \sum_{j=1}^{n} \int_{w_j^0}^{w_j^1} \bar{x}_j[\hat{w}_j(w_j)] dw_j$$

which is simply the sum of changes in the output market producer surpluses associated with respective changes from p_i^0 to p_i^1 (where all other output prices are fixed at p_k^1 for $k = 1, \ldots, i - 1$, and at p_k^0 for $k = i + 1, \ldots, m$ and all input prices are held at initial levels), plus the sum of changes in the input market consumer surpluses associated with changes in the respective input prices from w_j^0 to w_j^1 (where all other input prices w_k are fixed at w_k^1 for $k = 1, \ldots, j - 1$ and at w_k^0 for $k = j + 1, \ldots, n$, and output prices are fixed at subsequent levels).

Thus, the overall change in quasi-rent can be evaluated by successively calculating the change in surplus over all markets for which prices change where supply or demand curves at each stage are conditioned on all previously considered changes (other prices are held at initial values) following the price path suggested by (A.8). Furthermore, because of path independence, it is a trivial extension of the foregoing results to show that the order in which price changes are considered is arbitrary and makes no difference with respect to the overall impact on rents.[15]

Another result immediately obtained is that the welfare impact of a single input price change can be completely measured in the associated factor market,

---

[15]One should note, however, that this property will not hold empirically unless estimated relationships are specified so as to satisfy certain theoretical constraints; see Section A.5.

or the welfare impact of a single output change can be completely measured in the associated output market even though the price change induces a shift in other output supplies and other factor demands. More generally, in the multiple-price-change case, all input markets for which prices do not change need not be considered in calculating the change in welfare.

A.2   EVALUATION OF A MULTIPLE PRICE CHANGE IN THE OUTPUT MARKET

Thus far, it is clear that producer welfare effects can be unambiguously and accurately measured using surplus concepts. However, knowledge of all supply and demand schedules for which prices change appears to be required before welfare impacts can be calculated. This section, however, shows that this is not necessarily so. This is first shown from the standpoint of an output market, in which case the change in quasi-rent is accurately measured by the change in an output market producer surplus regardless of which prices are changed as long as the output is a necessary output of the firm.

Consider a general price change from (p^0, w^0) to (p^1, w^1) and define a *necessary output* as one for which a shutdown price exists. The *shutdown price* for the necessary output in each case is one which is just low enough, given other prices, that the firm is induced to shut down.[16] Specifically and without loss of generality, suppose that the first output is a necessary output and define shutdown price for q_1 as

$$\hat{p}_1^{\,k} = \max \{p_1 ; \bar{x}\,(p_1, p_2^{\,k}, \ldots, p_m^{\,k}, w^k) = 0\}, \qquad k = 0, 1$$

In this case, using (A.5), the producer surplus in the output market for q_1 with prices (p^k, w^k) is

$$P_1^{\,k} = \int_{\hat{p}_1^{\,k}}^{p_1^{\,k}} \bar{q}_1(p_1, p_2^{\,k}, \ldots, p_m^{\,k}, w^k)\, dp_1$$

$$= \int_{\hat{p}_1^{\,k}}^{p_1^{\,k}} \frac{\partial R^k}{\partial p_1}\, dp_1 = \hat{R}^k(p_1^{\,k}) - \hat{R}^k(\hat{p}_1^{\,k}) \tag{A.9}$$

$$= R(p^k, w^k) \tag{A.10}$$

where $\hat{R}^k(p_1) = R(p_1, p_2^{\,k}, \ldots, p_m^{\,k}, w^k)$ and $\hat{R}^k(\hat{p}_1^{\,k}) = 0$ by definition (that is, quasi-rent must be zero if all input levels and thus all output levels are zero). Thus, the welfare effect of the multiple price range is captured completely by $P_1^1 - P_1^0$, the change in producer surplus in the market for the (necessary) output q_1. With this equivalence of producer surplus and quasi-rent, the inves-

---

[16] By admitting negative and possibly infinite shutdown prices, one can show that q_i is a necessary output if $q_i = 0$ requires $q_k = 0, k = 1, \ldots, m$, and/or $x_j = 0, j = 1, \ldots, n$.

tigator thus has alternatives as to whether to measure the impact of an input price change in the input or the output market.

For intuitive purposes, one might note that the result in (A.9) holds where $\hat{p}_1^k$ is simply defined as the maximum price where q_1 is not produced, $\hat{p}_1^k = \max \{p_1; \tilde{q}_1(p_1, p_2^k, \ldots, p_m^k, w^k) = 0\}$. However, in this case the change in producer surplus is

$$\Delta P_1 = P_1^1 - P_1^0 = R(p^1, w^1) - R(p^0, w^0) + \hat{R}^0(\hat{p}_1^0) - \hat{R}^1(\hat{p}_1^1)$$
$$= \Delta R + \hat{R}^0(\hat{p}_1^0) - \hat{R}^1(\hat{p}_1^1)$$

which does not measure the change in quasi-rent if $\hat{R}^0(\hat{p}_1^0) \neq \hat{R}^1(\hat{p}_1^1)$. In general, this will not be the case, since $\hat{R}^0(\hat{p}_1^0)$ is quasi-rent for the firm with prices $(\hat{p}_1^0, p_2^0, \ldots, p_m^0, w^0)$ and $\hat{R}^1(\hat{p}_1^1)$ is quasi-rent with prices $(\hat{p}_1^1, p_2^1, \ldots, p_m^1, w^1)$. This problem arises because all marginal adjustments are not reflected in the q_1 supply curve when the firm continues to operate or adjust at prices where $q_1 = 0$.

A.3   EVALUATION OF A MULTIPLE PRICE CHANGE IN A SINGLE-INPUT MARKET

An even wider range of alternatives is suggested by similarly integrating over quantities in input markets. In point of fact, it turns out that the impact of multiple price changes (including output prices) can also in certain cases be completely measured by using surplus concepts in any one of the input markets.

To see this, consider again a multiple price change from (p^0, w^0) to (p^1, w^1) and define a *necessary input* as one for which a shutdown price exists. The *shutdown price* in the case of a necessary input is one that is just high enough, given other prices, to induce the firm to cease all production.[17] Specifically, without loss of generality, suppose that the first input is a necessary input and define shutdown input price for x_1 as

$$\hat{w}_1^k = \min \{w_1; \tilde{x}(p^k, w_1, w_2^k, \ldots, w_n^k) = 0\}, \qquad k = 0, 1$$

---

[17]By admitting possibly infinite shutdown prices, one can show that x_j is a necessary input if $q_i(x_1, \ldots, x_{j-1}, 0, x_{j+1}, \ldots, x_n) = 0$ for $i = 1, \ldots, m$. Although this condition may not hold for all inputs, Ferguson, for example, after discussing alternative assumptions for production processes, concludes: "The more reasonable assumption seems to be that a positive usage of all inputs simultaneously is required to produce a positive output"; see Ferguson, *The Neoclassical Theory of Production and Distribution* (Cambridge, England: Cambridge University Press, 1969), p. 61.

Thus, using (A.6), the consumer surplus in the input market for x_1 with prices (p^k, w^k) is

$$C_1^k = \int_{w_1^k}^{\hat{w}_1^k} \tilde{x}_1(p^k, w_1, w_2^k, \ldots, w_n^k)dw_1$$

$$= -\int_{w_1^k}^{\hat{w}_1^k} \frac{\partial \tilde{R}^k}{\partial w_1} dw_1$$

$$= \tilde{R}^k(w_1^k) - \tilde{R}^k(\hat{w}_1^k) \tag{A.11}$$

$$= R(p^k, w^k) \tag{A.12}$$

where $\tilde{R}^k(w_1) = R(p^k, w_1, w_2^k, \ldots, w_n^k)$ and $\tilde{R}^k(\hat{w}_1^k) = 0$ by definition (since all input levels are zero at $\tilde{w}_1^k$). Thus, the welfare effect of a multiple price change is captured completely by $C_1^1 - C_1^0$, the change in consumer surplus in the market for a necessary input.

For intuitive purposes, one can note, as in the producer surplus case, that (A.11) holds even if x_1 is not a necessary input. But if $\tilde{R}^k(\hat{w}_1^k)$ is not zero, as it is when $\hat{w}_1^k$ represents a corresponding shutdown price, then $\tilde{R}^0(\hat{w}_1^0)$ will generally not be equal to $\tilde{R}^1(\hat{w}_1^1)$; each would represent quasi-rents under different sets of prices even though $\tilde{x}_1$ would be zero under each. This problem, as in the case of producer surplus, arises because all marginal adjustments are not reflected by the marginal valuations of x_1 embodied in its derived demand if the firm continues to operate or adjust at prices where $x_1 = 0$.

A.4   CONCLUSIONS AND AN EXAMPLE FOR THE NONSTOCHASTIC PRODUCTION CASE

Combining the results in (A.10) and (A.12) yields

$$R^k = P_i^k = C_j^k \tag{A.13}$$

and

$$\Delta R = \Delta P_i = \Delta C_j$$

where $\Delta R = R^1 - R^0$, $\Delta P_i = P_i^1 - P_i^0$, and $\Delta C_j = C_j^1 - C_j^0$ for all i and j such that q_i is a necessary output and x_j is a necessary input. The implications of these results are that the welfare impact of a policy which has possible multiple-price effects on a price-taking, profit-maximizing producer can be completely evaluated not only in any necessary output market but also in any input market for which the input is necessary in the production process—whether or not the corresponding market price is among those that change. The investigator may thus have some freedom to choose a market for evaluation based on ease of measurement and data availability. Further advantages of this result from the point of view of statistical measurement are discussed in Section 8.9.

To aid in intuition and give a concrete example of this result, consider a Cobb–Douglas production function (based on implicit fixed factors),

$$q = q(x_1, x_2) = Ax_1^{\alpha_1}x_2^{\alpha_2}, \qquad \alpha_1 > 0, \ \alpha_2 > 0, \ \alpha_1 + \alpha_2 < 1 \qquad \text{(A.14)}$$

where quasi-rent is

$$R = pAx_1^{\alpha_1}x_2^{\alpha_2} - w_1x_1 - w_2x_2 \qquad \text{(A.15)}$$

Obviously, from (A.14), one has $q(0, x_2) = q(x_1, 0) = 0$, so that both inputs are necessary. The output is trivially a necessary output in the single-product case. Solving first-order conditions, $\partial R/\partial x_i = 0$, $i = 1, 2$, for x_1 and x_2 and substituting into (A.14) yields

$$q = A\left(\frac{\alpha_1 pq}{w_1}\right)^{\alpha_1}\left(\frac{\alpha_2 pq}{w_2}\right)^{\alpha_2} = \left[Ap^{\alpha_1+\alpha_2}\left(\frac{\alpha_1}{w_1}\right)^{\alpha_1}\left(\frac{\alpha_2}{w_2}\right)^{\alpha_2}\right]^{1/(1-\alpha_1-\alpha_2)} \qquad \text{(A.16)}$$

Further substituting for q in first-order conditions, $x_i = \alpha_i pq/w_i$, $i = 1, 2$, one obtains profit maximizing derived demands,

$$x_i = \left[Ap\left(\frac{\alpha_i}{w_i}\right)^{1-\alpha_j}\left(\frac{\alpha_j}{w_j}\right)^{\alpha_j}\right]^{1/(1-\alpha_1-\alpha_2)}; \qquad i = 1, 2; \ \ j = 3 - i \qquad \text{(A.17)}$$

Finally, substituting derived demands into (A.15), one obtains

$$R = (1 - \alpha_1 - \alpha_2)\left[Ap\left(\frac{\alpha_1}{w_1}\right)^{\alpha_1}\left(\frac{\alpha_2}{w_2}\right)^{\alpha_1}\right]^{1/(1-\alpha_1-\alpha_2)} \qquad \text{(A.18)}$$

These results can be illustrated by computing producer surplus corresponding to the supply function in (A.16) and the consumer surpluses corresponding to demand functions in (A.17). One finds that producer surplus at prices (p_0, w_1^0, w_2^0) is

$$P = \int_0^{p_0}\left[Ap^{\alpha_1+\alpha_2}\left(\frac{\alpha_1}{w_1^0}\right)^{\alpha_1}\left(\frac{\alpha_2}{w_2^0}\right)^{\alpha_2}\right]^{1/(1-\alpha_1-\alpha_2)}dp$$

$$= (1 - \alpha_1 - \alpha_2)\left[Ap\left(\frac{\alpha_1}{w_1^0}\right)^{\alpha_1}\left(\frac{\alpha_2}{w_2^0}\right)^{\alpha_2}\right]^{1/(1-\alpha_1-\alpha_2)}\Bigg|_{p=0}^{p_0} = R(p_0, w_1^0, w_2^0)$$

since, from (A.16), the output shutdown price regardless of input prices is $\bar{p}_0 = 0$. Consumer surpluses at prices (p_0, w_1^0, w_2^0) are

$$C_i = \int_{w_i^0}^{\infty} \left[Ap_0 \left(\frac{\alpha_i}{w_i} \right)^{1-\alpha_j} \left(\frac{\alpha_j}{w_j^0} \right)^{\alpha_j} \right]^{1/(1-\alpha_1-\alpha_2)} dw_i$$

$$= (1 - \alpha_1 - \alpha_2) \left[Ap_0 \left(\frac{\alpha_i}{w_i} \right)^{\alpha_i} \left(\frac{\alpha_j}{w_j^0} \right)^{\alpha_j} \right]^{1/(1-\alpha_1-\alpha_2)} \Bigg|_{w_i=w_i^0}^{\infty}$$

$$= R(p_0, w_1^0, w_2^0); \qquad i = 1, 2; \quad j = 3 - i$$

thus verifying (A.13), since (A.17) implies input shutdown prices of $\hat{w}_i^0 = \infty$ regardless of other prices.

A.5 EMPIRICAL CONSIDERATIONS

The arguments of Section 8.9 suggest that the most accurate empirical approach to welfare analysis when the alternatives of Sections A.1 through A.3 are available is to choose the sequential approach of Section A.1. The reason is that these calculations can be made without extrapolating estimated supplies and/or demands far beyond the ranges in which data are observed. According to the results in Section A.1, the order or sequence of imposing price changes for purposes of welfare calculations should make no difference. Similarly, if welfare effects are evaluated completely in a single market, the results of Sections A.2 and A.3 imply that the choice of market should make no difference in results obtained.

From an empirical standpoint, however, one should note that the order in which price changes are considered or the choice of market for calculations will generally make a difference if product supplies and input demands are specified arbitrarily for purposes of estimation (for example, if all relationships are specified linearly and estimated independently). The reason this occurs is that, once estimated, the several supplies and demands may not relate to any conceivable underlying profit-maximization problem. This undesirable situation, where the researcher can arbitrarily influence results by choosing alternative orders of considering price changes or by choosing alternative markets as a basis for calculations, can be avoided in one of two practical ways.[18] Both involve specifying relationships so they necessarily relate to the same underlying profit-maximization problem upon estimation.

The first way, sometimes called the *primal approach*, is to specify a produc-

---

[18]A third way of avoiding this difficulty is to impose path independency (symmetry) conditions directly in estimation but such an approach is impractical except as a local approximation.

tion function form which satisfies the usual properties of a production function (concavity with positive first derivatives). Then, by solving the profit-maximization problem theoretically, the implied functional forms for all supplies and demands of the firm can be obtained. These supplies and demands, however, will generally contain common parameters [e.g., (A.16) and (A.17) both contain A, α_1, and α_2] so that independent estimation does not suffice. For example, estimates of A, α_1, and α_2 obtained from estimation of (A.16) may not match those obtained by independent estimation of (A.17). Instead, the resulting supply and demand specifications must be estimated jointly so that the necessary parameter constraints can be imposed across equations. When this is done, the same welfare effects are obtained empirically regardless of the order of considering price changes or choice of markets in making welfare calculations.

This first approach can be exemplified using the model in Section A.4. For example, one can start by specifying the production function in equation (A.14). Of course, one should be careful that the functional form chosen at this point is reasonable in view of the practical aspects of the problem considered. Once this is done, one can follow the derivation of equations (A.15) through (A.17), thus producing a specification for the supply equation and for each of the input demands which all relate to the same underlying profit-maximization problem. Then, using data for output and input prices and quantities, the supply equation in (A.16) and the two input demand equations in (A.17) can be estimated jointly producing estimates for A, α_1, and α_2. Again, if these three equations were estimated independently rather than jointly, each would probably lead to different estimates of the three parameters, and the welfare calculations could be arbitrarily altered by choosing alternative sets of parameter estimates.

The second approach to avoiding an arbitrary choice of results is based on *duality* theory and the pioneering work of Daniel McFadden.[19] Duality implies that there is a one-to-one relationship between production functions and profit (or quasi-rent) functions. In this context, the *profit function* is a function of input and output prices faced by the competitive firm and gives the maximum attainable profits under those prices. If some inputs are fixed, one may use the *restricted profit function* (or *quasi-rent function*) which specifies maximum short-run profit (or quasi rent) as a function of prices of output and variable inputs, given fixed input quantities. The right-hand side of equation (A.4) is a

---

[19]Although much of this development occurred in the late 1960s, the published work appears in Daniel McFadden, "Cost, Revenue, and Profit Functions," in *Production Economics: A Dual Approach to Theory and Applications,* 2 vols., ed. Melvyn Fuss and Daniel McFadden (Amsterdam: North-Holland Publishing Company, 1978). The entire two volumes by Fuss and McFadden develop and demonstrate issues related to this type of approach; see also Varian, *Microeconomic Analysis,* or Silberberg, *Structure of Economics.*

general profit or quasi-rent function, and the right-hand side of equation (A.18) is a specific example associated with the case of Section A.4.

The crux of the *dual approach* rests on the argument that it is no more arbitrary to start the analysis by choosing a specification for the profit function than it is to choose a specification for the production function. That is, profit functions under competition and nonstochastic prices characterize a firm's technology as completely as a production function under a certain set of regularity conditions.[20] Thus, specifying an arbitrary functional form for a profit function that satisfies these regularity conditions guarantees that the profit function is derivable as a result of some profit-maximization process with well-behaved technology.[21] Since profit functions so specified can be made more flexible while allowing analytic derivation of implied supply and demand specifications than with the primal approach, less stringent restrictions can be imposed on the related technology and market supply and demand relation-

---

[20]For a proof, see W. E. Diewert, "Applications of Duality Theory," in *Frontiers of Econometrics*, Vol. 2, ed. M. Intriligator and D. Kendrick (Amsterdam: North-Holland Publishing Company, 1974).

[21]These regularity conditions are that the profit function must be nondecreasing in output prices; nonincreasing in input prices; and continuous, convex, and homogeneous of degree 1 in all prices with $R = 0$ in shutdown cases; see *ibid.* and McFadden, "Cost." Some of the better known functional forms that can be used for these purposes are the translog form,

$$R = \exp\left(\alpha_0 + \sum_{i=1}^{k} \alpha_i \ln z_i + \sum_{i=1}^{k} \sum_{j=1}^{k} \beta_{ij} \ln z_i \ln z_j\right), \qquad \beta_{ij} = \beta_{ji}$$

the generalized Leontief form,

$$R = \sum_{i=1}^{k} \sum_{j=1}^{k} \beta_{ij} z_i^{\frac{1}{2}} z_j^{\frac{1}{2}}, \qquad \beta_{ij} = \beta_{ji}$$

the generalized Cobb–Douglas form,

$$R = \prod_{i=1}^{k} \prod_{j=1}^{k} \left(\frac{1}{2} z_i + \frac{1}{2} z_j\right)^{\beta_{ij}}, \qquad \beta_{ij} = \beta_{ji}$$

and the generalized quadratic mean form of order ρ,

$$R = \left(\sum_{i=1}^{k} \sum_{j=1}^{k} \beta_{ij} z_i^{\rho/2} z_j^{\rho/2}\right)^{1/\rho}, \qquad \beta_{ij} = \beta_{ji}$$

where $(z_1, \ldots, z_k) = (p_1, \ldots, p_m, w_1, \ldots, w_n)$. (Each of these functions is the homothetic version of the generalized functional forms. The more general forms are given in Appendix B, but homotheticity is a common assumption in the case of production.) In each case, certain restrictions must be placed on the parameter space to satisfy the regularity conditions. However, in each case second-order flexibility is attained for the profit or quasi-rent function for little, if any more computational difficulty than required in the primal approach with first-order flexibility; see W. E. Diewert, "Functional Forms for Profit and Transformation Functions," *Journal of Economic Theory*, Vol. 6 (1973), pp. 284–316; and Diewert, "Applications."

ships. The latter considerations may be crucial in welfare economics, as suggested by Sections 11.1 to 11.4.

Once the profit function is specified, the implied specifications for supplies and demands can be easily determined using (A.5) and (A.6), that is, by simply differentiating the profit or quasi-rent function with respect to the relevant output or input price. For example, suppose that one arbitrarily specifies a profit or quasi-rent function of the form in (A.18) as a starting point. Then differentiation with respect to output price obtains the supply specification in (A.16), and differentiation with respect to respective input prices obtains the demand specifications in (A.17). Thus, using data on input and output prices and quantities, the three equations in (A.16) and (A.17) can be estimated jointly to produce estimates of A, α_1, and α_2 which can subsequently be used for welfare calculations by substituting estimates into (A.18).

A.6 STOCHASTIC GENERALIZATIONS: RISK AVERSION AND EXPECTED UTILITY MAXIMIZATION

The results of Sections A.1 through A.3 can be generalized to consider the case where production and prices are stochastic, and similar results follow in most instances. To demonstrate these results, continue with the notation of Section A.1 with the corresponding assumptions regarding properties of production functions. For the moment, assume that production is nonstochastic but that prices are random with $E(p_i) = \bar{p}_i$, $i = 1, \ldots, m$, and $E(w_j) = \bar{w}_j$, $j = 1, \ldots, n$. To represent the producer's risk preferences following the intuition of Section 11.6, suppose that the producer possesses a utility function U defined on profit π with $\partial U/\partial \pi > 0$, $\partial^2 U/\partial \pi^2 < 0$. The producer's problem is thus to maximize

$$E\left[U\left(\sum_{i=1}^{m} p_i q_i(x) - \sum_{j=1}^{n} w_j x_j - \bar{K} \right) \right] \tag{A.19}$$

where $\bar{K}$ is any ex ante payment required of the firm, including fixed costs. The purpose and importance of $\bar{K}$ become apparent below.

First-order conditions for expected utility maximization are

$$E\left[U' \cdot \left(\sum_{i=1}^{m} p_i q_{ij}' - w_j \right) \right] = 0, \qquad j = 1, \ldots, n \tag{A.20}$$

where the arguments of $U' \equiv \partial U/\partial \pi$ and $q_{ij}' \equiv \partial q_i/\partial x_j$ are suppressed for notational convenience. Second-order conditions can be verified under assumptions outlined thus far. The solution to (A.20) can be written in principle as

$$x_j = \tilde{x}_j(\bar{p}, \bar{w}, \alpha, \bar{K}), \qquad j = 1, \ldots, n \tag{A.21}$$

$$q_i = q_i[\tilde{x}(\bar{p}, \bar{w}, \alpha, \bar{K})] = \tilde{q}_i(\bar{p}, \bar{w}, \alpha, \bar{K}), \qquad i = 1, \ldots, m \tag{A.22}$$

where α is a vector of parameters (moments about means) characterizing the stochastic properties of p and w other than their means such that $\partial \epsilon_i / \partial \bar{p}_i = 0$ for $i = 1, \ldots, m$ and $\partial \delta_j / \partial \bar{w}_j = 0$ for $j = 1, \ldots, n$, where $\epsilon_i \equiv p_i - \bar{p}_i$, $\delta_j \equiv w_j - \bar{w}_j$. Substituting (A.21) and (A.22) into (A.19) obtains the *indirect expected utility function*, which specifies maximum expected utility as a function of the stochastic properties of prices (including their means) and the ex ante payment,

$$V \equiv V(\bar{p}, \bar{w}, \alpha, K) \equiv E\left[U\left(\sum_{i=1}^{m} p_i \tilde{q}_i - \sum_{j=1}^{n} w_j \tilde{x}_j - \bar{K} \right) \right]$$

where the arguments of $\tilde{q}_i$ and $\tilde{x}_j$ are suppressed for convenience.

In this context, one finds using (A.20) or the envelope theorem that

$$\frac{\partial V}{\partial \bar{p}_i} = E(U' \cdot \tilde{q}_i) + E\left[U' \cdot \sum_{j=1}^{n} \left(\sum_{k=1}^{m} p_k q_{kj}' - w_j \right) \frac{\partial \tilde{x}_j}{\partial \bar{p}_i} \right]$$

$$= E(U') \cdot \tilde{q}_i \qquad\qquad \text{(A.23)}$$

and

$$\frac{\partial V}{\partial \bar{w}_j} = -E(U' \cdot \tilde{x}_j) + E\left[U' \cdot \sum_{k=1}^{n} \left(\sum_{i=1}^{m} p_i q_{ik}' - w_k \right) \frac{\partial \tilde{x}_k}{\partial \bar{w}_j} \right]$$

$$= -E(U') \cdot \tilde{x}_j \qquad\qquad \text{(A.24)}$$

where $\tilde{x}_j$ is an ex ante (thus nonstochastic) decision function for all j. Thus, to consider economic welfare, define $\hat{C}_i(\bar{p}_i^0, \bar{p}_i^1)$ as the compensating variation of a change in mean price for q_i from $\bar{p}_i^0$ to $\bar{p}_i^1$, which implies that

$$E\left\{ U\left[\sum_{i=1}^{m} (\bar{p}_i^1 + \epsilon_i) \cdot \tilde{q}_i(\bar{p}^1, \bar{w}, \alpha, \bar{K} + \hat{C}_i) \right. \right.$$

$$\left. - \sum_{j=1}^{n} w_j \cdot \tilde{x}_j(\bar{p}^1, \bar{w}, \alpha, \bar{K} + \hat{C}_i) - \bar{K} - \hat{C}_i \right]\right\}$$

$$\qquad\qquad \text{(A.25)}$$

$$= E\left\{ U\left[\sum_{i=1}^{m} (\bar{p}_i^0 + \epsilon_i) \cdot \tilde{q}_i(\bar{p}^0, \bar{w}, \alpha, \bar{K}) \right.\right.$$

$$\left.\left. - \sum_{j=1}^{n} w_j \cdot \tilde{x}_j(\bar{p}^0, \bar{w}, \alpha, \bar{K}) - \bar{K} \right]\right\} \equiv V_0$$

where $\bar{p}_k^1 = \bar{p}_k^0 = \bar{p}_k$ for $k \neq i$. Differentiating both sides of (A.25) with respect to the subsequent price $\bar{p}_i^1$ and using (A.23) yields

$$E(U') \cdot \tilde{q}_i(\bar{p}^1, \bar{w}, \alpha, \bar{K} + \hat{C}_i) - E\left(U' \cdot \frac{\partial \hat{C}_i}{\partial \bar{p}_i^1} \right) = 0 \qquad\qquad \text{(A.26)}$$

Assuming that $\hat{C}_i$ is an ex ante compensation, it must be nonstochastic, so that (A.26) implies that

$$\tilde{q}_i(\bar{p}^1, \bar{w}, \alpha, \bar{K} + \hat{C}_i) = \frac{\partial C_i}{\partial \bar{p}_i^{\;1}} \tag{A.27}$$

Also, since $\tilde{q}_i(\bar{p}^1, \bar{w}, \alpha, \bar{K} + \hat{C}_i)$ is a supply curve that varies $\hat{C}_i$ to maintain the initial expected utility level V_0, it may be reparametrized as

$$\tilde{q}_i(\bar{p}^1, \bar{w}, \alpha, V_0) \equiv \tilde{q}_i[\bar{p}^1, \bar{w}, \alpha, \bar{K} + \hat{C}_i(\bar{p}_i^{\;0}, \bar{p}_i^{\;1})] \tag{A.28}$$

Thus, using (A.27) and (A.28) and noting that $\hat{C}_i(\bar{p}_i^{\;0}, \bar{p}_i^{\;0}) = 0$, *the compensating variation of a change in mean output price is given by the change in producer surplus associated with the corresponding compensated supply curve conditioned on the initial expected utility level and taken as a function of mean price,*

$$\hat{C}_i(\bar{p}_i^{\;0}, \bar{p}_i^{\;1}) = \int_{\bar{p}_i^{\;0}}^{\bar{p}_i^{\;1}} \tilde{q}_i(\bar{p}, \bar{w}, \alpha, V_0)d\bar{p}_i \tag{A.29}$$

Additionally noting that $\hat{E}_i(\bar{p}_i^{\;1}, \bar{p}_i^{\;0}) = -\hat{C}_i(\bar{p}_i^{\;0}, \bar{p}_i^{\;1})$, where $\hat{E}_i(\bar{p}_i^{\;1}, \bar{p}_i^{\;0})$ is the equivalent variation of a mean output price change from $\bar{p}_i^{\;1}$ to $\bar{p}_i^{\;0}$, one finds that

$$\hat{E}_i(\bar{p}_i^{\;0}, \bar{p}_i^{\;1}) = \int_{\bar{p}_i^{\;0}}^{\bar{p}_i^{\;1}} \tilde{q}_i(\bar{p}, \bar{w}, \alpha, V_1)d\bar{p}_i \tag{A.30}$$

where $V_1 = V(\bar{p}^1, \bar{w}, \alpha, \bar{K})$. That is, *the equivalent variation of a mean output price change is given by the change in producer surplus associated with the corresponding compensated supply conditioned on the subsequent expected utility level and taken as a function of mean price.*

As suggested by this derivation, the compensating and equivalent variations no longer necessarily coincide in the producer case under risk, just as they do not coincide in the consumer case. The reason is that the size of the ex ante payment can affect the producer's aversion to risk. For example, after giving a producing firm a large amount of money, it may not be as averse to risk as before. This effect is manifested by a conditioning of supplies and demands on the ex ante payment or compensation. If supplies and demands do not depend on the ex ante payment, the compensating and equivalent variations coincide. In general, the two coincide only under *constant absolute risk aversion,* in which case $-U''/U' = r_a$, the coefficient of absolute risk aversion, is constant over all levels of profit.

To see this, one can differentiate (A.20) with respect to K and impose the condition that q_i does not depend on $\bar{K}$, which implies that

$$\sum_{i=1}^{m} E(U'' \cdot p_i) \cdot q_{ij}' = E(U'' \cdot w_j), \qquad j = 1, \ldots, n$$

as compared with the direct implications of (A.20),

$$\sum_{i=1}^{m} E(U' \cdot p_i) \cdot q_{ij}' = E(U' \cdot w_j), \qquad j = 1, \ldots, n$$

These two conditions on decisions are the same and imply that optimal decisions do not depend on $\bar{K}$ if U'' is a scalar multiple of U' (as under constant absolute risk aversion); and, furthermore, considering all possible price distributions, it is clear that this is the only condition under which optimal decisions do not change generally. Thus, the compensating and equivalent variations coincide; and supplies and demands do not depend on compensation (of fixed costs) if and only if absolute risk aversion is constant.

For empirical purposes, the assumption of constant absolute risk aversion is one that has been often used. For example, the mean-variance expected utility methodology suggested in Chapter 11 corresponds to constant absolute risk aversion, since decisions in such a framework do not depend on fixed costs or nonstochastic compensation payments. For empirical purposes, however, more general assumptions are possible. For example, if data are available on fixed costs, they give a basis for estimating the dependence of supplies and demands on fixed ex ante payments. One should also note for empirical purposes, however, that the utility function appropriately depends on initial wealth in addition to current profits when absolute risk aversion is not constant; changes in initial wealth supposedly enter the utility function in the same way as does an ex ante payment to the firm. Thus, data requirements become substantial when the assumption of constant absolute risk aversion is relaxed. Furthermore, upon estimation, one is faced with solution of the differential equation in (A.27) with boundary condition $\hat{C}_i(\bar{p}_i^0, \ \bar{p}_i^0) = 0$ in the case of compensating variation and $\hat{C}_i(\bar{p}_i^0, \ \bar{p}_i^1) = 0$ in the case of equivalent variation before welfare effects can be calculated.

Consider next the possibility of measuring the welfare effect of a mean input price change from, say, $\bar{w}_j^0$ to $\bar{w}_j^1$. If $\tilde{C}_j(\bar{w}_j^0, \ \bar{w}_j^1)$ measures the compensating variation, then by definition,

$$E\left\{ U\left[\sum_{i=1}^{m} p_i \cdot \tilde{q}_i(\bar{p}, \ \bar{w}^1, \ \alpha, \ \bar{K} + \tilde{C}_j) - \sum_{j=1}^{n} (\bar{w}_j^1 + \delta_j) \cdot \tilde{x}_j(\bar{p}, \ \bar{w}^1, \ \alpha, \ \bar{K} + \tilde{C}_j) - \bar{K} - \tilde{C}_j \right] \right\}$$

$$= E\left\{ U\left[\sum_{i=1}^{m} p_i \cdot \tilde{q}_i(\bar{p}, \ \bar{w}^0, \ \alpha, \ \bar{K}) - \sum_{j=1}^{n} (\bar{w}_j^0 + \delta_j) \cdot \tilde{x}_j(\bar{p}, \ \bar{w}^0, \ \alpha, \ \bar{K}) - \bar{K} \right] \right\} \qquad \textbf{(A.31)}$$

where $\bar{w}_k^1 = \bar{w}_k^0 = \bar{w}_k$ for $k \neq j$. Differentiating both sides of (A.31) with respect to the subsequent price $\bar{w}_j^1$ and using (A.24) implies that

$$-E(U') \cdot \tilde{x}_j(\bar{p}, \ \bar{w}^1, \ \alpha, \ \bar{K} + \tilde{C}_j) - E\left(U' \cdot \frac{\partial \tilde{C}_j}{\partial \bar{w}_j^1} \right) = 0 \qquad \textbf{(A.32)}$$

Again, if $\tilde{C}_j$ is an ex ante compensation and thus does not depend on randomness in prices, (A.32) implies that

$$\tilde{x}_j(\bar{p}, \bar{w}^1, \alpha, \bar{K} + \tilde{C}_j) = - \frac{\partial \tilde{C}_j}{\partial \bar{w}_j^1} \tag{A.33}$$

Also, since $\tilde{x}_j(\bar{p}, \bar{w}^1, \alpha, \bar{K} + \tilde{C}_j)$ is a demand curve that varies $\tilde{C}_j$ to hold expected utility at the initial level V_0, one can reparameterize as

$$\tilde{x}_j(\bar{p}, \bar{w}^1, \alpha, V_0) \equiv \tilde{x}_j(\bar{p}, \bar{w}^1, \alpha, \bar{K} + \tilde{C}_j) \tag{A.34}$$

Using (A.33) and (A.34) and noting that $\tilde{C}_j(\bar{w}_j^0, \bar{w}_j^0) = 0$ yields

$$\tilde{C}_j(\bar{w}_j^0, \bar{w}_j^1) = - \int_{\bar{w}_j^0}^{\bar{w}_j^1} \tilde{x}_j(\bar{p}, \bar{w}, \alpha, V_0) d\bar{w}_j \tag{A.35}$$

That is, *the compensating variation of a mean input price change is given by the change in consumer surplus associated with the corresponding compensated derived demand curve conditioned on the initial expected utility level and taken as a function of mean input price.* Similarly, noting that $\tilde{E}_j(\bar{w}_j^1, \bar{w}_j^0) = -\tilde{C}_j(\bar{w}_j^0, \bar{w}_j^1)$, where $\tilde{E}_j(\bar{w}_j^1, \bar{w}_j^0)$ is the equivalent variation of a mean input price change from $\bar{w}_j^1$ to $\bar{w}_j^0$, one finds that

$$\tilde{E}_j(\bar{w}_j^0, \bar{w}_j^1) = - \int_{\bar{w}_j^0}^{\bar{w}_j^1} \tilde{x}_j(\bar{p}, \bar{w}, \alpha, V_1) d\bar{w}_j \tag{A.36}$$

where $V_1 = V(\bar{p}, \bar{w}^1, \alpha, \bar{K})$. That is, *the equivalent variation of a mean input price change is given by the change in consumer surplus associated with the corresponding compensated derived demand curve conditioned on the subsequent expected utility level and taken as a function of mean input price.*

Again, the compensating and equivalent variations no longer coincide generally when risk is added to the producer problem. However, as shown above, optimal decisions generally do not depend on the ex ante payment and thus, derived demands do not depend on $\bar{K} + \tilde{C}_j$ in (A.33) if and only if absolute risk aversion is constant. Hence, under constant absolute risk aversion, the compensating and equivalent variations associated with mean input price changes also coincide. Again, comments similar to the supply estimation problem apply to empirical data needs in estimating derived demands when absolute risk aversion is not constant; and again solution of the differential equation in (A.33) is required before welfare effects can be calculated. The appropriate boundary condition is $\tilde{C}_j(\bar{w}_j^0, \bar{w}_j^0) = 0$ for calculating compensating variation and $\tilde{C}_j(\bar{w}_j^0, \bar{w}_j^1) = 0$ for calculating equivalent variation.

Coupling the results in (A.35) and (A.36) with the supply results in (A.29) and (A.30) implies that any general change in some or all mean prices can be evaluated using essentially the sequential approach of Section A.1, where each mean price change is evaluated conditionally on all preceding mean price change considerations. However, ordinary supplies and demands can be used for these calculations if and only if absolute risk aversion is constant. If absolute risk aversion is not constant, the calculations must be based on compensated supplies and demands, and each mean price change consideration must be conditioned on compensation corresponding to all preceding mean price change considerations. This approach thus becomes somewhat impractical because it involves solution of a system of differential equations composed of (A.27) and (A.33) for $i = 1, \ldots, m$ and $j = 1, \ldots, n$. Section B.13 contains a similar case related to consumer welfare measurement.

Although the methodology described above gives a feasible approach in evaluating welfare change associated with mean price changes, it remains to consider the welfare effects of changes in risk or other parameters affecting the firm. To do this, suppose that output q_i is a necessary output in the sense that there exists a mean price $\hat{p}_i$ low enough to cause the firm to shut down. Specifically, for a general price-risk change from $(\bar{p}^0, \bar{w}^0, \alpha^0)$ to $(\bar{p}^1, \bar{w}^1, \alpha^1)$ where, without loss of generality, the first output is a necessary output, define

$$\hat{\bar{p}}_1^{\,k} = \max \{\bar{p}_1; \, \tilde{x}(\bar{p}_1, \bar{p}_2^{\,k}, \ldots, \bar{p}_m^{\,k}, \bar{w}^k, \alpha^k, \bar{K} + C_0) = 0\}, \qquad k = 0, 1$$

where C_0 is any compensation pertinent to the shutdown case. Then note that the compensating variation C of the overall change is given implicitly by

$$V(\bar{p}^1, \bar{w}^1, \alpha^1, \bar{K} + C) = V(\bar{p}^0, \bar{w}^0, \alpha^0, \bar{K})$$

For conceptual purposes, this change can be broken into several steps, where, first, the mean price $\bar{p}_1$ is changed from $\bar{p}_1^{\,0}$ to $\hat{\bar{p}}_1^{\,0}$, which forces a shutdown; then all parameters are changed from $(\hat{\bar{p}}_1^{\,0}, \bar{p}_2^{\,0}, \ldots, \bar{p}_m^{\,0}, \bar{w}^0, \alpha^0)$ to $(\hat{\bar{p}}_1^{\,1}, \bar{p}_2^{\,1}, \ldots, \bar{p}_m^{\,1}, \bar{w}^1, \alpha^1)$, which also corresponds to a shutdown; and finally, mean price $\bar{p}_1$ is changed from $\hat{\bar{p}}_1^{\,1}$ to $\bar{p}_1^{\,1}$. In this context, note that

$$\begin{aligned}
V(\bar{p}^1, \bar{w}^1, \alpha^1, \bar{K} + C_1 + C_2) &= V(\hat{\bar{p}}_1^{\,1}, \bar{p}_2^{\,1}, \ldots, \bar{p}_m^{\,1}, \bar{w}^1, \alpha^1, \bar{K} + C_1) \\
&= V(\hat{\bar{p}}_1^{\,0}, \bar{p}_2^{\,0}, \ldots, \bar{p}_m^{\,0}, \bar{w}^0, \alpha^0, \bar{K} + C_1) \quad \textbf{(A.37)} \\
&= V(\bar{p}^0, \bar{w}^0, \alpha^0, \bar{K}) = V_0
\end{aligned}$$

for some C_1, where $C = C_1 + C_2$ since the first two right hand sides of (A.37) each represent a shutdown case with $V = U(\bar{K} + C_1) = V_0$. Following (A.25) to (A.29) with respect to the third equality in (A.37) implies that

$$C_1 = - \int_{\hat{\bar{p}}_1^{\,0}}^{\bar{p}_1^{\,0}} \bar{q}_1(\bar{p}_1, \bar{p}_2^{\,0}, \ldots, \bar{p}_m^{\,0}, \bar{w}^0, \alpha^0, V_0) d\bar{p}_1 \qquad \textbf{(A.38)}$$

where $V_0 = V(\bar{p}^0, \bar{w}^0, \alpha^0, \bar{K})$. A similar application of (A.25) to (A.29) to the first equality in (A.37) where $\bar{K}$ is replaced by $\bar{K} + C_1$ also implies that

$$C_2 = \int_{\hat{\bar{p}}_1^1}^{\bar{p}_1^1} \bar{q}_1(\bar{p}_1, \bar{p}_2^1, \ldots, \bar{p}_m^1, \bar{w}^1, \alpha^1, V_0) d\bar{p}_1 \qquad \text{(A.39)}$$

since C_1 is the compensation that restores the initial expected utility level in the event of a shutdown following (A.37). *The overall compensating variation of the general change in parameters ($\bar{p}$, $\bar{w}$, or α) affecting the firm is thus given by the change in producer surplus associated with the compensated supply of a necessary (nonstochastic) output conditioned on the initial level of expected utility and taken as a function of the respective mean price* (that is, $C = C_1 + C_2$).

Of course, similar results can be attained for measuring equivalent variation except that the compensated supply curve must be conditioned on the terminal level of expected utility. Again, however, the compensating and equivalent variations will generally coincide if and only if absolute risk aversion is constant, in which case the foregoing conclusions hold with respect to ordinary supply curves.

Turning to the demand side, similar results are possible in the case of a necessary input, say x_1, for which

$$\hat{\bar{w}}_1^k = \min \{\bar{w}_1; \bar{x}(\bar{p}^k, \bar{w}_1, \bar{w}_2^k, \ldots, \bar{w}_n^k, \alpha^k, \bar{K} + C_0) = 0\}, \qquad k = 0, 1$$

where again C_0 is any compensation pertinent to the shutdown case. In this case,

$$\begin{aligned} V(\bar{p}^1, \bar{w}^1, \alpha^1, \bar{K} + C_1 + C_2) &= V(\bar{p}^1, \hat{\bar{w}}_1^1, \bar{w}_2^1, \ldots, \bar{w}_n^1, \alpha^1, \bar{K} + C_1) \\ &= V(\bar{p}^0, \hat{\bar{w}}_1^0, \bar{w}_2^0, \ldots, \bar{w}_n^0, \alpha^0, \bar{K} + C_1) \qquad \text{(A.40)} \\ &= V(\bar{p}^0, \bar{w}^0, \alpha^0, \bar{K}) = V_0 \end{aligned}$$

where again both sides of the second equality represent a shutdown case with $V = U(\bar{K} + C_1) = V_0$. Following (A.31) to (A.35) with respect to the third equality of (A.40) yields

$$C_1 = \int_{\hat{\bar{w}}_1^0}^{\bar{w}_1^0} \bar{x}(\bar{p}^0, \bar{w}_1, \bar{w}_2^0, \ldots, \bar{w}_n^0, \alpha^0, V_0) d\bar{w}_1$$

and a similar application to the first equality implies that

$$C_2 = -\int_{\hat{\bar{w}}_1^1}^{\bar{w}_1^1} \bar{x}(\bar{p}^1, \bar{w}_1, \bar{w}_2^1, \ldots, \bar{w}_n^1, \alpha^1, V_0) d\bar{w}_1$$

Thus, *the overall compensating variation of a general change in parameters ($\bar{p}$, $\bar{w}$, or α) affecting the firm is given by the change in consumer surplus associated with the compensated derived demand of a necessary input conditioned on the initial level of expected utility and taken as a function of the respective mean input price* (that is, $C = C_1 + C_2$). Again, similar results apply for measuring equivalent variation where the compensated derived demand is conditioned on the subsequent level of expected utility. And again, the compensating and equivalent variations coincide generally if and only if absolute risk aversion is constant, in which case the foregoing conclusions hold for ordinary, as well as compensated, derived demands.

Although the results with stochastic prices are quite similar to those with nonstochastic prices, the results are somewhat more troublesome if production is also stochastic. If production is stochastic, one can simply assume that the q_i functions are random and return to the derivation in (A.19), (A.20), and so on. The only difference that occurs is that $E(U' \cdot \tilde{q}_i) \neq E(U')E(\tilde{q}_1)$ unless the producer is risk neutral (U' constant), so the results in (A.23), (A.26) through (A.30), and (A.38) and (A.39) do not follow. Hence, welfare calculations based on expected supply curves are not justified. Alternatively, however, where x_1, . . . , x_n represent ex ante decisions, they must be made before observing the random components of prices or production and are thus nonstochastic from the standpoint of the decision maker. Thus, all the results above relating to welfare calculations associated with derived demands continue to hold and give a substantial basis for economic welfare analysis of producers under both stochastic prices and stochastic production.

Or, as another alternative, one could consider a random compensation *function* where compensation depends on the state of nature. Specifically, differentiating the equation

$$V(\bar{p}^1, \bar{w}, \alpha, \bar{K} + C_i) = V(\bar{p}^0, \bar{w}, \alpha, \bar{K}) = V_0$$

with respect to $\bar{p}_i{}^1$ obtains

$$E\left\{ U'\left[\tilde{q}_i(\bar{p}^1, \bar{w}, \alpha, \bar{K} + C_i) - \frac{\partial C_i}{\partial \bar{p}_i{}^1} \right] \right\} = 0$$

Thus, if

$$\tilde{q}_i(\bar{p}^1, \bar{w}, \alpha, \bar{K} + C_i) = \frac{\partial C_i}{\partial \bar{p}_i{}^1}$$

for every state of nature, then C_i determines a random compensation which keeps the producer's welfare position the same with or without the change for every state of nature. There is nothing intrinsically wrong with this type of compensation scheme. The major problem is simply operational. Namely, the compensation must be specified for the producer in advance (so it will affect his decisions), but it must be specified as depending on the basic states of nature rather than on the states of nature as manifested in the producer's decisions; otherwise, the producer may strategically alter his behavior in an attempt to influence the amount of compensation he receives. Thus, welfare calculations based on *ex post* supply curves may not be appropriate; rather, compensation should be based on what *ex post* supply curves would be without strategic behavior.

Finally, consider an extension of the empirical possibilities in Section A.5. Again, both primal and dual approaches are possible, but calculations are so tedious with the primal approach that it is practical only for very specific probability distributions and utility functions (for example, with normally distributed prices and exponential utility).[22]

In the context of the dual approach, however, one finds, using (A.19), (A.23), and (A.24), that

$$\frac{\partial V/\partial \bar{p}_i}{\partial V/\partial \bar{K}} = -\frac{E(U') \cdot \tilde{q}_i}{E(U')} = -\tilde{q}_i \tag{A.41}$$

when production is nonstochastic and

$$\frac{\partial V/\partial \bar{w}_j}{\partial V/\partial \bar{K}} = \frac{E(U') \cdot \tilde{x}_j}{E(U')} = \tilde{x}_j \tag{A.42}$$

whether or not production is stochastic. Thus, once an indirect expected utility function is arbitrarily specified, it is a simple matter to derive all the implied input demand specifications (and output supply specifications if production is nonstochastic) so that appropriate parameter restrictions can be applied across equations to ensure that all estimated equations relate to a common underlying expected utility maximization problem (so that implied welfare effects are unique, as they should be). One should note, however, that the literature to date has not developed appropriate regularity conditions which ensure that an arbitrarily specified indirect expected utility function relates to some plausible underlying expected utility maximization problem with plausible stochastic properties and well-behaved technology. Nevertheless, this approach appears to dominate arbitrary specification of supplies and demands, in which case the estimated equations may suggest nonunique welfare effects in addition to not relating to a plausible underlying problem. Furthermore, this approach avoids the need to solve differential equations in computing willingness to pay for various changes when absolute risk aversion is not constant since estimates of (A.41) and (A.42) for the various outputs and inputs of the firm generally provide sufficient information to compute the necessary compensation in the context of the initial specification for V using the approach of equation (A.37). See Section B.13 for a similar example in the case of the consumer problem.

---

[22]R. J. Freund, "The Introduction of Risk into a Programming Model," *Econometrica*, Vol. 24 (1956), pp. 253–63.

Appendix B

Welfare Measurement for Consumers and Resource Owners

The purpose of this appendix is to provide a rigorous mathematical analysis of consumer surplus as a measure of consumer welfare, consider alternative measures that can be justified in lieu of consumer surplus, and determine the practical applicability or accuracy of consumer surplus as a measure of the alternative concepts; these concepts are then extended to consider the resource owner's problem. Finally, cases with constrained quantities are considered and an alternative empirical approach is presented. Attention is first focused on measurement of welfare change for a single utility-maximizing consumer in a comparative static sense. Later the analysis is generalized to consider market aggregation of both consumer demand and resource supply.

A rigorous analysis of the conjectures of Marshall[1] and Hicks[2] discussed in Chapters 5 and 6 began with the work by Patinkin[3] and Samuelson.[4] Each of the

[1] Alfred Marshall, *Principles of Economics* (London: Macmillan & Co. Ltd., 1930).

[2] J. R. Hicks, *A Revision of Demand Theory* (Oxford: Clarendon Press, 1956).

[3] Don Patinkin, "Demand Curves and Consumer's Surplus," in *Measurement in Economics, Studies in Mathematical Economics and Econometrics in Memory of Yehuda Grunfeld,* ed. Carl F. Christ et al. (Stanford, Calif.: Stanford University Press, 1963), pp. 83–112.

[4] P. A. Samuelson, "Constancy of the Marginal Utility of Income," in *Studies in Mathematical Economics and Econometrics in Memory of Henry Schultz,* ed. Oscar Lange et al. (Chicago: University of Chicago Press, 1942), pp. 75–91.

latter authors was concerned with the implications and necessity of constant marginal utility of income as a condition leading to validity of consumer surplus in measuring the welfare change associated with a single price change. The problem of consumer welfare measurement with multiple price changes was introduced by Hotelling[5] and has been examined in some detail by Harberger,[6] Silberberg,[7] Burns,[8] Richter,[9] and Chipman and Moore.[10] Among these authors, Silberberg and Richter have cast great doubt on the usefulness of consumer surplus as a *money measure* of utility change because very stringent conditions are required for uniqueness of the measure (or path independence in prices and income). Harberger, however, has continued to argue that consumer surplus provides a reasonable approximation as a measure of consumer welfare. Alternatively, Burns has argued that the problem of path dependence is of little practical consequence, since all reasonable paths in price–income space lead to results that are bounded by the Hicksian compensating and equivalent variations. Richter has suggested, however, that because of path dependence problems, it is impossible to construct a broadly applicable money measure of utility change. Alternatively, he supports the abandonment of "money measures" of utility change in favor of using the well-defined "willingness-to-pay" concepts suggested by the Hicksian compensating and equivalent variations. He then suggests estimating the Hicksian measures directly using the expenditure function approach. Chipman and Moore derive conditions under which consumer surplus measures lead to correct rankings which embody the cases discussed by Silberberg and Richter, but they leave the question of aggregation open. Finally, however, the error bounds established by Willig on consumer surplus as an approximation of the Hicksian compensating and equivalent

---

[5]Harold Hotelling, "The General Welfare in Relation to Problems of Taxation and of Railway and Utility Rates," *Econometrica,* Vol. 6 (1938), pp. 242–69; reprinted in K. J. Arrow and T. Scitovsky, eds., *Readings in Welfare Economics* (Homewood, Ill., Richard D. Irwin, Inc., 1969).

[6]Arnold C. Harberger, "Three Basic Postulates for Applied Welfare Economics: An Interpretive Essay," *Journal of Economic Literature,* Vol. 9 (September 1971), pp. 785–97.

[7]Eugene Silberberg, "Duality and the Many Consumer's Surpluses," *American Economic Review,* Vol. 62, No. 5 (December 1972), pp. 942–51.

[8]Michael E. Burns, "On the Uniqueness of Consumer's Surplus and the Invariance of Economic Index Numbers," *The Manchester School of Economic and Social Studies,* Vol. 45, No. 1 (March 1977), pp. 41–61.

[9]Donald K. Richter, *Games Pythagoreans Play,* Department of Economics, University of Rochester Discussion Paper 74–3, 1974.

[10]John S. Chipman and James C. Moore, "Compensating Variation, Consumer's Surplus, and Welfare," *American Economic Review,* Vol. 70, No. 5 (December 1980), pp. 933–49; and Chipman and Moore, "The Scope of Consumer's Surplus Arguments," in *Evolution, Welfare, and Time in Economics: Essays in Honor of Nicholas Georgescu-Roegen,* ed. Anthony M. Tang et al. (Lexington, Mass.: Heath—Lexington Books, 1976), pp. 69–123.

variations in both the single consumer and aggregate cases suggest the alternative and, perhaps, more practical methodology originally proposed by Marshall and supported by Harberger. The derivation in this appendix roughly follows the order of the literature and arguments presented above.

B.1   THE PURE CONSUMER CASE

Consider a consumer with (ordinal) utility function $U(q_1, \ldots, q_n)$ assumed to be strictly increasing, quasi-concave, and twice differentiable in q_i.[11] The budget constraint is given by

$$m = \sum_{i=1}^{n} p_i q_i \qquad \text{(B.1)}$$

Hence, the consumer's problem of utility maximization can be solved by maximizing the Lagrangian,

$$U(q_1, \ldots, q_n) + \lambda \left(m - \sum_{i=1}^{n} p_i q_i \right)$$

First-order conditions for a maximum imply that

$$U_i \equiv \frac{\partial U}{\partial q_i} = \lambda p_i, \qquad i = 1, \ldots, n \qquad \text{(B.2)}$$

and (B.1) must hold at the optimum. Second-order conditions are satisfied under the quasi-concavity assumption above.[12] As pointed out by Samuelson,[13] the Lagrangian multiplier λ can be interpreted as the marginal utility of income. Furthermore, when second-order conditions hold, equations (B.1) and (B.2) can be solved for the ordinary demand functions,[14]

$$q_i = \bar{q}_i(p_1, \ldots, p_n, m), \qquad i = 1, \ldots, n \qquad \text{(B.3)}$$

---

[11]Quasi-concavity simply implies nonincreasing marginal rates of substitution or that indifference curves are nowhere concave to the origin; for a further explanation, see W. Zangwill, *Nonlinear Programming: A Unified Approach* (Englewood Cliffs, N.J.: Prentice-Hall, Inc., 1969), pp. 25–36.

[12]Throughout this appendix, it is assumed for simplicity and convenience that the maximum is attained at an interior point (i.e., one with all $q_1 > 0$). However, the results are not substantially altered when $q_i = 0$ at the optimum for some i.

[13]Samuelson, "Constancy."

[14]James M. Henderson and Richard E. Quandt, *Microeconomic Theory: A Mathematical Approach,* 2d ed. (New York: McGraw Hill Book Company, 1971), pp. 407, 408.

Substituting (B.3) into the utility function U yields

$$U \equiv U(\tilde{q}_1, \ldots, \tilde{q}_n) \equiv V(p_1, \ldots, p_n, m) \equiv V$$

where V is the indirect utility function. Note that for simplicity of notation, the tildes which appear above $q_1, \ldots, q_n$ will be omitted in the remainder of this appendix.

In this context one finds that the change in utility associated with a change in prices and income from $(p_1{}^0, \ldots, p_n{}^0, m_0)$ to $(p_1{}^1, \ldots, p_n{}^1, m_1)$ can be represented as a line integral,

$$\Delta U = V(p_1{}^1, \ldots, p_n{}^1, m_1) - V(p_1{}^0, \ldots, p_n{}^0, m_0)$$

$$= \int_L dV = \int_L \left(V_m dm + \sum_{i=1}^{n} V_i dp_i \right) \tag{B.4}$$

where $V_i \equiv \partial V/\partial p_i$, $V_m \equiv \partial V/\partial m \equiv \lambda$, and L represents some path of integration in price-income space. Also, substituting

$$dV = dU = \sum_{i=1}^{n} U_i dq_i$$

into (B.4) and using (B.2) yields

$$\Delta U = \int_L \sum_{i=1}^{n} U_i dq_i = \int_L \sum_{i=1}^{n} \lambda p_i dq_i \tag{B.5}$$

Now using the total differential of the budget constraint,

$$dm - \sum_{i=1}^{n} q_i dp_i = \sum_{i=1}^{n} p_i dq_i$$

equation (B.5) becomes

$$\Delta U = \int_L \lambda \left(dm - \sum_{i=1}^{n} q_i dp_i \right) \tag{B.6}$$

Note that this line integral gives an exact measure of utility change regardless of the path L.[15]

---

[15] A line integral between any two given points,

$$\int_L \sum_{i=1}^{n} g_i(z_1, \ldots, z_n) \, dz_i$$

However, some further modification is required before (B.6) becomes useful for empirical measurement of welfare change since the marginal utility of income λ is, in general, unobservable. Consequently, the attention of economists has focused on conditions under which (B.6) can be converted to a money measure of utility change. The usual approach in this context has been to assume λ "approximately" constant over the path L and thus divide (B.6) by λ to obtain the money measure $\Delta U/\lambda$. Alternatively, Silberberg[16] investigates the case where λ is not necessarily constant by converting the integrand of (B.6) to money terms through division by λ. Since $1/\lambda$ can be interpreted as "the imputed marginal rent associated with the level of utility at a point along $[L]$," Silberberg argues that this measure, S, can be regarded as the limit of a sum of marginal dollar rents associated with utility change *along a specified path*. Either way, the line integral of interest is

$$S = \int_L \left(dm - \sum_{i=1}^{n} q_i dp_i \right) \tag{B.7}$$

If λ is constant along L, then $S = \Delta U/\lambda$, whereas if λ is not constant, S is not proportional to ΔU but simply measures a particular imputed dollar gain assigned by the consumer to the utility change.

One must then consider the conditions under which λ can possibly be constant along L or, at least, conditions under which S is a unique measure. To do this, recall the Roy equation,[17]

is independent of the path L if

$$g_{ij} \equiv \frac{\partial g_i}{\partial z_j} = \frac{\partial g_j}{\partial z_i} \equiv g_{ji}, \qquad i, j = 1, \ldots, n$$

Equivalently, if there exists a function $f \equiv f(z_1, \ldots, z_n)$ such that

$$g_i \equiv f_i \equiv \frac{\partial f}{\partial z_i}, \qquad i = 1, \ldots, n$$

then the integrability conditions (for path independence) are automatically satisfied since

$$g_{ij} = \frac{\partial^2 f}{\partial z_i \, \partial z_j} = \frac{\partial^2 f}{\partial z_j \, \partial z_j} = g_{ji}$$

always holds; hence, the integrand is an exact differential and thus

$$\int_L \sum_{i=1}^{n} g_i \, (z_1, \ldots, z_n) \, dz_i = \int_L df = \Delta f$$

Clearly, by the construction in (B.4), the integrand in (B.6) is such an exact differential; see Arthur E. Danese, *Advanced Calculus* (Boston: Allyn and Bacon, Inc., 1965), pp. 123–29.

[16] Silberberg, "Duality."

[17] The Roy equation can be derived by noting that, at the optimum utility level U^*,

$$q_j = -\frac{V_j}{V_m}$$

Now, rearranging, one has

$$-\lambda q_j = V_j$$

since $V_m \equiv \lambda$, so that differentiation with respect to m yields

$$-\lambda \frac{\partial q_j}{\partial m} - q_j \frac{\partial \lambda}{\partial m} = \frac{\partial \lambda}{\partial p_j} \tag{B.8}$$

since, by definition,

$$\frac{\partial \lambda}{\partial p_j} \equiv \frac{\partial V_m}{\partial p_j} \equiv \frac{\partial^2 V}{\partial p_j \, \partial m} \equiv \frac{\partial V_j}{\partial m}$$

It is now evident that λ cannot be constant with respect to all prices and income since $\partial \lambda / \partial p_j = \partial \lambda / \partial m = 0$ implies from (B.8) that $\partial q_j / \partial m = 0$, but the budget constraint implies that

$$1 = \frac{\partial m}{\partial m} = \frac{\partial \sum_{i=1}^{n} p_i q_i}{\partial m} = \sum_{i=1}^{n} p_i \frac{\partial q_i}{\partial m}$$

which cannot hold if $\partial q_j / \partial m = 0$, $j = 1, \ldots , n$. Thus, at most, λ can be

$$U^* = U[\bar{q}_1 (p_1, \ldots , p_n, m), \ldots , \bar{q}_n (p_1, \ldots , p_n, m)]$$
$$= V(p_1, \ldots , p_n, m)$$

If the marginal utility of income is always positive, $V_m > 0$, then one can solve for an inverse function V^{-1} which expresses income as a function of prices and the utility level,

$$m = V^{-1}(p_1, \ldots , p_n, U^*)$$

Now substituting V^{-1} for m in the indirect utility function above yields the identity

$$U^* \equiv V[p_1, \ldots , p_n, V^{-1} (p_1, \ldots , p_n, U^*)]$$

Differentation with respect to p_j thus implies that

$$0 = V_j + V_m \frac{\partial V^{-1}}{\partial p_j} = V_j + V_m \frac{\partial m}{\partial p_j} = V_j + V_m q_j$$

The Roy equation follows immediately. The reader might note that the inverse function, V^{-1}, used here is simply the expenditure function commonly used to describe the minimum income necessary to attain a given utility level with a given set of prices; see Section B.4 for a more detailed explanation and a proof that $\partial m / \partial p_j = q_j$; also, see René Roy, "La Distribution due revenu entre les divers biens," *Econometrica*, Vol. 15, No. 3 (July 1947), pp. 205–25.

constant with respect to all prices but not income or with respect to income and, say, the first $n - 1$ prices. Samuelson interprets the former case as the Marshallian definition of the constancy of marginal utility of income, whereas the second case is associated with constancy of the marginal utility of "money" where the nth good is taken as a numéraire or money.[18] At any rate, it is clear that one must carefully specify with respect to which prices (and income) the marginal utility of income is supposed to be constant. Similarly, in examining path dependency, S cannot possibly be unique when all prices and income change. In fact, as shown in the following section, the various assumptions about the constancy of the marginal utility of income have a very close relationship with the path-dependency problem.

B.2   PATH DEPENDENCY

The integrand of (B.7) is not necessarily an exact differential; hence, one must verify the path-independence conditions,[19]

$$\frac{\partial q_i}{\partial m} = \frac{\partial(1)}{\partial p_i} \equiv 0, \qquad i = 1, \ldots, n \tag{B.9}$$

$$\frac{\partial q_i}{\partial p_j} = \frac{\partial q_i}{\partial p_i}, \qquad i, j = 1, \ldots, n \tag{B.10}$$

Obviously, all of the conditions above cannot hold simultaneously since (as in the proof that λ cannot be constant with respect to all prices and income) $\partial q_i/\partial m = 0, i = 1, \ldots, n$, implies that the budget constraint would be violated with a change in income, *ceteris paribus* (since income changes while consumption and prices do not change).

Since all the conditions in (B.9) and (B.10) cannot hold simultaneously, it has been necessary in the literature to constrain price and income changes to some subspace of price–income space. For example, Silberberg considers changes in all prices but holds income constant; hence, where $dm \equiv 0$, the integral in (B.7) becomes simply

$$S = -\int_L \sum_{i=1}^{n} q_i dp_i \tag{B.11}$$

---

[18]In the latter case it can easily be shown that the marginal utility of money and the marginal utility of income must always be the same (at equilibrium) since the first-order conditions in (B.2) imply that $U_n = \lambda$ if $p_n \equiv 1$.

[19]These conditions are derived by applying the material in footnote 15 to equation (B.7).

The relevant path-independency conditions are given by[20]

$$\frac{\partial q_i}{\partial p_j} = \frac{\partial q_j}{\partial p_i}, \qquad i, j = 1, \ldots, n. \tag{B.12}$$

Richter, on the other hand, considers the price of one good, q_n (the numéraire), fixed while all other prices and income may vary; in his case, (B.7) becomes

$$S = \int_L \left(dm - \sum_{i=1}^{n-1} q_i dp_i \right) \tag{B.13}$$

where $dp_n \equiv 0$ and path-independency conditions are[21]

$$\frac{\partial q_i}{\partial m} = 0, \qquad i = 1, \ldots, n - 1 \tag{B.14}$$

$$\frac{\partial q_i}{\partial p_j} = \frac{\partial q_j}{\partial p_i}, \qquad i, j = 1, \ldots, n - 1 \tag{B.15}$$

It is interesting to note in each of the cases above, however, that the path-independency conditions are conditions implied by constancy of the marginal utility of income λ under the alternative interpretations discussed by Samuelson. That is, the conditions for path independency are implied by the conditions under which λ can be factored out of (B.6) and placed in the left-hand denominator (i.e., where $S = \Delta U / \lambda$), obtaining (B.11) or (B.13) when $dm \equiv 0$ or $dp_n \equiv 0$, respectively. In point of fact, the path-independency conditions for (B.6) are[22]

$$\frac{\partial \lambda q_i}{\partial m} = \frac{\partial \lambda}{\partial p_i} \qquad i = 1, \ldots, n \tag{B.16}$$

$$\frac{\partial \lambda q_i}{\partial p_j} = \frac{\partial \lambda q_j}{\partial p_i} \qquad i, j = 1, \ldots, n \tag{B.17}$$

which must always hold (by construction) since the integrand is an exact differential of V. Assuming that $\partial \lambda / \partial p_i = 0$, $i = 1, \ldots, n$, as in the Silberberg case, thus yields (B.12) immediately from (B.17); assuming that $\partial \lambda / \partial m = 0$ and $\partial \lambda / \partial p_i = 0$, $i = 1, \ldots, n - 1$, as in the Richter case, yields (B.14) and (B.15) immediately from (B.16) and (B.17).[23] Conversely, however, one should also

---

[20] See footnote 15.

[21] Ibid.

[22] Ibid.

[23] Although neither Silberberg nor Richter makes this relationship clear, Richter is perhaps somewhat misleading since he explicitly assumes λ constant and then belabors the derivation of conditions for path independency which, as shown above, are immediate and hold automatically with constancy of λ.

note that path independence does not imply constancy of the marginal utility of income. Using the path-independence conditions in (B.14) and (B.15), for example, implies only that

$$q_i \frac{\partial \lambda}{\partial m} = \frac{\partial \lambda}{\partial p_i}, \qquad i = 1, \ldots, n - 1$$

$$q_i \frac{\partial \lambda}{\partial p_j} = q_j \frac{\partial \lambda}{\partial p_i}, \qquad i, j = 1, \ldots, n - 1$$

As Mishan has pointed out, this condition simply requires "that λ change at the same rate for each of the price changes (when connected by relative expenditures on the goods)."[24]

B.3   MONEY MEASURES OF UTILITY CHANGE AND CONSTANCY OF THE MARGINAL UTILITY OF INCOME FOR CONSUMERS

The Silberberg and Richter studies attempt to develop conditions under which consumer surplus concepts can be used to measure utility change in money terms. As they find, these conditions lead to some rather restrictive and, perhaps, unrealistic utility indifference maps. Silberberg finds that, in the case where all prices can change but income does not, path-independency conditions in (B.12) hold if and only if consumer utility is homothetic, which holds if and only if all income elasticities are unity (that is, the income-consumption paths are rays emanating from the origin).[25]

---

[24]E. J. Mishan, "The Plain Truth about Consumer Surplus," *Nationalokonomie Journal of Economics,* Vol. 37, No. 1–2 (Spring 1977), p. 12.

[25]To see the equivalence of path independency with the latter condition, one need merely consider the budget constraint in conjunction with the result (proved below) from path independency that income elasticities must be equal among all goods for which prices change. That is, if all prices change and hence all income elasticities are equal, a change in income will violate the budget constraint unless all income elasticities are unity. To see that path independence implies equality among income elasticities, note that (B.17) implies that

$$q_i \frac{\partial \lambda}{\partial p_j} + \lambda \frac{\partial q_i}{\partial p_j} = q_j \frac{\partial \lambda}{\partial p_i} + \lambda \frac{\partial q_j}{\partial p_j}$$

Hence, by path independence,

$$q_i \frac{\partial \lambda}{\partial p_j} = q_j \frac{\partial \lambda}{\partial p_i}$$

(Footnote continued on pg. 366)

In the Richter case, where one price is fixed, it can be shown that the conditions in (B.15) are implied by (B.14) since, by the Slutsky equation,[26]

$$\frac{\partial q_i}{\partial p_j} = \left(\frac{\partial q_i}{\partial p_j}\right)_{U \text{ const}} - q_j \frac{\partial q_i}{\partial m} = \left(\frac{\partial q_i}{\partial p_j}\right)_{U \text{ const}} = \left(\frac{\partial q_j}{\partial p_i}\right)_{U \text{ const}}$$

$$= \left(\frac{\partial q_j}{\partial p_i}\right)_{U \text{ const}} - q_i \frac{\partial q_j}{\partial m} = \frac{\partial q_j}{\partial p_i} \tag{B.18}$$

when $\partial q_i/\partial m = \partial q_j/\partial m = 0$. But (B.14) holds if and only if income elasticities are zero,[27] that is, income effects are zero for the first $n - 1$ goods; hence, all increases in income are spent entirely on one good—the numéraire q_n.

Clearly, the foregoing cases are too restrictive to provide an acceptable basis for applications of welfare economics generally. If, however, only a subset of prices and/or income change, the restrictions on utility surfaces and demand functions are reduced. That is, suppose (for simplicity) that only the first k prices—and possibly income—change with the imposition of some policy, say, from prices $(p_1^0, \ldots, p_k^0, p_{k+1}^0, \ldots, p_n^0)$ to prices $(p_1^1, \ldots, p_k^1, p_{k+1}^0, \ldots, p_n^0)$ and from income m_0 to m_1. Since the integrand in (B.6) is an exact differential, the value of the integral is independent of the path of integration, and one may choose an arbitrary path along which to evaluate it.

Consider, for example, the path where, first, income is changed and then the k prices are changed in order from initial to final values. For notational convenience, let

$$\hat{p}_0(m) \equiv (p_1^0, \ldots, p_n^0, m)$$

and

$$\hat{p}_i(p_i) \equiv (p_1^1, \ldots, p_{i-1}^1, p_i, p_{i+1}^0, \ldots, p_n^0) \tag{B.19}$$

Then the line integral in (B.6) can be written as a sum of intermediate line integrals and finally as a sum of ordinary definite integrals as follows:[28]

Now, multiplying both sides by $m/(q_i \cdot q_j)$ and using (B.8) yields

$$\frac{m}{q_i} \frac{\partial q_j}{\partial m} = \frac{m}{q_i} \frac{\partial q_i}{\partial m}$$

[26]The middle equality of (B.18) follows from the symmetry of the Hessian; see Henderson and Quandt, *Microeconomic Theory*, p. 36.

[27]Geometrically, the condition of zero income elasticities implies vertical income-consumption paths and is equivalent to the well-known case of vertically parallel indifference curves. See Figure 5.6 and the related discussion for the geometric interpretation.

[28]For example, see Danese, *Advanced Calculus*, p. 103.

$$\Delta U = \int \lambda \left(dm - \sum_{i=1}^{n} q_i dp_i \right)$$

$$= \int_{\hat{p}_0(m_0)}^{\hat{p}_0(m_1)} \lambda \left(dm - \sum_{i=1}^{n} q_i dp_i \right) + \sum_{j=1}^{k} \int_{\hat{p}_j(p_j^0)}^{\hat{p}_j(p_j^1)} \lambda \left(dm - \sum_{i=1}^{n} q_i dp_i \right) \qquad \text{(B.20)}$$

$$= \int_{m_0}^{m_1} \lambda[\hat{p}_0(m)] dm - \sum_{j=1}^{k} \int_{p_j^0}^{p_j^1} \lambda[\hat{p}_j(p_j), m_0] \, q_j[\hat{p}_j(p_j), m_0] dp_j$$

where, in the latter step, λ and q_j are written as explicitly depending on prices and income.

It can now be noted that, if λ is simply constant with respect to income and the k prices which change, it can be factored out and taken to the left side, obtaining the unique money measure of utility change:

$$S = \int_{m_0}^{m_1} dm - \sum_{j=1}^{k} \int_{p_j^0}^{p_j^1} q_j[\hat{p}_j(p_j), m_0] dp_j \qquad \text{(B.21)}$$

$$= \Delta m + \sum_{j=1}^{k} \Delta S_j \qquad \text{(B.22)}$$

where $\Delta S_j(\cdot, \cdot)$ represents the change in consumer surplus in market j as a function of initial and final price vectors given by

$$\Delta S_j[\hat{p}_j(p_j^0), \hat{p}_j(p_j^1)] \equiv \int_{p_j^0}^{p_j^1} q_j[\hat{p}_j(p_j), m_0] dp_j \qquad \text{(B.23)}$$

Furthermore, if income does not change from the initial to the final price–income position, the first right-hand term of equations (B.20) through (B.22) can be deleted; hence, constancy of λ with respect to income is not necessary.

The foregoing results imply that, whenever the marginal utility of income λ is constant with respect to only the prices (and income) that change, a money measure of utility change is obtained by adding (to the change in income) the changes in consumer surpluses in the markets where prices change. However, the consumer surpluses in successive markets must be evaluated along ordinary demand curves conditioned on all previously considered changes; since the methodology leading to (B.20) and (B.22) is path independent, the order of consideration of price changes (markets) makes no difference.

Clearly, these results imply that λ need only be constant with respect to the prices and/or income that changes between the initial and final states. These resulting conditions, which may be useful in certain specific situations, are, of course, much less restrictive than those developed by Samuelson, Silberberg, Richter, and others in their general cases. Nevertheless, it should be recognized that some strong restrictions are being placed on the utility function even in this less stringent case. For example, if income and any other price p_j are changing and, to attain a money measure, one assumes that $\partial\lambda/\partial m = \partial\lambda/\partial p_j = 0$, then using equation (B.8),

$$0 = \frac{\partial\lambda}{\partial p_j} = -\lambda\frac{\partial q_j}{\partial m} - q_j\frac{\partial\lambda}{\partial m} = -\lambda\frac{\partial q_j}{\partial m} \tag{B.24}$$

Hence, $\partial q_j/\partial m = 0$, so that zero income elasticities (or zero-income effects) are required for all prices that change.

If prices p_i and p_j change (regardless of whether or not income changes) and one correspondingly assumes that $\partial\lambda/\partial p_i = \partial\lambda/\partial p_j = 0$, then the first two equalities in (B.24) continue to hold for both i and j; hence,

$$\frac{1}{q_i}\frac{\partial q_i}{\partial m} = -\frac{1}{\lambda}\frac{\partial\lambda}{\partial m} = \frac{1}{q_j}\frac{\partial q_j}{\partial m}$$

which implies (multiplying through by m) that all income elasticities for prices that change must be the same (not necessarily unity or zero).

Finally, as a special case of (B.22), the early hypothesis of Marshall can be verified; namely, if the marginal utility of income is constant with respect to the single price p_j that is changed, then

$$\frac{\Delta U}{\lambda} = -\int_{p_j^0}^{p_j^1} q_j dp_j = \Delta S_j \tag{B.25}$$

Thus, the change in consumer surplus in that market alone is a unique money measure of utility change.[29]

In summary, it appears that there are two conditions under which a unique money measure of utility change can be established: (1) if $\partial q_i/\partial p_j = \partial q_j/\partial p_i$ for all pairs of prices that change[30] or (2) if λ is constant with respect to those

---

[29]Silberberg is perhaps unclear on this point because he indicates that the integral in (B.25), considered as a line integral, may be path dependent if all prices p_i, $i \neq j$, change along the path of integration even though they finally attain their initial values. This is indeed true when λ is not constant with respect to the prices (income) for which final values are different from the initial values. Clearly, however, by writing ΔU with an exact differential as integrand following (B.20), only constancy of λ with respect to p_j is required to obtain (B.25) as a definite integral. In effect, the ambiguity found by Silberberg results from looking for a money measure of utility change in a subspace (generated by all other price movements) in which utility does not change.

[30]Although not shown explicitly earlier, it is not necessary to hold income constant in case (1). As Silberberg has shown, integrating by parts yields

$$S = \int_L \sum_{i=1}^{n} p_i dq_i$$
$$= \sum_{i=1}^{n} p_i^1 q_i(p^1, m_1) - \sum_{i=1}^{n} p_i^0 q_i(p^0, m_0) - \int_L \sum_{i=1}^{n} q_i dp_i$$
$$= m_1 - m_0 - \int_L \sum_{i=1}^{n} q_i dp_i$$

Thus, only the conditions in (1) are necessary for path independence in this case.

prices and/or income that change. In the former case the utility function must be homothetic with respect to the goods for which prices change, while in either case income elasticities associated with all prices that change must be the same, and these must be zero if income changes.

Unfortunately, the simple conclusions relating to (B.20) through (B.22) in the general Silberberg case with all prices possibly changing and nonconstancy of λ are not possible. Unless the path-independency conditions in (B.9) and (B.10) are satisfied for the prices and/or income which are not identically fixed, an attempt to divide the integrands of (B.20) by λ turns out to correspond to only one of many possible paths in (B.11) or (B.13).

In view of these arguments, it has been suggested, by Burns,[31] for example, that the class of paths considered should be restricted in some way. As pointed out by Richter, however:

> . . . various characterizations of reasonable paths of integration do not really get around the difficulty. Most importantly, the creation of a money index of utility change is a comparative statics exercise. By the very nature of such exercises one should not have to appeal to the particular adjustment path followed, reasonable or otherwise, in defining the welfare change measure. . . . Why in a comparative statics analysis should the actual adjustment path between the two static equilibria have any theoretical importance? Why in a comparative statics analysis should any one path be more interesting than another path?[32]

Yet another difficulty is encountered in attempting to deal with a money measure of utility change. That is, suppose that one is successful in attaining a money measure of utility change for two consumers. One must then consider what basis is gained for investigating policy actions that affect both. In fact, one finds that much more restrictive assumptions are additionally required in order to answer such questions. For example, suppose that the policymaker simply seeks to maximize the sum of the two consumers' utilities. As explained in Section 6.1, this is not equivalent to maximizing the sum of their corresponding money measures of utility (unless their marginal utilities of income are identical). Indeed, if their marginal utilities are not identically equal, no method of aggregation of the two money measures of utility change consistent with the foregoing policymaking objective is apparent unless the respective marginal utilities of income are known. But marginal utilities of income can almost certainly not be measured or even estimated in practice. For example, consider one consumer with utility function U and another with utility function $\hat{U} \equiv 2U$; then all observed behavior by the two consumers will be identical because the utility functions carry only an ordinal significance (in this context), while the marginal utility of income for the second consumer will always be twice that of the first.

---

[31]Burns, "Uniqueness of Consumer's Surplus."

[32]Richter, *Games Pythagoreans Play.*

B.4 WILLINGNESS-TO-PAY MEASURES FOR CONSUMERS

Since it is seemingly impossible to develop a unique money measure of utility change that is generally applicable, this section turns to the alternative and less restrictive concepts of compensating and equivalent variation (suggested in Chapter 6) as measures of consumer welfare. These concepts can be investigated most easily in the following framework. Consider the counterpart (or dual) of the standard utility-maximization problem which, rather than maximizing utility, seeks to minimize consumer expenditures subject to a given utility level U:

$$\min_{q_1, \ldots, q_n} \sum_{i=1}^{n} p_i q_i \qquad (B.26)$$

subject to

$$U(q_1, \ldots, q_n) = \bar{U}$$
$$q_i \geq 0, \qquad i = 1, \ldots, n$$

Solving first-order conditions, one obtains the Hicksian compensated demand functions $\bar{q}_i(p_1, \ldots, p_n, \bar{U})$, which, for convenience, will be denoted by $\bar{q}_i(p, \bar{U})$, where $p \equiv (p_1, \ldots, p_n)$.[33] The expenditure function m, which gives minimum expenditure as a function of prices and utility level, is thus obtained by substituting compensated demands in the objective function of (B.26),

$$m(p, \bar{U}) = \sum_{i=1}^{n} p_i \bar{q}_i(p, \bar{U})$$

Consider now a change in prices and income from (p^0, m_0) to (p^1, m_1), which leads to a change in maximum utility from U^0 to U^1. In this context the Hicksian equivalent variation (E), that is, the amount of compensation that will leave the consumer in his or her subsequent welfare position in the absence of the change (where consumption adjustments are possible), is given by

$$E = m(p^0, U^1) - m_0 \qquad (B.27)$$

The Hicksian compensating variation (C), that is, the amount of compensation that will leave the consumer in his or her initial welfare position following the change (where consumption adjustments are possible) is

$$C = m_1 - m(p^1, U^0) \qquad (B.28)$$

---

[33] A clear explanation of this approach, as well as properties of the expenditure function, can be found in Daniel McFadden and Sidney G. Winter, *Lecture Notes on Consumer Theory,* University of California, Berkeley, Calif., 1968, pp. 36–42; or Hal Varian, *Microeconomic Analysis* (New York: W. W. Norton & Company, Inc., 1978).

To relate these definitions to the usual graphical analysis in quantity–quantity and price–quantity space, it can be noted that E and C correspond to the actual income change plus the areas to the left of the Hicksian compensated demand curves (and between prices) where the compensated demands are associated with final and initial utility levels, respectively.[34] To see this, note that

$$\frac{\partial m}{\partial p_j} = \bar{q}_j(p, \bar{U}) + \sum_{i=1}^{n} p_i \frac{\partial \bar{q}_i}{\partial p_j} \qquad \textbf{(B.29)}$$

But using (B.2) in (B.29) (which is basically an application of the envelope theorem) yields

$$\sum_{i=1}^{n} p_i \frac{\partial \bar{q}_i}{\partial p_j} = \frac{1}{\lambda} \sum_{i=1}^{n} \frac{\partial U}{\partial q_i} \frac{\partial \bar{q}_i}{\partial p_j} = \frac{1}{\lambda} \frac{d\bar{U}}{dp_j} = 0$$

where the third equality holds since

$$\bar{U} \equiv U[\bar{q}_1(p_1, \ldots, p_n, \bar{U}), \ldots, \bar{q}_n(p_1, \ldots, p_n, \bar{U})]$$

---

[34]As Bergson has pointed out, "the compensating and equivalent variations are nothing more than the 'true' magnitudes of real income variations that we seek to approximate when we compile index numbers of real income according to the Paasche formula, on the one hand, and the Laspeyres formula, on the other." Specifically, the Laspeyres and Paasche formulas correspond to the inner and outer cost differences, respectively, described in Section 5.1. The compensating and equivalent variations, on the other hand, correspond to the Laspeyres–Konyus and Paasche–Konyus formulas, respectively (Konyus indices are defined in terms of preferences for an individual consumer). Thus, as noted by Samuelson, the theory of consumer surplus is mathematically equivalent in many respects to the theory of index numbers; see Abram Bergson, "A Note on Consumer's Surplus," *Journal of Economic Literature*, Vol. 13, No. 1 (March 1975), p. 42; Herman Wold and Lars Jureen, *Demand Analysis: A Study in Econometrics* (New York: John Wiley & Sons, Inc., 1953); Paul A. Samuelson, *Foundations of Economic Analysis* (Cambridge, Mass.: Harvard University Press, 1947), p. 196; Burns, "Uniqueness of Consumer's Surplus"; and Burns, "A Note on the Concept and Measure of Consumer Surplus," *American Economic Review*, Vol. 63, No. 3 (June 1973), pp. 335–44.

Because the Paasche and Laspeyres variations (the outer and inner cost differences, respectively) bound consumer surplus for a single-price-change case (see Section 5.1), some have argued that, in lieu of calculating consumer surplus, one can simply calculate the Paasche and Laspeyres variations and use an average of the two as a measure of welfare change if the two are acceptably close to one another. One should beware of this practice, however, since the premise does not necessarily hold for a multiple price change, as pointed out (once again) by Samuelson and Swamy in the context of index number theory; see P. A. Samuelson and S. Swamy, "Invarient Economic Index Numbers and Canonical Duality: Survey and Synthesis," *American Economic Review*, Vol. 64, No. 4 (September 1974), pp. 566–93. A related discussion also appears in George W. McKenzie, "Consumer's Surplus without Apology: Comment," *American Economic Review*, Vol. 69, No. 3 (June 1979), pp. 465–68; and Robert D. Willig,"

is simply an identity. Hence, the partial derivatives of the expenditure function with respect to price,

$$\frac{\partial m}{\partial p_j} = \bar{q}_j(p, U) \tag{B.30}$$

are precisely the Hicksian compensated demands. Thus, using (B.30) to compute the area between prices and left of the compensated demand corresponding to utility level U^*, one finds that

$$m(p^0, U^*) - m(p^1, U^*) = -\int_L \sum_{j=1}^{n} \frac{\partial m(p, U^*)}{\partial p_j} dp_j \tag{B.31}$$

$$= -\int_L \sum_{j=1}^{n} \bar{q}_j(p, U^*) dp_j \tag{B.32}$$

where L denotes any path of integration in price space from p^0 to p^1. Since the integrand of (B.31) is an exact differential of m with respect to p, no path-dependency problems are encountered.[35]

To interpret E in (B.27) geometrically, note that the budget constraint, together with (B.32), implies that

$$E = m(p^0, U^1) - m_0 = m(p^0, U^1) - m(p^1, U^1) + m_1 - m_o$$

$$= m_1 - m_0 - \int_L \sum_{j=1}^{n} \bar{q}_j(p, U^1) dp_j$$

which upon following the same procedure leading to (B.20) through (B.22) yields

$$E = \Delta m - \sum_{j=1}^{n} \int_{p_j^0}^{p_j^1} \bar{q}_j[\hat{p}_j(p_j), U^1] dp_j \tag{B.33}$$

where $\hat{p}_j$ is defined by (B.19). Thus, the Hicksian equivalent variation is uniquely measured by adding to the actual change in income all the changes in areas left of the compensated demands where the compensated demand functions are all evaluated at the final utility level but successively conditioned on all previously considered price changes (conditioned on initial prices for the

---

Consumer's Surplus without Apology: Reply," *American Economic Review*, Vol. 69, No. 3 (June 1979), pp. 469–74.

[35] Also, it is well known from an economic standpoint that $\partial q_i/\partial p_j = \partial q_j/\partial p_i$ along an indifference surface (Henderson and Quandt, *Microeconomic Theory*, p. 36), and this is exactly the condition for path independency in (B.32) when U does not change along L; see footnote 15.

first good considered). Again, as in (B.22), the order of integration makes no difference.

To interpret C in (B.28) geometrically, note that the budget constraint and (B.32) imply that

$$C = m_1 - m(p^1, U^0) = m_1 - m_0 + m(p^0, U^0) - m(p^1, U^0)$$

$$= m_1 - m_0 - \int_L \sum_{j=1}^{n} \bar{q}_j(p, U^0) \, dp_j \qquad \textbf{(B.34)}$$

$$= \Delta m - \sum_{j=1}^{n} \int_{p_j{}^0}^{p_j{}^1} \bar{q}_j[\hat{p}_j(p_j), U^0] dp_j$$

Thus, the Hicksian compensating variation is uniquely measured by adding to the change in income all the changes left of compensated demands, where demands are successively conditioned on previously considered price changes; but in this case all demands are evaluated at the initial utility level.

Clearly, the Hicksian compensating and equivalent variations are not always equal. However, from (B.32) and (B.33), one finds that

$$E - C = \sum_{j=1}^{n} \int_{p_j{}^0}^{p_j{}^1} \{\bar{q}_j[\hat{p}_j(p_j), U^0] - \bar{q}_j[\hat{p}_j(p_j), U^1]\} dp_j$$

This difference is zero if and only if

$$\int_{p_j{}^0}^{p_j{}^1} \{\bar{q}_j[\hat{p}_j(p_j), U^0] - \bar{q}_j[\hat{p}_j(p_j), U^1]\} dp_j$$

$$= -\int_{p_j{}^0}^{p_j{}^1} \int_{U^0}^{U^1} \frac{\partial \bar{q}_j[\hat{p}_j(p_j), U]}{\partial U} \, dU \, dp_j = 0 \qquad \textbf{(B.35)}$$

for each price p_j that changes. But (B.35) holds if[36]

$$\left. \frac{\partial \bar{q}_j}{\partial U} \right|_{p \text{ const}} = \left. \frac{\partial q_j}{\partial m} \frac{\partial m}{\partial U} \right|_{p \text{ const}} = \frac{\partial q_j}{\partial m} \frac{1}{\lambda} = 0 \qquad \textbf{(B.36)}$$

which implies that $\partial q_j/\partial m = 0$ (zero-income effects) for all commodities for which prices change.[37] The condition in (B.36) also implies that compensated

---

[36]The second equality is apparent upon noting that, for any interior solution in commodity space,

$$\partial U/\partial m|_{p \text{ const}} = \frac{\partial V}{\partial m} = \lambda > 0$$

[37]Again, this cannot be the case and (B.37) cannot hold if all prices change since, as shown earlier, zero-income effects for all commodities are an impossibility. It is also clear, however, that E and C may be equal in specific instances when income effects are

demands $\bar{q}_j$ are independent of the utility level if and only if ordinary demands q_j are independent of income. Since, for example, $\bar{q}_j(p^0, U^0) = q_j(p^0, m_0)$, it must be the case that $\bar{q}_j = q_j$ for all income and utility levels if and only if $\partial q_j/\partial m = 0$. Comparing (B.22), (B.33), and (B.34), this implies that

$$\Delta m + \sum_{j=1}^{n} \Delta S_j = E = C \qquad \text{(B.37)}$$

where ΔS_j is defined as in (B.23) if and only if income effects are zero (income elasticities are zero) for all prices that change.[38]

B.5 PRACTICAL ASPECTS OF WILLINGNESS-TO-PAY MEASURES FOR CONSUMERS

It may appear at this point that adoption of willingness-to-pay measures gains little over the money-measure-of-utility-change approach. Indeed, the conditions for equivalence of E and C are as restrictive as the conditions that lead to a unique money-measure-of-utility change. However, in many practical cases, only one of these measures (E or C) is appropriate. Furthermore, the work of Willig[39] has produced results that greatly enhance the willingness-to-pay approach. This is accomplished by developing a general and reasonable set of conditions under which consumer surplus methodology leads to approximately the same measure of welfare change as suggested by compensating and equivalent variations—regardless of their equivalence.

The Willig results are particularly attractive since the estimation of consumer surplus is easier than direct estimation of compensating and equivalent variations when demands are arbitrarily specified. That is, estimation of consumer surplus simply requires calculating the area under an estimated ordinary demand curve, whereas estimation of compensating and equivalent variations can involve solution of a system of partial differential equations based on estimated demand functions; see Section B.13.

Consumer Surplus as an Approximation in the Single-Price-Change Case

Alternatively, one can use consumer surplus as a rather simple method of approximation. Errors of this approximation have been examined rigorously by

---

not zero if the inner integral of (B.35) is zero. This case cannot be ruled out, since $\partial q_j/\partial U$ may change signs over the path of integraton as q_j switches from, say, a superior to an inferior good.

[38]Technically, necessity of zero-income effects requires continuous second-order differentiability of $\bar{q}_j$ and q_j.

[39] Robert D. Willig, "Consumer's Surplus Without Apology," *American Economic Review,* Vol. 66, No. 4 (September 1976), pp. 589–97, and Willig, *Consumer's Surplus: A Rigorous Cookbook,* Technical Report No. 98 (Stanford University Press: Institute for Mathematical Studies in the Social Sciences, 1973).

Willig. This approach is first demonstrated in the case of a single price change. For simplicity, demands are represented by $q_i(p, m)$, where $p \equiv (p_1, \ldots, p_n)$ and the price change is from $p^0 \equiv (p_1^0, \ldots, p_n^0)$ to $p^1 \equiv (p_1^0, \ldots, p_{i-1}^0, p_i^1, p_{i+1}^0, \ldots, p_n^0)$, $p_i^1 \neq p_i^0$. Assuming that η_1 and η_2 are lower and upper bounds on income elasticity, $\eta \equiv (\partial q_i / \partial m) \cdot (m / q_i)$, over the region of price and income space for which changes are considered with $\eta_1 \neq 1 \neq \eta_2$,[40] results can be derived from the inequality[41]

$$\left(\frac{m_1}{m_0} \right)^{\eta_1} \leq \frac{q_i(p, m_1)}{q_i(p, m_0)} \leq \left(\frac{m_1}{m_0} \right)^{\eta_2} \tag{B.38}$$

Letting $m_1 = m(p, U^0)$, the relationship in (B.38) implies that

$$\left[\frac{m(p, U^0)}{m_0} \right]^{\eta_1} \leq \frac{q_i[p, m(p, U^0)]}{q_i(p, m_0)} \leq \left[\frac{m(p, U^0)}{m_0} \right]^{\eta_2}$$

Hence, substituting from (B.37) and rearranging implies that

$$q_i(p, m_0) \cdot m_0^{-\eta_1} \leq \frac{\partial m(p, U^0)}{\partial p_i} [m(p, U^0)]^{-\eta_1} = \frac{1}{1 - \eta_1} \frac{\partial [m(p, U^0)^{1-\eta_1}]}{\partial p_i} \tag{B.39}$$

and

$$\frac{1}{1 - \eta_2} \frac{\partial [m(p, U^0)^{1-\eta_2}]}{\partial p_i} = \frac{\partial m(p, U^0)}{\partial p_i} [m(p, U^0)]^{-\eta_2} \tag{B.40}$$

$$\leq q_i(p, m_0) \cdot m_0^{-\eta_2}$$

---

[40]In theory, the choice of η_1 and η_2 is quite arbitrary and, of course, the width of bounds obtained depends directly on the range of income elasticities assumed. In empirical application, however, econometric estimates of income elasticity are usually obtained, and choices of η_1 and η_2 can be made objectively depending on statistical results.

[41]This inequality follows from the mean value theorem upon representing m as $m \equiv e^t$; whence, for $y(t) \equiv \ln q_i(p, m)$, one has

$$\frac{dy}{dt} = \frac{dy}{dq_i} \frac{\partial q_i}{\partial m} \frac{dm}{dt} = \frac{1}{q_i} \frac{\partial q_i}{\partial m} e^t = \frac{\partial q_i}{\partial m} \frac{m}{q_i} = \eta$$

and thus $\eta_1 \leq dy/dt \leq \eta_2$ for $\ln m_0 \leq t \leq \ln m_1$, where (m_0, m_1) is the range of income considerations. By the mean value theorem (Danese, *Advanced Calculus*) there exists some $\bar{t}$ such that

$$\frac{dy(\bar{t})}{dt} = \frac{y(t_1) - y(t_0)}{t_1 - t_0}$$

Substituting the bounds on dy/dt and multiplying by $t_1 - t_0$ yields

$$\eta_1(t_1 - t_0) \leq y(t_1) - y(t_0) \leq \eta_2(t_1 - t_0)$$

The relationship in (B.38) follows upon noting that $t_i = \ln m_i$ and $y(t_i) = \ln q_i(p, m_i)$, $i = 0, 1$.

Integrating both sides of (B.39) and (B.40) then yields

$$-\Delta S_i \cdot m_0^{-\eta_1} = m_0^{-\eta_1} \int_{p_i^0}^{p_i^1} q_i(p, m_0)dp_i \leq \frac{[m(p^1, U^0)]^{1-\eta_1} - m_0^{1-\eta_1}}{1 - \eta_1} \tag{B.41}$$

$$\frac{[m(p^1, U^0)]^{1-\eta_2} - m_0^{1-\eta_2}}{1 - \eta_2} \leq m_0^{-\eta_2} \int_{p_i^0}^{p_i^1} q_i(p, m_0)dp_i = -\Delta S_i \cdot m_0^{-\eta_2} \tag{B.42}$$

where ΔS_i is again the corresponding change in consumer surplus as the price of q_i changes from p_i^0 to p_i^1 [recall that $m(p^0, U^0) \equiv m_0$]. From (B.42), one finds that

$$\left[\frac{m(p^1, U^0)}{m_0}\right]^{1-\eta_2} \gtrless 1 - \frac{\Delta S_i}{m_0}(1 - \eta_2) = 1 + s(\eta_2 - 1) \qquad \text{as } 1 - \eta_2 \gtrless 0$$

where $s \equiv \Delta S_i/m_0$; thus, taking roots of both sides for the case where $1 + s(\eta_2 - 1) > 0$ yields

$$\frac{m(p^1, U^0)}{m_0} \leq [1 + s(\eta_2 - 1)]^{1/(1-\eta_2)} \tag{B.43}$$

regardless of the sign of $1 - \eta_2$. A similar procedure using (B.41) also yields

$$\frac{m(p^1, U_0)}{m_0} > [1 + s(\eta_1 - 1)]^{1/(1-\eta_1)} \tag{B.44}$$

Using (B.28) where income does not change (i.e., $m_0 = m_1$) and subtracting $1 = m_0/m_0$ from both sides of (B.43) and (B.44) thus yields

$$[1 + s(\eta_2 - 1)]^{1/(1-\eta_2)} - 1 \geq \frac{m(p^1, U_0) - m_0}{m_0} = \frac{-C}{m_0} \geq [1 + s(\eta_1 - 1)]^{1/(1-\eta_1)} - 1$$

from which one can immediately conclude that

$$\epsilon_2^c \geq \frac{\Delta S_i - C}{|\Delta S_i|} \geq \epsilon_1^c \tag{B.45}$$

where[42]

$$\epsilon_k^c \equiv \frac{[1 + s(\eta_k - 1)]^{1/(1-\eta_k)} - 1 + s}{|s|}, \qquad k = 1, 2 \tag{B.46}$$

Thus, error bounds are obtained on the extent to which compensating variation is

---

[42]It may be noted that some signs and directions of inequality are different here than in Willig's case since his A and C are opposite in sign to the change in consumer surplus, ΔS_i, and the compensating variation C defined here.

approximated by the change in consumer surplus in the market where price changes.

Having derived the foregoing bounds relating to the Hicksian compensating variation, it is a simple matter to get similar bounds relating to the Hicksian equivalent variation. That is, if one simply reverses the role of p^0 and p^1 in (B.27), then, where $m_0 = m_1$, one finds that the equivalent variation of a price change from p^1 to p^0 is the negative of the compensating variation of a price change from p^0 to p^1. When this change is made, the sign of ΔS_i and thus s is also reversed. Hence, (B.45) holds where C, ΔS_i, and s are replaced by $-E$, $-\Delta S_i$, and $-s$, respectively:

$$\epsilon_2^e \geq \frac{E - \Delta S_i}{|\Delta S_i|} \geq \epsilon_1^e \tag{B.47}$$

where ϵ_k^e is defined similarly to ϵ_k^c in (B.46);

$$\epsilon_k^e \equiv \frac{[1 - s(\eta_k - 1)]^{1/(1-\eta_k)} - 1 - s}{|s|}, \qquad k = 1, 2 \tag{B.48}$$

Several interesting results are now apparent. First, bounds on the percentage error of the change in consumer surplus, as a measure of compensating or equivalent variation, can be simply calculated from information about the change in surplus (ΔS_i), income elasticity of demand (η), and base income (m_0).

Second, the error bounds provide information that can be useful in improving estimates of compensating and equivalent variations over simple use of ΔS_i. For example, if both error bounds are positive (negative), it is clear from (B.45) and (B.47) that a downward (upward) adjustment of ΔS_i would better approximate the compensating variation, and an upward (downward) adjustment would better approximate the equivalent variation.

These results can be better understood using a second-order Taylor series expansion,

$$(1 + t)^{1/(1-\eta)} \doteq 1 + \frac{t}{1 - \eta} + \frac{\eta t^2}{2(1 - \eta)^2}$$

where $t = s(\eta - 1)$ in (B.46) and $t = -s(\eta - 1)$ in (B.48), whence

$$\epsilon_k^c, \ \epsilon_k^e \doteq \frac{\eta_k |s|}{2} \equiv \hat{\epsilon}_k, \qquad k = 1, 2 \tag{B.49}$$

Using (B.49), one can thus approximate the true bounds on percentage errors. Furthermore, substituting these approximations in (B.45) and (B.47) leads to simple approximations of bounds on compensating and equivalent variation in terms of income elasticity, base income, and consumer surplus change, that is, where

$$\xi_2^c \equiv \Delta S_i - \epsilon_2^c \, |\Delta S_i| \leq C \leq \Delta S_i - \epsilon_1^c \, |\Delta S_i| \equiv \xi_1^c \qquad \text{(B.50)}$$

$$\xi_2^e \equiv \Delta S_i + \epsilon_2^e \, |\Delta S_i| \geq E \geq \Delta S_i + \epsilon_1^e \, |\Delta S_i| \equiv \xi_1^e \qquad \text{(B.51)}$$

The approximation in (B.49) implies that

$$\xi_k^c \doteq \Delta S_i - \hat{\epsilon}_k |\Delta S_i| = \Delta S_i - \frac{\eta_k (\Delta S_i)^2}{2m_0}, \qquad k = 1, 2 \qquad \text{(B.52)}$$

$$\xi_k^e \doteq \Delta S_i + \hat{\epsilon}_k |\Delta S_i| = \Delta S_i + \frac{\eta_k (\Delta S_i)^2}{2m^0}, \qquad k = 1, 2 \qquad \text{(B.53)}$$

This implies that the second right-hand member of (B.52) or (B.53) may be a reasonable correction factor that could be added to the change in consumer surplus to estimate compensating or equivalent variation, respectively.

The question that arises in this context is to what extent the foregoing approximations are useful and reasonably accurate. To see this, consider Appendix Table B.1, which is similar to that developed by Willig. This table compares the values of $\hat{\epsilon}$, ϵ^c, and ϵ^e and gives four types of information:

1. Comparison of the entries for different values of η but the same values of s leads to observation of the width of the interval defined by the error bounds in (B.45) and (B.47).

2. Observation of the second or third entries (in their absolute levels) indicates the (relative) error made in using consumer surplus change as a measure of compensating or equivalent variation.[43]

3. Comparison of the first with the second and third entries for any given values of η and s indicates the precision lost in computing error bounds by the rule of thumb in (B.49).

4. Observation of the difference in the first and the second or third entries thus also indicates the error that remains even when the consumer surplus estimate of compensating and equivalent variation is modified using the factors included in (B.52) and (B.53), that is, when variation is estimated by

$$\hat{C}^k \equiv \Delta S_i - \hat{\epsilon}_k |\Delta S_i| \qquad \text{(B.54)}$$

and equivalent variation is estimated by

$$\hat{E}^k \equiv \Delta S_i + \hat{\epsilon}_k \, |\Delta S_i| \qquad \text{(B.55)}$$

---

[43] The second entry corresponds to a (relative) overestimate of the compensating variation. The third entry corresponds to the relative underestimate of the equivalent variation.

APPENDIX TABLE B.1[a]

				s				
η	−0.10	−0.05	0.00	0.05	0.10	0.15	0.20	0.25
−1.01	−0.05050	−0.02525	0.00000	−0.02525	−0.05050	−0.07575	−0.10100	−0.12625
	−0.04597	−0.02405	0.00000	−0.02660	−0.05632	−0.08993	−0.12852	−0.17374
	−0.05632	−0.02660	0.00000	−0.02405	−0.04597	−0.06609	−0.08467	−0.10190
−0.8	−0.04000	−0.02000	0.00000	−0.02000	−0.04000	−0.06000	−0.08000	−0.10000
	−0.03687	−0.01917	0.00000	−0.02091	−0.04390	−0.06938	−0.09795	−0.13042
	−0.04390	−0.02091	0.00000	−0.01917	−0.03687	−0.05328	−0.06858	−0.08290
−0.6	−0.03000	−0.01500	0.00000	−0.01500	−0.03000	−0.04500	−0.06000	−0.07500
	−0.02798	−0.01447	0.00000	−0.01557	−0.03243	−0.05079	−0.07094	−0.09327
	−0.03243	−0.01557	0.00000	−0.01447	−0.02798	−0.04065	−0.05257	−0.06383
−0.4	−0.02000	−0.01000	0.00000	−0.01000	−0.02000	−0.03000	−0.04000	−0.05000
	−0.01888	−0.00971	0.00000	−0.01031	−0.02130	−0.03307	−0.04574	−0.05946
	−0.02130	−0.01031	0.00000	−0.00971	−0.01888	−0.02758	−0.03585	−0.04372
−0.2	−0.01000	−0.00500	0.00000	−0.00500	−0.01000	−0.01500	−0.02000	−0.02500
	−0.00956	−0.00488	0.00000	−0.00512	−0.01049	−0.01616	−0.02215	−0.02850
	−0.01049	−0.00512	0.00000	−0.00488	−0.00956	−0.01404	−0.01834	−0.02248
0.0	0.00000	0.00000	0.00000	0.00000	0.00000	0.00000	0.00000	0.00000
	0.00000	0.00000	0.00000	0.00000	0.00000	0.00000	0.00000	0.00000
	0.00000	0.00000	0.00000	0.00000	0.00000	0.00000	0.00000	0.00000
0.2	0.01000	0.00500	0.00000	0.00500	0.01000	0.01500	0.02000	0.02500
	0.00980	0.00494	0.00000	0.00504	0.01020	0.01547	0.02086	0.02637
	0.01020	0.00504	0.00000	0.00494	0.00980	0.01457	0.01925	0.02384
0.4	0.02000	0.01000	0.00000	0.01000	0.02000	0.03000	0.04000	0.05000
	0.01986	0.00996	0.00000	0.01003	0.02013	0.03030	0.04055	0.05087
	0.02013	0.01003	0.00000	0.00996	0.01986	0.02970	0.03948	0.04920
0.6	0.03000	0.01500	0.00000	0.01500	0.03000	0.04500	0.06000	0.07500
	0.03019	0.01504	0.00000	0.01494	0.02979	0.04454	0.05919	0.07373
	0.02979	0.01494	0.00000	0.01504	0.03019	0.04544	0.06079	0.07623
0.8	0.04000	0.02000	0.00000	0.02000	0.04000	0.06000	0.08000	0.10000
	0.04080	0.02019	0.00000	0.01979	0.03920	0.05822	0.07686	0.09512
	0.03920	0.01979	0.00000	0.02019	0.04080	0.06182	0.08326	0.10512
1.01	0.05050	0.02525	0.00000	0.02525	0.05050	0.07575	0.10100	0.12625
	0.05231	0.02586	0.00000	0.02489	0.04889	0.07209	0.09452	0.11623
	0.04889	0.02489	0.00000	0.02586	0.05231	0.07977	0.10829	0.13774
1.2	0.06000	0.03000	0.00000	0.03000	0.06000	0.09000	0.12000	0.15000
	0.06291	0.03071	0.00000	0.02933	0.05731	0.08406	0.10964	0.13410
	0.05731	0.02933	0.00000	0.03071	0.06291	0.09669	0.13216	0.16942
1.4	0.07000	0.03500	0.00000	0.03500	0.07000	0.10500	0.14000	0.17500
	0.07444	0.03608	0.00000	0.03397	0.06602	0.09627	0.12487	0.15194
	0.06602	0.03397	0.00000	0.03608	0.07444	0.11529	0.15886	0.20539
1.6	0.08000	0.04000	0.00000	0.04000	0.08000	0.12000	0.16000	0.20000
	0.08630	0.04152	0.00000	0.03858	0.07451	0.10805	0.13942	0.16881
	0.07451	0.03858	0.00000	0.04152	0.08630	0.13474	0.18726	0.24439
1.8	0.09000	0.04500	0.00000	0.04500	0.09000	0.13500	0.18000	0.22500
	0.09852	0.04703	0.00000	0.04313	0.08281	0.11943	0.15334	0.18480
	0.08281	0.04313	0.00000	0.04703	0.09852	0.15510	0.21757	0.28685
2.0	0.10000	0.05000	0.00000	0.05000	0.10000	0.15000	0.20000	0.25000
	0.11111	0.05263	0.00000	0.04761	0.09090	0.13043	0.16666	0.20000
	0.09090	0.04761	0.00000	0.05263	0.11111	0.17647	0.25000	0.33333

[a] Each group of three numbers includes

$$\hat{\epsilon} = \frac{\eta|s|}{2}, \quad \epsilon^c = \frac{[1 + (\eta - 1)s]^{1/(1-\eta)} - 1 + s}{|s|} \quad \text{and} \quad \epsilon^e = \frac{[1 - (\eta - 1)s]^{1/(1-\eta)} - 1 - s}{|s|}$$

respectively.

In the latter case the respective relative errors can be bounded using (B.50) and (B.51):

$$\hat{\epsilon}_k - \epsilon_2{}^c \leq \frac{C - \hat{C}^k}{|\Delta S_i|} \leq \hat{\epsilon}_k - \epsilon_1{}^c$$

$$\epsilon_2{}^e - \hat{\epsilon}_k \geq \frac{E - \hat{E}^k}{|\Delta S_i|} \geq \epsilon_1{}^e - \hat{\epsilon}_k$$

In the case where income elasticity is not constant, however, one may prefer to work with the median income elasticity rather than the two separate bounds for simplicity. Hence, the correction factor in (B.54) and (B.55) could be based on

$$\bar{\epsilon} \equiv \tfrac{1}{2} (\hat{\epsilon}_1 + \hat{\epsilon}_2)$$

rather than $\hat{\epsilon}_k$. Then, by linearity of $\hat{\epsilon}_k$ in η_{lk} in (B.49), one finds that

$$\bar{C} \equiv \tfrac{1}{2} (\hat{C}^1 + \hat{C}^2) \equiv \Delta S_i - \bar{\epsilon}|\Delta S_i| \qquad \text{(B.56)}$$
$$\bar{E} \equiv \tfrac{1}{2} (\hat{E}^1 + \hat{E}^2) \equiv \Delta S_i - \bar{\epsilon}|\Delta S_i| \qquad \text{(B.57)}$$

To use Appendix Table B.1 in this case, note from (B.45), (B.47), (B.56), and (B.57) that

$$\epsilon_2{}^c - \bar{\epsilon} \geq \frac{\bar{C} - C}{|\Delta S_i|} \geq \epsilon_1{}^c - \bar{\epsilon} \qquad \text{(B.58)}$$

$$\epsilon_2{}^e - \bar{\epsilon} \geq \frac{E - \bar{E}}{|\Delta S_i|} \geq \epsilon_1{}^e - \bar{\epsilon} \qquad \text{(B.59)}$$

An example can serve to demonstrate these points. Consider, first, the case where $\eta = \eta_1 = \eta_2 = 1.01$ and $s = 0.1$ (assuming for simplicity that income elasticity is constant). In this case the change in consumer surplus (see type 2 above) overestimates the compensating variation of a price fall by 4.889 percent but underestimates the equivalent variation by 5.231 percent. Second, using the rule of thumb in (B.49) to approximate these errors (see type 3 above), on the other hand, implies an approximate error of 5.049 percent in both cases, which is off by 0.160 percent in the former case and by 0.182 percent in the latter case. Finally, using Appendix Table B.1, the modified estimates in (B.54) and (B.55) are off by 0.160 and 0.182 percent, respectively, as a percentage of the change in surplus (see type 4 above). Of course, if $\epsilon_k{}^c$ and $\epsilon_k{}^e$ were used in (B.54) and (B.55), respectively, rather than $\hat{\epsilon}_k$, then no error results in the constant-elasticity case [in this case the inequalities in (B.50) and (B.51) become equalities]. Now suppose that $\eta_1 = 0.8$ and $\eta_2 = 1.2$, where $s =$

0.1. In this case (see type 1 above), one knows that the consumer surplus change overestimates the compensating variation by between 3.920 and 5.731 percent, so that the width of the error bound is 1.811 percent. For the underestimate of equivalent variation, the respective percentages are 4.080, 6.291, and 2.211. If one uses $\bar{C}$ in (B.56) to estimate compensating variation, then (B.58) implies a percentage error (in terms of consumer surplus) of between -1.080 and 0.731 percent, that is $[0.03920 - (0.040 + 0.060)/2] \times 100$ percent and $[0.05731 - (0.040 + 0.060)/2] \times 100$ percent. Similarly (B.59) implies percentage error bounds on $\bar{E}$ as an estimate of equivalent variation of between -0.920 and 1.291 percent, that is, $[0.04080 - (0.040 + 0.060)/2] \times 100$ percent and $[0.06291 - (0.040 - 0.060)/2] \times 100$ percent.

Consumer Surplus as an Approximation in the Multiple-Price-Change Case

Consider now the case of multiple price changes and the extent to which the sum of consumer surplus changes can be used to approximate the compensating or equivalent variations. Suppose that initial and final prices are given by $p^0 = (p_1^0, \ldots, p_n^0)$ and $p_n = (p_1^1, \ldots, p_n^1)$, respectively. For convenience, also, let income be unchanged, $m_0 = m_1$, with initial and final utility levels given by U^0 and U^n, respectively.[44] In this case,

$$C = m_0 - m(p^n, U^0)$$
$$E = m(p^0, U^n) - m_0$$

so the compensating and equivalent variations are clearly independent of the order in which the price changes are imposed (path independent). Although the sum of consumer surplus changes depends on the order in which price changes are considered, the same approach as that described above can be used to reach error bounds.

For notational purposes, let

$$p^i \equiv (p_1^1, \ldots, p_i^1, p_{i+1}^0, \ldots, p_n^0)$$

$$\Delta S_i = - \int_{p_i^0}^{p_i^1} q_i(p_1^1, \ldots, p_{i-1}^1, p_i, p_{i+1}^0, \ldots, p_n^0, m_0)dp_i$$

and let η_1^i and η_2^i be the minimum and maximum income elasticities associated with demand for the ith good. Finally, let $\eta_1 \equiv \min (\eta_1^1, \ldots, \eta_1^n)$ and $\eta_2 = \max (\eta_2^1, \ldots, \eta_2^n)$. One can deduce immediately from equations (B.41) and (B.42) that

$$-\Delta S_i \cdot m_0^{-\eta_1} \leq \frac{m(p^i, U^0)^{1-\eta_1} - m(p^{i-1}, U^0)^{1-\eta_1}}{1 - \eta_1} \qquad \text{(B.60)}$$

---

[44]If income changes, all the results derived below would continue to hold if the sum of consumer surplus changes were simply modified by adding the change in income.

$$\frac{m(p^i, U^0)^{1-\eta_2} - m(p^{i-1}, U^0)^{1-\eta_2}}{1 - \eta_2} \le -\Delta S_i \cdot m_0^{-\eta_2} \tag{B.61}$$

Hence, noting that $m_0 = m(p^0, U^0)$ and summing the inequalities in (B.60) and (B.61) for $i = 1, \ldots, n$ yields

$$-\sum_{i=1}^{n} \Delta S_i \cdot m_0^{-\eta_1} \le \frac{m(p^n, U^0)^{1-\eta_1} - m_0^{1-\eta_n}}{1 - \eta_1} \tag{B.62}$$

$$\frac{m(p^n, U^0)^{1-\eta_2} - m_0^{1-\eta_2}}{1 - \eta_2} \le -\sum_{i=1}^{n} \Delta S_i \cdot m_0^{-\eta_2} \tag{B.63}$$

Since (B.62) and (B.63) are identical to equations (B.41) and (B.42) except that ΔS_i and p^i are replaced by $\sum_{i=1}^{n} \Delta S_i$ and p^n, respectively, the results in (B.43) through (B.59) generalize similarly, where $s = \sum_{i=1}^{n} \Delta S_i / m_0$. Hence,

$$\epsilon_2^c \ge \frac{\sum_{i=1}^{n} \Delta S_i - C}{\left|\sum_{i=1}^{n} \Delta S_i\right|} \ge \epsilon_1^c$$

$$\epsilon_2^e \ge \frac{E - \sum_{i=1}^{n} \Delta S_i}{\left|\sum_{i=1}^{n} \Delta S_i\right|} \ge \epsilon_1^e$$

where ϵ_k^c and ϵ_k^e are defined by (B.46) and (B.48) as before. All the information in Appendix Table B.1 pertaining to the single-price-change case is thus also applicable with multiple price changes. That is, Appendix Table B.1 can be used to determine error bounds on the sum of consumer surplus changes (computed sequentially) or on such modified estimates as

$$\bar{C} \equiv \sum_{i=1}^{n} \Delta S_i - \bar{\epsilon}\left|\sum_{i=1}^{n} \Delta S_i\right|$$

$$\bar{E} \equiv \sum_{i=1}^{n} \Delta S_i + \bar{\epsilon}\left|\sum_{i=1}^{n} \Delta S_i\right|$$

corresponding to (B.56) and (B.57) as measures of compensating and equivalent variation.[45] Using this approach, however, compensating and equivalent

[45] In the latter case the bounds would be computed as in (B.58) and (B.59), where the denominator $|\Delta S_i|$ is replaced by $\left|\sum_{i=1}^{n} \Delta S_i\right|$.

variation cannot be computed accurately even with constant-income elasticities unless all income elasticities are the same (that is, $\eta_1{}^i = \eta_2{}^i = \eta$, $i = 1, \ldots, n$.)[46]

The foregoing bounds for multiple price changes can be useful when income elasticities do not differ greatly among the commodities for which prices change, but the bounds can be quite wide when income elasticities are quite different among the commodities for which prices change, as evidenced by Appendix Table B.1. Fortunately, tighter bounds can be computed for such cases, although the approach for doing so is laborious and unwieldy. The improvements are basically possible because the inequalities in (B.60) and (B.61) can be made tighter by using $\eta_1{}^i$ and $\eta_2{}^i$ rather than η_1 and η_2, respectively, in calculations relating to market i, as discussed in the following section.

Computation of Tight Error Bounds

The computation of tighter error bounds on the sum of consumer surplus changes (computed sequentially) as a measure of compensating and equivalent variation for cases of multiple price changes can be considered as follows. Suppose again that prices change from p^0 to p^n, where

$$p^i = (p_1{}^1, \ldots, p_i{}^1, p_{i+1}^0, \ldots, p_n{}^0), \qquad i = 0, \ldots, n$$

and again the initial and final utility levels are U^0 and U^n, respectively, and income does not change ($m_0 = m_1$). The change in surplus in market i where price changes are imposed sequentially is

$$\Delta S_i = - \int_{p_i{}^0}^{p_i{}^1} q_i(p_1{}^1, \ldots, p_{i-1}^1, p_i, p_{i+1}^0, \ldots, p_n{}^0, m_0) dp_i$$

whereas the change in consumer surplus associated with a simple price change from p^{i-1} to p^i with income level $m(p^{i-1}, U^0)$ is

$$\Delta S_i{}' = - \int_{p_i{}^0}^{p_i{}^1} q_i[p_1{}^1, \ldots, p_{i-1}^1, p_i, p_{i+1}^0, \ldots, p_n{}^0, m(p^{i-1}, U^0)] dp_i$$

---

[46]Following (B.50) and (B.51), where ΔS_i is replaced by $\displaystyle\sum_{i=1}^{n} \Delta S_i$, it is clear that

$$C = \sum_{i=1}^{n} \Delta S_i - \epsilon^c \left| \sum_{i=1}^{n} \Delta S_i \right|$$

$$E = \sum_{i=1}^{n} \Delta S_i + \epsilon^e \left| \sum_{i=1}^{n} \Delta S_i \right|$$

when $\eta_1 = \eta_2$ since $\epsilon_1{}^c = \epsilon_2{}^c \equiv \epsilon^c$ and $\epsilon_1{}^e = \epsilon_2{}^e \equiv \epsilon^e$. Hence, compensating and equivalent variation can be computed accurately, and this is true regardless of the order in which price changes are imposed. Interestingly, this corresponds to the result found earlier in investigating money measures of utility change, which indicated that the order of imposing price changes (choice of path) in computing the overall change in consumer surplus makes no difference when income elasticities are identical for all prices that change.

Now, let $\bar{m}_i = m(p^{i-1}, U^0)$ and use (B.50) for the case where initial income is $\bar{m}_i$ and prices change from p^{i-1} to p^i to find that

$$\Delta S_i' - \epsilon_{2i}^c |\Delta S_i'| \leq m(p^{i-1}, U^0) - m(p^i, U^0) \leq \Delta S_i' - \epsilon_{1i}^c |\Delta S_i'| \qquad \text{(B.64)}$$

where

$$\epsilon_{ki}^c \equiv \frac{[1 + s_i(\eta_k^i - 1)]^{1/(1-\eta_k^i)} - 1 + s_i}{|s_i|}, \qquad k = 1, 2$$

and

$$s_i \equiv \frac{\Delta S_i'}{\bar{m}_i}$$

Next, use (B.64) to find that

$$\xi_{2i}^c \leq m(p^{i-1}, U^0) - m(p^i, U^0) - \Delta S_i \leq \xi_{1i}^c$$

where

$$\xi_{ki}^c \equiv -\epsilon_{ki}^c |\Delta S_i'| + \Delta S_i' - \Delta S_i, \qquad k = 1, 2 \qquad \text{(B.65)}$$

Finally, summing over markets yields

$$\xi_2^j \equiv \sum_{i=1}^j \xi_{2i}^c \leq m_0 - m(p^j, U^0) - \sum_{i=1}^j \Delta S_i \leq \sum_{i=1}^j \xi_{1i}^c \equiv \xi_1^j, \qquad j = 1, \ldots, n \qquad \text{(B.66)}$$

which suggests

$$\xi_2^n \leq C - \sum_{i=1}^n \Delta S_i \leq \xi_1^n$$

as error bounds on the sum of consumer surplus changes as a measure of compensating variation.

The only problem with the bounds in (B.66) is that the necessary ξ_{ki}^c in (B.65) cannot be calculated on the basis of information that is normally available; one needs the unobservable demands which correspond to incomes $\bar{m}_i = m(p^{i-1}, U^0)$, respectively, to obtain the $\Delta S_i'$. It is thus necessary to derive bounds on ξ_{1i}^c and ξ_{2i}^c in terms of observable information.

Such an approach has been suggested by Willig. Using the relationship in (B.38), he notes that

$$\left[\frac{m(p^{i-1}, U^0)}{m_0}\right]^{\eta_2^i} \Delta S_i \geq \Delta S_i' \geq \left[\frac{m(p^{i-1}, U^0)}{m_0}\right]^{\eta_1^i} \Delta S_i \qquad \text{(B.67)}$$

for $p^i > p^{i-1}$ (that is, $p_i^1 > p_i^0$). Now, suppose that markets are ordered so that price increases in the first k markets but decreases in the the last $n - k$ markets. Then $m(p^{i-1}, U^0) \geq m(p^k, U^0)$ and $m_0 \geq m(p^k, U^0)$ for $i = k + 1, \ldots, n$. Again using (B.38), this implies that

$$m(p^k, U^0)^{\eta_2^{i}-\eta_1^{i}} \, m(p^{i-1}, U^0)^{\eta_1^{i}} \, m_0^{-\eta_2^{i}} \, \Delta S_i \geq \Delta S_i'$$
$$\geq m(p^k, U^0)^{\eta_1^{i}-\eta_2^{i}} \, m(p^{i-1}, U^0)^{\eta_2^{i}} \, m_0^{-\eta_1^{i}} \Delta S_i, \qquad i = k + 1, \ldots, n \tag{B.68}$$

Then one can further note from (B.66) that

$$m_0 - \xi_2^j - \sum_{i=1}^{j} \Delta S_i \geq m(p^j, U^0) \geq m_0 - \xi_1^j - \sum_{i=1}^{n} \Delta S_i$$

which, together with (B.67) and (B.68), is sufficient to bound $\Delta S_i'$ for $i = 1, \ldots, n$. The corresponding bounds for equivalent variation are derived similarly by noting that the equivalent variation of a change from p^n to p^0 is the negative of the compensated variation of a change from p^0 to p^n.

Although this is the spirit of the algorithm developed by Willig, it is perhaps impractical to attempt hand calculations of these bounds or to present a detailed analytic treatment of the algorithm. But a computer program can easily handle such calculations in empirical cases.

Conclusions for the Pure Consumer Case

It is difficult to reach general conclusions from the foregoing results. Apparently, if $|\eta_1 s|$ and $|\eta_2 s|$ are close together but large, then the change in consumer surplus, ΔS_i, will not be close to C and E; nevertheless, the modifications in (B.54) through (B.57) may be used. In fact, if $\eta_1 = \eta_2$, that is, the income elasticity for q_i is constant in the region of change, C and E can be calculated precisely in terms of ΔS_i using (B.54) and (B.55). In general, however, the extent to which the various approximations are useful depends on the particular application and the errors the investigator is willing to accept. As Willig claims, if the investigator is willing to accept up to about a 5 percent error, then consumer surplus change can be used without modification for all cases where $|\eta s/2| < 0.05$.[47] If, on the other hand, one is not willing to accept more than a 1 percent error, one must essentially require that $|\eta s/2| \leq 0.01$ to use the (unmodified) consumer surplus change. Whereas Willig's requirement may hold for most practical problems, the latter case does not. Alternatively, with constant (and equal) income elasticity (for all commodities for which prices change), one can avoid more than about a 1 percent error by using the corrected estimates in (B.54) and (B.55) for compensating and equivalent variation,

---

[47]Willig also requires that $|\Delta S_i/m_0| \leq 0.9$ to assure that $1 \pm s (\eta - 1) > 0$ but, as evidenced by Appendix Table B.1, this condition holds for essentially all practical cases.

respectively, as long as $|\eta s/2| \leq 0.1$. This is a broad enough condition to include most practical single-price-change, constant-elasticity cases. Finally, if income elasticity is not constant, one can avoid more than about a 2 percent error by using the modified estimates in (B.56) and (B.57) if $|\eta s/2| \leq 0.08$ and income elasticity changes by less than 50 percent, where η is the largest income elasticity (in absolute value) associated with goods for which prices change.

B.6.   THE CASE WITH CONSUMPTION AND LABOR SUPPLY

Consider next extending the mathematical analysis of Sections B.1 through B.5 to the case of resource ownership. The focus first turns to consideration of labor supply in this section and then the general problem is considered in Section B.10. Owing in large part to the work of Becker[48] and Mincer,[49] labor supply has come to be viewed as the mirror image of leisure demand. A decision to sell a marginal hour of labor in the marketplace is, in a manner of speaking, a decision not to buy the marginal hour of leisure. Viewing leisure as a consumption good, the framework above can thus be easily generalized to investigate welfare effects associated with labor and wages. At the same time, some important qualifications associated with the results in the pure consumer case relating to interdependence of consumption and labor decisions become apparent. That is, the derivation in Sections B.1 through B.5 is based on the assumption of fixed income. But, in fact, when a worker is faced with higher prices, he might react by working more for example, becoming more willing to work overtime, in which case income would increase and partially offset the erosion of increasing prices on his purchasing power. In point of fact, it turns out that the path-dependency notions of Section B.2 must be expanded to include wages as well as prices.

Consider a laborer-consumer with a twice-differentiable utility function $U(l, q_1, \ldots, q_n)$, where l is consumption of nonmarket time (leisure) and q_i is consumption of commodity i, $i = 1, \ldots, n$, per unit of time. Also, suppose that the total amount of time that can be allocated between work time (h) and leisure (l) is τ hours per unit of time (i.e., $\tau = h + l$). Then the budget constraint that equates income and expenditures becomes

$$\sum_{i=1}^{n} p_i q_i = w(\tau - l) + m^*$$

$$\text{(B.69)}$$

$$= w \cdot h + m^*$$

---

[48]Gary S. Becker, "A Theory of the Allocation of Time," *Economic Journal,* Vol. 75, No. 299 (September 1965), pp. 493–517.

[49]Jacob Mincer, "Market Prices, Opportunity Costs, and Income Effects," in *Measurement in Economics: Studies in Mathematical Economics and Econometrics in Memory of Yehuda Grunfeld,* ed. C. Christ et al. (Stanford, Calif.: Stanford University Press, 1963).

where w is the wage rate and m^* is exogenous income, that is, income resulting from the consumers' endowment of resources that affect consumption only through their income-earning ability (e.g., royalties).[50] The Lagrangian of the associated utility-maximization problem is thus

$$U(l, q_1, \ldots, q_n) + \lambda \left[w(\tau - l) + m^* - \sum_{i=1}^{n} p_i q_i \right]$$

and the associated first-order conditions for maximization imply that

$$U_i \equiv \frac{\partial U}{\partial q_i} = \lambda p_i, \qquad i = 1, \ldots, n$$

$$\tag{B.70}$$

$$U_o \equiv \frac{\partial U}{\partial l} = \lambda w$$

and that (B.69) must hold at the optimum. In this context, λ is again the marginal utility of income. Solving the first-order conditions yields ordinary demand equations,

$$q_i = \tilde{q}_i(w, p_1, \ldots, p_n, m^*), \qquad i = 1, \ldots, n \tag{B.71}$$

and a leisure demand equation,

$$l = \tilde{l}(w, p_1, \ldots, p_n, m^*) \tag{B.72}$$

which implies a labor supply function of the form

$$h = \tilde{h}(w, p_1, \ldots, p_n, m^*) \equiv \tau - \tilde{l}(w, p_1, \ldots, p_n, m^*)$$

Substituting (B.71) and (B.72) into the utility function also yields the indirect utility function,

$$V = V(w, p_1, \ldots, p_n, m^*) \equiv U(\tilde{l}, \tilde{q}_1, \ldots, \tilde{q}_n)$$

Again, tildes associated with $q_1, \ldots, q_n$, l, and h will be omitted for simplicity of notation.

Following the derivation of Section B.1, the change in utility associated with a wage–price–income change from $(w^0, p_1^0, \ldots, p_n^0, m_0^*)$ to $(w^1, p_1^1, \ldots, p_n^1, m_1^*)$ can be represented as a line integral,

---

[50] For a similar classification of income (although using the terms "earned" and "unearned" instead of "endogenous" and "exogenous"), see Michael Abbott and Orly Ashenfelter, "Labor Supply, Commodity Demand and the Allocation of Time," *Review of Economic Studies*, Vol. 63, No. 135 (October 1976), pp. 389–411.

$$\Delta U = \int_L dU$$

$$= \int_L \left(\sum_{i=1}^{n} U_i dq_i + U_o \, dl \right) \tag{B.73}$$

$$= \int_L \lambda \left(\sum_{i=1}^{n} p_i dq_i + w \, dl \right)$$

where L is some wage–price–income path between the two specified wage–price–income points. Differentiating the budget constraint in (B.69) totally,[51]

$$\sum_{i=1}^{n} p_i dq_i + \sum_{i=1}^{n} q_i dp_i = (\tau - l)dw - w \, dl + dm^*$$

and substituting into (B.73) thus yields

$$\Delta U = \int_L \lambda \left[(\tau - l)dw + dm^* - \sum_{i=1}^{n} q_i dp_i \right]$$

$$= \int_L \lambda \left(h \, dw + dm^* - \sum_{i=1}^{n} q_i dp_i \right) \tag{B.74}$$

Similar to the pure consumer case, (B.74) provides an exact measure of utility change regardless of path but is not meaningful for empirical measurement since the units of measurement are indeterminant in an ordinal utility world. Again, the suggestion has been to convert ΔU to money terms through a division by λ, the marginal utility of income.[52] The associated utility indicator,

$$S = \int_L \left(h \, dw + dm^* - \sum_{i=1}^{n} q_i dp_i \right) \tag{B.75}$$

however, possesses path-dependency problems. By analogy with the derivation in Section B.2 [e.g., let the indices in (B.9) and (B.10) range from 0 to n where $p_0 \equiv w$ and $q_0 \equiv -h$], conditions for path independence of (B.75) are

$$\frac{\partial q_i}{\partial w} = -\frac{\partial h}{\partial p_i} = \frac{\partial l}{\partial p_i} \qquad i = 1, \ldots, n \tag{B.76}$$

$$\frac{\partial q_i}{\partial p_j} = \frac{\partial q_j}{\partial p_i}, \qquad i, j = 1, \ldots, n \tag{B.77}$$

---

[51]For simplicity of notation, the tildes associated with $l, h, q_1, \ldots, q_n$ will not be included explicitly in the remainder of this appendix even though optimal adjustments to prices are assumed.

[52]See, for example, Burns, "Uniqueness of Consumer's Surplus."

$$\frac{\partial q_i}{\partial m^*} = 0, \qquad i = 1, \ldots, n \tag{B.78}$$

$$\frac{\partial h}{\partial m^*} = 0$$

B.7 MONEY MEASURES OF UTILITY CHANGE FOR LABOR SUPPLIERS

Obviously, all the path-independence conditions in (B.76), (B.77), and (B.78) cannot hold simultaneously; for example, a simple change in exogenous income holding prices and wages fixed would violate (B.69) according to (B.78), since the increase in income would not be offset by either reduced labor or increased allocation to possible consumer choices. This result amounts to recognizing, as in the pure consumer case (see Section B.1), that λ cannot be constant with respect to all prices (including wages) and income; that is, S in (B.75) does not differ from ΔU in (B.74) by a multiplicative constant.

An alternative suggested, for example, by Burns is to consider only those wage–price–income paths where some subset of prices, wage, and income is allowed to vary.[53] The results of this exercise are apparent by analogy with Section B.2. For example, if exogenous income m is held constant ($dm^* \equiv 0$), then (B.76) and (B.77) constitute path-independency conditions which, following the derivation in Section B.3, implies unitary income elasticities for all goods, including leisure. Alternatively, if other prices are also held constant, income elasticities need not be unitary but must be the same for all goods, including leisure.

Similarly, if the price of one commodity (a numéraire) is fixed ($dp_n \equiv 0$), the path-dependency conditions paralleling (B.14) and (B.15) are

$$\frac{\partial q_i}{\partial p_j} = \frac{\partial q_j}{\partial p_i}, \qquad i, j = 0, 1, \ldots, n - 1 \tag{B.79}$$

$$\frac{\partial q_i}{\partial m^*} = 0, \qquad i = 0, 1, \ldots, n - 1 \tag{B.80}$$

where $p_0 \equiv w$ and $q_0 \equiv -h$. The Slutsky equation in (B.18) applies for $i, j = 0, 1, \ldots, n - 1$ and implies that (B.79) holds automatically if (B.80) holds.[54] Hence, path independence is attained in the numéraire case with varying exogenous income if $\partial q_i/\partial m^* = 0$ for all goods other than the numéraire; that is, the

---

[53] Ibid.

[54] For a similar application of the Slutsky equation with respect to leisure, see Abbott and Ashenfelter, "Labor Supply."

exogenous income elasticity of all goods, including labor (leisure), is zero and any increase in income is spent entirely on the numéraire.[55] More specifically, if other prices are also held constant, exogenous income elasticities need only be zero for goods corresponding to prices that change, and increases in income would be spent entirely on goods for which prices do not change; the exogenous income elasticity of labor (leisure) must be zero in this case if wage changes are possible.

As Burns points out, the former case with fixed exogenous income requires homotheticity in the consumer's indifference map with respect to an origin determined by the amount of exogenous income (a zero origin if exogenous income is zero). The latter case with varying exogenous income, on the other hand, requires zero-income effects, which imply vertically parallel indifference curves with respect to commodities for which prices change.

B.8   WILLINGNESS-TO-PAY MEASURES OF UTILITY CHANGE FOR CONSUMER-LABORERS

Apparently, the restrictions associated with developing money measures of utility change in the labor market (where other prices may change) are quite restrictive, just as are those associated with the pure consumer case. Thus, one must conclude along with Burns that "appropriate conditions are . . . so restrictive as to preclude operational significance."[56] Again, the less restrictive concepts of compensating and equivalent variation provide a possible and more applicable alternative.

Consider the consumer-laborer's utility-maximization problem from the alternative viewpoint of minimizing the exogenous income required for a particular level of utility:[57]

$$\underset{q_0, \ldots, q_n}{\text{minimize}} \sum_{i=0}^{n} p_i q_i \tag{B.81}$$

subject to

$$U^*(q_0, \ldots, q_n) = \bar{U}$$

where, for notational simplicity, $p_0 \equiv w$, $q_0 \equiv -h$, and $U^*(h, q_1, \ldots, q_n) \equiv U(l, q_1, \ldots, q_n) \equiv U(\tau - h, q_1, \ldots, q_n)$.[58] Let the optimum value of the

---

[55] As Burns, "Uniqueness of Consumer's Surplus" shows, this condition also corresponds to additive separability of the numéraire in the consumer's utility function.

[56] Ibid., p. 50.

[57] For the moment, it is assumed that no corner solutions are obtained, so that inclusion of nonnegativity constraints for $h, q_1, \ldots, q_n$ is not necessary.

[58] In turning to a utility function defined on the amount of a good given up (leisure),

objective function of this problem be given by the function $m^*(p, \bar{U})$, where the * denotes dependence on p_0 (or w) as well as $p_1, \ldots, p_n$. The problem in (B.81) is thus the same for analytical purposes as in (B.26); the only difference is that the commodity set has been expanded to include labor (leisure). Hence, without repeating the lengthy derivation in Sections B.4 and B.5, a number of useful results for welfare measurement in the labor market become apparent.

Before discussing these results, it is first necessary to develop definitions and concepts that facilitate interpretation where factor sales and income are determined simultaneously together with consumption. For example, in interpreting results from Sections B.4 and B.5 in the context of this section, one must bear in mind that the function $m^*(p, \bar{U})$ is not an expenditure function in the traditional sense but rather a function specifying the amount of exogenous income necessary to attain utility level $\bar{U}$ with wage–price vector $p = (w, p_1, \ldots, p_n)$. The function $m^*(p, U)$ thus will be called a *pseudo-expenditure* function. In the case where $j = 0$, one can deduce from (B.30) that differentiation of the pseudo expenditure function with respect to the wage rate yields a compensated labor supply (in absolute value),

$$\frac{\partial m^*}{\partial w} \equiv \frac{\partial m^*}{\partial p_0} = \bar{q}_0(p, U) \equiv -\bar{h}(p, U) \tag{B.82}$$

which specifies the negative of the amount of labor required to attain utility level U with wage–price vector p. Of course, (B.82) also corresponds to the compensated leisure demand,

$$\bar{l}(p, U) \equiv \tau + \bar{q}_0(p, U) \equiv \tau - \bar{h}(p, U)$$

The equivalent variation of a wage–price–income change from (p^0, m_0^*) to (p^1, m_1^*) following (B.33) is

$$E = m^*(p^0, U^1) - m_0^*$$

$$= \Delta m^* - \sum_{j=0}^{n} \int_{p_j^0}^{p_j^1} \bar{q}_j[\hat{p}_j(p_j), U^1]dp_j \tag{B.83}$$

$$= \Delta m^* + \int_{w^0}^{w^1} \bar{h}[\hat{p}_0(w), U^1]dw - \sum_{j=1}^{n} \int_{p_j^0}^{p_j^1} \bar{q}_j[\hat{p}_j(p_j), U^1]dp_j$$

where

$$\hat{p}_j(p_j) \equiv (p_0^1, \ldots, p_{j-1}^1, p_j, p_{j+1}^0, \ldots, p_n^0, m_1^*)$$
$$w^0 = p_0^0$$

the framework of this section more closely parallels the seminal work of E. J. Mishan, "Rent as a Measure of Welfare Change," *American Economic Review*, Vol. 49, No. 3 (June 1959), pp. 386–95.

and

$$w^1 = p_0^1$$

Similarly, the compensating variation of a general wage–price–income change following (B.34) is

$$C = m_1^* - m^*(p^1, U^0)$$

$$= \Delta m^* - \sum_{j=0}^{n} \int_{p_j^0}^{p_j^1} \bar{q}_j[\hat{p}_j(p_j), U^0]dp_j \tag{B.84}$$

$$= \Delta m^* + \int_{w^0}^{w^1} \bar{h}[\hat{p}_0(w), U^0]dw - \sum_{j=1}^{n} \int_{p_j^0}^{p_j^1} \bar{q}_j[\hat{p}_j(p_j), U^0]dp_j$$

Thus, the compensating (equivalent) variation for a general wage–price–income change is uniquely measured by adding to the change in exogenous income the change in area left of compensated labor supply plus all the changes in areas left of compensated demands for consumption goods, where each demand or supply is evaluated at the initial (final) utility level but successively conditioned on previously considered wage or price changes. As in Section B.4, the order of integration theoretically makes no difference.

In the special case where only the wage rate changes ($dp_i \equiv 0, i = 1, \ldots, n$), these results indicate that the willingness to pay for a wage change in the labor market is, indeed, given by the change in area left of the compensated labor supply curve, where compensation corresponds to the initial (final) utility level in the case of compensating (equivalent) variation. The results are thus consistent with, but a generalization of, those by Mishan.[59]

As in the pure consumer case, it may again be noted that (B.35) holds for $j = 0, \ldots, n$, and hence $E = C$ if

$$\left.\frac{\partial \bar{q}_j}{\partial U}\right|_{p \text{ const}} = \left.\frac{\partial q_j}{\partial m^*}\right|_{p \text{ const}} = \frac{\partial q_j}{\partial m^*}\frac{1}{\lambda} = 0 \tag{B.85}$$

which implies that $\partial q_j/\partial m^* = 0, j = 0, \ldots, n$. The implication of (B.85) in this case is not that zero-income effects are required for all goods but that zero *exogenous* income effects are required; clearly, this condition is needed only for those goods for which prices change. The latter situation may be more apt to occur than the former. For example, suppose that a laborer-consumer draws exogenous income from investments but, as a matter of course, reinvests all investment income, thus seeking to finance all consumption from wage and salary income. In this case, zero exogenous income effects would hold for all consumption goods (assuming a dichotomy between consumption goods and

---

[59] Ibid.

investments). If any compensation is also treated as exogenous income, the equivalent and compensating variations for any multiple price change associated only with consumption goods would be identical and would be measured exactly by the sum of changes in surpluses associated with ordinary consumption demands and labor supply.[60]

B.9   APPROXIMATE MEASUREMENT OF WILLINGNESS TO PAY FOR CONSUMER-LABORERS

Whether or not the foregoing rationale permits exact measurement of willingness to pay using consumer-surplus concepts, the Willig approach can be extended in a straightforward manner to the laborer-consumer case. Hence, approximate measures of willingness to pay can be made with the consumer-surplus approach as long as exogenous income elasticities can be bounded and initial exogenous income can be measured and is not zero.

Consider first a single price (wage) change from $p^0 = (p_0{}^0, \ldots, p_n{}^0)$ to $p^1 = (p_0{}^0, \ldots, p_{i-1}^0, p_i{}^1 p_{i+1}^0, \ldots, p_n{}^0)$, $p_i{}^1 \neq p_i{}^0$. Suppose that $\eta_1{}^*$ and $\eta_2{}^*$ are lower and upper bounds, respectively, on the exogenous income elasticity, $\eta^* = (\partial q_i / \partial m^*) \cdot (m^*/q_i)$, over the region of wage–price–income space for which changes are considered, $\eta_1{}^* \neq 1 \neq \eta_2{}^*$. In this case the derivation of equations (B.37) through (B.59) can be repeated, simply substituting η^* for η and m^* for m. Note, however, in the case of a wage change ($i = 0$) that

$$\Delta S_0 = -\int_{p_0{}^0}^{p_0{}^1} q_0(p, m_0)dp_0$$

(B.86)

$$= \int_{w^0}^{w^1} h(p, m_0)dw$$

that is, ΔS_0 is precisely the change in the Marshallian surplus triangle or rent associated with labor supply. Hence, letting $i = 0$, the Willig results can be immediately extended to determine the usefulness of the Marshallian surplus associated with labor supply in measuring compensating and/or equivalent variation associated with a wage change.

Thus, the error bounds,

$$\epsilon_2{}^{c^\infty} \geq \frac{\Delta S_i - C}{|\Delta S_i|} \geq \epsilon_1{}^{c^\infty}$$

(B.87)

---

[60] As before, however, these measurements must be successively conditioned on previously considered price changes.

and

$$\epsilon_2{}^{e^\circ} \geq \frac{E - \Delta S_i}{|\Delta S_i|} \geq \epsilon_1{}^{e^\circ} \qquad (B.88)$$

on consumer (factor supplier) surplus as a measure of the compensating or equivalent variation of a price (wage) change follow directly from (B.45) and (B.47) except that the bounds are based on exogenous income and exogenous income elasticities, that is,

$$\epsilon_k{}^{c^\circ} = \frac{[1 + s^*(\eta_k^* - 1)]^{1/(1-\eta_k^\circ)} - 1 + s^*}{|s^*|}, \qquad k = 1, 2$$

and

$$\epsilon_k{}^{e^\circ} = \frac{[1 - s^*(\eta_k^* - 1)]^{1/(1-\eta_k^\circ)} - 1 - s^*}{|s^*|}, \qquad k = 1, 2$$

where $s^* = \Delta S_i / m_0^*$. Similarly, (B.87) and (B.88) suggest the possibility of modifying the surplus measure ΔS_i to obtain better estimates of compensating and equivalent variation. In point of fact, following (B.54) through (B.57) yields

$$\epsilon_2{}^{c^\circ} - \bar\epsilon^* \geq \frac{\bar C^* - C}{|\Delta S_i|} \geq \epsilon_1{}^{c^\circ} - \bar\epsilon^* \qquad (B.89)$$

and

$$\epsilon_2{}^{e^\circ} - \bar\epsilon^* \geq \frac{E - \bar E^*}{|\Delta S_i|} \geq \epsilon_1{}^{e^\circ} - \bar\epsilon^* \qquad (B.90)$$

where

$$\bar C^* = \Delta S_i - \bar\epsilon^* |\Delta S_i| \qquad (B.91)$$
$$\bar E^* = \Delta S_i + \bar\epsilon^* |\Delta S_i| \qquad (B.92)$$

$$\bar\epsilon^* = \frac{|s^*|}{4} (\eta_1^* + \eta_2^*) \qquad (B.93)$$

Appendix Table B.1 may again be used to investigate the magnitude of error in various cases. For example, if exogenous income elasticity is between 0 and 0.4 and the labor surplus change associated with a wage increase is 25 percent of exogenous income ($\eta_1^* = 0$, $\eta_2^* = 0.4$, $s^* = 0.25$), then Table B.1 implies that the labor surplus change overestimates the compensating variation by no more than 4.9 percent and underestimates the equivalent variation by no more than 5.1 percent.

B.10   FACTOR SUPPLY OF OTHER RESOURCES

As pointed out by Mishan, supply of other factors by consumers can be treated in the same way as labor supply.[61] That is, given a consumer's initial endowment of resources, which includes his time, suppose that a generalization of the utility function U^* is defined where quantities of goods may be either positive or negative, with negative amounts denoting sales, as in the case of labor, in Sections B.8 and B.9. The consumer's utility-maximization problem is thus to

$$\text{maximize } U^*(q_0, \ldots, q_n)$$

subject to

$$\sum_{i=0}^{n} p_i q_i = m^*$$

$$q_i \leq r_i, \quad i = 0, \ldots, n^* < n$$

where r_i represents the consumers' initial endowment of good i (e.g., $r_0 = \tau$). To determine willingness to pay for various alternative wage–price–income situations, this problem can be usefully reformulated as

$$\text{minimize } \sum_{i=0}^{n} p_i q_i$$

subject to

$$U^*(q_0, \ldots, q_n) = \bar{U}$$
$$q_i \leq r_i, \quad i = 0, \ldots, n^* < n$$

Upon solving the latter problem, one obtains compensated demand (supply) functions, $\bar{q}_i(p, \bar{U})$, $i = 0, \ldots, n$, depending on whether the positive (negative) regions of the functions are considered. Thus, a pseudo-expenditure function, which specifies the minimum amount of exogenous income necessary to make utility level $\bar{U}$ attainable with wage–price vector p, is

$$m^*(p, \bar{U}) = \sum_{i=0}^{n} p_i \bar{q}_i(p, \bar{U})$$

In this framework the results of the preceding section clearly generalize in a

---

[61] Mishan, "Rent."

straightforward fashion, so that sales of other factors besides labor present no further complications. Just as in (B.86), the term ΔS_i would represent a change in economic rent (or a change in the Marshallian surplus triangle left of the factor supply curve) for those goods sold rather than purchased. Similarly, the error bounds on surplus measures as a measure of compensating and equivalent variation in the single–price–change case would be given by (B.87) and (B.88), respectively. Also, the modified estimates in (B.91) and (B.92) would possess the improved error bounds in (B.89) and (B.90).

Furthermore, whether or not factors besides labor are sold, the Willig results can also be extended for the multiple–price–change case. Suppose that the wage–price vector changes from $p^0 = (p_0{}^0, \ldots, p_n{}^0)$ to $p^n = (p_0{}^1, \ldots, p_n{}^1)$ and the resulting utility level changes from U^0 to U^n. For notational purposes, let

$$\hat{p}_i(p_i) = (p_0{}^1, \ldots, p_{i-1}^1, p_i, p_{i+1}^0, \ldots, p_n{}^0)$$

and

$$\Delta S_i = -\int_{p_i{}^0}^{p_i{}^1} q_i[\hat{p}_i(p_i)]dp_i$$

where, for simplicity, $m_0{}^* = m_1{}^*$.[62] Finally, define $\eta_1{}^*$ and $\eta_2{}^*$ as the minimum and maximum exogenous income elasticities over all goods for which prices change, that is,

$$\eta_1{}^* = \min_{\substack{i = 0, \ldots, n \\ p^0 \leq p \leq p^n}} \frac{\partial q_i}{\partial m^*} \frac{m^*}{q_i} \tag{B.94}$$

and

$$\eta_2{}^* = \max_{\substack{i = 0, \ldots, n \\ p^0 \leq p \leq p^n}} \frac{\partial q_i}{\partial m^*} \frac{m^*}{q_i} \tag{B.95}$$

In this framework one can follow the derivation of (B.60) through (B.63), where η_i is replaced by $\eta_i{}^*$, m is replaced by m^*, and summations run over indices $0, \ldots, n$, to obtain

$$\epsilon_2{}^{c^0} \geq \frac{\sum_{i=0}^{n} \Delta S_i - C}{\left|\sum_{i=0}^{n} \Delta S_i\right|} \geq \epsilon_1{}^{c^0} \tag{B.96}$$

---

[62] Again, if exogenous income changes, the expressions below for compensating and equivalent variation would be modified by adding the change in exogenous income.

and

$$\epsilon_2^{e^\circ} \geq \frac{E - \sum_{i=0}^{n} \Delta S_i}{\left| \sum_{i=1}^{n} \Delta S_i \right|} \geq \epsilon_1^{e^\circ} \tag{B.97}$$

These results also suggest the modified estimates of compensating and equivalent variation given by

$$\bar{C}^* = \sum_{i=0}^{n} \Delta S_i - \bar{\epsilon}^* \left| \sum_{i=0}^{n} \Delta S_i \right| \tag{B.98}$$

and

$$\bar{E}^* = \sum_{i=0}^{n} \Delta S_i + \bar{\epsilon}^* \left| \sum_{i=0}^{n} \Delta S_i \right| \tag{B.99}$$

where $\bar{\epsilon}^*$ is defined as in (B.93) with $s^* = \sum_{i=0}^{n} \Delta S_i / m_0^*$ and, similarly, the tighter error bounds in (B.89) and (B.90) continue to hold where ΔS_i is replaced by $\sum_{i=0}^{n} \Delta S_i$.

Unlike the earlier cases, however, the bounds in (B.96) and (B.97) or even the tighter bounds associated with $\bar{C}^*$ in (B.98) and $\bar{E}^*$ in (B.99) are not as satisfactory, as indicated by the Willig results discussed in Section B.5. That is, in the case where factors are sold and consumption goods are purchased, the variation in income elasticities among commodities is likely to be much greater. For example, the exogenous income elasticity of labor may be zero (no less labor would be supplied with an increase in exogenous income), whereas the exogenous income elasticity for luxury consumption goods would be positive and greater than 1. Hence, if both wage and luxury-good prices change, then $\eta_1^* = 0$, $\eta_2^* > 1$; and the error bounds could become quite wide, as demonstrated by Table B.1, unless the ratio of surplus change to exogenous income s^* is small.

Alternatively, however, reasonable error bounds can be developed according to the derivation in (B.64) through (B.68) as long as variation of income elasticities for individual commodities is not great in the range of wage–price–income considerations. In conclusion, one may reiterate the final paragraph of Section B.5 with the minor modification that all reference to income must be replaced with reference to exogenous income. For example, if an investigator is willing to accept up to about a 5 percent error, then the surplus measure can be used without modification if $|\eta^* s^*/2| \leq 0.05$ for all goods with changing price. One can avoid more than about a 1 percent error by using the modified estimates in (B.98) and (B.99) if $|\eta^*s^*/2| \leq 0.08$ for all goods with changing price, and exogenous income elasticities with respect to individual commodities vary by less than 50 percent.

Finally, it is important to compare the general implications of the Willig results where all income is treated exogenously with the implications of the more realistic case where factor sales and consumption decisions are determined simultaneously. Comparing with the results in Section (B.5), it may be noted that the limits on ηs imposed in the pure consumer case for the same approximate validity statements as made above correspond exactly to those imposed on η^*s^* in this case, that is,

$$|\eta s| \leq 0.1$$

versus

$$|\eta^*s^*| \leq 0.1$$

In this context it is interesting to note that

$$\eta s = \frac{\partial q_j}{\partial m} \frac{m}{q_j}\bigg|_{q_j=q_j^*} \cdot \frac{\Sigma_i \Delta S_i}{m}$$

$$= \frac{\partial q_j}{\partial m} \frac{m^*}{q_j}\bigg|_{q_j=q_j^*} \cdot \frac{\Sigma_i \Delta S_i}{m^*}$$

(B.100)

where $\eta = (\partial q_j/\partial m) \cdot (m/q_j)|_{q_j=q_j^*}$ is the largest income elasticity associated with a good for which price changes. Hence, in the special case where the marginal effect of income on q_j is the same as the marginal effect of exogenous income on q_j (i.e., $\partial q_j/\partial m = \partial q_j/\partial m^*$), one finds $\eta s = \eta^*s^*$ from (B.100), so that the requirements for approximate application of surplus measures according to Willig's methods in Section B.5 are indeed valid even when factor supply decisions are interdependent with consumer demand decisions.[63]

---

[63]One may note that the condition $\partial q_i/\partial m = \partial q_i/\partial m^*$ under which the Willig approximation criteria are identical in the pure consumer and consumer–resource owner problems are exactly those under which a two-stage budgeting procedure is appropriate; these requirements have already been well developed in the theory of separability and require that consumption commodities and resources form two weakly separable groups. For example, in the consumer-laborer problem,

$$\max U(q_1, \ldots, q_n, l)$$

subject to

$$\sum_{i=1}^{n} p_i q_i + wl = m^* + w\tau$$

B.11 APPROXIMATE WILLINGNESS-TO-PAY MEASURES WITH QUANTITY RESTRICTIONS

Turning to the case where quantity restrictions must be considered (because of lumpiness, shortages, durable fixities, governmental controls, or government production of public goods), the Willig results have been extended in a recent paper by Randall and Stoll.[64] Suppose that the general consumer/resource owner attempts to

$$\underset{q_1, \ldots, q_n}{\text{maximize}} \quad U^*(q_1, \ldots, q_n)$$

subject to

$$\sum_{i=1}^{n} p_i q_i = m^*$$

$$q_i = q_i^0, \qquad i = 1, \ldots, n^* \leq n$$

the first-order conditions for maximization of the Lagrangian

$$U(q_1, \ldots, q_n, l) - \lambda \left[\sum_{i=1}^{n} p_i q_i + w(l - \tau) - m^* \right]$$

are

$$U_i - \lambda p_i = 0, \qquad i = 1, \ldots, n$$
$$U_l - \lambda w = 0$$

$$\sum_{i=1}^{n} p_i q_i + w(l - \tau) - m^* = 0$$

From these conditions, one finds that

$$\frac{U_i}{U_j} = \frac{p_i}{p_j}, \qquad i = j - 1; j = 2, \ldots, n$$

$$\sum_{i=1}^{n} p_i q_i = m$$

where $m \equiv m^* + w(\tau - l)$. When labor is weakly separable from all other goods [i.e., when $\partial(U_i/U_j)/\partial l = 0$ for $i, j = 1, \ldots, n$], the latter set of conditions depend on l only through m and thus uniquely determine demands of the form $q_i = q_i(p_1, \ldots, p_n, m)$, which depend on l only through m. Hence, $\partial q_i/\partial m^* = (\partial q_i/\partial m)(\partial m/\partial m^*) = \partial q_i/\partial m$. For most empirical work, leisure (labor) is assumed to be a separable commodity group at least implicitly; hence, a strong precedent exists as a basis for assuming the Willig approximation criteria are identical in the pure consumer and consumer-laborer problems. For a further discussion and review of separability, see Charles Blackorby, Daniel Primont, and R. Robert Russell, *Duality, Separability, and Functional Structure: Theory and Economic Applications* (New York: Elsevier/North-Holland, Inc., 1978).

[64] Alan Randall and John R. Stoll, "Consumer's Surplus in Commodity Space," *American Economic Review*, Vol. 70, No. 3 (June 1980), pp. 449–57.

where, for example, $q_1^0, \ldots, q_{n^*}^0$ are imposed quantities of $q_1, \ldots, q_{n^*}$. The dual of this problem is

$$\underset{q_1, \ldots, q_n}{\text{minimize}} \sum_{i=1}^{n} p_i q_i$$

subject to

$$U^*(q_1, \ldots, q_n) = \bar{U}$$
$$q_i = q_i^0, \qquad i = 1, \ldots, n^*$$

But this problem can be further simplified to the form

$$\underset{q_{n^*+1}, \ldots, q_n}{\text{minimize}} \sum_{i=n^*+1}^{n} p_i q_i$$

subject to

$$U^*(q_1^0, \ldots, q_{n^*}^0, q_{n^*+1}, \ldots, q_n) = \bar{U}$$

Obviously, for a given $q_0^0 \equiv (q_1^0, \ldots, q_{n^*}^0)$, this problem is mathematically equivalent to those considered previously, so that evaluation of price changes in other markets follows the procedures already outlined.

To evaluate the impact of a change in the quantity restriction q_0^0, note that solution of either of the latter two problems above leads to compensated demand (supply) functions, $\bar{q}_i(\tilde{p}, \bar{U}, q_0^0)$, where $\tilde{p} = (p_{n^*+1}, \ldots, p_n)$, that is $\tilde{p}$ does not include prices of restricted quantities. The pseudo-expenditure function specifying the minimum amount of exogenous income necessary to attain utility level $\bar{U}$ is

$$m^*(p, \bar{U}, q_0^0) = \sum_{i=1}^{n^*} p_i q_i^0 + \sum_{i=n^*+1}^{n} p_i \bar{q}_i(\tilde{p}, \bar{U}, q_0^0)$$

where $p = (p_1, \ldots, p_{n^*}, \tilde{p})$. Thus,

$$\frac{\partial m^*}{\partial q_j^0} = p_j + \sum_{i=n^*+1}^{n} p_i \frac{\partial \bar{q}_i}{\partial q_0^0}, \qquad j = 1, \ldots, n^* \qquad \text{(B.101)}$$

Note, however, that the Lagrangian of the first expenditure minimization problem above is

$$\sum_{i=1}^{n} p_i q_i - \phi[U(q_1, \ldots, q_n) - \bar{U}] - \sum_{i=1}^{n^*} \psi_i(q_i - q_i^0)$$

for which first-order conditions imply that

$$p_i = \phi U_i + \psi_i, \qquad i = 1, \ldots, n^* \tag{B.102}$$

$$p_i = \phi U_i, \qquad i = n^* + 1, \ldots, n \tag{B.103}$$

Substituting (B.102) and (B.103) into (B.101) yields

$$\frac{\partial m^*}{\partial q_j{}^0} = \psi_j + \phi \sum_{i=1}^{n} \frac{\partial U}{\partial q_i} \frac{\partial \bar{q}_i}{\partial q_0{}^0} = \psi_j + \phi \frac{d\bar{U}}{dq_0{}^0} = \psi_j, \qquad j = 1, \ldots, n^* \tag{B.104}$$

where, for convenience, $\partial \bar{q}_j / \partial q_j{}^0 = \partial q_j{}^0 / \partial q_j{}^0 = 1$ and $\partial \bar{q}_k / \partial q_j{}^0 = 0$ for $k, j = 1,$ $\ldots, n^*, k \neq j$. Furthermore, ψ_j may, in fact, be written as a function $\psi_j(p, \bar{U}, q_0{}^0)$ and, by the usual interpretation of a Lagrangian multiplier, represents the marginal value of a change in the associated restriction, $q_j{}^0$, or, in other words, the marginal value of consuming q_j given that price p_j must be paid for it. Since $\psi_j(p, \bar{U}, q_0{}^0)$ gives the marginal value of consuming an additional unit of q_j over and above its price when utility is held constant, this is precisely the vertical difference in the Hicksian compensated supply or demand of q_j in inverse form (value per unit as a function of quantity) and the price p_j.

Because of the mathematical equivalence of the second expenditure minimization problem above and those considered earlier, one again finds that

$$\frac{\partial m^*}{\partial p_i} = \bar{q}_i (\bar{p}, \bar{U}, q_0{}^0), \qquad i = n^* + 1, \ldots, n$$

for the cases where quantities are not restricted (which are Hicksian compensated demands in standard form); and somewhat trivially,

$$\frac{\partial m^*}{\partial p_j} = q_j{}^0$$

for those cases where quantities are restricted.

Next consider a change in prices, exogenous income, and quantity restrictions from $(p^0, m_0{}^*, q_0{}^0)$ to $(p^1, m_1{}^*, q_0{}^1)$ which leads to a change in maximum attainable utility from U^0 to U^1. In this context, the amount of compensation that leaves a consumer/resource supplier in the subsequent welfare position in the absence of a change is

$$E = m^*(p^0, U^1, q_0{}^0) - m_0{}^* \tag{B.105}$$

Similarly, the amount of compensation that leaves a consumer in the initial welfare position following a change is

$$C = m_1{}^* - m^*(p^1, U^0, q_0{}^1) \tag{B.106}$$

Note that these definitions do not strictly correspond to the Hicksian concepts of equivalent surplus or compensating surplus, since adjustment is allowed for some commodities and not for others.

In this case, one finds following the approach of Sections B.4 and B.8, but using (B.105) and (B.106), that

$$E = m_1^* - m_0^* + m^*(p^0, U^1, q_0^0) - m^*(p^1, U^1, q_0^1)$$

$$= m_1^* - m_0^* - \int_L \left[\sum_{i=1}^{n^\circ} \frac{\partial m^*}{\partial q_i} dq_i + \sum_{i=1}^{n} \frac{\partial m^*}{\partial p_i} dp_i \right]$$

$$= m_1^* - m_0^* - \int_L \left[\sum_{i=1}^{n^\circ} \psi_i(p, U^1, q_0) \, dq_i + \sum_{i=1}^{n^\circ} q_i dp_i \right.$$

$$\left. + \sum_{i=n^\circ+1}^{n} \bar{q}_i \, (\bar{p}, U_1, q_0) \, dp_i \right]$$

(B.107)

$$= m_1^* - m_0^* - \sum_{i=1}^{n^\circ} q_i^0(p_i^1 - p_i^0) - \sum_{i=1}^{n^\circ} \int_{q_i 0}^{q_i 1} \psi_i[p^1, U^1, \hat{q}_i(q_i)] \, dq_i$$

$$- \sum_{i=n^\circ+1}^{n} \int_{p_i 0}^{p_i 1} \bar{q}_i[\hat{p}_i(p_i), U^1, q_0^0] \, dp_i$$

and similarly that

$$C = m_1^* - m_0^* + m^*(p^0, U^0, q_0^0) - m^*(p^1, U^0, q_0^1)$$

$$= m_1^* - m_0^* - \sum_{i=1}^{n^\circ} q_i^1(p_i^1 - p_i^0) - \sum_{i=1}^{n^\circ} \int_{q_i 0}^{q_i 1} \psi_i[p^0, U^0, \hat{q}_i(q_i)] \, dq_i$$

(B.108)

$$- \sum_{i=n^\circ+1}^{n} \int_{p_i 0}^{p_i 1} \bar{q}_i[\hat{p}_i(p_i), U^0, q_0^1] \, dp_i$$

where L is any path of integration from (p^0, q_0^0) to (p^1, q_0^1) and $\hat{p}_i(p_i)$ is defined similarly to (B.19) with

$$\hat{p}_i(p_i) = (p_{n^*+1}^1, \ldots, p_{i-1}^1, p_i, p_{i+1}^0, \ldots, p_n^0)$$

where now

$$\hat{q}_i(q_i) = (q_1^1, \ldots, q_{i-1}^1, q_i, q_{i+1}^0, \ldots, q_{n^*}^0)$$

The implication of (B.107) and (B.108) is that a change in a quantity restriction is evaluated by the change in area below (above) the compensated demand (supply) curve, above (below) price, and left of quantity, whereas a price change for an unrestricted quantity is evaluated by the change in area below (above) the compensated demand (supply) curve and above (below) price. Any change in price for a restricted quantity acts essentially as an income change since that amount must be exactly compensated to leave the individual just as well off when adjustment is not possible. Again, these changes can be imposed sequentially along any arbitrary path from $(p^0, q_0{}^0)$ to $(p^1, q_0{}^1)$; but following Sections 6.7 or 7.7, the income changes and price changes that behave like income changes can be more easily imposed first in calculating the equivalent welfare measure, or last in calculating the compensation welfare measure when ordinary surplus approximations are to be used.

To consider the errors associated with using a consumer or producer surplus approximation in the case of a quantity restriction, suppose that only one quantity restriction, $q_1{}^0$, is imposed while all prices remain constant. Suppose that the ordinary demand curve in implicit form (with price as a function of quantity) is represented by

$$\tilde{p}_i(\tilde{p}, m^*, q_i{}^0)$$

and that the vertical distance between the ordinary demand curve and price is represented by

$$\tilde{\psi}_i(p, m^*, q_i{}^0) = \tilde{p}_i(\tilde{p}, m^*, q_i{}^0) - p_i$$

In this context, define price flexibility of income as

$$\phi^* = \frac{\partial \tilde{\psi}_i}{\partial m^*} \frac{m^*}{\tilde{\psi}_i}$$

Then further define $y(t) \equiv \ln \tilde{\psi}_i \ (p, m^*, q_i)$ and $m^* = e^t$ so that

$$\frac{dy}{dt} = \frac{dy}{d\tilde{\psi}_i} \frac{\partial \tilde{\psi}_i}{\partial m^*} \frac{dm^*}{dt} = \frac{1}{\tilde{\psi}_i} \frac{\partial \tilde{\psi}_i}{\partial m^*} e^t = \frac{\partial \tilde{\psi}_i}{\partial m^*} \frac{m^*}{\tilde{\psi}_i} = \phi^*$$

Following a similar procedure as used to derive (B.38), this implies that

$$\left(\frac{m_1{}^*}{m_0{}^*}\right)^{\phi_1{}^\circ} \leq \frac{\tilde{\psi}_i(p, m_1{}^*, q_i)}{\tilde{\psi}_i(p, m_0{}^*, q_i)} \leq \left(\frac{m_1{}^*}{m_0{}^*}\right)^{\phi_2{}^\circ}$$

where $\phi_1{}^*$ and $\phi_2{}^*$ are lower and upper bounds on price flexibility over the path of the quantity change. Then substituting $m^*(p, U^0, q_i)$ for $m_1{}^*$ and using (B.104) yields

$$\tilde{\psi}_i(p, m_0{}^*, q_i) \cdot (m_0{}^*)^{-\phi_1{}^*} \leq \frac{\partial m^*(p, U^0, q_i)}{\partial q_i} \, m^*(p, U^0, q_i)^{-\phi_1{}^*}$$

(B.109)

$$= \frac{\partial [m^*(p, U^0, q_i)^{1-\phi_1{}^\circ}]}{\partial q_i}$$

and

$$\frac{\partial[m^*(p, U^0, q_i)^{1-\phi_2^*}]}{\partial q_i} = \frac{\partial m^*(p, U^0, q_i)}{\partial q_i} \, m(p, U^0, q_i)^{-\phi_2^*}$$

(B.110)

$$\le \tilde{\psi}_i(p, m_0^*, q_i) \cdot (m_0^*)^{-\phi_2^*}$$

Integrating both sides of (B.109) and (B.110) thus yields

$$-\Delta S_i \cdot (m_0^*)^{-\phi_1^*} = (m_0^*)^{-\phi_1^*} \int_{q_i^0}^{q_i^1} \tilde{\psi}_i(p, m_0^*, q_i) \, dq_i$$

(B.111)

$$\le \frac{m^*(p, U^0, q_i^1)^{1-\phi_1^\circ} - (m_0^*)^{1-\phi_1^\circ}}{1 - \phi_1^*}$$

and

$$\frac{m^*(p, U^0, q_i^1)^{1-\phi_2^\circ} - (m_0^*)^{1-\phi_2^\circ}}{1 - \phi_2^*} \le (m_0^*)^{-\phi_2^*} \int_{q_i^0}^{q_i^1} \tilde{\psi}_i \, (p, m_0^*, q_i) \, dq_i$$

(B.112)

$$= -\Delta S_i \cdot (m_0^*)^{\phi_2^\circ}$$

where ΔS_i is obviously defined as in Section 7.9. Now following steps similar to those used in (B.41) through (B.44), one finds that

$$[1 + s_i^*(\phi_2^* - 1)]^{1/(1-\phi_2^*)} \ge \frac{m^*(p, U^0, q_i^1)}{m_0^*} \ge [1 + s_i^*(\phi_1^* - 1)]^{1/(1-\phi_1^*)}$$

and

$$\epsilon_2^c \ge \frac{\Delta S_i - C_s}{|\Delta S_i|} \ge \epsilon_1^c$$

(B.113)

where

$$\epsilon_k^c \equiv \frac{[1 + s_i^*(\phi_k^* - 1)]^{1/(1-\phi_k^*)} - 1 + s_i^*}{|s_i^*|}, \qquad k = 1, 2$$

(B.114)

and

$$s_i^* \equiv \frac{\Delta S_i}{m_0^*}$$

Similarly, one finds that

$$\epsilon_2^e \ge \frac{E_s - \Delta S_i}{|\Delta S_i|} \ge \epsilon_1^e$$

(B.115)

where

$$\epsilon_k^e \equiv \frac{[1 - s_i^*(\phi_k^* - 1)]^{1/(1-\phi_k^*)} - 1 - s_i^*}{|s_i^*|}, \qquad k = 1, 2 \qquad \textbf{(B.116)}$$

Obviously, comparing (B.113) and (B.115) with (B.87) and (B.88), all of the further approximation results in (B.89) through (B.92) hold for this case as well when $\bar{\epsilon}^* = |s_i^*| \cdot (\phi_1^* + \phi_2^*)/4$. Also, based on (B.114) and (B.116), Appendix Table B.1 may again be used in investigating the magnitude of error in various cases by simply replacing the role of η with ϕ. Thus, ϵ_k^c and ϵ_k^e are approximated by

$$\epsilon_k^c, \ \epsilon_k^e \doteq \frac{\phi_k^*|s_i^*|}{2} \equiv \hat{\epsilon}_k, \qquad k = 1, 2$$

so that more than about a 5 percent error is avoided by using consumer surplus change in place of a willingness to pay for changes in quantity restrictions so long as price flexibility times the surplus change relative to income is less than 0.1 in absolute value (i.e., $|\eta^*\phi^*/2| \leq 0.05$).

These results can also be readily extended to the case of simultaneous changes in many quantity restrictions and many prices. For example, suppose that

$$\hat{q}_i(q_i) \equiv (q_1^1, \ldots, q_{i-1}^1, q_i, q_{i+1}^0, \ldots, q_m^0)$$

$$\Delta S_i = -\int_{q_i^0}^{q_i^1} \psi_i[p^n, m_j^*, \hat{q}_i(q_i)]dq_i, \qquad i = 1, \ldots, n^*$$

$$\hat{p}_i(p) \equiv (p_1^j, \ldots, p_{n^*}^j, p_{n^*+1}^1, \ldots, p_{i-1}^1, p_i, p_{i+1}^0, \ldots, p_n^0)$$

$$\Delta S_i = -\int_{p_i^0}^{p_i^1} q_i[\hat{p}_i(p_i), m_j^*, q_0^0]dp_i, \qquad i = n^* + 1, \ldots, n$$

where $j = 0$ in the case of a compensating measure and $j = 1$ in the case of an equivalent measure. Thus, the total surplus change is $\sum_{i=1}^{n} \Delta S_i + m_1^* - m_0^* + \sum_{i=1}^{n^*} (p_i^0 - p_i^1) \cdot q_i^j$, following the methods of Sections 6.7 and 7.7, where actual income change (now also including expenditure effects of price changes for restricted quantities) is evaluated before (after) all other effects in computing equivalent (compensating) welfare measures. Here, the component $m_1^* - m_0^* + \sum_{i=1}^{n^*} (p_i^0 - p_i^1) \cdot q_i^j$ is without error, while bounds on the error associated with $\sum_{i=1}^{n} \Delta S_i$ follow from (B.60) through (B.63), where $m(p^i, U^0)$ is replaced by $m^*(p^i, U^0, q_0^0)$, and from (B.111) and (B.112), where

$$\phi_1{}^* \equiv \eta_1{}^* \equiv \min_L \left\{ \frac{\partial \psi_1}{\partial m^*} \frac{m^*}{\psi_1}, \ldots, \frac{\partial \psi_{n^*}}{\partial m^*} \frac{m^*}{\psi_{n^*}}, \frac{\partial q_{n^*+1}}{\partial m^*} \frac{m^*}{q_{n^*+1}}, \ldots, \frac{\partial q_n}{\partial m^*} \frac{m^*}{q_n} \right\}$$

(B.117)

$$\phi_2{}^* \equiv \eta_2{}^* \equiv \max_L \left\{ \frac{\partial \psi_1}{\partial m^*} \frac{m^*}{\psi_1}, \ldots, \frac{\partial \psi_{n^*}}{\partial m^*} \frac{m^*}{\psi_{n^*}}, \frac{\partial q_{n^*+1}}{\partial m^*} \frac{m^*}{q_{n^*+1}}, \ldots, \frac{\partial q_n}{\partial m^*} \frac{m^*}{q_n} \right\}$$

(B.118)

That is, the results associated with (B.96) through (B.99) hold for the cases where some markets are affected by changes in quantity restrictions and other markets are affected by price changes.

Again in this case, as in the earlier case of Section B.10, these results are not as comforting as the Willig results for the pure consumption case since the bounds defined by (B.117) and (B.118) may be quite wide; they include now not only income elasticities of goods sold and goods purchased but also price flexibilities of income with respect to both goods sold and goods purchased. Nevertheless, the approach of (B.64) through (B.68) is applicable and can lead to much narrower error bounds on the same surplus measure if variation of income elasticities and price flexibilities of income is not great for individual commodities. Thus, in general, one can avoid an error in measurement of more than about 5 percent for $\sum_{i=1}^{n} \Delta S_i$ as long as $|\eta^* s^*/2| \leq 0.05$ for all unrestricted goods with changing price and $|\phi^* s^*/2| \leq 0.05$ for all restricted goods with changing restrictions.

B.12 AGGREGATION OF WILLINGNESS TO PAY IN CONSUMER DEMAND AND RESOURCE SUPPLY

The purpose of this section is to briefly formalize the technical aspects of the argument that the area behind a market consumer demand curve or a market consumer resource supply curve can serve as an approximate welfare measure in the context of the willingness-to-pay approach. Following the approach set forth by Willig,[65] suppose that bounds similar to (B.87) and (B.88) are derived for each of J consumers for a particular price change from $p^0 = (p_0{}^0, \ldots, p_n{}^0)$ to $p^1 = (p_0{}^0, \ldots, p_{i-1}^0, p_i{}^1, p_{i+1}^0, \ldots, p_n{}^0)$,

$$\epsilon_{2j}{}^{c^*} \geq \frac{\Delta S_{ij} - C_j}{|\Delta S_{ij}|} \geq \epsilon_{1j}{}^{c^*}$$

(B.119)

---

[65]Robert Willig, *Consumer's Surplus: A Rigorous Cookbook,* Technical Report No. 98, Institute for Mathematical Studies in the Social Sciences (Stanford, Calif.: Stanford University Press, 1973).

$$\epsilon_{2j}^{e^\circ} \geq \frac{E_j - \Delta S_{ij}}{|\Delta S_{ij}|} \geq \epsilon_{1j}^{e^\circ} \tag{B.120}$$

where the j subscripts denote pertinence to consumer $j, j = 1, \ldots, J$. Since the market demand (supply) curve under competition, holding all other prices constant, can be regarded as a horizontal summation of individual demand (supply) curves, it follows immediately that the area behind the market demand (supply) curve is the summation of areas behind individual demand (supply) curves over all individuals. Hence, the change in area behind the market demand (supply) curve associated with any particular price change, ΔS_i, is the sum of changes in areas behind individual demand (supply) curves, that is,

$$\Delta S_i = \sum_{j=1}^{J} \Delta S_{ij}$$

Also, the willingness to pay of a group of individuals is the simple summation of individuals' willingness to pay (excluding possibilities of externalities). Hence, error bounds on changes in market surplus as a measure of compensating variation, C, or equivalent variation, E, for a group of individuals may be easily derived from (B.119) and (B.120):

$$\sum_{j=1}^{J} \epsilon_{2j}^{c^\circ}|\Delta S_{ij}| \geq \Delta S_i - C \geq \sum_{j=1}^{J} \epsilon_{1j}^{c^\circ}|\Delta S_{ij}| \tag{B.121}$$

$$\sum_{j=1}^{J} \epsilon_{2j}^{e^\circ}|\Delta S_{ij}| \geq E - \Delta S_i \geq \sum_{j=1}^{J} \epsilon_{1j}^{e^\circ}|\Delta S_{ij}| \tag{B.122}$$

or, converting to percentage terms,

$$\sum_{j=1}^{J} \epsilon_{2j}^{c^\circ}\gamma_j \geq \frac{\Delta S_i - C}{|\Delta S_i|} \geq \sum_{j=1}^{J} \epsilon_{1j}^{c^\circ}\gamma_j \tag{B.123}$$

$$\sum_{j=1}^{J} \epsilon_{2j}^{e^\circ}\gamma_j \geq \frac{E - \Delta S_i}{|\Delta S_i|} \geq \sum_{j=1}^{J} \epsilon_{1j}^{e^\circ}\gamma_j \tag{B.124}$$

where $\gamma_j = |\Delta S_{ij}|/|\Delta S_i|$ (note that $\Delta S_{i1}, \ldots, \Delta S_{iJ}$, and ΔS_i are all of the same sign since all consumers face the same prices). Thus, the percentage error bounds for market-level surplus changes as measures of C or E are simply weighted averages of corresponding individuals' percentage error bounds (note that $0 < \gamma_j < 1$ for $j = 1, \ldots, J$, and $\sum_{j=1}^{J} \gamma_j = 1$). From this it may be concluded that "if consumers are similar, then we can treat their aggregate as one individual."[66] Furthermore, even if consumers are not similar but their individual

---

[66] Ibid., p. 45.

percentage error bounds are not large (or if they are large for only an insignificant set of individuals), the market surplus measure serves a useful purpose
for measuring the compensating and equivalent variation of a single price
change.

Similarly, in the case of a multiple price change from $p^0 = (p_0^0, \ldots, p_n^0)$ to
$p^1 = (p_0^1, \ldots, p_n^1)$, one can easily deduce from (B.96) and (B.97) that

$$\sum_{j=1}^{J} \epsilon_{2j}^{c^\circ} \left| \sum_{i=0}^{n} \Delta S_{ij} \right| \geq \sum_{i=0}^{n} \Delta S_i - C \geq \sum_{j=1}^{J} \epsilon_{1j}^{c^\circ} \left| \sum_{i=0}^{n} \Delta S_{ij} \right|$$

$$\sum_{j=1}^{J} \epsilon_{2j}^{e^\circ} \left| \sum_{i=0}^{n} \Delta S_{ij} \right| \geq E - \sum_{i=0}^{n} \Delta S_i \geq \sum_{j=1}^{J} \epsilon_{1j}^{e^\circ} \left| \sum_{i=0}^{n} \Delta S_{ij} \right|$$

or that

$$\sum_{j=1}^{J} \epsilon_{2j}^{c^\circ} \gamma_j^* \geq \frac{\sum_{i=0}^{n} \Delta S_i - C}{\sum_{j=1}^{J} \left| \sum_{i=0}^{n} \Delta S_{ij} \right|} \geq \sum_{j=1}^{J} \epsilon_{1j}^{c^\circ} \gamma_j^* \qquad \textbf{(B.125)}$$

$$\sum_{j=1}^{J} \epsilon_{2j}^{e^\circ} \gamma_j^* \geq \frac{E - \sum_{i=0}^{n} \Delta S_i}{\sum_{j=1}^{J} \left| \sum_{i=0}^{n} \Delta S_{ij} \right|} \geq \sum_{j=1}^{J} \epsilon_{1j}^{e^\circ} \gamma_j^* \qquad \textbf{(B.126)}$$

where

$$\gamma_j^* = \frac{\left| \sum_{i=0}^{n} \Delta S_{ij} \right|}{\sum_{j=1}^{J} \left| \sum_{i=0}^{n} \Delta S_{ij} \right|}$$

Thus, if surpluses associated with consumption and/or resource supply are
useful for measuring compensating and equivalent variations at the individual
level of analysis, they are also reasonable at the market level of analysis. The
results of Willig thus suggest that the error made by using $\sum_{i=0}^{n} \Delta S_i$ as a measure
of compensating or equivalent variation will be no more than about 5 percent of
the sum of absolute surplus changes over all individuals as long as $|\eta_{2j}^* s_j^*/2| \leq$
0.05 for all individuals where $s_j^* = \Sigma_i \Delta S_{ij}/m_j^*$, m_j^* is the jth consumer's initial
exogenous income and η_{2j}^* is the jth consumer's maximum exogenous income

elasticity over all goods for which prices change in the range of price changes considered. Alternatively, using the result at the end of Section B.10, the same statement applies for endogenous income elasticities and endogenous initial income if both endogenous and exogenous income have the same marginal effects on consumption/resource supply decisions.

In the case that percentage errors associated with raw surpluses are too great or if additional precision is desired, the kinds of modifications in (B.98) and (B.99) can also be considered. For example, consider a single price change and suppose that $\underline{\eta s}$ and $\overline{\eta s}$ are the minimum and maximum values, respectively, that $\eta_j^*|s_j^*|$ can take over all consumers in the domain of price changes considered, that is,

$$\underline{\eta s} = \min_j \eta_{1j}^*|s_j^*| \tag{B.127}$$

$$\overline{\eta s} = \max_j \eta_{2j}^*|s_j^*| \tag{B.128}$$

where η_{1j}^* is the minimum exogenous income elasticity defined analogously to η_{2j}^* above. Using the approximation in (B.49) implies that

$$\min_j \epsilon_{1j}^{c°} \doteq \hat{\epsilon}_1^* \doteq \min_j \epsilon_{1j}^{e°} \tag{B.129}$$

$$\max_j \epsilon_{2j}^{c°} \doteq \hat{\epsilon}_2^* \doteq \max_j \epsilon_{2j}^{e°} \tag{B.130}$$

where $\hat{\epsilon}_1^* \equiv \underline{\eta s}/2$ and $\epsilon_2^* \equiv \overline{\eta s}/2$. Substituting into (B.123) and (B.124) then suggests that

$$\hat{\epsilon}_2^* \sum_{j=1}^{J} \gamma_j \geq \frac{\Delta S_i - C}{|\Delta S_i|} \geq \hat{\epsilon}_1^* \sum_{j=1}^{J} \gamma_j$$

$$\hat{\epsilon}_2^* \sum_{j=1}^{J} \gamma_j \geq \frac{E - \Delta S_i}{|\Delta S_i|} \geq \hat{\epsilon}_2^* \sum_{j=1}^{J} \gamma_j$$

Multiplying by $|\Delta S_i| \Big/ \sum_{j=1}^{J} \gamma_j$ thus verifies that $\hat{\epsilon}_1^*$ and $\hat{\epsilon}_2^*$ serve as approximate lower and upper bounds, respectively, on both $(\Delta S_i - C)/|\Delta S_i|$ and $(E - \Delta S_i)/|\Delta S_i|$ (note that $|\Delta S_i| = \sum_{j=1}^{J} |\Delta S_{ij}|$ since all ΔS_{ij} are of the same sign).

As suggested in Section B.5, these bounds can be fairly tight even though the magnitude of error may be sizable. Hence, improved estimates in such cases can be obtained following the approach in (B.89) to (B.93), that is, estimating compensating variation by

$$\bar{C}^* = \Delta S_i - \hat{\bar{\epsilon}}^* |\Delta S_i| \tag{B.131}$$

and equivalent variation by

$$\bar{E}^* = \Delta S_i + \hat{\bar{\epsilon}}^* |\Delta S_i| \tag{B.132}$$

where $\hat{\bar{\epsilon}}^* = (\hat{\epsilon}_1^* + \hat{\epsilon}_2^*)/2$. The associated approximate percentage error bounds would be $\pm (\hat{\epsilon}_1^* - \hat{\epsilon}_2^*)/2$. Using this procedure, one can thus avoid more than about 2 percent error if $|\eta_{2j}^* s_j^*/2| \le 0.08$ and exogenous income elasticities for individual consumers change by less than 50 percent in the domain of price changes under consideration.

Unfortunately, the construction of improved estimates becomes somewhat more cumbersome in the multiple-price-change case. To examine this possibility, suppose that $\hat{\epsilon}_1^*$ and $\hat{\epsilon}_2^*$ are defined as in equations (B.127) to (B.130) where minimums and maximums are also taken with respect to the set of goods for which prices change. Then substitution into (B.125) and (B.126) suggests in an analogous manner that $\hat{\epsilon}_1^*$ and $\hat{\epsilon}_2^*$ serve as approximate lower and upper bounds, respectively, on

$$\frac{\displaystyle\sum_{i=0}^{n} \Delta S_i - C}{\left| \displaystyle\sum_{j=1}^{J} \left| \displaystyle\sum_{i=0}^{n} \Delta S_{ij} \right| \right.}$$

and

$$\frac{E - \displaystyle\sum_{i=0}^{n} \Delta S_i}{\left| \displaystyle\sum_{j=1}^{J} \left| \displaystyle\sum_{i=0}^{n} \Delta S_{ij} \right| \right.}$$

In this case, however, modified estimates similar to (B.131) and (B.132) cannot be defined solely in terms of market-level measurements. That is, these approximate bounds would suggest modified estimates,

$$\sum_{i=0}^{n} \Delta S_i - \hat{\bar{\epsilon}}^* \sum_{j=1}^{J} \left| \sum_{i=0}^{n} \Delta S_{ij} \right|$$

$$\sum_{i=0}^{n} \Delta S_i + \hat{\bar{\epsilon}}^* \sum_{j=1}^{J} \left| \sum_{i=0}^{n} \Delta S_{ij} \right|$$

for compensating and equivalent variation, respectively. But ΔS_{ij} can be calculated only from information about individual consumers' demand curves. Only in the case that $\sum_{i=0}^{n} \Delta S_{ij}$ is of the same sign for all individuals does one find that

$$\left| \sum_{i=0}^{n} \Delta S_i \right| = \sum_{j=1}^{J} \left| \sum_{i=0}^{n} \Delta S_{ij} \right|$$

in which case the modified estimates (relying only on market surplus measurements),

$$\bar{C}^* = \sum_{i=0}^{n} \Delta S_i - \hat{\bar{\epsilon}}^* \left| \sum_{i=0}^{n} \Delta S_i \right| \tag{B.133}$$

$$\bar{E}^* = \sum_{i=0}^{n} \Delta S_i - \hat{\bar{\epsilon}}^* \left| \sum_{i=0}^{n} \Delta S_i \right| \tag{B.134}$$

with associated approximate error bounds of $\pm (\hat{\epsilon}_1^* - \hat{\epsilon}_2^*)/2$ are clearly suggested. If such is the case, however, application of arguments in Sections B.5 and B.10 again imply that more than about 2 percent error can be avoided even in the multiple-price-change case if $|\eta_{2j}^* s_j^*/2| \leq 0.08$ for $j = 1, \ldots, J$ and exogenous income elasticity varies by less than 50 percent among consumers and goods for which prices change. By application of the algorithm in (B.64) through (B.68), this requirement can be relaxed even further; that is, bounds can be computed, in effect, individually for each segment of the overall path in which exogenous income elasticities can be bounded. Also, if the marginal effects of endogenous and exogenous income on consumer decisions are the same, all requirements related to exogenous income above can be replaced by analogous requirements related to endogenous income or total income.

An important implication of the foregoing results is that disaggregation of consumer groups in measuring or estimating demand is sometimes desirable. That is, the tighter bounds associated with (B.133) and (B.134) are applicable only when all consumers in the relevant group have welfare effects in the same direction. The modifications in (B.133) and (B.134) may also lead to improvements over using raw surplus changes in most practical problems when such is not the case, but this is not necessarily so since the appropriate correction factor, $\hat{\bar{\epsilon}}^* \sum_{j=1}^{J} \left| \sum_{i=0}^{n} \Delta S_{ij} \right|$, may be near zero when surplus gains for some individuals offset the surplus losses for others. Thus, it behooves the practitioner of applied welfare economics to attempt measurement or estimation of demand within groups that are affected in the same direction by the set of wage–price changes under consideration, not only to increase distributional information available for policymaking purposes but also to increase accuracy. It is also intuitively clear at this point that any further possible disaggregation according to income elasticities is desirable and leads to smaller error bounds on the aggregate welfare effect.

B.13   DIRECT ESTIMATION OF COMPENSATING AND EQUIVALENT VARIATION

In some problems, direct estimation of compensating or equivalent variation is desirable because the Willig bounds are wider than satisfactory. There are two basic approaches to direct estimation of the compensating and equivalent variations. The first approach assumes that supply and demand equations are specified arbitrarily, in which case solution of a system of partial differential equations is necessary. The second approach involves deriving supply and demand specifications in terms of parameters of an underlying direct or indirect utility specification. Then, upon estimation of supplies and demands, the parameter estimates can be used in direct calculation of welfare effects based on the utility specification. With the latter of these approaches, supply and demand equations can be specified making exact calculations (aside from statistical errors in estimation) of the compensating and equivalent variations quite simple.

To obtain estimates of the willingness-to-pay measures directly when ordinary supply and demand equations are specified arbitrarily, one can substitute the pseudo-expenditure function m^* into estimates of ordinary supply and demand equations represented by $q_j(p, m^*)$, $j = 1, \ldots, n$, obtaining[67]

$$\bar{q}_j(p, \bar{U}) \equiv q_j[p, m^*(p, \bar{U})]$$

which is an identity by definition. Then equations such as (B.30) and (B.82) can be written as

$$\frac{\partial m^*(p, \bar{U})}{\partial p_j} = q_j[p, m^*(p, \bar{U})], \qquad j = 0, \ldots, n \qquad \textbf{(B.135)}$$

This system of partial differential equations can, in principle, be solved for the expenditure function as a function of price, given utility level $\bar{U}$. Considering a change in prices and exogenous income from (p^0, m_0^*) to (p^1, m_1^*) which leads to a change in (maximum) utility from U_0 to U_1, the Hicksian equivalent variation is calculated according to (B.83), where $m^*(p, U_1)$ is obtained by solving (B.135) with the boundary condition, $m^*(p^1, U_1) = m_1^*$; the Hicksian

---

[67] This relationship follows from duality between the standard utility-maximization problem and the expenditure-minimization problem, for example, in (B.81).

compensating variation is obtained using (B.84), where $m^*(p, U_0)$ is the solution of (B.135) corresponding to the boundary condition, $m^*(p^0, U_0) = m_0^*$. Unfortunately, however, it is often not possible to find an exact or analytic solution of (B.135), even with common functional properties such as linearity or log linearity.[68] Numerical methods are thus often necessary to obtain even approximate solutions of (B.135) for purposes of calculating compensating and equivalent variation.

Aside from the rather difficult computational problems encountered with this approach, another serious empirical problem must also be considered. That is, if the demand and supply equations are specified arbitrarily, they may not relate to a common underlying consumer utility-maximization problem. As a result, when welfare effects are calculated based on the solution of the differential equations, the estimated effects may be path dependent even though in theory they should be path independent. This path dependence, as in the producer case, can be avoided by ensuring that all supply and demand specifications relate to a common underlying consumer choice problem. But if this is done by means of specifying an underlying consumer utility-maximization problem, estimation of the parameters of supplies and demands can allow direct calculation of welfare effects in the context of the underlying utility specification.

In cases where demand and supply specifications are derived from an underlying utility specification, either a primal or dual approach can be used. With the primal approach, one begins by specifying a direct utility function with reasonable properties (e.g., continuous, nondecreasing, and quasiconcave in consumption goods, including items such as leisure). Then specifications for demands (and supplies) can be derived through maximization with fixed prices and (exogenous) income. Finally, once demands and supplies are estimated, the estimated parameters can be substituted into the utility specification for purposes of calculating compensating or equivalent variation.

To exemplify this approach, consider a simplistic pure consumer case with two goods where the direct utility function is a simple Cobb–Douglas form,

$$\max U(q_1, q_2) = A q_1^{\alpha_1} q_2^{\alpha_2}, \qquad 0 < \alpha_i < 1; i = 1, 2 \tag{B.136}$$

subject to

$$p_1 q_1 + p_2 q_2 = m$$

---

[68]Hause presents a general solution for the pure consumer case with linearity when income effects are zero, but that is the special case where compensated and ordinary demand curves coincide; hence, use of surplus measures is equivalent to use of compensating and equivalent variations. Analytic solutions are also presented for linearity and log linearity in the case with zero cross-price effects, but this is also a rather restrictive case; see John C. Hause, "The Theory of Welfare Cost Measurement," *Journal of Political Economy,* Vol. 83 (December 1975), pp. 1154, 1178.

Substituting for q_2 in $U(q_1, q_2)$ using the constraint and applying calculus yields from the first-order condition [for $\tilde{\alpha}_1 \equiv \alpha_1/(\alpha_1 + \alpha_2)$]

$$q_1(p, m) = \frac{\alpha_1}{\alpha_1 + \alpha_2} \frac{m}{p_1} \equiv \tilde{\alpha}_1 \frac{m}{p_1} \qquad (\text{B.137})$$

and substituting (B.137) into the constraint yields [for $\tilde{\alpha}_2 \equiv \alpha_2/(\alpha_1 + \alpha_2)$]

$$q_2(p, m) = \frac{\alpha_2}{\alpha_1 + \alpha_2} \frac{m}{p_2} \equiv \tilde{\alpha}_2 \frac{m}{p_2} \qquad (\text{B.138})$$

Thus, (B.137) and (B.138) give ordinary Marshallian demand specifications that necessarily relate to a common underlying consumer choice problem. These demand equations can then be estimated using data on prices, quantities, and income. In this special, overly simplified case, independent estimation of demands is possible because separate estimation cannot possibly yield parameter estimates for $\tilde{\alpha}_1$ and $\tilde{\alpha}_2$ which are inconsistent with one another. However, in general, constraints may be required across equations in estimation so that all estimated equations correspond to a unique choice of the parameters involved.

To evaluate compensating or equivalent variation in this case, one can substitute (B.137) and (B.138) into $U(q_1, q_2)$ in (B.136), obtaining the indirect utility function,

$$V = V(p, m) = U\left(\tilde{\alpha}_1 \frac{m}{p_1}, \tilde{\alpha}_2 \frac{m}{p_2}\right) = A\left(\frac{\alpha_1}{\alpha_1 + \alpha_2}\right)^{\alpha_1}\left(\frac{\alpha_2}{\alpha_1 + \alpha_2}\right)^{\alpha_2}\left(\frac{m}{p_1}\right)^{\alpha_1}\left(\frac{m}{p_2}\right)^{\alpha_2} \qquad (\text{B.139})$$

Then the compensating variation of a price–income change from (p^0, m_0) to (p^1, m_1) can be found by solving the equation

$$V(p^1, m_1 - C) = V(p^0, m_0) \qquad (\text{B.140})$$

for C which yields

$$C = m_1 - \left(\frac{p_1{}^1}{p_1{}^0}\right)^{\tilde{\alpha}_1}\left(\frac{p_2{}^1}{p_2{}^0}\right)^{\tilde{\alpha}_2} m_0$$

Thus, the compensating variation can be calculated without error aside from the usual problems of errors in estimating the parameters of demand in (B.137) and (B.138). Similarly, an exact equation for equivalent variation is obtained by solving the equation

$$V(p^1, m_1) = V(p^0, m_0 + E) \qquad (\text{B.141})$$

in which case similar comments apply.

Turning to the dual approach to specification of supplies and demands, the rationale is again much like that of the dual approach for producers in Section A.5. That is, because a duality exists between direct and indirect utility functions, it is no more arbitrary to specify a functional form for indirect utility than for direct utility as long as certain regularity conditions are satisfied which guarantee that an arbitrarily specified indirect utility function corresponds to some reasonable underlying utility function.[69] Once an indirect utility function is specified, the implied demands and supplies can be derived by application of Roy's identity (see Section B.1). Since this process involves simple differentiation rather than solution of a maximization problem as when one starts from a direct utility specification, greater flexibility can be attained in modeling consumer behavior. In particular, one can attain at least a second-order local approximation to any arbitrary, twice-differentiable indirect utility function using common forms, and thus no a priori constraints are placed on the various price and income elasticities at a base point.[70] Such an approximation is not

---

[69]These regularity conditions (corresponding to continuous, nondecreasing, quasiconcave direct utility) imply that the indirect utility function taken as a function of normalized prices, $p_i/m, i = 1, \ldots, n$, is continuous, nonincreasing, and quasi-convex; see Varian, *Macroeconomic Analysis*, or Blackorby, Primont, and Russell, *Duality*. Similar conditions are appropriate for the consumer/resource owner problem, where m is replaced by m^* and the set of commodities is expanded to include resources sold as well as quantities consumed.

[70]Some of the common functional forms used for an indirect utility function are the translog form,

$$V(p, m) = \exp\left[\alpha_0 + \sum_{i=1}^{n} \alpha_i \ln\left(\frac{p_i}{m}\right)\right.$$
$$\left. + \sum_{i=1}^{n} \sum_{j=1}^{n} \beta_{ij} \ln\left(\frac{p_i}{m}\right) \ln\left(\frac{p_j}{m}\right), \qquad \beta_{ij} = \beta_{ji}\right.$$

the generalized Leontief form,

$$V(p, m) = \alpha_0 + \sum_{i=1}^{n} \alpha_i \ln\left(\frac{p_i}{m}\right)$$
$$+ \sum_{i=1}^{n} \sum_{j=1}^{n} \beta_{ij} \left(\frac{p_i}{m}\right)^{1/2} \left(\frac{p_j}{m}\right)^{1/2}, \qquad \beta_{ij} = \beta_{ji}, \sum_{i=1}^{n} \alpha_i = 0$$

the generalized Cobb–Douglas form,

$$V(p, m) = \alpha_0 + \sum_{i=1}^{n} \alpha_i \ln\left(\frac{p_i}{m}\right)$$
$$+ \prod_{i=1}^{n} \prod_{j=1}^{n} \left(\frac{p_i}{2m} + \frac{p_j}{2m}\right)^{\beta_{ij}}, \qquad \beta_{ij} = \beta_{ji}$$

and the quadratic mean of order ρ form,

$$V(p, m) = \left[\sum_{i=1}^{n} \alpha_i \left(\frac{p_i}{m}\right)^{\rho/2} + \sum_{i=1}^{n} \sum_{j=1}^{n} \beta_{ij} \left(\frac{p_i}{m}\right)^{\rho/2} \left(\frac{p_j}{m}\right)^{\rho/2}\right]^{1/\rho}, \qquad \beta_{ij} = \beta_{ji}$$

In each case the parameter space can be constrained so that the appropriate regularity conditions hold; for further discussion, see Blackorby, Primont, and Russell, *Duality*.

(Footnote continued on pg. 416)

possible from a practical point of view with the direct approach because of the complexity of solving a maximization problem.

To exemplify the dual approach, suppose that one arbitrarily specifies an indirect utility function for a simple, two-good, pure consumer case as

$$V = V(p, m) = \tilde{A}\left(\frac{m}{p_1}\right)^{\alpha_1}\left(\frac{m}{p_2}\right)^{\alpha_2} \tag{B.142}$$

In this case,

$$\frac{\partial V}{\partial p_i} = -\alpha_i \tilde{A}\left(\frac{m}{p_1}\right)^{\alpha_1}\left(\frac{m}{p_2}\right)^{\alpha_2}\frac{1}{p_i}, \quad i = 1, 2$$

and

$$\frac{\partial V}{\partial m} = (\alpha_1 + \alpha_2)\,\tilde{A}\left(\frac{m}{p_1}\right)^{\alpha_1}\left(\frac{m}{p_2}\right)^{\alpha_2}\frac{1}{m}$$

so that use of Roy's identity implies that

$$q_i(p, m) = -\frac{\partial V/\partial p_i}{\partial V/\partial m} = \frac{\alpha_i}{\alpha_1 + \alpha_2}\frac{m}{p_i} \equiv \tilde{\alpha}_i\frac{m}{p_i}, \quad i = 1, 2 \tag{B.143}$$

Thus, the resulting demands are identical to those in (B.137) and (B.138), which verifies that they relate to a common underlying consumer choice problem. Upon estimation of the demand equations in (B.143), economic welfare analysis can proceed as in the direct utility example. The results are identical since (B.142) and (B.139) are identical functions when

$$\tilde{A} = A\left(\frac{\alpha_1}{\alpha_1 + \alpha_2}\right)^{\alpha_1}\left(\frac{\alpha_2}{\alpha_1 + \alpha_2}\right)^{\alpha_2}$$

and the welfare quantities do not depend on $\tilde{A}$. That is, estimates of the parameters of demands in (B.143) can be used to solve for the compensating variation C in (B.140) or the equivalent variation E in (B.141). Thus, errors in calculating the compensating and equivalent variations (aside from statistical errors in estimating demands) can be avoided with an approach that also yields the uniqueness of welfare estimates suggested by theory and that possesses the empirical flexibility advantages of the dual approach.

For an example of an application involving estimation of the first three of these forms, see E. R. Berndt, M. N. Darrough, and W. E. Diewert, "Flexible Functional Forms and Expenditure Distributions: An Application to Canadian Consumer Demand Functions," *International Economic Review*, Vol. 18, No. 3 (October 1977), pp. 651–75.

Appendix C

The Role of Producer Factor Fixity and Consumer Durables in Temporal Aggregation and Intertemporal Economic Welfare Analysis

This appendix provides a mathematical justification of the results exemplified in Section 4.7 and then introduces more general considerations which form the basis for dynamic economic welfare analysis for both producers and consumers. That is, concepts of dynamic economic welfare analysis are first developed for the special case where all future price changes are anticipated with certainty or, at least, where the producer believes this to be so. Since this assumption is unreasonable for many dynamic economic welfare analyses, however, the framework is generalized for the case where prices and optimal decisions in later time periods are subjectively random in the current decision-making period. The latter framework generalizes easily to handle the dynamic case of consumer decision making associated with durable purchases.

C.1 THE PRODUCER CASE WITH CERTAIN ANTICIPATED PRICES OR NAIVE PRICE EXPECTATIONS

The case where the producing firm believes its anticipations with certainty is worth considering as a special case for several reasons. First, in some industries, future price changes may be well anticipated under alternative policies, particularly where the policies affect prices directly. Second, futures markets may exist so that future prices can be essentially locked in or guaranteed. Third, this case is general enough to capture the generality allowed in some of the more popular empirical models. Finally, the limited generality of this case offers a useful intermediate step in moving to an understanding of the more general case in Section C.2.

Consider a single-product competitive firm with production function at time t given by

$$q_t = q_t(x_t, z_{t-1}^1, z_{t-2}^2, \ldots, z_{t-N}^N)$$

where x_t is a current variable input and z_t^n is the amount of fixed input n planned at time t, $n = 1, \ldots, N$; thus, z_t^1 must be planned one period in advance, z_t^2 must be planned two periods in advance, and so on. For example, in agricultural production a factor such as land is, for all intents and purposes, fixed after commencement of the growing season; but fertilizer may be varied at a later point in the growing season, and harvesting labor may be determined at the time of harvest. For simplicity of notation, only one input is included corresponding to each planning horizon in which a decision affecting period t must be made, but others could also be included without affecting the results below. As usual, suppose that q_t is increasing, concave, and second-order differentiable in all inputs.

In attempting to determine the appropriate levels of investments to undertake in planning production for future periods, as well as to determine the appropriate production decisions for the current period, a firm maximizing its discounted stream of profits or its discounted future wealth will maximize[1]

$$\Pi_t^T = \sum_{k=t}^{T} \pi_t^k \tag{C.1}$$

where

$$\pi_t^k = \delta^{k-t} p_k q_k - \delta^{k-t} w_k x_k - \sum_{n=1}^{k-t} \delta^{k-t-n} v_{k-n}^n z_{k-n}^n \tag{C.2}$$

---

[1]Note that, in this simple problem, current decisions have no direct or indirect effects on profits beyond period T; thus, the $T - t + 1$ period planning horizon (including periods t and T) is sufficient in maximizing profits over any longer life of the firm or wealth at any period beyond period T.

(note that $\sum_{n=1}^{0} y_t$ is defined to be zero for any series $\{y_t\}$ for simplicity of notation). In this context, p_t is the price of output in period t, w_t is the price of the variable input x_t in period t, v_t^n is the price of fixed input z_t^n in period t, δ is a discounting factor as discussed in Chapter 13, Π_t^T represents a $(T - t + 1)$-period quasi-rent (revenues minus costs excluding costs that have already been incurred before period t), and π_t^k represents quasi-rent at period k, where all inputs not yet fixed before period t are considered variable.

Because of the special separable structure of this problem (inputs affecting output in one period do not affect output in any other period), one can consider independent maximization of π_t^k for $k = t, \ldots, T$, for which first-order conditions are

$$\frac{\partial \pi_t^k}{\partial x_k} = \delta^{k-t}\left[p_k \frac{\partial q_k}{\partial x_k} - w_k \right] = 0 \tag{C.3}$$

$$\frac{\partial \pi_t^k}{\partial z_{k-n}^n} = \delta^{k-t} p_k \frac{\partial q_k}{\partial z_{k-n}^n} - \delta^{k-t-n} v_{k-n}^n = 0, \qquad n = 1, \ldots, k - t \tag{C.4}$$

which can be solved in principle for input demands and output supply

$$x_k = \tilde{x}_t^k(p_k, w_k, v_t^k, \bar{z}_t^k)$$
$$z_{k-n}^n = \tilde{z}_{k-n}^{n,t}(p_k, w_k, v_t^k, \bar{z}_t^k), \qquad n = 1, \ldots, k - t$$
$$q_k = \tilde{q}_t^k(p_k, w_k, v_t^k, \bar{z}_t^k) \equiv q_k(\tilde{x}_t^k, \tilde{z}_{k-1}^{1,t}, \ldots, \tilde{z}_t^{k-t,t}, \bar{z}_t^k)$$

where $v_t^k = (v_{k-1}^1, \ldots, v_t^{k-t})$ is a vector of fixed input prices affecting π_t^k, and $\bar{z}_t^k = (z_{t-1}^{k-t+1}, z_{t-2}^{k-t+2}, \ldots, z_{t-N}^N)$ is a vector of fixed input decisions affecting q_k which were made prior to time t.

In this context, one can define quasi-rent functions corresponding to (C.1) and (C.2):

$$\tilde{\Pi}_t^T = \sum_{k=t}^{T} \tilde{\pi}_t^k$$

and

$$\tilde{\pi}_t^k = \delta^{k-t} p_k \tilde{q}_t^k - \delta^{k-t} w_k \tilde{x}_t^k - \sum_{n=1}^{k-t} \delta^{k-t-n} v_{k-n}^n \tilde{z}_{k-n}^{n,t}$$

for which the envelope theorem [or (C.3) and (C.4)] implies that

$$\frac{\partial \tilde{\Pi}_t^T}{\partial p_k} = \frac{\partial \tilde{\pi}_t^k}{\partial p_k} = \delta^{k-t} \tilde{q}_t^k \tag{C.5}$$

$$\frac{\partial \tilde{\Pi}_t^T}{\partial w_k} = \frac{\partial \tilde{\pi}_t^k}{\partial w_k} = -\delta^{k-t} \tilde{x}_t^k \tag{C.6}$$

Now suppose that the current variable input is an essential input for production in the sense that one can define shutdown prices

$$\bar{p}_t^k = \max\{\bar{p}_k;\, \tilde{q}_t^k(\bar{p}_k, w_k, v_t^k, \bar{z}_t^k) = 0\}, \quad k = t, \ldots, T \tag{C.7}$$
$$\bar{w}_t^k = \min\{\bar{w}_k;\, \tilde{x}_t^k(p_k, \bar{w}_k, v_t^k, \bar{z}_t^k) = 0\}, \quad k = t, \ldots, T \tag{C.8}$$

where presumably $\tilde{q}_t^k = \tilde{x}_t^k = \bar{z}_{k-1}^{1,t} = \cdots = \bar{z}_t^{k-t,t} = 0$ in any case where at period t a production shutdown is planned for period k.

Using (C.5) and (C.7), one finds that

$$\pi_t^k = \delta^{k-t} \int_{\bar{p}_t^k}^{p_k} \tilde{q}_t^k \, dp_k = \delta^{k-t} \bar{P}_t^k$$

where $\bar{P}_t^k$ is the producer surplus associated with a one-period supply curve for a $(k - t + 1)$-period length of run [i.e., a one-period supply curve with $(k - t + 1)$-period foresight]. From this result, one finds that the welfare effect on a firm of changing the sequence of (all) prices over time periods $t, \ldots, T$ is

$$\Delta\Pi_t^T = \sum_{k=t}^T \Delta\bar{\pi}_t^k = \sum_{k=t}^T \delta^{k-t} \Delta\bar{P}_t^k \tag{C.9}$$

which verifies one of the results discussed in Section 4.7 (where $\delta = 1$ is assumed). In other words, under the assumptions of this section, *the welfare effect of any change on a firm is given by the discounted sum of producer surplus changes associated with respective supply curves of all relevant lengths of run* (as viewed from the initial point in time). Similarly, one finds, using (C.6) and (C.8), that

$$\pi_t^k = \delta^{k-t} \int_{w_k}^{\bar{w}_t^k} \tilde{x}_t^k \, dw_k = \delta^{k-t} \bar{C}_t^k$$

where $\bar{C}_t^k$ is the consumer surplus associated with the one-period variable input-derived demand curve for a $(k - t + 1)$-period length of run [that is, a $k - t + 1)$-period foresight]. From this result, the welfare effects of any general change in the temporal sequence of (output or input) prices facing a firm can also be measured by

$$\Delta\Pi_t^T = \sum_{k=t}^T \Delta\pi_t^k = \sum_{k=t}^T \delta^{k-t} \Delta\bar{C}_t^k \tag{C.10}$$

In other words, under the assumptions of this section, *the welfare effect of any change on a firm is given by the discounted sum of consumer surplus changes associated with variable input demand curves for a necessary input of all relevant lengths of run* (as viewed from the initial point in time).

Next, consider the alternative method of measurement suggested in Section

4.7. To do this, note that the condition in (C.3) can be solved in principle for (short-run) variable input demands as a function of output price, variable input price, and all fixed input quantities,

$$x_k = \hat{x}_k(p_k, w_k, z_k) \tag{C.11}$$

where $z_k = (z_{k-1}^1, \ldots, z_{k-N}^N)$. Substitution into the production function yields short-run (one-period length of run) supply relationships,

$$q_k = \hat{q}_k(p_k, w_k, z_k) \equiv q_k(\hat{x}_k, z_k) \tag{C.12}$$

Using (C.11) and (C.12), one can define short-run quasi-rent functions

$$\hat{\pi}_k = p_k \hat{q}_k - w_k \hat{x}_k$$

for which the envelope theorem [or use of (C.3)] implies that

$$\frac{\partial \hat{\pi}_k}{\partial p_k} = \hat{q}_k$$

$$\frac{\partial \hat{\pi}_k}{\partial w_k} = -\hat{x}_k$$

Again, assuming that the current variable input is an essential input for production regardless of earlier investment, one can define shutdown prices

$$\hat{p}_k = \max\{\bar{p}_k; \hat{q}_k(\bar{p}_k, w_k, z_k) = 0\}, \quad k = t, \ldots, T$$
$$\hat{w}_k = \min\{\bar{w}_k; \hat{x}_k(p_k, \bar{w}_k, z_k) = 0\}, \quad k = t, \ldots, T$$

which depend on levels of all fixed inputs affecting the relevant production period (as reflected by z_k). In this context, one finds that

$$\hat{\pi}_k = \int_{\hat{p}_k}^{p_k} \hat{q}_k \, dp_k = P_k \tag{C.13}$$

$$= \int_{w_k}^{\hat{w}_k} \hat{x}_k \, dw_k = C_k \tag{C.14}$$

where P_k and C_k are the producer and consumer surpluses associated with the short-run supply and variable input demand curves in period k, respectively; note that each depends on fixed input levels represented in z_k. Returning to (C.2) and using (C.13) and (C.14) thus yields

$$\pi_t^{\ k} = \delta^{k-t}\hat{\pi}_k - \sum_{n=1}^{k-t} \delta^{k-t-n} v_{k-n}^{\ n} z_{k-n}^{\ n}$$

$$= \delta^{k-t} P_k - \sum_{n=1}^{k-t} \delta^{k-t-n} I_{k-n}^{\ k}$$

$$= \delta^{k-t} C_k - \sum_{n=1}^{k-t} \delta^{k-t-n} I_{k-n}^{\ k}$$

so that the effect of any general change in the temporal sequence of (output or input) prices facing a firm can be measured by

$$\Delta\Pi_t^{\ T} = \sum_{k=t}^{T} \delta^{k-t} \Delta P_k - \sum_{k=t}^{T} \sum_{n=1}^{k-t} \delta^{k-t-n} \Delta I_{k-n}^{\ k} \tag{C.15}$$

$$= \sum_{k=t}^{T} \delta^{k-t} \Delta C_k - \sum_{k=1}^{T} \sum_{n=1}^{k-t} \delta^{k-t-n} \Delta I_{k-n}^{\ k} \tag{C.16}$$

where $I_{k-n}^{\ k} = v_{k-n}^{\ n} z_{k-n}^{\ n}$ represents investment undertaken at time $k - n$ in planning for production in period k. The result in (C.15) thus verifies and generalizes the graphical analysis of Section 4.7 which shows that *the welfare effect of any change affecting a firm over time can be measured by the (discounted) sum of changes in short-run producer surpluses minus the (discounted) sum of changes in investments.* The result in (C.16) shows that this result also holds for the demand side; namely, *the welfare effect in terms of willingness to pay of any change affecting a firm over time can be measured by the discounted sum of changes in short-run consumer surpluses associated with a necessary variable input minus the discounted sum of changes in investments.*

By comparison with (C.9) and (C.10), the advantages of the results in (C.15) and (C.16) are that they can be generalized easily for the case where the production function is not temporally separable (where each fixed input decision may affect output over several periods, including the current time period). However, the results in (C.9) and (C.10) are relatively more useful when the production function is temporally separable since changes in investments induced by a policy change may be observable only in an ex post sense; thus, direct use of (C.15) or (C.16) for ex ante policy analysis may not be feasible.

Interestingly, however, comparison of the results in, say, (C.9) and (C.15) yields a method for estimating changes in investment induced by a policy change affecting the temporal sequence of output prices when the production function is temporally separable even though quantities of fixed inputs and/or their prices are unobservable. To see this, note from (C.9) and (C.15) that

$$\sum_{k=t}^{T} \delta^{k-t}\Delta\tilde{P}_t^{\,k} = \sum_{k=t}^{T} \delta^{k-t}\Delta P_k - \sum_{k=t}^{T}\sum_{n=1}^{k-t} \delta^{k-t-n}I_{k-n}^{\,k}$$

Subtracting from this equation the same equation where T is replaced by $T - 1$ yields

$$\delta^{T-t}\Delta\tilde{P}_t^{\,T} = \delta^{T-t}\Delta P_T - \sum_{n=1}^{T-t} \delta^{T-t-n}\Delta I_{T-n}^{\,T} \tag{C.17}$$

which implies for $T = t + 1$ that

$$\Delta I_t^{\,t+1} = \delta(\Delta P_{t+1} - \Delta\tilde{P}_t^{\,t+1}) \tag{C.18}$$

Advancing (C.18) one period and substituting into (C.17) with $T = t + 2$ further implies that

$$\begin{aligned}
\Delta I_t^{\,t+2} &= \delta^2(\Delta P_{t+2} - \Delta\tilde{P}_t^{\,t+2}) - \delta^2(\Delta P_{t+2} - \Delta\tilde{P}_{t+1}^{\,t+2}) \\
&= \delta^2(\Delta\tilde{P}_{t+1}^{\,t+2} - \Delta P_t^{\,t+2})
\end{aligned} \tag{C.19}$$

Noting that $\Delta P_{t+1} = \Delta\tilde{P}_{t+1}^{\,t+1}$ and comparing (C.18) and (C.19) thus suggests the general result

$$\Delta I_t^{\,k} = \delta^{k-t}(\Delta\tilde{P}_{t+1}^{\,k} - \Delta\tilde{P}_t^{\,k}) \tag{C.20}$$

which can be verified by continuing to substitute results such as (C.18) and (C.19) into (C.17) as T is increased.

From the result in (C.20), one can use a dynamic supply relationship to estimate amounts of investment change by time period resulting from a change in the temporal sequence of output prices over time. Thus, useful information in terms of temporally disaggregated welfare effects as well as the overall effect can be developed. Similar results can also be developed in terms of variable input demand measurements. That is, using (C.10) in (C.16), one can follow the steps in (C.17) through (C.20), simply replacing P's with C's to find

$$\Delta I_t^{\,k} = \delta^{k-t}(\Delta\tilde{C}_{t+1}^{\,k} - \Delta\tilde{C}_t^{\,k}) \tag{C.21}$$

Thus, one can also use dynamic variable input demand equations to estimate temporal effects on investment of a change in the temporal sequence of variable input prices.

An example can suffice to demonstrate how, say, a dynamic supply equation can be used to estimate temporally disaggregated effects on investment. One of the most basic supply models representing the fixity of inputs is the Koyck model, where only a fraction β of the difference in desired production at time t and that planned previously can be made up by an additional year of planning; that is,

$$q_t^k - q_{t-1}^k = \beta(\bar{q}_t^k - q_{t-1}^k) \tag{C.22}$$

where desired production for time k is given by

$$\bar{q}_t^k = a_0 + b_0 p_k \tag{C.23}$$

and q_t^k represents the amount of production for time k planned at period t.[2] Substitution of (C.23) into (C.22) yields

$$q_t^k = a_0\beta + b_0\beta p_k + (1 - \beta)q_{t-1}^k \tag{C.24}$$

Then further substituting (C.24) with $t = k - 1$ into (C.24) with $t = k$, and so on [i.e., solving the difference equation in (C.24)] yields

$$q_t^k = a_t^k + b_t^k p_k \tag{C.25}$$

where

$$a_t^k = a_0\beta \sum_{j=0}^{k-t} (1 - \beta)^j + (1 - \beta)^{k-t+1}q_{t-1}^k$$

$$b_t^k = b_0\beta \sum_{j=0}^{k-t} (1 - \beta)^j$$

Thus, following (C.7),

$$\bar{p}_t^k = - \frac{a_t^k}{b_t^k}$$

and

$$\bar{P}_t^k = \int_{\bar{p}_t^k}^{p_k} (a_t^k + b_t^k p_k)dp_k$$

$$= a_t^k(p_k - \bar{p}_t^k) + \tfrac{1}{2} b_t^k[p_k^2 - (\bar{p}_t^k)^2]$$

$$= \tfrac{1}{2} b_t^k \left(p_k + \frac{a_t^k}{b_t^k}\right)^2 \tag{C.26}$$

Calculations, such as in (C.26) for a variety of t and k, then allow computation

---

[2]Although this is a somewhat unusual interpretation of the Koyck model, it is one adapted to the assumptions of this section. The more common interpretation supposes that a producer naively expects price for all future time periods to be the same as current price, and then expectations are revised each period. For the moment, however, the producer is supposed to anticipate future prices perfectly. Application in the more standard context is also accommodated by this modification, though, as shown below.

of changes in investment over time associated with alternative output price scenarios following (C.20); thus, the temporal disaggregation in (C.15) is feasible even when investment quantities or prices are not directly observable.[3]

Based on the results above, one can begin to consider generalizations for cases where future prices are not perfectly anticipated. For example, consider the common interpretation of the Koyck model where a producer naively expects prices for all future time periods to be the same as current prices (with certainty) even though expectations are revised each period as new prices are observed. In this case, (C.23) is replaced by

$$\bar{q}_t^k = a_0 + b_0 p_t$$

in which case (C.25) becomes the popular form

$$q_t^k = a_t^k + b_0 \beta \sum_{j=0}^{k-t} (1 - \beta)^j p_{k-j} \tag{C.27}$$

where a_t^k is as defined above.

Although this model has a somewhat different interpretation, the investment effects can be calculated in a similar manner. That is, if prices in this case were, by chance, to remain constant over future time periods according to naive expectations at time t, the calculations above are correct. But if that is what the producer expects, the firm will make the same investments at time t even though future prices may turn out to be different. Thus, ΔI_t^k can be calculated following (C.20), where $\tilde{P}_{t+1}^k$ and $\tilde{P}_t^k$ are calculated following (C.26) with p_k replaced by its naive expectation p_t; that is,

$$\Delta I_t^k = \delta^k (\Delta \tilde{P}_{t+1}^k - \Delta \tilde{P}_t^k) \tag{C.28}$$

where

$$\tilde{P}_{t+i}^k = \tfrac{1}{2} b_{t+i}^k \left(p_t + \frac{a_{t+i}^k}{b_{t+i}^k} \right)^2, \qquad i = 0, 1 \tag{C.29}$$

[Note also that a_{t+i}^k changes if q_{t-1}^k is affected by the change in the temporal price sequence under consideration, but these changes can be determined using (C.27).]

By supplementing the calculations in (C.28) and (C.29) with calculations of changes in short-run producer surpluses, $\Delta P_t \equiv \Delta \tilde{P}_t^t$, for all time periods affected by the temporal sequence of price changes, the approach in (C.15) for calculating total welfare effects becomes feasible even though calculations of $\tilde{P}_t^k$ and the related approach in (C.9) are not feasible when future price expecta-

---

[3]Of course, similar results are also possible on the input side by using (C.21) if a model similar to (C.22) and (C.23) is used to represent planned variable input usage.

tions are revised over time. Thus, for the general case where producers have naive expectations that all future prices will be the same as current prices, the results of this section justify a dynamic economic welfare methodology consisting of equations (C.15), (C.28), and

$$\tilde{P}_{t+i}^k = \int_{\tilde{p}_{t+i}^k}^{p_t} \tilde{q}_{t+i}^k(p_t, w_t, v_t^1, \ldots, v_t^{k-t-i}, \tilde{z}_{t+i}^k) dp_t$$

where

$$\tilde{p}_{t+i}^k = \max\{\tilde{p}_t; \tilde{q}_{t+i}^k(\tilde{p}_t, w_t, v_t^1, \ldots, v_t^{k-t-i}, \tilde{z}_{t+i}^k) = 0\}$$

While this section has investigated calculation of dynamic welfare effects on a producer in a rather special case, the general approach may be extended to many other cases as well (for example, to welfare analysis with many other types of dynamic supply equations).

C.2 INTERTEMPORAL ECONOMIC WELFARE ANALYSIS IN THE GENERAL PRODUCER CASE

Whereas the methodology described above is suitable for certain classes of problems, a more general framework is needed for economic welfare analysis in cases where producers recognize uncertainities regarding future prices. When uncertainties are introduced concerning future time periods, the dynamic producer problem takes on characteristics of the stochastic producer problem in Section A.6.

Consider a multiple-product competitive producer with intertemporal (or dynamic) production function given in implicit form by

$$f_t^T(q_t^T, \bar{q}^t) = 0$$

where

$$q_t^T = (q_T, q_{T-1}, \ldots, q_t)$$
$$q_t = (q_{1t}, \ldots, q_{Nt})$$
$$\bar{q}^t = (\bar{q}_{t-1}, \bar{q}_{t-2}, \ldots)$$
$$\bar{q}_t = (\bar{q}_{1t}, \ldots, \bar{q}_{Nt})$$

and q_{nt} (or $\bar{q}_{nt}$ if q_{nt} has already been decided) is the quantity of good n produced (used as input if negative) at time t; $\bar{q}_t$ is included to represent fixed input decisions made in previous periods. Also, assume that f_t^T is strictly decreasing, concave, and twice differentiable in q_t^T. In this context, consider the producer's problem of maximizing expected utility over a planning horizon from current time t to terminal time T (or maximization of the expected utility of wealth at terminal time T) given by

$$\max_{q_t^T} E_t[U(\pi_t - K_t, \ldots, \pi_T - K_T)] \qquad \text{(C.30)}$$

subject to

$$f_t^T(q_t^T, \bar{q}^t) = 0$$

where π_k is receipts less expenditures in time period k,

$$\pi_k = \sum_{n=1}^{N} p_{nk} q_{nk}$$

Here p_{nk} is the price of good n at time period k, which is a subjectively random variable; K_k is an ex ante payment required of the firm in period k (as in Section A.6); U is an intertemporal utility function associated with the planning horizon and is assumed to be strictly increasing, concave, and twice differentiable in π_t, $\ldots$, π_T; and E_t is the expectation operator associated with the subjective distribution at time t. Note that this expression of intertemporal preferences is much more general than the fixed rate of time discounting used in Section C.1. In completing the statement of the problem, suppose that the joint subjective distribution of prices $p_T^t = (p_t, \ldots, p_T)$ at time k is characterized completely by $\bar{p}_k^T = (\hat{p}_t^k, \ldots, \hat{p}_T^k)$ and α_k^T where $\hat{p}_t^k = (\bar{p}_{1t}^k, \ldots, \bar{p}_{Nt}^k)$, $\bar{p}_{nt}^k = E_k(p_{nt})$, and $\partial \epsilon_{nt}^k / \partial \bar{p}_{nt}^k = 0$ with $\epsilon_{nt}^k \equiv p_{nt} - \bar{p}_{nt}^k$ for all n and t. For added generality, one can also view α_k^T as characterizing any stochastic properties of the production function f_t^T not yet known at time k.

Using Bellman's optimality principle,[4] the problem in (C.30) can be solved by backward dynamic (stochastic) programming or, in other words, by solving the sequence of problems in each time period k, $k = T, T - 1, \ldots, t$, conditioned on decisions in earlier periods and assuming optimal decisions in later periods,[5]

$$\max_{q_k} \bar{U}_k \equiv E_k[U(\bar{\pi}_t - K_t, \ldots, \bar{\pi}_{k-1} - K_{k-1}, \pi_k - K_k, \\ \bar{\pi}_{k+1} - K_{k+1}, \ldots, \bar{\pi}_T - K_T)] \qquad \text{(C.31)}$$

---

[4]See, for example, R. Bellman and S. Dreyfus, *Applied Dynamic Programming* (Princeton, N.J.: Princeton University Press, 1962).

[5]Note that one cannot simply solve the problem in (C.30) directly for q_t^T ignoring the possibility of adjusting planned decisions in later periods as more price and production information become available. Such an approach is appropriate only if the decision maker proceeds naively as if the current subjective distribution of prices and production will not be modified with new information. The backward dynamic programming approach in (C.31), on the other hand, considers future optimal decisions as stochastic depending on new information that will be accumulated along the way.

subject to

$$\tilde{f}_k \equiv f_t^T(\tilde{q}_{k+1}^T, q_k, \tilde{q}^k) = 0 \tag{C.32}$$

where $\tilde{q}_h$ is the optimal decision vector resulting from the problem with $k = h$ and

$$\tilde{q}_h^T = (\tilde{q}_T, \tilde{q}_{T-1}, \ldots, \tilde{q}_h) \tag{C.33}$$

$$\tilde{\pi}_h = \sum_{n=1}^{N} p_{nh}\tilde{q}_{nh} \tag{C.34}$$

$$\tilde{\pi}_h = \sum_{n=1}^{N} p_{nh}q_{nh}$$

The Lagrangian associated with this problem is

$$L_k = E_k[U(\tilde{\pi}_t - K_t, \ldots, \tilde{\pi}_{k-1} - K_{k-1}, \pi_k - K_k, \tilde{\pi}_{k+1} - K_{k+1}, \ldots, \tilde{\pi}_T - K_T)] - \phi_k f_t^T(\tilde{q}_{k+1}^T, q_k, \tilde{q}^k)$$

and the associated first-order conditions for constrained optimization in addition to (C.32) are

$$\frac{\partial L_k}{\partial q_{nk}} = \frac{\partial \bar{U}_k}{\partial \pi_k} \frac{\partial \pi_k}{\partial q_{nk}} - \phi_k \frac{\partial \tilde{f}_k}{\partial q_{nk}} = 0, \qquad n = 1, \ldots, N \tag{C.35}$$

Second-order conditions are satisfied under the assumptions above. Hence, solution of (C.32) and (C.35) leads, in principle, to decision functions (supply if positive and demand in negative) of the form

$$q_{nk} = \tilde{q}_{nk}(\bar{p}_k^T, \alpha_k^T, \tilde{q}^k, K), \qquad n = 1, \ldots, N \tag{C.36}$$

where $K = (K_t, \ldots, K_T)$, which can be substituted into (C.31) through (C.34) to solve the problem where k is reduced by one in each successive step. Continuing in this manner for $k = T, T - 1, \ldots, t$ obtains the optimal decision functions in (C.36) for every time period in the planning horizon. Note, however, that $\tilde{q}_{nk}$ is generally a random variable at time t if $k > t$ since it depends on the subjective price distribution at time k which is not yet known at time t and on some random components of the production function not yet known at time t but which become known by time k. Note that, while the production function may induce a stochastic distribution on any q_{nk}, the related stochastic forces are assumed to become known by time k so that current production is subjectively nonstochastic.[6]

---

[6]This assumption is not restrictive if one assumes that all the related production

Using (C.34) and (C.36), one can define an indirect expected utility function

$$V_t(\bar{p}_t^T, \alpha_t^T, \bar{q}^t, K) \equiv E_t[U(\bar{\pi}_t - K_t, \ldots, \bar{\pi}_T - K_T) - \sum_{k=t}^{T} \phi_k \tilde{f}_t^T(\tilde{q}_t^T, \bar{q}^t)] \quad \text{(C.37)}$$

where the last term in brackets is included for convenience below even though it is zero for every state of nature (for every set of subjective distributions that can occur over time periods $t, \ldots, T$) by first-order conditions; that is, decisions in each period must be made to satisfy (C.32) so that $\tilde{f}_k = 0$ for every possible set of subjective distributions and corresponding decision functions. Note, however, that ϕ_k is generally a random variable at time $t < k$.

The remaining derivation then becomes closely analogous to the general case of Section A.6. That is, the current decisions in this problem play very much the same role as the input decisions in Section A.6, while the future decisions are random and must thus be treated as the production variables in the random production case of Section A.6. Specifically, by the envelope theorem [or use of (C.35)], one obtains

$$\frac{\partial V_t}{\partial \bar{p}_{ih}{}^t} = E_t(U_k \cdot \tilde{q}_{ih}) + E_t\left[\sum_{k=t}^{T} \left(\sum_{n=1}^{N} \frac{\partial L_k}{\partial q_{nk}} \frac{\partial \tilde{q}_{nk}}{\partial \bar{p}_{ih}{}^t} + \frac{\partial L_k}{\partial \phi_k} \frac{\partial \phi_k}{\partial \bar{p}_{ih}{}^t}\right)\right] \quad \text{(C.38)}$$

$$= E_t(U_h \cdot \tilde{q}_{ih}), \qquad i = 1, \ldots, N, \quad h = t, \ldots, T \quad \text{(C.39)}$$

where $U_h \equiv \partial U/\partial \pi_h$; note that (C.38) simplifies to (C.39) because the derivatives of L_k are zero for every state of nature by the first-order conditions. Also, since current decisions are nonstochastic with respect to the subjective distribution at time t, one finds that

$$\frac{\partial V_t}{\partial \bar{p}_{it}{}^t} = E_t(U_t) \cdot \tilde{q}_{it}, \qquad i = 1, \ldots, N \quad \text{(C.40)}$$

Using the result in (C.40), one can determine the compensating variation, $\hat{C}_{it}(\bar{p}_{it}{}^{t0}, \bar{p}_{it}{}^{t1})$, of any current subjective mean price change for good i from $\bar{p}_{it}{}^{t0}$

---

choices require decision in prior periods. For example, if all input decisions in a single-product case are made in a prior period, the random disturbance in production can be viewed as becoming known in the current period and then determining the amount of production through the production function constraint. Alternatively, one can assume at some notational expense that some current quantities are the result of other current, directly controlled decisions in a stochastic sense. In such a case, the result in (C.38) holds for all decisions, whereas (C.39) does not hold for decisions that are not directly controlled but result stochastically from other decisions (which is analogous to Section A.6).

to $\bar{p}_{it}^{t1}$. Using the approach in Section A.6, this compensating variation is defined by

$$V_t(\bar{p}_t^{T1}, \alpha_t^T, \bar{q}^t, K_t + \hat{C}_{it}, \bar{K}_t) = V_t(\bar{p}_t^{T0}, \alpha_t^T, \bar{q}^t, K_t, \bar{K}_t) = V_t^0 \qquad \text{(C.41)}$$

where $\bar{p}_t^{Tj} = (\hat{p}_t^{tj}, \hat{p}_{t+1}^t, \ldots, \hat{p}_T^t), \hat{p}_t^{tj} = (\hat{p}_{1t}^t, \ldots, \bar{p}_{it}^{tj}, \ldots, \bar{p}_{Nt}^t)$, and $\bar{K}_t = (K_{t+1}, \ldots, K_T)$. Differentiating both sides of (C.41) with respect to $\bar{p}_{it}^{t1}$ and using (C.37) and (C.40) implies that

$$E_t(U_t) \cdot \tilde{q}_{it}(\bar{p}_t^{T1}, \alpha_t^T, \bar{q}^t, K_t + \hat{C}_{it}, \bar{K}_t) - E_t\left(U_t \cdot \frac{\partial \hat{C}_{it}}{\partial \bar{p}_{it}^{t1}}\right) = 0$$

But if $\hat{C}_{it}$ is an ex ante compensation, it must be nonstochastic and thus $\partial \hat{C}_{it}/\partial p_{it}^{t1}$ factors out of the expectation, yielding

$$\tilde{q}_{it}(\bar{p}_t^{T1}, \alpha_t^T, \bar{q}^t, K_t + \hat{C}_{it}, \bar{K}_t) = \frac{\partial \hat{C}_{it}}{\partial \bar{p}_{it}^{t1}} \qquad \text{(C.42)}$$

Also, since $\hat{C}_{it}$ is determined so as to hold expected utility at its initial level, V_t^0, one may further define

$$\tilde{q}_{it}(\bar{p}_t^{T1}, \alpha_t^T, \bar{q}^t, V_t^0) \equiv \tilde{q}_{it}(\bar{p}_t^{T1}, \alpha_t^T, \bar{q}_t^t, K_t + \hat{C}_{it}, \bar{K}_t) \qquad \text{(C.43)}$$

which is a compensated supply equation (demand if negative) for good i at time t. Thus, since $\hat{C}_{it}(\bar{p}_{it}^{t0}, p_{it}^{t0}) = 0$, *the compensating variation of a current subjective mean price change is given by the change in producer (consumer) surplus associated with the corresponding current supply (demand) curve conditioned on initial expected utility and taken as a function of mean price.*

$$\hat{C}_{it}(\bar{p}_{it}^{t0}, \bar{p}_{it}^{t1}) = \int_{\bar{p}_{it}^{t0}}^{\bar{p}_{it}^{t1}} \tilde{q}_{it}(\bar{p}_t^T, \alpha_t^T, \bar{q}^t, V_t^0)dp_{it}^t$$

Interestingly, this is true even if the good in question is an investment good which may affect production in many different production periods, possibly including the current period.[7]

Additionally noting that $\hat{E}_{it}(\bar{p}_{it}^{t1}, \bar{p}_{it}^{t0}) = -\hat{C}_{it}(\bar{p}_{it}^{t0}, \bar{p}_{it}^{t1})$, where $\hat{E}_{it}(\bar{p}_{it}^{t1}, \bar{p}_{it}^{t0})$ is the equivalent variation of a current subjective mean price change for good i from $\bar{p}_{it}^{t1}$ to $\bar{p}_{it}^{t0}$, one finds that

$$\hat{E}_{it}(\bar{p}_{it}^{t0}, \bar{p}_{it}^{t1}) = \int_{\bar{p}_{it}^{t0}}^{\bar{p}_{it}^{t1}} \tilde{q}_{it}(\bar{p}_t^T, \alpha_t^T, \bar{q}^t, V_t^1)dp_{it}^t$$

---

[7]The reader familiar with putty-clay production theory may note that this concept of welfare measurement is sufficiently general to consider putty-clay capital which is employed in a productive capacity for a period of years and then disposed of or replaced with random timing depending on future developments.

where $V_t^1 = V_t(\bar{p}_t^{T1}, \alpha_t^T, \bar{q}^t, K_t, \bar{K})$. That is, *the equivalent variation of a current subjective mean price change is given by the change in producer (consumer) surplus associated with the corresponding current supply (demand) durve conditioned on the subsequent expected utility and taken as a function of mean price.* And this is true even though the good may be an investment good that affects many production periods.

Again, one may show, as in Section A.6, that this compensating and equivalent variation generally coincide if, and only if, absolute risk aversion is constant, at least in the initial time period when compensation is paid, that is,

$$r_{at} = - \frac{U_{tt}}{U_t}$$

where r_{at} is a constant and $\partial^2 U/\partial \pi_t^2 \equiv U_{tt}$. If absolute risk aversion is constant, supply or demand equations can be estimated without consideration of $K_t + \hat{C}_{it}$ or $\bar{K}$ in (C.42) or of V_t^0 in (C.43). Alternatively, if risk aversion is not constant, supply or demand functions of the form on the left side of (C.42) can be estimated using data on fixed costs, any ex ante transfers, and initial wealth which is included implicitly (in addition to data on fixed inputs and the parameters of the subjective distribution at time t). However, in this case computation of compensating or equivalent variation involves solution of the differential equation in (C.42) with boundary condition $\hat{C}_{it}(\bar{p}_{it}^{t0}, \bar{p}_{it}^{t0}) = 0$ in the former case and $\hat{C}_{it}(\bar{p}_{it}^{t0}, \bar{p}_{it}^{t1}) = 0$ in the latter case. Yet another approach is to begin with an arbitrary specification for the indirect expected utility function in (C.37) rather than an arbitrary specification of supplies and demands. Then, using duality, one can derive the implied supply and demand functions by calculating

$$\tilde{q}_{it} = - \frac{\partial V_t/\partial \bar{p}_{it}^t}{\partial V_t/\partial K_t}$$

which follows from (C.40) and direct calculation of $\partial V_t/\partial K_t$ using (C.37). Estimates of parameters of the resulting supplies and demands can then be used for direct calculation of compensating or equivalent variation from (C.41). With this approach, it is also a simple matter to consider common parameters among estimated equations so that the resulting supplies and demands all relate to a conceivable underlying producer problem.

Although the foregoing results are quite acceptable and offer a useful generalization in evaluating the welfare effects of current price changes that have lingering effects (the effects of many current price changes can be evaluated using a sequential approach corresponding to Section A.1), they are somewhat disturbing where policy changes affect prices over a number of time periods. The problem here is that future decisions are random by the current subjective distribution; thus, (C.39) does not simplify to (C.40). One possibility is thus to consider a random compensation function determined by the equation

$$V_t(\bar{p}_t^{T1}, \alpha_t^T, \bar{q}^T, K + \bar{C}_{ih}) = V_t(\bar{p}_t^{T0}, \alpha_t^T, \bar{q}^t, K) = V_t^0 \qquad \text{(C.44)}$$

where $\bar{p}_t^{Tj} = (\hat{p}_t^t, \ldots, \hat{p}_h^{tj}, \ldots, \hat{p}_T^t), \hat{p}_h^{tj} = (\bar{p}_{1h}^t, \ldots, \bar{p}_{ih}^{tj}, \ldots, \bar{p}_{Nh}^t)$, and $\bar{C}_{ih} = (0, \ldots, \hat{C}_{ih}, \ldots 0)$. Differentiating both sides of (C.44) with respect to $\bar{p}_{ik}^{t1}$ using (C.37) and (C.38) yields

$$E_t\left\{U_k \cdot \left[\bar{q}_{ik}(\bar{p}_t^{T1}, \alpha_k^T, \bar{q}^k, K + \bar{C}_{ih}) - \frac{\partial \hat{C}_{ih}}{\partial \bar{p}_{ih}^{t1}}\right]\right\} = 0$$

which holds if

$$\tilde{q}_{ik}(\bar{p}_k^{T1}, \alpha_k^T, \bar{q}^k, K + \bar{C}_{ih}) = \frac{\partial \hat{C}_{ih}}{\partial \bar{p}_{ik}^{t1}} \qquad \text{(C.45)}$$

for all states of nature. Thus,

$$\hat{C}_{ih}(\bar{p}_{ih}^{t0}, \bar{p}_{ih}^{t1}) = \int_{\bar{p}_{ih}^{t0}}^{\bar{p}_{ih}^{t1}} \tilde{q}_{ih}(\bar{p}_h^T, \alpha_h^T, \bar{\tilde{q}}^h, V_h^0) d\bar{p}_{ih}^t$$

where

$$\tilde{q}_{ih}(\bar{p}_h^T, \alpha_h^T, \bar{\tilde{q}}^h, V_h^0) \equiv \tilde{q}_{ih}(\bar{p}_h^T, \alpha_h^T, \bar{\tilde{q}}^h, K + \bar{C}_{ih})$$

and

$$V_h^0 = V(\bar{p}_h^{T0}, \alpha_h^T, \bar{\tilde{q}}^{h0}, K)$$

Note, however, that $\bar{q}^h$ depends on the mean price change which is anticipated at time $t, t + 1, \ldots, k - 1$ and thus takes into account any modifications of decisions prior to time k associated with the anticipated change. This dependence is represented by

$$\bar{\tilde{q}}^h = (\bar{q}_{h-1}, \ldots, \bar{q}_t, \bar{q}_{t-1}, \bar{q}_{t-2}, \ldots)$$

where $\bar{\tilde{q}}^{h0}$ is the particular $\bar{\tilde{q}}^h$ that occurs in the absence of the change.

In this context, $\tilde{q}_{ih}(\bar{p}_h^T, \alpha_h^T, \bar{\tilde{q}}^h, V_h^0)$ is clearly a supply (demand) relationship for good i in period h associated with an $h - t + 1$ length of run or, in other words, an $(h - t + 1)$-period subjective foresight. Also, the associated producer (consumer) surplus is random and depends on the state of nature resulting in period h. Thus, *the (random) compensating variation of a mean change in the period h price anticipated at time t is given by the period h producer (consumer) surplus change associated with compensated supply (demand) of $(h - t + 1)$-period foresight conditioned on utility expectations as of period h in the event of no change.*

Thus, a random compensation function is determined by solving (C.45) so that the effects of a mean price change for period $h > t$ can be evaluated for each possible state of nature with compensation paid in period h depending on the state of nature that actually occurs. Again, as in Section A.6, this type of compensation function suffers from an operational viewpoint because it is difficult to specify such a compensation scheme for which the parameters are declared in advance yet which is not vulnerable to strategic behavior of producers. Nevertheless, such evaluations are possible if a good ex ante model can be developed regarding how a decision maker reacts to proposed changes.

Of course, similar results can also be developed for evaluation of equivalent variation where the utility expectations as of period h are held at $V_h{}^1$,

$$V_h{}^1 = V(\bar{p}_h{}^{T1}, \alpha_h{}^T, \bar{\bar{q}}^{h1}, K)$$

and $\bar{\bar{q}}^{h1}$ is defined as the particular $\bar{\bar{q}}^h$ that occurs in the event of change. In this case the two welfare measures coincide generally if and only if absolute risk aversion in period h, $r_{ah} = -U_{hh}/U_h$, is constant. In other words, with constant risk aversion, the ordinary supplies and demands [with $(h - t + 1)$-period foresight] coincide with the respective compensated supplies and demands in period h, and neither depends on K_h or $\hat{C}_{ih}$.

If this is not the case, estimation of compensated supplies and demands and the associated welfare measures can be accomplished in one of two ways. First, one can estimate ordinary supplies or demands with $(h - t + 1)$-period foresight and then solve differential equations of the form $\bar{q}_{ih} = \partial \hat{C}_{ih}/\partial \bar{p}_{ih}{}'$ for compensated supplies and demands. These equations are complicated by the fact that $\bar{q}_{ih}$ depends on $\bar{p}_{ih}{}'$ not only directly through $\bar{p}_{ih}{}^h$ but also through $\bar{\bar{q}}^h$. Alternatively one can use the dual approach to specification and estimation by specifying an arbitrary functional form for $V_k = V(\bar{p}_k{}^T, \alpha_k{}^T, \bar{q}^k, K), k = t, \ldots ,$ h. Then functional forms for supplies and demands are obtained from

$$\tilde{q}_{ik} = -\frac{\partial V_k/\partial \bar{p}_{ik}{}^k}{\partial V_k/\partial K_k}, \qquad i = 1, \ldots , N; \quad k = t, \ldots , h$$

(which can be derived as shown above). If estimation of these equations sufficiently identifies the parameters of V_t, then $\hat{C}_{ih}$ can be calculated directly from (C.44) in empirical terms.

Combining the foregoing results for various combinations of changes thus gives a sequential methodology for evaluation of any *multiple mean price change* affecting a producer. However, further methodology is needed to evaluate changes in risk or other parameters in $\alpha_t{}^T$. One possibility for measuring the effects of more general changes is based on the concept of necessary inputs or necessary outputs. To examine this case, suppose that the input of good i at time t is necessary for operation of the firm in time periods $t, \ldots , T$ in the sense that one can define

$$\hat{p}_{it}{}' = \min \{\bar{p}_{it}{}'; (\tilde{q}_{1k}, \ldots, \tilde{q}_{Nk}) \equiv 0 \quad \text{for } k = t, \ldots, T\} \qquad \text{(C.46)}$$

where $\tilde{q}_{nk} \equiv \tilde{q}_{nk}(\bar{p}_t{}^T, \alpha_t{}^T, \bar{q}{}', K_t + C_0, \bar{K}_t) \equiv 0$ implies that $\tilde{q}_{nk}$ is zero for every state of nature and C_0 represents any current compensation relevant to the shutdown case. For a necessary output, one would simply replace the "min" in (C.46) with "max." In this context one can evaluate any general change in the intertemporal distribution of prices and production (including changes in risk) from $(\bar{p}_t{}^{T0}, \alpha_t{}^{T0})$ to $(\bar{p}_t{}^{T1}, \alpha_t{}^{T1})$ by using the approach in equation (A.37),

$$
\begin{aligned}
V_t[\bar{p}_t{}^{T1}(\bar{p}_{it}{}'), \alpha_t{}^{T1}, \bar{q}{}', K_t + C_1 + C_2, \bar{K}_t] &= V_t[\bar{p}_t{}^{T1}(\hat{p}_{it}{}'), \alpha_t{}^{T1}, \bar{q}{}', K_t + C_1, \bar{K}_t] \\
&= V_t[\bar{p}_t{}^{T0}(\hat{p}_{it}{}'), \alpha_t{}^{T0}, \bar{q}{}', K_t + C_1, \bar{K}_t] = V_t[\bar{p}_t{}^{T0}(\bar{p}_{it}{}'), \alpha_t{}^{T0}, \bar{q}{}', K_t, \bar{K}_t] = V_t{}^0
\end{aligned}
\qquad \text{(C.47)}
$$

where C_1 is compensation corresponding to an intertemporal shutdown, $\bar{p}_t{}^{Tj}(p_{it}{}') = [\hat{p}_t{}^{tj}(p_{it}{}'), \hat{p}_{t+1}{}^{tj}, \ldots, \hat{p}_T{}^{tj}], \hat{p}_t{}^{tj}(p_{it}{}') = (\bar{p}_{1t}{}^{tj}, \ldots, p_{it}{}', \ldots, \bar{p}_{Nt}{}^{tj})$, and $\hat{p}_{it}{}^{tj}$ is the shutdown mean price for good i at time t defined by (C.46) corresponding to other parameters contained in $(\bar{p}_t{}^{Tj}, \alpha_t{}^{Tj}), j = 1, 2$. Thus, using the approach in (C.42) and (C.43), one finds from (C.47) that

$$
\begin{aligned}
C = C_1 + C_2 = &- \int_{\hat{p}_{it}{}^{t0}}^{\bar{p}_{it}{}^{t0}} \tilde{q}_{it}[\bar{p}_t{}^{T0}(p_{it}{}'), \alpha_t{}^{T0}, \bar{q}{}', V_t{}^0] dp_{it}{}' \\
&+ \int_{\hat{p}_{it}{}^{t1}}^{\bar{p}_{it}{}^{t1}} q_{it}[\bar{p}_t{}^{T1}(p_{it}{}'), \alpha_t{}^{T1}, \bar{q}{}', V_t{}^0] dp_{it}{}'
\end{aligned}
\qquad \text{(C.48)}
$$

In other words, *the overall compensating variation of a general change in parameters affecting the firm intertemporally is given by the change in consumer (producer) surplus associated with the compensated demand (supply) at initial time and initial expected utility for any input (output) where purchases (sales) in the initial period are necessary for operation of the firm over the planning horizon.*

Of course, similar results can be developed for measuring equivalent variation where the compensated demands or supplies are simply conditioned on the subsequent expected utility level. Again, the compensating and equivalent variations will generally coincide if and only if absolute risk aversion is constant in the initial time period, in which case the compensated supply and demand curves coincide with the ordinary supply and demand curves.

Perhaps, cases are rare where one can identify an input (or output) such that purchases (or sales) in the initial time period are essential to operation of a firm over an entire planning horizon. More likely, one can identify inputs (or outputs) such that purchases (or sales) are essential to operation of the firm in each time period individually. This observation suggests a partitioning of parameter changes affecting a firm according to groupings of commodities and time periods such that one good at one time period in each group is essential among that group (meaning that no other good in the group would be bought or sold unless the essential good were also bought or sold), and no change in a partition of parameter changes associated with one group affects any other group when the firm does not buy or sell commodities in the first group. That is, suppose that a general change in parameters affecting a firm can be broken into steps $(\bar{p}_t^{Tj}, \alpha_t^{Tj})$, $j = 0, \ldots, J$, such that $j = 0$ represents the initial situation, $j = J$ represents the final situation, and each step corresponds to changing the parameters associated with one partition of the parameter set. Suppose, further that q_{ijh_j} is an essential input or output within the group of commodities associated with the jth change.

In this context, in the case of an essential input, define

$$\hat{p}_{ijh_j}^{tk} = \min\{\bar{p}_{ijh_j}^t; \tilde{q}_{ih}(\bar{p}_h^{Tk}, \alpha_h^{Tk}, \tilde{\bar{q}}^{hk}, K + C_k) \equiv 0, (i, h) \in G_j\}, \qquad k = j - 1, j$$

where G_j is the set of indices (i, h) included in group j and

$$\tilde{\bar{q}}^{hk} = (\tilde{q}_{h-1}^k, \ldots, \tilde{q}_t^k, \tilde{q}_{t-1}, \tilde{q}_{t-2}, \ldots)$$

with $\tilde{q}_\tau^k \equiv \tilde{q}_\tau(\bar{p}_t^{Tk}, \alpha_t^{Tk}, \tilde{\bar{q}}^{\tau k}, K + C_k)$. In the case of an essential output, one can simply replace the "min" with "max." Now, paralleling (C.47), note that

$$V_t[\bar{p}_t^{Tj}(\bar{p}_{ijh_j}^{tj}), \alpha_t^{Tj}, \bar{q}^t, K + C_j] = V_t[\bar{p}_t^{Tj}(\hat{p}_{ijh_j}^{tj}), \alpha_t^{Tj}, \bar{q}^t, K + C_{j-1} + \bar{C}_j]$$
$$= V_t[\bar{p}_t^{T,j-1}(\hat{p}_{ijh_j}^{t,j-1}), \alpha_t^{T,j-1}, \bar{q}^t, K + C_{j-1} + \bar{C}_j]$$
$$= V_t[\bar{p}_t^{T,j-1}(\bar{p}_{ijh_j}^{t,j-1}), \alpha_t^{T,j-1}, \bar{q}^t, K + C_{j-1}] = V_t^{j-1}$$

where $\bar{C}_j = (0, \ldots, \bar{C}_{ijh_j}, \ldots, 0)$ represents a period h_j compensation for losing access to markets $(i, h) \in G_j$ given parameters $(\bar{p}_t^{Tj}, \alpha_t^{Tj})$; $C_j - C_{j-1} = (0, \ldots, C_{ijh_j}, \ldots, 0)$ represents a period h_j compensation for the change from $(\bar{p}_t^{T,j-1}, \alpha_t^{T,j-1})$ to $(\bar{p}_t^{Tj}, \alpha_t^{Tj})$, $\bar{p}_t^{Tj}(p_{ih}^t) = [\hat{\bar{p}}_t^{tj}, \ldots, \hat{\bar{p}}_h^{tj}(p_{ih}^t), \ldots, \hat{\bar{p}}_T^{tj}]$, and $\hat{\bar{p}}_h^{tj}(p_{ih}^t) = (\bar{p}_{1k}^{tj}, \ldots, p_{ih}^t, \ldots, \bar{p}_{Nh}^{tj})$. Thus, paralleling (C.48) and using (C.45), one finds that

$$C_{ijh_j} = -\int_{\hat{p}_{ijh_j}^{t,j-1}}^{\bar{p}_{ijh_j}^{t,j-1}} \tilde{q}_{ijh_j}[\bar{p}_{h_j}^{T,j-1}(p_{ijh_j}^{t,j-1}), \alpha_{h_j}^{T,j-1}, \tilde{\bar{q}}^{h_j,j-1}, V_{h_j}^0]dp_{ijh_j}^{t,j-1}$$
$$+ \int_{\hat{p}_{ijh_j}^{tj}}^{\bar{p}_{ijh_j}^{tj}} \tilde{q}_{ijh_j}[\bar{p}_{h_j}^{Tj}(p_{ijh_j}^{tj}), \alpha_{h_j}^{Tj}, \tilde{\bar{q}}^{h_j,j}, V_{h_j}^0]dp_{ijh_j}^{tj}$$

This represents a stochastic compensation paid in period h_j depending on the state of nature at and before period h_j. These compensations can then be summed over $j = 1, \ldots, J$ to determine an overall intertemporal compensating variation, C_j, which possibly involves payments in several or all time periods. A crucial requirement in this result is that

$$V_t[\bar{p}_t^{tj}(\hat{p}_{ijh_j}^{tj}), \alpha_t^{Tj}, \bar{q}^t, K + C_{j-1} + \bar{C}_j] = V_t[\bar{p}_t^{T,j-1}(\hat{p}_{ijh_j}^{t,j-1}),$$
$$\alpha_t^{T,j-1}, \bar{q}^t, K + C_{j-1} + \bar{C}_j]$$

which is satisfied as long as no change in the jth partition of parameter changes affects $\tilde{q}_{ih}$ for $(i, h) \notin G_j$ when $\tilde{q}_{i',h'} = 0$ for $(i', h') \in G_j$. For example, if a firm is induced to switch from using petroleum-powered machinery to electrical equipment because of high petroleum prices, changes in petroleum price, the price of petroleum-using machinery, and risk associated with these prices would not affect the expected utility of the producer as long as petroleum prices remain high enough to keep the firm from using petroleum-powered machinery.

Based on these results, *the overall compensating variation of a general change in parameters affecting a producer intertemporally is given by the sum of changes in producer (consumer) surplus associated with compensated supplies (demands) at expected utility in the absence of change over all groups of goods where the calculations for each group are made in the market of the essential good in that group considering the partition of parameter changes relevant to that group.* This result justifies one of the more common approaches in dynamic producer problems. For example, suppose that the inputs used by a single-product producer can be partitioned into groups associated with the various production periods. Then a decision not to produce in a given period will imply nonuse of inputs affecting production in that period (that are not yet fixed). Thus, the compensating variation relevant to each time period h can be determined as the change in producer surplus associated with compensated output supply in period h with $(h - t + 1)$-period foresight. Of course, the component of compensation associated with any period $h > t$ would be stochastic depending on the state of nature occurring at and before period h. Again, similar results can be developed for the case of equivalent variation, and the two coincide generally if and only if absolute risk aversion is constant in each time period.

The results for dynamic economic welfare analysis in the general producer case are thus partially encouraging and partially disturbing. Several approaches can be used for examining the effects of current policy changes on current plus future periods and, in particular, the empirical accuracy of the sequential approach of welfare calculations is possible if the data permit. However, the effects of changes in policy for future periods, in general, can only be evaluated in terms of producer and consumer surpluses if some current input is necessary for operation of the firm over the planning horizon (or a similar approach can be developed if some subset of current inputs as a group are necessary for operation of the firm over the planning horizon) or if stochastic compensation schemes are considered.

C.3   INTERTEMPORAL ECONOMIC WELFARE ANALYSIS IN THE GENERAL CONSUMER CASE

The general dynamic consumer case is important in empirical analyses that are related to durable choice. When a consumer makes a decision to buy a car, for example, the decision is based, in part, on price expectations for gasoline, maintenance, and resale in future periods. Thus, the choice of a *consumer durable*—that is, a consumer good used over more than just the current period of consumption—is very much akin to the choice of a fixed input for a producer. An additional generalization of the consumer problem, which has become popular, is based on the theory of household production (see Section 13.3). In this theory the consumer is viewed as producing some of his or her consumption goods at home using durables as well as other goods and services. For example, warmth for a house is produced by combining, say, electricity or natural gas with a (durable) furnace. Thus, the consumer also possesses a production function, much like a producer.

To consider these various generalities, suppose that a consumer possesses a production function given in implicit form by

$$f_t^T(q_t^T, \bar{q}^t) = 0$$

where q_t^T and $\bar{q}^t$ are denoted as in Section C.2. In this case, $\bar{q}^t$ represents any fixity in the household production function or carryover due to previous durable choices. As in the producer case, suppose that f_t^T is strictly decreasing, concave, and twice differentiable in q_t^T. Suppose, also, that the consumer possesses an intertemporal utility function, $U(q_t^T)$, corresponding to a planning horizon from period t to period T, where U is assumed to be strictly increasing, concave, and twice differentiable in q_t^T. The consumer's problem of maximizing expected utility over the planning horizon is thus

$$\max_{q_t^T} E_t[U(q_t^T)]$$

subject to

$$\sum_{n=1}^{N} p_{nk} q_{nk} = m_k^*, \qquad k = t, \ldots, T$$

$$f_t^T(q_t^T, \bar{q}^t) = 0$$

where m_k^* is exogenous income for the consumer in period k; note that any savings by the consumer from one period to another can be handled through the "production" function. Again, suppose that the parameters of the subjective distribution of prices and household production at time k is denoted by $\bar{p}_k^T$ and α_k^T, as in Section C.2.

As in the producer case, this problem can be solved by backward dynamic (stochastic) programming, that is, by solving the sequence of problems conditioned on earlier decisions and assuming optimal later decisions, $k = T, T - 1, \ldots, t,$

$$\max_{q_k} \bar{U}_k \equiv E_k[U(\bar{q}_t, \ldots, \bar{q}_{k-1}, q_k, \bar{q}_{k+1}, \ldots, \bar{q}_T)] \qquad \textbf{(C.49)}$$

subject to

$$\sum_{n=1}^{N} p_{nk}q_{nk} = m_k^* \tag{C.50}$$

$$\tilde{f}_k \equiv f_t^T(\tilde{q}_{k+1}^T, q_k, \bar{q}^k) = 0 \tag{C.51}$$

where $\tilde{q}_{k+1}^T$ is defined as in (C.33). The Lagrangian associated with this problem is

$$L_k = E_k[U(\bar{q}_t, \ldots, \bar{q}_{k-1}, q_k, \tilde{q}_{k+1}, \ldots, \tilde{q}_T)]$$

$$- \lambda_k\left(\sum_{i=1}^{N} p_{ik}q_{ik} - m_k^*\right) - \phi_k f_t^T(\tilde{q}_{k+1}^T, q_k, \bar{q}^k)$$

so that first-order conditions for constrained maximization in addition to (C.50) and (C.51) are

$$\frac{\partial L_k}{\partial q_{nk}} = \frac{\partial \bar{U}_k}{\partial q_{nk}} - \lambda_k p_{nk} - \phi_k \frac{\partial \tilde{f}_k}{\partial q_{nk}} = 0, \qquad n = 1, \ldots, N \tag{C.52}$$

Note that second-order conditions are satisfied under the assumptions given above. Hence, solution of (C.50) through (C.52) leads, in principle, to demand equations (supply if negative) of the form

$$\tilde{q}_{nk}(\bar{p}_k^T, \alpha_k^T, \bar{q}^k, m^*), \qquad n = 1, \ldots, N \tag{C.53}$$

where $m^* = (m_t^*, \ldots, m_T^*)$. These decision functions can then be substituted into (C.49) through (C.51) to solve the problem where k is reduced by one in each successive step. Continuing in this manner for $k = T, T - 1, \ldots, t$, thus yields the optimal decisions in (C.53) for every time period in the planning horizon, although q_{nk} is generally a random variable at time t if $k > t$ as in the producer case.

At this point, one can define an indirect expected utility function for the consumer of the form

$$V_t(\bar{p}_t^T, \alpha_t^T, \bar{q}^t, m^*) \equiv E_t\left[U(\bar{q}_t, \ldots, \bar{q}_T)\right.$$

$$\left. - \sum_{k=t}^{T} \lambda_k\left(\sum_{i=1}^{N} p_{ik}\tilde{q}_{ik} - m_k^*\right) - \sum_{k=t}^{T} \phi_k f_t^T(\bar{q}_t^T, \bar{q}^t)\right] \tag{C.54}$$

The last two terms in the brackets are included for convenience below even though they are zero for every state of nature by the first-order conditions. Note, however, that λ_k, $\tilde{q}_{ik}$, and ϕ_k are individually random variables at time $t < k$ in general. Using the envelope theorem [or (C.52)], and assuming that

$E_t[E_k(z_k)] = E_t(z_k)$ for any variable z_k which is stochastic according to the subjective distribution at time $k > t$, one obtains

$$\frac{\partial V_t}{\partial \bar{p}_{ih}{}'} = -E_t(\lambda_h \cdot \tilde{q}_{ih}) + E_t\left[\sum_{k=t}^{T}\left(\sum_{n=1}^{N} \frac{\partial L_k}{\partial q_{nk}} \frac{\partial \tilde{q}_{nk}}{\partial \bar{p}_{ih}{}'} + \frac{\partial L_k}{\partial \lambda_k} \frac{\partial \lambda_k}{\partial \bar{p}_{ih}{}'} + \frac{\partial L_k}{\partial \phi_k} \frac{\partial \phi_k}{\partial \bar{p}_{ih}{}'}\right)\right]$$

$$= -E_t(\lambda_h \cdot \tilde{q}_{ih}), \qquad i = 1, \ldots, N, \quad h = t, \ldots, T \qquad \textbf{(C.55)}$$

because the derivatives of L_k are zero for every state of nature by the first-order conditions. Also, assuming that current decisions are nonstochastic with respect to the subjective distribution at time t following the production function assumptions of the producer case, one has

$$\frac{\partial V_t}{\partial \bar{p}_{it}{}'} = -E(\lambda_t) \cdot q_{it} \qquad \textbf{(C.56)}$$

Using the result in (C.56), the compensating variation, $\tilde{C}_i(\bar{p}_{it}{}^{t0}, \bar{p}_{it}{}^{t1})$, of any current subjective mean price change for good i from $\bar{p}_{it}{}^{t0}$ to $\bar{p}_{it}{}^{t1}$ can be determined. This compensating variation is defined by

$$V_t(\bar{p}_t{}^{T1}, \alpha_t{}^T, \bar{q}^t, m_t^* + \tilde{C}_{it}, \bar{m}_t^*) = V_t(\bar{p}_t{}^{T0}, \alpha_t{}^T, \bar{q}^t, m_t^*, \bar{m}_t^*) = V_t^0 \qquad \textbf{(C.57)}$$

where $\bar{p}_t{}^{Tj} = (\hat{p}_t{}^{tj}, \hat{p}_{t+1}^t, \ldots, \hat{p}_T^t)$, $\hat{p}_t{}^{tj} = (\bar{p}_{1t}{}', \ldots, \bar{p}_{it}{}^{tj}, \ldots, \bar{p}_{Nt}{}')$, and $\bar{m}_t^* = (m_{t+1}^*, \ldots, m_T^*)$. Differentiating both sides of (C.57) with respect to $\bar{p}_{it}{}^{t1}$ and using (C.54) and (C.56) implies that

$$-E(\lambda_t) \cdot \tilde{q}_{it}(\bar{p}_t{}^{T1}, \alpha_t{}^T, \bar{q}^t, m_t^* + \tilde{C}_{it}, \bar{m}_t^*) + E\left(\lambda_t \frac{\partial \tilde{C}_{it}}{\partial \bar{p}_{it}{}^{t1}}\right) = 0 \qquad \textbf{(C.58)}$$

where m_t^* in (C.54) is replaced by $m_t^* + \tilde{C}_{it}$ as specified in (C.57). If $\tilde{C}_{it}$ is an ex ante, thus nonstochastic, compensation at time t then (C.58) yields

$$\tilde{q}_{it}(\bar{p}_t{}^{T1}, \alpha_t{}^T, \bar{q}^t, m_t^* + \tilde{C}_{it}, \bar{m}_t^*) = \frac{\partial \tilde{C}_{it}}{\partial \bar{p}_{it}{}^{t1}} \qquad \textbf{(C.59)}$$

which can be reparameterized following (C.57) as

$$\tilde{q}_{it}(\bar{p}_t{}^{T1}, \alpha_t{}^T, \bar{q}^t, V_t^0) \equiv \tilde{q}_{it}(\bar{p}_t{}^{T1}, \alpha_t{}^T, \bar{q}^t, m_t^* + \tilde{C}_{it}, \bar{m}_t^*) \qquad \textbf{(C.60)}$$

Note that $\tilde{q}_{it}$ is thus a compensated demand equation (supply if negative) for good i at time t. Thus, since $\tilde{C}_{it}(\bar{p}_{it}{}^{t0}, \bar{p}_{it}{}^{t0}) = 0$, *the compensating variation of a current subjective mean price change is given by the change in consumer (producer) surplus associated with the corresponding current demand (supply) curve conditioned on initial expected utility and taken as a function of mean price,*

$$\tilde{C}_{it}(\bar{p}_{it}{}^{t0}, \bar{p}_{it}{}^{t1}) = \int_{\bar{p}_{it}{}^{t0}}^{\bar{p}_{it}{}^{t1}} \bar{q}_{it}(\bar{p}_t{}^T, \alpha_t{}^T, \bar{q}^t, V_t{}^0) dp_{it}{}^t$$

This result holds not only for current consumption goods but also for durables with long-lived use.

Additionally noting that $\tilde{E}_{it}(\bar{p}_{it}{}^{t1}, \bar{p}_{it}{}^{t0}) = -\tilde{C}_{it}(\bar{p}_{it}{}^{t0}, \bar{p}_{it}{}^{t1})$, where $\tilde{E}_{it}(\bar{p}_{it}{}^{t1}, \bar{p}_{it}{}^{t0})$ is the equivalent variation of a current subjective mean price change for good i from $\bar{p}_{it}{}^{t1}$ to $\bar{p}_{it}{}^{t0}$, one finds that

$$\tilde{E}_{it}(\bar{p}_{it}{}^{t0}, \bar{p}_{it}{}^{t1}) = \int_{\bar{p}_{it}{}^{t0}}^{\bar{p}_{it}{}^{t1}} \bar{q}_{it}(\bar{p}_t{}^T, \alpha_t{}^T, \bar{q}^t, V_t{}^1) dp_{it}{}^t$$

where $V_t{}^1 = V(\bar{p}_t{}^{T1}, \alpha_t{}^T, \bar{q}^t, m_t*, \bar{m}_t*)$. That is, *the equivalent variation of a current subjective mean price change is given by the change in consumer (producer) surplus associated with the corresponding current demand (supply) curve conditioned on the subsequent expected utility and taken as a function of mean price.* Again, this result holds for durables as well as current consumption.

Clearly, from (C.59) and (C.60), the compensating and equivalent variations will coincide generally only if the current-income effects in current demand are zero. In this case welfare effects can be calculated using ordinary consumer demands and supplies which would not depend on current income. Of course, as in Appendix B, this condition is implausible for all commodities jointly. Alternatively, compensating or equivalent variation can be calculated by solving the differential equation in (C.59) with boundary condition $\tilde{C}_{it}(\bar{p}_{it}{}^{t0}, \bar{p}_{it}{}^{t0}) = 0$ in the former case and $\tilde{C}_{it}(\bar{p}_{it}{}^{t0}, \bar{p}_{it}{}^{t1}) = 0$ in the latter case. Yet another approach is to begin from an arbitrary specification for the indirect expected utility function rather than an arbitrary specification of demands and supplies.[8] Then, using duality, one can derive the implied specifications for demands and supplies using a generalized version of Roy's identity. That is, using (C.56) and direct calculation from (C.54), one finds that

$$-\frac{\partial V_t / \partial \bar{p}_{it}{}^t}{\partial V_t / \partial m_t*} = \frac{E_t(\lambda_t) \cdot \bar{q}_{it}}{E_t(\lambda_t)} = \bar{q}_{it} \qquad \text{(C.61)}$$

Estimates of the parameters in the resulting demand and supply specifications then allow direct calculation of compensating or equivalent variation by an approach similar to that discussed in Section B.13. Furthermore, with this approach, it is a simple matter to consider common parameters among estimated equations so that the resulting empirical supplies and demands all relate to a conceivable underlying consumer problem.

---

[8] As in the general dynamic stochastic producer case, however, the appropriate regularity conditions, which such arbitrary specifications must satisfy for plausibility, have not been developed.

Turning to the problem of evaluating welfare effects of policy changes that affect future period prices, the compensation calculation is complicated by the fact that (C.55) does not simplify to something like (C.56) if $h > t$. As a result, an ex ante compensation at time t for a change in prices at time h is not a simple calculation. Alternatively, one can consider a stochastic compensation scheme where the compensation for a price change at time h is paid at time h according to a formula specified at time t involving the state of nature that occurs at (and before) time h. That is, suppose that the compensating variation of a subjective price change for good i at time h foreseen at time t is given by $\tilde{C}_{ih}(\bar{p}_{ih}^{t0}, \bar{p}_{ih}^{t1})$, where $\tilde{C}_{ih}$ is defined by

$$V_t(\bar{p}_t^{T1}, \alpha_t^T, \bar{q}^t, m^* + \bar{C}_i) = V_t(\bar{p}_t^{T0}, \alpha_t^T, \bar{q}^t, m^*) = V_t^0 \qquad \text{(C.62)}$$

and $\bar{C}_i = (0, \ldots, \tilde{C}_{ih}, \ldots, 0)$ with $\bar{p}_t^{Tj} = (\hat{p}_t^t, \ldots, \hat{p}_h^{tj}, \ldots, \hat{p}_T^t)$, $\hat{p}_h^{tj} = (\bar{p}_{1h}^t, \ldots, \bar{p}_{ih}^{tj}, \ldots, \bar{p}_{Nh}^t)$. Then differentiating (C.62) with respect to $\bar{p}_{ih}^t$ and using (C.54) and (C.55) yields

$$-E_t \left[E_h(\lambda_h \cdot \tilde{q}_{ih}) - E_h \left(\lambda_h \frac{\partial \tilde{C}_{ih}}{\partial \bar{p}_{ih}^t} \right) \right] = 0 \qquad \text{(C.63)}$$

which simplifies to

$$-E_t \left[E_h(\lambda_j) \left(\tilde{q}_{ih} - \frac{\partial \tilde{C}_{ih}}{\partial \bar{p}_{ih}^t} \right) \right] = 0$$

Thus, a random compensation scheme can be determined by choosing C_{ih} so that $\tilde{q}_{ih} = \partial \tilde{C}_{ih} / \partial \bar{p}_{ih}^t$ for every state of nature, which implies that

$$\tilde{C}_{ih}(\bar{p}_{ih}^{t0}, \bar{p}_{ih}^{t1}) = \int_{\bar{p}_{ih}^{t0}}^{\bar{p}_{ih}^{t1}} \tilde{q}_{ih}(\bar{p}_h^T, \alpha_h^T, \tilde{\bar{q}}^h, V_h^0) d\bar{p}_{ih}^t \qquad \text{(C.64)}$$

where

$$\tilde{q}_{ih}(\bar{p}_h^T, \alpha_h^T, \tilde{\bar{q}}^h, V_h^0) \equiv \tilde{q}_{ih}(\bar{p}_h^T, \alpha_h^T, \tilde{\bar{q}}^h, m^* + \bar{C}_i) \qquad \text{(C.65)}$$

and

$$V_h^0 = V(\bar{p}_h^{T0}, \alpha_h^T, \tilde{\bar{q}}^{h0}, m^*)$$

Note, however, that $\bar{q}^h$ depends on the mean price change that is anticipated at time $t, t + 1, \ldots, k - 1$ and thus takes into account any modifications of durable purchases prior to time k associated with the change. To represent this dependence, define

$$\tilde{\bar{q}}^h = (\tilde{q}_{h-1}, \ldots, \tilde{q}_t, \bar{q}_{t-1}, \bar{q}_{t-2}, \ldots)$$

where, by previous definition, $\tilde{q}_k$ depends on the subjective distribution of future prices (p_{ih}) at times $k < h$. Specifically, define $\bar{\tilde{q}}^{h0}$ as the series of decisions prior to h without the change.

In this context, the demand (supply) curve in (C.65) is clearly a one-period demand (supply) for an $(h - t + 1)$-period length of run [that is, an $(h - t + 1)$-period foresight]. Hence, *the (random) compensating variation of a mean change in period h price anticipated at time t is given by the period h consumer (producer) surplus change associated with compensated demand (supply), respectively, with $(h - t + 1)$-period foresight and conditioned on utility expectations as of period h in the event of no change.* A similar statement also holds for evaluation of equivalent variation by simply replacing V_h^0 by V_h^1 in (C.65), where

$$V_h^1 = V(\bar{p}_h^{T1}, \alpha_h^T, \bar{\tilde{q}}^{h1}, m^*)$$

and $\bar{\tilde{q}}^{h1}$ is defined as the series of decisions that would occur prior to h in the event of change.

Again, the two welfare measures coincide generally if and only if time h income effects are zero in $\tilde{q}_{ih}$, so that ordinary demands and supplies suffice for calculating welfare effects. Otherwise, as in the producer case, one must solve differential equations at time h of the form $\tilde{q}_{ih} = \partial \tilde{C}_{ih}/\partial \bar{p}_{ih}^t$ or use the dual approach to specification and estimation following application of a generalized version of Roy's identity at time h.

Combining the foregoing results for the consumer case thus gives a complete methodology for sequential evaluation of any *multiple mean price change* affecting a consumer over time. However, further methods are needed to evaluate changes in risk or other parameters in α_t^T. One possibility in this case, if the assumption of Section 7.10 is applicable, is to define a withdrawal price by (C.46) in the case of a consumption good [or the "min" in (C.46) is replaced by "max" in the case of defining a withdrawal price for a resource good sold by the consumer]. That is, assuming that good i is a consumption good always consumed in positive amounts (or a resource good always sold in positive amounts), as long as any other goods are bought or sold by the consumer, one can define a withdrawal price at which the consumer withdraws from the set of markets in the economy in question. For example, the withdrawal price could be a price at which the consumer will migrate from one economy (for example, country) to another. Thus, using (C.47) where K_t and $\bar{K}_t$ are replaced by m_t^* and $\bar{m}_t^*$ to define the compensating variation of any general change in parameters affecting the consumer, one can use (C.64) and (C.65) to derive (C.48) just as in the producer case. Thus, *the overall compensating variation of a general change in parameters affecting a consumer intertemporally is given by the change in consumer (producer) surplus associated with the compensated demand (supply) at initial time and at expected utility in absence of change for any good for which initial purchases (sales) are essential for the entire planning* *horizon.* An example of the latter case would be where a consumer is induced to migrate to another economy in the initial period and, once moved, does not consider returning within the planning horizon. Of course, similar results hold in calculating equivalent variation where compensated supply or demand is evaluated at the expected utility level occurring in the event of the change.

Alternatively, suppose that the set of changes affecting the consumer can be partitioned according to groupings of commodities and time periods so that one good at one time period in each group is essential to consumption (resource sales) within that group (meaning that no other good in the group would be bought or sold unless the essential good in the group were also bought or sold), and no change in a partition of parameter changes associated with one group affects any other group when the consumer does not buy or sell commodities in the first group. Then the foregoing result can be generalized by considering stochastic compensation associated with later periods. Thus, *just as in the producer case, the overall compensating variation of a general change in parameters affecting a consumer intertemporally is given by the sum of changes in consumer (producer) surplus associated with compensated demands (supplies) at expected utility in the event of change over all groups of goods where the calculations for each group are made in the market of the essential good in that group considering the partition of parameter changes relevant to that group.* For example, if the sale of labor is essential to any consumer market activity in corresponding time periods, the effect of a general change affecting the consumer that can be partitioned by the time period of effect (after compensation) would be given by the sum of changes in producer surplus associated with compensated labor supply over all time periods in the planning horizon. Of course, any supply or demand for period h used in such calculations is based on $(h - t + 1)$-period foresight and the associated change in producer or consumer surplus is viewed as a stochastic compensation in period h depending on the state of nature that occurs in (and prior to) period h. Again, all these statements carry through for evaluating equivalent variation as well where all compensated supplies and demands are evaluated at the expected utility occurring in the event of change.

C.4   IMPLICATIONS FOR SOCIAL DISCOUNTING

With these results, a fairly extensive methodology exists for evaluating intertemporal welfare effects on either producers or consumers. The results in Sections C.2 and C.3, however, skirt the issue of social discounting with risk by considering stochastic compensation in each period. An issue that is crucial in determining whether a project with effects over several time periods should be undertaken is how current nonstochastic effects should be weighed against future stochastic effects.

To do this, more intertemporal structure can be considered in the problems in (C.31) and (C.49). For example, considering only current nonstochastic compensation in (C.62), one can let $\bar{C}_i = (\tilde{C}_{it}, 0, \ldots, 0)$, so that, in place of (C.63), one finds that

$$-E_t\left[E_h(\lambda_h \cdot \tilde{q}_{ih}) - \lambda_t \frac{\partial \tilde{C}_{it}}{\partial \bar{p}_{ih}{}^t}\right] = 0 \tag{C.66}$$

Thus, if the marginal utility of income is constant within each time period (if λ_h and λ_t are constants) but differ by a factor δ^{h-t} because of personal discounting, then (C.66) implies that

$$\delta^{h-t}E_t[\tilde{q}_{ih}] = \frac{\partial \tilde{C}_{it}}{\partial \bar{p}_{ih}{}^t}$$

In other words, welfare calculations can be based on consumer (producer) surpluses in later periods associated with expected demand (supply) curves where surplus changes are discounted over time at personal discount rates.

Alternatively, a greater level of generality is apparently possible using duality. That is, differentiating both sides of (C.41) or (C.57) with respect to $\bar{p}_{ik}{}^{t1}$, where $\bar{p}_t{}^{Tj}$ is defined as in (C.44) or (C.62), yields

$$\frac{\partial V_t}{\partial \bar{p}_{ih}{}^{t1}} + \frac{\partial V_t}{\partial C_{it}} \frac{\partial C_{it}}{\partial \bar{p}_{ih}{}^{t1}} = 0$$

or

$$\frac{\partial C_{it}}{\partial \bar{p}_{ih}{}^{t1}} = -\frac{\partial V_t/\partial \bar{p}_{ih}{}^{t1}}{\partial V_t/\partial C_{it}} \tag{C.67}$$

where carets and tildes are suppressed for simplicity. Again, once a functional form for V_t is specified, the implied functional forms for current supplies and demands follow from (C.61). If estimation of these supplies and demands identifies all the parameters of V_t involved in (C.67), the necessary calculations for a nonstochastic ex ante compensation can be handled easily. Whether or not this approach is possible, however, depends on the intertemporal nature of V_t and on how V_t changes over time. The latter consideration can become important in inferring the parameters of V_t related to later time periods from estimates of supplies and demands in later time periods. If this approach is feasible, one need not rely on the approximations in Section 13.4 in questions of social discounting with risk; social risk preferences can be determined by aggregating over individuals.

Appendix D

Welfare Measures for Multimarket Equilibrium

As demonstrated in Chapter 4 and Appendix A, the producer surplus of a competitive supply curve conditioned on fixed input prices measures returns or quasi-rent on the associated fixed production factors; and the consumer surplus of a derived demand for inputs (conditioned on fixity of other input and output prices) measures returns or quasi-rent on fixed production factors of the production process using the input. These results suggest that, when one estimates supply and demand in an intermediate market and calculates the associated producer and consumer surplus under the stated conditions, the welfare quantities exactly measure quasi-rent for the two groups of firms involved in selling and buying in that market, respectively. That is, when all other prices facing the selling and buying firms are uninfluenced by their (group) actions, the ordinary surplus quantities do not include effects on other groups (e.g., final consumers) of which there would be none if all other prices were truly unaffected because of elastic supplies, etc.

In contrast to this extremely partial approach, a number of authors have attempted to approach welfare surpluses from a general equilibrium standpoint where all other prices in the economy are allowed to vary.[1] In a more recent

[1]For example, see Harry G. Johnson, "The Cost of Protection and the Scientific Tariff," *Journal of Political Economy,* Vol. 68, No. 4 (August 1960), pp. 327–45; and Melvin Krauss and David Winch, "Mishan on the Gains from Trade: Comment," *American Economic Review,* Vol. 61, No. 1 (March 1971), pp. 199, 200.

paper, Anderson shows that welfare changes can be determined by comparing the change in income arising from production (which, he notes, can be measured by the producer surplus triangle associated with an aggregate general equilibrium supply function for the whole economy) with the income effect of price changes in consumption (which, he notes, has been referred to as consumer surplus).[2]

Each of these approaches has serious shortcomings in applied welfare economics. In reality, the imposition of a quota, tax, and so on, in an intermediate market, such as for cattle or crude oil, may have a substantial effect on final consumption prices and quantities and conversely. Using partial methodology, these general equilibrium effects would be ignored; in many interesting problems this practice is unacceptable. On the other hand, measurement with the general equilibrium approach at the aggregate economy level "is far from our reach" because of the intractability of practically estimating responses of *all* prices and quantities in an economy.[3]

This appendix develops a framework that falls somewhere between the two cases noted above, in an effort to capture the essential generality of empirical problems while maintaining tractability as well as the capability of disaggregating welfare effects. The first part of the appendix considers the case of a vertically structured competitive sector of an economy where each industry in the sector produces a single product using one major variable input produced within the sector and a number of other variable inputs originating in other sectors of the economy. Any number of fixed production factors may originate either from within or outside the sector. Assuming that the sector is only one of many users of the other inputs, the prices in other sectors are assumed fixed or uninfluenced by the sector in question. However, the actions of any individual industry in the sector may affect all other prices and quantities within the sector. Later sections relax the vertical structure assumption and consider the case where prices and quantities in other sectors are also possibly altered as a result of intervention. In each of these cases, the welfare significance of the producer and consumer surplus associated with supply and demand curves that take account of equilibrium adjustments in other markets is considered.

D.1   THE CASE OF A SMALL VERTICALLY STRUCTURED SECTOR[4]

The development begins by building upon the results in Appendix A, which show that a producing firm's welfare position is reflected in both its input and

---

[2]James E. Anderson, "A Note on Welfare Surpluses and Gains from Trade in General Equilibrium," *American Economic Review,* Vol. 64, No. 4 (September 1974), pp. 758–62.

[3]Ibid., p. 762.

[4]The first part of this appendix draws heavily on the paper by Richard E. Just and

output markets when the associated input and output are necessary in the production process. As noted in Appendix A, Wisecarver,[5] Schmalensee,[6] and Anderson[7] began to investigate the relationship of surplus measures in input markets with those in output markets, but the cases considered thus far deal only with long-run equilibrium or infinitely elastic input supply, which disregards the producer side of the problem. The earlier of these four papers contained incorrect conclusions due to approximations, but eventually Anderson[8] showed that final market consumer surplus is the same as the input market consumer surplus when all producer quasi-rents are zero; and Schmalensee[9] showed that, for a final-goods industry with nonzero quasi-rents but perfectly elastic supply of its input, the consumer surplus in its input market is equal to the sum of producer and consumer surplus in its output market. Both Anderson and Schmalensee assumed perfect competition, a single input, and the existence of no distortions. Although the results due to Anderson[10] suggest extension of these propositions from the standpoint of aggregate welfare analysis, it was not made clear until the work of Just and Hueth[11] that interpretation of the usual surplus triangles with respect to individual market groups changes with market level. In point of fact, in their framework it is possible to examine disaggregate welfare impacts on each affected market group. Nevertheless, the disaggregated results are consistent with Anderson and show that the overall impact of introducing a distortion in some intermediate market is reflected by the sum of areas behind the general equilibrium supply and demand functions in that market.

Consumer Surplus in an Intermediate Market

Consider first the welfare significance of the triangle behind demand and above price in an intermediate market of a vertically structured sector. For notational convenience, assume that the industries in a sector are competitive and can be ordered so that each industry n producing q_n and facing output price

---

Darrell L. Hueth, "Multimarket Welfare Measurement," *American Economic Review*, Vol. 69, No. 5 (December 1979), pp. 947–54.

[5]Daniel Wisecarver, "The Social Costs of Input-Market Distortions," *American Economic Review*, Vol. 64, No. 3 (June 1974), pp. 359–72.

[6]Richard Schmalensee, "Consumer's Surplus and Producer's Goods," *American Economic Review*, Vol. 61, No. 4 (September 1971), pp. 682–87; Schmalensee, "Another Look at the Social Valuation of Input Price Changes," *American Economic Review*, Vol. 66, No. 1 (March 1976), pp. 239–43.

[7]James E. Anderson, "The Social Cost of Input Distortions: A Comment and a Generalization," *American Economic Review*, Vol. 66, No. 1 (March 1976), pp. 235–38.

[8]Ibid.

[9]Schmalensee, "Another Look."

[10]Anderson, "A Note on Welfare Surpluses."

[11]Just and Hueth, "Multimarket Welfare Measurement."

p_n, $n = 1, \ldots, N$, uses as variable factor inputs the product q_{n-1} produced at the preceding industry level in the sector plus some subset of inputs $x = (x_1, \ldots, x_m)$ with corresponding price vector $\gamma = (\gamma_1, \ldots, \gamma_m)$ produced in the rest of the economy. The restricted profit (quasi-rent) function for the industry is, thus,

$$R_n(\gamma, p) = p_n q_n{}^n(\gamma, p) - p_{n-1} q_{n-1}^n(\gamma, p) - \sum_{j=1}^{m} \gamma_j x_j{}^n(\gamma, p),$$

where profit-maximizing levels of output, input purchased within the sector, and inputs purchased from outside the sector at given prices are denoted by $q_n{}^n(\gamma, p)$, $q_{n-1}^n(\gamma, p)$, and $x_j{}^n(\gamma, p)$, respectively. Now suppose that prices in all industries in the sector are related through competition at the industry level so that, as price p_j is altered—perhaps by some government intervention—the entire price vector, $p = (p_1, \ldots, p_N)$, changes (monotonically) following $\bar{p}(p_j)$.[12] All inputs purchased from other industries, however, are available in elastic supply from the standpoint of the sector; hence, their prices do not change.

As pointed out by Mishan,[13] evaluation of the welfare impact of such a distortion in this case requires looking beyond the buyers and sellers in market j. Consider first the effects on any industry n in the sector where $j < n$. By the envelope theorem, one finds that[14]

$$\frac{\partial R_n}{\partial p_j} = q_n{}^n \frac{\partial \bar{p}_n}{\partial p_j} - q_{n-1}^n \frac{\partial \bar{p}_{n-1}}{\partial p_j}$$

Integration for a specific change from, say, $p_j{}^0$ to $p_j{}^1$ implies that

$$\Delta R_n = \int_{p_j{}^0}^{p_j{}^1} \frac{\partial R_n}{\partial p_j} \, dp_j = \int_{p_j{}^0}^{p_j{}^1} q_n{}^n \frac{\partial \bar{p}_n}{\partial p_j} \, dp_j - \int_{p_j{}^0}^{p_j{}^1} q_{n-1}^n \frac{\partial \bar{p}_{n-1}}{\partial p_j} \, dp_j \qquad \textbf{(D.1)}$$

where ΔR_n denotes the change in quasi-rents for industry n.

To interpret (D.1) when $j < n$, note that the first right-hand term is the change in area behind demand and above price in market n, denoted by ΔC_n,

$$\Delta C_n = - \int_{p_j{}^0}^{p_j{}^1} q_n{}^n \frac{\partial \bar{p}_n}{\partial p_j} \, dp_j = - \int_{\bar{p}_n(p_j{}^0)}^{\bar{p}_n(p_j{}^1)} q_n{}^n dp_n \qquad \textbf{(D.2)}$$

This is clear since, with $j < n$, integration in (D.1) is along equilibrium quan-

---

[12]The function $\bar{p}(p_j)$ can be determined in principle by solving the equations $q_n{}^n(r, p) = q_n^{n+1}(r, p)$, $n = 1, \ldots, j - 1, j + 1, \ldots, N$, for p as a function of p_j and r.

[13]E. J. Mishan, "What Is Producer's Surplus?" *American Economic Review*, Vol. 58, No. 5, Part 1 (December 1968), pp. 1269–82.

[14]For more details concerning application of the envelope theorem, see Appendix A.

tities in market n as the supply curve (influenced by p_j) is shifted. It should be noted, however, that ΔC_n is not calculated with respect to the usual ordinary demand curve. It is, in fact, calculated according to the equilibrium demand curve, which accounts for adjustments in other industries within the sector (assuming that prices in other sectors of the economy are truly unaffected by such changes).

To interpret the remaining right-hand term of (D.1) when $j < n$, note that integration is along equilibrium quantities in market $n - 1$ as input supply (influenced by p_j if $j < n - 1$ or represented by p_j if $j = n - 1$) is altered. Hence, the resulting integral represents the change in the area behind demand and above price in market $n - 1$,

$$\Delta C_{n-1} = -\int_{p_j^0}^{p_j^1} q_{n-1}^n \frac{\partial \bar{p}_{n-1}}{\partial p_j} \, dp_j = -\int_{\bar{p}_{n-1}(p_j^0)}^{\bar{p}_{n-1}(p_j^1)} q_{n-1}^n \, dp_{n-1} \tag{D.3}$$

Again, the reader should bear in mind that the relevant demand curve for input q_{n-1} is a general equilibrium demand rather than an ordinary demand (in the same sense as above).

Substituting equations (D.2) and (D.3) into (D.1) implies that

$$\Delta R_n = \Delta C_{n-1} - \Delta C_n, \qquad n = j + 1, \ldots, N \tag{D.4}$$

or, upon solving the difference equation for ΔC_j,

$$\Delta C_j = \sum_{n=j+1}^{N} \Delta R_n + \Delta C_N \tag{D.5}$$

where ΔC_N represents the change in final consumer surplus (associated with consumption of the sector's final product). Thus, the change in the "consumer surplus" triangle in market j associated with an alteration in price p_j measures the sum of changes in final-product consumer surplus plus quasi-rents for all industries (related by imperfectly elastic demands) involved in transforming the commodity traded in market j into final consumption form.

Of course, the welfare significance of ΔR_n is the same as in Mishan. On the other hand, the term ΔC_N may hold welfare significance either in the context of final consumption, as discussed in Chapter 5, 6, or 7, or where some industry $N + 1$ faces perfectly elastic demand for its output. In the latter case, ΔC_N merely measures the change in quasi-rent for that industry, and no further search (on the demand side) need be made for welfare effects of changing p_j.

Here it is interesting to note that the Schmalensee and Anderson results hold only in special cases. Anderson's derivation, assuming long-run competitive equilibrium (in which case $\Delta R_N = 0$), shows that $\Delta C_{N-1} = \Delta C_N$, so that consumer surplus can be measured in either the input or the output market. Schmalensee, on the other hand, assumed perfectly elastic input supply (that is, $j = N - 1$) and found that $\Delta C_N + \Delta R_N = \Delta C_{N-1}$. Since this is the case where Mishan's results suggest that producer surplus in market N measures quasi-rent for industry N, equation (D.4) reduces to Schmalensee's result that the input market consumer surplus is equivalent to the sum of producer and consumer surpluses in the output market.

Producer Surplus in an Intermediate Market

To interpret the change in the triangle area behind supply and below price in an intermediate market j denoted by ΔP_j, consider the effect of a similar change in p_j on market n where $j \geq n$. In this case, demand rather than supply in market n is affected by the change, so that integration in equation (D.1) is along equilibrium quantities supplied as demand (or output price if $j = n$) is altered. Hence,

$$\Delta P_n = \int_{p_j^0}^{p_j^1} q_n{}^n \frac{\partial \bar{p}_n}{\partial p_j} \, dp_j = \int_{\bar{p}_n(p_j^0)}^{\bar{p}_n(p_j^1)} q_n{}^n dp_n$$

and similarly for ΔP_{n-1},

$$\Delta P_{n-1} = \int_{p_j^0}^{p_j^1} q_{n-1}^n \frac{\partial \bar{p}_{n-1}}{\partial p_j} \, dp_j = \int_{\bar{p}_{n-1}(p_j^0)}^{\bar{p}_{n-1}(p_j^1)} q_{n-1}^n dp_{n-1}$$

which suggests that equation (D.1) can be rewritten as

$$\Delta R_n = \Delta P_n - \Delta P_{n-1}, \qquad n = 1, \ldots, J \tag{D.6}$$

Solving the difference equation in (D.6), one finds that

$$\Delta P_j = \Delta P_0 + \sum_{n=1}^{j} \Delta R_n \tag{D.7}$$

where ΔP_0 represents the change in the initial resource supplier's surplus. Thus, the change in the "producer surplus" triangle in market j associated with a change in p_j measures the sum of the change in initial resource supplier's surplus plus quasi-rents for all industries (related by imperfectly elastic supplies) involved in transforming the raw resource into the commodity at market level j.

Again, the welfare significance of ΔR_n is clear from Mishan, as discussed in Chapter 4. The welfare significance of ΔP_0, on the other hand, is clear from Chapter 7 in the case of a basic resource or again from Chapter 4 if there is an industry 0 facing perfectly elastic supply of *all* inputs. In the latter case, ΔP_0 simply measures the change in quasi-rent for industry 0, and no further search is needed (on the supply side) for welfare effects of changing p_j.

From the results in (D.4), (D.5), (D.6), and (D.7), the conclusions in Section

9.1 follow immediately. It is also a simple matter to extend this analysis to the case where distortions exist in some of the markets, but the procedure for doing so is similar to that presented in the following sections for the more general case, so no similar derivation is made here for the vertical market structure.

D.2 GENERAL EQUILIBRIUM WELFARE MEASUREMENT

In this section the analysis is extended to consider the possibilities for measuring the net social welfare effects due to introduction (or alteration) of a single distortion where *all* other sectors or markets in the economy are possibly altered as a result. This subject has been examined by Harberger.[15] He argues on the basis of Taylor series approximations to consumer surplus that all consumer effects can indeed be captured in a single market when no distortions exist in the rest of the economy; in the case where distortions exist elsewhere, he suggests that welfare effects in those markets must also be considered, although he does not make clear how this should be done.

In the development that follows, the Harberger thesis is brought more clearly into focus by developing the results rigorously without approximation (in the case of compensated consumer adjustments). It turns out that net private social welfare effects, as well as government effects, resulting directly from the new (or altered) distortion can be determined from equilibrium analysis in the market of interest. In some cases where existing distortions in the economy do not lead to market revenues or costs for government, the same results continue to hold (which is somewhat different from the implicit implications of Harberger's arguments). In any case, government effects directly associated with existing distortions in other markets must be considered, and in some cases private effects in other markets must also be considered.

Consider a competitive economy involving N goods $(q_1, \ldots, q_N)$, including basic resources, intermediate goods, and final goods (some goods may simultaneously fall into more than one of these categories), with fixed tastes and preferences for consumers and fixed technology for producers. Each of J consumers possessing utility function $U_j(q_{1j}, \ldots, q_{Nj})$ defined on respective personal consumption quantities $q_{1j}, \ldots, q_{Nj}$ and realizing exogenous income m_j^* seeks to maximize utility and thus possess an expenditure function m_j^* $(p_1, \ldots, p_N, \bar{U}_j)$ specifying the minimum exogenous income required to attain utility level $\bar{U}_j$ at prices $p_1, \ldots, p_N$ (where U_j is strictly increasing, concave, and twice differentiable in $q_{1j}, \ldots, q_{Nj}$). Where $\bar{q}_{nj}(p_1, \ldots, p_N, \bar{U}_j)$ represents

[15]A. C. Harberger, "Three Basic Postulates of Applied Welfare Economics: An Interpretive Essay," *Journal of Economic Literature,* Vol. 9, No. 3 (September 1971), pp. 785–97.

the associated compensated demand (or resource supply if negative) of commodity n by consumer j, one thus has

$$m_j^*(p_1, \ldots, p_N, \bar{U}_j) = \sum_{n=1}^{N} p_n \tilde{q}_{nj}(p_1, \ldots, p_N, \bar{U}_j)$$

Hence, by the envelope theorem,

$$\frac{\partial m_j^*}{\partial p_n} = \tilde{q}_{nj}(p_1, \ldots, p_N, \bar{U}_j)$$

Each of the K firms uses any subset of the N goods to produce any other subset of the N goods following its implicit production function $f_k(q_{1k}, \ldots, q_{Nk}) = 0$, where each argument q_{nk} of the production function f_k represents the net amount of good n produced in the production process (implying net use if $q_{nk} < 0$) by firm k. Competitive maximization of profits subject to the production function and any fixed inputs leads to restricted profit or quasi-rent function R_k,

$$R_k(p_1, \ldots, p_N) = \sum_{n=1}^{N} p_n \hat{q}_{nk}(p_1, \ldots, p_N)$$

where $\hat{q}_{nk}(p_1, \ldots, p_N)$ represents the net output supply (input demand if negative) of good n by firm k (assuming f_k is strictly decreasing, convex, and twice differentiable in $q_{1k}, \ldots, q_{Nk}$). Again, by the envelope theorem,

$$\frac{\partial R_k}{\partial p_n} = \hat{q}_{nk}(p_1, \ldots, p_N)$$

Now consider the introduction of a distortion in market m. Depending on the type of distortion introduced, define ϕ as the size of the ad valorem tax, size of the subsidy, level of the price ceiling, level of the price floor, and so on. In the case of quotas and price controls not enforced by government buy/sell activities, assume that some efficient rationing procedure is employed so that those actually involved in the market transactions which take place are those willing to pay more or those willing to sell for less than those who are not. Now let the equilibrium response of market price p_n, taking into account all equilibrium adjustments in other markets, be represented by a differentiable function $\bar{p}_n(\phi)$, thus specifying price p_n as a function of the distortion in market m, $n = 1, \ldots, N, n \neq m$. In the case of market m, it is necessary to specify two prices. Let $p_m^s(\phi)$ be a differentiable function specifying the price associated with marginal behavior of suppliers (e.g., the price excluding tax or the supply price that would lead to the same quantity supplied in the absence of a quota), and let $p_m^d(\phi)$ be a differentiable function specifying the price associated with marginal behavior of demanders (e.g., the price including tax, etc.). Specifically, define *supply price* $p_m{}^s(\phi)$ and *demand price* $p_m{}^d(\phi)$ as those prices which, together with prices $\bar{p}_n(\phi)$, $n = 1, \ldots, N$, $n \neq m$, lead to the same compensated equilibrium quantities supplied and demanded without distortions as are obtained in the distorted economy.[16] Of course, in other markets, which are not distorted, no such divergence in effective supply and demand prices occurs.

The existence of these two prices in market m in the case with an ad valorem tax or subsidy is obvious; supply price excludes taxes and includes subsidies, whereas demand price includes taxes and excludes subsidies. Similarly, in the case of monopoly, the demand price is the market price, whereas the price associated with the marginal behavior of the producing firm is its marginal cost (see Section 10.1). Or in the case of monopsony, the supply price is the market price, whereas the price associated with the marginal behavior of the buyer is his or her marginal revenue of product (see Section 10.2).[17]

Finally, consider the case of a quota on sales or a price floor where the rationing system limits the amount that each individual can sell or, alternatively, a quota on purchases or a price ceiling where the rationing system limits the amount of the good individuals can buy. Specifically, where $q_{mk} - \bar{q}_{mk}$ is the effective limitation placed on firm k, the profit-maximization problem is to

maximize $\sum_{n=1}^{N} p_n q_{nk}$ subject to $f_k(q_{1k}, \ldots, q_{Nk}) = 0$ and $q_{mk} = \bar{q}_{mk}$. The associated Lagrangian is

$$\sum_{n=1}^{N} p_n q_{nk} - \lambda_k \cdot f(q_{1k}, \ldots, q_{Nk}) - \zeta_{mk} \cdot (q_{mk} - \bar{q}_{mk})$$

for which first-order conditions for maximization include

$$p_n - \lambda_k \frac{\partial f}{\partial q_{nk}} = 0, \qquad n = 1, \ldots, N, n \neq m$$

$$p_m - \lambda_k \frac{\partial f}{\partial q_{mk}} - \zeta_{mk} = 0$$

---

[16] For a further discussion and graphical presentation of these concepts of prices, see Chapter 9.

[17] Generalizing this analysis to the case of dominant share price leadership oligopoly (Section 10.3) implies that the marginal behavior of all producers except those in the dominant share is also associated with the market price, whereas only the behavior of firms in the dominant share is related to their marginal cost. Or in the case of dominant-share price leadership oligopsony, the demand price for all buyers except those in the dominant share is the market price, whereas the marginal behavior of firms in the dominant share is associated with their marginal revenue of product. Although these generalizations are not considered explicitly below to avoid complication in notation, they can be easily accommodated.

Comparing these conditions with the corresponding first-order conditions in the absence of the limitation, that is,

$$p_n - \lambda \frac{\partial f}{\partial q_{nk}} = 0, \qquad n = 1, \ldots, N$$

reveals that constrained profit maximization with prices $p_1, \ldots, p_N$ leads to the same quantities supplied and demanded as unconstrained profit maximization with prices $p_1, \ldots, p_{m-1}, p_m - \zeta_{mk}, p_{m+1}, \ldots, p_N$. Thus, the good m supply or demand price, as the case may be, for firm k is $p_m - \zeta_{mk}$, which obviously exists under standard assumptions.

Similarly, where $q_{mj} = \bar{\bar{q}}_{mj}$ is the effective limitation placed on consumer j, the expenditure minimization problem is to minimize $\sum_{n=1}^{N} p_n q_{nj}$ subject to $U_j(q_{1j},$ $\ldots, q_{Nj}) = \bar{U}_j$ and $q_{mj} = \bar{\bar{q}}_{mj}$. The associated Lagrangian,

$$\sum_{n=1}^{N} p_n q_{nj} - \tilde{\lambda}_j \cdot (U_j - \bar{U}_j) - \tilde{\zeta}_{mj} \cdot (q_{mj} - \bar{\bar{q}}_{mj}),$$

has first-order conditions including

$$p_n - \tilde{\lambda}_j \frac{\partial U_j}{\partial q_{nj}} = 0, \qquad n = 1, \ldots, N, n \neq m$$

$$p_m - \tilde{\lambda}_j \frac{\partial U_j}{\partial q_{mj}} - \tilde{\zeta}_{mj} = 0$$

Comparing these conditions with the corresponding problem in the absence of the limitation, that is,

$$p_n - \tilde{\lambda}_j \frac{\partial U_j}{\partial q_{nj}} = 0, \qquad n = 1, \ldots, N$$

verifies that prices $p_1, \ldots, p_{m-1}, p_m - \tilde{\zeta}_{mj}, p_{m+1}, \ldots, p_N$ in the absence of the limitation lead to the same compensated quantities supplied and demanded as prices $p_1, \ldots, p_N$ in the presence of the limitation. Thus, the good m supply or demand price (depending on whether $\tilde{q}_{mj} < 0$ or $\tilde{q}_{mj} > 0$, respectively) for consumer j is $p_m - \tilde{\zeta}_{mj}$, which obviously exists under standard assumptions.

For the following analysis, any quota or rationing system associated with a price ceiling or floor is assumed to be imposed or altered with limited efficiency in the sense that $\zeta_{mk} = \tilde{\zeta}_{mj} = \zeta^s$ for all producers with $\hat{q}_{mk} > 0$ and all consumers with $\tilde{q}_{mk} < 0$ (i.e., for all net sellers of good m) or, alternatively, that $\zeta_{mk} = \tilde{\zeta}_{mj} = \zeta^d$ for all producers with $\hat{q}_{mk} < 0$ and all consumers with $\tilde{q}_{mk} > 0$ (i.e., for all net buyers of good m). Thus, the supply price in market m is $p_m - \zeta^s$, and the demand price in market m is $p_m - \zeta^d$. These assumptions ensure that those actually involved in market transactions have equal marginal willingness to pay or marginal willingness to sell since ζ_{mk} and $\tilde{\zeta}_{mj}$ represent such marginal values. One might note that this assumption of efficiency in the allocation of a market distortion can be relaxed by retaining individualized supply and demand prices, but any associated empirical work must also be individualized in so doing.

The Equilibrium Welfare Effects of Introducing a Single Distortion

Having verified the existence of the supply and demand price concepts defined above for a variety of common distortions, the general equilibrium effect of marginally changing the distortion ϕ (for example, from the free-market level) on each individual firm or consumer can be determined by substituting $\tilde{p}_n$, $n = 1, \ldots, N$, for all prices in the appropriate quasi-rent or expenditure function and then differentiating with respect to ϕ. By the envelope theorem (see Appendices A and B), one obtains

$$\frac{\partial R_k}{\partial \phi} = \sum_{n=1}^{N} \frac{\partial R_k}{\partial \tilde{p}_n} \frac{\partial \hat{p}_{nk}}{\partial \phi} = \sum_{n=1}^{N} \hat{q}_{nk}(\hat{p}_{1k}, \ldots, \hat{p}_{Nk}) \frac{\partial \hat{p}_{nk}}{\partial \phi} \tag{D.8}$$

$$\frac{\partial m_j^*}{\partial \phi} = \sum_{n=1}^{N} \frac{\partial m_j^*}{\partial \tilde{p}_n} \frac{\partial \tilde{p}_{nj}}{\partial \phi} = \sum_{n=1}^{N} \tilde{q}_{nj}(\tilde{p}_{1j}, \ldots, \tilde{p}_{Nj} \bar{U}_j) \frac{\partial \tilde{p}_{nj}}{\partial \phi} \tag{D.9}$$

where, for notational convenience, $\hat{p}_{mk} = p_m^s(\phi)$ for each firm producing good m ($\hat{q}_{mk} > 0$) and $\tilde{p}_{mj} = p_m^s(\phi)$ for each consumer supplying good m ($\tilde{q}_{mj} < 0$); $\hat{p}_{mk} = \hat{p}_{mj} = p_m^d(\phi)$ in the alternative cases with $\hat{p}_{nk} = \tilde{p}_{nj} = \tilde{p}_n$ for $n \neq m$.[18] Where ϕ_0 represents the level of the distortion corresponding to a free market, (e.g., $\phi_0 - 0$ in the case where ϕ_0 is an ad valorem tax) and where ϕ_1 is the level of the distortion to be introduced, the effect of the distortion can be determined by integration of (D.8) and (D.9),

$$\Delta R_k = \int_{\phi_0}^{\phi_1} \sum_{n=1}^{N} \hat{q}_{nk}(\hat{p}_{1k}, \ldots, \hat{p}_{Nk}) \frac{\partial \hat{p}_{nk}}{\partial \phi} d\phi \tag{D.10}$$

$$\Delta m_j^* = \int_{\phi_0}^{\phi_1} \sum_{n=1}^{N} \tilde{q}_{nj}(\tilde{p}_{1j}, \ldots, \tilde{p}_{Nj}, \bar{U}_j) \frac{\partial \tilde{p}_{nj}}{\partial \phi} d\phi \tag{D.11}$$

---

[18]This definition of $\tilde{p}_m$ may lead to a discontinuity in individual firm or consumer supplies and demands such that a marginal change in ϕ induces a switch from net buying to net selling, or vice versa. Nevertheless, practical examples of such cases are rare and, furthermore, in a large economy with essentially continuous income and production efficiency distributions among individuals, such a switch at the individual level is without substantive implication for the (competitive) market level of analysis. To be technically correct for all types of distortions, however, assume that production and utility functions are such that compensated changes never induce net buyers to become net sellers, or vice versa.

In the latter case, Δm_j^* represents the negative of the compensating or equivalent variation for consumer j, depending on whether $\bar{U}_j$ is defined as the equilibrium utility level of consumer j before or after the introduction of the distortion.

To determine the net social welfare effects ΔW of the new distortion, the individual welfare effects in (D.10) and (D.11) can be aggregated over all individuals and added to the difference in purchases and sales in market m which accrues to either producers, consumers, or government, depending on the type of distortion,

$$\Delta W = \sum_{k=1}^{K} \Delta R_k - \sum_{j=1}^{J} \Delta m_j^* + \Delta T_m$$

$$= \sum_{n=1}^{N} \int_{\phi_0}^{\phi_1} \left[\sum_{k=1}^{K} \hat{q}_{nk} \frac{\partial \hat{p}_{nk}}{\partial \phi} - \sum_{j=1}^{J} \tilde{q}_{nj} \frac{\partial \tilde{p}_{nj}}{\partial \phi} \right] d\phi + \Delta T_m$$

(D.12)

where

$$\Delta T_m = p_m^d(\phi^1) \cdot q_m^d(\phi^1) - p_m^s(\phi^1) \cdot q_m^s(\phi^1) - p_m^d(\phi^0) \cdot q_m^d(\phi^0) + p_m^s(\phi^0) \cdot q_m^s(\phi^0)$$

and the arguments ϕ^0 and ϕ^1 in each case denote compensated equilibrium prices or quantities before or after alteration of the distortion in market m, respectively. Note that ΔT_m represents the change in buyer expenditures less seller receipts (evaluated at demand and supply prices as defined above) with the change in distortion. Some group in the economy (consumers, producers, or government) must receive (give up, if negative) this change, as becomes clear below.

Changing variables of integration in (D.12) implies that

$$\int_{\phi_0}^{\phi_1} \left[\sum_{k=1}^{K} \hat{q}_{nk} \frac{\partial \hat{p}_{nk}}{\partial \phi} - \sum_{j=1}^{J} \tilde{q}_{nj} \frac{\partial \tilde{p}_{nj}}{\partial \phi} \right] d\phi = \int_{\phi_0}^{\phi_1} \left[\sum_{k=1}^{K} \hat{q}_{nk} - \sum_{j=1}^{J} \tilde{q}_{nj} \right] \frac{\partial \tilde{p}_n}{\partial \phi} d\phi$$

$$= \int_{\tilde{p}_n(\phi^0)}^{\tilde{p}_n(\phi^1)} \left[\sum_{k=1}^{K} \hat{q}_{nk} - \sum_{j=1}^{J} \tilde{q}_{nj} \right] dp_n = 0 \quad \text{(D.13)}$$

$$n = 1, \ldots, N, \quad n \neq m$$

since $\sum_{k=1}^{K} \hat{q}_{nk} - \sum_{j=1}^{J} \tilde{q}_{nj}$ simply represents the equilibrium sum of all supplies less the equilibrium sum of all demands at a particular set of prices. The sum must be zero in equilibrium. In the case of market m, on the other hand, one finds that

$$\int_{\phi_0}^{\phi_1} \left[\sum_{k=1}^{K} \hat{q}_{mk} \frac{\partial \hat{p}_{mk}}{\partial \phi} - \sum_{j=1}^{J} \tilde{q}_{mj} \frac{\partial \tilde{p}_{mj}}{\partial \phi} \right] d\phi = \int_{\phi_0}^{\phi_1} \left[q_m^s \frac{\partial p_m^s}{\partial \phi} - q_m^d \frac{\partial p_m^d}{\partial \phi} \right] d\phi$$

$$= \int_{p_m^{s(\phi_0)}}^{p_m^{s(\phi_1)}} q_m^s dp_m^s - \int_{p_m^{d(\phi_0)}}^{p_m^{d(\phi_1)}} q_m^d dp_m^d \qquad \textbf{(D.14)}$$

$$= \Delta P_m{}^* + \Delta C_m{}^*$$

where $\Delta P_m{}^*$ and $\Delta C_m{}^*$ are the changes in producer and consumer surplus associated, respectively, with the supply and demand prices and the general equilibrium supply and demand curves given by

$$q_m^s = \sum_{\substack{k=1 \\ \hat{a}_{mk}>0}}^{K} \hat{q}_{mk} - \sum_{\substack{j=1 \\ \tilde{a}_{mj}<0}}^{J} \tilde{q}_{mj} \qquad \textbf{(D.15)}$$

$$q_m^d = \sum_{\substack{j=1 \\ \tilde{a}_{mj}>0}}^{J} \tilde{q}_{mj} - \sum_{\substack{k=1 \\ \hat{a}_{mk}<0}}^{K} \hat{q}_{mk} \qquad \textbf{(D.16)}$$

In addition, one must consider ΔT_m, which is the change in receipts minus expenditures where receipts are calculated at supply price and expenditures are calculated at demand price. Specifically, ΔT_m is the change in tax revenues, change in subsidy expenditure, or change in producer quasi-rent or consumer expenditure not reflected by the supply and demand prices. Thus, from (D.12), (D.13), and (D.14), the total social welfare effects of a change in ϕ are captured completely in the distorted market by computing surpluses associated with equilibrium supply and demand curves in the distorted market which account for all associated price adjustments in the rest of the economy. The results discussed graphically in Section 9.3 thus follow immediately. From these results, it is also clear that the appropriate compensated general equilibrium curves for use in economic welfare calculations depend on the form of distortion only through its influence on the demand and supply prices.

Equilibrium Welfare Effects of a Distortion in an Otherwise Distorted Economy

The foregoing results are not of sufficient generality for practical purposes since one is not likely to encounter a problem where an economy is free of any distortions beyond the one for which change is considered. To carry the analysis to a practical level, consider the case where distortions possibly exist throughout the economy. That is, suppose that a distortion exists in principle in each market n (although possibly at a noneffective level) and can be represented by a scalar parameter ϕ_n, $n = 1, \ldots, N$. Also, suppose that a unique set of equilibrium prices is associated with each choice of distortions, $\phi = (\phi_1, \ldots, \phi_N)$, for each given distribution of exogenous income. That is, suppose that the supply price associated with the marginal behavior of suppliers in market n is denoted by $p_n^s(\phi)$ and suppose that the demand price associated with the marginal behavior of demanders in market n is denoted by $p_n^d(\phi)$, where both p_n^s and p_n^d are differentiable in ϕ_m, $n = 1, \ldots, N$. One can show the existence of such prices in the presence of several distortions following the same arguments as used above in the case where a single distortion was introduced.

Following the notation described above, one has

$$m_j^*(\bar{p}_{1j}, \ldots, \bar{p}_{Nj}, \bar{U}_j) = \sum_{n=1}^{N} \bar{p}_{nj}\bar{q}_{nj}$$

$$R_k(\hat{p}_{1k}, \ldots, \hat{p}_{Nk}) = \sum_{n=1}^{N} \hat{p}_{nk}\hat{q}_{nk}$$

where $\hat{p}_{nk} = \bar{p}_{nj} = p_n^s(\phi)$ for each firm k and consumer j that is a net seller of good n and $\hat{p}_{nk} = \bar{p}_{nj} = p_n^d(\phi)$ for each firm k and consumer j that is a net buyer of good n. These definitions again presuppose efficient rationing in the case of quotas, price ceilings, and price floors, so that the demanders (suppliers) gaining access to markets are those willing to pay more (receive less) at the margin than those who do not.[19]

Now suppose that the distortion in market m is altered from ϕ_m^0 to ϕ_m^1 while all other distortions remain unchanged. One finds in place of (D.8) and (D.9) that

$$\frac{\partial R_k}{\partial \phi_m} = \sum_{n=1}^{N} \hat{q}_{nk} \frac{\partial \hat{p}_{nk}}{\partial \phi_m}$$

$$\frac{\partial m_j^*}{\partial \phi_m} = \sum_{n=1}^{N} \bar{q}_{nj} \frac{\partial \bar{p}_{nj}}{\partial \phi_m}$$

Hence, in place of (D.12) one finds a net social welfare effect,

---

[19]This assumption can be easily relaxed with respect to distortions for which changes are not considered if any inefficiency in rationing can be represented by constraints imposed on individual decision makers. That is, individualized market access or market quotas can be represented by vectors of parameters which pertain to individual consumers or producers. Supplies, demands, quasi-rent functions, and expenditure functions of individuals then depend on these additional vectors of parameters. If they are unchanged, however, all the results below continue to hold. The assumption of efficient rationing with a quota or price control for which change is considered can also be relaxed, but only with considerable empirical detail, as discussed earlier.

$$\Delta W = \sum_{k=1}^{K} \Delta R_k - \sum_{j=1}^{J} \Delta m_j^* + \sum_{n=1}^{N} \Delta T_n$$

$$= \int_{\phi_m^0}^{\phi_m^1} \left[\sum_{k=1}^{K} \frac{\partial R_k}{\partial \phi_m} - \sum_{j=1}^{J} \frac{\partial m_j^*}{\partial \phi_m} \right] d\phi_m + \sum_{n=1}^{N} \Delta T_n \qquad \textbf{(D.17)}$$

$$= \sum_{n=1}^{N} \int_{\phi_m^0}^{\phi_m^1} \left[q_n^s \frac{\partial p_n^s}{\partial \phi_m} - q_n^d \frac{\partial p_n^d}{\partial \phi_m} \right] d\phi_m + \sum_{n=1}^{N} \Delta T_n$$

where ΔT_n is essentially a transfer effect the same as in (D.12),

$$\Delta T_n = p_n^d(\phi^1) \cdot q_n^d(\phi^1) - p_n^s(\phi^1) \cdot q_n^s(\phi^1) - p_n^d(\phi^0) \cdot q_n^d(\phi^0) + p_n^s(\phi^0) \cdot q_n^s(\phi^0)$$

and where q_n^s and q_n^d are defined as in (D.15) and (D.16) for each market n. The arguments ϕ^0 and ϕ^1 again determine compensated equilibrium prices or quantities in market n before or after alteration of the distortion, respectively. Specifically, ΔT_n measures the changes in receipts minus expenditures in market n, where receipts are evaluated at supply prices and expenditures are evaluated at demand prices.

The result in (D.17) can be interpreted by considering the type of distortion that exists in each market. Consider the effect

$$\Delta \tilde{S}_n = \int_{\phi_m^0}^{\phi_m^1} \left[q_n^s \frac{\partial p_n^s}{\partial \phi_m} - q_n^d \frac{\partial p_n^a}{\partial \phi_m} \right] d\phi_m \qquad \textbf{(D.18)}$$

in each market n of changing ϕ_m from ϕ_m^0 to ϕ_m^1, $n \neq m$. If distortions in any market n, $n \neq m$, are not effective, equilibrium prevails in that market, meaning that $q_n^s = q_n^d$ and $p_n^s = p_n^d$, so that $\partial p_n^s / \partial \phi_m = \partial p_n^d / \partial \phi_m$ and hence

$$\Delta \tilde{S}_n = \int_{\phi_m^0}^{\phi_m^1} (q_n^s - q_n^d) \frac{\partial p_n^d}{\partial \phi_m} d\phi_m = 0 \qquad \textbf{(D.19)}$$

since market n attains equilibrium for each level of the distortion in market m. Also, $\Delta T_n = 0$ in this case. Thus, effects in nondistorted markets are completely captured by equilibrium measurements only in distorted markets.[20]

Next, consider the case where an ad valorem tax exists at an effective level in market n. Then $p_n^d = p_n^s + t_n$, where t_n is the tax rate and equilibrium prevails in the presence of the tax in the sense that $q_n^s = q_n^d$. Hence, $\partial p_n^s / \partial \phi_m = \partial p_n^d / \partial \phi_m$ if the tax rate remains fixed, so that (D.19) continues to apply. From this result, one finds that private welfare effects can be captured com-

---

[20]This result was developed by Arnold C. Harberger. He argued essentially that explicit measurements are required only in distorted markets. The results below carry these considerations somewhat further by determining what special considerations are needed depending on the type of distortion; see Harberger, "Three Basic Postulates."

pletely without explicit measurements in markets with taxes. However, one must note that government tax revenues in such a market increase (decrease, if negative) by

$$\Delta T_n = t_n \left[q_n^s(\phi^1) - q_n^s(\phi^0) \right] = t_n \left[q_n^d(\phi^1) - q_n^d(\phi^0) \right]$$

Thus, whereas estimation of supply and demand in a market distorted by a tax (that does not change) is not necessary for measuring *private* welfare effects, some means of estimating the change in tax revenues is needed for measuring *social* welfare effects; one means of the latter is estimation of the effects on supply and demand in such a market.[21]

The case where a subsidy is distorting market n can be investigated similarly. In this case, $\bar{p}_n^d + s_n = \bar{p}_n^s$ and $q_n^s = q_n^d$ for each ϕ_m, where s_n is a subsidy paid by government per unit of sales in market n. Again, (D.19) applies, so that *private* welfare effects are completely captured without explicit measurement in markets distorted by subsidies (that do not change). However, government costs decrease (increase, if negative) by

$$\Delta T_n = s_n[q_n^s(\phi^0) - q_n^s(\phi^1)] = s_n[q_n^d(\phi^0) - q_n^d(\phi^1)]$$

Again, one means of estimating this effect is to estimate the effects on supply and demand in market n of changing ϕ_m.

Consider next the case where market n is distorted by the imposition of an effective quota on sales or purchases. If such a quota does not change as ϕ_m changes, then q_n^s and q_n^d do not change. Hence, $\Delta \tilde{S}_n$ in (D.18) becomes

$$\Delta \tilde{S}_n = q_n^s \cdot [p_n^s(\phi^1) - p_n^s(\phi^0)] - q_n^d \cdot [p_n^d(\phi^1) - p_n^d(\phi^0)]$$

However, since $q_n^s = q_n^d$ with a quota, one finds that $\Delta \tilde{S}_n = -\Delta T_n$, so that welfare effects on participants in markets with quotas are completely captured in markets with other types of distortions. Thus, no explicit measurements are required in markets distorted by unchanged quotas to evaluate the overall social welfare change associated with altering a distortion elsewhere.

Another distortion, of particular interest in stabilization problems, is the case where a given price level is enforced by means of a buffer stock adjustment. If such an enforced price level does not change as ϕ_m is changed, then p_n^s and p_n^d are constant, so that $\partial p_n^s/\partial \phi_m = \partial p_n^d/\partial \phi_m = 0$. Hence, from (D.18), $\Delta \tilde{S}_n = 0$. However,

$$\Delta T_n = p_n[q_n^s(\phi^0) - q_n^s(\phi^1) + q_n^d(\phi^1) - q_n^d(\phi^0)]$$

---

[21] For empirical purposes, however, since one need only measure the effects of ϕ_m on the equilibrium quantity in market n, estimation of a reduced-form equation describing equilibrium quantity suffices in lieu of estimation of both supply and demand in market n.

which represents a net cash transaction by government in altering the buffer stock level (where $p_n = p_n^s = p_n^d$). Thus, as in the case with taxes and subsidies, estimation of supply and demand in a market distorted by a government buffer stock activity is not necessary in evaluating the *private* welfare effects of altering some other distortion. However, some means of estimating quantity responses in markets distorted by government buffer stocks is necessary to evaluate the government and overall social welfare effect of any change in some other distortion.

Next, consider the case where market n has a government-imposed price floor with an efficient rationing mechanism. If the price floor does not change as ϕ_m changes, then $\partial p_n^d / \partial \phi_m = 0$. Hence, $\Delta \tilde{S}_n$ in (D.18) becomes

$$\Delta \tilde{S}_n = \int_{\phi_m^0}^{\phi_m^1} q_n^s \frac{\partial p_n^s}{\partial \phi_m} d\phi_m = \int_{p_n^s(\phi^0)}^{p_n^s(\phi^1)} q_n^s \, dp_n$$

Also, in this case, producers additionally gain

$$\Delta T_n = q_n(\phi^1) \cdot [p_n^d - p_n^s(\phi^1)] - q_n(\phi^0) \cdot [p_n^d - p_n^s(\phi^0)]$$

where $q_n(\phi^i) = q_n^s(\phi^i) = q_n^d(\phi^i)$, $i = 0, 1$. The evaluation of these two effects requires measurement of the response of both equilibrium supply and demand in market n to changes in ϕ_m.

Similarly, in the case of a price ceiling with an efficient rationing mechanism, one has $\partial p_n^s / \partial \phi_m = 0$ if the price ceiling is not changed as ϕ_m changes. Hence,

$$\Delta \tilde{S}_n = - \int_{p_n^d(\phi^0)}^{p_n^d(\phi^1)} q_n^d \, dp_n$$

and consumers additionally gain

$$\Delta T_n = q_n(\phi^0) \cdot [p_n^s - p_n^d(\phi^0)] - q_n(\phi^1) \cdot [p_n^s - p_n^d(\phi^1)]$$

Again, measurement of the response of both equilibrium supply and equilibrium demand in market n to changes in ϕ_m is required for equilibrium social welfare analysis.

Finally, consider the case where the distortion in market n is due to market power. This case also requires explicit measurement of both equilibrium supply and equilibrium demand in market n, where the equilibrium supply and demand are defined as those that would occur with competitive behavior (for example, equilibrium supply is the equilibrium marginal cost in the case of monopoly). One finds in this case that

$$\Delta \tilde{S}_n = \int_{p_n^s(\phi^0)}^{p_n^s(\phi^1)} q_n^s \, dp_n - \int_{p_n^d(\phi^0)}^{p_n^d(\phi^0)} q_n^d \, dp_n$$

where those exercising market power additionally gain

$$\Delta T_n = q_n(\phi^0) \cdot [p_n{}^s(\phi^0) - p_n{}^d(\phi^0)] - q_n(\phi^1) \cdot [p_n{}^s(\phi^1) - p_n{}^d(\phi^1)]$$

Thus, in the case of market power distortions, measurement of both equilibrium demand and equilibrium supply responses to changes in ϕ_m is necessary in calculating social welfare effects.

Having determined the measurements that are necessary in all markets except market m as the distortion in market m is altered, it remains to consider the necessary measurements in market m. For this case, one finds, using the notation in (D.18), that

$$\Delta \tilde{S}_m = \int_{p_m{}^{s(\phi^0)}}^{p_m{}^{s(\phi^1)}} q_m{}^s dp_m - \int_{p_m{}^{d(\phi^0)}}^{p_m{}^{d(\phi^1)}} q_m{}^d dp_m$$

In addition, ΔT_m must be considered, which leads to the same graphical results for the market in which the distortion is changed, as described graphically in Chapter 9.

With these results, a general equilibrium welfare methodology emerges for which the major limitation is simply the ability to measure equilibrium relationships empirically. However, some results for one further particular case are of interest in view of practical empirical possibilities.

The Case of a Segmented Economy

As discussed in Section 9.5, estimation of equilibrium welfare effects can be complicated by a combination of problems of multicollinearity and econometric identification. Multicollinearity of prices that respond to the same external forces can prevent estimation of partial (or ordinary) supply and demand relationships, whereas econometric identification of equilibrium supply and demand relationships, such as in equations (9.22) and (9.23), is not possible if the same set of determinants of the economy affects both equilibrium supply and equilibrium demand. There is, however, one set of circumstances where the latter problem clearly does not occur. This is when the demand side of a market can be isolated from the supply side of a market in a general equilibrium sense or, in other words, where any change affecting one side of a market cannot filter through a series of other markets, finally affecting the other side of the market.

To develop the results in this case, suppose that the first segment of the economy is composed of consumers $1, \ldots, J_1$ and producers $1, \ldots, K_1$, whereas the second segment of the economy is composed of consumers $J_1 + 1, \ldots, J$ and producers $K_1 + 1, \ldots, K$. Suppose that all individuals possibly participate in the market for q_1 but that only consumers $1, \ldots, J_1$ and producers $1, \ldots, K_1$ possibly participate in markets for $q_2, \ldots, q_{N_1}$; and only consumers $J_1 + 1, \ldots, J$ and producers $K_1 + 1, \ldots, K$ possibly participate in markets for $q_{N_1+1}, \ldots, q_N$. Following the notation of Section D.2, one can thus solve the equilibrium equations

$$\sum_{h=1}^{K_1} \hat{q}_{nk}(p_1, p_2, \ldots, p_{N_1}) - \sum_{j=1}^{J_1} \bar{q}_{nj}(p_1, p_2, \ldots, p_{N_1}, \bar{U}_j) = 0 \qquad \text{(D.20)}$$

for equilibrium prices $\tilde{p}_n(p_1)$ as a function of p_1, $n = 2, \ldots, N_1$; similarly, one can solve the equilibrium equations

$$\sum_{k=K_1+1}^{K} \hat{q}_{nk}(p_1, p_{N_1+1}, \ldots, p_N) - \sum_{j=J_1+1}^{J} \bar{q}_{nj}(p_1, p_{N_1+1}, \ldots, p_N, \bar{U}_j) = 0,$$

$$n = N_1 + 1, \ldots, N \qquad \text{(D.21)}$$

for equilibrium prices $\tilde{p}_n(p_1)$ as a function of p_1, $n = N_1 + 1, \ldots, N$. Thus, one finds that the equilibrium net q_1 supply (demand, if negative) of the first segment of the economy, given by

$$q_{11}(p_1) \equiv \sum_{k=1}^{K_1} \hat{q}_{1k}(p_1, \bar{p}_2, \ldots, \bar{p}_{v_1}) - \sum_{j=1}^{J_1} \bar{q}_{1j}(p_1, \bar{p}_2, \ldots, \bar{p}_{N_1}, \bar{U}_j)$$

does not depend on phenomena in the other segment of the economy except through the price of q_1; similarly, the equilibrium net q_1 supply of the second segment,

$$q_{12}(p_1) \equiv \sum_{k=K_1+1}^{K} \hat{q}_{1k}(p_1, \bar{p}_{N_1+1}, \ldots, \bar{p}_N) - \sum_{j=J_1+1}^{J} \bar{q}_{1j}(p_1, \bar{p}_{N_1+1}, \ldots, \bar{p}_N, \bar{U}_j)$$

does not depend on phenomena in the first segment of the economy except through the price of q_1.

In this case, one finds, using (D.20), that the overall welfare effect of changing the price of q_1 from $p_{11}{}^0$ to $p_{11}{}^1$ for the first segment of the economy is

$$\sum_{k=1}^{K_1} \Delta R_k + \sum_{j=1}^{J_1} \Delta m_j^* = \sum_{n=1}^{N_1} \int_{p_{11}{}^0}^{p_{11}{}^1} \left[\sum_{k=1}^{K_1} \hat{q}_{nk} \frac{\partial \bar{p}_n}{\partial p_1} - \sum_{j=1}^{J_1} \bar{q}_{nj} \frac{\partial \bar{p}_n}{\partial p_1} \right] dp_1$$

$$= \int_{p_{11}{}^0}^{p_{11}{}^1} q_{11} dp_1$$

and similarly, using (D.21), the overall welfare effect of changing the q_1 price from $p_{12}{}^0$ to $p_{12}{}^1$ for the second segment of the economy is

$$\sum_{k=K_1+1}^{K} \Delta R_k + \sum_{j=J_1+1}^{J} \Delta m_j^* = \int_{p_{12}{}^0}^{p_{12}{}^1} q_{12} dp_1$$

Thus, for any policy change that causes the q_1 price associated with marginal behavior of the first (second) segment of the economy to change from p_{11}^0 to p_{11}^1 (p_{12}^0 to p_{12}^1), the overall social welfare effect is

$$\Delta W = \sum_{i=1}^{2} \int_{p_{1i}^0}^{p_{1i}^1} q_{1i}dp_1 + \Delta T_1$$

where ΔT_1 is a transfer effect to government or to one segment or the other,

$$\Delta T_1 = \sum_{i=1}^{2} [p_{1i}^0 q_{1i}(p_{1i}^0) - p_{1i}^1 q_{1i}(p_{1i}^1)]$$

In other words, the change in producer (consumer) surplus for the net supplying (demanding) segment of the economy measures the net welfare effect in terms of willingness to pay over individuals in that segment.[22] These results thus make estimation of general equilibrium supply and demand and some limited distributional calculations possible in some empirical cases where multicollinearity prevents estimation of partial (or ordinary) supply and demand relationships. Further potential for using these results in practical empirical cases is discussed in Section 9.5.

D.3 THE BOADWAY PARADOX

Based on simple graphical analysis, Robin W. Boadway has developed a result which apparently shows that use of compensating (or equivalent) variation leads to an implausible decision criterion when general equilibrium adjustments are considered.[23] E. J. Mishan later developed results which apparently resolved the conflict raised by Boadway, but pointed out another *apparent* problem with the compensating or equivalent variation criterion.[24] Since the conclusions in each of these papers are counterintuitive and very disturbing because of the qualifications they seem to place on the use of compensating and equivalent variation in general equilibrium welfare analysis, a resolution of the conflict is needed. The results of Section D.2 are useful for this purpose since they correspond to a much more general model than that used by Boadway and Mishan.

First, consider the Boadway result in Figure D.1 for a two-good, two-person economy with individuals A and B and goods q and m, where a fixed bundle of goods represented by O_B is available for distribution. Boadway considers the

---

[22]Of course, these results can also be generalized to consider existing distortions in other markets, as demonstrated for the general case above.

[23]Robin W. Boadway, "The Welfare Foundations of Cost–Benefit Analysis," *The Economic Journal,* Vol. 84, No. 336 (December 1974), pp. 926–39.

[24]E. J. Mishan, "The Use of Compensating and Equivalent Variation in Cost–Benefit Analysis," *Economica,* Vol. 43, No. 170 (May 1976), pp. 185–97.

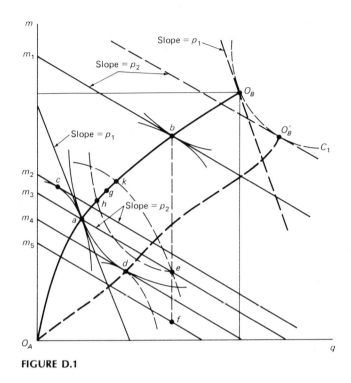

FIGURE D.1

case of a purely redistributive movement along the contract curve $O_A O_B$ from point a to point b. Since both points represent Pareto optima, the results in Chapter 3 suggest that no compensation scheme exists supporting either the move from point a to point b, or vice versa. Hence, the net compensating variation of the move should be zero.

Boadway, however, adds prices to the problem. Suppose that the price of m is unity both before and after the change, whereas the price of q is p_1 in the initial state at point a and is p_2 in the subsequent state at point b. In this case the constructs of Section 5.3 imply a compensating variation of $m_1 - m_4$ for individual A and a compensating variation of $m_2 - m_1$ for individual B since points c and d are the subsequent choices of individuals A and B, respectively, which return both individuals to initial welfare levels by means of compensation in m if price remains at p_2. The sum of these compensating variations is thus $m_2 - m_4 > 0$, which contradicts the results in Chapter 3 for the pure barter economy. This seeming contradiction and apparent inconsistency in the compensating (equivalent) variation criterion is called the Boadway paradox.

Mishan has shown that Boadway's reasoning is incorrect, however, because his subsequent compensated equilibrium where individual A is at point d and individual B is at point c does not correspond to the initial bundle of goods O_B but to some other bundle O_B' on the Scitovsky indifference curve C_1 (which holds both utility levels the same as with distribution of the initial bundle O_B at point a). Thus, the gain in moving from O_B to O_B' with price p_1 (or the gain in moving from O_B' to O_B with price p_2) is not surprising.

Mishan attempts to resolve this paradox by arguing that the compensating variation should be made by comparison of point b with a compensated point which satisfies the physical constraints associated with availability of goods (i.e., a compensated point that is some allocation of O_B). He suggests that point a is the appropriate point for comparison with point b, so that at subsequent price p_2 the compensating variation for individual A is $m_1 - m_3$, which is just exactly offset by the compensating variation, $m_3 - m_1$, for individual B. However, he does not give adequate justification for choosing point a.

To see that his resolution is not generally correct, suppose that the change is made from point a to point b, and then individual A is required to compensate individual B by an amount $m_3 - m_1$. This moves the distribution of goods to point e. But from point e, the initial utility levels cannot possibly be attained by subsequent equilibrium adjustments in the case of Figure D.1; that is, individual A will not agree to any trade that leads to point a, because point a is on a lower indifference curve for individual A than is point e. Free trading following such compensation would lead to equilibrium at some point g between points h and k on the contract curve (where both individuals are better off than at point e). And incidentally, the new prices that result at point g will be associated with a price line tangent to indifference curves for both individuals at point g. Alternatively, suppose that there is some point f directly below point b such that free trading from point f leads to equilibrium at point a; then the correct measure of willingness to pay is the vertical distance between points b and f. This then correctly resolves the Boadway paradox. The compensating variations are $m_1 - m_5$ for individual A and $m_5 - m_1$ for individual B; the net effect is indeed zero, as Mishan asserts and as the barter analysis of Chapter 3 suggests, even though the necessary amount of compensation is different than Mishan argues.[25]

The problem with Mishan's "resolution" of the Boadway paradox is that he ignores the possibility of equilibrium price adjustments following compensation by maintaining a price p_2 at which neither consumer is comfortable with his or her consumption bundle. Neither consumer can satisfy the usual marginal conditions of equilibrium (see Section 2.5), although perhaps neither can find a trading partner in attempting to make all desired adjustments. And incidentally,

---

[25] It is interesting to compare this analysis to that in Figure 3.3, which deals with the Scitovsky reversal paradox. The reversal paradox arises because compensation is not actually paid (which is similar in this respect to the Boadway Paradox). But clearly in Figure 3.3 compensation could be paid to make everyone *actually* better off. This is possible in Figure 3.3 because second best bundles are being compared. In the Boadway case, by definition, everyone cannot be made better off and on further reflection, his compensation is not potentially possible since after adjustment the means for compensation do not exist.

there is no reason to assume that free trade, even at price p_2 from point e, will lead to point a; for example, individual A would be inclined to stop trading at some point to the right of point a on the ae segment.[26]

Two points are worth noting here. First, Mishan is correct that the appropriate measures of compensation must satisfy the physical accounting constraints, so that compensation is indeed feasible. That such physical constraints are satisfied in Section D.2 is obvious, for example, in (D.13). Second, however, compensation must be based *not* on what an individual thinks he or she is willing to pay in a partial sense where all prices (other than a directly distorted price) do not change but on what an individual would be willing to pay if he or she could foresee all accompanying equilibrium adjustments. Mishan's analysis does not fully account for the latter point, but clearly compensation is based on equilibrium price adjustments in Section D.2, since $\hat{q}_{nk}$ and $\bar{q}_{nj}$ depend on equilibrium prices $\bar{p}_i^s$ or $\bar{p}_i^d$, $i = 1, \ldots, N$.

Mishan has proceeded further to point out another seeming paradox based on his misleading concept of general equilibrium compensation as depicted in Figure D.2. Consider the case where both the distribution of goods and the bundle of goods available for distribution changes; the latter may take place along a production possibilities curve PP' as in Figure 2.4 or 2.7. Suppose, initially, that production is at point O_B with distribution at point a, but a change is considered to production at point O_B' with distribution at point b. Again, suppose that the price of m is unity in both cases, so that the initial equilibrium price of q is p_1 and the equilibrium price of q after the change is p_2. Finally, suppose that C_1 is the Scitovsky indifference curve associated with the distribution of output bundle O_B at point a and C_2 is the Scitovsky indifference curve associated with the distribution of output bundle O_B' at point b. Thus, both the initial and terminal situations represent first-best states, so that the results of Chapter 3 imply that no compensation scheme is possible such that one state is preferred to the other.

The Mishan measures, however, imply that the compensating variation for individual A is $m_3 - m_5$, and the compensating variation for individual B is $m_5 - m_4$, for a net gain of $m_3 - m_4$. The latter compensating variation is determined by shifting point b to point d and then to point c as the origin of the indifference map for individual B is shifted from point O_B' to point e and then to point O_B. The net gain of $m_3 - m_4$ corresponds by construction to $m_1 - m_2$, which simply amounts to the difference in values of bundles O_B' and O_B evaluated at price p_2. A similar contradiction with the results of Chapter 3 for the barter economy is obtained (in the case of Figure D.2) by moving back to bundle O_B distributed at

---

[26]The latter point is the reason why Mishan's analysis is not correct, even when the change involves controlling prices. That is, if the change involves fixing both prices so that their ratio is p_2, equilibrium is no longer possible after compensation (given the way Figure D.1 is drawn), and the issue of compensation cannot be decided without imposing further restrictions or incorporating a theory of disequilibrium.

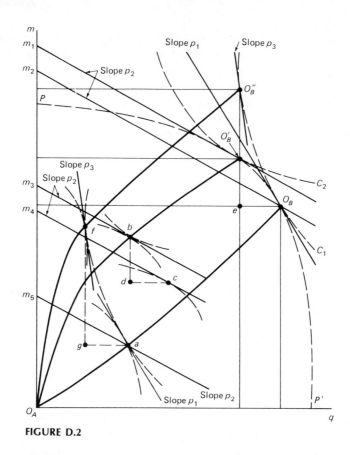

FIGURE D.2

point a since the value of bundle O_B exceeds that of bundle O_B' when both are evaluated at price p_1.

Again, the problem with the apparent inconsistency raised by Mishan is due to a lack of consideration of equilibrium price adjustments following compensation; since price p_2 would not be retained with compensation, the initial bundle O_B cannot generally be evaluated at price p_2 for purposes of comparison. In point of fact, any compensation scheme that restores both individuals to their original utility levels must correspond to a bundle of goods along Scitovsky curve C_1, with distribution at some point along the indifference curve for individual A that passes through point a. If compensation is paid only in m, then the sum of compensating variations must be a negative amount given by the vertical distance between O_B' and O_B''; if the total amount of q is held constant and the total amount of m is changed following the change from O_B to O_B', then movement from O_B' to O_B'' is the only way that both individuals can be restored to their initial utility levels. Furthermore, the compensation for individuals A and B which yields a net negative compensation of the distance between O_B' and O_B'' must be one such that subsequent equilibrium adjustments (in moving

468

to the contract curve in the Edgeworth box associated with O_B'') lead to the distribution of bundle O_B'' at point f corresponding to Scitovsky curve C_1 (where $ga = eO_B$ and $gf = eO_B''$). The resulting price of q following the change with compensation is thus p_3.

With these considerations, the paradox raised by Mishan is resolved. From Figure D.2 it is clear that a positive sum of compensating variations can never be generated in moving from one first-best state to another since the Scitovsky curve at the initial bundle by definition does not intersect the production possibilities frontier. Alternatively, the analysis in Figure D.2 can be extended to the case where the initial state corresponds to efficient distribution of a given bundle, but the corresponding Scitovsky indifference curve is not tangent to the production possibilities curve. In this case, one can show that a positive sum of compensating variations is generated by moving to any production bundle above the corresponding Scitovsky curve (with efficient distribution), since the point O_B'' will then lie directly below O_B'. Similarly, the other results in Chapter 3 for the barter economy carry through in a market economy where compensation is paid in income and equilibrium adjustments follow compensation.

D.4   EMPIRICAL CONSIDERATIONS

Aside from the empirical considerations discussed in Chapter 9 and Section D.2, another important consideration suggested by the results in this appendix has to do with estimating partial market supply and demand relationships in such a way that the sum of partial welfare effects over all markets is equal to the implied general equilibrium effects. As indicated in Section 9.5, two approaches are possible in analyzing equilibrium economic welfare effects. One way is to attempt estimation of general equilibrium supply and demand in the market for which a change in policy is considered (as well as any other distorted markets for which effects of the change must be considered). In so doing, one obtains only an overall welfare effect, with no information regarding the distribution of effects or the necessary extent of compensation needed to make any indicated changes Pareto preferable. And, of course, to undertake such changes without compensation involves a value judgment in ignorance because income distribution is altered in an unknown way.

The alternative approach which can provide needed distributional information is to estimate a system of partial supply and demand relationships for all markets where substantive effects may occur. Equilibrium distributional effects can then be determined by solving the system of supply and demand equations for equilibrium prices before and after a contemplated change and then evaluating partial welfare effects on each market group using the methodology of Chapters 4 through 7 as generalized by the aggregation in Chapter 8.[27]

---

[27]In estimation of these supplies and demands, prices in markets among the group of markets included empirically would be considered as endogenous, whereas any prices

However, when such a system of supplies and demands is estimated, one can solve for implied equilibrium supply and demand for the market in which a change is contemplated. Thus, one must be concerned that the implied equilibrium welfare effect is, indeed, the sum of the implied partial welfare effects, as the theory in Section D.2 indicates. Otherwise, the economic welfare analyst can arbitrarily influence the estimated overall welfare effects by choosing to use either the implied equilibrium welfare effect or the sum of partial effects over all included (affected) market groups. Furthermore, the added distributional information is hard to interpret if the disaggregated effects do not sum to the total effect.

This problem of inconsistency in estimated partial and general welfare effects can be avoided by ensuring that certain theoretical relationships exist among the supplies and demands that relate to common groups of decision makers. Thus, the problem here is closely related to the empirical considerations in Sections A.5 and B.13 respectively. That is, suppose that a single group of decision makers is solely responsible for both the demand for q_1 and the supply of q_2. Then the estimated demand relationship for q_1 and the estimated supply relationship for q_2 must result from the same producer or consumer decision problem or must be an aggregation of such relationships that result from common underlying decision problems. If this condition is not satisfied, then even the partial effects are ambiguous, as indicated in Sections A.5 and B.13; thus, potential inconsistency with implied equilibrium effects is obvious.

Again, the two approaches paralleling those outlined in Sections A.5 and B.13 are possible for avoiding these problems. With the primal approach, direct utility and production functional forms are specified for consumers and producers, respectively. Then implied functional forms for supply and demand are generated by utility or profit maximization, as the case may be. Finally, these functions must be aggregated over consumers and producers so that the existence of common parameters in different supplies and demands can be considered in estimation of market relationships. With this approach, the theoretical results of Section D.2 guarantee that partial effects will sum to the implied equilibrium effect.

With the dual approach, one begins by specifying functional forms for the indirect utility functions of consumers and the indirect profit or quasi-rent functions of producers. Then the implied individual supply and demand functional forms can be derived as in Sections A.5 and B.13. Finally, these functional forms must be aggregated over producers and consumers to obtain functional forms for market supplies and demands in which the existence of

---

from other markets would be considered as exogenous. The latter assumption would be appropriate if, indeed, no substantive effects of the contemplated change occur outside the group of markets considered empirically. One must be careful in this distinction, however, because a very small price effect in a distant market can have a substantive effect if it is imposed on a very large volume of trade.

common parameters is evident and can be considered in estimation.[28] Again, with this approach the theoretical results of Section D.2 guarantee that partial effects will sum to the implied overall equilibrium effect. Thus, based on these additional empirical needs and the relative tractability of the dual approach, duality appears to hold important possibilities for measurement of equilibrium welfare effects in empirical policy analysis.

D.5　FURTHER GENERALIZATIONS WITH RISK AND INTERTEMPORAL CONSIDERATIONS

It remains to generalize the equilibrium welfare analysis of this appendix for the case of dynamic considerations in producer and consumer adjustment and/or where decision makers recognize uncertainties regarding prices or production processes. This can be done by combining the framework of Sections C.2 and C.3 with the concept of equilibrium in (current) prices discussed in Section D.2.

Consider a competitive economy involving N goods traded in each time period from current time t to some future time horizon T. Each of J consumers possesses an intertemporal utility function, $\tilde{U}_j(\tilde{q}_{tj}^T)$, an intertemporal household production function, $\tilde{f}_{tj}^T(\tilde{q}_{tj}^T, \bar{q}_j^t) = 0$, and budget constraints $\sum_{n=1}^{N} p_{nh} \tilde{q}_{nhj} = m_{hj}^*$, $h = t, \ldots, T$, where definitions are the same as in Section C.3 except that tildes are added to denote reference to consumers and j subscripts are added to refer to specific consumers. Similarly, each of K producers possesses an intertemporal utility function, $\hat{U}_k(\pi_{tk} - K_{tk}, \ldots, \pi_{Tk} - K_{Tk})$, and an intertemporal production function, $\hat{f}_{tk}^T(\hat{q}_{tk}^T, \bar{q}_k^t) = 0$ where $\pi_{hk} = \sum_{n=1}^{N} p_{nh}\hat{q}_{nhk}$ and all other definitions are the same as in Section C.2 except that carets are added to denote reference to producers and k subscripts are added to refer to specific producers.

---

[28]Summing functional forms over many decision makers is impractical for empirical purposes unless some parameters are common to groups of decision makers; otherwise, the number of parameters requiring estimation can be econometrically intractable. For example, a common approach is to assume that all individuals in a group have the same utility or production (profit) function where possibly additional variables are added to explain differences in tastes or production efficiency. Then market relationships are obtained either by multiplying individual demands and supplies by the number of individuals in the group (if efficiency or taste variables are not included) or by integrating the implied individual supply and demand relationships with respect to the distribution of efficiency or taste shifters over individuals in the group. For an application of the latter approach where differences in taste are associated with income, see E. R. Berndt, M. N. Darrough, and W. E. Diewert, "Flexible Functional Forms and Expenditure Distributions: An Application to Canadian Consumer Demand Functions," *International Economic Review*, Vol. 18, No. 3 (October 1977), pp. 651–75.

Now consider imposing a policy change which alters the subjective distribution from $\hat{\bar{p}}_{tj}{}^0$, $\hat{\alpha}_{tj}{}^0$ to $\hat{\bar{p}}_{tj}{}^1$, $\hat{\alpha}_{tj}{}^1$ for each consumer j and from $\hat{\bar{p}}_{tk}{}^0$, $\hat{\alpha}_{tk}{}^0$ to $\hat{\bar{p}}_{tk}{}^1$, $\hat{\alpha}_{tk}{}^1$ for each producer k. Under these conditions, one can solve for equilibrium prices in each successive time period by equating the sum of supplies to the sum of demands in all markets (assuming the existence of short-run equilibrium).[29] Then the welfare analysis for each individual consumer or producer can be carried out following Sections C.2 and C.3. Alternatively, welfare effects can be determined for *groups* of individuals following the results in Sections C.2 and C.3 since areas behind market supplies and demands are the sum of areas behind supplies and demands of individuals involved in the market, respectively (see Chapter 8). That is, the results in Sections C.2 and C.3 hold for groups of individuals where the demands and supplies are market supplies and demands by those groups.[30] For these purposes, however, one must note that the appropriate market supply and demand relationships for such calculations are the compensated relationships; areas behind ordinary supplies and demands have relevance only insofar as they approximate areas behind compensated supplies and demands (such as in the producer case of constant absolute risk aversion where ordinary and compensated curves coincide).

With these generalizations the meaning of areas behind equilibrium supplies and demands is a more difficult issue. For example, one can show in a static context that the general conclusions of Section D.2 for interpretation of areas behind general equilibrium curves hold if production is nonstochastic or stochastic but predetermined and if all decision makers are risk neutral or risk (represented by the α_t of Sections C.2 and C.3) is held constant for all decision makers.[31] But in general equilibrium, the assumption that risks remain fixed

---

[29]If conditions are such that the equilibrium is not unique, then the welfare analysis can be performed only if one can determine from observed data which equilibrium is appropriate.

[30]One must bear in mind, however, that such market supplies and demands may be sensitive to distribution among the groups of income or fixed costs or other determinants.

[31]To see this, suppose that C_i is the compensation required by individual i for some change in a policy instrument from ϕ_0 to ϕ_1 which changes expected prices from $\bar{p}_{ti}{}^0$ to $\bar{p}_{ti}{}^1$ and other parameters from $\alpha_{ti}{}^0$ to $\alpha_{ti}{}^1$. The welfare effect for the individual can be represented as

$$C_i = \int_L dC_i = \int_{\phi_0}^{\phi_1} \sum_{n=1}^{N} \frac{\partial C_i}{\partial \bar{p}_{nti}} \frac{\partial \bar{p}_{nti}}{\partial \phi} d\phi + \int_{L_\alpha} dC_i$$

where L is any path of integration from $\bar{p}_{ti}{}^0$, $\alpha_{ti}{}^0$ to $\bar{p}_{ti}{}^1 > \alpha_{ti}{}^0$ and L_α is any path of integration from $\alpha_{ti}{}^0$ to $\alpha_{ti}{}^1$. The latter term is trivially zero if $\alpha_{ti}{}^0 = \alpha_{ti}{}^1$ or if the individual is risk neutral in which case C_i does not depend on α_{ti}. Thus, using the results in Sections A.6 or C.2 and C.3, $\partial C_i / \partial \bar{p}_{nti}$ can be replaced by supplies or demands $\bar{q}_{nti}$ to obtain

$$C_i = \int_{\phi_0}^{\phi_1} \sum_{n=1}^{N} \bar{q}_{nti} \frac{\partial \bar{p}_{nti}}{\partial \phi} d\phi$$

when altering policy is difficult to accept. And as shown in Appendix A, not even areas behind all ordinary curves hold direct welfare significance when production is currently stochastic. Furthermore, as shown in Appendix C, areas behind ordinary curves in a present time period cannot always capture future welfare effects. Thus, it is not surprising that results in Section D.2 do not generalize in a straightforward manner to provide interpretation of areas behind general equilibrium curves in all cases.

---

where $\bar{q}_{nti}$ is a compensated supply or demand curve such as in (C.43) or (C.60). From this point, the analysis can proceed as in Section D.2 since this result is the same as in equation (D.10) where C_k and $\bar{q}_{nti}$ are substituted for ΔR_k and $\hat{q}_{nk}$ for producers and C_j and $\bar{q}_{ntj}$ are substituted for $-\Delta m_j{}^*$ and $-\tilde{q}_{nj}$ for consumers, respectively.

Bibliography

Abbott, Michael, and Orley Ashenfelter, "Labour Supply, Commodity Demand and the Allocation of Time," *Review of Economic Studies,* 43, no. 135 (October 1976), 389–411.

Addison, John T., and W. Stanley Siebert, *The Market for Labor: An Analytical Treatment.* Santa Monica, Calif.: Goodyear Publishing Company, Inc., 1979.

Anderson, J. E., "The Social Cost of Input Distortions: A Comment and a Generalization," *American Economic Review,* 66, no. 1 (March 1976), 235–38.

———, "A Note on Welfare Surpluses and Gains from Trade in General Equilibrium," *American Economic Review,* 64, no. 4 (September 1974), 758–62.

Anderson, James, and John G. Riley, "International Trade with Fluctuating Prices," *International Economic Review,* 17, no. 1 (February 1976), 76–97.

Arrow, K. J., *Social Choice and Individual Values.* New York: John Wiley & Sons, Inc., 1951.

Arrow, K. J., "The Organization of Economic Activity: Issues Pertinent to the Choice of Market Versus Nonmarket Allocation," in *Public Expenditures and Policy Analysis,* eds. J. Margolis and Robert H. Haveman. Chicago: Markham Publishing Company, 1970.

Arrow, K. J., and F. Hahn, *Competitive Equilibrium Analysis.* San Francisco: Holden-Day, Inc., 1971.

Arrow, K. J., and R. C. Lind, "Uncertainty and the Evaluation of Public Investment Decisions," *American Economic Review,* 60, no. 3 (June 1970), 364–78.

474

Atkinson, A. B., "On the Measurement of Inequality," *Journal of Economic Theory,* 2, no. 3 (September 1970), 244–63.

Bailey, M. J., "The Interpretation and Application of the Compensation Principle," *Economic Journal,* 64, no. 253 (March 1954), 39–52.

Bator, F. M., "The Anatomy of Market Failure," *Quarterly Journal of Economics,* 72, no. 3 (August 1958), 351–79.

Baumol, W., and W. Oates, "The Use of Standards and Prices for Protection of the Environment," *Swedish Journal of Economics,* 73, no. 1 (March 1971), 42–54.

Becker, Gary S., "A Theory of the Allocation of Time," *Economic Journal,* 75, no. 299 (September 1965), 493–517.

Bellman, R., and S. Dreyfus, *Applied Dynamic Programming.* Princeton, N.J.: Princeton University Press, 1962.

Bentham, Jeremy, *Principles of Morals and Legislation* (1823 ed.). New York: Doubleday Book Company, 1961.

Bergson, Abram, "A Note on Consumer's Surplus," *Journal of Economic Literature,* 13, no. 1 (March 1975), 42.

———, "A Reformulation of Certain Aspects of Welfare Economics," *Quarterly Journal of Economics* 52 (February 1938), 310–34.

Berndt, E. R., M. N. Darrough, and W. E. Diewert, "Flexible Functional Form and Expenditure Distributions: An Application to Canadian Consumer Demand Functions," *International Economic Review,* 18, no. 3 (October 1977), 651–75.

Bhagwati, Jagdish, "The Pure Theory of International Trade: A Survey," in American Economic Association and Royal Economic Society, *Surveys of Economic Theory,* 2 (New York: AEA/RES, 1965), 213.

Bieri, Jurg, and Andrew Schmitz, "Export Instability, Monopoly Power and Welfare," *Journal of International Economics,* 3, no. 4 (November 1973), 389–96.

———, "Market Intermediaries and Price Instability: Some Welfare Implications," *American Journal of Agricultural Economics,* 56, no. 2 (May 1974), 280–85.

Blackorby, Charles, Daniel Primont, and R. Robert Russell, *Duality, Separability, and Functional Structure: Theory and Economic Applications.* New York: Elsevier/North Holland, Inc., 1978.

Boadway, Robin W., "The Welfare Foundations of Cost-Benefit Analysis," *Economic Journal,* 84, no. 336 (December 1974), 926–39.

Bohm, Peter, "An Approach to the Problems of Estimating Demand for Public Goods," *Swedish Journal of Economics,* 73, no. 1 (March 1971), 94–105.

Brookshire, David S., Berry C. Ives, and William D. Schultze, "The Valuation of Aesthetic Preferences," *Journal of Environmental Economics and Management,* 3, no. 4 (December 1976), 325–46.

Brown, Gardner M., and Henry O. Pollakowski, "Economic Valuation of Shoreline," *Review of Economics and Statistics,* 59 (August 1977), 272–78.

Buchanan, J., "External Diseconomies, Corrective Taxes, and Market Structure," *American Economic Review,* 59, no. 1 (March 1969), 174–77.

Burns, Michael E., "A Note on the Concept and Measure of Consumer Surplus," *American Economic Review,* 63, no. 3 (June 1973), 335–44.

———, "On the Uniqueness of Consumer's Surplus and the Invariance of Economic Index Numbers," *The Manchester School of Economic and Social Studies,* 45, no. 1 (March 1977), 41–61.

Burt, Oscar R., "Optimal Resource Use Over Time with an Application to Groundwater," *Management Science,* 11 (1964), 80–93.

Burt, O. R., and D. Brewer, "Estimates of Net Social Benefits for Outdoor Recreation," *Econometrica,* 39, no. 5 (September 1971), 813–27.

Burt, O. R., and R. G. Cummings, "Production and Investment Natural Resource Industries," *American Economic Review,* 60, no. 4 (1973), 576–90.

Burt, Oscar R., Won W. Koo, and Norman J. Dudley, "Optimal Stochastic Control of U.S. Wheat Stocks and Exports," *American Journal of Agricultural Economics,* 62, no. 2 (May 1980), 172–87.

Carter, Colin C., Nancy Gallini, and Andrew Schmitz, "Producer-Consumer Trade-Offs in Export Cartels," *American Journal of Agricultural Economics,* 62, no. 4 (November 1980), 812–18.

Carter, Colin, Darrell Hueth, John Mamer, and Andrew Schmitz, "Labor Strikes and the Price of Lettuce," *Western Journal of Agricultural Economics,* 6, no. 1 (July 1981), 1–13.

Cesario, Frank J., "Value of Time in Recreation Benefit Studies," *Land Economics,* 55, no. 1 (February 1976), 32–41.

Chipman, John S., and James C. Moore, "Compensating Variation, Consumer's Surplus, and Welfare," *American Economic Review,* 70, no. 5 (December 1980), 933–49.

————, "The Scope of Consumer's Surplus Arguments," in *Evolution, Welfare, and Time in Economics: Essays in Honor of Nicholas Georgescu-Roegen,* ed. Anthony M. Tang et al. Lexington, Mass.: Heath-Lexington Books, 1976, 69–123.

Ciriacy-Wantrup, S. V., *Resource Conservation: Economics and Policies.* Berkeley: University of California Press, 1952.

Clark, Colin W., *Mathematical Bioeconomics: The Optimum Management of Renewable Resources.* New York: John Wiley & Sons, Inc., 1976.

Clawson, Marion, and Jack L. Knetsch, *Economics of Outdoor Recreation.* Baltimore: Johns Hopkins University Press, 1966.

Coase, R. H., "The Problem of Social Cost," *Journal of Law and Economics,* 3 (October 1960), 1–44.

Cochrane, Willard W., and Yigal Danin, *Reserve Stock Grain Models: The World and United States, 1975–1985.* Minnesota Agricultural Experiment Station Technical Bulletin No. 305, 1976.

Cohen, Kalman J., and Richard M. Cyert, *Theory of the Firm: Resource Allocation in a Market Economy.* Englewood Cliffs, N.J.: Prentice-Hall, Inc., 1965.

Comanor, William S., and Harvey Leibenstein, "Allocative Efficiency, X-Efficiency and the Measurement of Welfare Losses, *Economica,* 36, no. 143 (August 1969), 304–09.

Cowling, Keith, and Dennis C. Mueller, "The Social Costs of Monopoly Power," *Economic Journal,* 88, no. 352 (December 1978), 740.

Crosson, P. R., R. G. Cummings, and K. D. Frederick, *Selected Water Management Issues in Latin America.* Baltimore: Johns Hopkins University Press, 1978.

Cummings, R. G., "Some Extensions of the Economic Theory of Exhaustible Resources," *Western Economic Journal,* 7 (September 1969), 201–10.

Currie, John M, John A. Murphy, and Andrew Schmitz, "The Concept of Economic Surplus and Its Use in Economic Analysis," *Economic Journal,* 81, (December 1971), 741–99.

Dales, J. H., *Pollution, Property, and Prices.* Toronto, Canada: University of Toronto Press, 1968.

Danese, Arthur E., *Advanced Calculus.* Boston: Allyn and Bacon, Inc., 1965.

Dardis, Rachel, and Janet Dennisson, "The Welfare Costs of Alternative Methods of Protecting Raw Wool in the United States," *American Journal of Agricultural Economics,* 51, no. 2 (May 1969), 303–19.

d'Arge, Ralph, William Schultze, and David Brookshire, *Benefit-Cost Evaluation of Long Term Future Effects: The Case of CO,* University of Wyoming Resource and Environmental Economics Laboratory Research Paper No. 13, April 1980.

Dasgupta, Partha, and Geoffrey Heal, "The Optimal Depletion of Exhaustible Resources," *The Review of Economic Studies: Symposium on the Economics of Exhaustible Resources,* 1974, 3–28.

David, Elizabeth L., "Lake Shore Property Values: A Guide to Public Investment in Recreation," *Water Resources Research,* 4, no. 4 (August 1968), 697–707.

Davis, O. A., and A. B. Whinston, "Welfare Economics and the Theory of the Second Best," *Review of Economic Studies,* 32 (1965), 1–14.

———, "Piecemeal Policy and the Theory of Second Best," *Review of Economic Studies,* 34 (1967), 323–31.

Diewert, W. E., "Applications of Duality Theory," in *Frontiers of Econometrics,* vol. 2, ed. M. Intriligator and D. Kendrick. Amsterdam: North-Holland Publishing Company, 1974.

———, "Functional Forms for Profit and Transformation Functions," *Journal of Economic Theory,* 6 (1973), 284–316.

Draper, N. R., H. Smith, *Applied Regression Analysis.* New York: John Wiley & Sons, Inc., 1966.

Dupuit, J., "On the Measurement of Utility of Public Works," *Annals des Ponts et Chaussees,* Second Series, 8 (1844).

Eckstein, O. "A Survey of the Theory of Public Expenditure," and "Reply," *Public Finances: Needs, Sources, and Utilization.* Princeton, N.J.: National Bureau of Economic Research, 1961, 493–504.

———, *Water-Resource Development: The Economics of Project Evaluation.* Cambridge, Mass.: Harvard University Press, 1961.

Evenson, R. E., P. E. Waggoner, and V. W. Ruttan, "Economic Benefit from Research: An Example from Agriculture," *Science,* 205 (September 14, 1979), 1101–7.

Ferguson, C. E., *The Neoclassical Theory of Production and Distribution.* Cambridge, England: Cambridge University Press, 1969.

———, *Microeconomic Theory.* Homewood, Ill.: Richard D. Irwin, Inc., 1969.

Fisher, Anthony C., "On Measures of Natural Resource Scarcity," in *Scarcity and Growth Reconsidered,* ed. V. Kerry Smith. Baltimore: Johns Hopkins University Press, 1979.

Freund, R. J., "The Introduction of Risk into a Programming Model," *Econometrica,* 24 (1956), 253–63.

Friedman, Milton, and Rose Friedman, *Free to Choose.* New York: Harcourt, Brace, and Jovanovich, 1980.

Fuss, M., and D. McFadden, *Production Economics: A Dual Approach to Theory and Applications,* vols. 1, 2. Amsterdam: North-Holland Publishing Company, 1978.

Goldberger, Arthur S., *Econometric Theory.* New York: John Wiley & Sons, Inc., 1964.

Goran, Karl, and Ronald Wyzga, *Economic Measurement of Environmental Damage.* Paris: Organisation for Economic Cooperation and Development, 1976.

Gorman, W. M., "The Intransitivity of Certain Criteria Used in Welfare Economics," *Oxford Economic Papers,* New Series, 7, no. 1 (February 1955), 25–35.

Hanemann, W. Michael, "Quality Changes, Consumer's Surplus, and Hedonic Price Indices," Department of Agricultural and Resource Economics Working Paper No. 116, University of California, Berkeley, 1980.

———, "Water Quality and the Demand for Recreation," Agricultural and Resource Economics Working Paper No. 164, University of California, Berkeley, March 1981.

Harberger, Arnold C., "Three Basic Postulates of Applied Welfare Economics: An Interpretive Essay," *Journal of Economic Literature,* 9, no. 3 (September 1971), 785–97.

———, "Monopoly and Resource Allocation," *American Economic Review, Proceedings,* 44 (May 1954), 77–87.

Hause, John C., "The Theory of Welfare Cost Measurement," *Journal of Political Economy,* 83 (December 1975), 1154–78.

Haveman, Robert H., "The Opportunity Cost of Displaced Private Spending and the Social Discount Rate," *Water Resources Research,* 5, no. 5 (October 1969).

Hazell, P. B. R., and P. L. Scandizzo, "Market Intervention Policies When Production Is Risky," *American Journal of Agricultural Economics,* 57, no. 4 (November 1975), 641–49.

———, "Optimal Price Intervention Policies When Production Is Risky," *Risk, Uncertainty and Agricultural Development,* ed. James A. Roumasset, Jean-Marc Boussard, and Inderjit Singh. Philippines: Southeast Asian Regional Center for Graduate Study and Research in Agriculture. New York: Agricultural Development Council, 1979.

Henderson, James M., and Richard E. Quandt, *Microeconomic Theory: A Mathematical Approach* (2nd ed.). New York: McGraw-Hill Book Company, 1971.

Herfindahl, O. C., and A. V. Kneese, *Economic Theory of Natural Resources.* Columbus, Ohio: Charles E. Merrill Publishing Company, 1974.

Hicks, J. R., "The Foundations of Welfare Economics," *Economic Journal,* 49, no. 196 (December 1939), 696–712.

———, "The Four Consumers' Surpluses," *Review of Economic Studies,* XI, no. 1 (Winter 1943), 31–41.

———, "The Rehabilitation of Consumer's Surplus," *Review of Ecomonic Studies,* 8 (February 1940–41), 112.

———, *A Revision of Demand Theory.* Oxford England: Clarendon Press, 1956.

Hirshleifer, Jack, "Investment Decision under Uncertainty: Applications of the State Preference Approach," *Quarterly Journal of Economics,* 80, no. 2 (May 1966), 270–75.

———, *Price Theory and Applications.* Englewood Cliffs, N.J.: Prentice-Hall, Inc., 1976.

Hirshleifer, Jack, James C. De Haven, and Jerome W. Milliman, *Water Supply: Economics, Technology, and Policy.* Chicago: University of Chicago Press, 1960.

Hochman, Eithan, David Zilberman, and Richard E. Just, "Internalization in a Stochastic Pollution Model," *Water Resources Research,* 13, no. 6 (December 1977), 877–81.

Hoos, Sidney (ed.), *Agricultural Marketing Boards: An International Perspective.* Cambridge, Mass.: Ballinger Publishing Company, 1979.

Hotelling, H., "Economics of Exhaustible Resources," *Journal of Political Economy,* 39 (April 1931), 137–75.

———, "The General Welfare in Relation to Problems of Taxation and of Railway and Utility Rates," *Econometrica,* 6 (1938), 242–69.

Howe, Charles W., *Natural Resource Economics: Issues, Analysis, and Policy.* New York: John Wiley & Sons, Inc., 1979.

Howe, Charles W., and K. William Easter, *Interbasin Transfers of Water: Economic Issues and Impacts.* Baltimore: Johns Hopkins University Press, 1971.

Hueth, Darrell L., and Andrew Schmitz, "International Trade in Intermediate and Final Goods: Some Welfare Implications of Destabilized Prices," *Quarterly Journal of Economics,* 86, no. 3 (August 1972), 351–65.

Intriligator, Michael D., *Econometric Models, Techniques, and Applications.* Englewood Cliffs, N.J.: Prentice-Hall, Inc., 1978.

Johnson, Harry G., "The Cost of Protection and the Scientific Tariff," *Journal of Political Economy,* 68, no. 4 (August 1960), 327–45.

Just, Richard E., "Theoretical and Empirical Considerations in Agricultural Buffer Stock Policy under the Food and Agriculture Act of 1977," prepared for the U.S. General Accounting Office, Washington, DC, 1981.

Just, Richard E., Andrew Schmitz, and David Zilberman, "Price Controls and Optimal Export Policies under Alternative Market Structures," *American Economic Review,* 69, no. 4 (September 1979), 706–14.

Just, Richard E., Ernst Lutz, Andrew Schmitz, and Stephen Turnovsky, "The Distribution of Welfare Gains from International Price Stabilization under Distortions," *American Journal of Agricultural Economics,* 59, no. 4, (November 1977), 652–61.

Just, Richard E., and Darrell L. Hueth, "Multimarket Welfare Measurement," *American Economic Review,* 69, no. 5 (December 1979), 947–54.

Just, Richard E., and David Zilberman, "Asymmetry of Taxes and Subsidies in Regulating Stochastic Mishap," *Quarterly Journal of Economics,* 93, no. 1 (February 1979), 139–48.

Just, Richard E., and J. Arne Hallam, "Functional Flexibility in Analysis of Commodity Price Stabilization Policy," *Proceedings, Journal of the American Statistical Association,* Business and Economic Statistics Section, 1978, 177–86.

Just, Richard E., and Wen S. Chern, "Tomatoes, Technology, and Oligopsony," *Bell Journal of Economics,* 11, no. 2 (Autumn 1980), 584–602.

Kaldor, Nicholas, "Welfare Propositions of Economics and Interpersonal Comparisons of Utility," *The Economic Journal,* 49, no. 195 (September 1939), 549–52.

Knetch, Jack L., "Economics of Including Recreation as a Purpose of Eastern Water Projects," *Journal of Farm Economics,* 46, no. 5 (December 1964), 1148–57.

Konandreas, Panos A., and Andrew Schmitz, "Welfare Implications of Grain Price Stabilization: Some Empirical Evidence for the United States," *American Journal of Agricultural Economics,* 60, no. 1 (February 1978), 74–84.

Krauss, Melvin, and David Winch, "Mishan on the Gains from Trade: Comment," *American Economic Review,* 61, no. 1 (March 1971), 199, 200.

Krutilla, John V., "Reflections of an Applied Welfare Economist," presidential address at the Annual Meeting of the Association of Environmental and Resource Economists, Denver, Colorado, September 1980.

Krutilla, John V., and Anthony C. Fisher, *The Economics of Natural Environments.* Baltimore: Johns Hopkins University Press, 1978.

Krutilla, John V., and Otto Eckstein, *Multiple Purpose River Development.* Baltimore: Johns Hopkins University Press, 1958.

Kurz, Mordecai, "An Experimental Approach to the Determination of the Demand for Public Goods," *Journal of Public Economics,* 3 (1974), 329–48.

Lancaster, K. J., "A New Approach to Consumer Theory," *Journal of Political Economy,* 74, no. 2 (April 1966), 132–57.

Lee, Dwight R., "Price Controls, Binding Constraints, and Intertemporal Economic Decision Making," *Journal of Political Economy,* 86, no. 2 (April 1978), 293–302.

Leftwich, Richard H., *The Price System and Resource Allocation,* (7th ed.). Hinsdale, Ill.: The Dryden Press, 1979.

Lerner, Abba P., "Statics and Dynamics in Social Economics," *Economic Journal,* 47 (June 1937), 80.

———, "The Concept of Monopoly and the Measurement of Monopoly Power," *Review of Economic Studies,* 1, nos. 1–3 (1933–34), 157–75.

Lipsey, R. G., and R. K. Lancaster, "The General Theory of the Second Best," *Review of Economic Studies,* 24 (1956–57), 11–32.

Mansfield, E., J. Rapoport, A. Romeo, E. Villani, S. Wagner, and F. Husic, *The Production and Application of New Industrial Technology.* New York: W. W. Norton & Company Inc., 1977.

Marglin, S., "The Social Rate of Discount and the Optimal Rate of Investment," *Quarterly Journal of Economics,* 77 (1963), 95–111.

Marshall, Alfred, *Principles of Economics.* London: Macmillan & Company Ltd., 1930.

Massell, B. F., "Price Stabilization and Welfare," *Quarterly Journal of Economics,* 83, no. 2 (May 1969), 285–97.

McConnell, K., "Some Problems in Estimating the Demand for Outdoor Recreation," *American Journal of Agricultural Economics,* 57, no. 2 (May 1975), 330–34.

McFadden, Daniel, "Cost, Revenue, and Profit Functions," in *Production Economics: A Dual Approach to Theory and Applications,* 2 vols., eds. Melvyn Fuss and Daniel McFadden. Amsterdam: North-Holland Publishing Company, 1978.

McFadden, Daniel, and Sidney G. Winter. *Lecture Notes on Consumer Theory,* University of California, Berkeley, 1968.

McInnerney, John, "The Simple Analytics of Natural Resource Economics," *British Journal of Agricultural Economics,* 27, no. 1 (1976), 31–52.

McKenzie, George W., "Consumer's Surplus without Apology: Comment," *American Economic Review,* 69, no. 3 (June 1979), 465–68.

Michael, R. T., and G. S. Becker, "On the New Theory of Consumer Behavior," *Swedish Journal of Economics,* 75 (1973).

Mincer, Jacob, "Market Prices, Opportunity Costs, and Income Effects," in *Measurement in Economics: Studies in Mathematical Economics and Econometrics in Memory of Yehuda Grunfeld,* ed. C. Christ et al. Stanford, Calif.: Stanford University Press, 1963.

Mishan, E. J., "Rent as a Measure of Welfare Change," *American Economic Review,* 49, no. 3 (June 1959), 394.

———, "The Plain Truth about Consumer Surplus," *Nationalokonomie Journal of Economics,* 37, nos. 1, 2 (Spring 1977), 1–24.

———, "The Use of Compensating and Equivalent Variation in Cost-Benefit Analysis," *Economica,* 43, no. 170 (May 1976), 185–97.

———, "Welfare Criteria: Resolution of a Paradox," *Economic Journal,* 83, no. 331 (September 1973), 747–48.

———, "What Is Producer's Surplus?" *American Economic Review,* 58, no. 5, part 1 (December 1968), 1279.

———, *Cost-Benefit Analysis: An Introduction.* New York: Praeger Publishers, Inc., 1971.

———, *Cost-Benefit Analysis* (2nd ed.). New York: Praeger Publishers, Inc., 1976.

Mueller, Dennis C., *Public Choice.* London: Cambridge University Press, 1979.

Nicholson, Walter, *Microeconomic Theory: Basic Principles and Extensions* (2nd ed.), Chapter 6. Hinsdale, Ill.: The Dryden Press, 1978.

Nozick, R., *Anarchy, State and Utopia.* New York: Basic Books, Inc., 1974.

Oi, W. Y., "The Desirability of Price Instability under Perfect Competition," *Econometrica,* 27, no. 1 (January 1961), 58–64.

Ordover, Janusz A., "Understanding Economic Justice: Some Recent Developments in Pure and Applied Welfare Economics," in *Economic Perspectives,* ed., Maurice B. Ballabon, p. 56. New York: Harwood Academic Publishers, 1979.

Pareto, Vilfredo, *Cours d' Economie Politique,* 2, Lausanne, 1896.

Patinkin, Don, "Demand Curves and Consumer's Surplus," in *Measurement in Economics, Studies in Mathematical Economics and Econometrics in Memory of Yehuda Grunfeld,* ed., Carl F. Christ et al. Stanford, Calif: Stanford University Press, 1963, 83–112.

Pendse, Dilip, and J. B. Wyckoff, "Scope for Valuation of Environmental Goods," *Land Economics,* 50, no. 1 (February 1974), 89–92.

Pfouts, R. W., "A Critique of Some Recent Contributions to the Theory of Consumer's Surplus," *Southern Economic Journal,* 19 (1953), 315.

Phlips, L., *Applied Consumption Analysis.* Amsterdam: North-Holland Publishing Company, 1974.

Pigou, A. C., *The Economics of Welfare.* London: Macmillan & Company Ltd., 1952.

Polinsky, A. Mitchell, and Daniel L. Rubinfeld, "Property Values and the Benefits of Environmental Improvements: Theory and Measurement," in *Public Economics and the Quality of Life,* ed. Lowdon Wingo and Alan Evans. Baltimore: Johns Hopkins University Press, 1977.

Polinsky, A. Mitchell, and Steven Shavell, "Amenities and Property Values in a Model of an Urban Area," *Journal of Public Economics,* 5, nos. 1, 2 (January-February 1976), 119–29.

Posner, Richard, "Oligopoly and the Antitrust Laws: A Suggested Approach," *Stanford Law Review,* 21 (June 1969), 1562–1606.

Quirk, James, and Rubin Saposnik, *Introduction to General Equilibrium Theory and Welfare Economics.* New York: McGraw-Hill Book Company, 1968.

Randall, Alan, Berry C. Ives, and Clyde Eastman, "Bidding Games for Evaluation of Aesthetic Environmental Improvement," *Journal of Environmental Economics and Management,* 1, no. 2 (August 1974), 132–49.

Randall, Alan, and John R. Stoll, "Consumer's Surplus in Commodity Space," *American Economic Review,* 71, no. 3 (June 1980), 449–57.

Rausser, Gordon C., and John W. Freebairn, "Estimation of Policy Preference Functions: An Application to U.S. Beef Import Quotas," *Review of Economics and Statistics,* 56, no. 4 (November 1974), 437–49.

Rawls, J., *A Theory of Justice.* New York: Oxford University Press, 1971.

Rees, Albert, "The Effects of Unions on Resource Allocation," in *Readings in Labor Market Analysis,* ed. John F. Burton, Jr., et al. New York: Holt, Rinehart, and Winston, 1971.

Reutlinger, Shlomo, "A Simulation Model for Evaluating Worldwide Buffer Stocks of Wheat," *American Journal of Agricultural Economics,* 58, no. 1 (February 1976), 1–12.

Ricardo, David, *The Principles of Political Economy and Taxation.* London: Macmillan & Company Ltd., 1829.

Richter, Donald K., *Games Pythagoreans Play,* Department of Economics, University of Rochester Discussion Paper 74-3 (1974).

Riordan, C. "General Multistage Marginal Cost Dynamic Programming Model for the Optimizations of Investment-Pricing Decisions," *Water Resources Research,* 7, no. 2 (April 1971), 245–53.

———, "Multistage Marginal Cost Model of Investment-Pricing Decisions: Application to Urban Water Supply Treatment Facilities," *Water Resources Research,* 7, no. 3 (June 1971), 463–78.

Roy, René, "La Distribution du revenu Entre les divers biens," *Econometrica,* 15, no. 3 (July 1947), 205–25.

Samuelson, P. A., "Constancy of the Marginal Utility of Income," *Studies in Mathematical Economics and Econometrics in Memory of Henry Schultz,* ed. O. Lange et al. Chicago: University of Chicago Press, 1942.

———, "Evaluation of Real National Income," *Oxford Economic Papers*, New Series, 2, no. 1 (January 1950), 1–29.

———, "Social Indifference Curves," *Quarterly Journal of Economics*, LXX, no. 1 (February 1956), 1–22.

———, "The Consumer Does Benefit from Feasible Price Stability," *Quarterly Journal of Economics*, 86, no. 3 (August 1972), 476–493.

———, "The Pure Theory of Public Expenditure," *Review of Economics and Statistics*, 36, no. 4 (November 1954), 387–89.

———, *Foundations of Economic Analysis*. Cambridge, Mass.: Harvard University Press, 1947.

Samuelson, P. A., and S. Swamy, "Invariant Economic Index Numbers and Canonical Duality: Survey and Synthesis," *American Economic Review*, 64, no. 4 (September 1974), 566–93.

Samuelson, P. A., and W. Vickrey, "Discussion," *American Economic Review, Proceedings,* 59 (1964), 88–96.

Schaefer, Elmer, "Passing-On Theory in Antitrust Treble Damage Actions: An Economic and Legal Analysis," *William and Mary Law Review*, 16, no. 4 (Summer 1975), 883–936.

Scherer, F. M., *Industrial Market Structure and Market Performance*. Chicago: Rand McNally and Company, 1970.

Schmalensee, Richard, "Another Look at the Social Valuation of Input Price Changes," *American Economic Review*, 66, no. 1 (March 1976), 237–43.

———, "Consumer's Surplus and Producer's Goods," *American Economic Review*, 61, no. 4 (September 1971), 682–87.

Schmitz, Andrew, Alex F. McCalla, D. O. Mitchell, and Colin C. Carter, *Grain Export Cartels*. Cambridge, Mass.: Ballinger Publishing Company, forthcoming, 1981.

Schmitz, Andrew, and David Seckler, "Mechanized Agriculture and Social Welfare: The Case of the Tomato Harvester," *American Journal of Agricultural Economics*, 52, no. 4 (November 1970), 569–77.

Schultze, W. D., R. C. d'Arge, and D. S. Brookshire, "Valuing Environmental Commodities: Some Recent Experiments," *Land Economics*, 57, no. 2 (May 1981), 151–72.

Schwartzman, David, "The Burden of Monopoly," *Journal of Political Economy*, 68, no. 6 (December 1960), 627–30.

Scitovsky, T., "A Note on Welfare Propositions in Economics," *Review of Economic Studies*, 9, no. 1 (November 1941), 77–88.

Scott, A. D., "Notes on User Cost," *Economic Journal*, 63, no. 250 (1953), 68–84.

———, *Natural Resources: The Economics of Conservation*. Canada: University of Toronto Press, 1955.

Sen, A. K., *Collective Choice and Social Welfare*. Edinburgh: Oliver & Boyd, Ltd., 1970.

———, *On Economic Inequality*. Oxford: Clarendon Press, 1973.

Sharples, J. A., R. L. Walker, and R. W. Slaughter, Jr., "Buffer Stock Management for Wheat Price Stabilization," Commodity Economics Division Economic Research Service, U.S. Department of Agriculture, Washington, DC, 1976.

Silberberg, Eugene, "Duality and the Many Consumer Surpluses," *American Economic Review*, 62, no. 5 (December 1972), 942–52.

———, *The Structure of Economics: A Mathematical Analysis*. New York: McGraw-Hill Book Company, 1978.

Smith, Adam, *Wealth of Nations,* 2 vols., ed. Edwin Cannan. London: Methuen and Company Ltd., 1904.

Smith, Vernon L., "On Models of Commercial Fishing," *Journal of Political Economy, 77,* no. 2 (March-April 1969), 181–98.

Solow, R. M., "Intergenerational Equity and Exhaustible Resources," *Review of Economic Studies: Symposium on the Economics of Exhaustible Resources, 1974.*

Stigler, George J., *The Theory of Price.* New York: The Macmillan Company, 1952.

Strand, I. E., and D. L. Hueth, "A Management Model for a Multispecies Fishery," in *Economic Impacts of Extended Fisheries Jurisdiction,* ed. Lee G. Anderson. Ann Arbor, Mich.: Ann Arbor Science Publishers, Inc., 1977.

Strauss, Robert P., and G. David Hughes, "A New Approach to the Demand for Public Goods," *Journal of Public Economics, 6,* no. 3 (October 1976), 191–204.

Taylor, C. Robert, and Hovav Talpaz, "Approximately Optimal Carryover Levels for Wheat in the United States," *American Journal of Agricultural Economics, 61,* no. 1 (February 1979), 32–40.

Theil, Henri, *Principles of Econometrics,* Chapter 9. New York: John Wiley & Sons, Inc., 1971.

Thurow, Lester C., *The Zero-Sum Society: Distribution and the Possibilities for Economic Change.* New York: Basic Books, Inc., 1980.

Tisdell, C., "Uncertainty, Instability, and Expected Profit," *Econometrica, 31,* nos. 1, 2 (January-April 1963), 243–47.

Tobin, James, "Comment on Borch and Feldstein," *Review of Economic Studies, 360,* no. 105 (January 1969), 13, 14.

Turnovsky, S. J., "The Distribution of Welfare Gains from Price Stabilization: A Survey of Some Theoretical Issues," *Stabilizing World Commodity Markets,* ed. F. G. Adams and S. A. Klein. Lexington, Mass.: Heath-Lexington Books, 1978, 119–48.

————, "The Distribution of Welfare Gains from Price Stabilization: The Case of Multiplicative Disturbances," *International Economic Review, 17,* no. 1 (1976), 133–48.

Turnovsky, Stephen, H. Shalit, and Andrew Schmitz, "Consumer's Surplus, Price Instability and Consumer Welfare," *Econometrica, 48,* no. 1 (January 1980), 135–52.

U.S. International Trade Commission, *Conditions of Competition in U.S. Markets between Domestic and Foreign Live Cattle and Cattle Meat Fit for Human Consumption,* no. 842 (1977), 1–126.

van den Doel, Hans, *Democracy and Welfare Economics.* London: Cambridge University Press, 1979.

Varian, Hal R., *Microeconomic Analysis.* New York: W. W. Norton & Company, Inc., July 1978.

Warren-Boulton, F. R., "Vertical Control by Labor Unions, *American Economic Review,* 67 (June 1977), 309–22.

Waugh, Frederick V., "Does the Consumer Benefit from Price Instability?" *Quarterly Journal of Economics, 58,* no. 4 (August 1944), 602–14.

Weitzman, Martin, L., "Prices vs. Quantities," *Review of Economic Studies, 41,* no. 128 (October 1974), 477–91.

Williamson, Oliver E., "Economies as an Antitrust Defense: The Welfare Trade-Offs," *American Economic Review, 58,* no. 1 (March 1968), 18–36.

Willig, Robert D., "Consumer's Surplus Without Apology," *American Economic Review, 66,* no. 4 (September 1976), 589–97.

————, *Consumer's Surplus: A Rigorous Cookbook,* Technical Report No. 98, Stanford University Press: Institute for Mathematical Studies in the Social Sciences, 1973.

Wisecarver, Daniel, "The Social Cost of Input Distortions: A Comment and a Generalization," *American Economic Review,* 66, no. 1 (March 1976), 235–38.

Wold, Herman, and Lars Jureen, *Demand Analysis: A Study in Econometrics.* New York: John Wiley & Sons, Inc., 1953.

Worcester, D. A., Jr., "Innovations in the Calculations of Welfare Loss to Monopoly," *Western Economic Journal,* 7 (September 1969), 234–43.

Zajac, E. E., "An Elementary Road Map of Integrability and Consumer's Surplus." Murray Hill, N.J.: Bell Telephone Laboratories, Inc., 1976.

Zangwill, W., *Nonlinear Programming: A Unified Approach,* Englewood Cliffs, N.J.: Prentice-Hall, Inc., 1969.

Zwart, A. C., and K. D. Mielke, "The Influence of Domestic Pricing Policies and Buffer Stocks on Price Stability in the World Wheat Industry," *American Journal of Agricultural Economics,* 61, no. 3 (August 1979), 434–47.

Author Index

Subject Index

488